California's Great Cabernets

*The Wine Spectator's
Ultimate Guide
for Consumers, Collectors and Investors*

By James Laube

WINE SPECTATOR PRESS
San Francisco, California

Published by Wine Spectator Press
A Division of M. Shanken Communications, Inc./West
Opera Plaza Suite 2014
601 Van Ness Avenue
San Francisco, CA 94102
(415) 673-2040, (415) 673-0103 (fax)

M. Shanken Communications, Inc. also publishes *The Wine Spectator*, *Impact*, *Impact International*, *Market Watch*, *Impact Research Reports*, *Leaders*, *Impact Yearbook*, *Market Watch Creative Adbook*, *The Wine Spectator's Wine Country Guide*, and sponsors the Impact Marketing Seminars and the California and New York Wine Experiences. Headquarters office at 387 Park Avenue South, New York, NY 10016, (212) 684-4224, (212) 684-5424 (fax)

First Edition
2nd Printing, 1990

Book and jacket design by Kathy McGilvery
Grapes illustration by Dorothy Reinhardt

Distributed to the Book Trade by Sterling Publishing Co., New York, NY

Manufactured in the United States of America
ISBN 0-918076-71-4

To My Parents, Ed and Jean Laube, Who Encouraged Me to Write About Things That Are Important to Me, and to Cheryl, For All Her Enthusiasm and Support.

FOREWORD

I may be too close to the subject to take an objective view of its value, but I believe that *California's Great Cabernets* will become a landmark book.

In the past 20 years, there has been a solid upward curve of interest in this subject. I remember well the early 1970s when few outside the trade (and I might add, few inside the trade) knew what Cabernet Sauvignon was, and fewer, how to pronounce it. It was not until perhaps 10 years ago that wine merchants, restaurateurs and the wine-consuming public began to understand the magic and nobility of this classic grape. Cabernet Sauvignon came of age in America during the 1980s.

Why this book and why now? When I told a knowledgeable friend in the wine trade about this project he responded, "a whole book on Cabernet — you gotta be nuts!" This response jogged my memory back to when *The Wine Spectator* was acquired in 1979. Many of my friends reacted, "You what? You bought a publication that writes about wine and comes out *twice* a month. You gotta be nuts!"

Maybe the vision then was too early, maybe not. But the vitality of *The Wine Spectator* today is self-evident.

I feel the same excitement and conviction today with regard to *California's Great Cabernets*.

Over the years, I have read many magazine essays about Cabernet wines. I never found the depth of information I was looking for. I wanted to know more about the winemaker, the vineyards and the resulting product. Its taste, its texture, its mouth-feel, its future. And I wanted to hear the truth, or a man's uncompromising interpretation of the truth, not soapsuds.

I believe that this book achieves all of the above and more.

With this book Jim Laube will earn his rightful position as a leading authority on the subject of California wine. This pleases me a great deal, since Laube, now a senior editor, has been writing for *The Wine Spectator* since 1980. I have watched his progress and his diligence. Those who know him personally know of his quiet demeanor. He's quite likable. When he speaks it's because he has something to say. He evokes respect and trust.

Laube has been drinking, studying and writing about wine for more than a decade. He also lives in the Napa Valley — a tough place to be living if you have written a truthful book on Cabernet Sauvignon and plan to continue to live there after the book is published. And yet I had faith that he could see and taste the truth, and write the truth even if it meant dislodging myths and egos, and hurting the feelings of people he sincerely likes.

This book has teeth, which in the wine-book world is a rather rare occurrence (except in the case of Robert Parker and one or two others), especially given the volume of wine books published each year.

There are several important parts of this book that I would like to bring to your attention. First and foremost, *virtually all* of the wines tasted and rated in this book were tasted blind.

Second, whereas Laube may have tasted these wines several or many times over the years, the ratings are his tasting notes and scores from tastings within the past nine months. All of the reviews are current and therefore more meaningful to the reader.

Third, if you are a fan of a particular Cabernet producer and it is not part of this book, do not assume it was overlooked. It wasn't. It simply means that the wine in question did not meet the book's criteria. Laube focused only on those Cabernets that reached a certain standard of quality and would be of interest to you because of their ageability and collectibility potential.

The purpose of this book is not to be nice to California winemakers. Or to serve as a useful public-relations tool. Enough such sources already exist.

Once you get beyond the ratings of the more than 1,200 wines reviewed in this book, as well as the ratings of the vintages, perhaps the most useful section is the chapter that classifies the reviewed wines into five "growths" similar to those used in the 1855 Classification of Bordeaux wine.

This chapter tells it all. How each of the wines really stack up. In it you will likely see one or two fifth growths that you feel certain should be first growths, and perhaps vice versa. The purpose here was not to create controversy or attack these wines perched on high by popularity or skillful publicity. What mattered were the tasting notes — of wines tasted blind — along with realistic and demanding views of the wine, its winemaker, the vineyards and most of all its future.

There is also a rather hard-edged "collectibility rating" of selected Cabernets in Chapter V. Here Laube goes a step further and trims down the group of 17 first-growth wines into a tightly clustered collection of 12 wines that are regarded as the ultimate collectibles. These wines enjoy a collectibility rating of AAA. Some of the other highly regarded wines receive AA or A ratings.

As wine is a living, evolving and changing product so do wines and winemakers travel roads to either higher or lower levels. Please accept this reference book in that spirit. It is our intention to update, revise and refine this book every two or three years. No doubt in the next edition there will be some jockeying around of wines as winemakers change jobs, vineyards are bought and sold and techniques are perfected.

I could not conclude this foreword without two final thoughts.

First, I believe that this book will serve to raise the reputation, stature and acceptability of California Cabernet around the world. I believe this book contains sufficient integrity and will be viewed as such when read by unbiased and knowledgeable consumers and the wine trade.

Second, for all of Laube's good intent and long hours, this book could not have happened without a team spirit and commitment from the members of *The Wine Spectator* staff — from the computer programmer to the many other staff members involved in research, editing, proofreading and production.

I would especially like to note the inspiration of the project director, *Wine Spectator* president Greg Walter, who spent endless hours keeping the book on track and on the truck to the printer.

I am as proud as proud can be of *The Wine Spectator* team. And I know that Jim Laube feels the same way. Enjoy.

Marvin R. Shanken
Editor and Publisher
The Wine Spectator
Quogue, New York
August 1989

ACKNOWLEDGMENTS

A good many people have come to my aid in researching and writing this book. At the top of my list I want to thank the entire staff of *The Wine Spectator*. It's a great organization of enthusiastic and professional people who are serious (but not too serious) about wine. From that family, a special thanks to Kathy McGilvery for designing the book and cover, Donna Marianno Morris, Liza Gross and their production staff for putting it together, copy editors Lisa King and Catherine Miller for cleaning up my prose, Mark Norris for keeping track of all the wines, tasting notes, scores and prices, and Ray Bush for organizing both regular and special tastings. I would also like to single out *Wine Spectator* editors and tasting panel members Jim Gordon and Harvey Steiman for helping edit the book, sharing their insights and experience on Cabernet and lending encouragement and support.

Many people in the wine industry have unselfishly shared their time and knowledge about wine with me and, I am grateful for that education. I owe a debt of gratitude to every vintner in this book for providing their wines, especially some of the older, rare bottles that are hard to come by. I also wish to thank their staffs for helping compile all the facts and figures about their wines. In particular I would like to single out the following for all their help along the way: André Tchelistcheff, Robert and Tim Mondavi, Tom Selfridge, Dennis Fife, John Richburg, Bill Hill, Charlie and Chuck Wagner, Bernard Portet, Gary Andrus, Al Brounstein, Paul Draper, Jim Barrett, Jerry Luper, Zelma Long, Marcus and Anne Moller-Racke, Bob Craig, Marty Lee, Legh Knowles, Christian Moueix, Chuck Carpy, Mike Grgich, Bob Travers, Joe Heitz, Dick Steltzner, Warren Winiarski, Tom Ferrell, John Thacher, Justin Meyer, Louis P. and Mike Martini, Mike Richmond, Patrick Campbell, Randy Dunn, Tony Soter, Ric Forman, Jim Allen, Joseph Phelps, Bruce Neyers, John Shafer, Donn Chappellet, Peter Mondavi, Ed Sbragia, Tom Burgess, Henry Mathieson, Ken Burnap, Tom Jordan, Francis Coppola, Gil Nickel, Steve Girard, Reverdy Johnson, Randy Mason, Bob Pepi, Joan Smith, Koerner Rombauer, Dennis Groth, Philip Togni, Dick Grace, Nils Venge, Bryan del Bondio, Su Hua Newton, Jack Stuart, John Williams, Mike Robbins, Roy and Walt Raymond, Dan

Duckhorn, Agustin Huneeus and the late Myron Nightingale.

Beyond winemakers, John Skupny, Dennis Bowker, Barney Rhodes, Haskell Norman, John Gay, Tom May, Milt Eisele, Harvey Posert, Andy Blue, Fred Dame, Bob Dwyer and Tor Kenward all contributed wine and/or thoughts on Cabernet that enhanced my understanding and appreciation of the subject. Bill Heintz was invaluable in his help with historical research and perspective.

I owe a great debt of gratitude to Greg Walter, president of *The Wine Spectator*, who in addition to being a good friend and confidant, supervised all aspects of this book and proved a constant source of moral support and critical analysis while keeping this project moving.

Finally I want to thank Marvin Shanken, my editor and publisher, who proved just how much he loves California Cabernet by lending his total and complete support to this project from start to finish.

Last but not least, thanks to my wife, Cheryl, for all her enthusiasm and enduring this *Year of Cabernet*, and my children, Dwight and Margaux, for letting Dad work uninterrupted (most of the time) in his office.

All authors should be so fortunate to be in such fine company.

CONTENTS

INTRODUCTION

If you drink, collect or invest in California Cabernet Sauvignon, this book's for you. I enjoy many different wines from all over the world and do not prefer one region, grape or style to another, but it was a bottle of Cabernet Sauvignon that first made me take notice of all the complexities and nuances a wine could offer.

I remember how clear and simple it seemed the day I realized there really was a difference between cork-finished jug wines and a fine bottle of Cabernet Sauvignon. The year was 1974. I was attending graduate school in history at San Diego State University, living at the beach in Cardiff-by-the-Sea. The local wine merchant down the hill had noted our enthusiasm for wine and steered me and my roommates away from the half-gallon bottles into generic burgundies and chablis, for which we were grateful.

The next step up was to varietal wines, and the first stop was Cabernet Sauvignon, a tricky name to pronounce at first but a name worth remembering. The first Cabernet that really struck me as wonderfully unique was the Heitz Cellar Napa Valley. The Heitz house style is unmistakable to those who regularly drink these Cabernets. The spicy cedar aromas and fruit flavors are complex, and the texture is rich and supple. The wine can be a fantastic drinking experience. After that revelation, we became more curious and quizzed the merchant about what might be finer. This time he introduced us to Heitz Martha's Vineyard 1968. It cost about $9 — nearly twice what we'd been paying for a bottle — but it was infinitely better, incredibly delicious, thick, concentrated and enormously complex, a wine that kept you coming back for one more glass and secretly praying that the bottle never emptied. I drank more than my share of Heitz Martha's 1968 that year, never stopping to think that putting a few bottles away in my closet might bring even greater rewards.

The research continued. The mantle above the fireplace was cluttered with empty mementos, now from Louis M. Martini, Beaulieu, Simi and others. Soon the top of the refrigerator was in a similar state of disorder. I remember thinking the day we moved from the beach house that we sure drank a lot of Heitz.

The next year started a series of trips to visit the Napa and Sonoma wineries, which opened a whole new vista of discovery and taste. The more I tasted the more opinions I formed, with mental snapshots of specific wines I liked and those that were less appealing. In 1978 I began to jot down notes. By then I had moved from San Diego to Napa, where I worked as a reporter in the Napa news bureau for a daily newspaper based in Vallejo. Napa Valley became my beat. Soon my assignment was to write about trends and developments in the wine and grape industries. The first vintage I covered was 1978, and it was a great harvest. One day my editor asked me to write about one of my favorite wines. By this time I had many but decided to call on Joe Heitz. It didn't take him long to figure out how little I knew about wine. He indulged me for more than an hour, answering questions and letting me taste a few of his wines.

I've been keeping track of wines ever since. I have no formal education or training with wine, but I'm not so sure that it's necessary. The opportunity I have been given is far greater: direct exposure to the great wines and winemakers of the world in their vineyards, cellars, homes and châteaux, as well as working with and tasting with some of the finest wine journalists in the business. In a decade of writing about wine, I have been fortunate to travel to and write about the wines of Bordeaux, Burgundy, the Loire Valley, the Rhône Valley, Germany, Italy, Spain, Australia, Mexico, Oregon, Long Island and California. At *The Wine Spectator* each year we taste between 3,000 and 4,000 of the world's finest wines, which allows me to examine the wines and vintages on a regular basis.

California is blessed with a great climate for winegrowing. Many of the world's noble grapes perform exceptionally well, resulting in wines of world-class stature. Cabernet Sauvignon has long been the king of the reds, the most consistently excellent, ageworthy and collectible wine grown in the Golden State. With time one hopes the enormous progress with Pinot Noir, Merlot, Zinfandel and recently the Rhône varieties will reach equally elevated heights, but for now Cabernet is the undisputed champion.

The thought of writing a book on California Cabernet has for the past few years been a fascinating topic to me, both from a historical perspective — reviewing older vintages — as well as from a journalist/critic's view of current wines. That concept is the genesis of this book.

This is a golden age for California Cabernet Sauvignon. Never in its history has California Cabernet Sauvignon been so popular with the American wine-drinking public or so well made. The current selection of wines now available from the 1984, 1985 and 1986 vintages rank among the very finest, yielding a wealth of magnificent wines for those with a casual interest in good drinking, collectors who cherish prized wines from great estates in outstanding vintages and investors who buy wine with the idea of reselling it at some future date.

My goal with this book is to identify California's finest Cabernet producers, the top wines from the top vintages and best growing areas. *California's Great Cabernets* is written with specific advice for consumers, collectors and investors who enjoy drinking Cabernet and are interested in buying wines either currently available on the market, sold at auction or soon to be released. I have attempted to review as many old California Cabernets as possible, both for historical documentation about which were the past great wines and producers and as reference material for people who either have these wines in their collections or want to buy them at retail or auction.

The vast majority of the more than 1,200 wines reviewed in this book were tasted from September 1988 to May 1989. Since moving to Napa in 1978 I have been fortunate to have had the opportunity to follow many of California's leading Cabernets up close, from the vineyards to the winery, pulled out of barrel and poured from the bottle into the glass. Many of the older vintages are very rare. Until the mid-1970s, production of most California Cabernet was extremely limited. Few producers made more than 2,000 cases. Even today buying classified

Bordeaux from the great 1961 or 1966 vintages is considerably easier than finding Cabernet from the 1968 or 1970 vintages. For most wineries production of superpremium Cabernet is closer in quantity to that of Burgundy or the Rhône than Bordeaux.

Finally, this book is in a sense a tribute to California's leading Cabernet producers, for it recognizes their many accomplishments with this magnificent wine.

JEL
August 1989
Napa, Calif.

How To Use This Book

The tasting notes and analysis of the more than 1,200 Cabernets reviewed in this book, along with descriptions of the individual wines, vintages and top Cabernet regions, are designed to help wine lovers make the most intelligent buying decisions about Cabernet Sauvignon, whether for drinking with tonight's dinner, cellaring for 10 to 20 years or buying or selling at a future date.

Tasting wine is a highly subjective matter. Everyone has his own taste and preferences for style, flavor, personality and character. The most objective way to judge wine is through blind tastings, where the identity of the wine is not known. The process for selecting the Cabernets reviewed in this book was based not only on blind tastings but on my own personal knowledge and experience in tasting these wines during the past decade. Most of these blind tastings were conducted at the editorial offices of *The Wine Spectator* in San Francisco. After years of tracking these wines with tasting notes, I went back in the past nine months and retasted as many of them as possible in vertical tastings to evaluate their quality and consistency of style. In a few instances, with older, rare bottles, I have only had occasion to taste them once or twice and sometimes not under blind conditions.

The surest way to evaluate effectively the quality of a wine is to taste it as many times as possible, beginning from barrel samples and continuing through its development. Numerous tastings of a wine allow you to measure both your and the wine's consistency. There is a saying among wine aficionados that people change more than the wines. What that means is our experiences with wine change more than any single bottle does. Beyond tastings, in which the wines are spit out, wines need to be consumed (yes, swallowed) for full appreciation. I am skeptical of critics who taste scores of wines and base their evaluations on how well the wine showed in a blind tasting without having drunk it at dinner. I have tasted most of the Cabernets in this book since the 1974 vintage on at least five occasions; many of them I have been fortunate to drink as well.

Clearly some wines and vintages are easier to judge than others. In recent years, the

1984 and 1985 Cabernets were especially delicious out of the barrel, and they continue to offer wonderful, seductive fruit flavors and fine, integrated tannins now that they're in bottle. The 1986 and 1987 vintages proved a shade more tannic and angular, making initial evaluations more challenging. The 1983 vintage in particular stands out as one of the toughest in recent years. Many of these wines were hard and tannic, uneven in quality. Making a summary judgment on a vintage like 1983 is infinitely more difficult, for wines (and vintages) can have a boomerang effect: Just when you think you know where they're going and have them neatly pegged, they can zoom back from out of the blue to startle or amaze you. If there is one vital message to remember about tasting wine, it is this: Friends and critics may steer you to or away from wines, but ultimately your taste is your own. Trust your own palate.

What To Look For in Great Cabernets

In the world of wines, Cabernet Sauvignon is distinct and readily identifiable, with its deep purple-red color, alluring black cherry, plum, currant and herb aromas, rich concentration of fruit and firm, sometimes mouth-puckering tannins. Like all wines, it constantly changes and evolves as it matures. What distinguishes the great wines from the good ones is that the great ones improve with age. A few Cabernets tasted for this book were unimpressive early on, either in barrel samples or right after bottling. Mayacamas Cabernet is a notoriously slow developer that many people dismiss as too tannic or too blunt, only to discover years down the road what they missed. This is also true of highly tannic first growth Bordeaux. But most of the great wines taste great right from the start.

In sampling infant Cabernets out of barrels, one expects an unfinished product that may be coarse, tannic or rough around the edges. But in general I look for many characteristics that are the same as those of a finished, polished bottle: depth and purity of color, the degree of ripeness, richness, concentration and breadth of fruit flavor, the balance of acidity and tannins and the length of fruit persistence on the aftertaste, when the wine is no longer on your palate. Of all these components, the most important is the fruit, for that affects the overall flavor, personality and character of the wine. When Cabernet is unripe, it tastes green, tart, leafy or vegetal. In rainy harvests, an earthy, watery and sometimes moldy quality can be evident.

When the Cabernet vine is allowed to overproduce, intense herbaceous and vegetal flavors dominate; when it overripens, prune and raisin flavors are apparent, often accompanied by strong alcoholic aromas and a hot finish. When Cabernet is picked at optimum ripeness, it offers a broad array of intense, sharply focused black currant, black cherry, plum and berry flavors along with spicy nuances of mint, anise or cedar and on occasion bell pepper flavors. The presence and intensity of these and other aromas and flavors — such as flowers, coffee or chocolate — combine to give a great Cabernet complexity. If any one component is too strong or dominant, it can detract from the overall impression of the wine and in that context can be a defect.

Cabernets that smell predominantly of green beans or pickles are to my taste flawed. If a Cabernet smells like ripe berries but offers little in the way of additional flavor or aroma, it is considered simple and correct; not unpleasant by any means, but given Cabernet's propensity for complexity and nuance, the best wines go well beyond direct, unsophisticated flavors.

When rooted in the right soil and climate, it is Cabernet's nature to be intense and concentrated. The small, purplish berries have a low ratio of juice to skin, which holds the grape's flavor and accounts for its high level of tannin. California Cabernet benefits from blending with other grapes, most notably Merlot and Cabernet Franc, in a fashion similar to — but not identical to — that of Bordeaux.

The biggest difference is that many of California's top Cabernets — Heitz Martha's Vineyard, Caymus Special Selection and Dunn Howell Mountain, to name just three — are 100 percent Cabernet, and each is enormously complex and ageworthy. The reasons for blending in Bordeaux are several. The grapes not only complement each other in flavor but also guard against total crop failure, for each has different ripening patterns, and most importantly they achieve complexity and finesse in the wines. In California, crop failure is rarely a threat; overproduction and overripening are more common concerns.

Cabernet ripens easily in a healthy, hearty, vigorous fashion, so much so that some winemakers believe it is too assertive and is best tempered by Merlot or Cabernet Franc. Increasingly the trend is toward more intermingling of varieties, but much less is known about the proper soil and climatic conditions for Merlot and Cabernet Franc. Early assumptions were that what is right for Cabernet is also correct for Merlot. But often Merlot offered flavors and textures that were as astringent as Cabernet and did not provide the supple softness and fruity flavors desired. Moreover, because Merlot is highly productive, in rich California soils it yields large crops of grapes that are often extremely herbal and not appealing to those who want to add fruit and polish to their wines. The planting of Cabernet Franc is still in the discovery stage with a shade more than 1,000 acres statewide, a small fraction compared to the more than 22,000 acres planted to Cabernet and nearly 3,000 acres of Merlot. But early results show promise, and it is in great demand.

Cabernet, along with California's winemakers, likes oak. Virtually everyone now uses it. When Cabernet ages in small casks it takes on additional toast, vanilla and cedar flavors along with wood tannins that can add structure to the wine. However, too much of a good thing can also ruin a wine, particularly a young one that lacks richness and concentration. The proper proportion of oak can give a wine spice and texture while allowing it to mature. Oak aging is a natural process of oxidation, which in a brash young Cabernet can take some of the sharp edges off the texture and mouth-feel. Oak — old, new, French or American — has been around for half a century, but only in the past two decades have California winemakers come to grips with its best use. The current trend is toward more new French oak for shorter lengths of barrel aging, but it is far from unanimous. The Heitz Martha's, Caymus Special Selection and Dunn Howell Mountain are all aged for extended periods of up to four years in a mixture of some new oak but mostly used, neutral barrels.

As California Cabernets mature, the color changes from the deep red-purple, sometimes inky hues to ruby-red and garnet tones and then finally to pale garnet shades. California Cabernets are typically very ripe when harvested and seldom lack color. While color in general is a important factor in visually analyzing the health and maturity of a wine, in California it is less vital than either the aromas or flavors. A California Cabernet can maintain a healthy depth of color even when it has begun to lose its flavor and zest.

With age, Cabernet's fresh, clean black cherry, currant and plum flavors begin to evolve; the aromas change from readily identifiable fruits to less precise yet more complex and appealing aromas, known as bottle bouquet. This begins five to seven years after the vintage. Older California Cabernets often display an assortment of sun-dried fruit aromas and flavors that echo cherry, plum, prune, anise and even sun-dried tomato with all its seasoned spice.

Cabernet at its best is a balancing act that allows for the intensity and power of the Cabernet grape without letting it overwhelm. There is no one way to produce a great Cabernet, but those that fall short of that measure most often lack balance and harmony.

HOW THE WINES WERE CHOSEN

Since 1978 I have made a conscious effort to taste as many Cabernets as possible. This book is the distillation of thousands of tasting notes scribbled on note pads, scraps of paper, matchbooks and menus and lately tracked by computer. The emphasis the past five years has been to zero in on the cream of the crop, Cabernets with track records of excellence and reputations for greatness; a secondary motive is to forecast a few of the new rising stars. It would be easy to explain the criteria for selection if all Cabernets were estate grown and each producer made just one wine, but that is not the case in California. The following factors were considered and given weight in selecting the wines.

Producer and Overall Quality: This is of foremost consideration. The producer's name on the label is the greatest guarantee of quality. Appellations, vineyards and estate bottling are important factors, but not as crucial as who made the wine and what's in the bottle.

Track Record of Excellence: How good are the wines from vintage to vintage within a framework of consistency in style? Wines with track records of 10 vintages or more of consistently high quality are worthy of special consideration, for they have demonstrated continuity. Five vintages of fine quality put a wine in the worth-watching category.

Consistency of Style: How precise and consistent is the style from year to year? Again, a wine, winery or winemaker's track record with a deliberate style ensures consistency. The key to evaluating consistency begins with fully understanding the style, whether it's effusively fruity, enormously concentrated, supple and elegant, lavishly oaked, intensely tannic or otherwise distinct. Consistent styles render wines with more similarities than differences from year to year and are most often affected by the quality and character of the vintage, not changes in winemaking techniques or styles.

Private Reserve or Special Selection: In most instances I concentrated on each winery's top-of-the-line Cabernet. For several producers that meant focusing on the Private Reserve, Reserve or Special Selection bottling, wines designated as higher in quality than other bottlings by the wineries even though their regular Cabernet may be notably fine, too.

Estate Bottled: A guarantee of authenticity and often superior quality. Ownership and control of winemaking from vineyard to the bottle is increasingly important in California, for it ensures a constant source of grapes and offers the greatest potential for consistency of style. Wines that are not estate bottled or vineyard designated are less likely to be consistent in style or quality from year to year. Wineries that use different sources of grapes each year face a greater challenge in achieving uniformity of style. The majority of the wines included in this book are estate bottled.

Two Wines From One Winery: A handful of producers make more than one wine from the same estate. Caymus bottles two Cabernets, including a Special Selection, from its Rutherford estate, and both are superb. Stag's Leap Wine Cellars also makes two estate-bottled Cabernets from the same vineyard. One is a proprietary bottling called Cask 23, which is only produced in years where superior quality is evident. Clos Du Val and Pine Ridge also produce reserve wines in select years from estate-grown grapes.

Vineyard Designations: Special consideration was given to Cabernets of excellent quality that bear vineyard designations, such as Heitz Martha's Vineyard or Joseph Phelps Eisele, which ensure the same grape source every year. This is very similar to estate bottled except that the winery does not necessarily own the vineyard. In some instances, a winery does own the vineyard; Diamond Creek produces at least three different vineyard-designated wines from its estate vineyards. For many wineries, vineyard-designated wines are their finest, showing superior quality and character to other bottlings, which are usually blends of grapes grown in different locations.

Rare or Older Vintages: I have tried to include as many old vintages as possible, particularly in situations where a winery produced a regular Cabernet before introducing a Reserve or vineyard-designated wine, or a winery produced a special, one-time bottling that is worthy of attention. For instance, in 1979 Beringer did not produce a Private Reserve but did bottle a State Lane Cabernet, which proved to be an exceptional wine and is included.

Vineyards: Quality and track record of the vineyard often predate a wine brand. Vineyards such as Steltzner, Spottswoode, Olive Hill (B.R. Cohn) and the Hess Collection have been providing first-rate grapes to other wineries longer than they have been making wines under their own labels. Steltzner Vineyards sold grapes to several Napa Valley wineries for years before releasing wines under its own brand.

Winemakers: A factor in some instances. Ric Forman, Philip Togni, Tony Soter (Spottswoode and Etude) and Jerry Luper (Freemark Abbey, Château Montelena, Diamond Creek and Rutherford Hill) are among those who have long, distinguished careers as winemakers that bear directly on their experience with Cabernet and the quality of their new wines. Moreover, the role of the winemaker in establishing a style is important, particularly early on. It typically takes 10 years to fully establish a style and know how a wine will age. For example, a wine produced in 1990 will be bottled in 1992 and released in 1994. How good that wine tastes in the next four to six years and beyond is the strongest indicator of its overall quality and aging potential. In instances where a winery blends grapes from several vineyards, the winemaker is usually the arbiter of quality and style. Once a winery establishes a style and consistent source of grapes, there is less a winemaker must do, which is why established European châteaux consider the job of winemaker more as a caretaker than a creator.

HOW THE BOOK IS ORGANIZED

This book is designed for easy reference. It is divided into six chapters, beginning with Chapter I, Cabernet in California: An Informal History; Chapter II, The Vineyards: The Lay of the Land; and Chapter III, The Vintages: 1933 to 1988. While all the wines selected for this book are superior in quality, some are simply better than others. Chapter IV, A Classification: Ranking the Cabernets, is my classification of the Cabernets in this book based on the overall quality and track records of the producers. Chapter V, Cabernet Strategies: Collecting and Investing, is a guide to my top Cabernet selections for collecting as well as general advice on investing in Cabernet for resale. In Chapter V, I also describe the Collectibility Rating. Chapter VI, Winery Profiles and Tasting Notes, is the heart of this book. Within this section, each of the wineries and wines selected for this book is presented in alphabetical order along with the following data:

Classification: One of five categories, first through fifth growth, denoting the overall quality of the wine.

Collectibility Rating: One of four categories — AAA, AA, A or No rating. Cabernets with AAA rating are the ones I believe are the top collectible wines with track records for excellence, the best candidates for long-term cellaring and appreciation in value. The wines rated AA or A are a notch or two below the AAA category. Most of the wines in this book have not been given a rating, but that does not necessarily reflect on their quality.

Best Vintages: Summary of the best vintages for the wine.

At a Glance: Facts and figures about the winery: the owner, address and phone number for ordering wine, founding date, winemaker and number of years in service, first Cabernet vintage, total Cabernet production (as distinguished from a single specific wine chosen for this book), Cabernet acres owned (which includes Merlot and Cabernet Franc), average age of vines, vineyard makeup and time and type of oak used for aging. Many of the producers in this book produce more than one Cabernet. See "How the Wines Were Chosen" above.

Winery Profile: A brief history of the winery, vintages and summary of tasting note reviews along with descriptions of the style and character of the Cabernet Sauvignons.

Tasting Notes: A review of each wine, its flavor and style, and how it fits in the context of the other wines produced and the different vintages; for example, how good a wine is it, using the 100-point scale, and how it rates when compared both with other wines produced and vintages.

For each of the Cabernets, this additional data is included:

Cases Produced: Information provided by wineries.

Release Price: What the wine sold for at retail on release.

Current Price: Estimated market value today, based on information provided by wineries along with data from the retail market and auctions as of June 1989. The value today is an approximation of what you can expect to pay for that particular wine, not what you can expect to sell it for. Retailers typically mark up prices by 33 percent to 50 percent. For more on this topic see Chapter V, Cabernet Strategies: Collecting and Investing.

Drink: My estimate of when each wine will be at its best for drinking. Just when a Cabernet is in its prime depends entirely on personal preference. There is no exact moment when it crosses over from being immature and into its prime or begins to decline. Luckily most California Cabernets are readily enjoyable on release and are fully mature within five to eight years of the vintage. The Drink window is at best a guideline of when to drink the wine before it begins to decline. Wines 15 years and older are mature and ready to drink.

Score: A numerical rating from 50 to 100 points based on *The Wine Spectator* 100-point scale. The ratings indicate how good or great the wines are today. With younger wines, I have factored in how good I think the wine will be based on my research and experience. Careful readers of *The Wine Spectator* will notice that some wines have different scores and tasting notes than the ones that appeared in the magazine. This reflects my personal preferences as distinguished from *The Wine Spectator* tasting panel's, as well as a revisionist look at the wines. As important as the score is, I consider the tasting note the most accurate reflection of how good the wine is, for the notes deal with aesthetics, not numbers.

About the Rating System

It's important to read carefully what the numbers indicate about the quality of a wine. Scores gauge how much the critic likes or dislikes a wine, but far too often the tasting note description is overlooked and consumers dismiss a good wine because it scores in the 70s. The best wines to concentrate on are those with the highest scores, but wines that are good are just that and should not be ignored. The scale is as follows:

The Wine Spectator's 100-Point Scale

95-100	Classic, a wine of extraordinary character
90-94	Excellent, a wine of superior quality and style
80-89	Very Good, a wine with special qualities
70-79	Good, a fine example of its type that may have minor flaws
60-69	Fair, a drinkable wine but not recommended
50-59	Poor, an undrinkable wine, best to avoid

Final Thoughts on Tasting

Bottle variation is a fact of life with wine. In researching this book, I have encountered significant bottle variation, particularly with older vintages. In most instances, the degree of variation is modest and quite likely caused by storage conditions; a wine stored at a steady 55 degrees Fahrenheit will age more slowly and longer than one kept at 70 degrees. In other instances, wines pulled from the same case differed in quality. I have done my best to retaste any wines where bottle variation appeared to be a reason for concern. In most cases, I have given the wine the benefit of the doubt and published the more complimentary review and score. In cases where bottle variation proved problematic, I have indicated such in the note; several of these wines I have recommended consumers avoid.

As much as I tried to include every great Cabernet Sauvignon produced in California in the past 50 years for purposes of historical documentation, many are missing. The wineries and wines selected for this book for the most part represent the most comprehensive review of the finest Cabernet Sauvignons being produced in California today.

Old California Cabernets are very rare, but on occasion can be found at auction, through classified ads in wine magazines or in select fine-wine shops. I would recommend that if you have never tried a wine from the 1940s, 1950s or 1960s and have the opportunity, do so by all means, even if it means paying the going price.

The experience of tasting what happens to a great bottle of Cabernet is well worth it and may help you decide whether laying wines down for years is right for you.

CHAPTER I

CABERNET IN CALIFORNIA: AN INFORMAL HISTORY

The Cabernet Sauvignon grape has been a part of California's winemaking heritage for 150 years. The first vines were grown in Southern California in the 1830s by Jean Louis Vignes, a Bordeaux native who imported Cabernet cuttings and planted them in what is now the heart of Los Angeles. Vignes brought with him other unspecified grape varieties, but given his origins and interest in the fine red wines of Bordeaux, it is quite likely that he also imported Merlot, Cabernet Franc, Malbec and Petit Verdot with the idea of producing a claret-style wine. The precise date of Vignes' first vintage is uncertain, but evidence points to 1837. According to one account, in 1857 Vignes advertised some of his wine as being 20 years old.

The origins of Cabernet Sauvignon in Bordeaux predates California's first plantings by nearly a century, although it did not become the preferred grape until after 1815. Although extremely rare, bottles of Château Margaux from the 1770s are occasionally poured at tastings, as are ancient bottles from Château Lafite and Château Latour from the same era. America's early fascination with Bordeaux included a keen interest by President Thomas Jefferson, who bought wines from Château Margaux and had his initials engraved on the bottles. By the early 1800s, Cabernet was widely planted throughout the Médoc and Graves, along with other varieties such as Malbec, Merlot and Cabernet Franc in early attempts to determine which grapes performed better in different soils. Grape variety selection was based on soil compatibility.

Clearly Merlot performed better in some soils than Cabernet and vice versa. That process of grape selection proved convenient because of the grapes' different flowering, ripening and maturity patterns, along with varying crop size, flavor and aromatic components, texture and mouth-feel. While Cabernet budded later, yielded smaller crops of intensely flavored and richly tannic wines, Merlot in Bordeaux threw larger crops and tasted more supple, more forward and much fruitier. Merlot's great weakness is that it buds and flowers in early spring and is susceptible to frosts and *coulure*, a condition in which grape embryos fail to develop, resulting in crop loss or failure. Cabernet and Merlot together combine to offer greater richness and depth of flavor, a silkier texture and fruitier aromas. It is important to note that while Cabernet Sauvignon is considered the preeminent grape of Bordeaux, it accounts for only one-quarter of the vineyards; Merlot is more widely planted, accounting for nearly half the acreage. While typical Bordeaux reds contain significant portions of both grapes, Cabernet Sauvignon is most widely planted in the Médoc and is the dominate grape in the great first growths Château Lafite-Rothschild, Château Mouton-Rothschild and Château Latour in the commune of Pauillac and Château Margaux in the Margaux commune.

What sets the great wines of the Médoc and California apart from the many other fine wines of the world is their incredible complexity of aroma and flavor and amazing longevity. To a great extent, the ability of these wines to age for decades, or even centuries, is largely due to the character of the Cabernet Sauvignon grape. At first tannic and mouth-puckering, with deep red and purple hues, Cabernet Sauvignon is a hearty, durable grape that grows vigorously in many climates and is easy to harvest. Its hard wood vine allows it to survive severe spring frosts, but it ripens late in the summer or fall, which can pose a problem in rainy harvests. The Cabernet grape is a small, thick-skinned berry that hangs in a loose cluster, which makes it less susceptible to bunch rot after rains. When properly cultivated in warm but not hot climates, it yields wines of great richness, depth, intensity, concentration and structure. The aromas and flavors in the finest Cabernets are ripe black currant, black cherry, plum and occasionally raspberry, which are often floral or chocolatey in their youth. Those flavors are often accompanied by the spicy nuances of mint, anise, clove and cedar, along with the herbal notes of bell pepper and olive. With age, tea and tobacco notes can often be found. Cabernet vines planted in the wrong climate, or allowed to overproduce can lead to pronounced vegetal flavors, which I consider to be a flaw in the flavor of the wine. This occurs in Bordeaux as well as certain parts of California.

In the early 1850s, Charles LeFranc, another Frenchman from Bordeaux, began planting Cabernet and other Bordeaux varieties and making wine in the Santa Clara Valley. LeFranc preferred a blend in the style and grape proportions of the famed Château Margaux, which is typically 70 percent Cabernet. In the 1860s, Count Agoston Haraszthy of Hungary, founder of Buena Vista Winery in Sonoma and a leading importer of grape-vine cuttings from Europe, probably introduced Cabernet Sauvignon to California's North Coast.

In those days, California wines were not known by varietal names, as they are today. Claret, the English term for red Bordeaux, was the preferred terminology for many of California's Cabernet-based or blended wines. In the years that followed, Bordeaux-style wines heavily reliant on Cabernet Sauvignon became the most prized red wines in California. There is less evidence of the use of Merlot or other Bordeaux varieties, but it is almost certain that these varieties were used, given the character and makeup of classic Bordeaux reds. At Inglenook in the late 1800s both the terms "California Claret" and "Médoc-Type" appeared on the labels of wines that, according to winery records, were predominantly Cabernet Sauvignon. But true to the Bordeaux tradition of blending, it is likely that at least a small percentage of Zinfandel and other hearty red varietals were included in the blend. Louis M. Martini almost always added a dollop of Zinfandel to his Cabernets well into the 1950s.

How good were the wines? Apparently they were excellent by international standards. California wineries claimed a number of medals at the wine competition at the Paris Exposition in 1900. Some of the winners were Beringer Brothers, Gundlach Bundschu Wine Co. and the To-Kalon Wine Co. of Oakville, a vineyard that is now owned by the Robert Mondavi Winery. The oldest California "Cabernet" I have tasted is the 1897 Inglenook California Claret Médoc-Type, which in June 1989 displayed wonderfully mature aromas and flavors that developed in the glass for more than an hour.

As promising as the future appeared for California wine, there was trouble ahead. The Prohibitionist movement, which began with anti-alcohol campaigns and laws dating back to the original 13 colonies, continued to gain momentum in the 1800s. Dozens of towns and counties throughout the East, Midwest and South voted themselves "dry" by banning alcoholic beverages. Also, between 1860 and 1900, the root louse phylloxera caused widespread damage to California and Europe's vineyards. New forms of resistant rootstock were planted around the turn of the century, but with the passage of Prohibition, which lasted from 1919 to 1933, the sale of alcoholic beverages was outlawed. Although many California wineries produced Cabernet between 1900 and 1919, these wines are extremely rare.

A few wineries survived Prohibition, keeping vineyards alive by selling grapes to home winemakers and producing altar wines for communion and other religious ceremonies. A loophole in the law allowed citizens to produce wine at home. Wine bricks, packages of pressed grapes, were sold with a yeast pill and a printed warning not to add the yeast because it would convert the grapes into wine. But most of the vineyards were either abandoned or replanted to other agricultural products and the value of land plummeted.

With repeal on Dec. 5, 1933, a fragile industry began its revival in the midst of the Great Depression. Somehow Inglenook managed a spectacular 1933 Cabernet, no doubt produced with the full confidence that repeal would pass and become law. In the 1930s and 1940s the California wine industry began the long, arduous process of replanting vines, rebuilding wineries and reintroducing wine to a generally uninterested and unappreciative American populace. In many states strict regulations controlled the distribution of wine, and many counties remained "dry." In other states high taxes were imposed on wine.

Phylloxera and Prohibition had taken their toll in the vineyards. When André Tchelistcheff arrived in Napa Valley from France in 1937, he estimated that there were fewer than 100 acres of Cabernet grapes planted in Napa Valley; 60 acres is probably a more accurate figure. Tchelistcheff, then the winemaker for Beaulieu Vineyard, oversaw BV's 35 to 40 acres of Cabernet vines; Beringer and Inglenook also bottled Cabernet from small Napa Valley plantings, as did Larkmead and a few others. In 1936 La Questa Winery in Woodside, on the peninsula south of San Francisco, produced a Cabernet that on occasion has turned up for sale at auction. Louis M. Martini struggled to find Cabernet grapes and ended up buying the Monte Rosso vineyard in Sonoma Valley in 1937.

Demand for California Cabernet could hardly have been an incentive for vintners of the era. Beaulieu Vineyard's first bottling of Georges de Latour Private Reserve Cabernet 1936, which sold for around $1.50 in 1940, commanded the same price or less 15 years later.

Winemaking conditions were abhorrent, with widespread bacteriological, mold and spoilage problems affecting many wines. Vineyards were infected by diseases such as red leaf virus, which provided pretty splashes of red and orange grape leaves in the fall, but were in reality a sign that vines were seriously ill. Consumers of the era faced some hard choices as well; terribly flawed wines were commonplace. Dessert wines were infinitely more popular since sweetness concealed defects.

But a number of wineries were determined to succeed with winemaking and Cabernet in particular. By the mid-1940s Charles Krug Winery began making Cabernet each vintage, joining Inglenook, Martini, Beringer and Beaulieu. All were producing superb Cabernets that were comparable in quality and style, and they became California's first collectibles. Inglenook was the classic California château, making severe selections with its wine, aging Cabernet in 1,000-gallon oak casks and producing deep, rich, long-aging Cabernets from its estate vineyard in Rutherford. Beaulieu was the classic Bordeaux-style château, a beautiful estate with elegant, ageworthy Cabernets aged in small American oak. Louis M. Martini was the master blender, selecting lots of grapes from various districts and creating wines of great harmony through blending. Charles Krug Cabernets epitomized the full force and intensity of rich, ripe California Cabernet. Of the four it was the least elegant and refined, but it displayed the purest flavor of abundantly ripe grapes.

In the late 1940s and early 1950s, American servicemen and women returned from Europe and World War II with heightened interest in drinking wine and producing it. California's climate and "land of opportunity" promotions attracted refugees from the East Coast and Midwest. Among the newcomers were ethnic wine drinkers, fans of French, German, Spanish and Italian wines, which ensured a larger wine-drinking audience.

The viticultural and enological research carried on at the University of California at Davis and then Fresno State College raised the quality standards in both the vineyards and the wines, both of which improved significantly. Renewed efforts toward planting the right grapes in the proper soils and climates were undertaken during this era, although choice spots for Cabernet had already been staked out in the Oakville-Rutherford corridor of Napa Valley as well as in the hills and mountains throughout the North Coast. Increasingly California wines were cleaner, fresher, better balanced and more complex.

In 1959 a group of scientists began home winemaking on weekends in the Santa Cruz Mountains. Later they became more serious and formed Ridge Vineyards, bottling a wine with the estate vineyard, Monte Bello, on the label. In the 1960s the first new wave of vintners in Napa Valley joined the old guard; people such as Joe Heitz and Robert Mondavi came from within the ranks and established new wineries with their names on bottles of Cabernet that sold for $5 to $8, staggering price increases compared to the $3 to $4 price tags in years before. Later in the decade Chappellet Vineyard and Freemark Abbey opened for business, followed by Diamond Creek, Spring Mountain, Cuvaison and Sterling.

In the 1970s, the back-to-nature, back-to-the-land movement lured a number of wine fanciers to the business; wine as a lifestyle and investment opportunity appealed to others. In the early 1970s the wine boom exploded with new Cabernet producers such as Kenwood, Stags' Leap Winery, Burgess, Caymus, Clos Du Val, Franciscan, Mount Eden, Silver Oak Cellars, Stag's Leap Wine Cellars, Cakebread, Mount Veeder, Joseph Phelps and Stonegate. There were dozens more Cabernet aficionados that followed in the 1970s and on into the 1980s, spreading beyond Napa Valley into Sonoma Valley and Alexander Valley in Sonoma County.

While there were many winemaking advances and sensational vintages in the 1960s and 1970s, perhaps the single most important event took place at the Paris Tasting of 1976 in France. In both divisions, judged by esteemed French wine critics, California wines triumphed over their French counterparts. In the Cabernet-Bordeaux pairing, Stag's Leap Wine Cellars 1973 Cabernet, the winery's second vintage, placed first ahead of Château Mouton-Rothschild 1970, Château Haut-Brion 1970 and Château Montrose 1970. In fifth place was Ridge Monte Bello 1971, followed by Château Léoville-Las Cases 1971, Mayacamas 1971, Clos Du Val 1972, Heitz Martha's Vineyard 1970 and Freemark Abbey 1969. In 1986, a *Wine Spectator* re-creation of that tasting produced the following results, rankings beginning with the highest scoring wines: Heitz Martha's Vineyard 1970, Mayacamas 1971, Ridge Monte Bello 1971, Stag's Leap Wine Cellars 1973, Clos Du Val 1972, Montrose 1970, Mouton-Rothschild 1970, Léoville-Las Cases 1971, Freemark Abbey 1969 and Haut-Brion 1970. The most striking feature of that tasting was that the extra decade of bottle age had actually been kinder to the California Cabernets than the Bordeaux. In 1980, four years after the Paris tasting,

Baron Philippe de Rothschild, owner of Mouton-Rothschild, realized a dream to make wine in California, joining forces with Robert Mondavi to create Opus One, which applied both French and California winemaking technologies and styles to California Cabernet Sauvignon and marked the beginning of a new wave of foreign investment in California.

Today America's wine drinkers are keenly aware of the exceptionally high level of quality of California's Cabernets. More recently, California Cabernet has earned a reputation in the international wine community. It is not uncommon to compare and contrast California Cabernets with the finest Bordeaux reds. Moreover, a number of Bordeaux's leading vintners, including Christian Moueix of Château Pétrus, have found the California climate and soil so conducive to producing rich, complex, dramatic Cabernets, that they have invested in vineyards and now produce their own California Cabernet.

How do Cabernet and Bordeaux compare? All things considered, quite well. Although the soils, climates and winemaking techniques are different, the results are often close in quality. While the focus of this book is on California's great Cabernets, each year I evaluate scores of Bordeaux reds from current and older vintages. I have also participated in numerous blind tastings where California Cabernets were poured side by side with great Bordeaux, and frequently they are indistinguishable from each other. While comparative tastings are fun and can be instructive, the wines deserve to be evaluated and appreciated on their own merits. With the possible exception of the first growths of the Médoc and a Pomerol or two made from Merlot, the very finest California Cabernets are consistently close in quality with the classified-growth Bordeaux.

In the 1980s, one could make a case that California Cabernet and Bordeaux are closer in quality and style than ever before. In California, many wineries have moved away from 100 percent varietal wines, increasingly finding that Merlot and Cabernet Franc add elegance, finesse and complexity to the purer flavor of Cabernet. They have also moved away from varietal names, many preferring proprietary names like Insignia and Dominus. The use of new French oak barrels for aging wines is the industry standard.

Many new techniques for vine training have their genesis in Bordeaux, as do vinification practices such as extended grape-skin maceration during fermentation. Perhaps most significantly the exchange of ideas and techniques by California and Bordeaux winemakers has grown through joint ventures such as Opus One and Dominus and through the desire to improve the overall quality of wine.

On more than one occasion, I have heard famous winemakers from prestigious Bordeaux châteaux describe their 1982 vintage as "California" in style, an apparent reference to the richness and ripeness of the wines. The current vintages of Bordeaux are also more accessible, which may be the result of climatic conditions or a conscious effort to make the wines more palatable early on. Many of Bordeaux's finest winemakers credit the academic and technical expertise that they learned in California as being beneficial to the quality of their vineyards and wines. California vintners have always looked to Bordeaux for direction with Cabernet Sauvignon. Only in the past decade has the impact of the California wine industry begun to influence the great European wine centers. Today much of the knowledge and expertise in grape growing and winemaking technology originates in California. One hundred and fifty years after the first Cabernet vines from Bordeaux were planted in California, the pendulum of interest has begun to swing the other way.

CHAPTER II
THE VINEYARDS:
THE LAY OF THE LAND

C alifornia's winemaking pioneers knew exactly what they were doing when they began planting Cabernet Sauvignon. They recognized the importance of soil and climate in producing fine Bordeaux-style wines and early on identified the finest land for Cabernet Sauvignon vines.

Not surprisingly many of the original wineries founded in the 1800s were in ideal Cabernet country such as Napa Valley, Alexander Valley, Sonoma Valley and the Santa Cruz Mountains. A century after the first great Inglenook Clarets were produced in Rutherford, the heart of Napa Valley remains California's most celebrated Cabernet district. While Cabernet flourishes in each of those districts, where vineyards consistently yield deep, rich, complex and ageworthy wines, Napa Valley remains the heart of Cabernet country with its vast array of producers and concentration of superb vineyards. Napa Valley combines a strong sense of tradition with cutting-edge innovation and leadership. Several factors contribute to this identity, including Napa Valley's long history of excellence with Cabernet, the compact size of the valley and, most importantly, the accessibility of prime agricultural soil and climate, as well as winemakers who are willing to strive for perfection with their wines.

THE CLIMATE

The factors that led the early winemakers to Napa Valley and other Northern California appellations were undoubtedly the climate, soil and availability of land. The rich, fertile soils were perfect for rooting vigorous vines, as George Yount discovered in 1838. But unlike hotter regions in California, where winemaking experiments were being undertaken by Spanish missionaries and European immigrants, the climate in Napa Valley provided the ideal balance

CABERNET-BLEND GRAPES: ACRES BY COUNTY

County	Cabernet Sauvignon (acres)	Merlot (acres)	Cabernet Franc (acres)	Total Acres	Maximum Production* Cases
Napa	6,884	966	407	8,257	1,981,680
Sonoma	5,091	629	239	5,959	1,430,160
Monterey	2,746	267	65	3,078	738,720
San Luis Obispo	1,181	65	32	1,278	306,720
Mendocino	1,001	71	61	1,133	271,920
Subtotal	16,903	1,998	804	19,705	4,729,200
Other counties	5,485	655	97	6,237	1,496,880
Total	22,388	2,653	901	25,942	6,226,080

*Note: Calculation is based on four tons per acre and 60 cases per ton. Chart does not take into account varietal Merlot bottlings, which would take away from the total Cabernet Sauvignon production.
SOURCE: CALIFORNIA DEPARTMENT OF FOOD AND AGRICULTURE

between the warmth necessary to ripen the late-blooming Cabernet grape and the cool maritime influence of the Pacific Ocean and San Pablo Bay that allowed the grapes to mature slowly and evenly without overripening.

It is perhaps the climate more than the soil that has the greatest influence on the quality of Cabernet Sauvignon in Northern California. In comparison with Bordeaux, where the soils are widely diverse and somewhat meager, California's are rich and fertile. There are distinct variations in the soil types in California, just as there are differences in rootstocks, grape clones, vineyard practices, vinification techniques and oak barrels (heavy or light toast, French or American), but it is the Pacific Ocean to the west of California's coastal valleys that creates the milder, Mediterranean climate and protects the narrow valleys and mountaintops from the baking temperatures of the Central Valley. The Central Valley and Pacific Ocean work together in shaping the Northern California climate. As temperatures rise in the vast Central Valley, it creates a vacuum effect that pulls the cool, damp, foggy air from the brisk ocean waters. There are days when the Bay Area's natural air conditioner fails and the weather is scorching. Even on those sizzling summer afternoons, the temperature at night almost always drops to significantly cooler levels, providing temporary relief to the Cabernet vines.

The maritime climate is not exclusive to the counties of Napa and Sonoma, but extends southward to the Santa Cruz Mountains, where a similar proximity to the Pacific Ocean and San Francisco Bay ensure the regularity of cooling coastal breezes. If anything the Santa Cruz Mountains are cooler, and vines there struggle to ripen in mild years. The most dramatic presentation of how the Bay Area's air conditioning works can be experienced by standing on the Golden Gate Bridge on a summer afternoon when the cold fog whips in under the bridge from the coast and into the surrounding bay. Once you leave San Francisco for wine country the temperatures get progressively warmer. The farther north and inland you go the hotter the weather.

The principal appellations featured in this book — Napa Valley and its subappellations, Alexander Valley, Sonoma Valley and the Santa Cruz Mountains — have climates that are more alike than dissimilar. The North Coast valleys are narrow and framed by hills and moun-

GREAT CABERNET REGIONS

On the following pages are maps of the regions discussed in this chapter. Each map locates the wineries reviewed in this book, and the various estate and independent vineyards.

Briefly, the maps cover the following areas: Map 1: Yountville, Stags Leap, Mount Veeder; Map 2: Oakville, Rutherford; Map 3: St. Helena, Calistoga, Spring Mountain, Diamond Mountain, Howell Mountain; Map 4: Alexander Valley, Dry Creek Valley; Map 5: Sonoma Valley, Carneros; Map 6: Santa Cruz Mountains, Paso Robles.

MAP LEGEND

 Winery

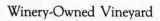 Independent Vineyard

Winery-Owned Vineyard

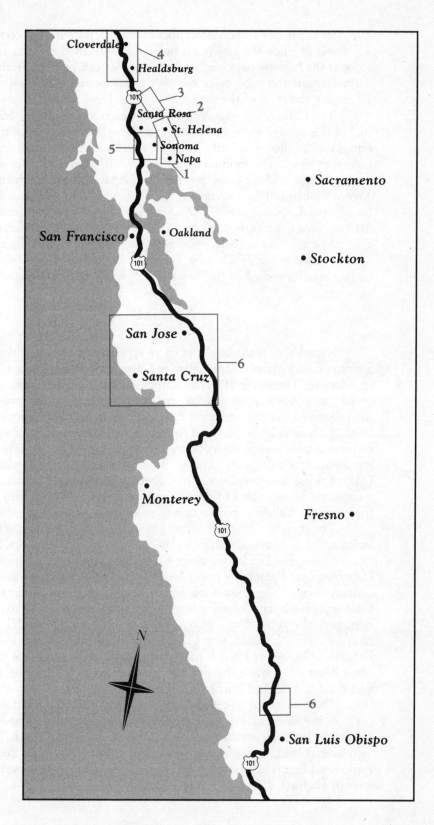

tains that rise several hundred feet above sea level, trapping the cool night air and then acting as funnels to guide the afternoon breezes inland. In the Santa Cruz Mountains, the folds between the hills are narrower, and the weather can be considerably cooler. The discussions of appellations and subappellations that follow concentrate on specific vineyards and estates that typify the style of the area.

The Cabernet Acreage chart shows the counties with the most Cabernet vines planted. Included is acreage for both Merlot and Cabernet Franc. What this chart shows is the maximum case production if all Cabernet, Merlot and Cabernet Franc grapes were made into Cabernet wines. The formula used for converting acres to cases assumes a conservative four tons per acre and 60 cases per ton. In Napa County, for instance, the total Cabernet/Merlot/Cabernet Franc average is 8,257. At four tons per acre, 33,028 tons of grapes could be harvested, resulting in 1,981,680 cases. Using the same formula, Sonoma County ranks behind Napa County, with a potential of 1,430,160 cases. California's leading Cabernet areas charted here have a capacity of more than 4.7 million cases. By comparison, the number of wines chosen is highly selective. For instance, the total number of cases from one vintage of the wines reviewed in this book was 519,477 in 1986 and 559,166 in 1985.

Napa Valley

Napa Valley is the largest of these appellations as well as the biggest Cabernet district; Sonoma County rivals Napa Valley in Cabernet acreage, but it is spread throughout several appellations. The whole of Napa County, except the outer limits near Lake Berryessa, is part of the Napa Valley appellation by law. In reality there are distinct climatic differences within the valley and the outlying areas of Pope Valley, Wooden Valley and Chiles Valley. But the heart of Napa Valley is the Napa River watershed, a slender valley framed by mountains that stretches 30 miles north from the city of Napa to Calistoga. At its broadest point near Oakville, it is about four miles wide. Roughly 31,000 acres are rooted to vines in Napa; approximately 7,000 of those acres are devoted to Cabernet and its sister grapes. If you use the formula for a conservative estimate of four tons per acre (280,000 tons) and 60 cases of wine per ton, the potential Cabernet production is more than 1.6 million cases.

The styles of Cabernet coming from the different subappellations are becoming more individualist as vineyards mature and winemakers refine their styles, but Napa Valley is nowhere near as diverse as Bordeaux, where the stylistic distinctions between Pauillac, dominated by Cabernet, and Pomerol, where Merlot is prevalent, are considerable. Within Napa Valley, Carneros-Napa Valley, Howell Mountain, Stags Leap District and Mount Veeder are viticultural areas approved by the federal government. A complex proposal to create four new subappellations from the valley floor is also under consideration by the U.S. Bureau of Alcohol, Tobacco and Firearms. It would create Oakville and Rutherford districts and, within those, an Oakville Bench and Rutherford Bench roughly extending from the Napa River west. If approved, the Napa River will provide the east-west split between the Oakville and Rutherford communes and the Oakville and Rutherford benches to the west.

The issue of the so-called Rutherford Bench is controversial. Advocates generally identify it as the vineyard area west of either Highway 29 or the Napa River and extending from Yountville to St. Helena. Critics disapprove of the word "bench," a specific geographic term for elevated land, and question whether a geographic bench exists. Historically the use of Rutherford Bench began in the mid-1970s when some writers used it to refer to the vineyards west of Highway 29.

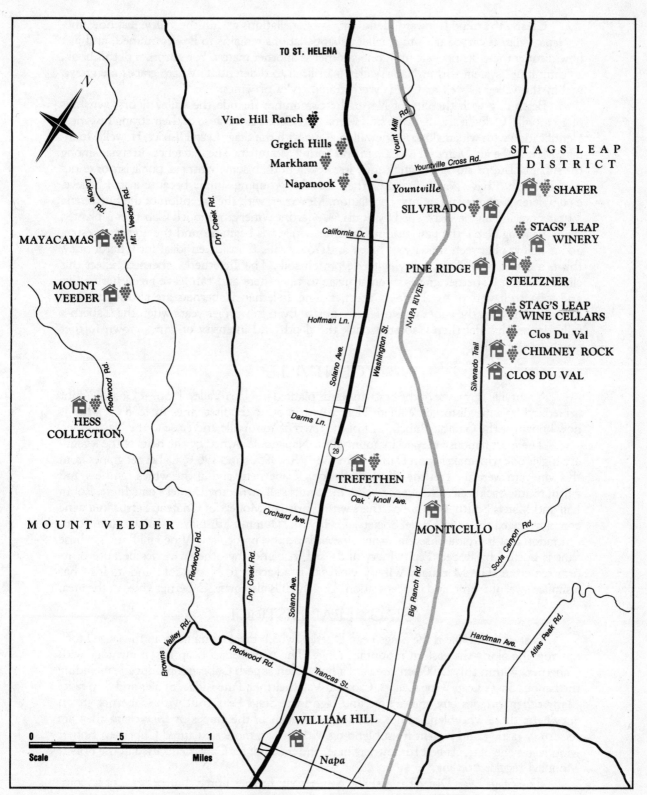

MAP 1: NAPA-YOUNTVILLE-STAGS LEAP

Clearly the trend is toward identifying subappellations within the valley. Just how finely Napa Valley is carved up into smaller subappellations remains to be determined, and just how distinct these districts are from one another is another matter. For purposes of this book, a "commune" system within Napa Valley is utilized to differentiate where grapes are grown within the valley as well as to analyze regional styles of wines.

Beginning with the city of Napa, the communes include the valley floor townships of Yountville, Oakville, Rutherford, St. Helena and Calistoga because of their strong historical identification with winemaking in the valley, along with the Stags Leap District, Howell Mountain, Mount Veeder, Diamond Mountain and Spring Mountain. The differences in styles among the subappellations are often significantly less apparent than some vintners, publicists or critics might preach. I have not included Carneros in this grouping simply because it is, I believe, a completely separate and unique appellation. Moreover, with the exception of the fine Buena Vista estate and a vineyard owned by Louis M. Martini Winery, not much Cabernet is planted there. Leaving Napa, the first serious Cabernet vineyards begin around the Trefethen estate about halfway between the city of Napa and Yountville. Considered ideal for Chardonnay, this is a cooler part of the valley, with deep, rich soils. The Trefethen Cabernets reflect this climatic effect; Cabernet grapes often struggle to ripen here and can leave green herb, olive and tobacco flavors of barely ripe Cabernet. The Trefethen Cabernets are also lighter and more elegant than the wines grown farther north. Even in warmer years when the Cabernet fully ripens, the Trefethen Cabernets lack the depth and intensity of wines grown further north in the valley.

YOUNTVILLE

Yountville is the site of the first vineyards planted in Napa Valley. Pioneer George Yount is credited by wine historian William Heintz with rooting the first vines in 1838 on what is now known as the Gamble Ranch, east of the town of Yountville and close to the Napa River.

The most famous vineyard in Yountville is Napanook, owned by the heirs of the legendary Inglenook winemaker John Daniel Jr. In the 1940s, 1950s and 1960s, Cabernet grapes from this vineyard were used in the classic Inglenook Cabernets, giving the wines richness and a firm tannic backbone. The Napanook Vineyard is still owned by Daniel's daughters, Robin Lail and Marcia Smith, who are partners with Christian Moueix of Château Pétrus in a wine company called the John Daniel Society. Their wine, Dominus, displays the rich, tannic concentration that is typical of several other vineyards nearby, particularly Vine Hill Ranch, whose fruit is bottled by Robert Pepi winery and used in blends by other wineries because of its firm structure. The Markham Winery vineyard is adjacent to Napanook, and its fruit has a similar level of tannin and concentration. Grgich Hills also owns Cabernet vines in the area.

STAGS LEAP DISTRICT

East of Yountville is the Stags Leap District, which takes its name from the jagged rock outcropping along the eastern mountain range. The name Stags Leap is synonymous with Cabernet. Within this 2,700-acre area are a half dozen superb Cabernet producers, including the famous Stag's Leap Wine Cellars, Clos Du Val, Steltzner, Pine Ridge, Shafer and Silverado. Many other wineries buy grapes here and blend the Stags Leap fruit with Cabernet grown elsewhere; those who blend either cannot get enough of the grapes or they claim they are too fruity tasting and benefit from blending with firmer, more structured Cabernet. Robert Mondavi is one of the largest landowners here, and much of his Cabernet is used in the Robert Mondavi regular bottling.

The Stags Leap District is a shade cooler than further north, but because of its loca-

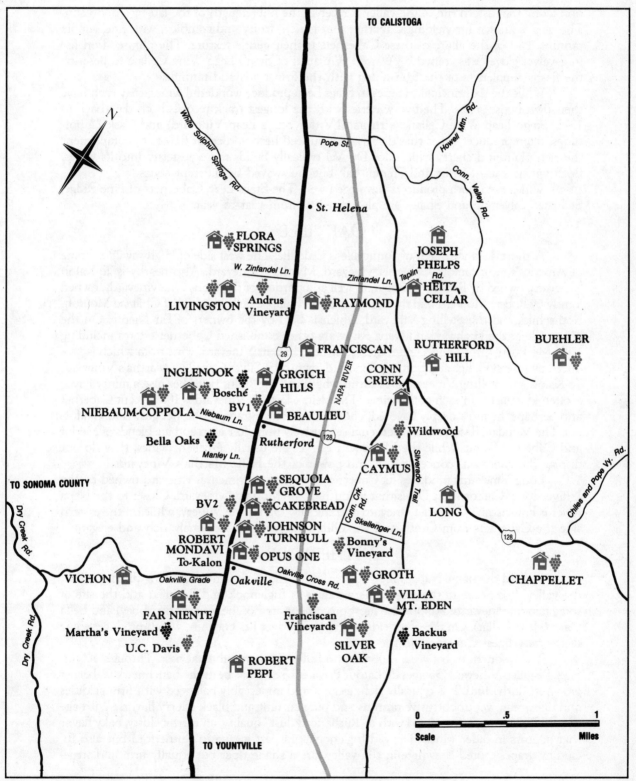

TO CALISTOGA

White Sulphur Springs Rd.

Pope St.

Howell Mtn. Rd.

Conn. Valley Rd.

• St. Helena

FLORA
SPRINGS

JOSEPH
PHELPS
Rd.

W. Zinfandel Ln.

Zinfandel Ln.

Taplin

HEITZ
CELLAR

LIVINGSTON   Andrus
Vineyard   RAYMOND

BUEHLER

29   FRANCISCAN

RUTHERFORD
HILL

INGLENOOK   GRGICH
HILLS

CONN
CREEK

Bosché

BV1

NIEBAUM-COPPOLA   Niebaum Ln.   BEAULIEU

NAPA RIVER

Wildwood

Bella Oaks

Rutherford   128

Manley Ln.

CAYMUS

Silverado Trail

Chiles and Pope Vy. Rd.

TO SONOMA COUNTY

Dry Creek Rd.

SEQUOIA
GROVE

BV2   CAKEBREAD

Conn. Crk. Rd.

Skellenger Ln.

LONG

JOHNSON
TURNBULL

ROBERT
MONDAVI   OPUS ONE

Bonny's
Vineyard

128

To-Kalon

VICHON

Oakville Grade   Oakville   Oakville Cross Rd.

GROTH

CHAPPELLET

FAR NIENTE

VILLA
MT. EDEN

Dry Creek Rd.

Martha's Vineyard
U.C. Davis

Franciscan
Vineyards

Backus
Vineyard

ROBERT
PEPI

SILVER
OAK

TO YOUNTVILLE

0   .5   1

Scale   Miles

MAP 2: OAKVILLE-RUTHERFORD

tion along the eastern rim of the valley it receives the full strength of the late-afternoon sun. The area is known for yielding Cabernet that is rich, fruity and complex, with fine, supple tannins. Part of the allure of these Cabernets is their gentle texture. The phrase "iron fist in a velvet glove" was coined by Warren Winiarski of Stag's Leap Wine Cellars to describe the fleshy suppleness of the fruit along with the firm acids and tannins.

While the six principal wineries in Stags Leap produce wonderful wines, they each have their own house styles. The two wineries with the longest track records both date back to 1972. Stag's Leap Wine Cellars, with its SLV (for Stag's Leap Vineyard) and Cask 23 bottlings, often produces wines that display pronounced herb and cedar flavors to complement the rich plum and cherry fruit. Clos Du Val typically builds more austerity into its wines. Both wineries use Merlot and French oak but are swayed by different styles.

Wines from both producers have aged well. The Stags Leap Cabernets of Pine Ridge, Steltzner, Silverado and Shafer are also excellent from year to year.

OAKVILLE

A short distance north of Yountville is Oakville. The west side of Highway 29 is home of America's most famous Cabernet vineyard, Martha's Vineyard. Also nearby is To-Kalon Vineyard, owned by Robert Mondavi, as well as a portion of the Opus One vineyards, owned jointly by Robert Mondavi and the family of Baron Philippe de Rothschild of Château Mouton-Rothschild, and the Stelling Vineyard, which is held by the owners of Far Niente. On the other side of the Highway and Napa River are other established Cabernet estates including Villa Mt. Eden, Groth and Girard, along with the Backus Vineyard, wine from which is produced by Joseph Phelps and Bonny's Vineyard, owned by Silver Oak. The Martha's Vineyard, To-Kalon and Stelling Vineyard area forms what I call the "mint belt," because a minty flavor is often identifiable in each of the wines. The Heitz Martha's Vineyard is 100 percent Cabernet and perhaps the most deeply flavored, enormously concentrated Cabernet grown in California. The Mondavi Reserve Cabernets come exclusively from To-Kalon and are blends of Merlot and Cabernet Franc. While the Mondavi Reserves are usually excellent wines, they do not display the enormous concentration and power of the Heitz Martha's Vineyards.

Long Vineyards produces its Cabernet from an experimental vineyard owned by the University of California at Davis that is south of the Mondavi vineyard. Closer to the Napa River is Franciscan's Cabernet vineyard and the new Opus One Winery, while on the eastern side the Cabernets from Groth and the Girard Reserves are extremely rich and elegant.

RUTHERFORD

Beyond the name Napa Valley, Rutherford is the most famous growing district within the valley. It is home to the great winery estates of Inglenook and Beaulieu and the site of some famous vineyards. Among the most prominent are Bosché (Freemark Abbey) and Bella Oaks (Heitz Cellar). On the other side of the Napa River lies Caymus, which produces some of the very finest Cabernets in the state.

The distinctions between Oakville and Rutherford are subtle at best. Through 50 vintages Beaulieu Vineyard Georges de Latour Private Reserve has been the benchmark Cabernet grown in Rutherford. It is typically rich, elegant and impeccably balanced with firm acidities and tight, lean, yet unobtrusive tannins and pure currant and black cherry flavors. With age the old BVs are often associated with a "Rutherford dust" quality, an earthy, dusty, oaky flavor that appears in older wines. The old Inglenooks, in part grown in Rutherford but also including grapes rooted elsewhere in the valley, are a shade riper but equally firm and struc-

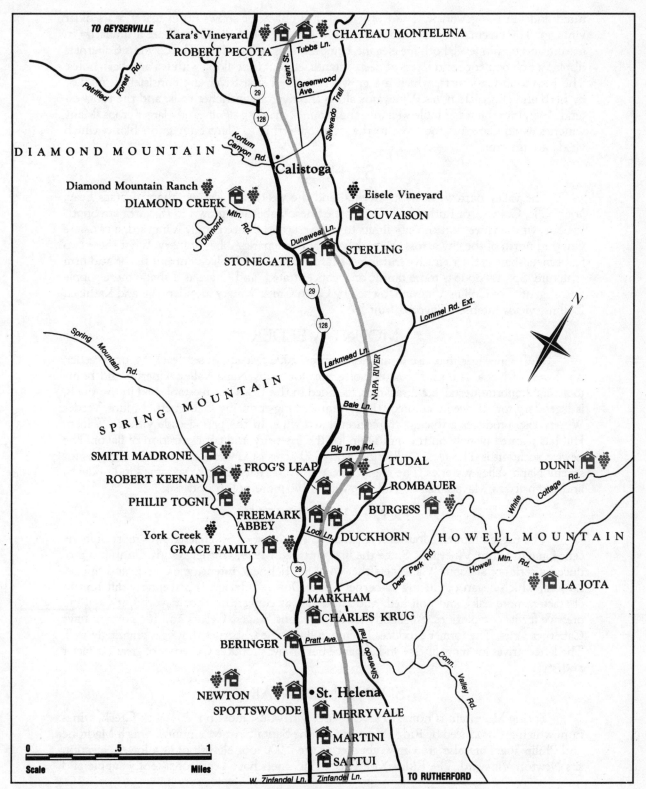

MAP 3: CALISTOGA-ST. HELENA

tured and just as ageworthy. The Rutherford dust character shows up in many of its older vintages. The Freemark Abbey Cabernet Bosché and Heitz Bella Oaks share a similarity in texture and tannin level; both are elegant, complex, long-aging wines. The Caymus Cabernets display a rich opulence and layers of deep, intense, elegant fruit along with tea and herb notes. The Raymond Cabernets, which are grown near the Napa River, are consistently marked by herb and chocolate notes. Vineyards along the river are in richer soils, and the roots extend down into the water table well into the summer, yielding significantly larger crops. Many wineries avoid Cabernet too close to the river, preferring to plant Sauvignon Blanc, which yields a large crop.

ST. HELENA

The valley narrows near St. Helena, and the weather is warmer than in Stags Leap, Yountville, Oakville or Rutherford. Two of the finest Cabernets grown in this area are Spottswoode, whose vines skirt the city limits to the west, and Grace Family Vineyard, a two-acre vineyard north of the city across the highway from Freemark Abbey Winery. What these two Cabernets share is their effusive fruitiness, sharply defined rich black currant flavor and firm structure. Spottswoode is more tannic and concentrated, and Grace is a shade more supple and elegant. The Collins Vineyard, owned by Conn Creek Winery founders Bill and Kathleen Collins, yields intensely flavored fruit.

MOUNT VEEDER

With vineyards that rise to an elevation of 2,000 feet above sea level, Mount Veeder, northwest of Napa, is both the source of grapes for many Napa Valley wineries and home to several important estates. Mayacamas, founded in the 1800s but reestablished in the 1950s, is legendary for its deeply colored, richly tannic, long-enduring Cabernets. Mount Veeder Winery also produces a thick, rich, concentrated wine. In the past decade vintner William Hill has planted heavily on the mountain for the intensity and concentration of flavor. The newest addition is The Hess Collection, with 130 acres of Cabernet, a source of grapes for several Napa Valley wineries. The Hess Collection Cabernets display the same kind of depth and intensity as Mayacamas or Hill but with a bit more polish and oak.

HOWELL MOUNTAIN

The rugged Howell Mountain appellation northeast of St. Helena owes most of its recent fame to Dunn Vineyards. Since the first vintage in 1979, vintner Randy Dunn has produced a series of awesome Cabernets that combine richness, intensity, elegance and finesse. La Jota, which began producing Cabernet under Dunn's tutelage, is perceptibly different in character, more oaky and polished, and while not as concentrated or flavorful, it's still impressive for its complexities. At slightly lower elevations Burgess Cellars and Ric Forman have Cabernet vines. The former produces intense, full-throttle Cabernet that ages amazingly well. The latter strives for more finesse and elegance but always produces Cabernet of great character and style.

SPRING MOUNTAIN

Spring Mountain is home to several large vineyards, most notably York Creek, wines from which are produced by Ridge Vineyards in the Santa Cruz Mountains. Smith Madrone and Philip Togni are also growing Cabernet at the 2,000-foot elevation; at a lower elevation sits Newton Vineyard. The Ridge York Creek Cabernets have been consistently supple and

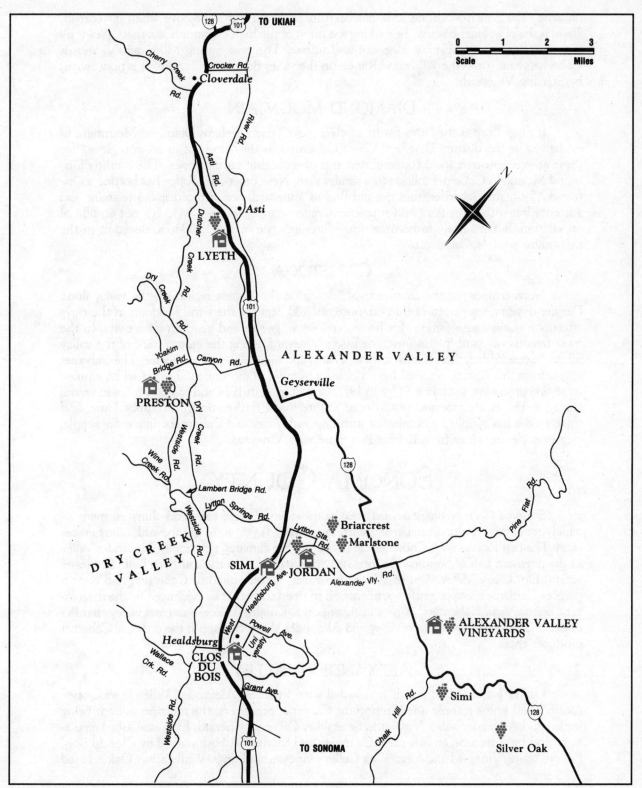

MAP 4: ALEXANDER AND DRY CREEK VALLEYS

pleasing. The Smith-Madrone style has been inconsistent but impressive when it's correct. Togni is the newcomer but may be making the finest of the high-elevation Cabernets. Newton's Cabernet features complexity, elegance and finesse. The best Spring Mountain Vineyards Cabernets came from the Wildwood Ranch on the valley floor near Caymus. It is now owned by Sterling Vineyards.

DIAMOND MOUNTAIN

If Stags Leap is the "iron fist in a velvet glove," then perhaps Diamond Mountain, as evidenced by the distinct Diamond Creek Cabernets, is the "steel fist in an iron glove," for these are very austere, lean, concentrated and often highly tannic wines. The Sterling Diamond Mountain Cabernet follows in a similar vein. Newcomer Pine Ridge has bottled a Diamond Mountain Cabernet from the old Roddis Vineyard, and it too displays restraint and austerity but with more flesh and suppleness, reflecting Pine Ridge's style. It's not an official appellation, but it's likely to become one. Vineyards rise to the 1,500-foot elevation in the mountains west of Calistoga.

CALISTOGA

Northernmost of the communes, Calistoga is the hottest region on the valley floor. Despite daytime temperatures that often exceed 100 degrees, the wind kicks up in the early afternoon. Calistoga is famous for its mineral water, geyser and geothermal activity. In the most famous vineyard in this area, the Eisele Vineyard, along the eastern side of the valley off the Silverado Trail, there is often a distinct earth and mineral flavor in the wine. The Cabernet grapes from this 40-acre vineyard have yielded a number of monumental wines when vinified by several producers, including Ridge in 1971, Conn Creek in 1974 and Joseph Phelps in several vintages. The estate vineyard of Château Montelena is farther north off Tubbs Lane, and since 1978 it has supplied a number of stunning, richly flavored Cabernets. In a more supple, elegant style are wines from Robert Pecota's Kara's Vineyard.

SONOMA COUNTY

Sonoma County has vineyard areas with widely diverse soils and climates, many of which are approved viticultural areas. With more than 31,000 acres in vineyard, many grapes excel. The best locations for Cabernet are in the warmer climates, principally Alexander Valley in the northern half of Sonoma County and Sonoma Valley in the southern half. To a lesser extent, Dry Creek Valley, west of Alexander Valley, is well suited to Cabernet, and certain parts of Carneros are apparently warm enough to ripen Cabernet as evidenced by the magnificent Buena Vista Cabernets. A promising region is Knights Valley, a narrow valley that lies north of Calistoga between Napa Valley and Alexander Valley. Beringer is the principal Cabernet producer there.

ALEXANDER VALLEY

Unlike Napa Valley, which is crowded with wineries, Alexander Valley is wide-open country and home to only a few important Cabernet producers, the most prominent being Jordan and Alexander Valley Vineyards. Several key Cabernet vineyards have established reputations and track records, among them Briarcrest and Marlstone, both owned by Clos du Bois, Robert Young Vineyard and Silver Oak Cellar's vineyard holdings. While Silver Oak is based

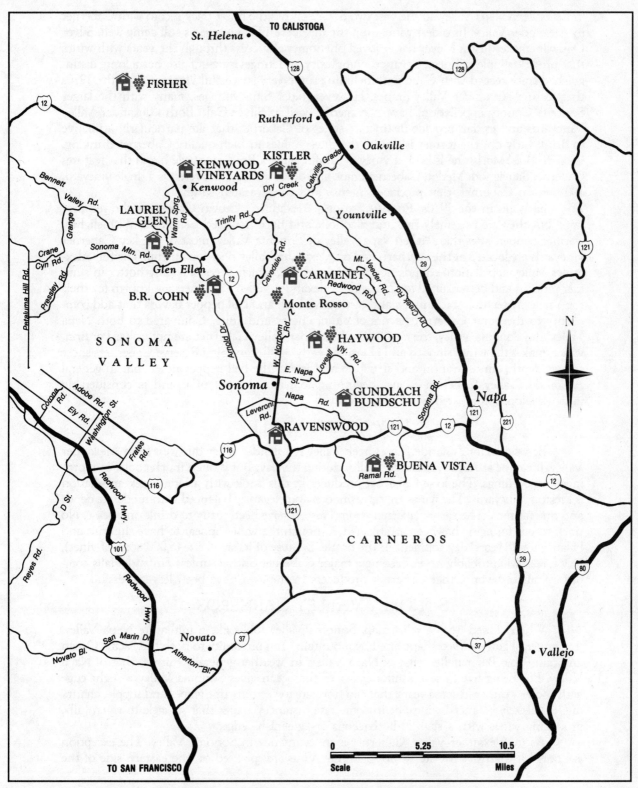

TO CALISTOGA

St. Helena

128

128

FISHER

12

Rutherford

Oakville

121

KENWOOD VINEYARDS
Kenwood

KISTLER

Dry Creek

Oakville Grade

Bennett

Valley Rd.

Grange

LAUREL GLEN

Warm Sprg. Rd.

Trinity Rd.

Yountville

Crane Cyn Rd.

Sonoma Mtn. Rd.

Glen Ellen

Pressley Rd.

12

Cavedale Rd.

CARMENET

Redwood Rd.

Mt. Veeder Rd.

29

B.R. COHN

Arnold Dr.

Monte Rosso

Dry Creek Rd.

N

Petaluma Hill Rd.

SONOMA
VALLEY

W. Napa Rd.

HAYWOOD

Lovell Vly. Rd.

E. Napa St.

Sonoma

Napa Rd.

GUNDLACH BUNDSCHU

Sonoma Rd.

Napa

121

221

Corona Rd.

Adobe Rd.

Ely Rd.

Washington St.

Frates Rd.

Leveroni Rd.

RAVENSWOOD

121

12

116

D St.

BUENA VISTA
Ramal Rd.

101

116

121

Reyes Rd.

Redwood Hwy.

CARNEROS

29

80

San Marin Dr.

Novato

37

37

Vallejo

Novato Bl.

Atherton Bl.

TO SAN FRANCISCO

0   5.25   10.5

Scale   Miles

MAP 5: SONOMA VALLEY-CARNEROS

in Oakville in Napa Valley, in the past two decades it has the finest track record with Cabernet in Alexander Valley. Its oldest wine, from the mediocre 1972 vintage, is still aging well. Silver Oak winemaker Justin Meyer has enjoyed phenomenal success through the years with wines that provide supple richness, elegance, complexity and longevity. Simi also has a long, distinguished track record with Cabernet, including some very successful vintages from the 1970s that feature Alexander Valley grapes. However, older Simi vintages, many with the larger Sonoma County appellation, have not aged as well as Silver Oak. Both Alexander Valley Vineyards and Jordan provide distinctive styles of Cabernet that are particularly attractive to drink early on; the former is one of the finest values in high-quality Cabernet drinking. Clos du Bois' Marlstone is both a vineyard and a wine, a Bordeaux-style blend that features Cabernet Sauvignon, Merlot, Cabernet Franc and other varieties. Briarcrest is a single vineyard, 100 percent Cabernet, that produces intense and concentrated wines.

Early on in the 1970s, Rodney Strong's Alexander's Crown Cabernets showed promise, but they are extremely ripe and alcoholic and have not aged well at all. With slightly warmer temperatures than either Napa Valley or Sonoma Valley, most of the key Cabernet vineyards are located at the southern end of Alexander Valley near Chalk Hill. The full Alexander Valley appellation extends north to Cloverdale, which is considerably hotter in summer months and better suited for Zinfandel. Alexander Valley Cabernets are known for their round, fleshy texture, soft tannins and distinctive herb and bell pepper flavors that add complexity to the purer Cabernet flavors of plum, cherry and anise. Compared to both Napa Valley and Sonoma Valley, the tannins in Alexander Valley Cabernet are not as hard or firm, which makes the wines smooth and charming early on. Recent Simi Reserve Cabernets show greater depth, concentration and structure and less of the bell pepper notes, but in general Alexander Valley Cabernet is just beginning to realize its potential and is considerably underdeveloped compared with Napa Valley.

DRY CREEK VALLEY

Best suited for Zinfandel, Dry Creek Valley is a slender valley due west from Alexander Valley. It can be as hot as Alexander Valley during the days but is often much cooler in mornings and evenings. The lone Cabernet producer in this book with a Dry Creek appellation is Preston Vineyards. The wines are ripe, smooth and elegantly balanced with moderate depth and fine tannins. The early Cabernets from Preston have been ready to drink on release. No track record for aging has been established, although the wines appear to have the fruit and balance for 10 years' development in the bottle. Because of its small size (6,000 acres of vines), Dry Creek will probably never become a major Cabernet district, unless Zinfandel falls completely out of favor. Other Cabernet producers in the area have been less successful.

SONOMA VALLEY-CARNEROS

When viewed from a relief map, Sonoma Valley looks like a miniature Napa Valley. Its slender, slightly curved shape lined by mountains and proximity to both the Pacific Ocean and San Pablo Bay parallels that of Napa Valley. Its weather generally mirrors that of Napa Valley. But being five to seven miles closer to the ocean gives Sonoma Valley a slight edge with cooler weather in some years; that can translate to perfectly ripe grapes and supple, charming, exquisitely balanced wines, or in some rare instances grapes that struggle to ripen fully, producing wines with a slightly herbaceous or "greenish" edge.

As in Alexander Valley, Cabernet is in its infancy in Sonoma Valley. The exception is Louis M. Martini's Monte Rosso Cabernet Vineyard, planted on the eastern side of the

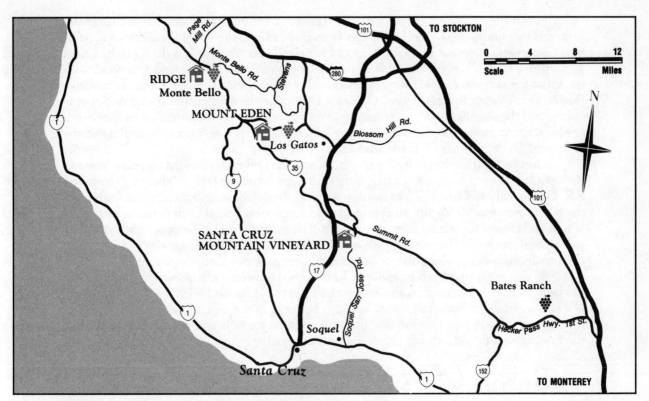

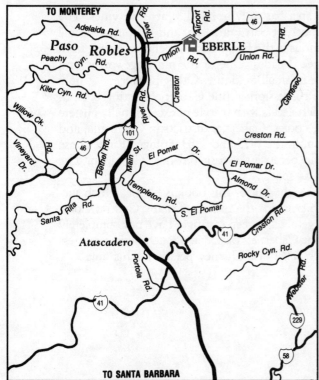

MAP 6: SANTA CRUZ MOUNTAINS-SOUTH

valley in the late 1930s. For most of the 50 years the Martinis have been harvesting grapes from this mountainside vineyard they have been blended into the Martini California appellation Cabernets. In recent vintages, a special Monte Rosso bottling has distinguished itself as Martini's finest. Buena Vista, California's oldest commercial winery, and Kenwood, with its Artist Series, have excelled with Sonoma Valley grapes since the late 1970s. Technically, Buena Vista's estate lies in the cool Carneros District at the southernmost end of Sonoma Valley, and the elegance and concentration of its Private Reserve (earlier called Special Selection) Cabernets makes you wonder why more wineries don't try Cabernet in what has become known as Pinot Noir and Chardonnay country.

Gundlach Bundschu, culling grapes from both Batto Ranch vineyard and now its estate Rhinefarm Vineyard, has a decade of history with Sonoma Valley fruit. Midway up the valley, B.R. Cohn, with its Olive Hill Vineyard, is making absolutely stunning Cabernets, while up the hill on Sonoma Mountain, an approved viticultural area, Laurel Glen makes astonishingly rich and elegant Cabernets from an eastward-facing slope. Across the valley and next door to Monte Rosso is the Carmenet estate, which is yielding rich, tannic, ageworthy Cabernets; a short distance north along the same mountain range is the Kistler estate; both the 1985 and 1986 Cabernets have been exceptional. Ravenswood is based south of Sonoma and recently has been focusing more on Sonoma Valley; the Pickberry Vineyard is on Sonoma Mountain and is superior to the Sonoma County bottlings before it. In the hills above the city of Sonoma is Haywood Winery's estate vineyard; the style so far is for rich and tannic Cabernets, but the first vintage in 1980 shows promise with each tasting.

SANTA CRUZ MOUNTAINS AND SOUTH

The Santa Cruz Mountains viticultural area has only about 100 acres in vines. The rugged terrain lies west of San Jose, 50 miles south of San Francisco, and is home to some superb Cabernet vineyards. By far the most famous is the Ridge Monte Bello vineyard, from which Ridge has been producing wines for three decades. One of the most ageworthy and complex of all California Cabernets, it is made in small amounts. Other producers of note from this region are Mount Eden, which has a succession of fine Cabernets dating back to 1972, and Santa Cruz Mountain Vineyard, which excels with a style of exceptionally austere Cabernet from the Bates Ranch. It is one of the coolest Cabernet districts in California, and in one out of five vintages the grapes barely ripen. In the 1979 and 1983 vintages, Ridge chose not to bottle a vineyard-designated Monte Bello because the fruit did not fully ripen. The quality of wines from the region as a whole was spotty.

The lone Cabernet from south of Monterey chosen for this book is Eberle, which succeeds with ripe, balanced, flavorful Cabernet that avoids the pitfalls of many Central Coast and South Central Coast Cabernets that are vegetal and green tasting. I have not completely given up on Monterey County either, but so far the Cabernets display too much herbaceousness and dense vegetal flavors to persuade me. Both Jekel and Durney persist in this area.

CHAPTER III
THE VINTAGES: 1933 TO 1988

With the recent succession of exquisite vintages from 1984 through 1987, California winemakers and Cabernet fanciers are enjoying an embarrassment of riches. At no other time in modern history have so many sensational vintages and so many superlative Cabernets been available on the market. Consumers should have a field day stocking up on the delicious 1984, 1985 and 1986 vintages, most of which are either currently available or will be released soon. The 1987 vintage, and to a lesser degree the 1988 vintage, also hold great promise for the immediate future.

This chapter is a summary guide to California Cabernet vintages from 1933 to 1988, with ratings based on *The Wine Spectator* 100-point scale. In the text that follows, a summary of each vintage covers the highlights and weather conditions, along with "price trends," wines selected as barometers of where prices are headed. A listing of all wines tasted for this book arranged by vintage can be found in Appendix 3 at the rear of this book. Appendix 4 contains a vintage chart for Cabernet, and Appendix 5 ranks all 55 vintages covered in this book in order of their ratings, best to worst.

A vintage overview is one of the fundamental tools in determining whether to buy the wines from that year. Weather patterns have the greatest single impact on influencing the style and character of wines. While California has a reputation for uniformly fine weather, the quality and style for each vintage varies significantly. In cold, rainy vintages, the wines can be diluted. When it's extremely hot, wines take on a ripe, fruity, sometimes raisiny quality. Knowing what the weather was like, both during the growing season and harvest, is critical in assessing the quality of a vintage year.

Collectors concentrate on great vintages like 1974, 1978, 1984, 1985 and 1986, for these are the wines that develop in the bottle and show the greatest appreciation in quality and price. Vintage summaries are just that; in sensational years, poor wines can be made, and in fair years great wines are often made. In this section, the vintages have been divided into six categories:

Classic   *(95-100 points)*
Excellent   *(90-94)*
Very Good *(80-89)*
Good   *(70-79)*
Fair   *(60-69)*
Poor   *(50-59)*

In rating the vintages, I have relied both on my own tasting experience, which is strong in the years 1966 through 1988, and on informed opinions from winemakers and collectors; virtually all of the wines reviewed in this book have been tasted within the past year. I have tasted dozens of Cabernets from the years 1933 to 1965, but I am too young to have known these wines in their youth. I have therefore attributed part of my rating to those who grew grapes and made wines in those eras, like André Tchelistcheff and Robert Mondavi as well as to skilled collectors such as Bernard Rhodes. Comments on vintages prior to 1970 relate primarily to Napa Valley. The overall rating given a vintage applies to all Cabernets produced that year and is not limited to the wines reviewed in this book.

One of the fascinating aspects of collecting and drinking Cabernets from different vintages is to learn how they develop, when they exceed expectations and when they fail. Anyone who has spent even a small amount of time analyzing wines such as Cabernet knows how often one can be surprised by a wine that was written off years ago or disappointed by a wine laid down in the cellar as a sure thing. Tchelistcheff once described his amazement with the 1948 Beaulieu Vineyard Private Reserve bottling this way:

> "This vintage may well be described as the unpredictable miracle of the century. Extremely cold growing temperatures delayed the harvest until late October. At first the wine showed no promise. Then, suddenly, after five years of bottle aging, it radically changed its individual aging ability and created an outstanding wine with a very light body, high fragrance and outstanding smoothness."

In each of the vintage summaries, I have generalized about when the wines should be drunk or how well or long they should age. These are estimates based on my own experience; more detailed analysis of each wine is included with the specific tasting notes in each winery's profile (see Chapter VI). Vintages older than 1966, in general, should be fully mature and consumed. Most of the Cabernets from the late 1970s are largely unavailable, and Cabernets from 1933 to 1966 are very rare. Vintage summaries for those years are provided as a context for which to evaluate and compare the current vintages. And now, the vintages:

1988: VERY GOOD (85)
SMALL CROP, UNEVEN QUALITY, SOME TRIUMPHS

The early line on 1988 is that it will not live up to the exceptionally high standards of its four predecessors. Skepticism about quality revolves around uneven grape sets (when grape clusters form), and ripening for both Cabernet and Merlot, coupled with a crop of below-average size. Because of that, vintners expect the wines to vary greatly in quality. A warm but not too hot growing season allowed grapes to ripen fully without getting overripe. That may translate into many very good to excellent wines and a few sensational ones, particularly among wineries that rigorously select their best lots for their finest bottlings. Based on limited barrel samplings, the 1988s showed fine balance, good, deep colors, lean, tight structure and firm but not heavy tannins. With a small crop for the second consecutive vintage and production off by 15 percent to 25 percent, prices may well hover in the range of the 1986 and 1987 vintages. Handicapping a vintage this early on is risky, but for now the 1988s don't appear to be long agers. This vintage, however, may fall into the sleeper category and surprise many with some charming wines and a few sensational bottlings. Consumers will have to shop carefully.

Price Trends: Expect 1988s to rival 1987s in price.

1987: EXCELLENT (92)
DEEP, CONCENTRATED, TANNIC, AGEWORTHY

A short crop of exceptional quality, the 1987 Cabernets in barrel tastings show a great concentration and depth of fruit, ripe, rich, complex, pure Cabernet flavors and firm tannins that promise a long life. What sets the 1987s apart from most recent Cabernet vintages is the unusually high level of thick tannins. Behind the 1987s' tannic veneer is an abundance of ripe, complex, full-bodied fruit flavors that are extremely concentrated and appear to have the aging potential for 15 to 20 years. A sharply reduced Merlot crop contributes to the firmness of these wines as well as tonnage being off by 20 percent to 40 percent in most vineyards. Climatic conditions in spring and early summer contributed to the smaller crop by reducing the size of clusters, resulting in uncommonly small, concentrated berries. The best wines of the vintage appears to come from the heart and hills of Napa Valley, where the wines early on showed better than those from the Stags Leap District, Sonoma Valley, Alexander Valley or the Santa Cruz Mountains. Because of the short crop and extremely high quality, prices for 1987s may well exceed those of the 1985 and 1986 vintages.

Below is a list of the 1987 barrel tasting results for the producers profiled in this book, listed by rating. (These wines are also included in Appendix 3: All Wines Tasted by Vintage.)

CLASSIC (95-100)

Beringer Vineyards Private Reserve, Grace Family Vineyard, Grgich Hills Cellars, Robert Keenan Winery, Spottswoode Winery, Sterling Vineyards Reserve

EXCELLENT (90-94)

Beaulieu Vineyard Private Reserve, Beringer Vineyards Chabot Vineyard, Buehler Vineyards, Carmenet Vineyard, Caymus Vineyards Estate, Château Montelena Winery, Conn Creek Winery, Conn Creek Winery Private Reserve, Diamond Creek Vineyards Gravelly Meadow, Diamond Creek Vineyards Red Rock Terrace, Dominus Estate, Dunn Vineyards Howell Mountain, Dunn Vineyards Napa Valley, Far Niente Winery, Flora Springs, Girard Winery, Girard Winery Reserve, Groth Vineyards and Winery, Hess Collection Winery Estate, William Hill Winery Reserve, Inglenook-Napa Valley Reserve Cask, Iron Horse Vineyards, Johnson Turnbull Vineyards Vineyard Selection 67, La Jota Wine Co., Laurel Glen Vineyard, Livingston Vineyards, Louis M. Martini Winery Monte Rosso, Robert Mondavi Winery Reserve, Newton Vineyard, Pine Ridge Winery Rutherford Cuvée, Ravenswood Sonoma County, Santa Cruz Mountain Vineyard Bates Ranch, Silverado Vineyards, Simi Winery Reserve, Stag's Leap

Wine Cellars Cask 23, Trefethen Vineyards Reserve, Vichon Winery SLD, Villa Mt. Eden Winery

VERY GOOD (80-89)

Chappellet Vineyard, Chimney Rock Wine Cellars, Clos Du Val Estate, Diamond Creek Vineyards Volcanic Hill, Duckhorn Vineyards, Fisher Vineyards Coach Insignia, Franciscan Vineyards Meritage, Gundlach Bundschu Winery, Haywood Winery, Johnson Turnbull Vineyards, Lakespring Winery, Monticello Cellars Reserve, Mount Eden Vineyards, Robert Pecota Winery Kara's Vineyard, Joseph Phelps Vineyards Backus Vineyard, Joseph Phelps Vineyards Eisele Vineyard, Pine Ridge Winery Diamond Mountain, Pine Ridge Winery Andrus Reserve, Pine Ridge Winery Pine Ridge Stags Leap Vineyard, Ridge Vineyards Monte Bello, Shafer Vineyards Hillside Select, Stag's Leap Wine Cellars SLV, Steltzner Vineyards, Sterling Vineyards Diamond Mountain Ranch

Price Trends: Similar to 1986 because of reduced quantity.

1986: CLASSIC (95)
FIRM, RICH, STRUCTURED, GREAT DEPTH

1986 ranks as one of the greatest vintages in California history. The superb Cabernets produced in this vintage place it in the same class as 1968, 1970 and 1985 and a shade above 1974, 1978, 1979 and 1984. The 1986s are deep, sharply focused, richly flavored wines that have the concentration and balance for midterm to long-term aging. The 1986s do not have the immediate seductive allure of the sensational 1985s or the fleshy, richly fruity 1984s, but they are extremely close in quality to the 1985s and with time a good many of the wines produced in 1986 may well exceed their 1985 counterparts.

The superb quality of this vintage was evident from the harvest conditions, particularly the principal North Coast appellations of Napa Valley, Sonoma Valley and Alexander Valley. Heavy winter rains led to widespread flooding in the North Coast, particularly in the Napa Valley, followed by a normal, uneventful spring, an even set with full clusters and a textbook growing season complemented by warm, balanced weather that avoided extremes. An above-average crop was harvested at full maturity without any rain.

The breadth and depth of quality of the vintage is further evident by its success in all of the major growing regions. The 1986 vintage for Sonoma Valley was extremely impressive. Across the board the wines produced from this appellation were outstanding, particularly B.R. Cohn, Buena Vista Private Reserve, Carmenet and Kenwood Artist Series. In Napa Valley, the Yountville, Oakville, Rutherford and Calistoga areas were superb, slightly overshadowing Stags Leap District and the Santa Cruz Mountains farther south, the main exception being the stunning Santa Cruz Mountain Vineyards Bates Ranch Cabernet. The mountain-grown wines in Napa Valley were also magnificent. Among the superstars of the vintage from Napa Valley are the Caymus Special Selection, Joseph Phelps Insignia and Eisele, Diamond Creek Volcanic Hill and Red Rock Terrace vineyards, Johnson Turnbull Vintage Selection 82, William Hill Gold Label Reserve, Beringer Private Reserve, Robert Mondavi Reserve, Opus One and Spottswoode. In general, the 1986s should begin drinking well between 1994 and 2000, but the cream of the crop have the aging potential to continue developing for 15 to 25 years and in a few instances even longer. Because many of these wines were released in 1989, there has been little price movement; many of the wines have yet to be released and do not have set prices.

Price Trends: (release price/current price)
Carmenet: $20/$20
William Hill Reserve: $24.50/$24.50
Robert Keenan: $18/$18
Laurel Glen: $20/$25
Spottswoode: $30/$30

1985: CLASSIC (97)
GREAT DEPTH, EXQUISITE BALANCE, COMPLEX, AGEWORTHY

With perfect weather and ideal growing conditions, the 1985 vintage is in my view the greatest vintage in California history. Uniformly the Cabernets are beautifully defined, rich and elegant and deeply concentrated. Although it is difficult to compare older vintages with current ones, the sheer number of great wines in the 1980s' vintages surpasses those of the 1960s and 1970s. By that measure, 1985 emerges by a slight edge as the greatest vintage. From the moment winemakers began harvesting the 1985 crop, they were enthusiastic about its quality and potential. What distinguishes the 1985 from other vintages is the impeccable balance, generous, supple, clean, ripe fruit and the fine, integrated tannins that are smooth, firm, broad and polished without any coarse or harsh texture. The fruit from the 1985 vintage is extremely rich and complex with layers of distinct, pure Cabernet flavors. Unlike the 1984 vintage, where a few wines are overly ripe and jammy, the top 1985s show a perfect level of ripeness that makes them seductive to drink now but almost guarantees they will develop and improve in the bottle for a good 15 to 25 years. Weather conditions were textbook perfect, with a cool, wet winter, mild spring, good set of full, tight clusters, and warm, even temperatures throughout the summer, allowing vintners to harvest the fruit at optimum sugar and acidity levels.

The greatness of this vintage is further evidenced by the depth and breadth throughout California's major Cabernet districts, notably the Stags Leap District, Oakville and Rutherford communes and Sonoma and Alexander valleys; for many wineries the 1985 vintage is the finest on record. In Napa Valley, 1985 proved a monumental vintage for Caymus Special Selection, Stag's Leap Wine Cellars Cask 23, Heitz Martha's Vineyard, Sterling Reserve, Joseph Phelps Insignia, Opus One, Hess Collection, Beringer Private Reserve, Château Montelena, Beaulieu Private Reserve, Spottswoode, Dominus, Grace Family Vineyard and Inglenook Reserve Cask, as well as for Ridge Monte Bello in the Santa Cruz Mountains and Silver Oak Cellar in Alexander Valley.

Because of the exceptionally high level of quality, the 1985 vintage is destined to become one of California's most sought-after vintages. Many of the wines listed below and reviewed in this book are already on sale. Consumers interested in acquiring these wines should act quickly as most 1985s will not remain on the market for very long. A handful of Private Reserve and special vineyard-designated wines, such as Heitz Martha's Vineyard, will be available in 1990 and beyond. If there is one vintage to concentrate on, 1985 is it. There's little price movement yet, but it is expected that demand will send prices upward fast.

Price Trends: (release price/current price)
B.R. Cohn: $16/$22
Laurel Glen: $18/$35
Robert Mondavi Reserve: $40/$40
Ridge Monte Bello: $40/$50

Spottswoode: $25/$35
Sterling Reserve: $30/$38

1984: EXCELLENT (94)
RIPE, OPULENT, FLESHY, CHARMING

Were it not for the three sensational vintages that followed, 1984 would rank along with 1968 and 1970 as among the finest vintages in California history. The earliest harvest on record, the 1984 vintage was a short, hot one, uninterrupted by rain or adverse weather. A mild winter and spring led to an above-normal crop of effusively fruity, opulent, concentrated yet fleshy wines with a seductive allure that for many aficionados typifies California Cabernet at its finest. In many ways the 1984 vintage is similar to both 1974 and 1978. In all three years the wines are very ripe and jam-packed with gorgeous fruit. The 1984s are unmistakably very ripe, but they are also extremely well balanced with crisp acidities and firm tannins that promise to age well for up to two decades.

Once again the greatness of the vintage is substantiated by both the number of outstanding wines and the uniformly high quality throughout the key Cabernet districts. The top five wines of the vintage are absolutely stunning, with incredible layers of rich, supple, compact fruit and impeccable balance that should sustain them for a full two decades. Not surprisingly they are wines from among the very finest Cabernet producers, including the top wine of the vintage, the Caymus Special Selection, followed closely by Heitz Martha's Vineyard, which is the finest bottling since 1974, Dunn Howell Mountain, Ridge Monte Bello and Diamond Creek Red Rock Terrace. The list of great wines runs long and deep with very few disappointments.

Most of the 1984s are already on the market; a few have long since sold out, so consumers should move quickly to secure whatever top-flight wines remain. A handful, such as Simi Reserve and Niebaum-Coppola Rubicon, are not scheduled for release until 1990 or later.

Price Trends: (release price/current price)
Beaulieu Private Reserve: $25/$28
Beringer Private Reserve: $25/$31
Château Montelena: $20/$25
Dunn Howell Mountain: $25/$85
Opus One: $50/$55
Ridge Monte Bello: $35/$60

1983: VERY GOOD (81)
LEAN, AUSTERE, TANNIC, UNEVEN QUALITY

The 1983 vintage produced some of the most austere and tannic Cabernets in recent history. Overall quality of the vintage was very erratic, ranging from thin, watery, excessively sharp and tannic wines to a respectable selection of wines that had enough fruit concentration and depth of flavor to match up to the gritty tannins. Heavy winter rains made for a larger-than-normal crop in what was a long, cool, even growing season until harvest time when sporadic weather patterns provided rain, which diluted some grapes and the subsequent wines, and a heat spell, which dehydrated others, resulting in the unusually high levels of tannin. The vintage proved so difficult in some regions, particularly the Santa Cruz Mountains and Alexander Valley, that leading producers, such as Ridge and Simi, did not release their premier wines, the Ridge Monte Bello and Simi Reserve, for public consumption. The Cabernets that were successful should be slow to develop and long, sturdy agers; some may have the tannic strength to endure 20 to 25 years. The vast majority, however, will never offer much appeal and always display the sharp, astringent, tannic edge. The top handful of wines all came from the Napa Valley and featured Dunn Napa Valley and Howell Mountain, Inglenook's Reunion, Newton, Château Montelena, Groth Reserve and Grace Family.

Price Trends: (release price/current price)
Caymus Estate: $15/$30
Château Montelena: $18/$26
Grgich Hills: $17/$23
Heitz Martha's Vineyard: $32.50/$42
Inglenook Reunion: $33/$40

1982: GOOD (78)
HUGE CROP, UNEVEN QUALITY, AUSTERE STYLE

Despite some showy wines of early appeal, the 1982 vintage has been a curious, somewhat disappointing one. A huge crop was picked under good conditions, but rain at harvest adversely affected a number of wines, and an earthy, diluted, sometimes watery quality is showing up in the wines now. Even the very best Cabernets of the vintage are lean and austere, with tight, sharply focused flavors that are evolving very slowly, not showing any of the bright, effusively fruity character often found in these wines. The stars of the vintage are undoubtedly Dunn Vineyard's Howell Mountain and Napa Valley bottlings, two massive but elegant wines that have the depth and concentration of pure, rich fruit to endure a full two decades. Caymus Special Selection, Château Montelena, Beringer Private Reserve, St. Clement and Inglenook Reserve Cask round out the choicest picks. Many of the 1982s are close to maturity, but because they have been slow to develop these wines can also sustain further cellaring.

Price Trends: (release price/current price)
Beaulieu Private Reserve: $24/$32
Caymus Estate: $14/$33
Château Montelena: $16/$33
William Hill Reserve: $18/$32
St. Clement: $13.50/$33

1981: VERY GOOD (85)
CHARMING, FRUITY, ELEGANT, BALANCED

Until the 1984 vintage, the 1981 harvest was the earliest on record in California, but it has been largely overlooked by critics because of overly enthusiastic reviews for the 1980 vintage. The 1981 growing season was warm to hot from start to finish, with some Cabernet vineyards fully ripe at the end of August and early September. The great appeal of the 1981s was their suppleness and forward, rich, fruity style. Most were ready to drink on release, and up until recently this appeared to be a vintage that would develop rapidly. In general, that remains true, but in recent tastings some of the 1981s are showing more tannic strength and backbone than was earlier evident. Still most of the wines are at or very close to their peak and should be consumed within the next three to five years. Caymus Special Selection and Inglenook Reserve Cask are the top two wines of the vintage, overshadowing Diamond Creek Volcanic Hill, Laurel Glen, Joseph Phelps Insignia, Pine Ridge Stags Leap Vineyard and Ridge Monte Bello.

Price Trends: (release price/current price)
Beaulieu Private Reserve: $24/$30
Caymus Special Selection: $35/$60
Heitz Martha's Vineyard: $30/$50
Opus One: $50/$90
Ridge Monte Bello: $24/$45

1980: VERY GOOD (84)
LARGE CROP, VERY RIPE AND FRUITY, AGING WELL

At harvest time, California vintners were wildly enthusiastic about the 1980 vintage. After a long, cool growing season, a heat wave in September pushed sugar levels and fully ripened a large, bountiful crop. Much of the vintners' joy stemmed from the size of the crop, which ensured full production after a 1979 vintage that was partly spoiled by harvest rains. But vintners were also euphoric over what they thought might be another vintage in the mold of the monumental 1978. There were some valid parallels, both in the large crop loads and the full-bodied, effusively fruity character of the wines. While there were some superb wines, including a stunning Pine Ridge Andrus Reserve, 1980 is a very good and not outstanding vintage of wines that are now fully mature. The 1980s are ripe, fleshy, concentrated wines with high alcohol and of good depth and structure. The wines are generally pleasantly balanced with acidities and tannins, and the best wines of the vintage feature bold, dramatic, rich flavors and the staying power to develop for up to two decades. Besides the Pine Ridge, the elite featured the Beaulieu Private Reserve, Opus One, Grace Family Vineyard, Heitz Bella Oaks and Conn Creek Collins Vineyard. Because of the 1978 and 1979 vintage, which turned out better than critics projected, 1980 is held in less esteem than either and only rates as average for collecting wines.

Price Trends: (release price/current price)
Beaulieu Private Reserve: $24/$35
Chappellet: $18/$28
Opus One: $50/$130
Silver Oak Alexander Valley: $18/$45
Sterling Reserve: $27.50/$37

1979: VERY GOOD (88)
AUSTERE, ELEGANT, STRUCTURED, AGEWORTHY

The 1979 vintage has always lived in the shadow of the fantastic 1978 harvest, but despite radically different growing seasons the best wines from each vintage are very close in quality. The 1978 crop is considered one of the best of the 1970s, primarily because it was a huge crop of fully developed fruit, by far the largest since 1974, and it came at a time when California Cabernet was gaining in popularity. The 1979 vintage was considerably cooler than 1978, and it rained heavily at the tail end of the harvest, producing many doomsayers. But even in that atmosphere, there were many vintners who preferred the 1979s because of the milder growing season and the balance, elegance and finesse in the wines. Some even predicted that in the long run 1979, with its deceptively tannic wines, would overshadow the overripe 1978s, and after a full decade of running neck and neck, the two vintages are still very close in quality, and 1979 has begun to win greater respect. The cool growing season allowed the Cabernet crop to ripen fully without allowing overly alcoholic wines. Only in the Santa Cruz Mountains was it a disaster; Ridge Monte Bello was declassified and sold under a separate bottling, and other producers in that region also experienced hardships with their crops. Those who did harvest their crops before the rains generally produced very elegant, austere, balanced wines with fine depth, intensity, delicate flavors and finesse, although tonnage was off by 10 percent to 20 percent and many grapes were left hanging in the vineyard. Caymus Special Selection ranks as the top wine of the vintage. Diamond Creek Volcanic Hill First Pick, Mayacamas, William Hill Gold Label Reserve, Heitz Martha's Vineyard, Freemark Abbey Bosché were close behind. Uneven in quality overall, the 1979s have been slow to evolve and because of their fine balance are drinking well now. The top wines have the aging potential to last another decade or more.

Price Trends: (release price/current price)
Beaulieu Private Reserve: $21/$43
Caymus Special Selection: $30/$85
Clos Du Val: $12.50/$45
Heitz Martha's Vineyard: $25/$60
William Hill: $18/$55

1978: EXCELLENT (93)
RIPE, INTENSE, POWERFUL, AGEWORTHY

The 1970s decade provided several wonderful vintages, but none surpassed 1978 for sheer intensity, power, richness and depth. A near-perfect growing season was warm and mild and then hot at harvest, producing immensely ripe, deeply colored, richly tannic wines that are still developing. In 1978 California winemakers were looking for ripeness and intense varietal character in their grapes — many wineries paid growers bonuses for high sugar content — and in 1978 they got what they paid for. Only on later reflection did some of the wines seem overblown and overpowering for some critics and winemakers, resulting in a move that began in 1979 and 1980 toward wines of less extract and varietal intensity and greater harmony and finesse.

With the possible exceptions of the 1974 and 1985 vintages, no vintage in California history has received as much publicity and come under such careful scrutiny as 1978. The 1978s will always have critics who find the enormous concentration of fruit, high alcohol levels and firm tannins excessive, but as a whole the vintage has lived up to its reputation. Most of the wines are now fully mature and ready to drink; a handful still need time to evolve, and a few have already passed their peak. Because of its reputation and the number of great wines produced, 1978 is a key vintage for collectors. At the top of the class is the Diamond Creek Lake Vineyard Cabernet, produced from a 0.75-acre vineyard and sold through the Napa Valley Wine Auction. This wine is extremely rare; I have only seen it sold in one or two locations. A notch below are the magnificent Caymus Special Selection, Joseph Phelps Eisele Vineyard, Diamond Creek Volcanic Hill and William Hill Gold Label Reserve.

Price Trends: (release price/current price)
Beringer Private Reserve: $15/$44
Caymus Special Selection: $30/$90
Clos Du Val: $12/$40
William Hill: $16.25/$60
Robert Mondavi Reserve: $40/$58

1977: VERY GOOD (82)
DROUGHT YEAR, SMALL CROP, ELEGANT, CHARMING

The second year of a two-year drought in California, 1977 generally produced more elegant, supple, charming wines than 1976, when the grapes became dehydrated, yielding intense, jammy, awkward fruit and harsh, biting tannins. In both years, crop yields were off considerably. Vintners and growers were better prepared for the second year; many vintners watered their vineyards during the winter and spring, resulting in wines that had more supple, generous fruit flavors and less harsh tannins. Rain at harvest affected vineyards where fruit remained on the vines. For Château Montelena, Ridge Monte Bello and Sterling Reserve, 1977 proved an exceptional vintage; each of these wines can stand further cellaring. There are another two dozen Cabernets that were highly successful, but most are fully developed and ready to drink. The majority have already begun to decline.

Price Trends: (release price/current price)
Beaulieu Private Reserve: $16/$46
Château Montelena Napa Valley: $12/$65
Heitz Martha's Vineyard: $30/$75
Ridge Monte Bello: $40/$80
Silver Oak Alexander Valley: $14/$85

1976: GOOD (75)
DROUGHT YEAR, INTENSE, JAMMY, TANNIC, UNBALANCED

The two-year drought that began in 1976 resulted in some of the most intense, jammy, alcoholic, tannic and unbalanced wines in modern times. They are also among the most curious, for many still have loads of ripe, chewy, chunky fruit and drying tannins.

One wonders what will finally happen to these wines as the fruit dries out or the tannins begin to ease and soften. Only the Joseph Phelps Insignia, Caymus Special Selection and Château Montelena North Coast are outstanding. Many others are very good but clumsy and unevolved. Because of the uneven quality and awkward style, the 1976s have limited appeal. In most instances they were more fun to drink years ago. Now the overripe, jammy plum flavors play off the harsh, biting tannins. One day these wines may be more interesting, but it's doubtful they will improve much beyond what they now are. This has never been a vintage for serious collecting, and only a dozen are worth trying.

Price Trends: (release price/current price)
Beaulieu Private Reserve: $19/$60
Château Montelena: $10/$75
Freemark Abbey Bosché: $12.50/$45
Heitz Martha's Vineyard: $30/$75
Ridge Monte Bello: $15/$65

1975: Very Good (86)
Charming, Supple, Elegant, Balanced

Coming in the wake of the monumental 1974 vintage, 1975 never stood much of a chance for full recognition. Completely different in style from the ripe, opulent, heady 1974s, the 1975s are more elegant, fruity, supple, charming and better balanced wines that for the most part have already fully evolved and should be drunk within the next few years. By far the greatest wine produced this vintage is the Joseph Phelps Eisele, a bold, rich, dramatic wine that ranks in the top dozen ever produced. It can still be cellared for up to a decade. The Diamond Creek Volcanic Hill, Caymus Special Selection and Heitz Martha's Vineyard are the crème de la crème. Because the 1974 vintage received so much attention and the 1975s were lighter and fruitier, few collectors have concentrated on 1975s.

Price Trends: (release price/current price)
Beaulieu Private Reserve: $16/$50
Caymus Special Selection: $22/$175
Heitz Martha's Vineyard: $25/$100
Silver Oak Alexander Valley: $10/$95

1974: Excellent (91)
Bold, Rich, Opulent, Dramatic

The 1974 vintage put California Cabernet on the map. Both the 1968 and 1970 vintages were superior in quality, but with the 1974 vintage, the number of Cabernet producers expanded dramatically, demonstrating the breadth and depth of the vintage and exposing the wines to a wider national audience. When the 1974s came to market in 1978, Stag's Leap Wine Cellars 1973 had won the Paris tasting of 1976, where an upstart California producer had upstaged the great Bordeaux. Interest in California wine was keen.

The 1974 crop was large, the result of increased plantings in the late 1960s and early 1970s, but also because climatic conditions were ideal, allowing for a full crop that matured slowly and evenly. If there is an Achilles' heel to the vintage it is that many of the Cabernets were overblown, excessively ripe, jammy and alcoholic, verging on unbalanced. The best wines of the vintage displayed uncommon depth, intensity, concentration and power with rich, explosive, complex fruit and a smooth, thick, supple texture. The Heitz Martha's Vineyard is one of a handful of the greatest Cabernets ever produced in California, with incredible depth, richness, concentration and durability. It has the potential to age 30 years or longer.

Also sensational that vintage were the Mayacamas, Conn Creek (produced from Eisele Vineyard grapes), Silver Oak Cellar North Coast (Alexander Valley), Ridge Monte Bello and Robert Mondavi Reserve. Most of the 1974s matured early on, but the best can still be cellared another decade. With the vintage's lofty reputation, 1974s are in great demand among collectors. The top wines, such as the Heitz Martha's Vineyard, now sell for $200.

Price Trends: (release price/current price)
Clos Du Val: $7.50/$75
Heitz Martha's Vineyard: $25/$200
Robert Mondavi Reserve: $30/$95
Ridge Monte Bello: $12/$140
Silver Oak North Coast (Alexander Valley): $8/$135

1973: VERY GOOD (87)
ELEGANT, CHARMING, SUBTLE, BALANCED

After fair 1971 and 1972 vintages, the 1973 should have been welcomed with open arms. Neither of the previous vintages provided anything more than a handful of first-rate wines, but the 1973 crop was clean and balanced, yielding wines of elegance, finesse, subtlety and charm that were best appreciated early on. Even the best wines of the vintage, the Caymus Estate, Conn Creek from Steltzner Vineyard, Heitz Martha's Vineyard, Mount Eden, Mount Veeder and Clos Du Val, are at their peaks and not likely to improve. Few collectors bother with these wines; they're not deep, concentrated or tannic but merely enjoyable at this stage. Best to drink them soon.

Price Trends: (release price/current price)
Freemark Abbey: $8/$70
Heitz Martha's Vineyard: $11/$120
Robert Mondavi Reserve: $7/$150
Ridge Monte Bello: $10/$110
Stag's Leap Wine Cellars: $6/$135
Sterling Reserve: $10/$70

1972: FAIR (67)
RAINY, SIMPLE, WATERY, UNINSPIRED

Were it not for the remarkable Clos Du Val and the debut bottlings by Caymus, Silver Oak Cellars and Diamond Creek, there is little worth remembering about 1972. Rain ruined what had been an odd, difficult vintage. Most of the wines were decent but have become increasingly diluted and watery with age. The Clos Du Val remains sensational. Caymus' first vintage was also successful, and the wine is still drinking well, as is the Silver Oak North Coast. But their best days have passed, and if you still have these wines in your collection, now is the time to drink them. The Clos Du Val, Caymus and Silver Oak bottlings have added value as collectibles since they are the first vintage from these fine producers.

Price Trends: (release price/current price)
Caymus: $4.50/$110
Clos Du Val: $6/$100
Freemark Abbey Bosché: $6/$30
Ridge Monte Bello: $10/$100
Silver Oak North Coast: $7/$160

1971: FAIR (68)
RAINY HARVEST, POOR QUALITY, MEDIOCRE

Along with the mediocre 1972 vintage, 1971 was one of the worst in the past 25 years. Cool weather at bud break limited the formation of berries, then there were mildew problems and finally rain at harvest. Somehow Robert Mondavi Reserve saved the vintage from total disaster, with a stunning 1971 that is fully mature now, amazingly rich and complex and capable of further aging. Mayacamas, Freemark Abbey Bosché and Ridge Monte Bello are the only others even worth considering, and they were better five years ago. The Mondavi Reserve is also the first bottling of that wine; a good portion of it is Cabernet Franc.

Price Trends: (release price/current price)
Mayacamas: $8/$80
Robert Mondavi Reserve: $12/$130
Ridge Monte Bello: $10/$145

1970: CLASSIC (95)
DEEP, COMPLEX, ELEGANT, AGEWORTHY

Severe spring frosts reduced the crop by nearly half, but 1970 proved a fantastic vintage of incredibly rich, elegant, complex wines that are still holding up quite well. While 1970 lacks the breadth of producers in 1974 and 1978, the top Cabernets from this vintage possess exquisite balance and fine, sharply focused flavors of great depth, persistence and longevity. The stars of the vintage are Heitz Martha's Vineyard, a massive but elegant wine; Mayacamas, which is just reaching its peak; Ridge Monte Bello, which can last another decade; Beaulieu Private Reserve, which has reached a lofty plateau; Chappellet, which ranks as the finest Cabernet ever produced at that winery; and the Freemark Abbey Bosché.

Price Trends: (release price/current price)
Beaulieu Private Reserve: $8/$130
Chappellet: $7.50/$160
Heitz Martha's Vineyard: $12.75/$275
Mayacamas: $8/$130
Ridge Monte Bello: $10/$190

1969: EXCELLENT (92)
ELEGANT, SUPPLE, BALANCED, CHARMING

Overshadowed by the extraordinary 1968 and 1970 vintages, 1969 is one of the most underrated vintages in modern times. A number of truly magnificent wines were produced that year, and they continue to develop extremely well. After the enormous concentration of the 1968s, the 1969 displayed more finesse, supple charm and impeccable balance. Heitz Martha's Vineyard, Ridge Monte Bello, Beaulieu Private Reserve and Mayacamas are the standouts; each of these wines can stand another decade of cellaring but are at their best now. This vintage is greatly underappreciated in quality.

Price Trends: (release price/current price)
Beaulieu Private Reserve: $6.50/$120
Chappellet: $10/$150
Heitz Martha's Vineyard: $12.75/$275
Ridge Monte Bello: $7.50/$200

1968: CLASSIC (96)
RICH, CONCENTRATED, POWERFUL, TANNIC

The 1968 vintage produced rich, deep, powerful Cabernets, none more so than the stunning Heitz Martha's Vineyard, which even today shows no sign of losing its intensity, concentration or beautifully defined fruit. Spring frosts and warm to hot temperatures resulted in very ripe, deeply perfumed and high-extract wines that peaked early and continued to develop for 15 years. Most of the 1968s are past their peak; the Heitz Martha's Vineyard, Mayacamas, Ridge and Chappellet still have ample tannin for cellaring. Others, such as the Robert Mondavi, are declining but still fine to drink. Collectors have zeroed in on the Heitz and now pay $325 a bottle, up from $9.50 on release. Clearly, this is the vintage of the decade.

Price Trends: (release price/current price)
Beaulieu Private Reserve: $6/$150
Chappellet: $5.50/$100
Heitz Martha's Vineyard: $9.50/$375
Louis M. Martini Special Selection: $6/$95
Ridge Monte Bello: $7.50/$190

1967: VERY GOOD (82)
ELEGANT, SUPPLE, BALANCED, EARLY CHARM

Sandwiched between two vastly superior vintages, 1966 and 1968, the 1967s never received much fanfare. They lacked the ripeness and concentration of the other two vintages, but they were especially charming and delicate to drink early on. Most are well past their primes, but the Heitz Martha's Vineyard, Beaulieu Private Reserve and Robert Mondavi provide intriguing drinking.

Price Trends: (release price/current price)
Beaulieu Private Reserve: $5.25/$120
Heitz Martha's Vineyard: $7.50/$300
Robert Mondavi: $5/$100

1966: EXCELLENT (91)
RICH, COMPLEX, BALANCED, DELIGHTFUL

Cabernets from the 1966 vintage are now well past their primes, the lone exception being the rich, elegant Heitz Martha's Vineyard, but they were absolutely delicious for the first decade after release. More concentrated than the 1967s, they displayed greater depth and complexity, but they never had the tannins or extract for long-term cellaring. 1966 marked the first Robert Mondavi and Heitz Martha's bottlings, both of which rate high as collectibles.

Price Trends: (release price/current price)
Beaulieu Private Reserve: $5.25/$140
Heitz Martha's Vineyard: $8/$425
Robert Mondavi: $5/$165

1965: VERY GOOD (83)
RIPE, BALANCED, CHARMING, SERVICEABLE

In the aftermath of the excellent 1964 vintage, the 1965s were very good, useful for drinking but not wines to lay away. From a limited field, the Charles Krug Vintage Select, Ridge Monte Bello and Beaulieu Private Reserve remain appreciatory.

Price Trends: (release price/current price)
Charles Krug Vintage Select: $5/$80
Ridge Monte Bello: $6.50/$275

1964: EXCELLENT (91)
RIPE, COMPLEX, BALANCED, ENDURING

Despite an extremely short crop reduced by spring frosts, 1964 proved an exceptional vintage. It was so superb that all 24,000 cases of Beaulieu were bottled under the Private Reserve label. Ridge Monte Bello is the best of wines that have shown uniformly well.

Price Trends: (release price/current price)
Beaulieu Private Reserve: $4.25/$145
Ridge Monte Bello: $6.50/$300

1963: FAIR (69)
FROST, SHORT CROP, UNEVEN QUALITY, NOT MEMORABLE

This was the last of three frost-damaged vintages, and the 1963s I have tasted have never impressed me, though there are those who see merit in the wines. Undoubtedly they were better in earlier times.

Price Trends: (release price/current price)
Mayacamas: $2/$150

1962: FAIR (69)
FROST DAMAGE, MEDIOCRE VINTAGE, UNINSPIRING

Much like the 1961 and the 1962, this vintage was a frost victim that produced no memorable wines, though Charles Krug Vintage Select remains interesting.

64

Price Trends: (release price/current price)
Beaulieu Private Reserve: $3.50/$140

1961: GOOD (71)
SEVERE FROSTS, DECENT QUALITY, PAST THEIR PRIME

Because of a severe spring frost, between 50 percent and 75 percent of the crop was lost in 1961. But the Charles Krug Vintage Select is superb and has been for a number of years, while Louis M. Martini and Beaulieu Private Reserve have held their own.

Price Trends: (release price/current price)
Beaulieu Private Reserve: $3.50/$200

1960: VERY GOOD (84)
FRUITY, ELEGANT, BALANCED, COMMENDABLE

The wines were widely admired by winemakers of the era for their elegance and structure, but I have only limited experience tasting wines from this vintage. Both the Inglenook and Charles Krug remain healthy, though past their prime.

Price Trends: (release price/current price)
Inglenook Cask: $2.75/$140

1959: VERY GOOD (87)
ELEGANT, BALANCED, COMPLEX, ENDURING

The 1959 vintage gets good marks from vintners of the era, but in my tastings the wines have shown exceptionally well and much better than any vintage since 1964. Three of the Big Four — Louis M. Martini Special Selection, Beaulieu Private Reserve and Charles Krug Vintage Select — are more than holding their own. They are very satisfactory and continue to impress.

Price Trends: (release price/current price)
Beaulieu Private Reserve: $2.50/$350

1958: CLASSIC (95)
AMAZINGLY YOUTHFUL, COMPLEX, ELEGANT, AGEWORTHY

The 1958 vintage has long been held in great regard, and the wines, especially from the Big Four, continue to demonstrate why this is considered one of California's classics. The Beaulieu Vineyard Private Reserve is a monumental wine, rich, complex and delicate, while the Inglenook Cask is remarkably fruity as it celebrates its 30th birthday. The Louis M. Martini and Charles Krug Vintage Select are also exceptional wines, aging gracefully. Despite limited production, this remains a highly collectible vintage because the wines are in such fine condition.

Price Trends: (release price/current price)
Beaulieu Private Reserve: $3/$400
Charles Krug Vintage Select: $2/$465

1957: GOOD (78)
ELEGANT, BALANCED, FRUITY, UNEVEN QUALITY

My best experience is with the 1957 Louis M. Martini, which is an amazing wine with enormous complexity and finesse. At the time, 1957 was considered only good; Martini's is excellent.

Price Trends: (release price/current price)
Louis M. Martini Special Selection: $3.50/$175

1956: VERY GOOD (86)
SUPPLE, BALANCED, COMPLEX, AGEWORTHY

While only considered average by vintners of the era, both the Charles Krug Vintage Select and Beaulieu Vineyard Private Reserve are exceptional wines that continue to impress. Not far off the pace, though fading, is the Louis M. Martini Private Reserve.

Price Trends: (release price/current price)
Beaulieu Private Reserve: $2.50/$600
Charles Krug Vintage Select: $1.40/$590

1955: VERY GOOD (89)
GREAT DEPTH, BALANCE, FINESSE, AGEABILITY

The 1955 vintage gets high marks from most vintners. The Inglenook is a classic, one of the winery's finest, while the Louis M. Martini Special Selection is also excellent.

Price Trends: (release price/current price)
Inglenook: $1.85/$375
Louis M. Martini: $2.50/$190

1954: VERY GOOD (85)
ELEGANT, BALANCED, CHARMING

Though it's considered a very good vintage by Tchelistcheff, particularly for Inglenook and Beaulieu, I have no recent experience with any wines from this vintage and have included no notes or prices.

1953: FAIR (67)
DECENT, DRINKABLE, BUT NOT NOTABLE

This vintage is remembered by old-timers in Napa Valley for the "Freeze of '53." Both temperatures and rainfall were extreme, and nearly half the grape crop was lost in freezing weather. The first wind machine, installed near Calistoga, reportedly saved one vineyard from frost. Wines were only fair, according to Tchelistcheff. I have no tasting notes.

1952: VERY GOOD (85)
SEVERE FROSTS, LOW EXPECTATIONS, BUT SOUND WINES

In one of the most damaging frost seasons on record, freezing weather destroyed about half the crop in Napa Valley, and vintners considered it only average in quality. My experience is limited to the Louis M. Martini Special Selection and Charles Krug Vintage Select, both of which were outstanding and are cause to believe some superior wines were made.

Price Trends: (release price/current price)
Charles Krug: $1.26/$750
Louis M. Martini: $2.50/$450

1951: EXCELLENT (94)
GREAT DEPTH, CHARACTER, BALANCE, AGEWORTHY

Along with 1958, 1951 is considered one of the top vintages of the 1950s. Milder weather allowed for a fuller crop, and unlike the following years there was no substantial frost damage. The Beaulieu Private Reserve remains a classic and one of the top California collectibles. Both the Louis M. Martini and Charles Krug Vintage Select bottlings showed fine in tastings.

Price Trends: (release price/current price)
Beaulieu Private Reserve: $1.82/$950
Charles Krug Vintage Select: $1.25/$700
Louis M. Martini Special Selection: $2/$275

1950: EXCELLENT (90)
FINE DEPTH, CHARACTER, AGEABILITY

Along with 1951, Tchelistcheff considers this a great vintage, producing wines of strength and durability. My only experience is with Charles Krug Vintage Select, which showed very well when tasted in 1985.

Price Trends: (release price/current price)
Charles Krug Vintage Select: $1.25/$500

1949: VERY GOOD (86)
HEAVY FROST, FIRM, STRUCTURED, AGEWORTHY

Despite another heavy spring frost, the 1949 vintage produced well-structured Cabernets that aged well. The Inglenook Cask is the finest example from that vintage that I have tasted. Beaulieu Private Reserve was also very good, according to Tchelistcheff, but I have never tasted it.

Price Trends: (release price/current price)
Inglenook Cask: $1.49/$750

1948: FAIR (69)
WET SPRING, LOW SUGARS, COOL HARVEST, UNEVEN QUALITY

The 1948 vintage was plagued by adversity; droughtlike conditions prevailed until March when 14 days of rain in Napa delayed development of the vines. Grapes were harvested in cool conditions and were slightly underripe. Despite that, the 1948 Beaulieu Private Reserve is like a claret, elegant and understated, and it has held up extremely well.

Price Trends: (release price/current price)
Beaulieu Private Reserve: $1.82/$800

1947: VERY GOOD (85)
WARM YEAR, ELEGANT, BALANCED, AGEWORTHY

Both the Beaulieu Vineyard Private Reserve and Louis M. Martini Special Selection are ample evidence that this was more than simply a good harvest. Both wines are still in excellent condition. The vintage's reputation, however, was only good; frosts were a factor.

Price Trends: (release price/current price)
Beaulieu Private Reserve: $1.82/$1,000
Louis M. Martini Special Selection: $1.50/$750

1946: EXCELLENT (91)
HEAVY FROSTS, EARLY HARVEST, DEEPLY FLAVORED, EARLY MATURING

Tchelistcheff described 1946 as an "unbelievable vintage" with "great wines that didn't last in the bottle." Growing conditions were considered ideal despite some frost damage; harvest in Napa began in August. Beaulieu Private Reserve, Charles Krug Vintage Select and Inglenook are all exceptional bottles of wine that merit special attention. This was the first vintage for Charles Krug Vintage Select.

Price Trends: (release price/current price)
Beaulieu Private Reserve: $1.47/$1,000
Inglenook: $1.49/$1,100
Charles Krug Vintage Select: $1/$750

1945: Very Good (84)
Elegant, Gentle, Delicate

My only experience with 1945 is with the Louis M. Martini Special Selection, and it has faded. Heavy winter rains led to a potentially large crop, but frosts cut yields.

Price Trends: (release price/current price)
Louis M. Martini Special Selection: $1.50/$400

1944: Good (78)
Heavy Frosts, Good Season, Decent Wines

The 1944 vintage is considered good. Heavy frosts affected the crops, and the wines were rated fair to good. My experience with this vintage has been better; both the Charles Krug Cabernet, the first under the new Cesare Mondavi regime (not Vintage Select), and Beaulieu Private Reserve are superb, drinking quite well.

Price Trends: (release price/current price)
Beaulieu Private Reserve: $1.47/$1,100
Charles Krug: $1/$800

1943: Good (79)
Wet Winter, Spring Frosts, Good Crop, Average Quality

This was a mediocre to good vintage with ample rainfall and minimal frost damage, according to the record books, but the Inglenook 1943 is magnificent, while the Louis M. Martini Private Reserve Villa del Rey is fading.

Price Trends: (release price/current price)
Inglenook: $1.49/$1,000
Louis M. Martini Private Reserve: $1.50/$400

1942: Very Good (88)
Ripe, Balanced, Aging Well

My only exposure to the 1942 vintage is the Beaulieu Private Reserve, which in 1989 was truly sensational considering winemaker Tchelistcheff rated the vintage as only good.

Price Trends: (release price/current price)
Beaulieu Private Reserve: $1.45/$1,200

1941: Very Good (89)
Rich, Deep, Concentrated, Ageworthy

The decade of the 1940s began with a string of terrific wines, most notably in my experience with the sensational Inglenook 1941. I've been fortunate to taste the 1941 on several occasions, and each time it has shown outstanding depth, richness and concentration with enormous fruit flavors, a wonderful floral and mature-fruit bouquet and the kind of persistence that makes me believe it can last another 20 years. It is the only wine in this book to receive 100 points. The 1941 vintage was apparently a very warm to hot year. The 1941 Inglenook is above 14 percent alcohol, yet because of the richness and concentration of fruit, the wine is in perfect balance. The Beaulieu Private Reserve is also very fine, although it is in decline and does not have the stamina of the Inglenook.

Price Trends: (release price/current price)
Beaulieu Private Reserve: $1.45/$1,200
Inglenook: $1.49/$1,400

1940: EXCELLENT (90)

I have no notes on this vintage, only reflections by contemporaries who rate it extremely high.

1939: VERY GOOD (87)
RIPE, BALANCED, AGEWORTHY

Although rated as simply good by Tchelistcheff and others, my experience with Cabernets from this vintage has been encouraging. The Louis M. Martini Special Reserve was fine in my last tasting of it, while the Beaulieu Private Reserve was fighting off old age.

Price Trends: (release price/current price)
Beaulieu Private Reserve: $1.45/$1,500
Louis M. Martini Special Reserve: $1.25/$1,000

1938: VERY GOOD (80)

No notes, only reminiscences.

1937: VERY GOOD (80)

I have tried two Cabernets from this vintage, the Beringer and Larkmead, both of which had aged quite gracefully. The Larkmead in particular was deep and rich and lasted for several hours in the glass.

1936: EXCELLENT (90)

This is the first vintage of Beaulieu Private Reserve. I tried it once years ago and was amazed how well it had aged. I have no recent notes, and it is not included in this book. It's extremely rare and very valuable as a collectible.

1935: GOOD (79)

The Simi 1935 is memorable for its vitality.

1934: EXCELLENT (91)

I have no notes, but this vintage is considered excellent by Tchelistcheff and others who drank the wines for decades.

1933: EXCELLENT (91)

My only experience with the 1933 vintage is the memorable Inglenook. It is simply sensational even today, with great depth of color, intensity and complexity, developing for up to two hours. This vintage has to rate as excellent, coming so soon after repeal of Prohibition.

Price Trends: (release price/current price)
Inglenook: $1.30/$1,600

CHAPTER IV
A CLASSIFICATION: RANKING THE CABERNETS

In creating a California Cabernet Classification, my principal consideration was overall quality and consistency of quality over time. The rankings have nothing to do with price or reputation, but are based on more than 5,000 tasting notes, including a comprehensive review within the past year.

Not all classifications are created equal. The most famous classification is the 1855 classification of the Médoc, in which 61 great Bordeaux châteaux were ranked in five tiers, first through fifth growths. The principal criteria in this ranking were prices paid for the château's wines and the château's reputation for quality.

For all its validity then, the 1855 classification is now outdated. The classification's greatest use is as a historical document. It is still widely respected by the Bordeaux wine trade and many connoisseurs. Many of the top-rated châteaux have maintained their reputations, particularly the first and second growths, but many have declined in quality.

Most California vintners resist the idea of a classification of California Cabernets or any other wines. Their concern relates to both the youth of the industry and the rigid nature of the 1855 classification of the Médoc and the influence it has maintained on prices. Winemakers' egos are also involved. No one wants to have his wine regarded as anything less than first class, or have his wine locked into a fixed classification.

It is doubtful that a classification of California Cabernet will ever be undertaken by the California wine industry. Whatever classifications do arise will probably come from the ranks of professional wine critics and historians who have spent the time tasting and analyzing the quality of the wines over a period of years, or have compiled information on the wines based on retail prices, auction prices, appreciation in value or other criteria.

My purpose in creating this California Cabernet classification is twofold. First, I hope to put the top California Cabernets from 1933 to 1986 in historical perspective, as the 1855 classification of the Médoc did in its time. Second, I have tried to sort out for consumers the quality of the wines and how they rank. My classification, which follows, utilizes the French language of first through fifth growths because it is common among wine connoisseurs. While I do believe there is a quality distinction between a first and a fifth growth, a fifth growth Cabernet is not a fifth-rate wine. All the wines that are included in this book were chosen because of their high level of quality. If a California Cabernet is not included in this book, it is simply because, in my opinion, it is not up to the minimum standard of quality that has been established.

This classification is not intended to last forever. A re-evaluation periodically is most appropriate. The classification is of individual wines, not wineries or estates, and is based on criteria that include: producer and overall quality, track record for excellence and longevity, and history of vineyard and winemaker (for more on the criteria, see "How the Wines Were Chosen" in the previous section, entitled "How to Use This Book"). Wineries that have one or more wines, such as Caymus and Caymus Special Selection and Clos Du Val and Clos Du Val Reserve, may be ranked differently. Finally, not every single wine in the book is classified according to quality. If a wine is not produced on a regular basis, it may or may not be included. For more detailed information on the specific producers and wines, along with a discussion of why they are classified as they are, refer to the winery profiles and tasting notes in Chapter VI.

A Classification of California Cabernets

First Growths

Beaulieu Vineyard Private Reserve	Inglenook Reserve Cask
Beringer Private Reserve	Mayacamas Vineyards
Caymus Special Selection	Robert Mondavi Reserve
Château Montelena	Opus One
Diamond Creek Gravelly Meadow	Joseph Phelps Eisele Vineyard
Diamond Creek Red Rock Terrace	Joseph Phelps Insignia
Diamond Creek Volcanic Hill	Ridge Monte Bello
Dunn Howell Mountain	Stag's Leap Wine Cellars Cask 23
Heitz Martha's Vineyard	

Second Growths

Buena Vista Private Reserve	Grace Family Vineyard
Burgess Vintage Selection	Groth Reserve
Caymus Estate	Hess Collection Winery
Clos Du Val Reserve	William Hill Gold Label Reserve
Clos Du Val Estate	Inglenook Reunion
Dominus Estate	Kenwood Artist Series
Duckhorn	Pine Ridge Andrus Reserve
Dunn Napa Valley	Silverado Vineyards
Forman Vineyard	Spottswoode Winery
Freemark Abbey Bosché	Sterling Reserve

THIRD GROWTHS

Beringer Chabot Vineyard
Carmenet
B.R. Cohn Winery
Far Niente Winery
Grgich Hills Cellar
Groth Estate
Heitz Bella Oaks Vineyard
Laurel Glen
Markham Vineyards
Louis Martini Monte Rosso

Niebaum-Coppola Rubicon
Pine Ridge Rutherford Cuvée
Pine Ridge Stags Leap Vineyard
Shafer Hillside Select
Shafer Estate
Silver Oak Cellar Alexander Valley
Simi Reserve
St. Clement
Stag's Leap Wine Cellars SLV
Steltzner Vineyards

FOURTH GROWTHS

Alexander Valley Vineyards
Buehler Vineyards
Chappellet
Conn Creek
Cuvaison Winery
Girard Reserve
Johnson Turnbull
Robert Keenan Winery
Charles Krug Vintage Select
Long Vineyards

Monticello Corley Reserve
Mount Eden Vineyards
Mount Veeder Winery
Newton Vineyard
Joseph Phelps Backus Vineyard
Ridge York Creek
Rombauer Le Meilleur du Chai
Santa Cruz Mountain Vineyard
Silver Oak Cellar Napa Valley
Sterling Diamond Mountain

FIFTH GROWTHS

Cakebread Cellars
Chimney Rock
Clos du Bois Marlstone
Clos du Bois Briarcrest
DeMoor Winery
Eberle Winery
Fisher Coach Insignia
Flora Springs Trilogy
Franciscan Reserve
Frog's Leap
Gundlach Bundschu
Haywood Winery
Iron Horse Vineyards
Jordan Vineyards and Winery
Kistler Vineyards
La Jota
Lakespring Winery
Livingston
Lyeth Winery
Merryvale

Robert Pecota Winery
Robert Pepi Winery
Preston Vineyard
Ravenswood
Raymond Private Reserve
Rombauer Napa Valley
Rutherford Hill Winery
V. Sattui Winery
Sequoia Grove Vineyards
Silver Oak Bonny's Vineyard
Smith Madrone Vineyard
Spring Mountain Vineyards
Stags' Leap Winery
Stonegate Winery
Philip Togni
Trefethen
Tudal Winery
Vichon Winery
Villa Mt. Eden

CHAPTER V

CABERNET STRATEGIES: COLLECTING AND INVESTING

Collecting California Cabernet has its rewards. The best Cabernets can easily improve for 10, 15 or 25 years. An investment in Cabernet for drinking offers the best of all worlds: Stockpiling cases for future consumption will save you money, and you'll benefit from enjoying the wines at their peak.

This chapter is devoted to collecting and investing strategies. True collectors strive to buy the very best Cabernets from the top vintages with the goal of drinking the wines themselves. The goal of investors is to buy wine and resell it at a profit at some later date. Quality is a factor in that decision, but price appreciation is far more important. At times collectors are investors. They may sell or trade older bottles of wine in order to buy new ones. Likewise an investor may buy 10 or 20 cases of a wine, stash two for drinking and resell the balance.

California Cabernet is worth collecting because it is in high demand and ages exceptionally well, gaining depth, complexity, richness and finesse with proper cellaring. It can also be a sound financial investment. In both instances, it's important to know which wines to concentrate on.

Buying California Cabernet used to be easy. Until 1978, there were only a dozen or so producers whose wines were worth collecting. Moreover, very few people invested in California wines because there was no market for older bottles. Classic Bordeaux reds provided greater investment opportunities and liquidity because they were frequently sold at London auction houses.

If you began collecting California Cabernets in the 1940s, 1950s or 1960s, you may still have a few dusty, old, prized bottles of Beaulieu Vineyard Private Reserve, Louis M. Martini, Inglenook and Charles Krug. If you've held on to those wines and aged them in a temperature-controlled environment, it is likely that they have greatly appreciated in value. Their value

CABERNET PRICE APPRECIATION BY VINTAGE

Vintage	Vintage Rating	Number Of Wines Reviewed	Average Release Price	Average Current Price	Percent Change
1986	95	112	$20.97	$21.09	0.57%
1985	97	125	$21.89	$24.69	12.79%
1984	94	121	$20.58	$27.69	34.54%
1983	81	111	$18.37	$26.50	44.25%
1982	78	109	$16.74	$29.40	75.62%
1981	85	89	$16.82	$33.25	97.68%
1980	84	87	$16.92	$37.63	122.39%
1979	88	70	$16.42	$42.84	160.90%
1978	93	70	$15.70	$52.55	234.71%
1977	82	51	$14.59	$46.58	219.25%
1976	75	36	$13.53	$56.08	314.48%
1975	86	33	$12.66	$69.54	449.28%
1974	91	32	$11.54	$86.87	652.77%
1973	87	21	$ 8.64	$90.66	949.30%
1972	67	18	$ 7.83	$84.11	974.20%
1971	68	9	$ 7.91	$72.22	813.02%
1970	95	11	$ 8.36	$125.45	1400.59%
1969	92	8	$ 8.65	$143.12	1554.56%
1968	96	9	$ 6.77	$150.00	2115.65%

Note: Vintage ratings from Chapter III

has soared since the days when you could buy them for $1.50 to $3 a bottle. If you laid away Inglenook 1933, the price has risen from $1.30 to $1,600 a bottle at auction. The Inglenook 1941 has increased in value from $1.49 to $1,400. Beaulieu Private Reserve 1939 sold for $1.45 the day it was released. Today expect to pay $1,500 a bottle.

Old bottles of California Cabernet are regularly sold at auction, but it's rare to see them sold in full case lots; more typically you can buy a bottle or two of a specific vintage. Wines from the 1930s to 1960s are scarce. There simply wasn't much wine produced, and most of it was consumed. Even in the mid-1960s, when Heitz began bottling Martha's Vineyard and Robert Mondavi introduced his first Cabernets, the production numbers were small. Heitz Martha's 1966 produced 392 cases; Mondavi's 1966 yielded 1,500 cases.

For collectors, the primary goal is to buy the best wines of the top vintages that are most likely to improve with age. Investors should study which wines appreciate in value the fastest. Sometimes the same wines can accomplish both goals, but often wines that are more frequently traded escalate faster in value than rarer, limited bottlings.

For example, Caymus Vineyards produces two Cabernets from its estate vineyard, an Estate and a Special Selection. In 1978, an excellent vintage in Napa Valley, the winery produced 2,600 cases of Estate and 600 cases of Special Selection. The Estate sold for $12 on release and now sells for $40. The Special Selection, a wine of superior quality, sold for $30 on release and now commands $65 a bottle. The Special Selection is the best wine for collecting because it is a richer, more dramatic and ageworthy wine. Early on the Estate is the best for investing because it has more than tripled in value, while the Special Selection has simply doubled. In the long run it is difficult to predict which will be more valuable. I suspect that the Special Selection will eventually be the more valuable of the two.

Another example of a wine that has shown great appreciation in value is Jordan Cabernet. It will not age as well or as long as either Caymus Estate or Special Selection. From the same 1978 vintage, a good but not great one in Alexander Valley, Jordan produced 58,000 cases, selling for $16 a bottle on release and trading for $70 a bottle today. Based on this appreciation, Jordan is a fine investment. The only caveat is that the Jordan style of Cabernet is not for long-term cellaring. It is a wine designed for restaurant sales, and while charming and complex on release, it is not meant to be cellared much longer than five to eight years. Many people who regularly drink Jordan, as I do, will find that the 1978 has already peaked in quality and begun to decline. The best explanation for the rapid price escalation of the Jordan, as compared to Caymus, is the Jordan 1978 has considerably more wine on the market and is more frequently traded than either the Caymus Estate or Special Selection, which tends to drive up prices. The Caymus Special Selection is a wine for collectors and connoisseurs who want to drink it, not resell it, mainly because it is seldom auctioned or sold.

Beyond buying specific wines for investment, it pays to concentrate on the best vintages, even those that may be overrated, for they tend to have the greatest appreciation in value.

In the Price Appreciation chart, figures show that using wines selected for this book, virtually all vintages have substantial price appreciation regardless of quality. For example, when comparing 1972 and 1973, the latter is clearly the superior vintage. Yet based on price tracking in this book, wines from the 1972 vintage have shown slightly greater price appreciation. In analyzing the data, 1972 was not only a poor vintage, but production was off substantially due to rain at harvest and prices started out lower than they did for 1973s. Yet despite a lower level of quality, 1972s have maintained value in the market. What this suggests to me is that old wines in general have significant value for investing, regardless of quality.

Looking at the 1974 and 1975 vintages, 1974 ranks slightly above 1975 in quality, but it rates substantially higher in price appreciation. This reflects the enormous popularity of the 1974s, but also suggests that perhaps the 1975s are undervalued in the market. In comparing 1978 and 1979, two vintages that are close in quality, 1978 is considered the better of the two and its value in the market is reflected by its considerable price appreciation. Again, that indicates the strong market pull of 1978s as well as 1979s perhaps being undervalued. In 1980 and 1981, two vintages of similar quality, 1980 shows greater price appreciation because it enjoys a better reputation. Buying 1981s gives you wines of similar quality at better prices.

COLLECTIBILITY

In general, all the Cabernet producers included in this book are exceptional choices for buying, drinking and cellaring. Clearly some Cabernets are better than others and will age longer, gaining greater depth, complexity and character than others. In the collectibility rating system that follows, I have selected Cabernets that I believe are the best Cabernets to concentrate on based on my research. In the rating system, three levels of collectibility are presented, using symbols like those used to rate bonds in the financial world — AAA,

AA and A — the latter being the highest rating and so on.

The Cabernets that receive the AAA rating are, in my view, the top collectibles. These are the wines that I believe will not only age the best over the longest period of time but will also show great appreciation in value and quality. Other factors, such as production, availability, track record of excellence, vineyard location and winemaker, are also weighed in the formula for selecting these wines. Below are some guidelines for collecting:

1. Concentrate on the top producers in the best vintages. In this book see Chapter IV on classifications, as well as Chapter III on vintages, which highlight the top vintages. Appendix 3 lists all wines tasted by vintage; Appendix 5 ranks all vintages by score, highest to lowest.

2. Focus on Cabernets with the best track record for aging and improving in the bottle. Wineries with at least a 10-year track record of excellence are the best bets. Estate-bottled Cabernets ensure the most consistency in quality from year to year. Wineries that don't own their vineyards or have long-term agreements to buy grapes from the same vineyard are less likely to produce consistent wines. That does not mean they may not produce fine wines, but styles are more likely to change with varying grape sources. The collectibility rating that follows is designed to address that issue.

3. Buy futures when offered, particularly in very good to outstanding vintages. If the wines you collect are scarce (see production figures for each winery), hard to find and appeal to your taste, make advance plans to buy them either as soon as they are released to the market or in any futures or pre-release offerings.

4. When buying at auction or retail, know as much as you can about the wine's prior storage history. Buying a 10-year-old Cabernet can be risky if you don't know where it's been cellared. Check the bottle level for ullage. If the wine level is down, that means air is getting in and oxidizing the wine.

5. Watch for the hot new wineries and their initial releases. Part of the excitement of the California Cabernet scene is discovering the new producers.

6. Oversized bottles, such as magnums, double magnums and imperials, are increasingly popular. Wine tends to age more slowly in larger bottles.

COLLECTIBILITY RATINGS FOR CALIFORNIA CABERNETS

AAA

Beaulieu Vineyard Private Reserve	Heitz Martha's Vineyard
Caymus Special Selection	Mayacamas Vineyards
Diamond Creek Gravelly Meadow	Joseph Phelps Eisele
Diamond Creek Red Rock Terrace	Joseph Phelps Insignia
Diamond Creek Volcanic Hill	Ridge Monte Bello
Dunn Howell Mountain	Stag's Leap Wine Cellars Cask 23

AA

Beringer Private Reserve	Inglenook Reserve Cask
Buena Vista Private Reserve	Inglenook Reunion
Burgess Vintage Selection	Kenwood Artist Series

Caymus Estate
Château Montelena
Clos Du Val Reserve
Dominus Estate
Duckhorn
Dunn Napa Valley
Forman Vineyard
Freemark Abbey Bosché
Grace Family Vineyard
William Hill Gold Label Reserve

Laurel Glen
Robert Mondavi Reserve
Niebaum-Coppola Rubicon
Opus One
Pine Ridge Andrus Reserve
Silver Oak Alexander Valley
Spottswoode Winery
Stag's Leap Wine Cellars SLV
Sterling Reserve

A

Beringer Chabot
Buehler Vineyards
Carmenet
Clos Du Val Estate
B.R. Cohn Winery
Far Niente Winery
Girard Reserve
Grgich Hills
Groth Reserve
Groth Estate
Heitz Bella Oaks Vineyard
Hess Collection Winery
Long Vineyards
Markham Vineyards
Louis M. Martini Monte Rosso

Mount Eden Vineyards
Mount Veeder Winery
Joseph Phelps Backus Vineyard
Pine Ridge Stags Leap Vineyard
Santa Cruz Mountain Vineyard
Shafer Hillside Select
Shafer Estate
Silver Oak Napa Valley
Silverado Vineyard
Simi Reserve
St. Clement Vineyards
Stag's Leap Wine Cellars SLV
Steltzner Vineyards
Philip Togni

INVESTING

Investing in Cabernet is like investing in general. There are always risks involved, but here are some guidelines for minimizing those risks.

1. Establish realistic goals for what you want to accomplish. Some wines will out-perform others. Others will struggle to keep pace with inflation.

2. Thoroughly research the subject, most importantly the wines you want to buy. Study their track records of price appreciation and evaluate the level of demand. This book is a guide to what has happened to prices in the past 55 years.

3. As with collecting, concentrate on the best vintages, but be more cautious with the high-priced wines unless you plan to hold them for a long time. When they are rare or irreplaceable, or demand exceeds supply, people are willing to pay huge premiums for special wines. Historically, there has always a market for fine wines.

4. Be aware that if you plan to resell your wine, each state has different laws. In some states it is illegal for private citizens to sell wine and a license is needed. Also, don't expect to receive retail prices. Retailers typically mark up prices by 25 percent to 50 percent. A wine you bought for $10 a bottle that is now retailing for $20 will probably only bring you $14

to $15, far less than the apparent gain. In the auction market, the seller usually gives up a 10 percent fee.

5. Don't hold on to a wine forever. Be prepared to sell. Remember that it's an investment and what you established as your goals. When a wine such as Jordan 1978 goes from $16 to $70, that is a healthy increase. Holding it another 10 years might not increase its value as fast. Also, if the wine has peaked, there is an added risk to holding the wine.

6. Storage and insurance are important considerations. If you're investing in Cabernet for resale in 10 years and have five to 10 cases of a specific wine, make sure that good temperature-controlled storage is part of your plan. If you don't have a large cellar, be prepared to pay for keeping your wine in a rented wine locker or warehouse. Wine needs to rest in a cool, dark environment, ideally between 55 and 65 degrees Fahrenheit. Insurance should be another factor to avoid loss from fire, theft or heat damage. In order to qualify for most insurance, you'll need a detailed inventory of your wine.

7. Keep up with your wine's development. Watch for reviews of older vintages and beware if the notes indicate your wine has peaked or is declining in quality. This shouldn't happen if you picked the right wine, but if it has peaked in quality, it's a good time to sell it.

8. If your investment fails to keep pace with inflation or match your goals, don't fret. You can always drink it.

Chapter VI

The Wineries and Wines: Profiles and Tasting Notes

Within this chapter each of the wineries chosen for this book is profiled along with tasting notes on their top Cabernets. Each of the wineries is classified, from first to fifth growths, denoting the overall quality of the producer, and given a collectibility rating from AAA, AA, A or No rating. The best vintages are underlined and a facts box is set off for reference. It tells you who owns the winery, their address and phone number, when they began Cabernet production, total Cabernet production, Cabernet acres owned, average vine age, vineyard composition and time and type of oak used for aging. Many producers in this book make more than one Cabernet. For more on the topic see "How The Wines Were Chosen" in the chapter "How To Use This Book." Each of the wines is described in a tasting note and ranked on the 100-point scale. There is also information about how many cases were produced, the release price and current price, when to drink the wines at their best.

ALEXANDER VALLEY VINEYARDS

Alexander Valley

CLASSIFICATION: *FOURTH GROWTH*

COLLECTIBILITY RATING: *Not rated*

BEST VINTAGES: *1986, 1985, 1984, 1983, 1982*

When it comes to consistency, quality and value, Alexander Valley Vineyards Cabernets rank among the best. These exceptionally well-made Cabernets are grown in a 64-acre parcel of the Wetzel family's vineyards in Alexander Valley. The style emphasizes rich, bold, concentrated fruit and rich, supple tannins. One of the most appealing features of Alexander Valley Vineyards Cabernets is their seductive charm for early drinking. While the Cabernets are among the first of the vintage to reach the market, they are typically brimming with sumptuous ripe fruit, herb and spice flavors and smooth, polished tannins, making them drinkable on release and for up to a decade. With age, the herb and chocolate flavors turn to cedar and tobacco, adding complexity to the wines.

The early vintages, including the first Cabernet, the 1975, are old and frail and not worth seeking out. The 1978 is fully mature, in slight decline, while the 1979, 1980 and 1981 are drinking well, particularly the 1979. Beginning with the 1982 vintage, Alexander Valley Vineyards has made some sensational wines. The 1982 shows more complexity and sophistication than previous bottlings, and the 1983 is highly successful for that vintage. The 1984 is by far the finest Alexander Valley Vineyards Cabernet ever produced, with incredibly rich, supple, complex and concentrated flavors. Both the 1985 and 1986 vintages are leaner, with harder edges. Production increased substantially with those two vintages, rising from 5,600 cases in 1984 to 15,000 cases in 1985 and 13,000 cases in 1986, which may account for the modest drop in quality.

TASTING NOTES

ALEXANDER VALLEY VINEYARDS, **Alexander Valley**

1986 ALEXANDER VALLEY VINEYARDS: The 1986 is a hard-edged, structured wine that's firm and lean, with good depth and intensity

---

AT A GLANCE

ALEXANDER VALLEY VINEYARDS
P.O. Box 175
Healdsburg, CA 94558
(707) 433-7209

Owners: The Wetzel family

Winemaker: Hank Wetzel (14 years)

Founded: 1975

First Cabernet vintage: 1975

Cabernet production: 14,000 cases

Cabernet acres owned: 64 acres

Average age of vines: 14 years

Vineyard makeup: Cabernet Sauvignon (50%), Merlot (50%)

Average wine makeup: Cabernet Sauvignon (88%), Merlot (12%)

Time in oak: 13 months

Type of oak: American, French

of flavor, firm tannins, delicious black cherry, plum and floral flavors that are reined in, similar in style to the fine 1985. Has the structure and balance to age. Drink 1992-1999. 13,522 cases produced. Release: $11.50. Current: $11.50. **88**

1985 ALEXANDER VALLEY VINEYARDS: Sleeker and more elegant than the 1984 but not quite as complex or dramatic, the 1985 is a very fine vintage, with complex herb, cedar, mineral and ripe plum flavors that are sharply focused and concentrated yet lacking the richness and depth of the 1984. Drink 1991-1997. 15,745 cases produced. Release: $11. Current: $12. **88**

1984 ALEXANDER VALLEY VINEYARDS: The finest Alexander Valley Vineyards bottling ever, with its remarkably rich, bold, supple and concentrated plum, black cherry and currant flavors that are complemented by herb, toast, chocolate and mineral notes. An amazingly flavorful and complex wine with layers of flavor and a measure of restraint. With its silky smooth texture, it's charming. Drink 1992-2000. 5,600 cases produced. Release: $10.50. Current: $13.50. **92**

1983 ALEXANDER VALLEY VINEYARDS: A highly successful 1983 that manages to combine a bouquet of mint and spice with focused, concentrated, reined-in Cabernet fruit, with generous black cherry, currant, herb and cigar box nuances that add complexity. The firm, tannic structure promises another eight to 10 years of development. Approachable now, but best in two to three years. Drink 1992-1998. 3,792 cases produced. Release: $10.50. Current: $14.50. **90**

1982 ALEXANDER VALLEY VINEYARDS: Still a very tightly wound, lean and concentrated wine that offers greater balance and sophistication than previous Alexander Valley Vineyards Cabernets, despite the mediocre quality of the vintage. The ripe plum, cherry and cedar flavors are well focused and long on the palate. Complex and intriguing, this wine still has room to grow. Drink 1990-1996. 3,987 cases produced. Release: $10. Current: $16. **90**

1981 ALEXANDER VALLEY VINEYARDS: Attractive for its balance and elegance, fully mature but capable of further development, exhibiting ripe plum, spice, cedar and anise notes that are rich and full-bodied. Drink 1990-1994. 3,625 cases produced. Release: $9. Current: $16. **87**

1980 ALEXANDER VALLEY VINEYARDS: Big, rich and very ripe, with road tar, cigar box, ripe plum and herb flavors that are crisp and lively. At its peak but can stand further cellaring. A shade overripe. Drink 1990-1994. 2,552 cases produced. Release: $9. Current: $16. **83**

1979 ALEXANDER VALLEY VINEYARDS: A very successful 1979 that is rich, full-bodied and complete, offering ripe, spicy plum, cherry and herb flavors that are well integrated and deep, with hints of cigar box on the nose. One of the best Alexander Valley Vineyards bottling to date; still developing. Drink 1990-1996. 2,819 cases produced. Release: $7. Current: $18. **86**

1978 ALEXANDER VALLEY VINEYARDS: Pretty Cabernet aromas but vegetal and herbal on the palate, with cigar box and tobacco notes and fading cherry and plum flavors that are drying out on the finish. Drink 1990-1993. 3,734 cases produced. Release: $6.50. Current: $20. **80**

1976 ALEXANDER VALLEY VINEYARDS: In two recent tastings, the 1976 showed unpleasant, odd, pungent, earthy, overripe flavors. Best to avoid. 2,080 cases produced. Release: $5.50. Current: $18. **60**

1975 ALEXANDER VALLEY VINEYARDS: Despite some pretty aromas, the 1975 is thin, tart and fading with faint hints of ripe plum and spicy herb flavors that linger on the palate. Drink 1990-1992. 3,416 cases produced. Release: $5.50. Current: $20. **75**

BEAULIEU VINEYARD

Georges de Latour Private Reserve, Rutherford, Napa Valley

CLASSIFICATION: *FIRST GROWTH*

COLLECTIBILITY RATING: AAA

BEST VINTAGES: *1986, 1985, 1984, 1980, 1979, 1978, 1970, 1969, 1968, 1958, 1956, 1951, 1947, 1946, 1944, 1942*

AT A GLANCE

BEAULIEU VINEYARD
P.O. Box 329
Rutherford, CA 94573
(707) 963-2411

Owner: Heublein Inc./Grand Metropolitan, England

Winemaker: Joel Aiken (5 years)

Founded: 1900

First Cabernet vintage: 1907
Private Reserve: 1936

Cabernet production: 200,000 cases
Private Reserve: 15,000 cases

Cabernet acres owned: 400

Average age of vines: 10 years

Vineyard makeup: Cabernet Sauvignon (100%)

Average wine makeup: Cabernet Sauvignon (100%)

Time in oak: 30 months

Type of oak: American

Beaulieu Vineyard Georges de Latour Private Reserve is undoubtedly the most famous and prestigious Cabernet Sauvignon produced in California. This richly flavored, elegant wine has proven to be a consistently excellent and amazingly ageworthy Cabernet as well as California's first and foremost collectible. Beaulieu, French for "beautiful place," was established in 1900 in Rutherford in Napa Valley and modeled after the great châteaux of Bordeaux, which Beaulieu's founder, French-born Georges de Latour, greatly admired.

With the release of the 1986 vintage in 1990, Beaulieu (BV) Private Reserve will celebrate its 50th anniversary of consecutive vintages produced from two of Napa Valley's greatest vineyards, BV No. 1 and BV No. 2, in Rutherford. By any winemaking standards, BV Private Reserve's track record of excellence is long and distinguished, dating back to its first vintage in 1936. No other California Cabernet can match BV's superb record for creating fine Cabernets.

Through 50 vintages there have been many peaks and only a few valleys. The great vintages from the 1930s and 1940s helped establish Napa Valley's Cabernet credentials. BV's winemaking style of elegance and finesse, shaped by the legendary André Tchelistcheff, influenced an entire school of winemakers from the 1950s to the present day, among them Joe Heitz, Mike Grgich (of Grgich Hills), Theo Rosenband (formerly of Sterling), Rob Davis (of Jordan), Jill Davis (of Buena Vista) and Tom Selfridge, currently BV's president. In the past year I have tasted many of the finest BV Private Reserves dating back to the 1940s, and they are still in wonderful condition.

Among the elite wines from the 1940s are the 1942, 1944 and 1946 vintages, and the monumental 1947 vintage, which ranks as one of California's classics. From the 1950s, the 1951, 1956 and the fabulous 1958 are still in pristine condition and are among the most sought-after wines as collectibles. In the 1960s, the 1964, 1966, 1968 and 1969 are magnificent wines that stand above the pack. The lowest point for BV in terms of quality came in the early 1970s. While the 1970 vintage is still an extraordinary wine, after that there are a string of weak vintages, specifically the 1974 vintage, which is already past its prime and fading. The 1975, 1976 and 1977 vintages were decent, well-made wines, but not among Napa Valley's best. With the 1978 vintage, BV returned to form, following with an excellent 1979 vintage. In the 1980s, the 1980, 1982, 1984, 1985 and 1986 vintages are all beautifully crafted wines and should go a long way toward erasing the quality-control question marks raised by the mediocre vintages of the early 1970s.

Beaulieu owes much of its prestige and reputation to de Latour and Tchelistcheff. De Latour had world-class wines in mind when he selected vineyard land in the heart of Napa Valley's finest Cabernet land. He planted his vineyards near the turn of the century, beginning with BV 1 and followed seven years later with BV 2. Each of the vineyards measures nearly 100 acres, and they are both on the western side of Highway 29, directly across the road from the winery.

In the early days, Cabernet Sauvignon vines made up only a small portion of the vineyard as the winery concentrated on producing sweet wines, which were in greater demand. Prohibition in the 1920s and early 1930s further restricted the winery's production to sales of sacramental wines. While Prohibition forced most Napa Valley wineries to close, and their vineyards were either uprooted, left barren or replanted to prune trees, Beaulieu thrived. Maintaining the vineyards gave Beaulieu a decided edge when repeal of Prohibition came in 1933 and the winery was able to resume commercial winemaking.

Under de Latour's direction, winemaker Leon Bonnet produced Beaulieu's first Private Reserve in 1936. A year later, while the wine aged in French oak barrels, Bonnet retired and de Latour began to search for a successor. While in Paris, de Latour met Tchelistcheff, a Russian-born, French-trained research enologist, whom he hired as winemaker. Tchelistcheff arrived in Napa Valley in 1938, bringing with him a sophisticated, worldly view of wine at a time when the California wine industry was in disarray and struggling to revive itself from Prohibition.

Tchelistcheff proved to be a bridge between European and California viticultural and winemaking practices. Through his experiences in France, Tchelistcheff understood many things about winemaking that were unheard of in California. Above all, he was a vineyardist who recognized the importance of soil, climate, location and vine maintenance in winegrowing. He also understood the significance of strict sanitation practices, which in the 1930s and 1940s posed serious problems for California wineries following repeal. A large percentage of the wines from that era were flawed by bacteria, spoilage and mold.

Tchelistcheff brought the science and chemistry of the lab closer to winemaking problems, operating his own lab in St. Helena and consulting with Robert and Peter Mondavi at Charles Krug Winery, Louis M. Martini, August Sebastiani and John Daniel of Inglenook. Along with his keen tasting abilities, he introduced to Napa Valley vintners new concepts on various yeast strains, cooler fermentation temperatures, malolactic fermentations and refinements on clarification, bottling and aging techniques.

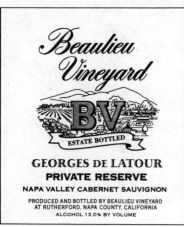

But he did not introduce small oak barrels to BV. That was a concept advanced by de Latour, who understood how the great French châteaux aged their wines. De Latour created the line of Private Reserve wines, a rigorous selection of BV's finest Cabernet lots aged in small oak barrels, but Tchelistcheff shaped the style and character through management of the vineyards and the use of American oak, which gave the BV wines a unique, spicy vanilla character. De Latour died before the first Private Reserve was bottled, but Tchelistcheff attached his name to the wine.

From the early vintages on, BV Private Reserves were the finest and purest expression of Rutherford Cabernet Beaulieu could produce. For each of the 50 consecutive vintages, BV No. 1 and No. 2 have been the sole grape sources for every Private Reserve bottling. What is rather extraordinary is just how consistent the vineyards and wine-making have been and how little changed at BV from vintage to vintage during Tchelistcheff's 36-year tenure.

From the outset the BV Private Reserve style emphasized understated elegance and refinement of flavor. Vintages varied radically in ripeness due to climatic deviations and apparently some diseased vines. But the BV Private Reserves rarely departed from the rich concentration of ripe fruit, delicate balance and fine tannins that made the wine eminently drinkable on release yet remarkably ageworthy, gaining elegance, complexity and finesse with age. In years when the grapes grew too ripe, Tchelistcheff employed what he called "château la pump" and claims he watered the fermenting grape musts to restore moisture that had evaporated from the berries. Often in cool vintages the grapes barely ripened beyond 21 degrees Brix, a factor some blame on vines afflicted by red leaf and leaf roll, two viruses that rob grapes of sugar except in very warm years. Despite these diseases, a good number of those wines aged very well.

Official production figures for BV Private Reserve have long been held as top-secret information, although it is known that annual case volume normally fluctuates between 7,000 and 15,000 cases and on occasion to more than 20,000. The 1964 vintage, for instance, was affected by a spring frost, which drastically reduced the size of the crop, but the quality was uniformly exceptional, and the entire Cabernet production of 25,000 cases was bottled as Private Reserve. Critics of BV claim its wines have suffered in quality since the winery's sale in 1969 to Heublein Inc., the huge food and beverage conglomerate, and one wonders whether attempts to stretch production in vintages like 1974, which produced a huge crop, resulted in a mediocre wine when many Napa Valley wineries made rich, opulent wines. If quality had remained mediocre, that theory might have gained credence, but the evidence of today's Private Reserves suggests otherwise.

Tchelistcheff retired after the 1972 vintage and after a brief succession of winemakers Tom Selfridge settled in as winemaker through the early 1980 vintages, before becoming president in 1983. Selfridge's philosophy has been to stay a steady course with BV Private Reserve through careful clone and rootstock selection and thorough selection of the best lots of wine.

Collectors and investors who have purchased BV Private Reserve over the years have seen the prices for these wines escalate. The 1951, which sold for $2 when released, has soared to $950 a bottle at auction. The 1968 Private Reserve has climbed in value from $6 to $150. BV Private Reserves from the 1930s are extremely rare. There is also tremendous demand for the sensational 1970 (Ronald Reagan's favorite wine) as well as for the 1974 and 1978; however, the 1974 is not holding up well in the bottle, and its future as a collectible is questionable.

BV Private Reserve remains one of California's top collectibles, particularly for older, rarer vintages, but competition from the scores of Napa Valley producers has altered its stature compared to the 1950s and 1960s, when there were only a handful of competitors. Based on the most recent vintages, 1984 through 1986, BV Private Reserve remains an excellent choice for cellaring, either for drinking or investment. The 1979 vintage, for instance, may prove to be a sleeper because it was a difficult vintage for many producers yet yielded a number of excellent, ageworthy wines that will take years to develop. BV Private Reserve is one of those wines. Beaulieu also makes an exceptional Rutherford bottling, which in some years is superb and worthy of cellaring; the Beau Tour bottling provides consistently good value.

TASTING NOTES

BEAULIEU VINEYARD, Private Reserve, Rutherford, Napa Valley

1986 BEAULIEU VINEYARD PRIVATE RESERVE: From another great vintage in Napa Valley and BV's third superlative vintage in a row, this is a remarkably deep, rich and concentrated wine, with beautifully defined black cherry and currant flavors supported by firm structure and fine tannins that promise a long life. This wine can stand more cellaring than either the 1984 or 1985. Drink 1995-2005. Not Released. **93**

1985 BEAULIEU VINEYARD PRIVATE RESERVE: This wine promises to be one of the great BVs of the decade. The 1985 vintage ranks as one of California's finest, and this wine has all the ingredients — rich, ripe, focused black cherry and currant flavors, fine, lean, elegant tannins, impeccable balance and a soft, gentle aftertaste that lingers. Typical of BV, it's ready to drink now but should improve for up to two decades. Drink 1995-2003. Not Released. **95**

1984 BEAULIEU VINEYARD PRIVATE RESERVE: A rich, seductive 1984 typical of the vintage, this wine is opulent by BV standards yet refined, with bright, supple black cherry, currant, vanilla and anise flavors that are complex and elegant. Should only get better. Drink 1994-2002. Release: $25. Current: $28. **91**

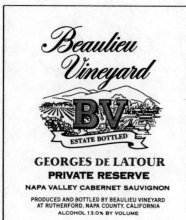

1983 BEAULIEU VINEYARD PRIVATE RESERVE: Lean and tannic like most 1983s, missing ripe, generous, delicate fruit, but the structure is fine, and the currant and herb flavors are nicely focused. An ager that may surprise after time in the cellar. Drink 1992-1997. Release: $24. Current: $28. **82**

1982 BEAULIEU VINEYARD PRIVATE RESERVE: A good candidate for the cellar, this is a hard, firm, closed wine that isn't showing much in the way of fruit now but has plenty of rich, concentrated black cherry and herb flavors and a firm tannic backbone. The finish is surprising, with pretty cherry flavors peeking through. A wine to watch in the cellar. Drink 1995-2005. Release: $24. Current: $32. **88**

1981 BEAULIEU VINEYARD PRIVATE RESERVE: A very pretty wine from an underrated vintage, beautifully balanced with rich plum, currant and spice nuances that are true to the BV character, finishing with herbs and berries. Not as rich and concentrated as the 1980 or 1982 but displaying the delicate balance that distinguishes BV. Has the potential to move up a notch or two. Drink 1993-2000. Release: $24. Current: $30. **87**

1980 BEAULIEU VINEYARD PRIVATE RESERVE: Massive by BV standards, this is an enormously rich, deep and concentrated wine, packed with generous currant, plum and black cherry flavors and a touch of mint and herbs. Like the 1979 it has been slow to evolve but has gorgeous fruit and impeccable balance. Delicious now but should only improve through the 1990s. Drink 1995-2005. Release: $24. Current: $35. **93**

1979 BEAULIEU VINEYARD PRIVATE RESERVE: This vintage has been slow to evolve because of the cool, rainy harvest, and it is still three or four years away from its peak. At first the herb, mint and spice aromas are curious, but the flavors are rich and concentrated, flanked by firm tannins and remarkable complexity. Fascinating to watch develop. Drink 1993-2000. Release: $21. Current: $43. **90**

1978 BEAULIEU VINEYARD PRIVATE RESERVE: Early on this wine seemed incredibly light and simple, but with each year and each tasting it has shown amazing improvement. Now it is easily the best BV since 1970, with layers of rich, concentrated, impeccably balanced plum, black cherry and cedar nuances that are crisp and lively on the palate. Still developing. Drink 1990-2000. Release: $19. Current: $45. **91**

1977 BEAULIEU VINEYARD PRIVATE RESERVE: Much better earlier on, this wine is fading fast, drying out and showing more tannin than most BVs. The lean cedar and spice flavors lack fruit and complexity. Best to drink up. Drink 1990-1991. Release: $16. Current: $46. **79**

1976 BEAULIEU VINEYARD PRIVATE RESERVE: This is a drought-year wine that is very ripe and concentrated but not overdone or raisiny. There are plenty of plum, spice, anise and black cherry flavors, and it tastes young and lively. Holding together very well. Drink 1990-1996. Release: $19. Current: $60. **86**

1975 BEAULIEU VINEYARD PRIVATE RESERVE: I have liked this wine and generally have given it good scores, rating it as the best BV since the 1970, but in the last two tastings it has taken on a damp, earthy, bitter quality and not shown much fruit beyond a hint of cherry and spice. Either these were bad bottles or it is sadly in decline. Drink 1990-1992. Release: $16. Current: $50. **79**

1974 BEAULIEU VINEYARD PRIVATE RESERVE: A great disappointment for a 1974, very mature in color and flavor, with a touch of sweet fruit up front but lacking depth and concentration. It tasted much better the day it was released. Drink 1990-1991. Release: $12. Current: $70. **79**

1973 BEAULIEU VINEYARD PRIVATE RESERVE: Better 10 years ago when it was fruity and elegant, this wine is in decline with fading, mature fruit and not much in the way of tannin. Drink 1990. Release: $9. Current: $50. **79**

1972 BEAULIEU VINEYARD PRIVATE RESERVE: From a wet, rainy vintage of mediocre wines, this wine is showing earthy flavors that are dry and tannic. Fading fast. Drink 1990. Release: $6. Current: $40. **73**

1971 BEAULIEU VINEYARD PRIVATE RESERVE: In decline but still drinkable; the fruit is drying out, leaving earthy, oxidized flavors and a slight vinegary quality on the finish. Drink 1990. Release: $8. Current: $60. **67**

1970 BEAULIEU VINEYARD PRIVATE RESERVE: Fantastic, deep, rich and full of ripe, concentrated fruit. Not quite as ripe or intense as the 1968 or 1969, but very elegant and powerful, with beautifully focused cedar, black cherry and plum flavors. Absolutely delicious now but should hold another five to seven years with ease. Drink 1990-1995. Release: $8. Current: $130. **95**

1969 BEAULIEU VINEYARD PRIVATE RESERVE: Doesn't quite have the intensity and concentration of the 1968, but this wine more than makes up for it in elegance, finesse and delicious complexities. The plum and black cherry aromas and flavors are ripe and supple, with cedar and anise notes on the finish. In perfect drinking condition now. Drink 1990-1995. Release: $6.50. Current: $120. **90**

1968 BEAULIEU VINEYARD PRIVATE RESERVE: Aging beautifully, with elegance and grace, 1968 was an exalted vintage in Napa, and this BV ranks among the elite, still offering rich, forward, well-integrated fruit with layers of anise, smoke, plum and black cherry flavors. Most of the tannins are resolved, leaving a long, lingering aftertaste. At its pinnacle. Drink 1990-1996. Release: $6. Current: $150. **91**

1967 BEAULIEU VINEYARD PRIVATE RESERVE: From a lighter vintage that produced elegant, subtle wines, this 1967 was at its peak a decade ago, with ripe, mature plum and cherry flavors and very delicate tannins. It's still hanging on, but it's best consumed soon. Drink 1990-1993. Release: $5.25. Current: $120. **85**

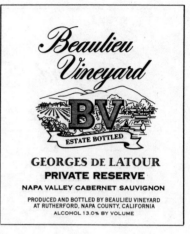

1966 BEAULIEU VINEYARD PRIVATE RESERVE: Another good vintage in Napa Valley and for BV, this wine defines BV elegance and finesse, with layers of pretty currant, cherry, anise and spice flavors, always supple and pleasing, beginning to show its wrinkles with age. Drink 1990-1994. Release: $5.25. Current: $140. **87**

1965 BEAULIEU VINEYARD PRIVATE RESERVE: A fine harvest in Napa Valley, the 1965 is fully mature, with well-integrated cherry, plum and Cabernet flavors. Still a trace of tannin left on the finish, but like most 1965s it is in decline. Drink 1990-1993. Release: $5.25. Current: $120. **85**

1964 BEAULIEU VINEYARD PRIVATE RESERVE: From a ripe vintage with high extract and muscle early on, it has begun to fade, and the flavors are turning from plum and cherry to cedar and anise. Spring frosts wiped out much of the crop, and the entire Cabernet production of 25,000 cases was bottled under the Private Reserve label. Drink 1990-1994. Release: $4.25. Current: $145. **84**

1963 BEAULIEU VINEYARD PRIVATE RESERVE: Only a decent vintage in Napa Valley, this wine was only a good bottle at its best and is now over the hill. Drink 1990. Release: $3.50. Current: $145. **70**

1962 BEAULIEU VINEYARD PRIVATE RESERVE: A mediocre vintage that yielded wines of early drinking charm. The only sampling I have had of this wine showed it to be frail and weakening, interesting but uninspiring. Drink 1990. Release: $3.50. Current: $140. **73**

1961 BEAULIEU VINEYARD PRIVATE RESERVE: In its heyday, a good, decent vintage marred by spring frosts that delayed bloom and a cool growing season. This wine reached only 21.5 degrees Brix and reflects the slightly unripe flavor. Having said that, it was nonetheless enjoyable on the three occasions I have tried it, though the last time it had begun to crumble. Drink 1990-1992. Release: $3.50. Current: $200. **78**

1959 BEAULIEU VINEYARD PRIVATE RESERVE: An excellent vintage in Napa Valley and a fine one for BV. Without quite the richness and concentration of the magnificent 1958, this is a more subtle, elegant wine that drank extremely well for the first two decades of its life but is now in decline. It's fully mature, with rich, smoky Cabernet fruit and hints of caramel on the finish. Drink 1990-1992. Release: $3.50. Current: $350. **89**

1958 BEAULIEU VINEYARD PRIVATE RESERVE: A monumental wine from an exceptional vintage, fully mature yet remarkably complex and well preserved, still showing plenty of ripe black cherry, currant and anise flavors and a touch of oak. Drink 1990-1994. Release: $3. Current: $400. **96**

1956 BEAULIEU VINEYARD PRIVATE RESERVE: From a lighter vintage, this wine has evolved into an elegant, delicate BV with tea, olive and spice aromas and spice, plum and cedar flavors that are fully mature and complex, with hints of black cherry and anise on the finish. Still drinking quite well and showing no signs of fading. Drink 1990-1991. Release: $2.50. Current: $600. **88**

1951 BEAULIEU VINEYARD PRIVATE RESERVE: Another in the ranks of BV's finest. More like an old claret than a California Cabernet, this '51 is holding its own quite nicely, beginning with a fully mature cedar and old claret bouquet that quickly develops into an elegant, complex wine with layers of complex fruit that carries through on the aftertaste. Drink 1990-1992. Release: $1.82. Current: $950. **90**

1948 BEAULIEU VINEYARD PRIVATE RESERVE: From a poor vintage, this wine never fully ripened, reaching only 21 degrees Brix, yet despite that it is quite pleasant and enjoyable, with plum, spice and black cherry flavors and a smoky aftertaste despite its frail condition. At its best years ago. Drink 1990-1992. Release: $1.82. Current: $800. **85**

1947 BEAULIEU VINEYARD PRIVATE RESERVE: From an excellent vintage, this wine shows incredible richness, complexity and harmony for a 40-year-old Cabernet. Even though it's past its peak, there is still much to admire in this amazing wine that seems suspended in time. Drink 1990-1995. Release: $1.82. Current: $1,000. **93**

1946 BEAULIEU VINEYARD PRIVATE RESERVE: In remarkably good condition for a 43-year-old wine, this 1946 still has plenty of ripe, supple fruit, and after an hour the aroma fully develops, with a pretty bouquet of anise, plum and cedar and plenty of flavor. Shows no sign of fading. Drink 1990-1994. Release: $1.47. Current: $1,000. **88**

1944 BEAULIEU VINEYARD PRIVATE RESERVE: Fully mature and past its prime but still holding together the one time I tried it. The bottle bouquet offers tar, anise and a hint of plum that more than captures your attention. Drink 1990-1992. Release: $1.47. Current: $1,100. **87**

1942 BEAULIEU VINEYARD PRIVATE RESERVE: Another healthy old-timer that's aging gracefully, with tar, earth and tea notes in the aroma and rich spice, currant, anise and black cherry on the palate. Fully mature, very complex and enjoyable, gaining in the glass for more than an hour. Drink 1990-1992. Release: $1.45. Current: $1,200. **87**

1941 BEAULIEU VINEYARD PRIVATE RESERVE: From a very ripe, alcoholic vintage, this wine when last tasted several years ago displayed a rich bouquet and mature, spicy anise flavors that were still in harmony. It's been ready to drink for years but was still hanging on. Drink 1990-1992. Release: $1.45. Current: $1,200. **85**

1939 BEAULIEU VINEYARD PRIVATE RESERVE: I have only had this wine once several years ago and then it was fully mature and in decline but still quite pleasant and fascinating, with spicy fruit and cedar aromas and an elegant aftertaste. This wine has great value as a collectible and provides a glimpse of how well California wines can age. Drink 1990. Release: $1.45. Current: $1,500. **82**

Beaulieu Vineyard

BV

ESTATE BOTTLED

GEORGES DE LATOUR
PRIVATE RESERVE
NAPA VALLEY CABERNET SAUVIGNON

PRODUCED AND BOTTLED BY BEAULIEU VINEYARD
AT RUTHERFORD, NAPA COUNTY, CALIFORNIA
ALCOHOL 13.0% BY VOLUME

BERINGER VINEYARDS

Private Reserve, St. Helena, Napa Valley
Chabot Vineyard, St Helena, Napa Valley

CLASSIFICATION:

Private Reserve: FIRST GROWTH

Chabot Vineyard: THIRD GROWTH

COLLECTIBILITY RATING:

Private Reserve: AA

Chabot Vineyard: A

BEST VINTAGES:

Private Reserve: 1986, 1985, 1984, 1982, 1981, 1978

Chabot Vineyard: 1986, 1985

AT A GLANCE

BERINGER VINEYARDS
P.O. Box 111
St. Helena, CA 94574
(707) 963-7115

Owner: Wine World Inc./Nestlé,
Switzerland

Winemaker: Ed Sbragia (12 years)

Founded: 1876

First Cabernet vintage: 1937
Private Reserve: 1977

Cabernet production: 58,000 cases
Private Reserve: 7,000 cases
Chabot Vineyard: 1,000 cases

Cabernet acres owned: 317
Private Reserve: 87
Chabot Vineyard: 29

Average age of vines: 15 years

Vineyard makeup: Cabernet Sauvignon (100%)

Average wine makeup: Cabernet
Sauvignon (100%)

Time in oak: 24 months

Type of oak: French (Nevers)

One of Napa Valley's oldest wineries, Beringer Vineyards in St. Helena has been making Cabernet on and off since 1937. The modern Beringer is a whole new institution, under the ownership of Nestlé, the Swiss food conglomerate, and the Labruyère family of Mâcon, France, since 1972. With the 1977 vintage, Beringer introduced its first Private Reserve bottling, entirely produced from the Lemmon Ranch (now called Chabot) Vineyard in the low hills east of St. Helena. In every vintage since, the Private Reserve has been a great wine, consistently outstanding, uniform in style and ranking among the finest produced in California.

The Beringer Private Reserve style, developed by Ed Sbragia, the current winemaker, and the late Myron Nightingale, emphasizes big, rich, bold, high-extract, 100 percent Cabernet laced with plenty of toasty oak and huge, polished tannins but with a sense of elegance and harmony. It's a dramatic style that ages well.

The 1977, from a drought year, has been drinking exceptionally well for most of its life and still has the depth and intensity to carry it another decade. The 1978 features explosive, ripe, thick fruit. No 1979 Private Reserve was bottled; however, a delicious 1979 was produced from the State Lane Vineyard between Oakville and Yountville and is included in these notes.

With the 1980 vintage, two Private Reserve bottlings were produced, one each from Lemmon-Chabot and State Lane; both are excellent. In 1981 Beringer returned to one Private Reserve that combined fruit from its best lots of Napa Valley fruit, incorporating both Lemmon-Chabot and State Lane along with other smaller lots. The 1982 was highly successful, richly flavored and complex, as was the 1983.

cessful, richly flavored and complex, as was the 1983.

Beginning with the 1984 vintage and carrying through to the 1986 vintage, Beringer's Private Reserve is at the very highest level of Cabernet in California. The 1984 features rich, ripe, explosive fruit, the 1985 shows incredible depth and complexity and the 1986 continues in the same style of deep, rich, powerful but seductive Cabernet. Beringer regularly produces about 1,000 cases of a Chabot Vineyard Cabernet, distinctive for its tightly focused, reined-in fruit and firm tannins. The Cabernet requires five to seven years to develop fully and has the aging potential for a decade or more. Beringer also makes 50,000 cases of Knights Valley Cabernet from its holdings in the slender Knights Valley area in Sonoma County, between Napa Valley and Alexander Valley to the north. It is consistently very good and an excellent value. The regular Beringer Napa Valley Cabernet is sound, but not in the class of the others.

TASTING NOTES

BERINGER VINEYARDS, Private Reserve, St. Helena, Napa Valley

1986 BERINGER VINEYARDS PRIVATE RESERVE: An enormously rich, deep and complex wine that rates among the vintage's finest. It is packed with delicious, concentrated currant, black cherry, anise, cassis and spice flavors, framed by a firm overlay of toasty oak and rigid, gutsy tannins, yet the flavors carry through with depth and persistence on the finish. A remarkable achievement. Drink 1995-2003. 4,000 cases produced. Not Released. **96**

1985 BERINGER VINEYARDS PRIVATE RESERVE: Incredibly rich, intense and sharply focused, brimming with bright, ripe, high-extract black cherry, currant, anise, chocolate and cedar flavors that are enormously deep and complex, supported by just the right amount of tannin and oak. One of the finest Beringer Private Reserves to date. Drink 1994-2004. 8,000 cases produced. Not Released. **96**

1984 BERINGER VINEYARDS PRIVATE RESERVE: A blockbuster of a Cabernet, massively proportioned, extremely rich and powerful, packed with ripe fruit and layers of cherry, cedar, chocolate and toasty vanilla. It's a mouthful of Cabernet that has a silky texture to stand up to the tannins. Ready now but best in four to five years. Drink 1993-2001. 8,000 cases produced. Release: $25. Current: $31. **94**

1983 BERINGER VINEYARDS PRIVATE RESERVE: A tribute to concentrated fruit. In a year of hard, tannic, charmless wines, Beringer managed a very delicate and delicious Cabernet. It has the 1983 trademarks — firmness, intensity and tannins — but plenty of ripe, concentrated fruit to stand up to them. Should age well. Drink 1994-2000. 8,000 cases produced. Release: $19. Current: $30. **89**

1982 BERINGER VINEYARDS PRIVATE RESERVE: Another immensely successful wine from what has proved to be a difficult vintage, richly flavored and deftly balanced, with lush cedar, chocolate, plum and currant flavors that are long and full on the finish. Drinkable now, it should peak in another two to three years. Drink 1992-1999. 4,000 cases produced. Release: $19. Current: $35. **92**

1981 BERINGER VINEYARDS PRIVATE RESERVE: A top-notch 1981 that was thoroughly delicious on release. With its broad, rich, supple fruit and delicate tannins, it has continued to improve with age and shows no sign of losing its charm. Drink 1990-1997. 3,000 cases produced. Release: $18. Current: $40. **91**

1980 BERINGER VINEYARDS PRIVATE RESERVE STATE LANE VINEYARD: Decidedly herbal, with cedar, tea and chocolate notes. High in extract, true to style, but somewhat less appealing than the Lemmon-Chabot; that's the real Private Reserve. Drink 1991-1997. 2,000 cases produced. Release: $15. Current: $40. **85**

1980 BERINGER VINEYARDS PRIVATE RESERVE LEMMON-CHABOT VINEYARD: Ripe, rich, lush and supple, fully mature, with layers of cedar, currant, herb and mint flavors that are well integrated and complex. Drink 1990-1997. 2,000 cases produced. Release: $20. Current: $42. **89**

1979 BERINGER VINEYARDS PRIVATE RESERVE STATE LANE VINEYARD: A highly successful 1979 that has been slow to evolve yet delicious all along the way, combining supple ripe current and spicy plum fruit with a touch of anise and oak. The texture is smooth and polished, finishing with a rich, smoky aftertaste. In perfect drinking condition. Drink 1990-1996. 2000 cases produced. Release: $15. Current: $42. **89**

1978 BERINGER VINEYARDS PRIVATE RESERVE LEMMON RANCH VINEYARD: A big, massive, richly concentrated wine with plenty of extract, flavor and muscle. Its layers of anise, cedar, plum, cherry and chocolate flavors thickly packed together with gutsy tannins should carry it another decade with ease. Despite its size, it is better balanced than the 1977. Drink 1990-1998. 3,000 cases produced. Release: $15. Current: $44. **92**

1977 BERINGER VINEYARDS PRIVATE RESERVE LEMMON RANCH VINEYARD: Fully mature, with complex chocolate, herb, cedar and currant flavors that are rich and smooth, picking up a trace of tannin on the finish. This wine has been drinking exceptionally well for several years yet appears to have the depth and intensity for another decade. Right now it's at its pinnacle. Drink 1990-1995. 2,500 cases produced. Release: $12. Current: $50. **88**

BERINGER VINEYARDS, Chabot Vineyard, St. Helena, Napa Valley

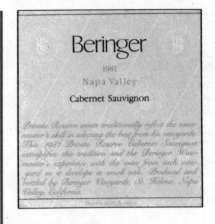

1986 BERINGER VINEYARDS CHABOT VINEYARD: Amazingly rich, complex and elegant, subtle yet intense, with sharply defined currant and cassis flavors, a pretty overlay of toasty oak and just the right amount of acid and tannin for it to age gracefully for a decade or more. The best Chabot bottling to date. Drink 1994-2002. 1,000 cases produced. Not Released. **93**

1985 BERINGER VINEYARDS CHABOT VINEYARD: Enticingly complex with delicious, tart black cherry, currant, earth and cedar flavors that are rich and supple. While this Chabot Vineyard is already approachable, it has the ideal balance of ingredients to improve for six to 10 years and beyond. Drink 1992-2000. 1,000 cases produced. Not Released. **91**

1984 BERINGER VINEYARDS CHABOT VINEYARD: A fine example of the rich, supple charm of the 1984 vintage, not as intense and backward as most bottlings from this vineyard. The bright plum, cherry and smoky anise flavors are attractive. Drink 1991-1997. 750 cases produced. Not Released. **87**

1983 BERINGER VINEYARDS CHABOT VINEYARD: Austere, with drying tannins and an ample core of herb, currant, cherry and cedar flavors. Needs time to unfold. Drink 1992-1998. 1,000 cases produced. Release: $27. Current: $27. **85**

1982 BERINGER VINEYARDS CHABOT VINEYARD: Intense yet elegant, packed with fresh, ripe, juicy currant and cherry flavors, accented with a touch of mint, firm, lean and tannic, a good candidate for another three years' cellaring. Drink 1993-2000. 1,200 cases produced. Release: $25. Current: $38. **89**

1981 BERINGER VINEYARDS CHABOT VINEYARD: Fully mature, with pure currant and berry flavors, ripe and full, with fine balance and plenty of mint and spice nuances. The tannins are deceptively soft. Drink 1990-1996. 1,000 cases produced. Release: $23. Current: $42. **87**

BUEHLER VINEYARDS
Napa Valley

CLASSIFICATION: *FOURTH GROWTH*

COLLECTIBILITY RATING: *A*

BEST VINTAGES: *1986, 1985, 1983*

AT A GLANCE
BUEHLER VINEYARDS
820 Greenfield Road
St. Helena, CA 94574
(707) 963-2155

Owner: John P. Buehler

Winemaker: John Buehler (11 years)

Founded: 1978

First Cabernet vintage: 1978

Cabernet production: 3,500 cases

Cabernet acres owned: 26

Average age of vines: 17 years

Vineyard makeup: Cabernet Sauvignon (100%)

Average wine makeup: Cabernet Sauvignon (100%)

Time in oak: 16 months

Type of oak: French, American

From its first vintage in 1978, Buehler Vineyards established a distinct style of explosively rich, powerful, opulent, deeply flavored Cabernets that are extremely concentrated and tannic. Buehler's Cabernets are not for everyone, for they are dramatic and flamboyant. The 1978 vintage produced an extremely ripe, jammy, 14 percent alcohol Cabernet that is intense and effusively fruity yet manages to remain in balance. It is still developing complexities. No 1979 was produced, and both the 1980 and 1981 Cabernets, while rich and tannic, lacked the drama of the 1978. The 1982 vintage was marred by extreme bottle variation and ranges from excellent to unpalatable.

Beginning with the 1983 vintage, however, Buehler has been on a steady course with its style. Both the 1985 and 1986 vintages are superlative and appear to have the components to age 15 to 20 years.

Buehler's 26-acre Cabernet vineyard is rooted on a gently sloping south-facing hillside in a narrow tuck of the hills east of Napa Valley. While it is technically in the Napa Valley, it has its own microclimate, which tends to be a shade warmer than Napa Valley, ideal for Buehler, which prefers that extra warmth to fully ripen its grapes.

The winery's output of Cabernet has increased from 224 cases in 1978 to nearly 4,000 with the 1986 vintage, yet prices for these exceptional Cabernets remain reasonable at $15. The distinctiveness and quality of the wines and their potential for longevity make them great values.

TASTING NOTES

BUEHLER VINEYARDS, Napa Valley

1986 BUEHLER VINEYARDS: Enormously tannic but with the richness and concentration of ripe fruit to stand up to it, with tremendous raspberry, cherry and spicy oak flavors that are complex and very promising. Structure bodes well for mid-term to long-term aging. Drink 1996-2005. 3,829 cases produced. Release: $15. Current: $15. **91**

1985 BUEHLER VINEYARDS: An extraordinary Cabernet from a great vintage, with beautifully defined, enormously complex fruit that unfolds with rich, ripe raspberry, cherry, currant, spice and pepper notes before the considerable tannins kick in. The best in the Buehler lineup so far, and consistently within the winery's style of bold, dramatic, ageworthy wines. Needs another five to seven years. Drink 1995-2004. 3,060 cases produced. Release: $14. Current: $16. **93**

1984 BUEHLER VINEYARDS: A rich, smooth, tannic 1984 in the Buehler style, with plenty of fresh, ripe fruit that offers hints of violets on the nose and black cherry and currant on the palate. This wine has shown better in previous tastings, and perhaps it is just closing up for a brief slumber. It needs another five years to allow the tannins to retreat. Drink 1995-2003. 2,639 cases produced. Release: $13. Current: $16. **87**

1983 BUEHLER VINEYARDS: This wine has very attractive features for a 1983, beginning with the pretty berry, earth and tar aromas and carrying through on the palate with rich, ripe, lush, well-focused raspberry and black cherry fruit, which stands up well to the dry tannins on the finish. Drink 1993-2001. 2,292 cases produced. Release: $12. Current: $20. **91**

1982 BUEHLER VINEYARDS: Tremendous bottle variation mars this vintage. On occasions it has been very bold and rich, with sturdy fruit, but it is often flawed by very woody, horsey flavors that are unacceptable. At its best it rates an 88; at its worst it rates a 63. Drink 1994-2004. 2,953 cases produced. Release: $12. Current: $30. **88**

1981 BUEHLER VINEYARDS: An even-handed if slightly tannic 1981 that is rich, ripe and earthy, with spicy fruit and firm, dry tannins on the finish. Lacks the dramatic flavors of some Buehler vintages, but it is a very good wine that should be even better in three to five years. Drink 1994-2000. 2,214 cases produced. Release: $11. Current: $20. **85**

1980 BUEHLER VINEYARDS: Another ripe, tannic wine with well-defined black cherry, earth and cedar flavors, finishing with a wallop of dry, mouth-puckering tannins. This wine is not as rich as other Buehler wines and needs more time for the tough edges to round out. Drink 1994-2002. 794 cases produced. Release: $10. Current: $25. **82**

1978 BUEHLER VINEYARDS: Buehler's first vintage, this is an extremely ripe and alcoholic (14 percent) wine that is effusively fruity, with jammy, well-defined black cherry and black currant flavors that are also remarkably elegant and well balanced. The flavors border on overpowering, but there is much to like in this wine. The tannins are in proportion. Drink 1990-1998. 224 cases produced. Release: $10. Current: $35. **87**

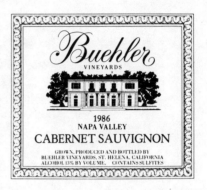

BUENA VISTA WINERY
Private Reserve, Carneros, Sonoma Valley
CLASSIFICATION: *SECOND GROWTH*

COLLECTIBILITY RATING: *AA*

BEST VINTAGES: *1986, 1985, 1984, 1979, 1978*

From one of California's coolest climates in the wind-swept Carneros District of southern Sonoma Valley, Buena Vista since 1978 has been producing brilliant Cabernets that age amazingly well and rank among the top Cabernets produced in Sonoma County. The Carneros climate, influenced by the cooling effects of San Pablo Bay to the south, is hailed as Chardonnay and Pinot Noir country, but Cabernet can do exceptionally well here as evidenced by the Buena Vista Special Selection Cabernets. Louis M. Martini Winery pioneered Carneros Cabernet, but fruit from Martini's La Loma Vineyard went into the Martini Cabernet blend.

The winery was founded in 1857 by Agoston Haraszthy of Hungary, who also probably introduced the Cabernet Sauvignon grape to California. Buena Vista was acquired in 1979 by A. Racke Co. of West Germany and is headed by President Marcus Moller-Racke and his wife, Vineyard Manager Anne Moller-Racke.

Buena Vista is the purest expression of Cabernet from Carneros, for despite the comparatively cool weather, Cabernet grapes rooted on south-facing hillsides receive enough warmth to ripen fully. The Cabernet crops are small, and the fruit is potent, with tart black cherry and currant flavors seasoned by herb and spice notes. Two prime examples are the 1978 and 1980 Special Selections, both abundantly ripe; the 1980 exceeds 14 percent alcohol, yet manages to remain in balance.

There is a sharp distinction between the early 1970s' Buena Vista Cabernets and those produced starting with the 1978 vintage. The 1974 through 1977 Buena Vistas are hardly worth seeking. They are mediocre wines at best and in most instances not worth drinking. With the 1978 Special Selection, a new era dawned at Buena Vista, as this vintage produced an exceptionally well-endowed wine that continues to improve in the bottle today. As excellent as the 1978 was, the 1979 proved better, displaying more elegance and finesse than the intensely ripe 1978, and aging even more gracefully. The 1980 offers jammy notes with plenty of flavor, and the 1981, 1982 and 1983 Cabernets are also very good.

With the 1984 vintage, however, Buena Vista begins another string of amazing wines, this time under the direction of winemaker Jill Davis. The 1984 is oozing with rich fruit, the 1985 is intense and elegant and the 1986 may become the finest Cabernet ever produced by Buena Vista, with thick, concentrated, intensely flavored fruit. Buena Vista's Cabernet vines are fully mature and consistently yield excellent fruit. Beginning with the 1981 vintage, the Special Selection designation became Private Reserve. The Buena Vista regular estate Cabernets are also especially well made and are an excellent value.

The consistently high quality and ageability of the Special Selection/Private Reserve Cabernets make them good investments for the cellar.

TASTING NOTES

BUENA VISTA WINERY, Private Reserve, Carneros, Sonoma Valley

1986 BUENA VISTA WINERY PRIVATE RESERVE: This wine, along with the 1985, is a candidate for the greatest Buena Vista Cabernet ever produced. It combines incredible richness, concentration and depth of flavor with ripe black cherry, plum, cedar and spicy oak flavors that are intense and powerful, yet with a measure of elegance and restraint. Great aftertaste. Years away from its full potential. Drink 1995-2005. 3,150 cases produced. Not Released. **93**

1985 BUENA VISTA WINERY PRIVATE RESERVE: With time this wine will surpass the magnificent 1984 with its intensity and depth of fresh, ripe, rich black cherry and cedar flavors that are just beginning to emerge from their tight coil. Tannins are integrated, and the finish is crisp, fruity and long. Defines elegance and finesse. Drink 1993-2000. 2,900 cases produced. Release: $18. Current: $18. **93**

1984 BUENA VISTA WINERY PRIVATE RESERVE: This wine is rich and seductive, oozing with fresh, ripe, beautifully focused black cherry, currant and spicy oak flavors. It is gorgeous, smooth, rich and supple, elegant and lively. Drinkable now and a good candidate for midterm cellaring. Drink 1990-1996. 2,700 cases produced. Release: $18. Current: $18. **90**

1983 BUENA VISTA WINERY PRIVATE RESERVE: The 1983 is impressive for its crisp, lively cherry aromas and flavors and absence of dry, hard tannins. Beautifully balanced, with plenty of complexity and hints of anise and cedar, this wine is perfectly enjoyable now and should hold for another decade. Drink 1990-1999. 3,500 cases produced. Release: $18. Current: $18. **87**

1982 BUENA VISTA WINERY PRIVATE RESERVE: An elegant, subdued Cabernet that grows on you. It's just beginning to open with complex cherry, cedar and oak flavors that need time to develop. A sleeper on its way up. Alluring now. Drink 1991-1996. 3,700 cases produced. Release: $18. Current: $30. **85**

1981 BUENA VISTA WINERY PRIVATE RESERVE (SPECIAL SELECTION): Not very showy early on, this wine continues to gain complexity and charm. It has a supple texture and bright cherry, cedar, earth and coffee flavors. The majority of the cases were bottled under the Private Reserve designation. Drink 1990-1995. 2,730 cases produced. Release: $18. Current: $32. **86**

1980 BUENA VISTA WINERY SPECIAL SELECTION: Extremely ripe and alcoholic, yet concentrated with plum, raisin and prune flavors that are rich and assertive. Well balanced, with fine tannins and hints of cedar and spice on the finish. Drink 1990-1996. 2,141 cases produced. Release: $18. Current: $35. **84**

1979 BUENA VISTA WINERY SPECIAL SELECTION: A very pretty 1979 with a pronounced toasty, cedary character and ripe currant and blackberry fruit underneath. It's elegant and refined, with great balance and length, but not the richness and extract of the 1978. Drink 1991-1996. 2,595 cases produced. Release: $18. Current: $50. **92**

1978 BUENA VISTA WINERY SPECIAL SELECTION: A wine that combines power with finesse, it is rich, ripe and fruity, loaded with fresh cherry, raspberry, spice and toasty oak flavors, very fine balance and great length, finishing with firm tannins. Approachable now but can still age another decade. Drink 1990-1996. 2,020 cases produced. Release: $18. Current: $60. **90**

1977 BUENA VISTA WINERY CASK 34: An improvement from the previous three vintages, the 1977 offers ripe plum flavors, but it's oaky, bitter and clumsy on the finish. Drink 1990. 2,146 cases produced. Release: $12. Current: $40. **72**

1976 BUENA VISTA WINERY: Losing its fruit now, with faint hints of ripe raisin flavors. Better seven years ago. Best to avoid. 994 cases produced. Release: $12. Current: $40. **66**

1975 BUENA VISTA WINERY: Very dense, weedy and vegetal, hardly reminiscent of Cabernet. Best to avoid. 3,864 cases produced. Release: $12. Current: $30. **64**

1974 BUENA VISTA WINERY CASK 25: Light and earthy, with green Cabernet flavors that are not very pleasant. Well past its prime. Best to avoid. 3,046 cases produced. Release: $12. Current: $40. **68**

BURGESS CELLARS
Vintage Selection, Napa Valley

CLASSIFICATION: *SECOND GROWTH*

COLLECTIBILITY RATING: *AA*

BEST VINTAGES: *1986, 1985, 1984, 1978, 1977, 1975*

Tom Burgess of Burgess Cellars has quietly and consistently produced some of the most richly textured, durable, ageworthy Cabernets in Napa Valley. Few would count Burgess among the Cabernet elite, but connoisseurs appreciate the stylistically robust and deeply flavored Burgess Vintage Selection Cabernets.

Burgess operates out of the old Souverain winery in a forested site on Howell Mountain where the late Lee Stewart first made Cabernets in the 1960s. Burgess is a fan of mountain-grown Cabernet and culls most of his fruit for his Vintage Selection bottling from the winery's 20-acre vineyard; the balance comes from purchased grapes. The early wines were 100 percent Cabernet, but in recent vintages about 10 percent each of Merlot and Cabernet Franc have been added to the blend, resulting in wines of greater finesse without sacrificing the hallmark Burgess style of firm, muscular, tannic wines.

Burgess' first Cabernet vintage came in 1972, but his top-of-the-line bottling Vintage Selection began in 1974 with a classic from that vintage, a deeply scented wine that has held up exceptionally well. In my last two tastings the 1974 had started to decline, so I would begin to drink it. The 1975 and 1976 vintages are also fully mature and ready to drink. The 1977 is marvelous, rich, smooth, thick and supple, while the 1978 is a great wine that still has room to grow. The vintages between 1979 and 1983 uphold the Burgess reputation for excellence, but the 1984 is one of the vintage's stars, with its extraordinary intensity and depth. The 1985 is another superb wine that is very close in quality to the 1984, and the 1986 is among the better efforts from a fine vintage.

Burgess's Cabernet production is nearly 7,000 cases. None of the wines, dating to 1974, has gone over the hill, making Burgess a safe bet for cellaring. At $18 a bottle on release, the Vintage Selection is a reasonably priced wine. Burgess' Zinfandel and Chardonnay, both made in similar rich, ripe, robust styles, are also superior wines. This is one of Napa Valley's unsung heroes.

AT A GLANCE
BURGESS CELLARS
1108 Deer Park Road
St. Helena, CA 94574
(707) 963-4766

Owners: Tom and Linda Burgess

Winemaker: Bill Sorenson (17 years)

Founded: 1972

First Cabernet vintage: 1972
   Vintage selection: 1974

Cabernet production: 7,000 cases

Cabernet acres owned: 20

Average age of vines: 10 years

Vineyard makeup: Cabernet Sauvignon (75%), Cabernet Franc (25%)

Average wine makeup: Cabernet Sauvignon (78%), Cabernet Franc (12%), Merlot (10%)

Time in oak: 33 months

Type of oak: French

BURGESS

1984
Napa Valley
Cabernet Sauvignon

Vintage Selection

PRODUCED AND BOTTLED BY BURGESS CELLARS
ST. HELENA, CALIFORNIA   ALCOHOL 13.0% BY VOLUME

TASTING NOTES

BURGESS CELLARS, Vintage Selection, Napa Valley

1986 BURGESS CELLARS VINTAGE SELECTION: Remarkably rich and fruity, the 1986 is well endowed with layers of cherry, berry, spice and cedar flavors. The tannins ensure a long life. Like most Burgess Cabernets, this wine should age quite well for a decade or more. Drink 1995-2004. 6,600 cases produced. Not Released. **91**

1985 BURGESS CELLARS VINTAGE SELECTION: An elegant, stylish 1985 brimming with ripe currant, cherry and cedar flavors that are rich, deep and concentrated, with fine tannins that smooth out on the finish. Fruit is pretty on the aftertaste. Drink 1992-2002. 6,600 cases produced. Release: $18. Current: $18. **93**

1984 BURGESS CELLARS VINTAGE SELECTION: A phenomenal 1984, firm, lean, rich and intense, with layers of concentrated plum, spice, currant and black cherry flavors offset by toasty oak. Not as fleshy as most '84s, this is an ager. The finish is long and vibrant. An intense wine that needs patience. Drink 1996-2006. 7,200 cases produced. Release: $17. Current: $19. **93**

1983 BURGESS CELLARS VINTAGE SELECTION: One of the more pleasant 1983s, this wine has vitality and crisp acidity to carry the ripe, lean, concentrated plum, currant and toasty oak flavors. The tannins on the finish are fine, allowing the fruity flavors to peek through. Has room to grow. Drink 1994-2002. 6,500 cases produced. Release: $17. Current: $21. **87**

1982 BURGESS CELLARS VINTAGE SELECTION: This wine may be a sleeper. Right now it's not showing much, but it's very rich and concentrated, tightly wound with plenty of cedar and currant flavors that are well focused, though not as vibrant as other Burgess vintages. The finish is supported by firm tannins, but they're not overpowering. Give it time. Drink 1994-2002. 8,300 cases produced. Release: $16. Current: $23. **88**

1981 BURGESS CELLARS VINTAGE SELECTION: A very impressive, intense, straightforward 1981 that is slow to develop. The rich cedar flavors add complexity to the ripe currant and spicy plum flavors, and then the oak and tannins kick in. Needs time to round out the rough spots. Drink 1993-2002. 6,900 cases produced. Release: $16. Current: $25. **88**

1980 BURGESS CELLARS VINTAGE SELECTION: A big, bold, dramatic 1980 with rich, ripe, concentrated plum, anise and currant flavors and firm, muscular tannins. Could use a little more finesse. With age that may come, but for now the tannins dominate. Drink 1994-2002. 5,800 cases produced. Release: $16. Current: $28. **88**

1979 BURGESS CELLARS VINTAGE SELECTION: Plenty of flavor for a 1979 and lots of tannin to shed too. The ripe plum flavors have an added minty component not found in other Burgess Cabernets, and while it's ripe and flavorful it lacks the richness of the great 1977 and 1978 vintages. The short finish gets dry from tannin. Drink 1993-1999. 2,800 cases produced. Release: $16. Current: $30. **87**

1978 BURGESS CELLARS VINTAGE SELECTION: A sensational 1978, this is an amazingly complex wine displaying a rich, earthy mineral note that adds to the ripe, supple plum and currant flavors. Not as tannic as the 1977, but beautifully proportioned, lively and full of flavor and vitality. Ready now but will hold. Drink 1992-2000. 2,800 cases produced. Release: $14. Current: $34. **93**

1977 BURGESS CELLARS VINTAGE SELECTION: A rich, young, bold and dramatic 1977 that is still improving, with complex earth, mineral, plum and currant flavors and crisp, vibrant acidity. Quite tannic. It's drinkable now but capable of aging another decade, maybe longer. A standout among 1977s. Drink 1992-2000. 3,000 cases produced. Release: $12. Current: $45. **92**

1976 BURGESS CELLARS VINTAGE SELECTION: A graceful 1976, ripe, supple, loaded with plum, currant and spicy anise flavors that are smooth and silky, finishing with plenty of flavor. Ready now but can still age. Drink 1991-1997. 2,200 cases produced. Release: $12. Current: $41. **87**

1975 BURGESS CELLARS VINTAGE SELECTION: Effusively fruity, rich and supple, with complex currant, spice, cedar and plum flavors that spread out and coat the palate, a silky texture and a long, smooth finish. Fully mature but will hold at this level for another five to eight years. Drink 1990-2000. 1,800 cases produced. Release: $9. Current: $45. **88**

1974 BURGESS CELLARS VINTAGE SELECTION: Fully mature now and ready to drink, this 1974 has ripe plum, black cherry, floral and cedar nuances, crisp acidity and firm tannins. Holding up well. Drink 1990-1996. 1,100 cases produced. Release: $9. Current: $50. **86**

BURGESS

1984
Napa Valley
Cabernet Sauvignon

Vintage Selection

PRODUCED AND BOTTLED BY BURGESS CELLARS
ST. HELENA, CALIFORNIA   ALCOHOL 13.0% BY VOLUME

CAKEBREAD CELLARS
Rutherford Reserve, Rutherford, Napa Valley

CLASSIFICATION: *FIFTH GROWTH*

COLLECTIBILITY RATING: *Not rated*

BEST VINTAGES:

Rutherford Reserve: 1983

Napa Valley: 1986, 1984, 1981

AT A GLANCE
CAKEBREAD CELLARS
P.O. Box 216
Rutherford, CA 94562
(707) 963-5221

Owners: Jack and Delores Cakebread

Winemaker: Bruce Cakebread
(11 years)

Founded: 1973

First Cabernet vintage: 1974

Cabernet production: 5,500 cases
Rutherford Reserve: 500 cases
Napa Valley: 5,000 cases

Cabernet acres owned: 45

Average age of vines: 6 years

Vineyard makeup: Cabernet Sauvignon (96%), Cabernet Franc (4%)

Average wine makeup:
Rutherford Reserve: Cabernet Sauvignon (90%), Cabernet Franc (10%)
Napa Valley: Cabernet Sauvignon (100%)

Time in oak:
Rutherford Reserve: 30 months
Napa Valley: 22 months

Type of oak: French (Limousin, Nevers)

Through its first dozen vintages, Cakebread's Cabernet style has swung radically, following a trend in Napa Valley away from ultraripe, lush, massively concentrated Cabernets of the 1970s to leaner, less opulent, more acidic wines of the 1980s. The two Cabernets of the 1978 vintage in particular were extremely ripe and luscious, displaying rich, jammy, alcoholic characteristics, and they are still drinking well today despite their style. Since the early 1980s, Cakebread has placed a greater emphasis on crispness and structure, in some instances sacrificing richness, concentration and flavor for correct, understated wines of rather modest character. The 1981 Cakebread, however, was remarkably well made, displaying richness and finesse, which was appealing early on. With the 1985 and 1986 vintage, the Cabernets show more flavor and depth.

Cakebread apparently has found markets for both styles. Beginning with the 1983 vintage, the Rutherford-based winery owned by Jack and Delores Cakebread produced two Cabernets. One is a Napa Valley bottling that is lean and elegant in a ready-to-drink, restaurant style for $18 (about 5,000 cases). The other is a Rutherford Reserve, offering more richness and depth, made with 10 percent Cabernet Franc. The Reserve is made in smaller quantities (300 to 700 cases) and at a much higher price (up to $35 for the 1983).

While Cakebread owns 45 acres of Cabernet near the winery, including a small plot of Cabernet Franc, the winery specializes in Sauvignon Blanc and also makes a Chardonnay. The Cabernets to date are not yet labeled "estate bottled." The winery purchases grapes from growers in the Yountville, Rutherford and Stags Leap districts. Production has risen to 5,500 cases of the two wines, but the level of quality has been irregular, the prices are high and the styles inconsistent. The 1984 offered plenty of rich flavor and early charm, but it is a notch below the top Cabernets from that vintage, and the 1985s, from a sensational year, are merely very good, safe and sound wines.

Moreover, there is little to distinguish the two 1985 bottlings, yet the Reserve will probably sell for twice as much as the regular.

TASTING NOTES

CAKEBREAD CELLARS, Various bottlings

1986 CAKEBREAD CELLARS: Fresh, clean and lively with plenty of concentrated black cherry, currant and plum flavors and a note of mintiness. Firm tannins and toasty oak bring up the rear. Drink 1992-1998. 5,000 cases produced. Release: $18. Current: $18. **89**

1985 CAKEBREAD CELLARS: This wine seems to represent a change from the thick, rich Cakebreads to a leaner, crisper style. Very elegant and pretty, with plum, currant, spice, cedar and tobacco notes, but the flavors lack richness and depth. For near-term drinking. Drink 1992-1996. 5,000 cases produced. Release: $17. Current: $17. **84**

1985 CAKEBREAD CELLARS RUTHERFORD RESERVE: A shade richer and more complex than the regular 1985, this wine is similar in character, with lean, crisp acidity and fresh, ripe plum flavors of medium depth. Approachable now, this wine should age well for a decade. Drink 1993-1998. 700 cases produced. Not Released. **85**

1984 CAKEBREAD CELLARS: An excellent 1984, with loads of rich vanilla, chocolate and black cherry flavors framed by supple tannins and a pretty aftertaste. Like most 1984s it's enticing now, but it has the intensity and concentration to improve for a decade. Drink 1992-2000. 5,000 cases produced. Release: $16. Current: $25. **89**

1983 CAKEBREAD CELLARS: A good 1983, but Cakebread's weakest vintage, this is a lean, thin, tannic wine whose ripe currant flavors can't quite match the tannins. Drink 1992-1995. 4,000 cases produced. Release: $16. Current: $25. **77**

1983 CAKEBREAD CELLARS RUTHERFORD RESERVE: A very elegantly balanced wine, lean and firm, with a pretty core of black cherry and currant flavors and fine tannins, offering more richness and body than the 1983 regular. Drink 1993-2000. 300 cases produced. Release: $35. Current: $35. **88**

1982 CAKEBREAD CELLARS: Fine potential for a 1982; hard and tannic like most wines from this vintage, but unlike most it has a pretty core of black cherry that's beginning to open up. Drink 1994-2000. 5,000 cases produced. Release: $16. Current: $35. **86.**

1981 CAKEBREAD CELLARS: This is a wine that grows on you, impressive for its balance and finesse, rich, lean and supple, with layers of thick currant and black cherry flavors that are fine are elegant on the finish. Charming now, not a long ager. Drink 1990-1995. 4,000 cases produced. Release: $16. Current: $50. **88**

Cakebread Cellars

NAPA VALLEY

Cabernet Sauvignon
1978

PRODUCED AND BOTTLED BY
CAKEBREAD CELLARS
RUTHERFORD, NAPA VALLEY, CALIFORNIA
ALCOHOL 14.8% BY VOLUME

Cakebread Cellars

NAPA VALLEY

Cabernet Sauvignon
1978

PRODUCED AND BOTTLED BY
CAKEBREAD CELLARS
RUTHERFORD, NAPA VALLEY, CALIFORNIA
ALCOHOL 14.8% BY VOLUME

1980 CAKEBREAD CELLARS: A very good 1980 that combines the rich, thick Cabernet fruit with a touch of elegance, but it's also fairly tannic and coarse on the finish. Needs more time to resolve the tannins. Drink 1993-2000. 4,000 cases produced. Release: $14. Current: $45. **84**

1979 CAKEBREAD CELLARS: A very refined 1979 that's a bit on the lean side, with earth, cedar and spicy currant flavors of medium body and weight, fine balance and a delicate aftertaste. Missing the richness of the top 1979s. Drink 1990-1995. 3,300 cases produced. Release: $13. Current: $45. **82**

1978 CAKEBREAD CELLARS: This has always been impressive for its thick, rich, concentrated texture, and there are plenty of ripe, spicy currant and black cherry flavors behind it. Aging gracefully, approaching maturity. Drink 1992-2000. 900 cases produced. Release: $12. Current: $60. **85**

1978 CAKEBREAD CELLARS LOT 2: This is a big, thick, rich, ripe, powerful wine (14.8 percent alcohol), intense, with concentrated black cherry, spice and currant flavors bordering on port-like. Despite all its weight, it's fairly elegant and has charm. Drink 1991-2000. 80 cases produced. Release: $12. Current: $100. **86**

CARMENET VINEYARD

Sonoma Valley

CLASSIFICATION: *THIRD GROWTH*

COLLECTIBILITY RATING: *A*

BEST VINTAGES: *1986, 1985, 1984*

Carmenet, situated in the sloping mountains that form the eastern border of Sonoma Valley, produces a Bordeaux-style blend that features mostly Cabernet Sauvignon with varying portions of Merlot and Cabernet Franc. Parts of the 57-acre Cabernet vineyard, which is a neighbor to Louis Martini Winery's Monte Rosso vineyard, were planted in the early 1970s when it was known as Glen Ellen Vineyard. Cabernets from the vineyard were produced by Ridge, Kistler and Chateau St. Jean.

Carmenet is the "Bordeaux connection" in the Chalone Inc. family of wineries. Chalone Inc., a publicly held wine company, owns Chalone and Acacia wineries, both Pinot Noir and Chardonnay specialists, along with part-interest in Edna Valley Vineyards and a percentage of the Domaines Rothschild wine empire.

From the first vintage in 1982, the Carmenet Red has been first-rate, improving with each vintage, gaining more elegance and finesse without sacrificing the Chalone Inc. house style of making rich, gutsy, tannic wines that are lavishly oaked in mostly new French barrels and built to age. Carmenet Red starts out sturdy, rough-hewn, chunky, oaky and coarse, but the flavors even out and offer remarkably ripe, deep and complex flavors.

AT A GLANCE
CARMENET VINEYARD
1700 Moon Mountain Road
Sonoma, CA 95476
(707) 996-5870

Owner: Chalone Inc.

Winemaker: Jeff Baker (8 years)

Founded: 1980

First Cabernet vintage: 1982

Cabernet production: 9,500 cases

Cabernet acres owned: 57

Average age of vines: 15 years

Vineyard makeup: Cabernet Sauvignon (76%), Cabernet Franc (14%), Merlot (10%)

Average wine makeup: Cabernet Sauvignon (87%), Merlot (8%), Cabernet Franc (5%)

Time in oak: 20 months

Type of oak: French

TASTING NOTES

CARMENET VINEYARD, Sonoma Valley

1986 CARMENET VINEYARD: From an excellent vintage in Sonoma Valley, this is Carmenet's finest effort to date. Everything is in sync, from the toasty vanilla and spicy plum aromas to the elegant, refined, sharply focused black cherry flavors. This wine has the richness, depth and concentration for midterm to long-term cellaring, and it's delicious already. Drink 1994-2005. 9,469 cases produced. Release: $20. Current: $20. **93**

1985
ESTATE BOTTLED

Carmenet

SONOMA VALLEY

CABERNET SAUVIGNON
Eighty-Seven Per Cent
MERLOT
Eight Per Cent
CABERNET FRANC
Five Per Cent

PRODUCED AND BOTTLED BY
CARMENET VINEYARD
A CHALONE PROPERTY
MAYACAMAS MOUNTAINS
SONOMA, CALIFORNIA USA
CONTAINS SULFITES • ALC. 12.9% BY VOL.

1985 CARMENET VINEYARD: A beautifully knit 1985 with layers of complex flavors, elegant balance and tannins and great length. This wine offers ripe plum and cherry flavors with vanilla and tobacco nuances on the finish. The tannins are fine and integrated, not showing much yet but are there for cellaring. Tempting now but can age a decade with ease. Drink 1994-2004. 6,040 cases produced. Release: $18.50. Current: $22. **91**

1984 CARMENET VINEYARD: An excellent 1984 that bears the stamp of the vintage with its rich, open, supple and generous fruit. The black cherry, currant and spice flavors are very concentrated and intense, finishing with fleshy-yet-firm tannins. Should age well for another decade or more, but because of its fleshy texture, you can begin drinking it earlier. Drink 1992-2004. 6,641 cases produced. Release: $16. Current: $30. **92**

1983 CARMENET VINEYARD: More austere than the 1982 but typical of the vintage, the 1983 is a tight, lean wine, not showing much fruit, with hints of mint and plum and drying tannins on the finish. With time it may gain elegance, but for now it needs cellaring for another five to eight years. Drink 1994-2004. 6,175 cases produced. Release: $17.50. Current: $25. **85**

1982 CARMENET VINEYARD: Carmenet's first vintage, this is a very sturdy, highly respectable 1982 that is lean, elegant and refined, with black cherry, herb, plum and tobacco notes along with plenty of concentration and tannins for cellaring. Drink 1993-2003. 5,348 cases produced. Release: $16. Current: $30. **87**

CAYMUS VINEYARDS
Special Selection, Rutherford, Napa Valley
Estate, Rutherford, Napa Valley

CLASSIFICATION:

Special Selection: FIRST GROWTH

Estate: SECOND GROWTH

COLLECTIBILITY RATING:

Special Selection: AAA

Estate: AA

BEST VINTAGES:

Special Selection: 1986, 1985, 1984, 1983, 1982, 1981, 1980,

1979, 1978, 1976, 1975

Estate: 1986, 1985, 1984, 1982, 1980, 1979, 1973

Caymus Vineyards is a name that is synonymous with classically proportioned, richly flavored Napa Valley Cabernets. Proprietor Charles Wagner considers Caymus California's most consistent producer of first-rate Cabernet, and that point is difficult to debate. Since 1972, when Wagner and his son Chuck produced their first vintage, Caymus has made an amazing line of distinctive, richly concentrated, ageworthy Cabernets from its 40-acre vineyard along the eastern outskirts of Rutherford. Moreover, the winery's flagship Cabernet, the Special Selection, has been one of the most sensational wines produced in California for more than a decade. Looking back at 16 vintages and 26 wines, including Special Selection bottlings, there was only one weak link, 1977, a drought year in which Caymus produced only a good wine. The rest of the lineup is flawless.

Charles Wagner, 77, is a Napa Valley original. A native of Rutherford, he has lived in the valley his entire life and is first and foremost a farmer. For years Wagner produced homemade wine and sold his grapes to Napa Valley wineries. In 1972 he produced his first 230 cases of Cabernet. The 1972 vintage was the poorest of the 1970s, yet Wagner managed to make a rich, flavorful Cabernet that is still drinking well today. In 1973 Caymus produced one of the top wines of the vintage, followed by a 1974 that was very good but not quite up to the best of that year. With the 1975 vintage, the year Randy Dunn joined the winemaking team, Caymus introduced its Special Selection, a wine chosen from the best barrels of wine each vintage and then given extended barrel aging of up to four years, a year longer than the Estate.

AT A GLANCE

CAYMUS VINEYARDS
P.O. Box 268
Rutherford, CA 94562
(707) 963-4204

Owners: The Wagner family

Winemaker: Charles & Chuck Wagner (17 years)

Founded: 1972

First Cabernet vintage: 1972
Special Selection: 1975

Cabernet production: 22,000 cases
Special Selection: 1,000 cases
Estate: 4,000 cases

Cabernet acres owned: 40

Average age of vines: 10 years

Vineyard makeup: Cabernet Sauvignon (96%), Cabernet Franc (3%), Malbec and Petit Verdot (1%)

Average wine makeup: Cabernet Sauvignon (100%)

Time in oak:
Special Selection: 48 months
Estate: 20 months

Type of oak:
Special Selection: French
Estate: French, American

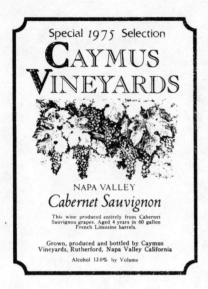

Special *1975* Selection
CAYMUS VINEYARDS

NAPA VALLEY
Cabernet Sauvignon

This wine produced entirely from Cabernet
Sauvignon grapes. Aged 4 years in 60 gallon
French Limosine barrels.

Grown, produced and bottled by Caymus
Vineyards, Rutherford, Napa Valley California

Alcohol 13.0% by Volume

Despite the high quality of both the Estate and Special Selection, the wines are genuinely distinct. While both are 100 percent Cabernet, rich and elegant, with intense, sharply focused fruit, the Special Selection is much deeper, richer and more intense; it is also more tannic and oaky. Connoisseurs debate which is the better wine, but in my tastings the Special Selection is clearly superior. In virtually every vintage it ranks ahead of the Estate bottling. The 1975, 1978, 1979, 1984, 1985 and 1986 Special Selections are colossal wines that have few peers. In each of those vintages, the Estate is also excellent, offering plenty of rich, well-defined herb and tea notes. The best Estate vintages remain 1973, 1979, 1980, 1982, 1984, 1985 and 1986.

Because of their long barrel aging, the Caymus Cabernets are drinkable early on. With age, the bright, fresh currant, cherry and chocolate flavors acquire an herbal-tea and cedary quality that adds complexity. In most years the Estate bottlings begin to drink well by the time they are six to 10 years old, and in superior vintages they can hold even longer. The Special Selection Cabernets need more time. The 1976 is ready to drink, but the 1975, while enjoyable, still has years of development left, as do the 1978 and 1979 bottlings. The 1985 Special Selection appears to be the finest Cabernet Caymus has ever produced, with phenomenal richness, depth, elegance and flavor, putting it a notch above the fantastic 1984. Stylistically, the 1986 falls between the 1984 and 1985.

Caymus' production of the Estate Cabernet hovers around 4,000 cases and represents an exceptional bottle of wine for $18 to $20. The Special Selection case volume has recently climbed from 600 to 1,000. Even at $35, it is well worth the price considering its truly unique character and limited availability. With the 1984 vintage, a third Cabernet was added to the lineup, the Napa Valley Cuvée bottling, made from grapes purchased in the valley but produced under the Wagners' careful attention. It, too is exceptionally fine.

TASTING NOTES

CAYMUS VINEYARDS, Special Selection, Rutherford, Napa Valley

1986 CAYMUS VINEYARDS SPECIAL SELECTION: From an excellent if not outstanding vintage, this 1986 Special Selection upholds the Caymus tradition, with incredibly forward fruit, elegance and sharply focused Cabernet flavors. The tannins are fine and integrated, and it's rich and flavorful, with fruit and oak lingering on the palate. Another triumph for Caymus. Drink 1995-2005. 1,000 cases produced. Not Released. **98**

1985 CAYMUS VINEYARDS SPECIAL SELECTION: This promises to be an extraordinary wine from a great vintage and the finest Special

Selection ever produced. The fruit is incredibly rich, complex and lively, with layers of cedar, plum, cassis and black cherry that gracefully unfold on the palate. The tannins are lean and, fine and mouthwatering, giving the wine a steely backbone and great length. Not as opulent as the 1984 but amazingly elegant and refined. Drink 1995-2009. 1,000 cases produced. Not Released. **99**

1984 CAYMUS VINEYARDS SPECIAL SELECTION: A magnificent wine, tight, lean and concentrated for an 1984, this is a definite ager in the finest Special Selection tradition. It's closed, hard and compact, with ripe plum and currant flavors dominated by the tannins and acidity. Needs only time for greatness. Drink 1995-2008. 1,000 cases produced. Release: $35. Current: $50. **98**

1983 CAYMUS VINEYARDS SPECIAL SELECTION: An excellent 1983, one of the vintage's finest, this intense, rich, concentrated wine is loaded with plum, currant, spice and toasty oak flavors, with crisp acidity and fine tannins. All you could want in elegance for cellaring. Drink 1993-2006. 1,100 cases produced. Release: $35. Current: $50. **91**

1982 CAYMUS VINEYARDS SPECIAL SELECTION: A massively structured, intense wine that is tight, hard and compact, years from drinking. It's loaded with ripe plum, currant, anise and oak flavors, firm, slightly coarse tannins and a pretty chocolate and caramel aftertaste. Everything's in place for greatness. Drink 1995-2006. 750 cases produced. Release: $35. Current: $65. **92**

1981 CAYMUS VINEYARDS SPECIAL SELECTION: Tight, firm, concentrated and tannic, this is an ager in the mold of the 1975 and 1978 vintages. The ripe plum, currant and black cherry flavors are closed and compact, requiring further aging before drinking, but it's beautiful, elegant and focused. Drink 1995-2006. 1,250 cases produced. Release: $35. Current: $60. **93**

1980 CAYMUS VINEYARDS SPECIAL SELECTION: A young wine on its way up, tight and lean, crisp, with ripe plum, cherry, currant and anise flavors that are elegant and stylish, finishing with a pretty aftertaste and great length. Fine tannins make it approachable now, but it should only get better. Drink 1993-2000. 750 cases produced. Release: $30. Current: $80. **92**

1979 CAYMUS VINEYARDS SPECIAL SELECTION: A gorgeous wine, rich, supple and complex, packed with ripe, vibrant currant, spice, cedar and anise flavors that are crisp, lively and long. One of the great 1979s as well as one of Caymus' finest. Nearing maturity and worth waiting for. Drink 1994-2006. 600 cases produced. Release: $30. Current: $85. **97**

1978 CAYMUS VINEYARDS SPECIAL SELECTION: A rich, bold, dramatic wine, complex and elegant, with layers of currant, earth, cedar, cherry and plum flavors that display uncommon depth and character, impeccable balance and great length. A magnificent wine that ranks among the greatest ever produced in California. Vibrant and tannic,

Special *1975* Selection
CAYMUS VINEYARDS

NAPA VALLEY
Cabernet Sauvignon

This wine produced entirely from Cabernet Sauvignon grapes. Aged 4 years in 60 gallon French Limosine barrels.

Grown, produced and bottled by Caymus Vineyards, Rutherford, Napa Valley California

Alcohol 13.0% by Volume

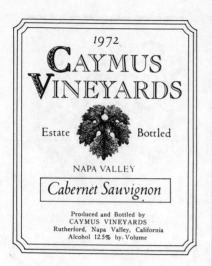

1972
CAYMUS
VINEYARDS

Estate   Bottled

NAPA VALLEY

Cabernet Sauvignon

Produced and Bottled by
CAYMUS VINEYARDS
Rutherford, Napa Valley, California
Alcohol 12.5% by. Volume

with years ahead. Drink 1994-2005. 600 cases produced. Release: $30. Current: $90. **97**

1976 CAYMUS VINEYARDS SPECIAL SELECTION: A successful 1976 that is rich and tannic, with a fair amount of oak and plenty of plum, currant and anise flavors. It's rather coarse, missing the elegance and finesse of the 1975 Special Selection, but it may soften with time. Nearing its peak. Drink 1993-1998. 270 cases produced. Release: $35. Current: $150. **90**

1975 CAYMUS VINEYARDS SPECIAL SELECTION: A magnificent wine, one of the great 1975s, as well as a one of Caymus's finest, this wine is deep and fragrant, loaded with fresh, ripe plum, cedar, currant and chocolate flavors that are supple and elegant, finishing with fine tannins and a pretty black currant and anise aftertaste. Lovely now but can age further. Drink 1992-2000. 180 cases produced. Release: $22. Current: $175. **92**

CAYMUS VINEYARDS, Estate, Rutherford, Napa Valley

1986 CAYMUS VINEYARDS ESTATE: This is a beautifully defined Rutherford Cabernet, rich, lean and elegant, with layers of spice, cedar, plum and black cherry flavors that echo on the palate. The tannins are there for aging but are in the background for now. Everything appears in place for greatness. Drink 1995-2005. 4,000 cases produced. Release: $22. Current: $22. **92**

1985 CAYMUS VINEYARDS ESTATE: With all of its richness and depth, this bottling defines the Caymus elegance. The flavors are lean, ripe and spicy, with layers of plum, currant, herb and cassis flavors and gentle, integrated tannins on the finish. Not as opulent as the 1984, it is nonetheless an excellent wine that should gain for another decade. Drink 1994-2003. 3,500 cases produced. Release: $18. Current: $28. **92**

1984 CAYMUS VINEYARDS ESTATE: Another excellent Caymus bottling from a fine vintage, this richly flavored, supple 1984 is packed with ripe plum, herb and currant flavors. The tannins, while thick, are smooth and fleshy. Tempting now but will age a decade with ease. Drink 1993-2002. 3,200 cases produced. Release: $16. Current: $30. **91**

1983 CAYMUS VINEYARDS ESTATE: In a difficult vintage that produced many lean, tannic, hard-as-nails wines, Caymus managed to produce a deep, concentrated, ageworthy wine. It's firm and hard, but there's a rich core of black currant, plum and spicy cherry flavors underneath, and the tannins, while firm and tight, are not overwhelmingly dry and biting. Put this one away for another five to 10 years; it should become polished and elegant. Drink 1994-2002. 3,000 cases produced. Release: $15. Current: $30. **87**

1982 CAYMUS VINEYARDS ESTATE: A rich, concentrated, compact wine, with bold ripe currant, plum and black cherry flavors that are beautifully focused and elegantly balanced, crisp acidity and firm yet supple tannins. The finish is long and fruity. Nearing maturity now but should age well for another decade. Drink 1993-2000. 4,200 cases produced. Release: $14. Current: $33. **90**

1981 CAYMUS VINEYARDS ESTATE: Ripe, forward and supple, with generous, fleshy plum, black cherry and cedar flavors, crisp, mouth-watering acidity and smooth, polished tannins. Impeccably balanced, elegant and refined. This wine is attractive for its drinkability now, but with its fine balance, lively acidity and fresh flavors, it's probably a good candidate for midterm cellaring. Drink 1990-1998. 3,200 cases produced. Release: $14. Current: $35. **88**

1980 CAYMUS VINEYARDS ESTATE: A deep, rich, concentrated wine with plenty of black cherry, currant and plum flavors, crisp acidity and tannins for a long life. At this point it is a shade less complex and flavorful than the 1979, but it has the same intensity and vibrancy on the palate. With time it may gain that additional measure of depth. Drink 1993-2000. 4,300 cases produced. Release: $12.50. Current: $35. **90**

1979 CAYMUS VINEYARDS ESTATE: This is a rich, elegant, concentrated wine, showing more intensity and depth of flavor than the 1978, more similar in character to the sensational 1973. The cedar, plum, vanilla and black cherry flavors are tightly knit and firm, and fine tannins give it a satiny texture. Pretty, complex earth and fruit flavors echo on the finish. Approachable now but capable of further aging. Drink 1992-1998. 2,700 cases produced. Release: $12. Current: $35. **92**

1978 CAYMUS VINEYARDS ESTATE: This wine is fully mature now, with black cherry, herb, earth and cedar flavors that are soft and elegant. There are enough tannins and fruit peeking through on the finish for further aging, but it's probably about as good as it's going to get. Drink 1990-1996. 2,600 cases produced. Release: $12. Current: $60. **87**

1977 CAYMUS VINEYARDS ESTATE: This wine is an apparent drought victim and not characteristic of Caymus. It's lighter in body and lacks the depth and intensity of every other Caymus vintage, and it's clearly a step below some of the finer 1977s. The mint and cedar flavors are simple and fade on the palate. Drink up. Drink 1990-1994. 1,700 cases produced. Release: $10. Current: $40. **77**

1976 CAYMUS VINEYARDS ESTATE: Offers ripe, supple plum and black cherry flavors; this elegantly balanced wine is now fully mature and ready to drink despite its deep color. While it can hold for another five to seven years, it is losing its intensity, and the finish is beginning to soften. Drink 1990-1995. 1,600 cases produced. Release: $10. Current: $60. **85**

1975 CAYMUS VINEYARDS ESTATE: An elegant yet generous wine, with black cherry, plum and spice flavors that offer depth, complexity and elegance. The fruit is fresh enough for further development. As

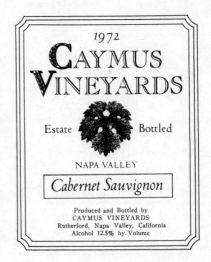

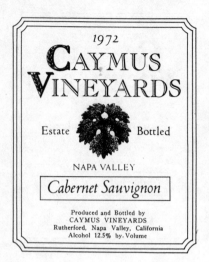

for quality, it falls between the 1973 and 1974. Drink 1990-1998. 1,300 cases produced. Release: $8.50. Current: $80. **89**

1974 CAYMUS VINEYARDS ESTATE: Very ripe and fruity on the nose but with less flavor coming through than the sensational 1973; it's a much less complex and elegant wine. The fruit seems hollow and less concentrated, and it comes across as sluggish on the finish. Still, it's a pretty fine wine, with black cherry and currant flavors and just enough tannin to carry it another five to 10 years. A step down in quality from the 1973, but it won't disappoint. Drink 1990-1996. 950 cases produced. Release: $7. Current: $110. **87**

1973 CAYMUS VINEYARDS ESTATE: Deliciously complex and elegant, with a beautiful bouquet of fruit and deep, rich flavors of black cherry, currant and anise. All silk and polish on the palate, long and lasting. In perfect condition now, with the color and depth to carry it another decade. Drink 1990-2000. 850 cases produced. Release: $6. Current: $120. **93**

1972 CAYMUS VINEYARDS ESTATE: Fully mature now but holding its own, a ripe, supple, elegantly balanced wine with anise, black cherry and cedar flavors that linger on the palate. Drink 1990-1993. 230 cases produced. Release: $4.50. Current: $110. **86**

CHAPPELLET VINEYARD

Reserve, Napa Valley
Estate, Napa Valley

CLASSIFICATION: *FOURTH GROWTH*

COLLECTIBILITY RATING: *Not rated*

BEST VINTAGES: *1986, 1985, 1980, 1978, 1970, 1969, 1968*

Chappellet Vineyard, founded in 1967 by Donn and Molly Chappellet, rose to prominence in the late 1960s on the merit of three successive vintages of rich, concentrated, ageworthy Cabernets. This winery on the forested hills east of Rutherford became one of the Napa Valley wineries to watch.

While the 1968, 1969 and 1970 vintages were remarkable for their depth and complexity, the wines of the mid-1970s and early 1980s were inconsistent, well below the top-echelon Napa Valley producers. The 1968, 1969 and 1970 have all aged exceptionally well, placing them among the top Cabernets produced in those vintages. The 1968 and 1969 are now both fully mature and at their drinking peaks, while the 1970 is still in magnificent condition and can stand further aging. As collectibles, the early Chappellet Cabernets all rank high because of their excellent quality and rather scarce supply. The 1968 vintage produced only 200 cases, the 1969 yielded 400 cases and the 1970, 700 cases. Prices for those early vintages have also soared; most notably the 1969, which sold for $10 on release and now is valued at $150 a bottle, and the 1970, which sold for $7.50 on release and is now valued at $160.

Beginning in the 1970s, as the winery expanded production, a succession of fair to mediocre vintages and a procession of winemakers, including Philip Togni, Joe Cafaro, Tony Soter and now Cathy Corison, resulted in considerably less-inspired Chappellet Cabernets than the first trio promised. In particular the 1973, 1974, 1975 and 1977 vintages, which were very good to excellent throughout Napa Valley, were only fair at Chappellet, and these wines have already declined in quality. The 1978 and 1980 vintages were both superb and showed Chappellet had regained its form, while the 1984, 1985 and 1986 vintages indicate Chappellet is fully back on track with its austere yet rich and concentrated style. The 1986 Reserve is the best Chappellet since the 1980, although not quite as dramatic as the monumental 1970, which remains the finest Chappellet has produced. While Chappellet is known for austere, tannic wines, they are not nearly as tannic as most mountain-grown Cabernets. With the 1986 Reserve, it appears Chappellet is adding more richness to its wines, which gives them a broader, more supple texture and more flavor.

AT A GLANCE

CHAPPELLET VINEYARD
1561 Sage Canyon Road
St. Helena, CA 94574
(707) 963-7136

Owner: Donn Chappellet

Winemaker: Cathy Corison (8 years)

Founded: 1967

First Cabernet vintage: 1968

Cabernet production: 6,000 cases

Cabernet acres owned: 36

Average age of vines: 20 years

Vineyard makeup: Cabernet Sauvignon (84%), Merlot (16%)

Average wine makeup: Cabernet Sauvignon (85%), Merlot (15%)

Time in oak: 22 months

Type of oak: French (Nevers, Tronçais, Allier)

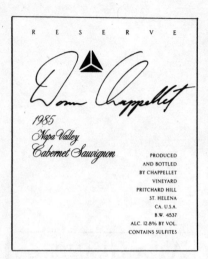

Production of Chappellet Cabernet has averaged 5,000 cases a year through 20 vintages, but has risen as high as 11,800 cases in 1982, 8,700 in 1983 and 8,000 in both 1981 and 1984. The entire Cabernet crop is grown in Chappellet's 36-acre vineyard on Pritchard Hill, which is 1,700 feet above sea level and overlooks Lake Hennessey and the surrounding hills. About 16 percent Merlot is added to the blend. Prices for current Chappellet releases are around $20 a bottle, but the winery has an honest practice of pricing according to its estimation of the vintage, so better vintages are priced higher than lesser ones. Cabernets with Donn Chappellet's signature and Reserve wines are designated only in superior years.

TASTING NOTES

CHAPPELLET VINEYARD, Various bottlings

1986 CHAPPELLET VINEYARD RESERVE: Chappellet's finest Cabernet since 1980 and one that belongs in the class of the late-1960s wines, this is a sharply defined wine with tart black cherry, anise and cedar flavors that are lean and elegant with firm tannins and a delicate aftertaste. Should be nearing its peak in five years. Drink 1994-2003. 6,000 cases produced. Not Released. **92**

1985 CHAPPELLET VINEYARD RESERVE: A very pretty wine, crisp, clean and elegant, laced with enticing, spicy cherry, currant and cedar flavors, impeccably balanced and with fine, supple tannins. This defines the Chappellet style of restrained elegance, balance, finesse and delicacy. It is not one of the rich, high-extract, massive wines that many wineries produced in 1985. This should be ready soon but is capable of midterm aging. Drink 1994-2000. 6,000 cases produced. Release: $20. Current: $20. **88**

1984 CHAPPELLET VINEYARD RESERVE: True to the Chappellet style, this is lean, tight and elegant, not as rich, fleshy and opulent as most of the 1984s but a very well-made wine nonetheless. The cedar, black cherry and spicy anise flavors are crisp and lively, and the tannins are fine and integrated. Enjoyable now but should improve in the next three to five years. Drink 1992-1996. 8,000 cases produced. Release: $18. Current: $23. **87**

1983 CHAPPELLET VINEYARD ESTATE: Typical of most '83s, lean, underdeveloped, simple and disproportionately tannic, this is a good, simple wine with herb, cedar and cherry flavors but not much depth or intensity. An average wine. Drink 1990-1995. 8,700 cases produced. Release: $12. Current: $15. **77**

1982 CHAPPELLET VINEYARD ESTATE: Light and herbal, with cherry flavor, this is a rather simple, ready-to-drink 1982 that is pleasant and delicate but missing the richness and concentration that the best 1982s possess. Drink 1990-1993. 11,800 cases produced. Release: $9.25. Current: $14. **80**

1981 CHAPPELLET VINEYARD ESTATE: This is a well-made, well-balanced if uninspired 1981, with a tight, lean framework and tart black cherry and cedar flavors that are a bit muted and closed, lacking the richness of the very fine 1980 bottling. Not too tannic. Drink 1990-1995. 8,000 cases produced. Release: $11. Current: $18. **79**

1980 CHAPPELLET VINEYARD ESTATE: A tightly wound, complex wine that is just beginning to reveal the depth and concentration of the rich black cherry, currant and cedar flavors of this very fine vintage. This is what one expects from Chappellet Cabernets: depth, concentration, elegance and flavor. Drink 1993-1998. 7,000 cases produced. Release: $18. Current: $28. **91**

1979 CHAPPELLET VINEYARD ESTATE: This is a hard, tannic, slightly green wine that is good but lacking in charm and depth of flavor. It appears to be a victim of the 1979 weather, which prevented many wines from reaching full maturity and developing the richness and breadth of flavor of the vintage's best wines. Drink 1990-1995. 6,400 cases produced. Release: $13. Current: $26. **79**

1978 CHAPPELLET VINEYARD ESTATE: This is one of Chappellet's finest Cabernets and clearly the best since the sensational 1970. It's tight, lean, concentrated and firmly structured, with rich, ripe currant, black cherry, cedar and pepper nuances. There's still plenty of tannin to resolve, but there is also ample fruit to match it. Drinkable now but should continue to improve. Drink 1992-1998. 7,000 cases produced. Release: $13. Current: $40. **88**

1977 CHAPPELLET VINEYARD ESTATE: The 1977 is very ripe and mature now, at its peak, with intense currant, anise and black cherry flavors and firm, drying tannins that are straightforward and rather simple, despite the intensity of flavor. Its major drawback is the dryness of the oak and tannin on the finish. Drink 1990-1994. 4,500 cases produced. Release: $12. Current: $33. **82**

1976 CHAPPELLET VINEYARD ESTATE: A shade past its prime, this 1976 is a good if simple wine that is fairly oaky and beginning to dry out. The ripe currant and anise flavors are fading on the palate. Better two years ago. Drink 1990. 4,500 cases produced. Release: $12. Current: $37. **76**

1975 CHAPPELLET VINEYARD ESTATE: Fully mature and enjoyable but only a shadow of its former self, this is a good wine that reached its peak several years ago but is holding its own. Its mature cedar, bark and black currant flavors are subtle and gentle. Just a hint of tannin remains. Drink 1990. 5,000 cases produced. Release: $10. Current: $45. **78**

1974 CHAPPELLET VINEYARD ESTATE: This wine is in a steep decline for a 1974, showing its age, with overly mature, oxidized flavors

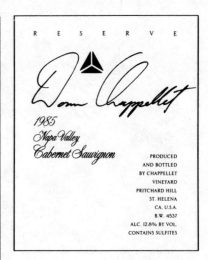

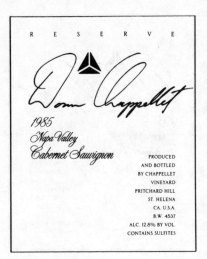

and just a faint hint of cedar and black cherry on the palate. Drink 1990. 3,500 cases produced. Release: $7.50. Current: $45. **70**

1973 CHAPPELLET VINEYARD ESTATE: On the downward side and fading fast, the 1973 has only a touch of life left, with mature cedar, herb and black currant flavors that vanish from the palate. Better five years ago, this wine should be consumed quickly. Drink 1990. 2,500 cases produced. Release: $7.50. Current: $65. **69**

1972 CHAPPELLET VINEYARD ESTATE: Faded now, with mature flavors of cedar and bark. Never a vintage for long-term aging anyway, this wine was best consumed five to seven years ago. A curiosity. Drink 1990. 1,500 cases produced. Release: $6.50. Current: $40. **67**

1971 CHAPPELLET VINEYARD ESTATE: Well past its prime, with oxidized, mature wine flavors, but this 1971 was once a very good wine from a mediocre vintage. Not much to look forward to if this one's still resting in your cellar. Drink 1990. 1,000 cases produced. Release: $7.50. Current: $80. **65**

1970 CHAPPELLET VINEYARD ESTATE: This is a beautifully knit, seamless Cabernet that defines the Chappellet style of understated elegance, delicate balance and finesse. This wine is fully mature now and on a lofty plateau, with rich, complex black cherry, earth and truffle nuances and a smooth smoke and anise aftertaste. Most of the tannin is gone, but this wine has the depth and character for another five to seven years. Drink 1990-1995. 700 cases produced. Release: $7.50. Current: $160. **93**

1969 CHAPPELLET VINEYARD ESTATE: Fully mature, this 1969 is drying out, with the ripe plum flavors giving way to dry, rich cedar flavors that are getting frail. Not likely to get much better. Drink 1990-1995. 400 cases produced. Release: $10. Current: $150. **87**

1968 CHAPPELLET VINEYARD ESTATE: Chappellet's first vintage, the 1968 is beginning to show its age, although it remains quite attractive, with rich cedar, berry, cherry and earth flavors that are tart and firm. While the flavors are mature, there are still hard tannins remaining. Lacks the delicacy and finesse of the 1970 vintage. Best consumed now, but it may surprise with further aging. Drink 1990-1996. 200 cases produced. Release: $5.50. Current: $100. **88**

CHATEAU MONTELENA

Estate, Calistoga, Napa Valley

CLASSIFICATION: *FIRST GROWTH*

COLLECTIBILITY RATING: *AA*

BEST VINTAGES:

Estate: 1986, 1985, 1984, 1983, 1982, 1978

Napa: 1977, 1974

North Coast: 1976

Sonoma: 1977

Château Montelena has one of the most consistently excellent and remarkable track records in California in producing rich, concentrated, elegant and ageworthy Cabernets. It is one of the surest, steadiest performers, with a style that is all its own yet classically Napa Valley. That the style has remained so deliberate and constant is a tribute to the winery and to its three winemakers, Mike Grgich (now of Grgich Hills), Jerry Luper (Freemark Abbey and Rutherford Hill) and current winemaker Bo Barrett.

Until 1978, when Château Montelena began its estate-bottled Cabernet from its 70-acre vineyard in Calistoga, the winery produced both a Napa Valley and Sonoma County Cabernet. Yet, despite disparate appellations, the Montelena style of elegance, grace and complexity shows through in all those bottlings, even today. There are numerous Cabernets to get excited about among the first 13 vintages, including the first vintage, a 1973 from Alexander Valley that remains an amazingly young and vibrant Cabernet, with ample fruit and intensity to carry it another decade. Both the 1974s are exceptional; the Sonoma County offers more ripe, opulent fruit than the bold, tannic Napa Valley bottling. The 1975 and 1976 are both in fine condition, and the 1976 North Coast is noteworthy for its smooth, supple texture. The 1977s again are both outstanding, but the Napa Valley Cabernet is incredibly thick and complex, still years from peaking. It ranks among the handful of great wines produced that year.

The 1978 estate defines Montelena's current valiant, gutsy style with its assertive black currant, cherry, mint and cedary oak complexities. The 1979 through 1981 vintages are also excellent. The 1982 is one of the standouts of that difficult vintage. The 1983 succeeds with richness and flavor when many Cabernets were thin and tannic, and the 1984 offers enormous power, concentration and finesse. The 1985 ranks as the

AT A GLANCE

CHATEAU MONTELENA
1429 Tubbs Lane
Calistoga, CA 94515
(707) 942-5105

Owner: Montelena Associates (General partner: James L. Barrett)

Winemaker: Bo Barrett (6 years)

Founded: 1882, reestablished: 1972

First Cabernet vintage: 1973
Estate: 1978

Cabernet production: 10,000 cases

Cabernet acres owned: 70

Average age of vines: 12 years

Vineyard makeup: Cabernet Sauvignon (90%), Cabernet Franc (10%)

Average wine makeup: Cabernet Sauignon (90%), Cabernet Franc (10%)

Time in oak: 24 months

Type of oak: French (Nevers)

finest Montelena ever produced, displaying uncommon richness, intensity, flavor and depth. The 1986 follows in that fine tradition.

Château Montelena's excellent performance has not gone unnoticed among connoisseurs who appreciate the sharply defined, beautifully balanced, enormously complex and ageworthy wines. The winery makes 10,000 cases of Cabernet in its old stone château at the foot of Mount St. Helena and is a must-have for any serious Cabernet aficionado.

TASTING NOTES

CHATEAU MONTELENA, Various bottlings

1986 CHATEAU MONTELENA ESTATE: An elegant and beautifully balanced 1986, rich, concentrated, complex and structured, a worthy successor to the superb 1984 and 1985 bottlings. The 1986 offers fresh, ripe, sharply focused black cherry, cassis and spicy oak flavors that are a shade more elegant and forward than either the 1984 or 1985. This wine is already drinking quite well but has the balance and depth for another eight to 15 years' development. Drink 1995-2004. 12,900 cases produced. Not Released. **93**

1985 CHATEAU MONTELENA ESTATE: Another magnificent wine that is amazingly rich and concentrated, packed with black cherry, currant, cedar and spice flavors and wrapped in thick tannins that promise a long life. It's massive but elegant, in need of six to eight years of cellaring before it's at its zenith. Finest bottling ever by Château Montelena. Drink 1996-2006. 9,723 cases produced. Release: $25. Current: $25. **95**

1984 CHATEAU MONTELENA ESTATE: An enormous wine that combines power and finesse with deep, rich, concentrated currant, black cherry and spicy plum flavors that are tight and closed now. Has the elegance and structure for long-term aging. One of the best 1984s and a great Montelena. Drink 1998-2006. 11,439 cases produced. Release: $20. Current: $25. **94**

1983 CHATEAU MONTELENA ESTATE: A very successful 1983 that is firm and tannic, built for cellaring. The rich, lean currant and cedar Cabernet flavors are sharply focused and offer great depth and intensity. Still too tannic to drink but should begin to soften in three to five years. Drink 1994-2002. 8,517 cases produced. Release: $18. Current: $26. **92**

1982 CHATEAU MONTELENA ESTATE: One of the standouts of the 1982 vintage, this wine is elegant and balanced, with black cherry, plum and currant aromas and flavors, backed with toasty oak. The tannins are fine, and the acidity is crisp, carrying the flavors a long way on the finish. Opening up now, but a good bet for another decade. Drink 1992-2002. 11,425 cases produced. Release: $16. Current: $33. **92.**

1981 CHATEAU MONTELENA ESTATE: A leaner, thinner version, lacking the richness, depth and fleshy texture of most vintages. Nevertheless, this is still a very good wine marked by a spicy, oaky, mineral flavor that overshadows the thin currant flavors and hard tannins. Drink 1990-1994. 7,144 cases produced. Release: $16. Current: $25. **80**

1980 CHATEAU MONTELENA ESTATE: A very good, well-made wine with generous, ripe fruit flavors and fine balance but lacking the added dimensions of richness, depth and complexity that distinguish the great Montelenas. This one might be a sleeper that surprises in the future, but for now it comes off as straightforward. Drink 1991-1997. 10,000 cases produced. Release: $16. Current: $40. **86**

1979 CHATEAU MONTELENA SONOMA COUNTY: A shade leaner and sleeker than the 1978 Sonoma but with similar character and flavor; the spicy black cherry, anise and mineral flavors combine to give this wine complexity and finesse. The last Sonoma bottling. Drink 1991-1998. 1,164 cases produced. Release: $14. Current: $45. **88**

1979 CHATEAU MONTELENA ESTATE: Very similar in character to the 1979 Sonoma, reflecting a consistency in winemaking style. It's a lean, elegant, sharply focused wine with black currant, mineral and cedar nuances that are rich and mature now but lacking the depth and concentration of the great Montelenas. This wine is still developing though drinkable now. Drink 1992-1998. 5,776 cases produced. Release: $16. Current: $45. **87**

1978 CHATEAU MONTELENA SONOMA COUNTY: Fully mature now, with pretty floral, black cherry and spice aromas, a gentle, rich, elegant texture and tannins that are soft and supple. The finish offers hints of mineral and anise. Complex and charming. Drink 1990-1996. 1,560 cases produced. Release: $12. Current: $50. **87**

1978 CHATEAU MONTELENA ESTATE: This is the first estate-bottled wine from Château Montelena, a rich, bold, dramatic Cabernet that is very concentrated and assertive, with deep black currant, cherry, mint and cedar flavors that are intense and still developing. Plenty of tannin for long-range cellaring. One of the great Montelenas, close to maturity. Drink 1993-2005. 7,500 cases produced. Release: $16. Current: $60. **93**

1977 CHATEAU MONTELENA SONOMA COUNTY: A smooth, polished, elegant wine with satiny texture and supple, generous plum and cherry flavors that are rich and ripe without being weighty, accented by a toasty, earthy note that adds complexity and depth to the finish. The soft, fine tannins provide accessibility now but are firm enough for further cellaring. Drink 1992-1999. 3,298 cases produced. Release: $12. Current: $65. **91.**

1977 CHATEAU MONTELENA NAPA VALLEY: This wine is bolder and richer with greater depth and complexity than the fine Sonoma bottling, with layers of ripe, concentrated currant, herb, plum and spice flavors that are young and vibrant. The tannins are smooth and soft

yet thick, which bodes well for further cellaring. One of the the standouts of the 1977 vintage. Drink 1995-2005. 3,800 cases produced. Release: $12. Current: $65. **94**

1976 CHATEAU MONTELENA NORTH COAST: An openly rich, fruity and seductive wine that is silky smooth on the palate, with layers of complex black cherry, currant, anise, cedar and earth flavors. The color is holding, and the tannins are softening, but the fruit is amazingly fresh and lively. This wine has been drinking exceptionally well for several years. Drink 1990-1995. 5,769 cases produced. Release: $10. Current: $75. **90**

1975 CHATEAU MONTELENA NORTH COAST: A lean, austere 1975 that is beginning to open up with beautifully focused black currant and cherry flavors that are rich and concentrated, backed with firm tannins, finishing with an earthy flavor. A very attractive wine that's lacking depth and complexity now but still has time to gain it. Drink 1993-2000. 6,675 cases produced. Release: $9. Current: $100. **86**

1974 CHATEAU MONTELENA SONOMA COUNTY: Very similar in character to the Napa Valley bottling, with its firm, tannic veneer, but this wine is showing more ripe, opulent plum, cherry and spice flavors that are youthful and straightforward. Approachable now but can stand aging and may move up a point or two. Drink 1992-2000. 6,000 cases produced. Release: $9. Current: $100. **87**

1974 CHATEAU MONTELENA NAPA VALLEY: A bold, rich and fruity 1974 with gutsy tannins, still tightly closed and evolving. The ripe black cherry, currant and spice flavors are youthful and fresh but overshadowed now by the tannins. Everything's in place for an outstanding wine, but it needs another five years. Drink 1993-2003. 1,100 cases produced. Release: $9. Current: $100. **90**

1973 CHATEAU MONTELENA SONOMA COUNTY: Château Montelena's first commercial Cabernet is a surprisingly youthful wine with a deep color, pretty floral and black currant aromas and fairly hard tannins. The black cherry and currant flavors are complemented by a spicy anise quality, but it's still tight and tart, and there's tannic grip on the finish. This wine still needs time to resolve its tannins. Drink 1990-2001. 3,000 cases produced. Release: $8.50. Current: $100. **87**

CHIMNEY ROCK WINE CELLARS

Stags Leap District, Napa Valley

CLASSIFICATION: *FIFTH GROWTH*

COLLECTIBILITY RATING: *Not rated*

BEST VINTAGES: *1986, 1985*

Chimney Rock is the Jordan of Napa Valley, producing fresh, fruity, elegant Cabernets that are meant to be consumed on release or within five years. While this Stags Leap District winery is not nearly as elaborate or expensive as Jordan, the winemaking philosophies are similar. Chimney Rock produces wines that are charming and complex the day they leave the winery, using fruit from its estate vineyards in Stags Leap. While the first vintage from 1984 was pleasant, the 1985 and 1986 vintages are both superior, displaying rich, ripe, elegant flavors that make the wines delicious to drink now. A new winery in Stags Leap north of Clos Du Val was completed in 1989 to process grapes from owner Sheldon "Hack" Wilson's 55 acres of Cabernet, Merlot and Cabernet Franc, which were once part of his Chimney Rock golf course.

TASTING NOTES

CHIMNEY ROCK WINE CELLARS, Stags Leap District, Napa Valley

1986 CHIMNEY ROCK WINE CELLARS: Already drinkable, this is a smooth, crisp, supple 1986 that is showing early signs of complexity with toasty oak, ripe currant, spice, anise and plum flavors of moderate depth and supple tannins on the finish. Elegant and delicious now but built for short-term to midterm aging. Drink 1990-1996. 5,700 cases produced. Release: $15. Current: $15. **86**

1985 CHIMNEY ROCK WINE CELLARS: A gorgeous 1985 that is rich and elegant, with layers of ripe black cherry, currant, spice and vanilla flavors that are crisp and lively, good depth and a pretty, lingering aftertaste of fruit and spice. Drink 1990-1997. 2,900 cases produced. Release: $15. Current: $15. **87**

1984 CHIMNEY ROCK WINE CELLARS: A light, elegant, fruity 1984 with crisp acidity and good balance, but for all its fruity complexities now, it is ultimately simple and straightforward, with a touch of cedar on the finish. Drink 1990-1996. 2,800 cases produced. Release: $15. Current: $15. **82**

AT A GLANCE

CHIMNEY ROCK WINE CELLARS
5320 Silverado Trail
Napa, CA 94558
(707) 257-2641

Owners: Sheldon "Hack" and Stella Wilson

Winemaker: Dave Fletcher (5 years)

Founded: 1984

First Cabernet vintage: 1984

Cabernet production: 5,700 cases

Cabernet acres owned: 55

Average age of vines: 9 years

Vineyard makeup: Cabernet Sauvignon (89%), Merlot (7%), Cabernet Franc (4%)

Average wine makeup: Cabernet Sauvignon (80%), Merlot (10%), Cabernet Franc (10%)

Time in oak: 18 months

Type of oak: French (Nevers)

CLOS DU BOIS WINERY

Briarcrest, Alexander Valley
Marlstone, Alexander Valley

CLASSIFICATION: *FIFTH GROWTH*

COLLECTIBILITY RATING: *Not rated*

BEST VINTAGES:

Briarcrest: 1984, 1981

Marlstone: 1985, 1984

Despite high prices and lofty reputations, neither of Clos du Bois' vineyard-designated reds, Marlstone or Briarcrest, has ever yielded a sensational wine. The two vineyards, both in Alexander Valley, came closest to excellence in 1984 and 1985, with wines that display uncommon richness, extract and complexity. But in other years the wines are often uneven. They age poorly and have not lived up to their reputations.

Marlstone, one of California's first proprietary blends, is from a 90-acre vineyard of the same name in Alexander Valley that is planted to the classic Bordeaux varieties — Cabernet Sauvignon, Merlot, Cabernet Franc, Malbec and Petit Verdot. The Marlstone bottling is a mixture of the best grapes from each vintage. The goal is to achieve complexity and depth through the blending of different grapes, but so far many of the wines lack complexity and pose serious questions as candidates for cellaring. Briarcrest, by comparison, measures 30 acres and is 100 percent Cabernet Sauvignon. It is an early ripening vineyard that yields small, intensely flavored grapes, and I believe it produces the better of the two wines, although a good many people I know are very fond of the Marlstone style.

The first Marlstone was produced in 1978 and was a blend of roughly half Cabernet and half Merlot. Since then the blend has changed, but it almost always relies on Cabernet as its base. That particular wine, the 1978, has aged very poorly. It is oxidized and frail, having spent three years in oak without possessing the richness and concentration to stand up to the wood. The 1979 is hard and tannic, and the fruit is drying out. The 1980 is overly ripe and raisiny. The 1981 is the best of the early vintages, with attractive fruit and better balance. It is ready to drink now. The 1982, from a wet vintage, is tough and tannic, not offering much hope for the future. The 1983 is another rain-at-harvest victim that even has Botrytis. The 1984 Marlstone is the best vintage yet, displaying the complexity and broad array of flavors one would would expect. It also appears to have the balance and finesse to improve in the cellar. The 1985 is similar in style, with lavish oak and herb notes.

The history of Briarcrest parallels that of Marlstone. The first vintage in 1980 has herb and bell pepper notes, while the 1981 is very successful, rich and intense and close to its peak. The 1982 Briarcrest has mossy, earthy flavors; it should be avoided. The 1983 is only a modest improvement, with shallow, rather uninteresting flavors. The 1984 shows more promise, with richer, more concentrated fruit and firm tannins that promise to age well. The 1985 is also well made, but perhaps a notch below the 1981 and 1984 bottlings.

Clos du Bois also produces a Alexander Valley Cabernet that is typically a good value in complex, early drinking Cabernet. The winery in Healdsburg was founded by Frank Woods and a group of investors, who sold it in 1988 to Hiram Walker.

TASTING NOTES

CLOS DU BOIS WINERY, Briarcrest, Alexander Valley

1985 CLOS DU BOIS WINERY BRIARCREST: Herbal and lavishly oaked, this is a very good but unexciting 1985. Considering the quality of the vintage, it is something of a disappointment. The flavors are muted by the oak, and what comes through is more herb and oak than fruit. Drink 1993-1998. 3,721 cases produced. Release: $16. Current: $16. **82**

1984 CLOS DU BOIS WINERY BRIARCREST: Similar in style to the excellent 1981, and the second-best Briarcrest to date, the 1984 exhibits ripe plum and cherry flavors and is laced with lavish oak and gritty tannins. Needs two to three years' cellaring to reach its peak. Drink 1993-2000. 1,711 cases produced. Release: $16. Current: $24. **87**

1983 CLOS DU BOIS WINERY BRIARCREST: From another troubled vintage, the 1983 is light and simple, with pure Cabernet flavors and a touch of honeyed Botrytis but not much in the way of richness or depth. May appeal to some. Drink 1990-1994. 1,122 cases produced. Release: $12. Current: $20. **74**

1982 CLOS DU BOIS WINERY BRIARCREST: An apparent victim of rain at harvest, this is a woody, cedary, mossy Cabernet without fruit, very dry and mossy on the finish. A flawed wine that should be avoided. 2,075 cases produced. Release: $12. Current: $25. **66**

1981 CLOS DU BOIS WINERY BRIARCREST: A very successful Briarcrest, rich and tannic, with intense, concentrated plum, currant and mint flavors that are firm and structured. Fruit echoes through on the finish. Near its peak now and a good candidate for cellaring throughout the decade. Drink 1991-1998. 2,095 cases produced. Release: $12. Current: $32. **88**

1980 CLOS DU BOIS WINERY BRIARCREST: Marked by distinct, vegetal herb and bell pepper flavors that overshadow the ripe plum notes. It's fully mature and should hold on for another five to eight years, but it has not gained complexity. Drink 1990-1995. 1,227 cases produced. Release: $12. Current: $32. **80**

CLOS DU BOIS WINERY, Marlstone, Alexander Valley

1985 CLOS DU BOIS WINERY MARLSTONE: Lavishly oaked, with pronounced herb and cedar flavors, rich and supple. Its concentrated olive, black cherry, anise and spice flavors are well balanced, with firm tannins. Tempting now but ageworthy for eight to 10 years. Drink 1992-1998. 5,917 cases produced. Release: $19.50. Current: $19.50. **88**

1984 CLOS DU BOIS WINERY MARLSTONE: By far the most complete, interesting and balanced Marlstone to date, the 1984 is an excellent wine from a fine vintage, offering rich, supple plum, anise, cherry and chocolate flavors flanked by firm tannins, ample oak and a measure of elegance and finesse that was missing in previous bottlings. Drink 1992-1997. 3,957 cases produced. Release: $19.50. Current: $24. **89**

1983 CLOS DU BOIS WINERY MARLSTONE: Very light in color with a touch of Botrytis on the palate, the 1983 is a victim of harvest rains and looks and smells more like Pinot Noir. Though a curiosity, some may find the honey-Cabernet flavors attractive. Drink 1990-1993. 1,600 cases produced. Release: $19.50. Current: $20. **70**

1982 CLOS DU BOIS WINERY MARLSTONE: Still firm and tough, with rugged tannins that dominate the cherry and herb flavors. It's one-dimensional and may never develop into anything more. Drink 1990-1994. 2,496 cases produced. Release: $16. Current: $16. **79**

1981 CLOS DU BOIS WINERY MARLSTONE: The best of the early Marlstone bottlings, offering ripe, rich black cherry and currant flavors that are broad and full with good depth and balance. Ready now and through the next five years. Drink 1990-1995. 1,005 cases produced. Release: $15. Current: $32. **85**

1980 CLOS DU BOIS WINERY MARLSTONE: Extremely ripe and raisiny, with an alcoholic finish and gritty tannins, a rambunctious wine laced with anise, ripe plum and cedar flavors. Overdone for my taste. Drink 1991-1998. 3,833 cases produced. Release: $15. Current: $32. **77**

1979 CLOS DU BOIS WINERY MARLSTONE: Hard and tannic and not likely to ever come around. Predominately Cabernet (79 percent) with herb, tar and spicy fruit flavors that are rapidly drying out. Drink 1990-1994. 3,395 cases produced. Release: $16. Current: $30. **75**

1978 CLOS DU BOIS WINERY MARLSTONE: Prematurely oxidized and falling apart, this wine spent nearly three years in oak and was never anything more than a good wine. Drink 1990. 3,129 cases produced. Release: $16. Current: $30. **72**

CLOS DU VAL WINE CO.

Reserve, Stags Leap District, Napa Valley
Estate, Stags Leap District, Napa Valley
Joli Val, Napa Valley

CLASSIFICATION:

Reserve: SECOND GROWTH

Estate: SECOND GROWTH

COLLECTIBILITY RATING:

Reserve: AA

Estate: A

BEST VINTAGES:

Reserve: 1985, 1982, 1979, 1978, 1973

Estate: 1986, 1985, 1984, 1979, 1978, 1977, 1974, 1972

Joli Val: 1986

F rom the outset, French-born Bernard Portet sought to establish Clos Du Val as a Bordeaux-style château, better known for wines of complexity, elegance and finesse than for Cabernets of intense varietal character. In a large way he has succeeded, for while the Clos Du Val wines are identifiably Cabernet Sauvignon, they are rarely pure expressions of that grape variety. Rather, as he would describe them, they are complete, harmonious wines of grace, complexity and deceptive strength created by blending Cabernet and Merlot.

The son of a former régisseur of Château Lafite, Portet came to Napa Valley in the early 1970s on a mission from John Goelet of New York to find land suitable for world-class wines. The area in Napa Valley that most appealed to Portet was the land just south of the rugged outcropping known as Stags Leap, where the soils are rich and deep and the air is somewhat cooler than farther north. Clos Du Val's Cabernet, Merlot and Cabernet Franc vines are rooted in 115 acres of land in a parcel that is adjacent to the vineyards of Warren Winiarski's Stag's Leap Wine Cellars. Despite the proximity of the two vineyards, the styles are quite different. Winiarski accentuates more varietal character, herbaceousness, depth, flesh and richness than Clos Du Val, which leans more toward understated elegance, austerity and refined flavors that take longer to develop. Portet produces three Cabernet bottlings at Clos Du Val: a reserve, the estate bottling and Joli Val, a new wine made from grapes purchased from in the Napa Valley.

AT A GLANCE

CLOS DU VAL WINE CO.
5330 Silverado Trail
Napa, CA 94558
(707) 252-6711

Owner: John Goelet

Winemaker: Bernard Portet (17 years)

Founded: 1972

First Cabernet vintage: 1972
Reserve: 1973
Estate: 1972
Joli Val: 1986

Cabernet production: 25,000 cases
Reserve: 2,000 cases (in some vintages)
Estate: 21,000 cases
Joli Val: 5,000 cases (in some vintages)

Cabernet acres owned: 115

Average age of vines: 17 years

Vineyard makeup: Cabernet Sauvignon (74%), Merlot (18%), Cabernet Franc (8%)

Average wine makeup:
Reserve: Cabernet Sauvignon (90%), Merlot (10%)
Estate: Cabernet Sauvignon (94%), Merlot (6%)
Joli Val: Cabernet Sauvignon (100%)

Time in oak: 22 months

Type of oak: French (Nevers)

Clos Du Val's first vintage was produced entirely from grapes grown in Steltzner Vineyard, another Stags Leap District property, and it was enormously successful considering the generally fair quality of the vintage. The 1972, which finished behind Stag's Leap Wine Cellars 1973 in the famous Paris Tasting of 1976, is still drinking exceptionally well and should last another eight to 10 years.

In 1973 Clos Du Val produced a wonderful estate bottling and its first reserve (produced only in vintages where there are clearly superior lots of wine), which is amazingly young and elegant today. Both the 1974 and 1975 vintages are fine examples of the Clos Du Val style, with Portet achieving elegance and concentration in 1974 and austerity and grace in 1975. The 1976 is overly ripe and uncommonly tannic, perhaps the result of Portet's using some Rutherford grapes to complement Clos Du Val's harvest, which was shortened by the drought. In 1977 the estate bottling is more appealing to me than the reserve, while in 1978 both bottlings are exceptional, with the reserve bottling ranking as one of the top two or three Clos Du Vals. The 1979 vintage proved another highly successful one for the estate and reserve; these wines should easily age to the year 2000 and beyond. In 1980 only one wine was produced, and it is big and full-bodied like most Cabernets of that vintage. The 1981 is the weakest in the entire lineup, but it is still a pleasant wine. With 1982 the two wines are similar in quality, with a slight edge going to the reserve for its depth and intensity. The 1983 is also very good, leaner and more tannic, followed by a rich, concentrated and deceptively powerful 1984 that should age well. The 1985 Reserve Clos Du Val may rival the 1978 and 1979 reserves as Clos Du Val's finest, while in 1986 both the Joli Val and estate bottlings are superb.

Through 15 vintages and 21 wines, Clos Du Val's accomplishments with Cabernet are quite apparent. None of the wines has fallen apart, but each has aged rather well and in some instances they appear to have the intensity, balance, depth and flavor to age 20 to 30 years. Production has risen to over 20,000 cases without sacrificing quality.

TASTING NOTES

CLOS DU VAL, Reserve, Stags Leap District, Napa Valley

1985 CLOS DU VAL RESERVE: A shade richer and more elegant than the 1985 estate, tightly wound and well defined, with bright cherry, cedar, anise and plum flavors that are long and satisfying. Because of its firm, concentrated structure, this reserve will need five to seven years before it nears its peak. If it's like other Clos Du Val Reserves, it should be a good candidate for 15 to 20 years of aging. Drink 1995-2006. 750 cases produced. Not Released. **94**

1982 CLOS DU VAL RESERVE: A shade less power and intensity than the 1978 and 1979 reserves, but still a breed apart. Very intense and concentrated, loaded with black cherry, currant and spicy oak flavors that are youthful and still a long way from peaking. One of the top 1982s. Drink 1997-2005. 2,600 cases produced. Release: $28. Current: $37. **90**

1979 CLOS DU VAL RESERVE: A magnificent, dramatic wine that is richer and deeper than the 1979 estate, combining intensity and power with a seam of elegance that highlights the concentrated plum, currant, anise and cedar flavors. Drink 1996-2008. 1,200 cases produced. Release: $25. Current: $55. **92**

1978 CLOS DU VAL RESERVE: A monumental 1978 that is big, rich and tannic, loaded with ripe, concentrated black cherry, currant, chocolate and spice flavors that are youthful and can stand up to the powerful tannins. Despite its strength, there's a gentle elegance to it. Approachable but needs more time. Drink 1993-2010. 2,400 cases produced. Release: $30. Current: $55. **94**

1977 CLOS DU VAL RESERVE: This is a lean, austere yet deceptively powerful Cabernet. It has a green, herbal, cedary quality that detracts slightly from the rich, concentrated currant and black cherry flavors. It's fully mature now but has the intensity to age another decade. Drink 1990-2001. 2,900 cases produced. Release: $20. Current: $53. **87**

1973 CLOS DU VAL RESERVE: An amazingly elegant wine that is aging gracefully, with richer, deeper, more concentrated flavors than the 1973 estate bottling. The lush chocolate, cinnamon and black cherry flavors are remarkably young and alive. At its peak now and for the next decade. Drink 1990-2000. 100 cases produced. Release: $10. Current: $100. **90**

CLOS DU VAL, Estate, Stags Leap District, Napa Valley

1986 CLOS DU VAL ESTATE: Deep, rich and concentrated, loaded with black cherry, currant and spicy cedar aromas, firm, fine tannins. Elegant and stylish, long and full on the finish. Should age gracefully into the 21st century. Drink 1994-2004. 21,000 cases produced. Release: $12.50. Current: $12.50. **92**

1985 CLOS DU VAL ESTATE: The 1985 has explosive fruit that is elegant and refined, sharply focused on the fresh, rich black cherry, currant and cedar flavors, with a touch more elegance and finesse than the 1984. The tannins are fine and integrated, offering subtlety and finesse on the finish. Alluring now but can age a decade or more. Appears to be the finest Clos Du Val estate bottling ever produced. Drink 1993-2005. 25,000 cases produced. Release: $16. Current: $16. **93**

1984 CLOS DU VAL ESTATE: Ripe, open and generous, the 1984 has black cherry and currant flavors that are broad and supple, with firm structure and hints of tobacco on the finish. With aeration it grows into a rich, concentrated yet elegant wine with a good measure of charm. Drink 1992-2004. 20,500 cases produced. Release: $15. Current: $16.50. **92**

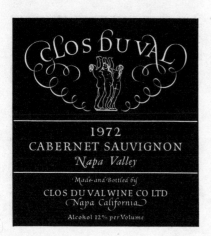

1983 CLOS DU VAL ESTATE: Surprisingly good for a 1983 despite its austere tannins and lean, compact black cherry, cedar and currant flavors. The finish is dry and tannic, like most 1983s, but this is better balanced than most. Drink 1994-2002. 23,500 cases produced. Release: $15. Current: $17.50. **86**

1982 CLOS DU VAL ESTATE: Similar in style to the 1980, this is a rich, elegant wine with cedar aromas and black cherry, currant and spice flavors supported by fine tannins and a long, lingering finish. Drinking well now but should age another decade. Drink 1992-2000. 21,000 cases produced. Release: $13.25. Current: $24. **88**

1981 CLOS DU VAL ESTATE: The weakest Clos Du Val, lean and austere, with herbaceous green bean and bell pepper flavors and biting tannins. It's less supple than most Clos Du Vals but is still a very good wine. Drink 1990-1996. 21,500 cases produced. Release: $12.50. Current: $25. **82**

1980 CLOS DU VAL ESTATE: A very impressive 1980 with a deep red color, rich, supple, elegant currant, cedar, black cherry and oak flavors that are warm and charming. Fine balance and good length on the finish. Drink 1990-1995. 17,400 cases produced. Release: $12.50. Current: $28. **88**

1979 CLOS DU VAL ESTATE: Similar in style to the elegant 1975 and 1977 vintages, lean and austere, with cedar, cinnamon, chocolate and currant flavors that are broad and supple. Still has a way to go. Drink 1990-2002. 15,400 cases produced. Release: $12.50. Current: $45. **90**

1978 CLOS DU VAL ESTATE: An excellent wine from a great vintage, this is a richly concentrated, deeply perfumed Cabernet loaded with sharply focused black cherry, currant, cedar and anise flavors that are complex and deep, with an underlying sense of elegance. This wine still has a great future. Drink 1990-2000. 14,000 cases produced. Release: $12. Current: $40. **92**

1977 CLOS DU VAL ESTATE: Similar in style to the elegant 1975 vintage with its understated elegance and finesse, the 1977 has beautifully focused black cherry and currant flavors and a rich and supple texture. Fine balance, still youthful and developing. It has the tannins and depth of fruit to carry it another decade. Drink 1990-2000. 14,700 cases produced. Release: $10. Current: $40. **89**

1976 CLOS DU VAL: Extremely ripe and raisiny, with earthy aromas that dry out on the palate. Despite the high level of concentration, this wine spent additional time in oak due to a glass strike that prevented Clos Du Val from bottling it sooner. One-third of the fruit came from Rutherford to augment the short crop in this drought year. Tannins may carry it another decade, but will the fruit survive? Drink 1990-1995. 6,800 cases produced. Release: $9. Current: $55. **82**

1975 CLOS DU VAL ESTATE: A lean, austere yet graceful 1975 that is excellent for its crisp, concentrated style and gentle fruit. Not as ripe and showy as most early Clos Du Val Cabernets, the cedar, black cherry and tobacco flavors offer subtlety and finesse, with hints of cinnamon on the finish. Drink 1990-2000. 9,300 cases produced. Release: $9. Current: $65. **89**

1974 CLOS DU VAL ESTATE: A very ripe, generous 1974 with tar, anise, black cherry, tea and spice flavors that are still quite concentrated, rich and deep. This wine has enough stuffing and tannin to carry it another decade. Fruit and tannin on the finish. Drink 1990-2000. 7,600 cases produced. Release: $7.50. Current: $75. **91**

1973 CLOS DU VAL ESTATE: Beautiful ripe fruit, polished tannins and supple texture, at its peak, with complex cherry, cedar and anise flavors, crisp acidity and fine tannins. The finish is a bit hard, but the acidity carries the cedar and tobacco flavors. Drink 1990-1995. 2,760 cases produced. Release: $6. Current: $70. **86**

1972 CLOS DU VAL ESTATE: Clos Du Val's first vintage is a masterpiece, especially given the many mediocre wines from this vintage. Still in great condition with a healthy red color and complex bouquet of fresh black currant and cherry flavors and a touch of spice. Complex, elegant, supple and still gaining. The fruit was from Steltzner Vineyard in Stags Leap. Drink 1990-1998. 3,500 cases produced. Release: $6. Current: $100. **90**

CLOS DU VAL, Joli Val, Napa Valley

1986 CLOS DU VAL JOLI VAL: A big, rich, concentrated yet elegant 1986, with rich black currant, cherry and cedary oak flavors, very aromatic, with fine structure and plenty of fruit and tannin on the finish. Drink 1994-2002. 5,000 cases produced. Not Released. **91**

B.R. COHN WINERY
Olive Hill Vineyard, Sonoma Valley
CLASSIFICATION: *THIRD GROWTH*

COLLECTIBILITY RATING: *A*

BEST VINTAGES: *1986, 1985, 1984*

In three vintages, B.R. Cohn has produced a trio of stunning Cabernets from his 40-acre Olive Hill Vineyard in the heart of Sonoma Valley. Rarely has a newcomer created such a stir. Proprietor Bruce Cohn, a manager of rock music groups, most notably the Doobie Brothers, used his earnings from that business to buy the Olive Hill Vineyard. For several years he sold grapes to producers such as Kenwood, Ravenswood and Gundlach Bundschu.

Cohn's first vintage under his own brand, the 1984, is distinctive for its rich, seductive fruit. The 1985 is a shade better, a touch more elegant, while the 1986 displays enormous concentration of fruit, with finesse and power. Because of the reputation of this excellent vineyard, Cohn is one of the state's promising new producers.

TASTING NOTES

B.R. COHN WINERY, Olive Hill Vineyard

1986 B.R. COHN WINERY OLIVE HILL VINEYARD: Enormous concentration of rich, ripe fruit, combining power and grace with intense black cherry and currant flavors, flanked by spice and rich cedar aromas from oak. Amazingly complex, with a lovely aftertaste. Drink 1993-2001. 2,400 cases produced. Release: $18. Current: $20. **94**

1985 B.R. COHN WINERY OLIVE HILL VINEYARD: This wine is rich, supple and satiny, with beautiful structure, great intensity and depth, and rich cassis, butter, toasty oak and spice flavors all wound together in a wonderful package with plenty of tannin. Impeccably balanced and ageworthy. Drink 1993-2000. 2,000 cases produced. Release: $16. Current: $22. **94**

1984 B.R. COHN WINERY OLIVE HILL VINEYARD: Cohn's first vintage, this is a seductive wine with rich, complex, distinctive black cherry, raspberry, cedar and tobacco flavors that are supple and opulent, framed by toasty oak and impeccably balanced. Drink 1991-1998. 900 cases produced. Release: $15. Current: $22. **93**

AT A GLANCE
B.R. COHN WINERY
P.O. Box 1673
Sonoma, CA 95476
(707) 938-4064

Owner: Bruce Cohn

Winemaker: John Speed (1 year)

Founded: 1984

First Cabernet vintage: 1984

Cabernet production: 2,400 cases

Cabernet acres owned: 40

Average age of vines: 12 years

Vineyard makeup: Cabernet Sauvignon (96%), Cabernet Franc (4%)

Average wine makeup: Cabernet Sauvignon (100%)

Time in oak: 24 months

Type of oak: French

Conn Creek Winery

Barrel Select Private Reserve, Napa Valley
Barrel Select, Napa Valley

CLASSIFICATION: *FOURTH GROWTH*

COLLECTIBILITY RATING: *Not rated*

BEST VINTAGES:

Barrel Select Private Reserve Collins Vineyard: 1984

Collins Vineyard Proprietor's Special Selection: 1980

Lot 2: 1978

Barrel Select Napa Valley: 1977, 1974, 1973

For a winery that owns virtually no Cabernet vines, Conn Creek Winery has succeeded in producing a number of memorable Cabernets, particularly in the 1970s. Its first two vintages were stunning, a magnificent 1973 from Steltzner Vineyard in the Stags Leap District and a monumental 1974 from the Eisele Vineyard near Calistoga. Both wines were produced by Lyncrest Winery before it went out of business. Bill Collins, founder of Conn Creek, bought the wines in barrel and bottled them under the Conn Creek label. There were other highlights in the 1970s for Conn Creek Cabernet, which came from the Collins' vineyard in St. Helena and Silverado Vineyard in the Stags Leap District. In addition to the 1973 and 1974, the winery made a rich, smooth, polished 1977 and a deeply concentrated 1978, Lot 2. No 1975 was made. In 1980, Conn Creek made two barrels of Cabernet from the Collins Vineyard near St. Helena, one that was sold to a bidder at the Napa Valley Wine Auction. It is an enormously rich, powerful, tannic wine that should age into the next decade.

In the 1980s the Conn Creek wines have continued to be very good and consistently well made, especially those from the Collins Vineyard, which produces high-extract, intensely flavored wines, although none of the more recent vintages have matched those from the 1970s. The 1985 Barrel Select Private Reserve, for example, is elegant and complex but lacks the depth and richness of the best wines from this sensational vintage.

The Conn Creek style has evolved from the rich, gutsy, tannic wines of the 1970s toward Cabernets that are more supple and elegant as well as lighter, making them more drinkable on release. There is also little difference stylistically between the Barrel Select and Barrel Select Private Reserve bottlings. What's more, the terminology is con-

AT A GLANCE

CONN CREEK WINERY
8711 Silverado Trail
St. Helena, CA 94574
(707) 963-5133

Owner: Stimson Lane/Château Ste. Michelle (U.S. Tobacco Co.)

Winemaker: Jeff Booth (1 year)

Founded: 1974

First Cabernet vintage: 1973

Cabernet production: 7,100 cases
Private Reserve: 1,100 cases
Napa Valley: 6,000 cases

Cabernet acres owned: 3

Average age of vines: 9 years

Vineyard makeup: Cabernet Sauvignon (100%)

Average wine makeup:
Private Reserve: Cabernet Sauvignon (91%), Merlot (6%), Cabernet Franc (3%)
Napa Valley: Cabernet Sauvignon (83%), Cabernet Franc (7%), Merlot (6%)

Time in oak: 18 months

Type of oak: French (Nevers)

fusing, because the terms are used inconsistently. Grapes in recent vintages have come from vineyards such as The Hess Collection on Mount Veeder, Spottswoode in St. Helena, Truchard near Napa, Honig in Rutherford, Chalk Hill in Sonoma County and Collins, which has a long-term contract to sell its grapes to Conn Creek.

In 1986 Conn Creek and Villa Mt. Eden were acquired by Stimson Lane/Château Ste. Michelle of Washington, itself owned by U.S. Tobacco Co. In 1987 André Tchelistcheff was hired as a winemaking consultant.

TASTING NOTES

CONN CREEK WINERY, Various bottlings

1986 CONN CREEK WINERY BARREL SELECT: This impressive wine from Conn Creek features the same bright, fresh, ripe and lively black cherry and black currant flavors as previous vintages. Not quite as rich as the 1985, it is a shade leaner, with fine tannins and a firm structure for midterm aging. Elegant and stylish, with a fruity aftertaste. Drink 1994-2000. 6,550 cases produced. Not Released. **87**

1985 CONN CREEK WINERY BARREL SELECT PRIVATE RESERVE: A shade deeper and more complex than the 1985 Barrel Select, but the differences are rather subtle at this point. The Private Reserve offers similar black cherry and black currant flavors and crisp acidity but not the kind of depth and concentration one expects from Private Reserve. Drink 1992-1997. 1,100 cases produced. Not Released. **87**

1985 CONN CREEK WINERY BARREL SELECT: An elegant, lean, fruity wine with ample fruit for midterm aging, but without the richness and concentration of the Private Reserve bottling. It's an elegant wine with layers of black cherry and currant flavors. Drink 1991-1995. 6,000 cases produced. Not Released. **85**

1984 CONN CREEK WINERY COLLINS VINEYARD PRIVATE RESERVE: Another excellent bottling from Collins Vineyard, richer, deeper and more concentrated that the 1984 Barrel Select, with layers of ripe black currant, black cherry and vanilla flavors that offer complexity and length. A higher level of extract and tannin should help this one age longer. Drink 1994-2002. 1,100 cases produced. Release: $23. Current: $23. **88**

1984 CONN CREEK WINERY BARREL SELECT LOT 79: Open and fruity, with ripe black currant, floral, black cherry and plum flavors that are delicious and tempting now. The forward, up-front fruit and crisp, lean tannins made it a good candidate for short-term to midterm cellaring. Drink 1991-1996. 4,450 cases produced. Release: $13. Current: $13. **86**

1983 CONN CREEK WINERY BARREL SELECT: A surprisingly good 1983 that offers enough ripe, supple fruit to match the drying tannins of this vintage. The key is the balance between cherry and plum flavors and the tannins, which are dry but not abrasive. Nearing its peak. Drink 1992-1996. 5,000 cases produced. Release: $13. Current: $15. **82**

1983 CONN CREEK WINERY COLLINS VINEYARD PROPRIETOR'S SPECIAL SELECTION: A fairly successful 1983 that avoids being overly tannic and manages to display enough ripe, intense cherry, plum, cedar and currant flavors to override the tannins. Close to maturity. Drink 1991-1997. 40 cases produced. Never released commercially; sold only at the Napa Valley Wine Auction. Current: $70. **87**

1982 CONN CREEK WINERY BARREL SELECT: A strong effort from a difficult vintage, full of ripe, elegant cherry flavors backed by firm, lean tannins. Together the fruit and tannins provide the kind of balance that should carry this wine another five to seven years. Drink 1992-1997. 7,100 cases produced. Release: $12. Current: $16. **85**

1982 CONN CREEK WINERY COLLINS VINEYARD PROPRIETOR'S SPECIAL SELECTION: Extremely austere and tannic, this wine will take a long time before it's smooth enough to drink. The fruit is hard, concentrated and tannic, with herb and black cherry flavors that are very dry on the finish. Only for the very patient. Drink 1995-2004. 40 cases produced. Never released commercially; sold only at the Napa Valley Wine Auction. Current: $70. **85**

1981 CONN CREEK WINERY: With age, this tight, lean wine has evolved into a richer and more complex bottling that offers spicy currant and black cherry flavors. Near its peak, it nonetheless has the depth and flavor intensity to carry it another five years. Drink 1990-1995. 5,700 cases produced. Release: $14. Current: $18. **85**

1981 CONN CREEK WINERY COLLINS VINEYARD PROPRIETOR'S SPECIAL SELECTION: A big, tannic, chunky 1981 with intense black currant, anise and plum flavors and firm, dry tannins. Has the structure and intensity but lacks finesse. Needs more time to soften; typical of the Collins Vineyard. Drink 1994-2002. 40 cases produced. Never released commercially; sold only at the Napa Valley Wine Auction. Current: $70. **86**

1980 CONN CREEK WINERY: Rich, ripe and fruity, with layers of plum, currant and black cherry flavors that are supported by firm, tight tannins, which promise to give this wine another eight to 10 years of life. While the fruit is softening, the tannins are firmly in place. Drink 1993-2000. 5,700 cases produced. Release: $13. Current: $28. **88**

1980 CONN CREEK WINERY COLLINS VINEYARD PROPRIETOR'S SPECIAL SELECTION: This is an enormously rich blockbuster of a wine, packed with ripe, thick, concentrated fruit flavors flanked by a wall of rich, thick tannins. Only two barrels were produced. It is so tannic that it should age another decade with ease yet has the intense fruit to stand up to it. Very impressive. Drink 1995-2004. 40 cases pro-

duced. Never released commercially; sold only at the Napa Valley Wine Auction. Current: $70. **93**

1979 CONN CREEK WINERY: A good if somewhat awkward 1979 that is still quite coarse and tannic, with grapy flavors that are ripe and straightforward and an earthy, minerally, slightly medicinal note on the finish that detracts. Drink 1993-1998. 6,270 cases produced. Release: $13. Current: $25. **77**

1978 CONN CREEK WINERY LOT 1: Impressive for its fresh, youthful, grapy, spicy fruit flavors and supple texture, this wine is enjoyable now for its rich fruit but appears to have enough flavor, structure and concentration for another five to 10 years. Not quite as complex as the best 1978s but nonetheless a very good bottling. Drink 1990-1998. 3,000 cases produced. Release: $12. Current: $35. **86**

1978 CONN CREEK WINERY LOT 2: A rich, smooth, elegant 1978 with more complexity than Lot 1; the well-focused black cherry, currant, spice and cedar flavors are crisp and mouthwatering. The tannins have softened, leaving a full, lush, delicate finish. At its peak now, but it has the intensity and flavor for another six to eight years. Drink 1990-2000. 2,500 cases produced. Release: $13. Current: $40. **92**

1977 CONN CREEK WINERY: A rich, young, elegant 1977 that is still on its way up, with generous, ripe, Cabernet fruit that is developing complexity. It still has tannin to shed. Drink 1991-1998. 2,000 cases produced. Release: $12. Current: $40. **90**

1976 CONN CREEK WINERY: Ripe without being overdone, with well-focused black cherry and currant flavors. This well-balanced wine has years of life left, missing only the sheer elegance and finesse of the best Conn Creek Cabernets. In fine drinking condition but can hold another five years. Drink 1990-1995. 2,000 cases produced. Release: $12. Current: $45. **86**

1974 CONN CREEK WINERY: From the great Eisele Vineyard near Calistoga, this 1974 is a rich yet elegant wine that continues to amaze me with its understated elegance and delicate complexities. It has none of the excesses of the vintage that led to many overly ripe, raisiny wines. This wine has remained sleek and complex, with sharply defined black currant, spice, mineral and oak flavors that are in harmony. There's still a trace of tannin on the finish, but this wine is in its prime and should hold there for another five years. Drink 1990-1998. 900 cases produced. Release: $9. Current: $70. **94**

1973 CONN CREEK WINERY: An amazingly fresh and fruity wine with rich black cherry, anise and raspberry flavors that taste as young as a five-year-old wine. Remarkably rich and elegant, with the tannins in perfect harmony. This wine is at its peak now but should hold another five to 10 years with ease. Crisp acidity carries the flavors on the finish. One of the best 1973s; from Steltzner Vineyard. Drink 1990-2000. 400 cases produced. Release: $9. Current: $70. **92**

CUVAISON WINERY

Calistoga, Napa Valley

CLASSIFICATION: *FOURTH GROWTH*

COLLECTIBILITY RATING: *Not rated*

BEST VINTAGES: *1986, 1985, 1984*

After a difficult period in the late 1970s and early 1980s, Cuvaison has settled on a style that emphasizes rich, concentrated fruit on a firm, lean, elegant framework. The 1986 vintage is clearly the finest Cabernet ever produced by this Swiss-owned winery near Calistoga. The 1984 and 1985 vintages showed dramatic improvement from the wines that preceded them.

I have never been a fan of their earlier Cabernets. Although one limited-edition, 400-case bottling of the 1975 that bore the signature of then-winemaker Philip Togni has been at times rich and seductive, the majority of the wines produced between 1976 and 1983 have been too ripe, oaky, alcoholic and unfriendly for my taste. The 1975 through 1983 Cabernets were produced almost entirely from mountain-grown grapes that were extremely ripe and raisiny, often with alcohol levels of 14 percent and higher. These wines are also extremely woody and often overly tannic, an exaggerated style that emerged in California in the 1970s when intense varietal character was a common goal among many winemakers. Some of these wines may come around with more time in the bottle, but I would not bet on it. The best wines to concentrate on are from the 1984, 1985 and 1986 vintages in which winemaker John Thacher turned from mountain-grown to valley floor grapes which the winery buys from independent growers. The 1986 in particular offers uncommon richness, depth and concentration with elegance and finesse. It should age exceptionally well and at $14 is a very good buy.

TASTING NOTES

CUVAISON WINERY, Calistoga, Napa Valley

1986 CUVAISON WINERY: The finest Cuvaison Cabernet ever produced, intense and weighty, combining deep, rich, concentrated black currant and cherry aromas and flavors with delicate herb and oak nuances, a firm structure, crisp acidity and firm tannins. Delicious now,

AT A GLANCE
CUVAISON WINERY
P.O. Box 384
Calistoga, CA 94515
(707) 942-6266

Owner: The Schmidheiny Family, Switzerland

Winemaker: John Thacher (7 years)

Founded: 1969

First Cabernet vintage: 1973

Cabernet production: 5,000 cases

Cabernet acres owned: None, 20 acres of Merlot

Average age of vines: 7 years

Vineyard makeup: Merlot (100%)

Average wine makeup: Cabernet Saugnon (85%), Merlot (10%), Cabernet Franc (5%)

Time in oak: 18 months

Type of oak: French (Nevers)

CUVAISON

Cabernet Sauvignon

Napa Valley

1984

ALC. 13.0% BY VOL.

but should age well for a decade and beyond. Drink 1993-2001. 5,000 cases produced. Release: $15. Current: $15. **93**

1985 CUVAISON WINERY: Similar in style to the excellent 1984, this is a shade leaner and more concentrated but very rich and complex, with toasty oak flavors to complement the ripe plum and cherry notes. The tannins are fine and elegant, making this wine delicious to drink now and through the next five to eight years. Drink 1992-1999. 3,000 cases produced. Release: $14. Current: $14. **90**

1984 CUVAISON WINERY: A vast improvement over its predecessors, the 1984 is rich and complex with layers of elegant cedar, currant and spicy cherry flavors that are lean and well focused with tannins in proportion to the fruit. A good candidate for midterm cellaring, it is also quite drinkable today. Drink 1991-1996. 3,000 cases produced. Release: $14. Current: $14. **89**

1983 CUVAISON WINERY: A disappointing Cuvaison that is lean, hard and tannic, lacking richness, grace and charm. It's one-dimensional and extremely austere. Drink 1990-1992. 2,000 cases produced. Release: $12. Current: $15. **75**

1982 CUVAISON WINERY: A big, intense, ripe and tannic 1982, young and assertive, with layers of plum, cedar, currant and anise flavors that still need five years to round out fully. Lacks the finesse and charm of the best from this vintage. Drink 1994-2000. 2,000 cases produced. Release: $11. Current: $15. **82**

1981 CUVAISON WINERY: Tannic and lean, with black cherry and plum notes, but it does not appear to have the concentration of fruit to stand up to the drying tannins. Drink 1993-1999. 6,000 cases produced. Release: $11. Current: $15. **74**

1980 CUVAISON WINERY: Although better balanced than the 1978 or 1979, the 1980 is nonetheless very ripe, woody and tannic, with a coarse texture. The ripe fruit is jammy, with peppery notes, but the finish is very dry and tannic. Drink 1994-2001. 5,000 cases produced. Release: $11. Current: $18. **77**

1979 CUVAISON WINERY: Intense, raw and tannic, much like the 1978 in style, with very ripe, raisiny flavors, high extract of fruit, tannins and wood, and a coarse, alcoholic texture. Not likely to improve. Drink 1993-2000. 5,000 cases produced. Release: $11. Current: $20. **75**

1978 CUVAISON WINERY: A hard, clumsy wine, bitterly tannic and oaky, that does not appear to have much of a future. It's ripe and raisiny, and the alcohol (14 percent) sticks out, too. If you wait for the tannins to disappear, it will be in the next century. Drink 1995-2002. 5,000 cases produced. Release: $10. Current: $20. **72**

1977 CUVAISON WINERY: A thick, tannic 1977 that is losing its fruit and has a hard, tannic shell. The ripe currant and anise flavors are dominated by the hard, woody tannins. Out of balance and not likely to regain it. Most of the fruit will be gone by the time the tannins fade. Drink 1992-1998. 6,000 cases produced. Release: $10. Current: $35. **79**

1976 CUVAISON WINERY: Typical of the 1976 vintage, ripe and raisiny with biting tannins, plenty of anise and plum but disjointed on the palate. Missing balance and finesse. Drink 1992-1996. 6,000 cases produced. Release: $10. Current: $35. **79**

1975 CUVAISON WINERY: Rich, ripe and supple, beginning to fade, but with pretty plum, anise and currant flavors along with mature coffee and herb notes. Still has a good dose of tannin on the finish. Drink 1990-1995. 5,000 cases produced. Release: $10. Current: $40. **79**

1975 CUVAISON WINERY PHILIP TOGNI SIGNATURE: A limited release of 400 cases and the best Cuvaison during Philip Togni's tenure. Made from Spring Mountain-grown fruit, it's very ripe and jammy, with plum, black currant and raisin notes, framed by generous oak flavors, crisp acidity and some heat on the finish. Despite its weight, it offers a measure of elegance on the palate. Has plenty of life left. Drink 1992-1998. 400 cases produced. Release: $40. Current: $60. **88**

AT A GLANCE
DEMOOR WINERY
7481 St. Helena Highway
Oakville, CA 94562
(707) 944-2565

Owner: Jacques deSchepper, Belgium

Winemaker: Aaron Mosley (11 years)

Founded: 1976

First Cabernet vintage: 1978

Cabernet production: 2,400 cases

Cabernet acres owned: none

Average age of vines: n/a

Vineyard makeup: n/a

Average wine makeup: Cabernet Sauvignon (94%), Cabernet Franc (6%)

Time in oak: 24 months

Type of oak: French, Yugoslavian

DEMOOR WINERY
Oakville, Napa Valley

CLASSIFICATION: *FIFTH GROWTH*

COLLECTIBILITY RATING: *Not rated*

BEST VINTAGES:

Owner's Selection: 1982

Napa Valley: 1984

Napa Cellars: 1978

The DeMoor Winery in Oakville is a low-key operation, but its Cabernets consistently have been first-rate, beginning with the first vintage in 1978. Founded in 1976 as Napa Cellars, the winery was acquired by the deSchepper family of Belgium in 1983, and it retained winemaker Aaron Mosley to oversee operations. DeMoor owns no Cabernet vineyards and buys grapes from various growers throughout the valley.

The DeMoor style emphasizes very ripe, sometimes jammy flavors with richness and intensity. The Cabernets are never shy and subdued, but packed with fresh, ripe fruit. The 1978 is drinking exceptionally well now and is rich, smooth and polished, with flavor and concentration to carry it another decade. Both 1979 and 1980 were very good but a step down from the 1978, while the 1981, 1982 and 1983 were also very good and typical of their vintages. The 1984 is effusively fruity and very attractive, the best wine since the 1978.

TASTING NOTES

DEMOOR WINERY, Oakville, Napa Valley

1985 DEMOOR WINERY: Despite the attractive flavors, it is surprisingly light and herbal, with modestly proportioned cedar, plum and spice flavors that do not match previous efforts. Inconsistent with the winery's style and the vintage, ready now. Drink 1991-1996. 1,800 cases produced. Release: $14. Current: $14. **79**

1984 DEMOOR WINERY: The best DeMoor since the excellent 1978, brimming with ripe, seductive fruit, with a smooth, supple texture and great length. The ripe black cherry, raspberry and jam flavors are rich and enticing. This wine is alluring to drink now but has all the ingredients to develop for a decade or more. Drink 1992-2002. 2,400 cases produced. Release: $14. Current: $16. **88**

1983 DeMOOR WINERY: Tight, firm and tannic, it manages to provide enough ripe, rich black cherry and raisin flavors to stand up to the hard tannins. A good candidate for the cellar. Drink 1995-2003. 2,400 cases produced. Release: $12. Current: $16. **86**

1982 DeMOOR WINERY OWNERS' SELECTION: Offers a shade more richness and depth than the regular bottling, very intense, tannic and concentrated with layers of spice, cedar, currant and cherry flavors that are tight and focused. Requires patience. Drink 1995-2003. 2,000 cases produced. Release: $12. Current: $19. **88**

1982 DeMOOR WINERY: The first bottling under the DeMoor label is earthy, tannic, toasty and well balanced, with tight, dense currant and chocolate flavors that will require another five to seven years to develop fully. Right now it's tight and closed. Drink 1994-2001. 1,000 cases produced. Release: $12. Current: $18. **86**

1981 NAPA CELLARS: Intensely fruity, with ripe, raisin, black cherry and currant flavors that are well proportioned, developing a silky smooth texture and finishing with a fresh, fruity aftertaste. Drink 1990-1997. 1,800 cases produced. Release: $12. Current: $25. **86**

1980 NAPA CELLARS: Very ripe and spicy, with currant, black cherry, tar, anise and raisin flavors that are showing some alcoholic heat. The tannins are resolved, but some may find the ripeness and alcohol excessive. Drink 1990-1996. 1,600 cases produced. Release: $12. Current: $20. **80**

1979 NAPA CELLARS: Another very ripe vintage, surprising for a 1979, with ripe currant, cherry and anise flavors that are framed by firm, drying tannins and an alcoholic finish. Despite the heat on the finish, this wine is fairly well balanced. Still needs time to shed its tannins. Drink 1990-1998. 1,600 cases produced. Release: $10. Current: $25. **85**

1978 NAPA CELLARS: Napa Cellars' first bottling, this is rich, smooth, elegant and complex, with attractive black cherry, currant, plum and anise notes and spicy vanilla and oak nuances that are long and smooth on the finish. At its peak now, with the supple tannins to age another eight to 10 years. Drink 1990-2000. 1,700 cases produced. Release: $10. Current: $28. **89**

DIAMOND CREEK VINEYARDS

Gravelly Meadow, Diamond Mountain, Napa Valley
Red Rock Terrace, Diamond Mountain, Napa Valley
Volcanic Hill, Diamond Mountain, Napa Valley
Lake Vineyard, Diamond Mountain, Napa Valley
Three Vineyard Blend, Diamond Mountain, Napa Valley

CLASSIFICATION: *FIRST GROWTH*

COLLECTIBILITY RATING: *AAA*

BEST VINTAGES:

Gravelly Meadow: 1986, 1985, 1984, 1983, 1982, 1980, 1979, 1978

Red Rock Terrace: 1986, 1985, 1984, 1981, 1979, 1978

Volcanic Hill: 1986, 1985, 1984, 1981, 1980, 1978, 1975

Lake: 1984, 1978

Diamond Creek Vineyards in Napa Valley is the most unique Cabernet vineyard in California. From its 660-foot elevation on Diamond Mountain southwest of Calistoga, this tiny, 3,000-case Cabernet specialist is actually four separate vineyards, each with a unique microclimate and identity, and each of which produces a distinct, long-lived Cabernet.

While Diamond Creek Cabernets are greatly admired by some connoisseurs and collectors, they are not for everyone. I doubt this winery has ever won many gold medals for its wines. Diamond Creek has a well-deserved reputation for austere, tannic, enormously concentrated wines, and while many people find these wines too extreme and tannic, it is exactly those qualities that appeal to Diamond Creek aficionados. For while these wines are hard, firm and unyielding, they are also beautifully crafted wines that are extremely concentrated, complex, flavorful and ageworthy.

Diamond Creek also created a unique marketing niche by producing three, and occasionally four, different Cabernets from the same estate, which provides connoisseurs with the ultimate study of the influences of *terroir* and microclimate from vintage to vintage. Moreover, no fan of these wines could collect one vineyard and ignore the others.

There has never been much Diamond Creek Cabernet to sell. Total production occasionally reaches 3,000 cases but is often closer to 2,000 cases, creating a tight supply-demand ratio. The largest vineyard is the 8-acre Volcanic Hill, a southerly facing vineyard on a sloping bed of chalky gray volcanic soil. Volcanic Hill is the most austere and tannic of the Diamond Creek bottlings, and it typically is the most backward and in need of the longest cellaring. But for all its austerity, it is extremely concentrated and flavorful. Up to 1,400 cases are produced in a good year.

Red Rock Terrace, a 7-acre vineyard on red-tinged, iron-rich soil, faces Volcanic Hill. It is northerly facing and slightly steeper, yielding a more elegant, polished Cabernet that still embraces the Diamond Creek style of concentration and tannic firmness. Production averages 750 cases.

Gravelly Meadow, a 5-acre vineyard, takes its name from its rocky, gravelly soil, which is extremely well drained. Gravelly Meadow typically displays an earthier quality than either Volcanic Hill or Red Rock Terrace, and it is the most forward of the three vineyards. Between 400 and 800 cases are produced.

Lake Vineyard is less than 1 acre and is named after a small, man-made pond nearby. Because of its size, the vineyard is usually blended into the Gravelly Meadow bottling. But in 1978, 1984 and 1987, the Lake Vineyard Cabernet was so spectacular that it was bottled separately.

The quality of Diamond Creek Cabernets is generally very high. While its early vintages were unusually tannic, the wines since 1978 have displayed more richness and fruit, a result of more mature vines, better vintages and modest winemaking modifications. While Diamond Creek's wines are tannic to begin with, they are also among the first Cabernets on the market, released just two years after harvest; other wineries hold their wines back three to four years for bottle age. Prices for Diamond Creek have also risen steadily in recent years, in part because of the limited supply but also because of the exceptional quality and high demand.

The first vintage in 1972 produced only 65 cases, followed by 150 cases in 1973, 742 in 1974, 972 in 1975 and 805 in 1976. Not until 1978 did the vines mature fully to produce at the capacity level of 3,000 cases. In 1972 only Red Rock Terrace and Volcanic Hill were bottled; fruit from Gravelly Meadow was blended with the two wines, and while the Volcanic Hill is drinking well considering the poor quality of the vintage, both bottles have greater value as collectibles because of their scant production and because they are Diamond Creek's first vintage. The 1974 vintage was the first exceptional one at Diamond Creek, and both the Gravelly Meadow and Volcanic Hill remain in fine condition.

In 1975, the Volcanic Hill eclipsed the other two in quality with a monumental wine that is amazingly rich and concentrated. All three 1976s were very good and close in quality. The 1977s were exceptional, particularly the Volcanic Hill, which ranks among the finest wines produced that year. In 1978 all four of the vineyards were sensational, in particular the Lake (99 points) and Volcanic Hill (95), and are still not fully mature. The 1979s are equally magnificent, with Volcanic Hill again rating slightly ahead of the other two vineyards. In 1980 all three vineyards yielded excellent wines, with the Gravelly Meadow ranked the highest. The 1981s are the most supple and forward Diamond Creeks

Gravelly Meadow

Napa **1975** Valley

Cabernet Sauvignon

grown and produced on diamond mountain by
DIAMOND CREEK VINEYARDS   CALISTOGA, CA.
BOTTLED BY DIAMOND CREEK WINERY, ST. HELENA, CA
ALCOHOL 12% BY VOLUME

and are drinkable today; all three are superior wines.

The 1982 vintage produced the largest crop at Diamond Creek before 1986, and while all three vineyards produced fine wines, they are a notch below Diamond Creek's best. Diamond Creek also produced a series of 1982 Special Selection bottlings from each vineyard designed for the restaurant trade. These wines received minimal egg white fining and are lighter and less flavorful than the regular bottlings. The Special Selection designation does not mean superior quality; rather it was an experiment that proved somewhat disappointing, and Diamond Creek has not attempted that since. The 1983s are typical of the vintage, hard, lean and tannic and probably long agers. Quality is close in the three bottlings. The 1984s are perhaps the finest ever produced at Diamond Creek, for they are the fruitiest, and they offer a measure of elegance and suppleness not usually found in these wines early on. They are also enormously rich and flavorful, with more than enough tannin to carry them for decades. A 50-case lot of a three-vineyard blend was also produced in 1984. The wine is an example of what Diamond Creek would taste like if all three vineyards were blended into one wine. The 1985 Diamond Creeks are also sublime wines, but they are leaner and firmer than the 1984s and will require more time to develop. The 1986 Diamond Creeks represent another phenomenal vintage, with enormously rich, concentrated wines that are also elegant and refined.

With so many excellent vintages to choose from, it's difficult to rank them, but in very tight formation here's one critic's view of the top five: 1984, 1986, 1978, 1985 and 1979.

With a cultlike following that snaps up cases in pre-release sales and distinctly styled wines that age on and on, Diamond Creek ranks as one of the top collectibles in California. Prices for new vintages are now at $30 to $40 a bottle and rising.

TASTING NOTES

DIAMOND CREEK VINEYARD, Gravelly Meadow, Diamond Mountain, Napa Valley

1986 DIAMOND CREEK VINEYARD GRAVELLY MEADOW: A lean, austere 1986 with very tight, concentrated earth, cedar and plum flavors that are very intense and deep. The fruit is lurking behind the dense tannins. A typically austere wine that ranks among the best Gravelly Meadows ever made. Drink 1997-2010. 795 cases produced. Release: $30. Current: $30. **94**

1985 DIAMOND CREEK VINEYARD GRAVELLY MEADOW: Extremely hard, tart and tannic, this is a very austere Gravelly Meadow that may well age 30 years. The cedar and black cherry flavors are so tight and concentrated that they won't be fully mature for 15 years. Drink 1995-2010. 736 cases produced. Release: $30. Current: $40. **92**

1984 DIAMOND CREEK VINEYARD GRAVELLY MEADOW: A touch earthier and more austere than the magnificent Red Rock Terrace, the 1984 Gravelly Meadow is nonetheless a sensational wine, rich and concentrated, with layers of lavish cedar, plum, currant and spice flavors that echo long. Tannic on the finish. Drink 1994-2007. 470 cases produced. Release: $25. Current: $40. **94**

1983 DIAMOND CREEK VINEYARD GRAVELLY MEADOW: Very complex and enticing, with earth, currant, spice and cherry flavors that are very well structured. More forward and accessible than most Diamond Creeks, it nonetheless needs the better part of another decade. Drink 1995-2004. 520 cases produced. Release: $20. Current: $25. **89**

1982 DIAMOND CREEK VINEYARD GRAVELLY MEADOW: Richer and more concentrated than the Red Rock Terrace bottling, this is a tight, complex, austere wine with plenty of cedar, earth, anise and black cherry flavors of great intensity and length. Tannins are in proportion for long aging. Drink 1995-2005. 404 cases produced. Release: $20. Current: $35. **89**

1982 DIAMOND CREEK VINEYARD GRAVELLY MEADOW SPECIAL SELECTION: Like the Red Rock Terrace Special Selection, the Gravelly Meadow received light egg white fining and is lighter in body and flavor with tart cherry, cedar and oak flavors backed by firm tannins. A shade better than the Red Rock Terrace Special Selection. Drink 1994-2000. 140 cases produced. Release: $20. Current: $35. **84**

1981 DIAMOND CREEK VINEYARD GRAVELLY MEADOW: Has an earthier style characteristic of the vineyard but with rich cedar, black cherry, currant and spice flavors that are a shade firmer than the Red Rock Terrace bottling. Still closed and tight, needs time. Drink 1995-2004. 656 cases produced. Release: $20. Current: $35. **89**

1980 DIAMOND CREEK VINEYARD GRAVELLY MEADOW: A richer, fuller, more complex wine than either the Red Rock Terrace or Volcanic Hill, the 1980 Gravelly Meadow displays layers of black cherry, currant and cedar flavors that are well integrated and intriguing, finishing with a touch of coffee and anise. Tannins bring up the rear. Drink 1996-2006. 460 cases produced. Release: $20. Current: $40. **92**

1979 DIAMOND CREEK VINEYARD GRAVELLY MEADOW: One of the most elegant and forward vintages from Diamond Creek, this is a spicy, earthy, cedary wine that is complex, with herb and black cherry flavors. Not nearly as tannic as previous vintages, this wine is approaching maturity but nonetheless will continue to drink well for another decade. Drink 1995-2005. 194 cases produced. Release: $15. Current: $60. **91**

1978 DIAMOND CREEK VINEYARD GRAVELLY MEADOW: A richer, more concentrated bottling than the Red Rock Terrace, packed with rich, ripe black cherry, currant and spice flavors that are very complex and austere, with hints of herbs, mint, anise and floral notes.

Lake

Napa **1984** Valley

Cabernet Sauvignon
grown, produced and bottled on diamond mountain by
DIAMOND CREEK VINEYARDS   CALISTOGA, CA.

ALCOHOL 12½% BY VOLUME

Amazingly complex. This wine has the tannin and structure for another decade or more. Drink 1995-2005. 315 cases produced. Release: $12.50. Current: $75. **93**

1977 DIAMOND CREEK VINEYARD GRAVELLY MEADOW: A durable 1977, the Gravelly Meadow is rich, thick and earthy, very concentrated, with layers of mineral, earth, currant and black cherry flavors that are very austere and in need of further cellaring. Drink 1994-2000. 422 cases produced. Release: $10. Current: $55. **89**

1976 DIAMOND CREEK VINEYARD GRAVELLY MEADOW: Ripe and forward for Diamond Creek, with fresh, ripe, concentrated cherry, earth and mineral flavors before the dry tannins kick in. Needs more time to soften and develop. Drink 1990-1999. 96 cases produced. Release: $9. Current: $90. **85**

1975 DIAMOND CREEK VINEYARD GRAVELLY MEADOW: In the context of the other wines, not quite as concentrated or tannic, nor quite as complex, yet this is still a sturdy, muscular wine with narrowly focused fruit, earth and mineral flavors supported by firm tannins. Almost ready. Drink 1991-2000. 95 cases produced. Release: $7.50. Current: $55. **85**

1974 DIAMOND CREEK VINEYARD GRAVELLY MEADOW: Considerably fruitier than the austere Volcanic Hill bottling, the Gravelly Meadow is nonetheless very dense, concentrated and complex with rich currant, cedar and spice flavors, finishing with firm, drying tannins. Approachable now but still has the depth and flavor for another three to five years. Drink 1990-1997. 105 cases produced. Release: $7.50. Current: $135. **88**

DIAMOND CREEK VINEYARD, Lake Vineyard, Diamond Mountain, Napa Valley

1984 DIAMOND CREEK VINEYARD LAKE: Only the second bottling from this vineyard, the 1984 is a rich, concentrated, elegant wine with complex cedar, currant, cinnamon, plum and vanilla flavors that are well integrated and very harmonious. Has crisp acidity on the finish and not quite the massive tannins of most Diamond Creeks. Drink 1995-2004. 130 cases produced. Release: $50. Current: $120. **92**

1978 DIAMOND CREEK VINEYARD LAKE: The finest Diamond Creek I've ever tasted and one of the greatest cabernets from California, this is the first bottling from the minuscule Lake Vineyard. It is a magnificent wine with beautiful currant, black cherry and floral aromas and rich, concentrated yet elegant flavors, finishing with cinnamon, spice and loads of ripe berry. Impeccably balanced, with tannins that are in proportion to the fruit, this is a simply sensational wine with a gorgeous, supple aftertaste that lingers. Drink 1994-2002. 25 cases produced. Release: $25. Current: $250. **99**

DIAMOND CREEK, Red Rock Terrace, Diamond Mountain, Napa Valley

1986 DIAMOND CREEK VINEYARD RED ROCK TERRACE: This ranks with 1984 as the greatest Red Rock Terrace ever produced, a remarkably rich, concentrated and elegant wine with layers of fresh, ripe plum, currant, spice and black cherry flavors that are simply delicious. The tannins are soft and fine. A long way from drinking. Drink 1999-2010. 970 cases produced. Release: $30. Current: $30. **96**

1985 DIAMOND CREEK VINEYARD RED ROCK TERRACE: The 1985 Red Rock Terrace is a very dense, earthy, concentrated wine with herb, juniper and spicy pepper notes to complement the currant and cedar flavors that turn hard and tannic on the finish. Drink 1996-2009. 643 cases produced. Release: $30. Current: $40. **93**

1984 DIAMOND CREEK VINEYARD RED ROCK TERRACE: By far the fruitiest vintage at Diamond Creek and in my view the most flavorful and complex vintage in Diamond Creek history. It is a very rich, concentrated yet supple wine, oozing with black cherry, currant, anise and vanilla flavors that linger long and full on the finish. An amazing wine that ranks among the very finest Diamond Creeks. Drink 1994-2006. 620 cases produced. Release: $25. Current: $40. **96**

1983 DIAMOND CREEK VINEYARD RED ROCK TERRACE: The 1983 Red Rock Terrace offers pretty, complex aromas of cedar, berries and spice but is rather closed and austere, showing hints of black cherry flavors. While tannic, it is well proportioned as 1983s go. Good depth and intensity on the aftertaste. Drink 1996-2005. 651 cases produced. Release: $20. Current: $25. **88**

1982 DIAMOND CREEK VINEYARD RED ROCK TERRACE: Tight, austere and closed, with hints of cedar, cherry, earth and spice flavors. One of Diamond Creek's lighter vintages, this is nonetheless balanced and built for another five years' cellaring. Drink 1995-2004. 753 cases produced. Release: $20. Current: $35. **87**

1982 DIAMOND CREEK VINEYARD RED ROCK TERRACE SPECIAL SELECTION: The Special Selection was an experimental bottling that was egg white fined as a restaurant wine with three egg whites per barrel, about half of normal. Drink 1993-1999. 192 cases produced. Release: $20. Current: $35. **80**

1981 DIAMOND CREEK VINEYARD RED ROCK TERRACE: The most elegant vintage from Diamond Creek, this is a rich, concentrated wine with ripe cherry, currant, earth and cedar flavors that are moderately tannic and elegantly balanced, finishing with fruit and spice. Ready sooner than most Diamond Creeks. Drink 1993-2002. 497 cases produced. Release: $20. Current: $35. **91**

1980 DIAMOND CREEK VINEYARD RED ROCK TERRACE: More herbaceous than previous Red Rock Terrace bottlings, the 1980 is a

Red Rock Terrace

Napa **1972** Valley

Cabernet Sauvignon

grown, produced and bottled on diamond mountain by

DIAMOND CREEK VINEYARDS   CALISTOGA, CA.

ALCOHOL 11¾% BY VOLUME

lean, firm wine that lacks the generous fruit of 1979 or 1978 but is still complex, with more cedar and tobacco notes. Plenty of tannin for aging. Drink 1994-2004. 591 cases produced. Release: $20. Current: $40. **86**

1979 DIAMOND CREEK VINEYARD RED ROCK TERRACE: The 1979 defines the elegance and sheer intensity of this vineyard. It's very lean yet well endowed, with ripe, spicy, layered fruit that is still a few years from reaching its pinnacle. In close running with the other two bottlings. Drink 1993-2000. 263 cases produced. Release: $15. Current: $60. **92**

1978 DIAMOND CREEK VINEYARD RED ROCK TERRACE: A remarkably rich and elegant 1978 offering delicate black cherry, currant and spicy cedar nuances, with hints of chocolate on the finish. A delicious, complex wine that is nearing its peak. Drink 1992-2004. 468 cases produced. Release: $12.50. Current: $75. **92**

1977 DIAMOND CREEK VINEYARD RED ROCK TERRACE FIRST PICK: A deliciously elegant and concentrated wine packed with firm tannins and layers of complex cedar, earth, spice and cherry aromas and flavors that are very tight and austere. Still needs five years. Drink 1994-2003. 238 cases produced. Release: $10. Current: $50. **88**

1977 DIAMOND CREEK VINEYARD RED ROCK TERRACE SECOND PICK: Considerably lighter and simpler than the First Pick, it lacks the ripe fruit and concentration of the other bottlings from this vintage and remains disproportionately tannic. Grapes from a second crop picked in November. Drink 1993-1996. 60 cases produced. Release: $10. Current: $40. **75**

1976 DIAMOND CREEK VINEYARD RED ROCK TERRACE: From a riper vintage, the 1976 Red Rock Terrace is rich and concentrated, with cherry and earth flavors. Still needs more time for the flavors to come through but holding up very well. Not quite as complex as the best from this difficult, overripe vintage. Drink 1990-1999. 283 cases produced. Release: $9. Current: $90. **85**

1975 DIAMOND CREEK VINEYARD RED ROCK TERRACE: A remarkably well-preserved 1975 that is very deep and concentrated, with rich currant, cherry and cedar aromas and a complex earthiness. Flavors are still evolving, and it's dry and tannic on the finish. Drink 1992-1997. 286 cases produced. Release: $7.50. Current: $75. **88**

1972 DIAMOND CREEK VINEYARD RED ROCK TERRACE: The 1972 vintage was a mediocre one in Napa Valley, and this wine is past its prime, with frail mature fruit and cedar and spice flavors. Most of the tannins have subsided too. Has more value as a collectible, since it is the first Diamond Creek Cabernet and only 25 cases were produced. Drink 1990-1992. 25 cases produced. Release: $7.50. Current: $200. **74**

DIAMOND CREEK, Volcanic Hill, Diamond Mountain, Napa Valley

1986 DIAMOND CREEK VINEYARD VOLCANIC HILL: Incredibly rich and concentrated, the 1986 Volcanic Hill rivals the 1986 Red Rock Terrace in quality. It is packed with layers of ripe plum, currant, cedar and vanilla flavors that are amazingly complex and structured. Dense and structured, it may be a wine for your children. Drink 1996-2012. 1,035 cases produced. Release: $30. Current: $30. **96**

1985 DIAMOND CREEK VINEYARD VOLCANIC HILL: Like the Red Rock Terrace and Gravelly Meadow, this is an enormously tannic and austere wine. A touch more black cherry and currant flavors are peeking through than in the Gravelly Meadow, but it has great structure, crisp acidity and firm tannins. Drink 1996-2010. 1,100 cases produced. Release: $30. Current: $40. **93**

1984 DIAMOND CREEK VINEYARD VOLCANIC HILL: The least showy of the three 1984s, the Volcanic Hill is typically austere and restrained on the nose and palate. It offers intense ripe plum, currant and vanilla flavors that are very complex but not quite as deep and intense as the Red Rock Terrace and Gravelly Meadow bottlings. Very tannic on the finish. Drink 1994-2007. 1,224 cases produced. Release: $25. Current: $40. **94**

1983 DIAMOND CREEK VINEYARD VOLCANIC HILL: Typically hard and austere, the 1983 Volcanic Hill is an amazingly rich and concentrated wine, with packed fruit and tannin and layers of vanilla, currant and chocolate. Needs time but should be a beauty. Best of the three vineyards. Drink 1996-2007. 1,442 cases produced. Release: $20. Current: $25. **89**

1982 DIAMOND CREEK VINEYARD VOLCANIC HILL: Extremely austere and tannic, a dense, tight, concentrated wine that may need a decade of cellaring. The tart cherry, cedar, earth and cranberry flavors are sharply defined and just beginning to open. Be patient. Drink 1997-2007. 1,420 cases produced. Release: $20. Current: $35. **89**

1982 DIAMOND CREEK VINEYARD VOLCANIC HILL SPECIAL SELECTION: Lighter and less flavorful, this Volcanic Hill Special Selection is much thinner and less interesting than most Diamond Creek bottlings. Drink 1993-1999. 258 cases produced. Release: $20. Current: $35. **79**

1981 DIAMOND CREEK VINEYARD VOLCANIC HILL: A big, rich, dense, structured 1981 that's very tight and concentrated, with hints of currant and cherry flavors and a touch of spice and earth on the finish. Tannic, but the tannins are softer and smoother than in most vintages. The best of the three bottlings, it is still a decade away from its peak. Drink 1996-2006. 1,026 cases produced. Release: $20. Current: $35. **92**

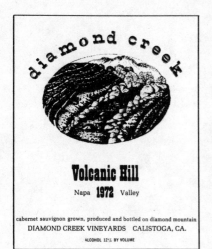

1980 DIAMOND CREEK VINEYARD VOLCANIC HILL: Like the other two vineyards, the Volcanic Hill in 1980 is more herbaceous, and for Volcanic Hill, more elegant. That doesn't mean it isn't tannic, but there are plenty of cedar, bell pepper and black cherry flavors. Austere and tannic on the finish. Give it another decade. Drink 1998-2008. 883 cases produced. Release: $20. Current: $40. **90**

1979 DIAMOND CREEK VINEYARD VOLCANIC HILL FIRST PICK: Another incredible Volcanic Hill bottling that rivals the sensational 1978, the 1979 is enormously deep, complex, rich and concentrated, packed with black cherry, earth, cedar and coffee flavors that are assertive and amazingly long. A very young wine that has a long, full life ahead. Drink 1994-2006. 50 cases produced. Release: $15. Current: $60. **95**

1979 DIAMOND CREEK VINEYARD VOLCANIC HILL SECOND PICK: Clearly the lesser of the two bottlings, the Second Pick came after the rains and is not as flavorful or complex as the First Pick bottling. This is a rather hard, lean, tannic wine with very tight and closed Cabernet fruit. With time it should be a bit more friendly, but now it's not showing much. Drink 1993-1999. 415 cases produced. Release: $15. Current: $40. **82**

1978 DIAMOND CREEK VINEYARD VOLCANIC HILL: A big, rich, dramatic 1978 that verifies the excellence of the vintage at Diamond Creek, it is extremely rich and concentrated, with full, dry tannins and generous black cherry, currant, cedar, coffee and earth flavors that are well integrated and complex. Still a long way from its pinnacle, this wine will benefit from further cellaring. One of the great Volcanic Hill bottlings. Drink 1993-2006. 503 cases produced. Release: $12.50. Current: $75. **95**

1977 DIAMOND CREEK VINEYARD VOLCANIC HILL: Distinct bottle variation; one bottle extremely horsey, basically unpalatable. In another tasting it was less horsey with complex cedar, cherry, herb and anise flavors, but not quite up to previous showings. Best to drink it now before the horsiness is overbearing. Drink 1992. 591 cases produced. Release: $10. Current: $45. **84**

1976 DIAMOND CREEK VINEYARD VOLCANIC HILL: Very close in quality to the other two vineyards, with fresh, ripe fruit that is hard and firm but aging well. Can be consumed now or in the next five years. Drink 1991-1999. 428 cases produced. Release: $9. Current: $90. **87**

1975 DIAMOND CREEK VINEYARD VOLCANIC HILL: The best of the three 1975 Diamond Creek bottlings and one of the finest of the vintage, this is an amazingly rich, elegant and concentrated wine that is just beginning to emerge from it tannic slumber. Its complex cedar, cherry and currant flavors are long and full on the finish. A beautifully crafted wine that should go another decade with ease. Drink 1993-2000. 571 cases produced. Release: $7.50. Current: $80. **93**

1974 DIAMOND CREEK VINEYARD VOLCANIC HILL: Still very deep in color and dense on the palate, packed with rich, dry, concentrated fruit that displays an earthy quality and hints of cherries, currants, spice and cedar. Given the level of tannin, this wine can age another six to 10 years. Drink 1992-2000. 485 cases produced. Release: $7.50. Current: $135. **87**

1973 DIAMOND CREEK VINEYARD VOLCANIC HILL: This is a remarkably rich, concentrated and tannic wine with ripe currant and cherry flavors flanked by a wall of tannins and earthiness on the finish. This wine can age further, but the fruit will be in jeopardy. Drink 1990-1996. 150 cases produced. Release: $7.50. Current: $200. **80**

1972 DIAMOND CREEK VINEYARD VOLCANIC HILL: Despite its age and the poor quality of the vintage, this wine is still in fine condition, with ripe plum, cherry and earth flavors that are rich and fully mature and firm, with dry tannins on the finish. Ready to drink or can age another five years. Good value as a collectible. Drink 1990-1995. 40 cases produced. Release: $7.50. Current: $200. **85**

DIAMOND CREEK, Three Vineyard Blend, Diamond Mountain, Napa Valley

1985 DIAMOND CREEK VINEYARD THREE VINEYARD BLEND: This unique blend has plenty of rich, ripe, concentrated fruit, with layers of plum, cedar, currant and spice flavors and firm tannins. Needs another decade. Drink 1998-2004. 10 cases produced. Release: $50. Current: $50. **89**

1984 DIAMOND CREEK VINEYARD THREE VINEYARD BLEND: Only 50 cases were produced from a second crop. This wine offers very ripe, sumptuous plum and black cherry flavors but not quite the tannic bite of other Diamond Creek bottlings from this vintage. Ready sooner than the others. Drink 1995-2000. 50 cases produced. Release: $50. Current: $50. **89**

1981 DIAMOND CREEK VINEYARD THREE VINEYARD BLEND: A second pick of the three vineyards in November. Very successful. It is rich and complex, with layers of cherry and currant flavors supported by firm, dry tannins and pretty cedar and currant notes on the aftertaste. Can stand some age. Drink 1995-2005. 15 cases produced. Release: $20. Current: $50. **90**

DOMINUS ESTATE

Napanook, Yountville, Napa Valley

CLASSIFICATION: *SECOND GROWTH*

COLLECTIBILITY RATING: AA

BEST VINTAGES: *1986, 1985, 1984*

AT A GLANCE

DOMINUS ESTATE
P.O. Box 3275
Yountville, CA 94599
(707) 944-8954

Owner: John Daniel Society (Christian Moueix, Robin Lail, Marcia Smith)

Winemaker: Christian Moueix (7 years)

Founded: 1982

First Cabernet vintage: 1983

Cabernet production: 6,300 cases

Cabernet acres owned: 41

Average age of vines: 15 years

Vineyard makeup: Cabernet Sauvignon (71%), Merlot (19%), Cabernet Franc (10%)

Average wine makeup: Cabernet Sauvignon (80%), Merlot (10%), Cabernet Franc (10%)

Time in oak: 18 months

Type of oak: French

Dominus is destined to be one of the great stars of Napa Valley. The Napanook Vineyard, due west from the town of Yountville, is one of the valley's finest, owned for decades by the family of former Inglenook winemaker John Daniel Jr. It provided the backbone for the classic, long-lived Inglenook Cabernets of the 1940s, 1950s and early 1960s. The winemaking ingenuity behind Dominus is that of the talented and insightful Christian Moueix, the brilliant general manager of Pomerol's famous Château Pétrus and other noteworthy estates.

The combination of Napanook, of which 41 acres are planted to Bordeaux varieties, and the winemaking of Moueix has already produced a quartet of superlative wines under the Dominus label, beginning with the 1983 vintage. Moueix's first attempt at Dominus came with the 1982 vintage, but when the grapes failed to meet his rigid standards, he waited another year. The 1983 Dominus began as an enormously tannic and rich wine that required an additional year of bottle age before its release. This caused it to be preceded to the marketplace by the 1984, a more supple, fruity and forward wine, but only in the context of the hugely tannic 1983. Both wines need a full hour's aeration for the aromas to develop. The 1984 displays a wider range of flavors than the narrowly focused 1983. With the 1985, Dominus reaches new heights, for this vintage fully demonstrates what Moueix can achieve with Dominus in a great year. The 1985 is a masterpiece, enticingly complex and elegant, with great richness and length. The 1986 is its near equal, deep, broad and rich.

Dominus is a wine collector's dream. While prices for Dominus are steep, beginning at $43 for the 1983, the wines have tremendous international appeal and will certainly be among the top collectibles. A second Cabernet from this vineyard, called Daniel Estate, is also produced, but so far it has not risen to the heights of Dominus. Moueix's partners are Robin Lail and Marcia Smith, Daniel's daughters and heirs to his estate. The partners sell a few tons of their Cabernet fruit to Inglenook for the Reunion bottling.

TASTING NOTES

DOMINUS ESTATE, Napanook, Yountville, Napa Valley

1986 DOMINUS ESTATE NAPANOOK: Deep, broad, rich, lush and tannic, another superior bottling. It's a shade less dramatic than the 1985 but more complex and complete than the 1984. The supple black cherry and currant flavors are supported by firm tannins. Overall, impeccably balanced and ageworthy. Drink 1995-2004. 6,300 cases produced. Not Released. **93**

1985 DOMINUS ESTATE NAPANOOK: By far the best Dominus so far, this is a rich, smooth, concentrated and enticingly seductive wine with layers of complexities and finesse. Its beautiful black cherry, currant and cedar aromas are supple and concentrated, with fine tannins on the palate. Great length, echoing complex flavors on the finish. At last, the masterpiece. Drink 1995-2005. 4,000 cases produced. Release: $45. Current: $45. **95**

1984 DOMINUS ESTATE NAPANOOK: Remarkably complex and forward, with layers of cedar, currant, anise and spice flavors bordered by firm yet supple tannins. It's already drinking quite well, especially with an hour's aeration. It should be at its peak in four to five years. Drink 1994-2002. 4,200 cases produced. Release: $40. Current: $45. **90**

1983 DOMINUS ESTATE NAPANOOK: Early on this was an enormously tannic wine, prompting Moueix to hold it an extra year, releasing it after the 1984. The additional bottle time helped soften the hard edge. It's still tannic, as are most 1983s, but has rich currant and black cherry flavors and a pretty overlay of cedary oak. Complex and balanced. Drink 1994-2002. 2,100 cases produced. Release: $43. Current: $43. **87**

AT A GLANCE
DUCKHORN VINEYARDS
3027 Silverado Trail
St. Helena, CA 94574
(707) 963-7108

Owner: Duckhorn Vineyards (Dan Duckhorn, president)

Winemaker: Tom Rinaldi (11 years)

Founded: 1976

First Cabernet vintage: 1978

Cabernet production: 4,000 cases

Cabernet acres owned: none

Average age of vines: n/a

Vineyard makeup: n/a

Average wine makeup: Cabernet Sauvignon (90%), Cabernet Franc (5%), Merlot (5%)

Time in oak: 20 months

Type of oak: French

DUCKHORN VINEYARDS
Napa Valley

CLASSIFICATION: *SECOND GROWTH*

COLLECTIBILITY RATING: *AA*

BEST VINTAGES: *1986, 1985, 1984, 1982, 1980, 1978*

Although perhaps better known for Merlot, Duckhorn Vineyards in St. Helena produces a magnificent Cabernet Sauvignon that mirrors its Merlot style — rich, deeply concentrated, firmly tannic wines that are made to age 10 to 15 years. Duckhorn does not own any Cabernet vineyards but relies on long-term agreements to buy grapes from prominent vineyards such as Spottswoode in St. Helena and The Hess Collection on Mount Veeder, along with grapes grown on Spring and Howell mountains. Without specific control over its vineyards, the exceptionally high quality of the Duckhorn Cabernets is tribute not only to the quality of the fruit, but also to the winemaking ingenuity of Dan Duckhorn and winemaker Tom Rinaldi.

From the first vintage in 1978, the Duckhorn style has emphasized ripe, concentrated, rich, deep, complex fruit flavors, and plenty of tannin and oak for structure and seasoning. The 1978, from a great vintage, has just reached its drinking peak, but it has the intensity and depth to carry it through the 1990s. No 1979 was produced, but with the 1980 vintage, Duckhorn made another dramatic Cabernet that is a few years away from maturity. The best Cabernets to date are the 1978, 1984, 1985 and 1986 bottlings. Production has reached 4,000 cases with the 1986 vintage, but prices remain reasonable considering the superior quality of the wines. If there is a weakness to the Duckhorn Cabernet program it is that the winery does not own its vineyards, and competition for top Napa Valley Cabernet is becoming keener and more expensive.

TASTING NOTES

DUCKHORN VINEYARDS, Napa Valley

1986 DUCKHORN VINEYARDS: More elegant and stylish than the 1985, loaded with beautifully focused fruit that is smooth and satiny with soft tannins. The rich, ripe black currant and cherry flavors have a touch of spice and pepper that adds to the complexity. May be

Duckhorn's finest. Drink 1995-2003. 4,000 cases produced. Release: $18. Current: $18. **94**

1985 DUCKHORN VINEYARDS: Sleeker and more elegant than the thick, chewy 1984 but still a massive concentration of rich, deep fruit and tannin. The compact black currant, cedar and plum flavors are dense and structured. More powerful than most 1985s, a long-term ager. The flavors are long and full. Drink 1996-2010. 2,800 cases produced. Release: $17.50. Current: $26. **92**

1984 DUCKHORN VINEYARDS: Deep and powerful, this is a massively concentrated, deep and tightly structured 1984 with loads of plum, black currant, cedar and earth flavors tightly woven together. More austere than most Napa Valley 1984s and not as ripe, but very well balanced. Needs time to soften, but this wine appears to have all the ingredients for greatness. Drink 1994-2004. 2,000 cases produced. Release: $17. Current: $30. **92**

1983 DUCKHORN VINEYARDS: A very complete and well-made wine with well-defined cedar, plum, cherry and anise flavors that are ripe, supple and elegant. Better balanced than most 1983s, yet it is dry on the finish. Could be a long-termer. Drink 1994-2000. 3,000 cases produced. Release: $16. Current: $30. **88**

1982 DUCKHORN VINEYARDS: Very impressive considering the vintage, displaying generous, ripe, supple, elegant fruit, layers of plum, black cherry and currant flavors and a touch of chocolate. Not quite the depth of 1978 and 1980, but still well balanced and proportioned. Drink 1992-1998. 3,800 cases produced. Release: $15. Current: $38. **90**

1981 DUCKHORN VINEYARDS: Firmer, leaner, more tannic and drier than the previous two vintages, the 1981 has an elegant core of ripe black currant and spice flavors that are very attractive. A little rough around the edges, it still needs time to shed tannins. Drink 1993-2000. 950 cases produced. Release: $15. Current: $45. **87**

1980 DUCKHORN VINEYARDS: Another remarkable wine that offers ripe, fleshy and elegant fruit, rich black cherry and currant flavors, with a touch of mint that adds a spicy quality. Mature now and very supple, but with depth and richness to carry it another decade. Drink 1992-2002. 1,600 cases produced. Release: $14. Current: $50. **91**

1978 DUCKHORN VINEYARDS: Duckhorn's first Cabernet, the 1978 has great harmony, elegance and finesse, offering rich, smooth and seductive black currant, cherry and anise flavors that are mature and harmonious. Tannins are round and smooth, and the finish is long and focused. Drinking well now but has the subtle intensity to age. Drink 1990-1998. 800 cases produced. Release: $10.50. Current: $85. **92**

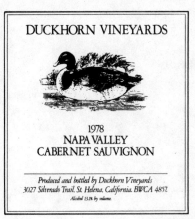

DUCKHORN VINEYARDS

1978
NAPA VALLEY
CABERNET SAUVIGNON

Produced and bottled by Duckhorn Vineyards
3027 Silverado Trail, St. Helena, California. BWCA 4857.
Alcohol 13.1% by volume.

DUNN VINEYARDS

Howell Mountain, Napa Valley
Napa Valley

CLASSIFICATION:
Howell Mountain: FIRST GROWTH
Napa Valley: SECOND GROWTH

COLLECTIBILITY RATING:
Howell Mountain: AAA
Napa Valley: AA

BEST VINTAGES:
Howell Mountain: 1986, 1984, 1983, 1982, 1981, 1980, 1979

Napa Valley: 1986, 1985, 1984, 1983, 1982

AT A GLANCE

DUNN VINEYARDS
805 White Cottage Road
Angwin, CA 94508
(707) 965-3642

Owners: Randy and Lori Dunn

Winemaker: Randy Dunn (10 years)

Founded: 1982

First Cabernet vintage: 1979
   Howell Mountain: 1979
   Napa Valley: 1982

Cabernet production: 4,000 cases
   Howell Mountain: 2,000 cases
   Napa Valley: 2,000 cases

Cabernet acres owned: 5

Average age of vines: 14 years

Vineyard makeup: Cabernet Sauvignon (100%)

Average wine makeup: Cabernet Sauvignon (100%)

Time in oak: 30 months

Type of oak: French

The emergence of Dunn Vineyards Howell Mountain Cabernet has been one of the most sensational developments in the 1980s. A century ago Howell Mountain vineyards flourished, but it wasn't until the first Dunn Cabernets hit the market in the early 1980s that people again began to take notice of the potential of this area. Winemaker Randy Dunn, who for 10 years was winemaker at Caymus, produced his first vintage in 1979, a massively proportioned, richly flavored, thick and tannic Cabernet that has evolved into a magnificent bottle of wine. Early on, skeptics doubted whether these hugely tannic, intensely fruity wines would ever age and develop. Now, a decade later, Napa Valley vintners are clamoring to acquire potential vineyard sites on Howell Mountain, and much of that is due to Dunn's tremendous accomplishment.

Dunn produces two Cabernets, one from Howell Mountain, where he owns 5 acres of Cabernet and leases a parcel of similar size, and a Napa Valley bottling. The Howell Mountain Cabernet is typically denser and more tannic than the Napa Valley bottling, which is produced from purchased grapes throughout Napa Valley through contracts with growers, yet both share the Dunn style of massively concentrated fruit on an elegant framework. Both the Howell Mountain and Napa Valley bottlings display sharply focused, amazingly rich black cherry, currant, earth and spice flavors, framed by thick yet soft and supple tannins. All of the Napa Valley bottlings have been outstanding, while only the 1985 bottling from Howell Mountain has missed that lofty mark, but not by much. The 1979 Howell Mountain is nearing full maturity, developing a broad array of flavors, yet with the depth and intensity to sustain it another decade. The 1982 and 1984 Howell Mountain Cabernets ranked among the finest in those two vintages.

Production for each bottling reached 2,000 cases with the 1986 vintage, but high demand and exceptionally high quality have made in the wines very scarce. The best way to buy the wine is through the winery mailing list.

TASTING NOTES

DUNN VINEYARDS, Howell Mountain, Napa Valley

1986 DUNN VINEYARDS HOWELL MOUNTAIN: Like every bottling of Dunn Cabernet, the 1986 Howell Mountain is an amazingly rich, deep, concentrated and elegant wine, loaded with layers of ripe black currant, raspberry, cherry and spice flavors that unfold on the palate. While the early Dunn Howell Mountains were extremely tannic, the 1986 is somewhat less so but still quite deep and ageworthy. The sharply defined fruit makes this wine appealing now, but it will only get better in the next decade. Drink 1993-2000. 2,000 cases produced. Release: $30. Current: $30. **94**

1985 DUNN VINEYARDS HOWELL MOUNTAIN: This has been the least-impressive of the Dunn Howell Mountain Cabernets because of its dense earthiness and green olive qualities, which depart from the black cherry and currant flavors of previous vintages. Despite that, there is still pretty Cabernet fruit in this wine, and it's balanced with crisp acidity and firm if slightly dry tannins. I'd give it the benefit of the doubt but age it five to seven years. Drink 1995-2002. 1,800 cases produced. Release: $30. Current: $60. **89**

1984 DUNN VINEYARDS HOWELL MOUNTAIN: A fabulous wine with amazing complexity and depth, rich yet elegant mineral, earth, spice, currant and cherry flavors that are supple and silky and a burst of toasty fruit complexities on the finish. Has the richness and concentration of the best 1984s along with an underlying of elegance and finesse. Drink 1996-2002. 1,800 cases produced. Release: $25. Current: $85. **97**

1983 DUNN VINEYARDS HOWELL MOUNTAIN: This is a huge, chewy, massively tannic 1983, but unlike most wines from this tannic vintage, it is packed with enough fresh ripe fruit and toasty oak to stand up to the tannins. The black currant and spicy mineral flavors linger on the finish. Drink 1995-2005. 1,600 cases produced. Release: $18. Current: $90. **92**

1982 DUNN VINEYARDS HOWELL MOUNTAIN: A massive yet elegant wine, clearly the top wine of this uneven vintage, very rich and concentrated, offering focused black cherry and currant flavors that echo long and full on the palate. I have enjoyed this wine a dozen times, and each time come away extremely impressed. Drink 1992-2000. 1,800 cases produced. Release: $15. Current: $130. **95**

1981 DUNN VINEYARDS HOWELL MOUNTAIN: A softer, more supple Howell Mountain, this wine offers rich, ripe, concentrated black currant, spice and toasty oak flavors in an elegant, appealing style. Charming now but should gain with time. Drink 1991-1996. 940 cases produced. Release: $14. Current: $150. **90**

1980 DUNN VINEYARDS HOWELL MOUNTAIN: A big, rich, dramatic wine, much like the 1979 with its tart, mouthwatering black cherry and raspberry flavors that are long and elegant, with firm tannins. Another star of the vintage. Drink 1993-2000. 825 cases produced. Release: $13. Current: $170. **92**

1979 DUNN VINEYARDS HOWELL MOUNTAIN: One of the best of the vintage, this 1979, Dunn's first, is a delicious, elegant, concentrated wine loaded with pretty raspberry, cranberry and black cherry flavors that are tart and clean and beginning to soften. Drink 1990-1997. 660 cases produced. Release: $12.50. Current: $160. **91**

DUNN VINEYARDS, Napa Valley

1986 DUNN VINEYARDS NAPA VALLEY: Remarkable for its rich, deep, tightly concentrated fruit, the 1986 Napa Valley is another sensational bottling by Dunn. It exhibits tremendous cherry, black currant, anise and cedar flavors that are lean and sharply focused, framed by tight tannins and finishing with great length. Drink 1993-2000. 2,000 cases produced. Release: $27. Current: $27. **93**

1985 DUNN VINEYARDS NAPA VALLEY: From an excellent vintage, the 1985 displays rich, sharply focused raspberry, cherry and currant flavors that are enormously concentrated and tightly packed together, framed by firm yet unobtrusive tannins that let the flavors sail on through. Drink 1992-2000. 2,000 cases produced. Release: $20. Current: $45. **94**

1984 DUNN VINEYARDS NAPA VALLEY: Another big, rich, muscular wine, tightly packed with fresh, ripe, rich cherry, berry, earth and cedar flavors that are persistent from start to finish. True to the vintage, the texture is smooth and supple and so are the tannins. Drink 1994-2004. 2,100 cases produced. Release: $18. Current: $55. **93**

1983 DUNN VINEYARDS NAPA VALLEY: In a vintage marked by extremely hard, lean, tannic Cabernets, Dunn succeeded with both his bottlings. The 1983 Napa Valley offers delicious cherry, plum, cassis and toasty oak flavors enlivened by crisp acidity and rich, deep, supple tannins. A magnificent achievement for a 1983. Drink 1994-2004. 1,500 cases produced. Release: $15. Current: $60. **95**

1982 DUNN VINEYARDS NAPA VALLEY: Similar in style to the fabulous Howell Mountain bottling, this too is an exceptional wine that is rich, concentrated and complex, with tart black cherry, currant and cedar flavors that are beginning to open. Firm but supple tannins on the finish bode well for aging. Drink 1992-2000. 1,250 cases produced. Release: $13. Current: $85. **94**

EBERLE WINERY
Reserve, Paso Robles
Estate, Paso Robles

CLASSIFICATION: *FIFTH GROWTH*
COLLECTIBILITY RATING: *Not rated*

BEST VINTAGES: *1985, 1984*

Eberle Winery in Paso Robles is proving Cabernet Sauvignon can be grown in the South Central Coast area with excellent results. While many of the Cabernets grown in this region are excessively herbal and vegetal, the Eberle Cabernets have succeeded in adding more currant and berry flavors. The 1979, Eberle's first vintage, is delicate, with tea, herb and black cherry notes, drinking quite well. The 1980 estate, 1981 reserve and 1982 estate were less impressive; however, the 1981 regular is gaining complexity. The 1984, 1985 and 1986 show more character; the 1985 is the best bottling so far. In my experience the Eberle Cabernets are best enjoyed on release. They do not appear to gain significantly from lengthy bottle aging.

TASTING NOTES

EBERLE WINERY, Various bottlings

1986 EBERLE WINERY: Rich, concentrated and tannic, it will need three to five years for the ripe cherry, herb, earth and cedar flavors to develop fully. A very well-made wine that offers depth and complexity. Drink 1993-1997. 4,196 cases produced. Release: $12. Current: $12. **85**

1985 EBERLE WINERY: Eberle's finest, a superb wine that combines richness, intensity, depth and concentration with firm tannins and impeccable balance. The ripe black cherry, spice and currant flavors are wrapped in thick tannins, with hints of bell pepper echoing on the finish. Enticing now but better in three years. Drink 1992-1998. 2,814 cases produced. Release: $12. Current: $14. **89**

1984 EBERLE WINERY: Dense, tannic and concentrated but balanced with herb, pepper and black cherry flavors that carry through on the finish. Needs time to soften. Drink 1992-1996. 3,013 cases produced. Release: $12. Current: $17. **86**

AT A GLANCE
EBERLE WINERY
Highway 46 East
Paso Robles, CA 93446
(805) 238-9607

Owner: Eberle Winery (Gary Eberle, general partner)

Winemaker: Gary Eberle (10 years)

Founded: 1984

First Cabernet vintage: 1979

Cabernet production: 3,500 cases

Cabernet acres owned: 25

Average age of vines: 12 years

Vineyard makeup: Cabernet Sauvignon (100%)

Average wine makeup: Cabernet Sauvignon (100%)

Time in oak: 21 months

Type of oak: French

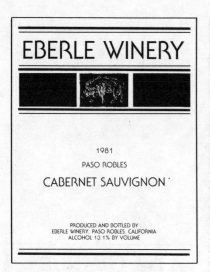

EBERLE WINERY

1981

PASO ROBLES

CABERNET SAUVIGNON

PRODUCED AND BOTTLED BY
EBERLE WINERY, PASO ROBLES, CALIFORNIA
ALCOHOL 13.1% BY VOLUME

1983 EBERLE WINERY: A rich, well-made 1983 with black cherry, currant and chocolate notes and very good balance and depth. This wine is drinking well now but appears to have the flavor and depth for further development. Drink 1991-1994. 2,800 cases produced. Release: $10. Current: $18. **84**

1982 EBERLE WINERY RESERVE: Similar to the 1982 Estate, with concentrated earth and vegetal flavors and excessive tannins. Does not appear to have enough fruit to stand up to the tannin. Drink 1991-1996. 76 cases produced. Release: $25. Current: $30. **71**

1982 EBERLE WINERY: Dry, earthy and tannic, lacking the ripe fruit found in other vintages. It's drinkable but unexciting. Drink 1990-1994. 2,500 cases produced. Release: $10. Current: $24. **72**

1981 EBERLE WINERY RESERVE: A shade more richness than the 1981 Estate but also a bit less flavor. The cedar, herb and cherry flavors are attractive, but ultimately they come across as one-dimensional. Can stand further cellaring. Drink 1991-1995. 191 cases produced. Release: $25. Current: $35. **80**

1981 EBERLE WINERY: An attractive wine that is becoming more complex. The tart black cherry and cedar flavors have taken on an anise quality that makes the wine more interesting. Tannins are softening. Drink 1990-1994. 2,500 cases produced. Release: $10. Current: $24. **85**

1980 EBERLE WINERY: Earthy and pungent, with fully mature herb, plum and spicy cherry flavors. Has the tannin for further aging, but the flavors are verging on herbaceousness. Drink 1990-1994. 2,000 cases produced. Release: $10. Current: $24. **78**

1979 EBERLE WINERY: Eberle's first vintage is fully mature and quite pleasant, with delicate tea, herb, black cherry and spicy cedar notes, moderate tannins and good length. Impressive for its elegance and balance. Drink 1990-1995. 1,000 cases produced. Release: $10. Current: $25. **82**

FAR NIENTE WINERY

Oakville, Napa Valley

CLASSIFICATION: *THIRD GROWTH*

COLLECTIBILITY RATING: *A*

BEST VINTAGES: *1986, 1985, 1984*

Far Niente is situated on some of the finest Cabernet land in Napa Valley. Founded in 1979 by Gil Nickel, its most prominent neighbors are the famous Martha's Vineyard, which is bottled under the Heitz Wine Cellar label, and Robert Mondavi Winery's To-Kalon Vineyard, the source of Mondavi's Reserve Cabernet wines. While the first two vintages from Far Niente (which means "without a care" in Italian), 1982 and 1983, were hard, austere, and tannic, the three subsequent bottlings are all exceptional wines, rich and concentrated showing both the promise of this vineyard and the potential of these wines for long-term aging.

The 1982 vintage proved troublesome for many Napa Valley wineries because of rain at harvest, and some of the wet, earthy flavors are showing in the 1982 Far Niente. The 1983 vintage produced unusually lean, tannic wines, and the Far Niente is rather typical of that vintage. Beginning with the 1984 vintage, Far Niente captures more richness, depth, flavor and character in its Cabernets. The 1984, while supple and ripe, has the intensity and complexity of flavor for midterm to long-term aging. The 1985 Far Niente shows an earthier style that is also more elegant and refined yet shows the depth and concentration for cellaring. The 1986 is similar to the 1985, with its elegant style and firm structure. Both wines should rival the 1984 in quality.

Far Niente's Cabernets include about 22 percent Cabernet Franc and Merlot grown in the 45-acre Stelling Vineyard directly behind the renovated 19th-century stone winery. Case production has climbed from 3,000 in 1982 to 12,000 in 1986. The current price of $27.50 for the 1986 vintage is high, reflecting the winery's view of the quality of its vineyard.

AT A GLANCE

FAR NIENTE WINERY
P.O. Box 327
Oakville, CA 94562
(707) 944-2861

Owner: Gil Nickel

Winemaker: Dirk Hampson (7 years)

Founded: 1979

First Cabernet vintage: 1982

Cabernet production: 10,000 cases

Cabernet acres owned: 45

Average age of vines: 11 years

Vineyard makeup: Cabernet Sauvignon (75%), Cabernet Franc (19%), Merlot (6%)

Average wine makeup: Cabernet Sauvignon (78%), Cabernet Franc (20%), Merlot (2%)

Time in oak: 18 months

Type of oak: French

TASTING NOTES

FAR NIENTE WINERY, Oakville, Napa Valley

1986 FAR NIENTE: With time, this elegant 1986 will rival the 1985 in quality, for while it is firmer and more structured now, there are ample black cherry, cedar, pepper and anise flavors coming through to give it depth and intricacy. Needs four or five years, then it should be near its pinnacle. Drink 1995-2003. 12,000 cases produced. Release: $27.50. Current: $30. **91**

1985 FAR NIENTE: Decidedly earthier yet more elegant than other Far Nientes to date, the 1985 combines the ripe cherry flavors with mineral, cedar and vanilla notes. Rich, elegant and complex, this wine has a supple texture that makes it appealing, but it has the depth and character for a decade's aging. Drink 1994-2002. 10,000 cases produced. Release: $28. Current: $28. **92**

1984 FAR NIENTE: Riper, fleshier and more open, the 1984 is attractive for its rich, supple, sharply focused black cherry, plum and currant flavors and soft tannins. There is plenty of depth and intensity behind the fruit, making it a good candidate for cellaring. Still needs three to five years to reach its peak. Drink 1994-2002. 8,500 cases produced. Release: $25. Current: $30. **92**

1983 FAR NIENTE: Austere and dry as 1983s go but with some attractive Cabernet fruit as well, with hints of berries, cherries and plums, framed with cedary oak and finishing with dry tannins. Evolving, slowly but surely. Drink 1993-2000. 5,500 cases produced. Release: $25. Current: $32. **87**

1982 FAR NIENTE: Far Niente's first vintage remains a hard, tannic wine that will require patience for the rough-hewn tannins to subside. There are pretty Cabernet aromas and flavors, hints of berries and cherries, but also wet earth and bark notes that muddle the flavor. Drink 1993-1999. 3,000 cases produced. Release: $25. Current: $35. **82**

FISHER VINEYARDS
Coach Insignia, Sonoma County

CLASSIFICATION: *FIFTH GROWTH*
COLLECTIBILITY RATING: *Not rated*
BEST VINTAGES: *1986, 1985, 1984*

Fisher Vineyards is nestled in a picturesque hillside property in the Mayacamas Mountains near the Napa-Sonoma county line, where most of its Cabernet Sauvignon grapes are planted on gently sloping, westerly facing hills. Fisher's Coach Insignia is its flagship Cabernet, representing the finest grapes and Cabernet that Fisher produces. The Coach Insignia, which takes its name from Fisher's "Body By Fisher" automotive company, is unique: Technically it is an estate-bottled wine, but because Fisher's vineyards are situated in two counties, it cannot be labeled as such, even though 95 percent of the grapes used in the wine are grown by Fisher in the two vineyards. The principal vineyard is at the winery in the Mayacamas and the other one on the Napa Valley floor near Rutherford. The blend, 95 percent Cabernet, is typically 75 percent Sonoma County and 25 percent Napa Valley.

In three vintages, the Coach Insignia has displayed tight, rich, concentrated flavors in an elegant, delicate style that strives more for finesse and refinement than power or intensity. To date, all three bottlings have been excellent, with the 1985 and 1986 vintages offering a shade more depth and complexity. While the 1984 still needs three to five years' cellaring, the Coach Insignia Cabernets should drink well through 10 to 15 years and longer in superior vintages.

AT A GLANCE
FISHER VINEYARDS
6200 St. Helena Road
Santa Rosa, CA 95404
(707) 539-7511

Owner: Fred Fisher

Winemaker: Henryk Gasiewicz (6 years)

Founded: 1979

First Cabernet vintage: 1979

Cabernet production: 1,500 cases

Cabernet acres owned: 29

Average age of vines: 10 years

Vineyard makeup: Cabernet Sauvignon (79%), Merlot (14%), Cabernet Franc (7%)

Average wine makeup: Cabernet Sauvignon (95%), Merlot (5%)

Time in oak: 22 months

Type of oak: French (Nevers)

TASTING NOTES

FISHER VINEYARDS, Coach Insignia, Sonoma County

1986 FISHER VINEYARDS COACH INSIGNIA: On a par with the 1985, this wine succeeds in the Coach Insignia style. The rich currant and black cherry flavors are tight and concentrated, with firm but subtle tannins in the background. Drinkable now but can stand a decade in the cellar. Drink 1993-2000. 1,500 cases produced. Release: $20. Current: $20. **90**

1985 FISHER VINEYARDS COACH INSIGNIA: A shade better than the excellent 1984, the 1985 offers more richness and complexity in

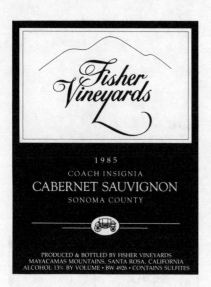

the same lean, crisp, well-defined style, with firm tannins that linger in the background. Plenty of ripe currant, black cherry and cedar nuances offer depth and dimension. Drink 1993-2000. 1,200 cases produced. Release: $18. Current: $20. **90**

1984 FISHER VINEYARDS COACH INSIGNIA: A very tight and sharply focused wine with tart black cherry, raspberry and currant flavors, supported by fine, lean, firm but unobtrusive tannins. Impressive for its well-defined Cabernet fruit. Approachable now but should only improve in the next five to seven years. Drink 1992-1999. 1,200 cases produced. Release: $18. Current: $25. **89**

FLORA SPRINGS WINE CO.

Trilogy, Rutherford, Napa Valley
Estate, Napa Valley

CLASSIFICATION: *FIFTH GROWTH*
COLLECTIBILITY RATING: *Not rated*

BEST VINTAGES:

Trilogy: 1985

Estate: 1985

With Trilogy, a Bordeaux-style blend of Cabernet Sauvignon, Merlot and Cabernet Franc, Flora Springs hopes to break into the top echelon of California proprietary wines. The first three vintages, 1984, 1985 and 1986, have been very good but short of outstanding, lacking the kind of richness, concentration and complexity one expects for $30 or more. Of the three vintages, the 1985 is best.

The 1985 Estate Cabernet shows more richness and depth than previous bottlings, a good sign that this winery has found a style that can accommodate more flavor and character. The winery has 156 acres of Cabernet, making it one of Napa Valley's largest Cabernet vineyard owners.

TASTING NOTES

FLORA SPRINGS WINE CO., Trilogy, Rutherford, Napa Valley

1986 FLORA SPRINGS WINE CO. TRILOGY: Similar in style and character to the 1985, with layers of fresh black cherry, currant, earth and raspberry flavors, but it's lean and acidic, without the concentration for greatness. Drink 1993-1998. 1,400 cases produced. Release: $33. Current: $33. **85**

1985 FLORA SPRINGS WINE CO. TRILOGY: A crisp, lean, elegant and complex wine of moderate depth and intensity, displaying layers of cedar, chocolate, currant and spice, supported by firm, dry tannins. A much better wine than the 1984, this one will be ready to drink within the next two years and should gain complexity for the next decade. Drink 1992-1998. 1,200 cases produced. Release: $30. Current: $30. **88**

AT A GLANCE

FLORA SPRINGS WINE CO.
1978 W. Zinfandel Lane
St. Helena, CA 94574
(707) 963-5711

Owners: The Komes and Garvey families

Winemaker: Ken Deis (9 years)

Founded: 1978

First Cabernet vintage: 1978
Trilogy: 1984
Estate: 1978

Cabernet production: 4,700 cases
Trilogy: 1,200 cases
Estate: 3,500 cases

Cabernet acres owned: 156

Average age of vines: 15 years

Vineyard makeup: Cabernet Sauvignon (74%), Merlot (19%), Cabernet Franc (7%)

Average wine makeup:
Trilogy: Cabernet Sauvignon (33%), Merlot (33%), Cabernet Franc (33%)
Estate: Cabernet Sauvignon (92%), Merlot (7%), Cabernet Franc (1%)

Time in oak: 22 months

Type of oak: French (Limousin, Nevers, Tronçais)

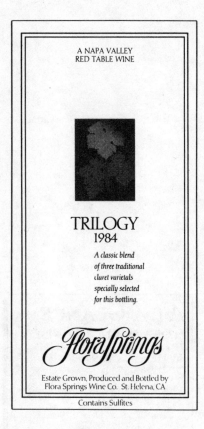

A NAPA VALLEY
RED TABLE WINE

TRILOGY
1984

*A classic blend
of three traditional
claret varietals
specially selected
for this bottling.*

Flora Springs

Estate Grown, Produced and Bottled by
Flora Springs Wine Co. St. Helena, CA

Contains Sulfites

1984 FLORA SPRINGS WINE CO. TRILOGY: Ripe and supple, with currant, spice and black cherry flavors, with crisp acidity and moderate tannins. A well-made wine with complexity and finesse but lacking in depth and character. Drink 1992-1998. 700 cases produced. Release: $30. Current: $35. **84**

FLORA SPRINGS WINE CO., Estate, Napa Valley

1986 FLORA SPRINGS WINE CO. ESTATE: Disappointing for a 1986, considering the excellent quality of this vintage. This wine is thin, lean and uninspiring, with shallow fruit and uninteresting flavors. Drink 1990-1994. 3,500 cases produced. Not Released. **77**

1985 FLORA SPRINGS WINE CO. ESTATE: A delicious 1985 that's ready to drink now, with ripe, rich, supple currant, black cherry and plum flavors and smooth tannins. Charming now but can age another decade. Drink 1991-1999. 4,000 cases produced. Release: $15. Current: $15. **88**

1984 FLORA SPRINGS WINE CO. ESTATE: A ripe, supple and fruity 1984, with plum, currant and berry flavors that are fat and opulent, supported by crisp acidity and supple tannins. Drink 1990-1996. 3,000 cases produced. Release: $13. Current: $18. **85**

1980 FLORA SPRINGS WINE CO. ESTATE: A big, fat, rich and supple 1980 with layers of ripe plum, currant, herb and anise flavors and smooth, supple tannins, but also a bit of acidity on the finish. Attractive now for its opulence and fleshiness; only the acidity on the finish detracts. Drink 1990-1996. 1,200 cases produced. Release: $12. Current: $20. **85**

FORMAN VINEYARD
Napa Valley

CLASSIFICATION: *SECOND GROWTH*

COLLECTIBILITY RATING: *AA*

BEST VINTAGES: *1986, 1985, 1984, 1983*

Ric Forman is one of California's whiz-kid winemakers who rose to fame at age 24 with Sterling Vineyards, where he spent the late 1960s and 1970s as the architect of the Sterling Reserve Cabernets and Sterling Merlot. After a five-year stint with Newton Vineyards, Forman founded his own Napa Valley winery, specializing in Chardonnay and Cabernet Sauvignon, the latter grown in his 23-acre hillside vineyard in the hills east of St. Helena. Forman's Cabernet is a blend of 75 percent Cabernet Sauvignon, 15 percent Merlot and 10 percent Cabernet Franc.

Forman emphasizes rich, concentrated, beautifully focused Cabernet fruit in a sleek, lean, elegant style with a measure of finesse and complexity that weaves a thread through the first four vintages. The 1983, Forman's first vintage, succeeds in balancing fruit with dry tannins typical of that year. The 1984 is more forward and opulent, drinking well already, while the 1985 is simply delicious, a fine wine from a great vintage. The 1986 is also superb, not quite as seductive as the 1984 and 1985 vintages, but showing more structure. Each of these wines has the potential for 10 to 15 years' cellaring, but they also drink well early on.

Case production of Forman Cabernet hovers around 1,600, but with high demand and limited supply these wines are difficult to find in many markets. A good portion of the Cabernet is sold through a winery mailing list.

AT A GLANCE
FORMAN VINEYARD
P.O. Box 343
St. Helena, CA 94574
(707) 963-0234

Owner: Ric Forman

Winemaker: Ric Forman (6 years)

Founded: 1983

First Cabernet vintage: 1983

Cabernet production: 1,600 cases

Cabernet acres owned: 23 acres

Average age of vines: 10 years

Vineyard makeup: Cabernet Sauvignon (75%), Merlot (15%), Cabernet Franc (10%)

Average wine makeup: Cabernet Sauvignon (75%), Merlot (15%), Cabernet Franc (10%)

Time in oak: 20 months

Type of oak: French

TASTING NOTES

FORMAN VINEYARD, Napa Valley

1986 FORMAN VINEYARD: A beautifully sculpted wine, rich and cedary, with vibrant currant, plum and spice flavors that are lean and concentrated, finishing with firm tannins. A seamless wine that's approachable now but will only get better. A safe bet for midterm cellaring. Drink 1995-2004. 1,800 cases produced. Release: $20. Current: $20. **93**

1985 FORMAN VINEYARD: Very rich and cedary, with a touch of elegance and finesse, great depth of currant, spice and plum flavors, finishing with fine, smooth tannins. A classic '85, well defined, focused, long and complex. Pretty to drink right now but should hold well for midterm aging. Drink 1994-2002. 1,600 cases produced. Release: $18. Current: $30. **93**

1984 FORMAN VINEYARD: Rich, forward and delicious, a splendid Cabernet with supple, layered black cherry, currant and anise flavors framed by toasty oak and smooth tannins. Because of its fleshy texture, this wine is seductively charming now but has the stuffing to age a decade and beyond. Drink 1992-2000. 1,000 cases produced. Release: $18. Current: $35. **92**

1983 FORMAN VINEYARD: An impressive debut wine for Forman from a difficult vintage, the 1983 is crisp and lean, with sharply defined, richly textured Cabernet fruit that will be at its best in five to seven years. The currant and black cherry flavors echo through the finish, and it's not too tannic. Drink 1994-2001. 600 cases produced. Release: $15.50. Current: $45. **90**

FRANCISCAN VINEYARDS
Library Selection, Oakville, Napa Valley
Meritage, Oakville, Napa Valley
Reserve, Oakville, Napa Valley

CLASSIFICATION: *FIFTH GROWTH*
COLLECTIBILITY RATING: *Not rated*

BEST VINTAGES:

Library Selection: 1985

Meritage: 1985

Reserve: 1985, 1984

With prime Cabernet acreage in Oakville, Franciscan currently provides one of the greatest values in Cabernet drinking. In two decades this winery, founded in 1972, has had its up and downs, with ownership changing hands several times. The current owners, the Eckes Corp. of West Germany and Agustin Huneeus, have stabilized the winery and focused on providing rich, fruity, elegantly balanced wines that drink well on release and are very reasonably priced; they are not long-aging wines and should be cellared no more than five years.

The Franciscan Cabernets, which come from a vineyard near the Napa River and the new Opus One vineyard, are typically characterized by distinctive herb, spice and currant flavors and the judicious use of oak. Earlier vintages displayed similar flavors but were marked by the spicy vanilla notes of American oak. Older Franciscan Reserve vintages have endured but not gained complexity. The best recent offerings include the 1984 Reserve and three 1985 bottlings using the Reserve, Library Selection and Meritage designations. 1986 also looks promising. While prices for the Reserve and Meritage blends are approaching $18 to $20, the regular Franciscan Oakville Estate Cabernet provides excellent drinking and in many instances is barely discernible from the higher-priced Reserve bottling. The Eckes-Huneeus partnership also owns Estancia, a brand that produces excellent Cabernet at good prices from vineyards in Alexander Valley, and recently purchased Mount Veeder Winery.

AT A GLANCE
FRANCISCAN VINEYARDS
1178 Galleron Road
St. Helena, CA 94574
(707) 963-7111

Owners: Eckes Corp., West Germany/Agustin Huneeus

Winemaker: Greg Upton (4 years)

Founded: 1972

First Cabernet vintage: 1974
  Library Selection: 1985
  Meritage: 1985
  Reserve: 1975

Cabernet production: 13,000 cases
  Library Selection: 2,000 cases
  Meritage: 450 cases
  Reserve: 1,800 cases

Cabernet acres owned: 102

Average age of vines: 17 years

Vineyard makeup: Cabernet Sauvignon (62%), Merlot (38%)

Average wine makeup:
  Library Selection: Cabernet Sauvignon (85%), Merlot (15%)
  Meritage: Cabernet Sauvignon (60%), Merlot (40%)
  Reserve: Cabernet Sauvignon (85%), Merlot (15%)

Time in oak: 18 months

Type of oak: French

TASTING NOTES

FRANCISCAN VINEYARDS, Various bottlings

1985 FRANCISCAN VINEYARDS LIBRARY SELECTION: Ripe, rich, firm and concentrated, displaying hard tannins and deep flavors of ripe black cherry, currant and spicy oak and an intense, full-bodied aftertaste. Drink 1990-1996. 2,000 cases produced. Release: $17.50. Current: $17.50. **88**

1985 FRANCISCAN VINEYARDS MERITAGE: Distinctive for its depth and richness, a Bordeaux blend of Cabernet, Merlot and Cabernet Franc, which displays a firm tannic backbone and herb, cherry and cedar flavors that are well orchestrated. This wine has the intensity and concentration to develop over the next decade. Best to cellar it three to five years. Drink 1993-2000. 450 cases produced. Release: $20. Current: $20. **89**

1985 FRANCISCAN VINEYARDS RESERVE: A first-rate effort, crisp and lively, with well-defined fruit, hints of currants, plums and cherries and a delicate touch of oak. The acidity carries the flavors and the tannins are in proportion. Drink 1991-1997. 1,800 cases produced. Release: $18. Current: $18. **87**

1984 FRANCISCAN VINEYARDS PRIVATE RESERVE: A delicious wine to drink now, ripe, rich and supple, displaying lush black currant, cherry, cedar and plum flavors that spread out on the palate. Not too tannic, it nonetheless has the depth and intensity for another four to six years in the cellar. Drink 1990-1996. 5,400 cases produced. Release: $9. Current: $12. **87**

1983 FRANCISCAN VINEYARDS PRIVATE RESERVE: Intense, firm and tannic, with a pretty core of currant, herb and cherry flavors scented by cedary oak. A wine that is near maturity despite the tannins. Drink 1993-1998. 3,000 cases produced. Release: $8.50. Current: $14. **85**

1979 FRANCISCAN VINEYARDS: Fully mature and in decline, the 1979 offers mature herb flavors that taste oaky and smooth. Ulitmately simple and enjoyable but nothing special. Drink 1990. 9,000 cases produced. Release: $8.50. Current: $18. **79**

1978 FRANCISCAN VINEYARDS RESERVE: A shade past its prime, exhibiting oak, herb and olive flavors that are smooth and mellow, with nearly all the tannins resolved. Best to drink it now before it gets any older. Drink 1990-1992. 4,000 cases produced. Release: $15. Current: $20. **78**

1975 FRANCISCAN VINEYARDS RESERVE: Fully mature and in decline. The last time I tried the 1975, it was out of a magnum and was quite pleasant, with mature cedar, olive, herb and currant flavors. The tannins had faded, and it was ready to drink. Drink 1990. 3,000 cases produced. Release: $12. Current: $32. **82**

FREEMARK ABBEY WINERY

Bosché, Rutherford, Napa Valley

CLASSIFICATION: *SECOND GROWTH*

COLLECTIBILITY RATING: *AA*

BEST VINTAGES: *1986, 1985, 1984, 1979, 1978, 1975, 1974, 1970*

Along with Beaulieu Vineyard Private Reserve and Inglenook Cask, Freemark Abbey Bosché is perhaps the truest embodiment of Rutherford-style Cabernet. The 21-acre Bosché vineyard has its own traits, but it shares more with those two great wines than others grown in the Rutherford area, particularly its slow aging curve — it requires more time in the bottle to reach its peak. For years the fruit from the Bosché vineyard contributed to the BV Private Reserves, and BV set aside special lots bottled especially for proprietor John Bosché. But in 1968 that policy was discontinued, and Bosché contacted Chuck Carpy at Freemark Abbey about buying his grapes. It didn't take Carpy long to recognize the greatness of this vineyard, and after an experimental barrel was produced in 1968, along with three separate trial bottlings with different mixes with and without Merlot, Freemark Abbey took over production of all the Bosché grapes. In 1989 all three 1968 bottlings were in terrific condition, particularly the final blend, which included 15 percent Merlot, that Carpy and then-winemaker Brad Webb chose for the style.

The trademark of Freemark Abbey Bosché is its understated elegance, depth and longevity. It takes a good six to eight years for its full richness, finesse and complexity to emerge, and then the ripe, supple black cherry and currant flavors gradually become more silky and polished, holding on for years. With fine yet firm tannins, Bosché is never overpowering but has a subtle intensity that becomes more apparent and enjoyable with age. Now approaching its 20th anniversary, the 1970 remains one of the great wines of that extraordinary vintage, marking the beginning of winemaker Jerry Luper's tenure (through 1975) with Freemark Abbey. The 1971 and 1972 bottlings are also superior considering the vintages, while in 1973, 1974 and 1975, the Bosché is excellent. The drought-year 1976 is a bit chunky and tannic but still pleasant, while the 1977 is all polish and silk, drinking at its peak now. The 1978 and 1979 are to my taste the best of the early lot, eclipsing the 1970, but not by much. From 1980 to 1984 Bosché is very fine, but with the 1985 it reaches another lofty plateau, fol-

AT A GLANCE

FREEMARK ABBEY WINERY
P.O. Box 410
St. Helena, CA 94574
(707) 963-9694

Owners: Charles Carpy, Laurie Wood, Brad Webb, Jim Warren, Bill Jaeger, Dick Heggie, John Bryan

Winemaker: Ted Edwards (5 years)

Founded: 1935, reestablished: 1967

First Cabernet vintage: 1967
Bosché: 1970

Cabernet production: 14,000 cases
Bosché: 3,500 cases

Cabernet acres owned: 82
Bosché Vineyard: 21

Average age of vines: 10 years

Vineyard makeup: Cabernet Sauvignon (83%), Merlot (13%), Cabernet Franc (4%)
Bosché Vineyard: Cabernet Sauvignon (85%), Merlot (15%)

Average wine makeup: Cabernet Sauvignon (86%), Merlot (14%)

Time in oak: 23 months

Type of oak: French (Nevers)

lowed by 1986, which may well rival the 1985 in the long run. Looking back at 17 vintages, Bosché Vineyard is as consistent as any Napa Valley Cabernet and is one of the surest bets for greatness in the cellar.

TASTING NOTES

FREEMARK ABBEY WINERY, Bosché, Rutherford, Napa Valley

1986 FREEMARK ABBEY WINERY BOSCHE: Firm, rich and concentrated, with floral, plum and black cherry aromas, the 1986 is another terrific bottling, with excellent structure, balance and depth of flavor and the Bosché touch of elegance and finesse. Drink 1994-2002. 4,000 cases produced. Not Released. **90**

1985 FREEMARK ABBEY WINERY BOSCHE: The 1985 is an exceptional wine and clearly the finest Bosché since the late 1970s. It is firm, rich and deeply concentrated, with sharply defined plum, black cherry, spice and cedary oak flavors that are tight, tannic and long. Showing early signs of complexity as well as excellent aging potential through the next decade. Drink 1995-2005. 3,500 cases produced. Release: $24. Current: $24. **93**

1984 FREEMARK ABBEY WINERY BOSCHE: A big, rich, dramatic Bosché, packed with fresh, ripe plum, cherry and spice flavors, firm tannins and crisp acidity. Needs time to soften but has the balance and elegance of the best Boschés, along with a touch more strength. Drink 1995-2003. 3,076 cases produced. Release: $20. Current: $20. **88**

1983 FREEMARK ABBEY WINERY BOSCHE: Hard, tannic and austere but with a rich core of ripe currant and plum flavors that are well balanced and capable of aging. This wine is already gaining grace and suppleness on the palate, a tribute to winemaking in this difficult vintage. Drink 1995-2003. 2,860 cases produced. Release: $18. Current: $18. **86**

1982 FREEMARK ABBEY WINERY BOSCHE: Tough, lean and tannic with herb and cherry flavors, but it's still elegant, with a decent core of spice and currant. The finish is dry and hard, but this one should age well. Drink 1996-2002. 3,592 cases produced. Release: $15. Current: $26. **88**

1981 FREEMARK ABBEY WINERY BOSCHE: Has pretty black cherry flavors and is leaner and more compact on the palate than the nose suggests, lacking complexity and depth. The fruit is clean and ripe and the wine is balanced, but it's not very generous, finishing with crisp acidity and firm tannins. Drink 1994-2000. 2,704 cases produced. Release: $14. Current: $24. **86**

1980 FREEMARK ABBEY WINERY BOSCHE: Rich and ripe, blunter and more awkward than the silky smooth 1978 and 1979 bottlings, but it has all the ingredients for greatness: rich, sharply defined fruit, a touch of herb, cherry and anise flavors and just the right amount of tannin for aging. Drink 1990-1996. 2,740 cases produced. Release: $14.50. Current: $36. **88**

1979 FREEMARK ABBEY WINERY BOSCHE: Firm, rich, thick and intense, the 1979 is an ideal successor to the superb 1978 Bosché, a shade more restrained and refined and less opulent, but perhaps a slightly longer-lived wine. Drinking exceptionally well now, with layers of black cherry, cedar, currant and spice. Beautifully tailored, long on the finish. Drink 1990-1997. 2,982 cases produced. Release: $12. Current: $30. **93**

1978 FREEMARK ABBEY WINERY BOSCHE: Elegant and subtle, with a distinctive smoky edge to the ripe currant, black cherry and spicy herb flavors. The fruit is rich and concentrated, and the acidity and tannins are in perfect proportion for drinking now or during the next five years. Drink 1990-1995. 3,908 cases produced. Release: $12.50. Current: $35. **93**

1977 FREEMARK ABBEY WINERY BOSCHE: Classic Cabernet from a vintage that yielded elegant, polished, supple wines. Has been drinking well its whole life and is now in peak condition, displaying ripe cherry, currant and herb nuances. Drink 1990-1994. 3,532 cases produced. Release: $12.50. Current: $25. **88**

1976 FREEMARK ABBEY WINERY BOSCHE: A drought-year wine that is ripe, jammy and chunky on the palate, pleasant but not quite displaying the balance and elegance of the best Boschés. Enough tannin for another five to seven years, but it's doubtful it will ever have the silky polish of most wines from this vineyard. Drink 1990-1994. 3,109 cases produced. Release: $12.50. Current: $45. **85**

1975 FREEMARK ABBEY WINERY BOSCHE: One of the top 1975s, with rich black cherry, plum and jam notes and floral aromas flanked by firm tannins and plenty of oak. The underlying sense of elegance comes through on the finish, where it is long and persistent. Drink 1990-1995. 2,632 cases produced. Release: $10. Current: $48. **90**

1974 FREEMARK ABBEY WINERY BOSCHE: A big, rich, ripe and sturdy Cabernet for Bosché, the 1974 tastes very complete, elegant and flavorful, with cedar, black cherry and plum flavors. At times it tastes like it's beginning to decline, yet on other occasions it displays the strength and intensity for another decade. Drink 1990-1998. 4,127 cases produced. Release: $7.75. Current: $75. **91**

1973 FREEMARK ABBEY WINERY BOSCHE: From a vintage that produced many elegant Cabernets, the 1973 is rich, smooth, deep and elegant, with cedar, currant and black cherry flavors, finishing with smoky cedar notes. In perfect condition now. Drink 1990-1993. 3,495 cases produced. Release: $8. Current: $70. **88**

1978
NAPA VALLEY
CABERNET
BOSCHÉ
(Cabernet Sauvignon)

PRODUCED AND BOTTLED BY
FREEMARK ABBEY WINERY, ST. HELENA, CALIFORNIA, USA

Alcohol 13.0% by volume

1972 FREEMARK ABBEY WINERY BOSCHE: This wine, from a light, rainy vintage, drank especially well early on but is now in decline yet very enjoyable. The mature cedar and earth flavors compete with the the ripe, mature, elegant fruit. Drink 1990-1992. 3,183 cases produced. Release: $6. Current: $30. **80**

1971 FREEMARK ABBEY WINERY BOSCHE: For a difficult vintage, the 1971 is an extraordinary wine that has aged extremely well. It's fully mature and elegant, with complex toast, cedar and mature plum and currant flavors. Drink 1990. 1,015 cases produced. Release: $6.75. Current: $40. **86**

1970 FREEMARK ABBEY WINERY BOSCHE: Amazingly rich and elegant, with supple cedar, black cherry and currant flavors, smooth tannins and a long, delicious finish. Complex and enticing, aging quite gracefully. First commercial Bosché bottling. Drink 1990. 424 cases produced. Release: $8.75. Current: $100. **91**

FROG'S LEAP WINERY

Napa Valley

CLASSIFICATION: *FIFTH GROWTH*

COLLECTIBILITY RATING: *Not rated*

BEST VINTAGES: *1986, 1984*

Despite the frivolity of its name, Frog's Leap is serious about Cabernet Sauvignon. Winemaker John Williams honed his skills at Spring Mountain before founding Frog's Leap as a Sauvignon Blanc specialist. Beginning with 1982, Frog's Leap has released five vintages of Cabernet, and two, the 1984 and 1986, have been sensational. The 1982 was successful, while the 1983 was lean and tart. The 1984 offers delicious layers of rich, ripe, supple Cabernet fruit. The 1985 has an herbaceous edge to it and not quite the fleshy opulence of 1984 or 1986. The two are similar in style, but the 1986 is better.

Frog's Leap owns 8 acres of Cabernet in Rutherford but buys most of its grapes from independent growers. Case production has reached 3,000 cases, but prices have remained rather modest at between $10 and $14 for new releases. The 1986, Frog's Leap's finest effort to date, is $14.

TASTING NOTES

FROG'S LEAP WINERY, Napa Valley

1986 FROG'S LEAP WINERY: A marvelous 1986, rich and expansive, with a fragrant, complex bouquet of fruit and flowers and rich, concentrated, elegant flavors that echo black currant, cherry, plum and spice on a long, full finish. Best yet from Frog's Leap. Drink 1993-1999. 2,600 cases produced. Release: $14. Current: $14. **94**

1985 FROG'S LEAP WINERY: Unusual green pepper and herbaceous notes runs through the black cherry flavors, adding another dimension. Plenty of stiff tannins and fine structure, but the flavors are just a bit off the mark. Needs more time in the bottle. Drink 1992-1998. 2,300 cases produced. Release: $12. Current: $12. **85**

1984 FROG'S LEAP WINERY: A wonderfully delicious wine, rich, smooth and supple, with tiers of currant, black cherry, cinnamon and cedar flavors that unfold on the palate, finishing with rich, deep, con-

AT A GLANCE

FROG'S LEAP WINERY
3358 St. Helena Highway
St. Helena, CA 94574
(707) 963-4704

Owners: John and Julie Williams, Larry Turley

Winemaker: John Williams (8 years)

Founded: 1981

First Cabernet vintage: 1982

Cabernet production: 2,500 cases

Cabernet acres owned: 8

Average age of vines: 12 years

Vineyard makeup: Cabernet Sauvignon (100%)

Average wine makeup: Cabernet Sauvignon (100%)

Time in oak: 20 months

Type of oak: French (Nevers)

FROG'S LEAP

1982
CABERNET SAUVIGNON
NAPA VALLEY

CELLARED AND BOTTLED BY FROG'S LEAP
ST HELENA, CALIFORNIA • ALCOHOL 12.7% BY VOL.

centrated tannins and a pretty fruit aftertaste. Lovely now but can age up to a decade. Drink 1991-1997. 1,900 cases produced. Release: $10. Current: $25. **92**

1983 FROG'S LEAP WINERY: Lean and tart, with sharp, light black cherry, earth and currant flavors of moderate depth. A good but unexciting 1983 that is rapidly approaching full maturity. Drink 1990-1994. 1,100 cases produced. Release: $10. Current: $20. **80**

1982 FROG'S LEAP WINERY: Quite successful given the vintage, with rich, elegant black cherry, cedar and spice flavors that are smooth and harmonious, finishing with a trace of tannin and a touch of tobacco. Drink 1990-1996. 900 cases produced. Release: $9. Current: $25. **87**

GIRARD WINERY

Reserve, Oakville, Napa Valley

CLASSIFICATION: *FOURTH GROWTH*

COLLECTIBILITY RATING: A

BEST VINTAGES:

Reserve: 1986, 1984

Estate: 1980

One of Napa Valley's most underrated Cabernet producers is Girard, located east of Oakville on the Silverado Trail. The Girard Reserve, made from Girard's 24-acre vineyard, is a rich, explosively fruity Cabernet that has been consistent from year to year, back to the first vintage in 1980. The 1980 is brimming with fresh, ripe fruit, making it one of the top wines of the vintage. The 1981 is a shade leaner but still successful, followed by a thick, dense, tannic 1982 that will require cellaring another four to five years and will probably age through 2004. In 1983 the first Reserve bottling was produced. The 1983 is a bit leaner and more tannic, followed by a massively proportioned 1984 Reserve that is built to age. The 1985 Reserve is a fine Cabernet, not quite as opulent as the 1984, but with time it may rival it. The 1986 Reserve is another exceptional bottling.

Girard also makes a regular Napa Valley bottling, and it too is often of superior quality, at a lower price than the Reserve. Girard Reserve Cabernet is produced in limited quantities, usually 500 to 600 cases. Considering the high quality and limited supply, it will soon become a prestigious and sought-after bottling.

TASTING NOTES

GIRARD WINERY, Reserve, Oakville, Napa Valley

1986 GIRARD WINERY RESERVE: Firm, structured and tightly wound, this wine exhibits deep, rich, intense anise, cherry, black currant and plum flavors with crisp acidity and tannins that bode well for aging. Another terrific Reserve bottling by Girard. Drink 1994-2002. 584 cases produced. Not Released. **91**

1985 GIRARD WINERY RESERVE: Elegant, rich, and complex, with firm, dry tannins and plenty of delicious plum, currant, spice and oak

AT A GLANCE

GIRARD WINERY
P.O. Box 105
Oakville, CA 94562
(707) 944-8577

Owner: Girard Winery (Steven Girard, President)

Winemaker: Mark Smith (1 year)

Founded: 1980

First Cabernet vintage: 1980
Reserve: 1983

Cabernet production: 2,500 cases
Reserve: 550 cases

Cabernet acres owned: 24

Average age of vines: 16 years

Vineyard makeup: Cabernet Sauvignon (95%), Cabernet Franc (5%)

Average wine makeup: Cabernet Sauvignon (100%)

Time in oak: 16 months

Type of oak: French (Allier)

flavors in a narrowly focused, well-crafted wine. Has all the ingredients for greatness but needs time to come together. Approachable now but better in five to 10 years. Drink 1993-2000. 480 cases produced. Release: $25. Current: $25. **89**

1984 GIRARD WINERY RESERVE: A massively concentrated 1984 with rich, ripe, opulent fruit and thick, integrated tannins. The ripe plum, currant and black cherry flavors are sharply focused and supported by a wallop of thick, chewy tannins. The texture is smooth and supple, like many 1984s, but it has a firmer structure and harder tannins than most from this vintage. Drink 1994-2004. 684 cases produced. Release: $25. Current: $25. **92**

1983 GIRARD WINERY RESERVE: Lean, austere, dry and tannic, with a supple texture and ripe, concentrated plum, currant and mint flavors that need several more years to mellow. Better balanced than most 1983s, an ager. Drink 1994-2000. 548 cases produced. Release: $18. Current: $20. **87**

1982 GIRARD WINERY ESTATE: Big, thick, rich and chewy, with robust tannins that are dry and firm. The rich black currant, anise and plum flavors are ripe and well focused, and the finish gets dry and tannic. Definitely a wine to lay away for another few years. Drink 1994-2004. 2,107 cases produced. Release: $12.50. Current: $30. **87**

1981 GIRARD WINERY ESTATE: A shade leaner and drier than the outstanding 1980, this wine has similar rich black currant and herb flavors, but it's more tannic and drier on the palate. Drink 1993-2000. 1,595 cases produced. Release: $12.50. Current: $20. **86**

1980 GIRARD WINERY ESTATE: One of the great 1980s, this is an exquisitely balanced, beautifully defined wine with deep color and rich, ripe, elegant black currant, plum, anise and spice flavors that are long and seductive on the finish. Ready now but can age another decade with ease. Drink 1991-2000. 1,480 cases produced. Release: $11. Current: $25. **92**

GRACE FAMILY VINEYARD
St. Helena, Napa Valley

CLASSIFICATION: *SECOND GROWTH*

COLLECTIBILITY RATING: *AA*

BEST VINTAGES: *1986, 1985, 1984, 1983, 1982, 1980, 1979*

W hen the Grace family produced its first Cabernet from its tiny 1-acre vineyard in St. Helena, it became an overnight sensation in Napa Valley. That first wine, a 1978, was wonderfully elegant and effusively fruity. The two-year-old vines that produced it came from cuttings taken from the Bosché Vineyard in Rutherford.

Charlie Wagner of Caymus Vineyards tasted the grapes before harvest and decided they were so good that he inaugurated a special bottling under the Caymus Vineyards label.

The next five vintages, through 1985, were produced and bottled at Caymus under the direction of Wagner. Beginning in 1983, Dick and Ann Grace launched their own label and later built a handsome winery adjacent to their home to handle their minuscule production.

The Grace Cabernets have been nothing short of sensational in each of the first nine vintages. The 1978 set the style, with its rich, intense cassis and black cherry flavors and supple, elegant structure. While the 1978 did not have the richness and concentration of subsequent vintages, it has remained in top form a decade after it was harvested. It is now fully mature and ready to drink.

The 1978 was followed by an incredibly rich, smooth, supple and complex 1979 and a big, deep, concentrated 1980. The 1981 vintage provided an effusively fruity wine that is attractive for its suppleness and forward fruit. The 1982 ranks among the top wines of that difficult vintage. It is slowly evolving, gaining complexity and depth. The 1983 is a sensational bottling, defining the Grace Vineyard richness and elegance, with layers of fruit complexity. The 1984, 1985 and 1986 vintages continue in that tradition, combining lavish Cabernet fruit of amazing richness, opulence and depth.

There has never been much Grace Family Vineyard Cabernet to go around with a typical harvest producing a mere eight barrels (150 cases). It is extremely expensive, selling for $50 a bottle through a winery mailing list. The Grace Cabernets have sold for astronomical prices at the Napa Valley Wine Auction, where they have been offered in special, limited-edition oversized bottles. Grace has since planted a second acre of Cabernet, adjacent to the original 1-acre plot, which should double production to 300 cases. Because of the exceptionally high quality

AT A GLANCE
GRACE FAMILY VINEYARDS
1210 Rockland Road
St. Helena, CA 94574
(707) 963-0808

Owners: Dick and Ann Grace

Winemaker: Dick Grace (4 years)

Founded: 1987

First Cabernet vintage: 1978

Cabernet production: 150 cases

Cabernet acres owned: 2

Average age of vines: 10 years

Vineyard makeup: Cabernet Sauvignon (100%)

Average wine makeup: Cabernet Sauvignon (100%)

Time in oak: 36 months

Type of oak: French (Limousin, Nevers)

Napa Valley
Cabernet Sauvignon
Produced entirely of Cabernet Sauvignon grapes
from the Grace Family Vineyard, this wine was aged in
excess of 3½ years in French Limousin barrels.
PRODUCED & BOTTLED BY GRACE FAMILY WINERY
RUTHERFORD, NAPA VALLEY, CALIFORNIA
ALCOHOL 13.2% BY VOLUME

of the wine and extremely limited availability, the Grace Cabernets rate high as collectibles. They are delicious on release and age well for a decade.

TASTING NOTES

GRACE FAMILY VINEYARD, St. Helena, Napa Valley

1986 GRACE FAMILY VINEYARD: Just beginning to open, with rich, elegant chocolate, plum, currant and black cherry flavors and the kind of firm structure and rich texture that promise to age well. The tannins sneak up on the finish. Needs three to five years before drinking. Drink 1994-2003. 150 cases produced. Release: $40. Current: $40. **93**

1985 GRACE FAMILY VINEYARD: Grace's finest effort to date, this is an amazingly complex and elegant 1985, offering rich, concentrated, beautifully defined fruit, layers of cassis, currant and plum flavors and a touch of anise and toasty oak on the finish. It's delicious now but should only get better for the next decade. Drink 1993-2004. 126 cases produced. Release: $50. Current: $90. **95**

1984 GRACE FAMILY VINEYARD: Enticingly generous and forward, the 1984 is a deep, rich, lush Cabernet with complex layers of plum, cassis and cherry flavors that are framed by toasty French oak. The tannins are soft and fleshy, making it quite seductive to drink now, but the richness and depth promise further development. Drink 1994-2004. 150 cases produced. Release: $38. Current: $125. **92**

1983 GRACE FAMILY VINEYARD: Sleek and elegant, an exceptional bottling, amazingly rich and supple, deep and concentrated, with pretty black cherry and currant flavors. Everything's in place for greatness, with crisp acidity and ample tannins. Should age another decade with ease. Drink 1994-2002. 175 cases produced. Release: $38. Current: $130. **91**

1982 GRACE FAMILY VINEYARD: Showing more French oak than previous vintages, the 1982 is lean, tight and delicate, with plenty of sharply focused plum, cassis and currant flavors. With time it should develop more nuance and depth. Drink 1993-1999. 225 cases produced. Release: $31. Current: $155. **89**

1981 GRACE FAMILY VINEYARD: Effusively fruity and forward, with elegant, supple cherry and plum aromas and flavors that lack the concentration of Grace's finest. Needs more time, but it's close to its peak. Drink 1992-1998. 185 cases produced. Release: $28. Current: $150. **88**

1980 GRACE FAMILY VINEYARD: This is a big, rich, concentrated wine that has the Grace elegance but offers more extract and stuffing. Offers sharply focused, rich black cherry and plum flavors, with layers of cedar and vanilla that add complexity. Drink 1993-2002. 183 cases produced. Release: $25. Current: $275. **92**

1979 GRACE FAMILY VINEYARD: A very special wine that defines the Grace vineyard's richness, suppleness and elegance. More elegant and focused than the 1978, this wine displays rich chocolate, plum and cherry flavors that are delicately balanced, finishing long and full. For the lucky few who have a bottle, this one is ready now and for the next six to 10 years. Drink 1991-2000. 56 cases produced. Release: $20. Current: $150. **92**

1978 GRACE FAMILY VINEYARD: Extremely impressive for a second-year crop, this 1978 bottled under the Caymus label features complex, elegant spice, cassis, currant and black cherry flavors and firm tannins. It's in perfect drinking condition now, but my last tasting showed signs that the fruit is fading. Best consumed now, although it ranks high as a collectible. Drink 1990-1995. 48 cases produced. Release: $20. Current: $275. **86**

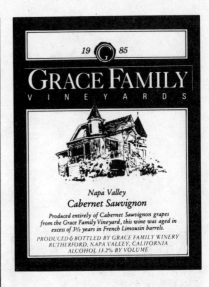

GRGICH HILLS CELLAR
Napa Valley

CLASSIFICATION: *THIRD GROWTH*

COLLECTIBILITY RATING: *A*

BEST VINTAGES: *1986, 1985, 1984, 1980*

AT A GLANCE
GRGICH HILLS CELLAR
P.O. Box 450
Rutherford, CA 94573
(707) 963-2784

Owners: Miljenko Grgich and Austin Hills

Winemaker: Mike Grgich (12 years)

Founded: 1977

First Cabernet vintage: 1980

Cabernet production: 10,000 cases

Cabernet acres owned: 43

Average age of vines: 14 years

Vineyard makeup: Cabernet Sauvignon (92%), Cabernet Franc (4%), Merlot (4%)

Average wine makeup: Cabernet Sauvignon (92%), Cabernet Franc (4%), Merlot (4%)

Time in oak: 24 months

Type of oak: French

Miljenko (Mike) Grgich of Grgich Hills Cellar in Napa Valley is known as a Chardonnay specialist for his rich, toasty, intensely concentrated Chardonnays. But Chardonnay is only part the story, for Grgich, a native of Croatia, Yugoslavia, is also a master with Cabernet Sauvignon, having worked for years at Beaulieu Vineyard under André Tchelistcheff and later as the first winemaker at Château Montelena. The Grgich Hills Cabernets receive only a portion of the attention they deserve, for they are rich, supple, beautifully sculpted wines that are sumptuous to drink on release yet display the intensity of fruit flavor and delicate balance for mid- to long-range cellaring. Grgich's partner is Austin Hills, an heir to the Hills Brothers coffee fortune.

Grgich Hills' first Cabernet, from the 1980 vintage, is distinctive for its ripe, opulent, polished fruit. The 1981, 1982 and 1983 vintages are somewhat leaner but still fine wines. With the 1984 vintage, Grgich has created a bold, rich, delicious Cabernet that ranks among the top wines of the vintage. The 1985 and 1986 vintages are also sublime.

Grgich's principal Cabernet vineyard is in Yountville near Napanook (Dominus) and Markham. Production has quietly climbed to 10,000 cases and at $17 represents a good value.

TASTING NOTES
GRGICH HILLS CELLAR, Yountville, Napa Valley

1986 GRGICH HILLS CELLAR: Deep, rich, concentrated and elegant, with sharply focused black currant and spicy cedar flavors that are tightly wound and framed by firm tannins. Fits in perfectly with the Grgich Cabernet portfolio. It is a beautifully structured wine with flavors to carry it a decade. Drink 1994-2002. 10,000 cases produced. Not Released. **91**

1985 GRGICH HILLS CELLAR: A superb 1985 that fits the mold of the vintage, with its sleek, elegant, beautifully focused black currant, cherry and plum flavors that are fresh, crisp and lively. Wonderful already but a good cellar candidate. Drink 1994-2005. 10,000 cases produced. Not Released. **92**

1984 GRGICH HILLS CELLAR: The best Grgich Hills to date, a bold, rich, concentrated wine with generous ripe currant and black cherry flavors that are supple, intense and richly textured, finishing with crisp acidity and great length. Delicious now but should hold up well for midterm aging. Drink 1993-2005. 10,000 cases produced. Release: $17. Current: $17. **94**

1983 GRGICH HILLS CELLAR: Ripe, full and fairly tannic, with bright plum and black cherry flavors, very well balanced for a 1983. It has enough intense, rich fruit to stand up to the drying tannins. A good candidate for cellaring. Drink 1994-2003. 10,000 cases produced. Release: $17. Current: $23. **88**

1982 GRGICH HILLS CELLAR: The 1982 splits the difference between the 1980 and 1981 vintages, with its firm, lean structure and ripe, fleshy plum, currant and anise flavors. Well proportioned and ready to drink soon, finishing with a touch of oak and tannin. Drink 1992-1998. 3,000 cases produced. Release: $17. Current: $28. **87**

1981 GRGICH HILLS CELLAR: Lean and supple, with herb, bell pepper and ripe plum flavors, this is a very good, true-to-form 1981, more herbaceous than the 1980 but not too tannic, ready to drink now or during the next five to seven years. Drink 1991-1997. 2,000 cases produced. Release: $17. Current: $28. **86**

1980 GRGICH HILLS CELLAR: Typical of the best from this vintage, the 1980 is very ripe, smooth, polished and complex, oozing with rich, fleshy plum and black cherry flavors, supple tannins and a tasty finish. Nearing its peak; should remain in good condition for five to seven years. Drink 1991-2000. 2,000 cases produced. Release: $16. Current: $32. **90**

GROTH VINEYARDS AND WINERY

Reserve, Oakville, Napa Valley
Estate, Oakville, Napa Valley

CLASSIFICATION:
  Reserve: SECOND GROWTH
  Estate: THIRD GROWTH
COLLECTIBILITY RATING:
  Reserve: A
  Estate: A

BEST VINTAGES:
  Reserve: 1986, 1985, 1984, 1983

  Estate: 1986, 1985, 1984

<table>
<tr><td colspan="2">

AT A GLANCE

**GROTH VINEYARDS
AND WINERY**
P.O. Box 412
Oakville, CA 94562
(707) 255-7466

Owners: Dennis and Judy Groth

Winemaker: Nils Venge (7 years)

Founded: 1983

First Cabernet vintage: 1982
  Reserve: 1983

Cabernet production: 8,000 cases
  Reserve: 500 cases
  Estate: 7,500 cases

Cabernet acres owned: 87

Average age of vines: 14 years

Vineyard makeup: Cabernet Sauvignon (86%), Merlot (14%)

Average wine makeup: Cabernet Sauvignon (85%), Merlot (15%)

Time in oak: 18 months

Type of oak: French (Nevers, Allier)

</td></tr>
</table>

With an excellent 87-acre Cabernet vineyard in Oakville and a skilled winemaker in Nils Venge, formerly of Villa Mt. Eden, Groth is one of the brightest new Cabernet producers in Napa Valley. Owner Dennis Groth, a former Atari Computer executive, made his first vintage in 1982, producing a rich, harmonious wine in a troubled vintage. Since then the wines have only gotten better. The Groth Cabernets feature rich, supple, opulent and elegant flavors, characteristic of the Oakville area, and Venge's style, which he honed at Villa Mt. Eden beginning with the 1974 vintage. Venge's Cabernets are complex and concentrated but never overly tannic.

Beginning with the 1983 vintage, Groth began producing a Reserve bottling, which spends extra time in oak barrels and has added dimensions of richness, depth and complexity over the regular estate bottling; however, both are consistently excellent wines, and neither should be overlooked. Since 1983, all of the Groth Cabernets have been outstanding. The 1984s are effusively fruity, rich and supple, in sync with the vintage. The 1985s display a measure of elegance and finesse, while the 1986 is deep, rich and concentrated, a good candidate for midterm cellaring.

Groth has made vineyards a strong priority, and production has climbed to 8,000 cases. All the winemaking successes have been achieved without building a winery, although Groth has a site selected in Oakville.

Tasting Notes

Groth Vineyards and Winery, Reserve, Oakville, Napa Valley

1986 GROTH VINEYARDS & WINERY RESERVE: Enticing for its richness and elegance, the 1986 Reserve is blessed with layers of ripe plum and currant fruit, lavish cedar, oak and chocolate nuances that combine to offer depth and complexity. Because of its delicacy and balance, it's drinkable now but should be great for a decade. Long, crisp finish. Drink 1993-2003. 475 cases produced. Not Released. **93**

1985 GROTH VINEYARDS & WINERY RESERVE: A shade richer and more concentrated than the 1985 estate, this wine is thick and concentrated, packed with young, intense, vibrant, supple fruit, layers of black cherry, currant, juniper berry and spicy oak that are deep and complex. Because of the enormous fruit concentration, this wine will require patience. Hold for seven to eight years, and drink the 1985 estate in the meantime. Drink 1996-2004. 500 cases produced. Not Released. **93**

1984 GROTH VINEYARDS & WINERY RESERVE: Fruitier than the delicious 1984 estate, this wine is packed with fresh, ripe, concentrated layers of black cherry, blueberry, currant and anise flavors, along with a hint of jam, all in a supple, elegant, seductive style. A charmer all the way. Drink 1992-2000. 500 cases produced. Release: $25. Current: $25. **94**

1983 GROTH VINEYARDS & WINERY RESERVE: Has all the ingredients a reserve wine should have over the regular bottling, with added dimensions of richness, concentration and depth. This wine is one of the vintage's standouts, a firm, richly textured wine with complex toasty oak, ripe black cherry and currant flavors, finishing with anise and berry aftertastes. Has the tannins for long-term aging. Drink 1996-2004. 200 cases produced. Release: $25. Current: $30. **92**

Groth Vineyards and Winery, Estate, Oakville, Napa Valley

1986 GROTH VINEYARDS & WINERY: Deep, rich and structured, this is an outstanding 1986, with a firm backbone of oak and tannin and a pretty core of supple plum, currant and spice flavors. The balance of fruit and oak is precise and elegant, and the depth of flavor makes it an excellent candidate for midterm aging. Drink 1994-2001. 6,400 cases produced. Release: $18. Current: $18. **92**

1985 GROTH VINEYARDS & WINERY: A very elegant, complex, seamless 1985 that is rich with ripe black cherry, currant, plum and anise flavors, firm yet supple tannins and mouthwatering acidity. Its fine structure makes it attractive to drink now but should ensure midterm aging. Pretty aftertaste, with subtlety and finesse. Drink 1994-2002. 7,800 cases produced. Release: $16. Current: $16. **91**

1984 GROTH VINEYARDS & WINERY: Effusively fruity with gorgeous layers of black cherry, currant, raspberry and spicy anise in a supple, elegant, charming style. Like most 1984s it's supple and ready to drink, but the concentration, depth of flavor and fine balance bode well for midterm aging. Drink 1993-2000. 6,500 cases produced. Release: $14. Current: $18. **92**

1983 GROTH VINEYARDS & WINERY: A very attractive 1983 in the lean, tannic style of the vintage, but the 1983 Groth shows better concentration and balance than most, with fine tannins that don't bite. Plenty of currant, black cherry, anise and toasty oak flavors to contemplate, yet no one sticks out. Has all the ingredients for midterm aging. Drink 1994-2000. 10,000 cases produced. Release: $13. Current: $21. **88**

1982 GROTH VINEYARDS & WINERY: Groth's first vintage, the 1982 is a very harmonious wine and one of the best 1982s, rich and dramatic, with supple, layered currant, anise, black cherry and cedar flavors that are balanced and long. Fine tannins are rounding out. Ready soon. Drink 1992-1998. 7,000 cases produced. Release: $13. Current: $24. **88**

GUNDLACH BUNDSCHU WINERY

Rhinefarm, Sonoma Valley

CLASSIFICATION: *FIFTH GROWTH*

COLLECTIBILITY RATING: *Not rated*

BEST VINTAGES:

Rhinefarm Reserve: 1981

Rhinefarm: 1986, 1985

Batto Ranch: 1981, 1977

Founded in 1858 by Jacob Gundlach and Charles Bundschu, this winery near the town of Sonoma first produced wines under the Bacchus Wines label a century ago. Following Gundlach's death, Bundschu operated the winery and the Rhinefarm vineyard, but the 1906 earthquake destroyed the stone winery, and Prohibition put an end to Bundschu's winemaking. Bundschu's grandson, Jim Bundschu, inherited the winery and reopened it in the 1970s, making its first Cabernet in 1974. Since then the Gundlach Bundschu Cabernets have come from two principal vineyards, the Batto Ranch and the Rhinefarm, both in Sonoma Valley.

The oldest notes I have come from the 1977 Batto Ranch, and it remains one of the more impressive 1977s. The 1979 and 1980 were less successful, but the 1981 and 1981 Reserve were both highly successful bottlings. Also in 1981 Gundlach Bundschu began producing a Rhinefarm bottling that has since become the winery's sole vineyard-designated bottling. The 1982 and 1983 bottlings from both Batto and Rhinefarm were merely good and not up to standards, while in 1984 the Rhinefarm is clearly the superior bottling. The 1984 Batto is the last under Gundlach Bundschu; Cabernet from that vineyard is now being bottled by Gundlach Bundschu winemaker Lance Cutler under his own label. The 1985 Rhinefarm is by far the finest wine ever produced by this old winery, defining its style of richness, elegance and finesse. The 1986 is a worthy successor. At $9 on release, the 1985 Rhinefarm Cabernet is one of the greatest values in California Cabernet. Release price for the 1986 is $12, still very reasonable.

AT A GLANCE

GUNDLACH BUNDSCHU WINERY
P.O. Box 1
Vineburg, CA 95467
(707) 938-5277

Owner: Jim Bundschu

Winemaker: Lance Cutler (11 years)

Founded: 1858, reestablished: 1970

First Cabernet vintage: 1974
Rhinefarm: 1981

Cabernet production: 6,000 cases
Rhinefarm: 5,000 cases

Cabernet acres owned: 25

Average age of vines: 16 years

Vineyard makeup: Cabernet Sauvignon (100%)

Average wine makeup: Cabernet Sauvignon (100%)

Time in oak: 13 months

Type of oak: French, American

TASTING NOTES

GUNDLACH BUNDSCHU WINERY, **Rhinefarm, Sonoma Valley**

1986 GUNDLACH BUNDSCHU WINERY RHINEFARM: Delicious, with beautifully focused fruit and lots of currant, black cherry, spice and vanilla flavors that are intense and lively. The tannins are in proportion for midterm cellaring, but it's alluring already. Drink 1993-1998. 5,000 cases produced. Release: $12. Current: $12. **89**

1985 GUNDLACH BUNDSCHU WINERY RHINEFARM: A smooth, sumptuous wine that ranks as Gundlach Bundschu's finest, offering layers of rich vanilla, chocolate, currant and spicy berry flavors that are long and full, with supple tannins and crisp acidity. Tempting now but should hold up well for a decade or more. Drink 1992-2000. 5,000 cases produced. Release: $9. Current: $10. **91**

1984 GUNDLACH BUNDSCHU WINERY RHINEFARM: Attractive, ripe, forward plum and black cherry flavors and a lean, firm structure. The tannin level should ensure its development in the next five years, but it lacks the richness and concentration for greatness or long-term cellaring. Drink 1992-1997. 5,000 cases produced. Release: $9. Current: $10. **85**

1983 GUNDLACH BUNDSCHU WINERY RHINEFARM: From a troubled vintage, this is a lean, tannic, simple Cabernet with light plum flavors. Decent to drink but lacks the richness and concentration of most Gundlach Bundschu efforts. Drink 1991-1994. 4,500 cases produced. Release: $9. Current: $12. **73**

1982 GUNDLACH BUNDSCHU WINERY RHINEFARM: A weak, disappointing vintage for Gundlach Bundschu, this wine is minty, vegetal and lacking in appeal. Best to avoid. 4,500 cases produced. Release: $9. Current: $13. **65**

1981 GUNDLACH BUNDSCHU WINERY RHINEFARM VINTAGE RESERVE: Has slowly developed into a rich, concentrated wine, with deep chocolate, bell pepper, currant and tobacco flavors and an abundance of rich, thick tannins and oak. Still five years from full maturity. Drink 1994-2002. 800 cases produced. Release: $20. Current: $26. **90**

1981 GUNDLACH BUNDSCHU WINERY: Intense and concentrated, with ripe pepper and berry flavors that are a bit coarse and tannic for a 1981 but still in balance. Give it three to five more years, then it should be more palatable. Drink 1994-1999. 4,000 cases produced. Release: $7. Current: $20. **84**

GUNDLACH BUNDSCHU WINERY, Batto Ranch, Sonoma Valley

1984 GUNDLACH BUNDSCHU WINERY BATTO RANCH: Surprisingly light and simple considering the amazingly rich, ripe and concentrated Cabernets made in 1984. This wine is already drinkable, with light Cabernet and cedar flavors that are ultimately plain. Disappointing. Drink 1990-1991. 800 cases produced. Release: $14. Current: $16. **79**

1983 GUNDLACH BUNDSCHU WINERY BATTO RANCH: Avoids

being overly tannic for a 1983, simple and light, lacking the richness and concentration of the best wines. Enjoyable but uninspired. Drink 1990-1993. 1,000 cases produced. Release: $10. Current: $15. **77**

1982 GUNDLACH BUNDSCHU WINERY BATTO RANCH: Of average quality and somewhat bland, with earthy, diluted flavors, an apparent rain victim. It's drinkable and technically correct, but the flavors leave much to be desired. Drink 1990-1992. 1,000 cases produced. Release: $10. Current: $18. **70**

1981 GUNDLACH BUNDSCHU WINERY BATTO RANCH: This has always been one of Gundlach Bundschu's best drinking wines for its elegance, delicacy and sharply defined fruit. It's fully developed now, with complex, supple black cherry, anise and cedar notes that have the last vestige of tannins on the finish. Drink 1990-1993. 950 cases produced. Release: $10. Current: $18. **88**

1980 GUNDLACH BUNDSCHU WINERY BATTO RANCH: Light and fruity for a 1980, not overly ripe but rather simple and elegant, with pepper, black cherry and jam flavors of moderate depth and intensity. Lacks the richness and concentration of the top 1980s. Drink 1990-1993. 950 cases produced. Release: $8. Current: $20. **80**

1979 GUNDLACH BUNDSCHU WINERY BATTO RANCH: A satisfying, elegant 1979 marked by simple cedar, anise and pepper flavors of moderate depth. This wine is fully mature. Drink 1990-1993. 900 cases produced. Release: $8. Current: $22. **80**

1977 GUNDLACH BUNDSCHU WINERY BATTO RANCH: One of the more stylish and elegant 1977s, this wine is at its peak now, with lovely, rich, supple fruit and enticing aromas of anise, black cherry and spice, smooth and velvety on the palate. Drink 1990-1995. 900 cases produced. Release: $8. Current: $24. **89**

HAYWOOD WINERY

Sonoma Valley

CLASSIFICATION: *FIFTH GROWTH*
COLLECTIBILITY RATING: *Not rated*
BEST VINTAGES: *1986, 1985, 1984*

H aywood, a hillside vineyard outside the city of Sonoma founded by former contractor Peter Haywood, produces rich yet fairly tannic Cabernets in a style that has limited appeal. The wines to date have had plenty of everything — extract, concentration and flavor — but they lack elegance and finesse, making them difficult to drink early on; they are best cellared for four or five years. Even then they lean toward the tannic side. The best Cabernets have been the most recent ones, in 1984, 1985 and 1986, each displaying a rich core of deeply concentrated and tannic fruit. The first vintage, 1980, is still evolving, picking up some nice complexities. The weakest vintages are the 1982 and 1983, neither of which has much charm. The winery's 17 acres are planted to Cabernet and Merlot.

AT A GLANCE

HAYWOOD WINERY
18701 Gehricke Road
Sonoma, CA 94576
(707) 996-4298

Owners: Peter Haywood, Rudy and Georgia Tulipani

Winemaker: Peter Haywood (9 years)

Founded: 1979

First Cabernet vintage: 1980

Cabernet production: 2,600 cases

Cabernet acres owned: 17

Average age of vines: 13 years

Vineyard makeup: Cabernet Sauvignon (88%), Merlot (12%)

Average wine makeup: Cabernet Sauvignon (88%), Merlot (12%)

Time in oak: 16 months

Type of oak: French (Nevers, Allier)

TASTING NOTES

HAYWOOD WINERY, Sonoma Valley

1986 HAYWOOD WINERY: Haywood's finest ever, the 1986 offers beautifully defined, rich, ripe black cherry and currant flavors that are intense and lively, loaded with fresh, snappy fruit. Better balanced than previous vintages and noticeably less tannic. It's approachable now but best in three to five years. Drink 1994-2003. 2,612 cases produced. Release: $16. Current: $16. **91**

1985 HAYWOOD WINERY: Another richly tannic offering from Haywood, the 1985 has a pretty core of sharply focused black cherry and currant flavors along with a hint of anise, but the tannins bite down hard on the finish. Patience required. Drink 1996-2004. 2,141 cases produced. Release: $14.50. Current: $14.50. **89**

1984 HAYWOOD WINERY: Ripe but fairly tannic as 1984s go, this bottling has ripe plum and currant flavors, but the tannins clamp down hard on the palate and dominate the finish. Will require more patience than most 1984s. Best in five to six years. Drink 1995-2002. 856 cases produced. Release: $12.50. Current: $20. **88**

1983 HAYWOOD WINERY: Lean, hard and tannic, tastes overly acidified, without the richness and depth of fruit to stand up to the tannins and sharp acidity. Needs years to round out. Drink 1995-2003. 711 cases produced. Release: $12.50. Current: $20. **77**

1982 HAYWOOD WINERY: Earthy, with juniper berry and currant flavors, the 1982 manages to bring enough ripe fruit to the forefront to offset the drying tannins. In three to five years the tannins should be resolved, but is there enough richness in the fruit to still make it interesting? Drink 1994-2000. 608 cases produced. Release: $11. Current: $20. **79**

1981 HAYWOOD WINERY: With not quite the breadth of flavor of the 1980, the 1981 is nonetheless similar in style, with thick, rich plum, mineral and earth flavors with prune notes in the background. The richness of the fruit comes through on the finish, although it still needs three to five years to soften. Drink 1994-2001. 1,081 cases produced. Release: $11. Current: $20. **85**

1980 HAYWOOD WINERY: Haywood's first vintage, a rich, ripe, thick, dense, tannic Cabernet with an assortment of earth, mineral, tar, anise and plum flavors that border on pruney. All in all it's balanced but chunky, with a weedy black currant and slightly metallic finish. Still needs time but near maturity. Drink 1992-1999. 570 cases produced. Release: $9.75. Current: $12. **86**

HEITZ WINE CELLARS

Martha's Vineyard, Oakville, Napa Valley
Bella Oaks Vineyard, Rutherford, Napa Valley,

CLASSIFICATION:
Martha's Vineyard: FIRST GROWTH
Bella Oaks Vineyard: THIRD GROWTH

COLLECTIBILITY RATING:
Martha's Vineyard: AAA
Bella Oaks Vineyard: A

BEST VINTAGES:
Martha's Vineyard: 1985, 1984, 1979, 1978, 1977, 1975,
1974, 1973, 1970, 1969, 1968, 1966

Bella Oaks Vineyard: 1985, 1981, 1980, 1977

AT A GLANCE

HEITZ WINE CELLARS
500 Taplin Road
St. Helena, CA 94574
(707) 963-3542

Owner: Heitz Wine Cellars (Joe Heitz, president)

Winemaker: Joe Heitz (28 years)

Founded: 1961

First Cabernet vintage: 1965
   Martha's Vineyard: 1966
   Bella Oaks Vineyard: 1976

Cabernet production: 13,000 cases
   Martha's Vineyard: 4,300 cases
   Bella Oaks Vineyard: 3,500 cases

Cabernet acres owned: 70
   Martha's Vineyard: 34
   Bella Oaks Vineyard: 17

Average age of vines: 15 years

Vineyard makeup: Cabernet Sauvignon (100%)

Average wine makeup: Cabernet Sauvignon (100%)

Time in oak: 42 months

Type of oak: French (Limousin), American

Martha's Vineyard, nestled up against the hills west of Oakville, is perhaps the most famous Cabernet vineyard in America. The fruit from this 34-acre vineyard, owned by independent growers Tom and Martha May, has always been vinified and bottled under the direction of an equally renowned winemaker, Joe Heitz, proprietor of Heitz Wine Cellars. Since 1966 Heitz Martha's Vineyard has ranked among the elite of California Cabernet year after year, making it one of the wines most sought-after by connoisseurs, who appreciate it for its richness, concentration and ageability, and by collectors, who recognize it as the most famous Cabernet in America.

To hear Tom May and Heitz discuss Martha's Vineyard, there is nothing particularly special about this gravelly loam vineyard flanked by a row of shaggy eucalyptus trees. May is a gentleman farmer who oversees care of the vineyard and has a handshake agreement to sell the grapes to Heitz, who insists he does nothing special other than take good care of the grapes.

The first 12 acres of the vineyard were planted in 1961 by Bernard and Belle Rhodes, who sold it to the Mays two years later in 1963. When the Rhodeses moved from their home on the property, they left a bottle of Heitz Champagne in the refrigerator as a gift for the Mays. When the Mays moved in, they found the bottle and later contacted Heitz to see if he was interested in buying the grapes.

Heitz, a U.C.-Davis enology graduate, was familiar with Oakville's soil, climate and grapes, having worked as a winemaker at Beaulieu from 1951 to 1959 under the direction of André Tchelistcheff before founding his own winery in 1961. Later both the Mays and Rhodeses became shareholders in the Heitz winery, a closely held corporation, along with wine writer and author Bob Thompson of St. Helena and a group of Kaiser Hospital physicians who invested money to help finance the winery operations. Agreements to buy the Martha's Vineyard grapes, and later the Cabernet from the Rhodeses' Bella Oaks Vineyard in Rutherford, are informal, non-binding agreements. Heitz and his wife, Alice, own a controlling interest in Heitz Wine Cellars and run the business with their children, Kathleen, David and Rollie.

The first Martha's crop in 1965 was bottled under the Heitz label without a vineyard designation, but the following vintage the quality was so exceptional that the name Martha's Vineyard appeared on the label and has for every vintage since, except 1971, when Heitz determined the quality did not warrant a separate bottling.

Heitz Martha's Vineyard is a textbook example of how a winemaker's style coincides with the character of the vineyard. Martha's Vineyard Cabernet is 100 percent Cabernet, very ripe and full-bodied, distinctive for its rich, enormously concentrated, gutsy character and complex, spicy flavors of mint, herb, currant and cherry. The Heitz style of Cabernet is unmistakable, bringing all those elements to the forefront in the aroma and flavor, emphasizing the thick, firm, intense flavor of the fruit, then seasoning it through a regimen of barrel aging in new and used French and American casks. When released in its fifth year, after three and a half years in oak and one year in the bottle, the wine has all its vitality, depth and power plus a subtle measure of polish that takes the edge off the tannins and makes the wine perfectly drinkable on release.

Through two decades of vintages, the Martha's Vineyard character comes across as strong and definitive, placing it almost always at or near the top among California's Cabernets. In 1966, 1967, 1968, 1969, 1970 and 1974 it is the highest-ranking Cabernet of the vintage in this book. In 1973, 1975, 1979, 1984 and 1985, the Martha's places within the top three wines of each vintage. No other Cabernet can rival that track record.

What's remarkable about the Martha's Vineyard Cabernets are not only the complex, distinctive mint, chocolate and cherry flavors, but how incredibly well they age. The 1966 is fully mature yet has the depth and flavor to sustain it another decade. The 1967, while not in the class of the 1966, is more delicate and elegant, aging gracefully. The 1968 is by far the finest Cabernet made from that exceptional vintage, and it ranks as one of the all-time greats made in California, deep, rich, complex and concentrated. The 1969 is another first-class wine, a shade more elegant than the 1968 but just as complex and pleasing in its own way.

In 1970 another monumental bottling was produced, and this wine still needs five to seven years before it peaks. The 1972 vintage is the weakest Martha's ever produced, yet is still pleasant, while the 1973 returns to top form with a flavorful, elegant wine. The 1974, made

by Heitz's son David when Joe was bedridden with a back injury, features a special commemorative label of the Heitz residence. It is incredibly rich and dramatic, perhaps another five years from reaching its zenith, ranking with the 1968 as one of the top Heitz Martha's ever made. The 1975 Martha's is superb, paling only by comparison with the incredible 1974, while the 1976 is very ripe and tannic, missing the impeccable balance and silky texture of most Martha's. The 1977 is mature and elegant, drinkable now, while the 1978 is similar in style, not quite the powerhouse one might expect in this very ripe, opulent vintage. The 1979 returns to the deeply intense and concentrated style and needs another five years cellaring for prime drinking.

The 1980 and 1981 are both very fine, more forward and less massive in structure, while the 1982 is tight and lean, in need of further aging. The 1983 is very successful, with Heitz managing to soften the tannins and produce a fairly approachable yet ageworthy wine. The 1984 is the best since the 1974, with explosive fruit and great concentration. Heitz believes the 1985 is one of the best Cabernets he's ever produced, and this bottling will sport a special label like the 1974 design.

Bella Oaks Vineyard, planted in the mid-1970s, is a few miles north of Martha's Vineyard. While Heitz employs nearly identical winemaking techniques for both wines and typically bottles them within a month of each other, Bella Oaks and Martha's are different and distinct. The Cabernets from the 17-acre Bella Oaks Vineyard are rich, elegant and flavorful, a shade less concentrated and tannic than the Martha's and without the power or the spicy mint quality. They also reach maturity sooner than the Martha's Vineyard wines. In some vintages, such as 1977 and 1980, the Bella Oaks can be marginally more appealing than the Martha's, which makes it fascinating to drink the two wines together. In a decade of vintages, however, Bella Oaks wines have yet to show the explosive fruit and sheer power of the Martha's. The first vintage in 1976 is drinking well now, while the 1977 is one of the top five 1977s. The 1978 is ripe and generous, ready to drink now and through the 1990s. No 1979 was produced because a swarm of insects wiped out the crop, but in 1980 Bella Oaks is again charming, rich and packed with fruit. The 1981 is elegant and refined, tight and complex, followed by the 1982 and 1983 vintages, which show some bottle variation. The 1984 is a fairly controversial bottling. I have tried this wine on at least eight occasions, at times finding it musty and corky, yet on other occasions it appeared fine. With the 1985 vintage, Heitz has produced the finest Bella Oaks since 1980, a rich, sharply focused wine with wonderful black cherry and spicy mint notes.

While Martha's remains the benchmark for most California Cabernets, as well as a price trendsetter and one of the state's top collectibles, Bella Oaks is equally worthy of attention because of its high quality and the association with the Heitz brand and house style. Not to be ignored or overlooked is the Heitz Napa Valley bottling, which often features fruit from both the two premier vineyards, along with fruit from Heitz's own 70-acre vineyard in Rutherford along the Silverado Trail near Conn Dam Road.

TASTING NOTES

HEITZ WINE CELLAR, Martha's Vineyard, Oakville, Napa Valley

1985 HEITZ WINE CELLAR MARTHA'S VINEYARD: A truly magnificent Cabernet. In two tastings in July 1989, this deeply colored wine showed powerful aromas of currant, mint, spice and plum, wonderfully rich, elegant, supple and concentrated fruit flavors and the smooth, polished tannins and impeccable balance for which Heitz's Cabernets are renowned. Because the 1985 won't be sold until early 1990, this wine will undergo substantial development in the bottle, no doubt for the better. Destined to join the ranks of the great Martha's of 1968, 1970, 1974 and 1984 as uncommonly spectacular wines. No release price yet, but $45-$50 is not an unreasonable guess. Drink 1995-2010. 4,848 cases produced. Not Released. **98**

1984 HEITZ WINE CELLAR MARTHA'S VINEYARD: The greatest Martha's since 1974, this a beautifully defined, richly concentrated Cabernet, with deep, complex, vibrant black cherry, currant, cedar and creamy vanilla flavors that are impeccably balanced and delicious. The aftertaste echoes the black cherry and spicy vanilla flavors. Drink 1997-2007. 4,421 cases produced. Release: $40. Current: $40. **97**

1983 HEITZ WINE CELLAR MARTHA'S VINEYARD: The 1983 is very well balanced and surprisingly supple for the vintage, with chocolate, currant and plum flavors that pick up the firm, hard tannins on the finish. The firm concentration and tannins promise good aging. Drink 1997-2005. 4,356 cases produced. Release: $32.50. Current: $42. **89**

1982 HEITZ WINE CELLAR MARTHA'S VINEYARD: A young, raw and woody Martha's, with a rich core of intense yet closed fruit. The mint and chocolate flavors are deep and firm, and there is a suppleness developing on the palate. The finish is quite tannic. Drink 1996-2003. 5,100 cases produced. Release: $30. Current: $45. **88**

1981 HEITZ WINE CELLAR MARTHA'S VINEYARD: Deep and intense for a 1981, this wine offers a rich concentration of ripe currant, plum and cherry flavors with cedar and mint notes. Great harmony, balance, finesse and depth; not the aftertaste of the best Martha's, but has time to develop it. Drink 1997-2004. 3,113 cases produced. Release: $30. Current: $50. **89**

1980 HEITZ WINE CELLAR MARTHA'S VINEYARD: Very forward and flavorful, with ripe, generous, bright cherry, plum, anise and cedar nuances that are beautifully focused and very long on the finish. Drink 1996-2006. 2,966 cases produced. Release: $30. Current: $55. **89**

1979 HEITZ WINE CELLAR MARTHA'S VINEYARD: A rich, bold,

notes. Beautifully balanced and built to age. Drink 1994-2004. 5,469 cases produced. Release: $25. Current: $60. **93**

1978 HEITZ WINE CELLAR MARTHA'S VINEYARD: More supple and elegant than most Napa Valley 1978s, this is a rich, intense, complex wine with great harmony and finesse, displaying cedar, coffee, currant and plum flavors and fine tannins that are well integrated and softening. Drink 1994-2002. 5,000 cases produced. Release: $22. Current: $75. **91**

1977 HEITZ WINE CELLAR MARTHA'S VINEYARD: A graceful, elegant 1977 that is ready to drink, this Martha's bottling has generous ripe cherry, plum and currant flavors, a nice overlay of peppery, cedary oak and fine balance and length. It's supple and closer to maturity than many other Martha's. Drink 1991-2000. 2,800 cases produced. Release: $30. Current: $75. **90**

1976 HEITZ WINE CELLAR MARTHA'S VINEYARD: Very ripe and tannic wine from a drought year, lacking the exquisite balance of other Martha's bottlings. It is nonetheless very concentrated, full of plum and currant flavors and a good dose of tannin. Needs cellaring. Drink 1995-2004. 1,664 cases produced. Release: $30. Current: $75. **85**

1975 HEITZ WINE CELLAR MARTHA'S VINEYARD: The 1975 pales only when compared to the monumental 1974, for it is a rich, supple, elegant Martha's that is still on its way up, displaying intense, concentrated, ripe currant, cedar, chocolate and cherry flavors that are just beginning to soften. Classic Heitz with a beautiful follow-through on the finish. Drink 1993-2003. 4,895 cases produced. Release: $25. Current: $100. **92**

1974 HEITZ WINE CELLAR MARTHA'S VINEYARD: Along with the 1968, the greatest Heitz Martha's Vineyard ever produced, this is a massive wine packed with explosive cedar, currant, chocolate and spice flavors that are very complex and intense. Beautifully crafted, it can age another decade with ease and grace. Amazing concentration of fruit and finesse, combined with great harmony and deft balance. Drink 1994-2008. 4,543 cases produced. Release: $25. Current: $200. **99**

1973 HEITZ WINE CELLAR MARTHA'S VINEYARD: An impressive 1973 for its rich core of cedar, chocolate and currant flavors and smooth, supple texture. This wine is fully mature but still has a firm wall of tannins and great intensity that should carry it through the decade. Finishes with a long, elegant aftertaste. Drink 1991-2000. 2,329 cases produced. Release: $11. Current: $120. **92**

1972 HEITZ WINE CELLAR MARTHA'S VINEYARD: The weakest Martha's Vineyard ever produced, it is still a good wine from a mediocre vintage, though it is now beginning to oxidize, and the currant, cedar and chocolate flavors are beginning to fade. Drink 1990-1994. 1,445 cases produced. Release: $12.75. Current: $100. **79**

1970 HEITZ WINE CELLAR MARTHA'S VINEYARD: A stunning

dramatic Martha's and one of the best wines of the vintage, intense yet elegant and supple, with rounder, smoother tannins than most 1979s. It has a long, gorgeous aftertaste that echoes the mint, fruit and floral wine that is still young, extremely intense and concentrated, tightly wrapped in firm tannins that are just beginning to mellow, allowing the full fragrance and opulence of this dramatic wine to develop. The deep, rich cherry flavors are beautifully focused, with great strength and persistence. While it's delicious to drink now, it may still be a few years from its peak. Drink 1993-2005. 866 cases produced. Release: $12.75. Current: $275. **98**

1969 HEITZ WINE CELLAR MARTHA'S VINEYARD: Another terrific Martha's bottling, trimmer and more elegant than 1966 or 1968, but with great intensity of flavor and depth and the characteristic Martha's mintiness that complements the rich currant and cherry flavors. Great length on the finish, holding up extremely well. Heitz's current favorite. Drink 1990-1995. 1,016 cases produced. Release: $12.75. Current: $275. **93**

1968 HEITZ WINE CELLAR MARTHA'S VINEYARD: A big, deep, extremely rich and concentrated wine, one of the greatest California Cabernets ever produced. Even at 20 years of age it has great strength and intensity and is packed with complex, ripe currant, cedar and spice flavors that are fully mature, with great persistence and depth of flavor on the finish. A stunning wine. Drink 1990-1998. 749 cases produced. Release: $9.50. Current: $375. **99**

1967 HEITZ WINE CELLAR MARTHA'S VINEYARD: Holding up well for a 1967, with pronounced earth and bark aromas, a lean body and tart, bright cherry, cedar and spice flavors that are mouthwatering on the finish. The last vestige of tannin is fading on the finish. Drink 1990-1995. 2,208 cases produced. Release: $7.50. Current: $300. **86**

1966 HEITZ WINE CELLAR MARTHA'S VINEYARD: The first Martha's Vineyard is a great, seemingly timeless wine that is at the top of its class and still developing. It offers the intense Martha's character of complex currant, earth, mint and cherry flavors and a delicate touch of cedar and cinnamon on the finish. Perfectly balanced. Drink now or in the next decade. Drink 1990-1997. 392 cases produced. Release: $8. Current: $425. **92**

HEITZ WINE CELLAR, Bella Oaks Vineyard, Rutherford, Napa Valley

1985 HEITZ WINE CELLAR BELLA OAKS VINEYARD: The best Bella Oaks since 1980, the 1985 is rich, deep and concentrated, with bright, vivid black cherry, spice and mint notes, firm yet elegant, with a long, clean, crisp finish that echoes cherry and cedar. Approachable now, but wait three to five years; then it should age well for up to 15. Drink 1994-2003. 4,037 cases produced. Not Released. **92**

1984 HEITZ WINE CELLAR BELLA OAKS VINEYARD: I have tasted this wine eight times and have noticed tremendous bottle variation. At its best it tasted delicious, with ripe, supple, elegant black cherry flavors, a fine overlay of toasty oak and a sense of delicacy and finesse. On several other occasions it has tasted extremely woody, musty and earthy, barely palatable. On that basis, it's recommended with caution. Drink 1994-2002. 2,944 cases produced. Release: $25. Current: $25. **86**

1983 HEITZ WINE CELLAR BELLA OAKS VINEYARD: A toastier style, with chocolate, currant and black cherry flavors that are rich and concentrated, better balanced than most 1983s, but needs time to soften as the tannins are strong and persistent. Drink 1994-2001. 2,944 cases produced. Release: $15. Current: $25. **86**

1982 HEITZ WINE CELLAR BELLA OAKS VINEYARD: The 1982 is a subtle, closed wine built for cellaring, with its tight, rich, concentrated fruit flavors. More herbal than previous Bella Oaks bottlings, it has cedar, plum, and currant flavors that are long. Needs time to soften. Drink 1993-2000. 2,944 cases produced. Release: $16. Current: $30. **85**

1981 HEITZ WINE CELLAR BELLA OAKS VINEYARD: Very elegant and refined, typical of the vintage, displaying ripe cherry, plum and cranberry flavors and a cedary richness on the finish. Tightly wound, lean and firm, it's drinking very well now. Drink 1992-1999. 3,225 cases produced. Release: $16. Current: $38. **90**

1980 HEITZ WINE CELLAR BELLA OAKS VINEYARD: A big, rich, dramatic wine with fruit galore, packed with ripe, explosive layers of currant, black cherry and toasty oak flavors, finishing with a strong aftertaste. Needs further aging. Drink 1994-2004. 2,280 cases produced. Release: $20. Current: $45. **93**

1978 HEITZ WINE CELLAR BELLA OAKS VINEYARD: Riper and more generous than the 1977, with more flesh than structure, this is a very pretty 1978, with ripe plum, cherry and spice flavors that are opulent and fleshy. Ready now. Drink 1990-1998. 4,837 cases produced. Release: $15. Current: $40. **89**

1977 HEITZ WINE CELLAR BELLA OAKS VINEYARD: With beautiful aromas and complex flavors, the 1977 has been drinking well for several years and is fully mature now. The rich, ripe black cherry, cranberry and spicy cedar nuances are supple and elegant on the palate, finishing with grace, balance and great length. Drink 1991-1997. 4,185 cases produced. Release: $30. Current: $57. **91**

1976 HEITZ WINE CELLAR BELLA OAKS VINEYARD: The first Bella Oaks bottling is a young, lively, harmonious wine, with ripe plum and currant flavors, crisp acidity, lean concentration and a supple texture developing on the palate. At its peak and beginning to dry out. Drink 1991-1996. 895 cases produced. Release: $30. Current: $62. **85**

HESS COLLECTION WINERY

Reserve, Mount Veeder, Napa Valley
Estate, Mount Veeder, Napa Valley

CLASSIFICATION: *SECOND GROWTH*

COLLECTIBILITY RATING: **A**

BEST VINTAGES:

Reserve: 1986, 1984

Estate: 1986, 1985

With 130 acres of Cabernet, Merlot and Cabernet Franc and a dedicated winemaking staff, the Hess Collection Winery on Mount Veeder promises to be one of the bright new stars of the 1990s. Already the first four releases from Swiss entrepreneur Donald Hess's winery have been first-rate. The first release is the 1983, a lean, austere wine, followed by a richer, more concentrated 1983 Reserve. In 1984 most of the Cabernet was sold in bulk, a decision the winery regrets, and only 250 cases were produced of the amazingly rich, smooth and concentrated wine. The 1985 vintage yielded another sensational Cabernet, deep, supple and concentrated, with a toasty oak overlay. All of the 1985 was bottled under the Hess Collection label; no reserve was produced. Both of the 1986s are excellent, showing the Hess style of richness, concentration, power and finesse. While these wines promise to age well for 10 to 15 years, they are not made in the style of neighboring Mayacamas or Mount Veeder wines, which are typically more austere and tannic and less showy early on in their lives.

Production is projected to climb to 25,000 cases in the next decade. Currently Hess, owner of the Valser mineral water company of Switzerland, is only using a small portion of his Cabernet grapes for the Hess Collection wines, of which nearly 12,000 cases of regular and reserve were produced in 1986. Nearly a dozen Napa Valley wineries, including Duckhorn, Beaulieu and St. Clement, buy grapes from Hess's vineyards, but as the winery expands fewer wineries will be able to rely on this superb fruit.

AT A GLANCE

HESS COLLECTION WINERY
P.O. Box 4140
Napa, CA 94558
(707) 255-1144

Owner: Donald Hess

Winemaker: Randle Johnson (7 years)

Founded: 1983

First Cabernet vintage: 1983

Cabernet production: 12,000 cases
  Reserve: 2,000
  Estate: 10,000

Cabernet acres owned: 130

Average age of vines: 10 years

Vineyard makeup: Cabernet Sauvignon (65%), Merlot (23%), Cabernet Franc (12%)

Average wine makeup:
  Reserve: Cabernet Sauvignon (100%)
  Estate: Cabernet Sauvignon (65%), Merlot (23%), Cabernet Franc (12%)

Time in oak: 22 months

Type of oak: French (Tronçais, Allier, Vosges)

TASTING NOTES

HESS COLLECTION WINERY, **Various bottlings**

1986 HESS COLLECTION WINERY RESERVE: The 1986 Reserve should rival the 1985 with time, for it is amazingly rich, supple, deep

THE HESS
COLLECTION
NAPA VALLEY CABERNET SAUVIGNON
1985
PRODUCED & BOTTLED BY THE HESS COLLECTION WINERY
RUTHERFORD, CALIFORNIA USA
ALCOHOL 12.5% BY VOLUME

and concentrated, with tiers of black cherry, currant and toasty French oak. Has the structure and definition for years of cellaring. Approachable in five years. Drink 1995-2003. 2,000 cases produced. Not Released. **93**

1986 HESS COLLECTION WINERY ESTATE: The 1986 is another highly successful vintage for Hess, with the regular bottling offering rich, smooth, elegant fruit, with layers of well-defined black cherry, currant and toasty oak flavors that are beautifully integrated. Drink 1994-2000. 10,000 cases produced. Release: $14. Current: $14. **91**

1985 HESS COLLECTION WINERY ESTATE: The 1985 has evolved into a sensational bottle of wine that is lavishly oaked, rich, smooth, supple and concentrated, with great depth and intensity of delicious black cherry, cedar, vanilla and anise flavors that are long and full. Clearly one of the top wines of this great vintage. Drink 1994-2002. 5,000 cases produced. Release: $13. Current: $13. **96**

1984 HESS COLLECTION WINERY RESERVE: All 250 cases of the 1984 Hess Collection were bottled under the Reserve designation. It is an amazingly rich and concentrated wine with beautifully focused black cherry, currant and anise flavors that are smooth and supple. The tannins are fine and soft but thick enough to carry this one through the decade. Because of its opulence, it's delicious to drink already. Rare, because most of the wine was sold off in bulk. Drink 1992-2000. 250 cases produced. Release: $22. Current: $30. **93**

1983 HESS COLLECTION WINERY RESERVE: Considerably richer and more concentrated than the regular bottling, it is nonetheless lean and austere, with better structure and sharply defined black cherry and currant flavors. Drink 1990-1997. 250 cases produced. Release: $22. Current: $30. **88**

1983 HESS COLLECTION WINERY ESTATE: A lean, austere wine typical of the vintage, offering ripe cherry, currant and cedar flavors of moderate depth and intensity. Well made and evenly balanced, ready to drink soon. Drink 1990-1995. 900 cases produced. Release: $13. Current: $18. **84**

WILLIAM HILL WINERY

Gold Label Reserve, Napa Valley

CLASSIFICATION: *SECOND GROWTH*

COLLECTIBILITY RATING: *AA*

BEST VINTAGES: *1986, 1985, 1984, 1982, 1979, 1978*

Wwilliam Hill is a true believer in mountain-grown Cabernet for its rich, intense, deeply concentrated fruit and great aging potential. With the 1978 vintage, Hill, a native of Oklahoma who began his career in Napa wine developing vineyards, introduced his first Cabernet from Mount Veeder vineyards, an explosive wine that combines incredible richness, intensity, complexity and depth. It is just now beginning to reach full maturity and is one of the finest wines from the great 1978 vintage, capable of developing for another decade.

Each of the subsequent vintages has been equally impressive in the rich, intense, concentrated Hill style, making this winery one of the most promising producers to emerge from the 1970s. The 1979 vintage has developed into a wine of remarkable finesse and elegance, with wonderful aromas. The 1980 is more forward and is already beginning to drink quite well. The 1981 is still developing and drinking well, while the 1982 is distinctive for its firm concentration and tart fruit. The 1983 is typical of the vintage, hard, lean, firm and tannic, while the 1984 has outstanding potential yet is still tight and closed. The 1985 is another exceptional vintage for Hill, while the 1986 has the potential to be the finest yet, perhaps with time even exceeding the phenomenal 1978.

The 1978 through 1983 vintages were 100 percent Cabernet exclusively from Mount Veeder. Beginning with the 1984 vintage, a portion of the fruit has come from Hill's vineyard a few miles north of Napa along the Silverado Trail near the Silverado Country Club, a cool area that suits Hill's preference for Cabernet. The winery owns 70 acres of Cabernet and bottles its best wine under the Gold Label Reserve designation. A second Silver Label Cabernet is also very good and ageworthy but not up to the quality of the Gold Label. Prices and production have steadily risen; 13,595 cases of the 1986 were produced, selling for $24.50 a bottle.

AT A GLANCE

WILLIAM HILL WINERY
P.O. Box 3989
Napa, CA 94558
(707) 224-6565

Owner: William Hill, general partner

Winemaker: William Hill (13 years)

Founded: 1976

First Cabernet vintage: 1976

Cabernet production: 22,000 cases
Gold Label Reserve: 13,000 cases

Cabernet acres owned: 70

Average age of vines: 13 years

Vineyard makeup: Cabernet Sauvignon (100%)

Average wine makeup: Cabernet Sauvignon (100%)

Time in oak: 20 months

Type of oak: French, American

TASTING NOTES

WILLIAM HILL WINERY, Gold Label Reserve, Napa Valley

1986 WILLIAM HILL WINERY GOLD LABEL RESERVE: Hill's best since 1978, the 1986 is a big, bold, rich and dramatic wine with great intensity and concentration of fruit, packed with black cherry and peppery currant flavors and framed with spicy oak. It's structured for midterm to long-term aging, but the tannins are refined and in perfect balance. Drink 1996-2006. 13,595 cases produced. Release: $24.50. Current: $24.50. **95**

1985 WILLIAM HILL WINERY GOLD LABEL RESERVE: An exceptional 1985 that ranks among Hill's best, this is a very rich, intense and concentrated wine that will need a decade to mature fully. It's packed with ripe black cherry and spicy currant flavors with hints of toasty oak. Tannins are integrated and should guarantee a long life. Drink 1995-2005. 10,204 cases produced. Release: $22.50. Current: $22.50. **94**

1984 WILLIAM HILL WINERY GOLD LABEL RESERVE: Very tight and concentrated for a 1984, packed with ripe black currant and cherry flavors that are just beginning to peek through. This wine needs time to develop but shows plenty of potential. Drink 1994-2002. 7,752 cases produced. Release: $18.25. Current: $26. **91**

1983 WILLIAM HILL WINERY GOLD LABEL: Typical 1983, tight, lean, hard and tannic, but better balanced than most. Hard to predict how it will evolve, but with time it could develop into an elegant wine. Could use a shade more concentration. Drink 1994-1999. 8,405 cases produced. Release: $18.25. Current: $25. **85**

1982 WILLIAM HILL WINERY GOLD LABEL: One of the finer 1982s, very tight and concentrated, with firm tannins. It's packed with black cherry, currant and spicy cedar flavors that are tart and hard on the finish. Everything's in place for greatness, but this wine needs time. Drink 1994-2002. 11,907 cases produced. Release: $18. Current: $32. **90**

1981 WILLIAM HILL WINERY GOLD LABEL: A very pretty wine with ripe black cherry and currant flavors, but it lacks the complexity, concentration and finesse of the other Hill wines. Still, there's plenty to like, and with time it may gain more character. Drink 1990-1995. 5,772 cases produced. Release: $16.25. Current: $34. **85**

1980 WILLIAM HILL WINERY GOLD LABEL: Plenty of ripe black cherry and currant flavors with herb and spicy cedar notes, an elegant wine from a ripe vintage that is beginning to drink well. There's still a trace of tannin on the finish, but it's ready. Drink 1990-1996. 4,961 cases produced. Release: $18.25. Current: $36. **87**

1979 WILLIAM HILL WINERY GOLD LABEL: This is a remarkably elegant and seductive 1979, with suppleness, finesse and complexity, classic cedar and cigar box aromas and ripe, rich black cherry, currant and spice notes. The texture is satiny smooth. Great now but it has the structure and concentration for another decade, maybe longer. Drink 1990-2000. 4,412 cases produced. Release: $18. Current: $45. **93**

1978 WILLIAM HILL WINERY GOLD LABEL: William Hill's first major commercial release, this is an amazingly rich and concentrated wine that is packed with ripe black cherry and currant flavors, framed by toasty oak and mineral nuances. Continues to gain complexity and depth with every year. It's nearing its peak now and needs about an hour's aeration before drinking. Drink 1991-1997. 4,451 cases produced. Release: $16.25. Current: $60. **95**

INGLENOOK-NAPA VALLEY

Reserve Cask, Rutherford, Napa Valley
Reunion, Napa Valley

CLASSIFICATION:
Reserve Cask: FIRST GROWTH
Reunion: SECOND GROWTH

COLLECTIBILITY RATING:
Reserve Cask: AA
Reunion: AA

BEST VINTAGES:
Reserve Cask: 1986, 1985, 1984, 1982, 1981, 1958, 1955

Reunion: 1986, 1985, 1984, 1983

Napa Valley: 1946, 1941, 1933, 1897

AT A GLANCE

INGLENOOK-NAPA VALLEY
P.O. Box 402
Rutherford, CA 94573
(707) 967-3300

Owner: Heublein Inc./Grand
Metropolitan, England

Winemaker: John Richburg (10 years)

Founded: 1879, reestablished: 1933

First Cabernet vintage: Late 1880s
Reserve Cask: 1949
Reunion: 1983

Cabernet production: 50,000 cases
Reserve Cask: 8,000 cases
Reunion: 3,500 cases

Cabernet acres owned: 69

Average age of vines: 10 years

Vineyard makeup: Cabernet Sauvignon (55%), Merlot (45%)

Average wine makeup:
Reserve Cask: Cabernet Sauvignon (91%), Merlot (9%)
Reunion: Cabernet Sauvignon (93%), Cabernet Franc (4%), Merlot (3%)

Time in oak: 20 months

Type of oak: French, American

After a slump in quality in the late 1960s and early 1970s, Inglenook-Napa Valley has clearly reestablished itself as a producer of deeply concentrated, beautifully proportioned, ageworthy Cabernets. Now with two fine bottlings, the Inglenook Cask Reserve and Reunion, a proprietary blend, Inglenook-Napa Valley once again ranks in the upper echelon of Napa Valley Cabernet houses.

Founded in 1879 by Finnish fur trader Gustave Niebaum, Inglenook first rose to prominence in the late 1800s and early 1900s. After searching for suitable vineyard land, Niebaum settled in Rutherford, where he built a handsome stone winery that still stands on the Inglenook property. An ambitious, energetic man, Niebaum imported large oak casks from Germany to age his red wines, and they won numerous medals at international wine competitions. Niebaum's goal was to produce great wines at any cost. The oldest California Cabernet I've tried, an Inglenook 1897 Claret Médoc-Type made by Niebaum, remains in fine condition for its age, ample evidence that California Cabernets do age exceptionally well. The smoky anise, cedar, tar and tea aromas add complexity to the fading prune and plum flavors. Niebaum died in 1908, 12 years before Prohibition closed the winery.

Inglenook reopened in 1933 under the direction of Carl Bundschu, a partner in Bacchus Wines of Sonoma. Amazingly, in the first vintage after repeal, Inglenook produced a stunning 1933 with a deep, dark color, and rich, complex, concentrated fruit that has aged gloriously. In 1939 John Daniel Jr., Niebaum's grandnephew, took over, marking the beginning of an era that would extend to 1964 when he sold Inglenook to Allied Grape Growers, which later became a part of United Vintners and later Heublein.

Under Daniel and winemaker George Deuer, Inglenook's Cabernets rivaled and in many instances surpassed those produced across the highway at Beaulieu and Louis M. Martini. By many accounts, Daniel maintained exceptionally high quality-control standards, with severe evaluations of the wines. His motto was "Pride, not Profits." Daniel's greatest achievement may well be the succession of fabulous wines from the 1940s, most notably the extraordinary 1941 Cabernet, which manages to combine magnificently powerful, ripe, complex fruit with a sense of elegance and finesse that promises to age another 15 to 20 years. When the Cabernets failed to meet his standards they were sold off in bulk, as in the 1945 and 1947 vintages. Daniel was the only vintner in Napa Valley who would "declassify" a vintage, according to André Tchelistcheff. Inglenook had carved out a style of its own, using the old casks for aging the Cabernets. Daniel refused to use small oak, the way Tchelistcheff did at BV, but he was not afraid to blend in other grapes, such as Zinfandel, to add color or body to a wine. The old Inglenook Cabernets were riper, fruitier and less oaky than the BVs, often more alcoholic, exceeding 14 percent at times, but exceptionally durable.

In 1946 Daniel purchased Napanook, due west of Yountville, and began incorporating grapes from that vineyard in the 1949 vintage, the first vintage to bear the "Cask" designation. In the late 1940s, the three key vineyards — Napanook, the Inglenook Home Vineyard in front of the winery and the old Niebaum estate (now owned by filmmaker Francis Coppola and called Niebaum-Coppola) adjacent to the Home Vineyard — combined to make the great Cask bottlings. The marvelous vintages of 1940s extended into the 1950s. Although somewhat less dense and dramatic, the 1955 and 1958 vintages are superlative.

The excellence of the Cabernets in the three decades from the 1930s to the 1950s may be attributable to the full maturity of the vines planted in the early 1930s, but in the 1960s things began to unravel at Inglenook and there was a noticeable period of decline. Although some of the Cabernets drank well early on, none have aged as wonderfully as their predecessors, and by 1967, United Vintners sold the Niebaum property; in 1970 Daniel died and left Napanook to his heirs who are now partners in Dominus, and Inglenook was left with only the Home Vineyard, roughly 72 acres and only partially planted to Cabernet. In the late 1960s and 1970s, under the Heublein corporate umbrella, which also included Beaulieu, Inglenook began to expand, increasing production of its Napa Valley wines and introducing an Inglenook Navalle line of low-priced jug wines and a line of vintage-dated varietals. By the mid-1980s the winery in Rutherford had attached "Napa Valley" to its name to avoid confusion.

In years like 1968, 1970, and 1974, when some Napa Valley wineries produced rich, deeply concentrated, monumental wines, Ingle-

nook's were light and simple, maturing fast and fading after a decade. My notes reflect a turnaround in 1977, when Inglenook produced an attractive bottling, followed by a fine 1978. The 1979 Centennial drank well for its first five to seven years but is now fading. The 1980 Cask, under the winemaking direction of current winemaker John Richburg, marks an even more vivid improvement over previous efforts. In 1983 the Reunion bottling, bringing back the three classic vineyards, fully demonstrates the dedication and direction of Inglenook-Napa Valley.

Because of the decline in quality from the 1960s to the late 1970s, Inglenook lost most of its prestige. There are still many skeptics who remain unconvinced, but that number is rapidly dwindling. Both the Cask Reserve and Reunion have been nothing short of excellent recently as Inglenook attempts to recapture its glorious past.

TASTING NOTES

INGLENOOK-NAPA VALLEY, Reserve Cask, Rutherford, Napa Valley

1986 INGLENOOK-NAPA VALLEY RESERVE CASK: The 1986 is a rich, concentrated wine with smoky cedar, currant and black cherry flavors that are tightly focused, firmly tannic and well structured for aging. Classic claret style, complex and understated. Drink 1996-2004. 6,000 cases produced. Not Released. **92**

1985 INGLENOOK-NAPA VALLEY RESERVE CASK: Beautifully balanced, with layers of rich, elegant, concentrated plum, cherry, currant and spice flavors supported by firm, lean yet structured tannins. Promises to be a long-lived Cabernet in the finest Cask tradition. Fruit echoes on the finish. Impeccable balance. Drink 1994-2002. 10,388 cases produced. Not Released. **95**

1984 INGLENOOK-NAPA VALLEY RESERVE CASK: Possesses the finest traits of the vintage, with fresh, ripe, supple fruit and firm tannins that promise long aging potential. This wine is oozing with complex black cherry, currant, plum and spice flavors. Despite its fleshy, forward flavors, this wine has the depth and intensity for midterm aging. Tempting now, but should hold a decade or more. Drink 1992-2002. 5,237 cases produced. Not Released. **92**

1983 INGLENOOK-NAPA VALLEY RESERVE CASK: Firm, lean and compact, will benefit from cellaring. Right now it's very tight and hard, with hints of black cherry and currant flavors beginning to emerge. Needs another three to five years for the tannins to soften. Drink 1994-2000. 11,188 cases produced. Release: $15.50. Current: $19. **89**

1982 INGLENOOK-NAPA VALLEY RESERVE CASK: A tight, austere 1982 that is quite tannic and will require another decade before reaching its peak. It is very rich and concentrated, with black currant, plum and mint flavors buried underneath the firm tannins. The flavors are complex and the wine is perfectly balanced. With time it should be sensational; one of the best 1982s. Drink 1994-2001. 4,631 cases produced. Release: $22. Current: $28. **91**

1981 INGLENOOK-NAPA VALLEY RESERVE CASK: Developing very well, with rich, ripe, supple, generous cassis and black cherry flavors, just the right amount of tannin and a long, complex aftertaste that is persistent. Alluring now but will age another decade. Drink 1992-2000. 12,115 cases produced. Release: $15.50. Current: $20. **93**

1980 INGLENOOK-NAPA VALLEY RESERVE CASK: The 1980 Reserve Cask marks Inglenook's comeback. It is a rich, concentrated yet supple wine with ripe currant, black cherry and spicy oak flavors that are supple and fruity on the finish. At its peak and capable of holding. Drink 1991-1996. 9,305 cases produced. Release: $15.50. Current: $22. **88**

1979 INGLENOOK CASK: Fully mature, with light cedar notes, the 1979 is on its descent, a simple, pleasant wine that falls short of the best wines from this vintage. Drink 1990. 2,672 cases produced. Release: $10.75. Current: $23. **77**

1978 INGLENOOK CASK: This wine has been drinking exceptionally well for several years and is at its peak now, with generous ripe plum and anise flavors that have shed most of their tannins. Ripe and fruity on the finish. Drink 1990-1994. 11,969 cases produced. Release: $9.25. Current: $26. **86**

1977 INGLENOOK CASK: The first bottle to throw sediment in nearly a decade. A very pleasing and elegant 1977 with layers of plum and spice flavors that are perfect for drinking now. The first in a long while for Inglenook that breaks out of mediocrity. Drink 1990-1994. 6,291 cases produced. Release: $8.75. Current: $23. **84**

1976 INGLENOOK CASK: Earthy, vegetal and pungent, the fruit is gone in this wine, leaving mature wine flavors that are not very attractive. Better seven years ago, but still drinkable. Drink 1990. 4,147 cases produced. Release: $8.75. Current: $19. **72**

1974 INGLENOOK CASK: Fully mature, elegant and balanced, with supple, smooth, delicate cedar, anise, black cherry and plum flavors, finishing with good length. Complex, ready to drink. Drink 1990-1995. 11,864 cases produced. Release: $9. Current: $45. **86**

1973 INGLENOOK CASK: Dense and vegetal, an uninspired 1973 lacking depth or character. Appears stripped and fined to death. A restaurant wine before its time? 6,494 cases produced. Release: $8. Current: $39. **67**

1972 INGLENOOK CASK: Like most from this rain-plagued year, this 1972 is thin, watery and vegetal, best consumed in the 1970s. Best to avoid. 7,278 cases produced. Release: $7. Current: $44. **67**

1971 INGLENOOK CASK: Past its prime and fading, this was a pleasant wine eight to 10 years ago, but it has lost most of its fruit. It's

drinkable, with light anise notes, but only as a curiosity. Drink 1990-1991. 2,978 cases produced. Release: $6.50. Current: $50. **73**

1970 INGLENOOK CASK: Mature, elegant and supple, but simple by comparison to the old Inglenooks, still enjoyable for its black cherry, currant and anise flavors. Drink it soon while the flavors are still vibrant. Drink 1990-1995. 8,109 cases produced. Release: $6.50. Current: $75. **85**

1969 INGLENOOK CASK: A very successful 1969, despite the previous three vintages, this wine fully developed 10 years ago but has held its depth and fruit despite a mild decline. Drink 1990-1992. 12,508 cases produced. Release: $6.50. Current: $80. **80**

1968 INGLENOOK CASK: Fully developed and beginning to decline, but there are still pretty floral, plum and spicy cherry flavors that are delicate and elegant, finishing with good length and a touch of Rutherford dust. Drink 1990-1995. 5,218 cases produced. Release: $6. Current: $90. **85**

1967 INGLENOOK CASK: Light and simple, fully mature with spicy anise notes that fade on the palate. Now only a shadow of its former self. Drink 1990. 4,194 cases produced. Release: $6. Current: $60. **73**

1966 INGLENOOK CASK: Its best years are behind it now, but this was once a deliciously elegant wine with complex flavors. Now it is very mature and delicate, enjoyable but only a faded memory of its peak. Drink 1990. 3,190 cases produced. Release: $5.75. Current: $95. **73**

1960 INGLENOOK CASK: The fruit is beginning to fade, and it has been better in earlier years. The fruit is lean and elegant, with faded tannins. Drink 1990. Estimated 2,000 cases produced. Release: $2.75. Current: $140. **80**

1958 INGLENOOK CASK: Ripe and forward, fully mature, a delicious wine from a great vintage, with mint, cherry and spice flavors, plenty of depth and finesse and a long, persistent finish. Young for its age, perhaps the last of the great Daniel Cabernets. Drink 1990. Estimated 2,000 cases produced. Release: $2.50. Current: $300. **94**

1955 INGLENOOK CASK: Great balance and depth from a fine vintage, ripe and mature, with rich cedar, herb, olive and plum flavors that are intense and lively and a long, full finish. Drinking exceptionally well and appears to have the depth and flavors for another decade. Drink 1990. Estimated 2,000 cases produced. Release: $1.85. Current: $375. **93**

1949 INGLENOOK CASK: A wonderful bouquet of dried fruit and flowers, the 1949 wraps up the fabulous 1940s for Inglenook, with smooth, rich, supple, fully mature fruit that tastes like liquid anise, supplemented with plum, currant, smoke and cherry flavors. The aftertaste of spice and mint goes on and on. Drink 1990-1993. Estimated 2,000 cases produced. Release: $1.49. Current: $750. **92**

1946 INGLENOOK NAPA VALLEY: Another extremely ripe, big, chewy, chunky Cabernet that is fully developed, with wonderful black cherry, anise, cedar and plum flavors that are complex and redolent on the palate. Beautifully scented dried fruit flavors echo on the finish, along with some volatile acidity. Drink 1990-1995. Estimated 7,000 cases produced. Release: $1.49. Current: $1,100. **87**

1943 INGLENOOK NAPA VALLEY: Earthy, with a slight mustiness that cleans up, the 1943 is another of the terrific vintages of the 1940s for Inglenook. The tart plum, anise and black cherry flavors are fully mature and have been for a decade, yet they still ring true. It's tight, lean and elegant, but what a wonderful wine. Drinking exceptionally well. Drink 1990-1995. Estimated 6,000 cases produced. Release: $1.49. Current: $1,000. **91**

1941 INGLENOOK NAPA VALLEY: Absolutely sensational and undoubtedly one of the greatest California Cabernets ever produced, the 1941 is the kind of wine that comes around once, maybe twice, in a lifetime. This wine is amazing for its youthful vitality, incredible depth and complexity of flavor and staying power. Few wines in the world ever achieve this height of intensity, and it appears to have the stamina to last another 20 to 30 years. From an extremely ripe vintage, the raisin, plum, currant, herb and tea flavors are very concentrated and sharply defined, yet integrated and harmonious, with a long, full aftertaste. What's more, it's shown consistently well in several tastings. Who says California wines don't age? Drink 1990-2005. Estimated 5,000 cases produced. Release: $1.49. Current: $1,400. **100**

1933 INGLENOOK NAPA VALLEY: In fantastic condition, with a healthy deep-red garnet color, wonderful spice, mint, rose petal and mature plum aromas, complex, with rich, elegant, faded plum, rose petal and spice flavors that turn to chocolate, cedar and coffee with aeration. Drinking incredibly well. Drink 1990. Estimated 5,000 cases produced. Release: $1.30. Current: $1,600. **95**

1897 INGLENOOK CLARET-MEDOC TYPE: One of the oldest California Cabernets in existence, this treasure is still hanging on, providing a wealth of information and insight into how California Cabernets age. A blend of Cabernet with a dollop of Zinfandel, it reflects the Bordeaux heritage in its name and still offers smoke, anise, orange and tea notes to complement the fading black cherry and ripe plum flavors. Very light in color, it gained in the glass for more than an hour. Short of perfection, yet brilliant in its own way. Drink 1990-1995. Estimated 2,000 cases produced. **87**

INGLENOOK-NAPA VALLEY, Reunion, Rutherford, Napa Valley

1986 INGLENOOK-NAPA VALLEY REUNION: A shade richer and more tannic than the Reserve Cask bottling, with complex cedar, black cherry, currant and anise flavors. Very tight and backward now but

with excellent aging potential. Needs time to soften. Drink 1996-2006. 4,251 cases produced. Not Released. **92**

1985 INGLENOOK-NAPA VALLEY REUNION: Despite the initial austerity of the 1985, this is the finest Reunion to date. It is concentrated, with spicy black cherry, currant and cedary oak flavors and fine tannins. Beautifully defined Cabernet, with richness, complexity, elegance and finesse. Drink 1993-2000. 3,602 cases produced. Release: $35. Current: $35. **94**

1984 INGLENOOK-NAPA VALLEY REUNION: A magnificent 1984, elegant, concentrated and complex, with layers of bright black cherry, currant, anise and spice flavors that are intense and delicate, firm, fine tannins and a long, full finish that echoes on and on. Graceful and refined now but with the intensity and depth for mid-range aging. Drink 1993-2000. 2,932 cases produced. Release: $35. Current: $35. **92**

1983 INGLENOOK-NAPA VALLEY REUNION: The first Reunion bottling is one of the standouts of the vintage. It's very rich, concentrated and tannic, but underneath that veneer is sharply defined fruit that is firm and muscular. This wine is evolving slowly. Drink 1993-2001. 1,991 cases produced. Release: $33. Current: $40. **93**

IRON HORSE VINEYARDS

Cabernets, Alexander Valley

CLASSIFICATION: *FIFTH GROWTH*

COLLECTIBILITY RATING: *Not rated*

BEST VINTAGES:

Cabernets: 1986, 1985

Alexander Valley: 1979

Iron Horse's second Cabernet vintage, 1979, produced a wonderfully rich, supple, concentrated wine that was loaded with fruit and complexities. In the early 1980s the winery's style shifted toward more elegant, restaurant-style wines that, while quite pleasing, elegant and drinkable, lacked the character of the magnificent 1979. Both the 1985 and 1986 "Cabernets," a brand name for a blend of Cabernet Sauvignon and Cabernet Franc, show a shade more richness and vitality, which is encouraging. In general the Iron Horse Cabernets are best on release when the fruit is lively and fresh. The 1979 is worth seeking out.

The winery is owned by Barry and Audrey Sterling, and the Tancer family, who managed the vineyards prior to becoming partners in Iron Horse.

TASTING NOTES

IRON HORSE VINEYARDS, Alexander Valley

1986 IRON HORSE VINEYARDS CABERNETS: Appears to be the finest Cabernet since the exceptional 1979 bottling, offering richness, extract and concentration. With rich, ripe, complex plum, floral, cedar and spice flavors, this is a delicious wine now but should age well throughout the 1990s. Drink 1993-2000. 3,500 cases produced. Release: $17.50. Current: $17.50. **88**

1985 IRON HORSE VINEYARDS CABERNETS: Delicate, complex and beautifully balanced, with ripe black cherry, currant, cedar and spice flavors that are moderately rich, supple tannins and a pretty floral aftertaste. Approachable now because of the fine tannins and attractive fruit. Drink 1992-1999. 3,000 cases produced. Release: $16. Current: $16.50. **87**

AT A GLANCE

IRON HORSE VINEYARDS
9786 Ross Station Road
Sebastopol, CA 95472
(707) 887-1507

Owners: The Sterling and Tancer families

Winemaker: Forrest Tancer (11 years)

Founded: 1978

First Cabernet vintage: 1978
Cabernets: 1985

Cabernet production: 3,000 cases

Cabernet acres owned: 22

Average age of vines: 14 years

Vineyard makeup: Cabernet Sauvignon (73%), Cabernet Franc (27%)

Average wine makeup:
Cabernets: Cabernet Sauvignon (70%), Cabernet Franc (30%)

Time in oak: 14 months

Type of oak: French (Nevers, Allier)

1984 IRON HORSE VINEYARDS: A very good 1984 but not nearly as rich and opulent as the top Cabernets from this vintage, offering ripe plum, currant, black cherry and cedary anise flavors in a moderately rich, well-balanced, easy-to-drink style. Ready soon. Drink 1992-1998. 1,900 cases produced. Release: $14. Current: $16. **86**

1983 IRON HORSE VINEYARDS: One of the more agreeable 1983s, a very good wine that exhibits spicy cherry, currant and cedary oak flavors that, while not especially rich or concentrated, are well focused and elegant. Needs three to five years for tannins to soften. Drink 1992-1997. 2,000 cases produced. Release: $12. Current: $15.50. **82**

1982 IRON HORSE VINEYARDS: A fairly typical 1982 that is well balanced, with ripe black cherry, herb and currant flavors that are tight and closed now, finishing with firm tannins. Needs time to soften. Drink 1994-1999. 2,500 cases produced. Release: $12. Current: $18. **83**

1981 IRON HORSE VINEYARDS: Lean, tart and hard, with a green, unripe quality, a curious wine that has become more awkward since release. There are ripe plum and cedar flavors that give it complexity, but it's difficult to predict whether this wine will grow out of its unripe flavor. Better to give it some time. Drink 1992-1998. 1,700 cases produced. Release: $12. Current: $15.50. **79**

1980 IRON HORSE VINEYARDS: Very young, ripe and generous, offering straightforward black cherry and currant flavors that are mildly tannic, finishing with elegance and delicacy. It's mature now but can age another five to seven years. Drink 1992-1998. 1,000 cases produced. Release: $12. Current: $20. **86**

1979 IRON HORSE VINEYARDS: A young, lively Cabernet with rich, supple, delicate cherry, raspberry and chocolate flavors, firm structure, gentle intensity and understated elegance. Plenty of vitality in this wine. It's ready now but should last throughout the 1990s. Gaining every step of the way. Drink 1992-1998. 1,000 cases produced. Release: $12. Current: $25. **91**

1978 IRON HORSE VINEYARDS: At its peak, with mature herb, cedar, plum and spice flavors that offer a modest amount of complexity and delicacy. Drink 1990-1994. 1,250 cases produced. Release: $12. Current: $25. **80**

JOHNSON TURNBULL VINEYARDS

Vineyard Selection 67, Oakville, Napa Valley
Estate, Oakville, Napa Valley

CLASSIFICATION: *FOURTH GROWTH*

COLLECTIBILITY RATING: *Not rated*

BEST VINTAGES:

Vineyard Selection 67: 1986

Vineyard Selection 82: 1986

Estate: 1984, 1983

Johnson Turnbull owns 20 acres of Cabernet and Cabernet Franc in Oakville. Until the 1986 vintage, the Johnson Turnbull Cabernets featured a distinct minty, spicy, bay leaf flavor that added complexity to the wines. Vintages from 1979 to 1985 all display that herbal quality, along with ample plum and currant notes.

With the 1986 vintage, Johnson Turnbull has released two Cabernets, one identified as Vineyard Selection 67, which possesses the characteristic minty aroma, while the other, Vineyard Selection 82, features more berry and currant flavors.

Minty and herbal qualities in Cabernet are not pleasing to everyone. At times the mint and bay leaf flavors become so pronounced that the wine smells more like oregano. I prefer the spice notes in modest proportions, more as seasoning than as the dominant flavor, so Vineyard Selection 82 is more to my liking, with its sharply focused, effusively fruity style and seductive character. The owners of Johnson Turnbull apparently believe otherwise, for the Vineyard Selection 67 is $20, compared to $14.50 for the Selection 82. The Selection 67 is dense and thick, with bay leaf and currant flavors, probably a dream wine for those who prefer that style.

Through eight vintages, the 1983 and 1984 vintages have shown the best. The 1983 succeeds by not being too tannic in a tannic vintage. The 1984 is supple and complex. The 1979, the first vintage, is near maturity, lean and elegant, while the 1980 is spicy, with oregano and herb notes. The 1981 is the best balanced of the first three vintages but is fairly tannic and needs more time. The 1982 is tight and lean. The 1985 is much harder and more austere than most Cabernets from this vintage. In several tastings it has not shown the richness or depth of the top wines.

AT A GLANCE

JOHNSON TURNBULL VINEYARDS
P.O. Box 410
Oakville, CA 94562
(707) 963-5839

Owners: The Johnson and Turnbull families

Founded: 1979

Winemaker: Kirstin Belair (4 years)

First Cabernet vintage: 1979

Cabernet production: 3,200 cases
Vineyard Selection 67: 1,200 cases
Estate: 2,000 cases

Cabernet acres owned: 20

Average age of vines: 10 years

Vineyard makeup: Cabernet Sauvignon (92%), Cabernet Franc (8%)

Average wine makeup:
Vineyard Selection 67: Cabernet Sauvignon (100%)
Estate: Cabernet Sauvignon (91%), Cabernet Franc (9%)

Time in oak: 21 months

Type of oak: French, American

1986

JOHNSON
TURNBULL

Cabernet
Sauvignon

Napa Valley
Vineyard Selection 67

Estate bottled by
Johnson Turnbull Vineyards
Oakville, California
ALCOHOL 13.2% BY VOLUME
CONTAINS SULFITES

TASTING NOTES

JOHNSON TURNBULL VINEYARDS, Various bottlings

1986 JOHNSON TURNBULL VINEYARDS VINEYARD SELECTION 67: A denser, thicker bottling than the Vineyard Selection 82, this wine has the herb, bay leaf and spice notes that characterized earlier Johnson Turnbull vintages. It is less opulent and fruity but still well balanced. Drink 1995-2005. 1,280 cases produced. Release: $20. Current: $20. **87**

1986 JOHNSON TURNBULL VINEYARDS VINEYARD SELECTION 82: One of the stars of the 1986 vintage, this is an effusively fruity, rich and seductive wine that is elegant and refined, with spicy berry, cherry and currant flavors, fine, supple tannins and a pretty aftertaste that lingers. Tasty now but can age a decade. By far the most dramatic and impressive Johnson Turnbull bottling. Drink 1992-2000. 1,540 cases produced. Release: $14.50. Current: $14.50. **95**

1985 JOHNSON TURNBULL VINEYARDS ESTATE: Harder and more austere than most 1985s, this is a tight, closed wine that is firmly structured and not showing much richness or depth at this point. It has the Johnson Turnbull spiciness and has shed some of its earlier woodiness, but it does not offer the charm of earlier wines. It may simply require patience. Drink 1994-2000. 2,350 cases produced. Release: $14.50. Current: $17.50. **83**

1984 JOHNSON TURNBULL VINEYARDS ESTATE: Supple and generous, the friendliest Johnson Turnbull for current drinking, the 1984 has an added dimension of complexity, with a rich, fleshy, opulent texture and spicy herb flavors. There is also a generous dose of plum, currant and cherry flavors that echo on the finish. Approachable now but can age. Drink 1993-1999. 1,825 cases produced. Release: $14.50. Current: $18. **90**

1983 JOHNSON TURNBULL VINEYARDS ESTATE: Lean and delicate for a 1983 and not overpowered by tannins, this is a well-focused, spicy, currant-flavored wine that offers subtlety and finesse in a very distinguished style. Needs time to soften. Drink 1993-1998. 1,300 cases produced. Release: $12.50. Current: $18. **88**

1982 JOHNSON TURNBULL VINEYARDS ESTATE: A very subdued Johnson Turnbull that is a good wine but lacks the opulence, richness and complexity of other vintages. The flavors are reined in, making it simple and unexciting. Needs time to shed tannins; maybe then it will show more fruit. Drink 1994-1998. 2,275 cases produced. Release: $12.50. Current: $18. **82**

1981 JOHNSON TURNBULL VINEYARDS ESTATE: The best balanced and most structured of the early Johnson Turnbull wines, with ample currant and plum flavors to complement the toned-down spiciness that dominates the 1979 and 1980 vintages. Too firm and tannic to drink now; needs another five years. Drink 1995-2000. 1,250 cases produced. Release: $12. Current: $20. **87**

1980 JOHNSON TURNBULL VINEYARDS ESTATE: Spicy, rich and full-bodied, a shade deeper than the 1979 but with similar mint, oregano and complex herb flavors, this wine is typical of the 1980 vintage with its suppleness and opulence. Has the tannin for another decade. Drink 1994-2000. 1,100 cases produced. Release: $12. Current: $26. **87**

1979 JOHNSON TURNBULL VINEYARDS ESTATE: Minty, tart, lean and elegant, with spicy bay leaf, herb and cassis flavors that linger on the palate, finishing with fine yet firm tannins. Nearing its peak, it can age another five to seven years. Drink 1993-1998. 450 cases produced. Release: $10.50. Current: $26. **85**

1986

JOHNSON
TURNBULL

Cabernet
Sauvignon

Napa Valley
Vineyard Selection 67

Estate bottled by
Johnson Turnbull Vineyards
Oakville, California
ALCOHOL 13.2% BY VOLUME
CONTAINS SULFITES

JORDAN VINEYARD AND WINERY

Estate, Alexander Valley

CLASSIFICATION: *FIFTH GROWTH*
COLLECTIBILITY RATING: *Not rated*
BEST VINTAGES: *1986, 1985, 1984*

AT A GLANCE

**JORDAN VINEYARD
AND WINERY**
**1474 Alexander Valley Road
(P.O. Box 878)
Healdsburg, CA 95448
(707) 433-6955**

Owner: Tom Jordan

Winemaker: Rob Davis (13 years)

Founded: 1976

First Cabernet vintage: 1976

Cabernet production: 55,000 cases

Cabernet acres owned: 188

Average age of vines: 15 years

Vineyard makeup: Cabernet Sauvignon (72%), Merlot (5%), Cabernet Franc (3%)

Average wine makeup: Cabernet Sauvignon (87%), Merlot (13%)

Time in oak: 12 months

Type of oak: French, American

The beauty of Jordan Cabernet is its supple elegance, complex fruit and early drinking charm. These are not Cabernets to lay away for 10 or 20 years. The secret to enjoying them is to drink them on release and during the next three to five years, for they are styled for immediate consumption, offering layers of fresh, ripe, spicy fruit framed by delicate French oak and hints of herbs and wild flowers.

Jordan enjoys an exalted reputation among many consumers. Proprietor Tom Jordan, a Denver oil entrepreneur, spent a small fortune on vineyards and built a lavish, Bordeaux-style château with state-of-the-art equipment to create claret like that of the Médoc. From the first vintage in 1976, Jordan's refreshing style was quite apparent. The 1976 vintage in California yielded extremely ripe, tannic wines that were sometimes unbalanced. The Jordan was magnificent, all silk and polish, with spicy cinnamon, currant and plum flavors, smooth, supple tannins and the kind of seductive allure that won immediate acclaim in the marketplace, particularly in restaurants. Both the 1976 and 1977 came from purchased fruit grown in Alexander Valley, and they both drank exceptionally well for their first five years. In 1978 Jordan produced its first estate-bottled Cabernet from grapes grown on low-lying land near the Russian River.

It has always perplexed critics as to why Tom Jordan preferred the lowlands to the hills surrounding his mansion, for proximity to the river can lead to excessive vine growth and potentially huge crops. But no one can argue with the success of his wines. Volume has soared to 55,000 cases from 188 acres of Cabernet, Merlot and a dollop of Cabernet Franc, making Jordan one of the largest producers of estate-grown Cabernet in California. The 1978 proved successful, as did the 1979, 1980 and 1981 vintages, aging on the same curve as the first two bottlings. The 1982 and 1983 bottlings have been the most disappointing for me, for neither was a particularly good vintage. The 1984, 1985 and 1986 Jordans are perfect examples of the house style, with the latter showing more richness and concentration but all the pretty spice and currant nuances that make the Jordan Cabernets so delicious. With the 1986, winemaker Rob Davis may be trying to extract more fruit and tannin for longer aging, but for now it's best to drink them early. I know of many collectors and investors who are holding on to these wines in hopes of aging them 10 or 20 years or earning great returns on investment by reselling the wines, but I think they will be disappointed.

TASTING NOTES

JORDAN VINEYARD AND WINERY, Alexander Valley

1986 JORDAN VINEYARD AND WINERY: With more richness and concentration than in past vintages, the 1986 Jordan is the best Cabernet to date from this producer. It is true to the Jordan style of rich, ripe, complex wines that are supple and forward enough to drink on release, yet this wine has an added measure of depth, concentration and tannin that should ensure that it develops longer than most Jordans. The cherry, plum, cedar and anise flavors are elegant and attractive. Drink 1990-1995. 58,000 cases produced. Not Released. **88**

1985 JORDAN VINEYARD AND WINERY: A sleek, smooth, supple 1985 with lovely black cherry, herb and plum flavors of moderate depth and intensity. Delicious now or in the next three years, but then it will begin to shed some of its fruit. Drink 1990-1994. 53,698 cases produced. Release: $19.50. Current: $19.50. **85**

1984 JORDAN VINEYARD AND WINERY: Ripe, supple and fleshy, with layers of complex black cherry, currant and plum flavors that are fresh and lively. This wine is at its peak and should be enjoyed now, for it lacks the depth and intensity for much further aging. Drink 1990-1993. 50,500 cases produced. Release: $19. Current: $25. **86**

1983 JORDAN VINEYARD AND WINERY: The 1983 was not very successful for Jordan, and it is beginning to lose its fruit and appeal. The ripe plum and cedar nuances lack depth and intensity. This wine is best consumed now; don't expect it to go much further. Drink 1990-1992. 51,400 cases produced. Release: $18. Current: $30. **78**

1982 JORDAN VINEYARD AND WINERY: A disappointing rain-plagued vintage, the 1982 is light, watery and earthy now after drinking well on release in 1986. Drink 1990-1991. 50,800 cases produced. Release: $18. Current: $36. **73**

1981 JORDAN VINEYARD AND WINERY: This 1981, like its predecessors, was better three to five years ago but now has begun to fade, losing its intensity and fruit. It is still displaying elegant plum, black cherry and anise flavors. Fully mature. Drink 1990-1994. 47,000 cases produced. Release: $17. Current: $40. **84**

1980 JORDAN VINEYARD AND WINERY: The 1980 has peaked and is now rather simple, with grapy, herbal aromas and spicy plum flavors

that fade on the palate. Better three to five years ago. Drink 1990-1992. 56,400 cases produced. Release: $17. Current: $45. **80**

1979 JORDAN VINEYARD AND WINERY: Leaning toward the vegetal end of the Cabernet spectrum, this wine is ready to drink, with most of the tannins having faded. Drink 1990-1992. 47,000 cases produced. Release: $16. Current: $50. **79**

1978 JORDAN VINEYARD AND WINERY: A shade past its prime, the ripe, supple fruit has begun to decline, leaving simple plum and spice flavors that are enjoyable now. Should not be cellared much longer. Drink 1990-1993. 58,000 cases produced. Release: $16. Current: $70. **81**

1977 JORDAN VINEYARD AND WINERY: Like the 1976, 1977 was delicious early on, but it has seen better days. It was especially fine in the early 1980s soon after its release. This wine has faded, leaving light herb, bell pepper and plum flavors that are simple and easy to drink. Drink 1990-1992. 35,000 cases produced. Release: $14. Current: $70. **77**

1976 JORDAN VINEYARD AND WINERY: The 1976 was amazingly complex and seductive on release in 1980, with layers of cinnamon, plum, currant and spice, and it avoided being overripe, as were many 1976s. It has since faded, losing most of its fruit, although it remains pleasant, with light plum and herb flavors. Valuable as a collectible; Jordan's first vintage. Drink 1990-1992. 35,000 cases produced. Release: $10. Current: $70. **79**

ROBERT KEENAN WINERY

St. Helena, Napa Valley

CLASSIFICATION: *FOURTH GROWTH*
COLLECTIBILITY RATING: *Not rated*
BEST VINTAGES: *1986, 1984, 1983, 1982*

After a string of high-extract, overly tannic and excessively oaky wines in the late 1970s, Robert Keenan Winery has redefined its style with an impressive series of opulent, polished Cabernets that are quite attractive. I have never been a fan of the 1977 to 1980 Keenan wines, for they were bitterly tannic and woody, and despite their high extract, it is extremely doubtful they will ever evolve into mellow, harmonious wines.

From 1981 on, however, Keenan has a very respectable, consistent track record. The 1982 is lean and elegant and should age well throughout the 1990s, while the 1983 succeeds by matching enough fruit to the tannins in a tannic vintage. The 1984 is a blockbuster, loaded with fruit, followed by a lean, fine 1985 that will need time to evolve. The 1986 is another monumental, classically proportioned California Cabernet, teeming with ripe, fleshy fruit that makes it seductive to drink now. At $16 it represents a good drinking value.

TASTING NOTES

ROBERT KEENAN WINERY, St. Helena, Napa Valley

1986 ROBERT KEENAN WINERY: A classic California Cabernet that combines rich, ripe fruit with firm tannins and toasty French oak for a wine of depth and complexity. This wine is loaded with ripe, fleshy fruit and pretty black cherry nuances. The tannins are fine and supple, with a long, full finish. Alluring now, it should hold up well for midterm cellaring. Drink 1992-2000. 3,395 cases produced. Release: $16.50. Current: $16.50. **94**

1985 ROBERT KEENAN WINERY: A surprisingly lean and elegant 1985 considering the richness and depth of the 1984 and 1986 Keenans. There is much to like in this wine, with its ripe cherry, plum and cedar flavors. It's well balanced and offers a toasty oak overlay, but it lacks the depth and concentration for greatness. Tannins are fine and integrated, making this wine approachable soon. Drink 1993-1998. 2,400 cases produced. Release: $15. Current: $15. **86**

AT A GLANCE

ROBERT KEENAN WINERY
3660 Spring Mountain Road
St. Helena, CA 94574
(707) 963-9177

Owners: Ann and Robert Keenan

Winemaker: Rob Hunter (4 years)

Founded: 1977

First Cabernet vintage: 1977

Cabernet production: 3,000 cases

Cabernet acres owned: 18

Average age of vines: 12 years

Vineyard makeup: Cabernet Sauvignon (67%), Merlot (33%)

Average wine makeup: Cabernet Sauvignon (89%), Merlot (6%), Cabernet Franc (5%)

Time in oak: 18 months

Type of oak: French (Nevers)

CABERNET SAUVIGNON
Napa Valley
1984

Produced and Bottled by
Robert Keenan Winery, Spring Mt. St. Helena, Ca.
ALCOHOL 13% BY VOLUME

1984 ROBERT KEENAN WINERY: A very successful 1984 and Keenan's finest to date, this is a big, rich, supple wine with loads of ripe currant, cedar and black cherry flavors and a thick, smooth, supple texture that makes it attractive to drink now. There's enough concentration and tannin for midterm cellaring. Drink 1994-2002. 3,500 cases produced. Release: $13.50. Current: $30. **92**

1983 ROBERT KEENAN WINERY: A tight, lean 1983 that strikes a balance between the rich, ripe currant and plum flavors and the firm tannins. This is a wine that will require another five to seven years' cellaring to reach its peak. Drink 1995-2000. 3,400 cases produced. Release: $11. Current: $18. **87**

1982 ROBERT KEENAN WINERY: An elegant and well-balanced 1982, lean and concentrated, with layers of ripe plum, currant and cedar flavors that are complex and well structured. Not nearly as tannic as previous Keenans, this is a good candidate for midterm to long-term cellaring. Drink 1993-2000. 2,900 cases produced. Release: $10. Current: $20. **88**

1981 ROBERT KEENAN WINERY: True-to-form Keenan, with very ripe fruit and dry, oaky tannins. Better balanced than most, with ripe black cherry, currant and spicy cedar notes, finishing with dry, oaky tannins. Still needs time but should age well. Drink 1993-1999. 3,298 cases produced. Release: $13.50. Current: $22. **84**

1980 ROBERT KEENAN WINERY: Unusually dry and tannic for a 1980 but typical of Keenan's style in this era. There's a core of ripe plum and black cherry underneath the dryness that is pretty and elegant, but the tannins continue to dominate. Better balanced than previous vintages but still quite dry. Drink 1993-2000. 3,272 cases produced. Release: $13.50. Current: $23. **80**

1979 ROBERT KEENAN WINERY: A mouthful of Cabernet with a wallop of tannin, this 1979 strives for extract and depth. It has ripe, floral plum flavors, but then the thick, dry tannins take over, masking the fruit and leaving an unpleasant aftertaste of tannin and stems. Undrinkable now, but its future is borderline. Drink 1994-2000. 2,460 cases produced. Release: $12. Current: $30. **74**

1978 ROBERT KEENAN WINERY: An unbalanced wine, thick and ripe, with straightforward plum and currant flavors that are unusually coarse. Tannins dry out the finish. It is questionable whether it will ever come around. Drink 1994-2000. 2,044 cases produced. Release: $12. Current: $40. **74**

1977 ROBERT KEENAN WINERY: This is a big, thick, dense 1977, with hard, tannic, cedary oak flavors overpowering the ripe fruit underneath. It's also clumsy, with unusual barnyard flavors that are very blunt and unappetizing. Best to avoid. 843 cases produced. Release: $12. Current: $50. **69**

KENWOOD VINEYARDS
Artist Series, Sonoma Valley

CLASSIFICATION: *SECOND GROWTH*
COLLECTIBILITY RATING: *AA*
BEST VINTAGES: *1986, 1985, 1984, 1981, 1979, 1978*

Beginning with the 1975 vintage, Kenwood began producing separate lots of superior Cabernet and bottling them under the Artist Series label, a concept borrowed from Château Mouton-Rothschild, using a different label each year.

While the 1975 was a decent wine early on, it has now faded. But the 1975's reputation and value have been greatly enhanced by the controversy that surrounded its label. The first label painting, called "The Naked Lady," by David Lance Goines, was rejected by the Bureau of Alcohol, Tobacco and Firearms on grounds of indecency. Only a few cases of the wine were given this label, and a few bottles are occasionally sold at auction. The Naked Lady bottling is now worth upwards of $250. Goines returned with a second label, a skeleton of the same lady lying on a hillside, which the BATF again rejected. This label is also rare and valuable since it was never sold by from the winery. A third rendering of the label simply shows the hillside. It sells for $175 a bottle.

The quality of both the Cabernet and the art has greatly improved over the years under the direction of winemaker Michael Lee and marketing director Marty Lee, an art collector who selects the image for the label each year. The 1975 and 1976 vintages were produced from Sonoma County fruit and fermented in old redwood tanks before being aged in used American oak barrels. Both of those vintages are in decline.

Beginning in 1977, Kenwood narrowed its selection to Sonoma Valley grapes and in 1978, produced the first in a series of excellent Cabernets. The 1978 shows grace and elegance and continues to be impressive. The 1979 was equally successful, with complex fruit and another decade of aging potential. The 1980 is a step down in quality. Early on it appeared to have the depth and richness to sustain it more than a decade, but in recent tastings it has taken on a weedy, herbal quality that strays from the mainstream currant and black cherry flavors of Cabernet.

With the 1981, Kenwood began using more French oak, including a number of new barrels, and continued to refine its style. The 1982 is tight and lean and should develop through the 1990s. The 1983 is crisp and lean, and the 1984 is rich, full, deep and concentrated, the

AT A GLANCE
KENWOOD VINEYARDS
9592 Sonoma Highway
Kenwood, CA 95452
(707) 833-5891

Owners: John Sheela, Michael Lee, Martin Lee, Neil Knott

Winemaker: Michael Lee (8 years)

Founded: 1970

First Cabernet vintage: 1970
Artist Series: 1975

Cabernet production: 19,000 cases
Artist Series: 3,000 cases

Cabernet acres owned: 18 acres

Average age of vines: 15 years

Vineyard makeup: Cabernet Sauvignon (100%)

Average wine makeup: Cabernet Sauvignon (85%), Merlot (10%), Cabernet Franc (5%)

Time in oak: 24 months

Type of oak: French (Nevers)

KENWOOD

Sonoma Valley

CABERNET SAUVIGNON

1979

PRODUCED & BOTTLED BY KENWOOD VINEYARDS
KENWOOD, CALIFORNIA

Artist Series   Alc. 12.9% by Vol.

finest effort to date. The 1985 is a shade leaner and firmer, true to the vintage.

Prices for the Artist Series have risen to $30 a bottle, but production hovers around 3,000 cases, and the quality remains very high, making it one of the top Sonoma Cabernets. The early bottles have greater value as collectibles than for drinking. Kenwood makes 19,000 cases of Cabernet from mostly purchased fruit, including a Jack London Vineyard bottling that since 1983 has shown dramatic improvement and is of excellent quality, and a Sonoma County bottling that represents good drinking value. Neither is in the same class as the Artist Series.

TASTING NOTES

KENWOOD VINEYARDS, Artist Series, Sonoma Valley

1986 KENWOOD VINEYARDS ARTIST SERIES: Along with the sensational 1984, the 1986 Artist Series ranks as the finest Cabernet ever produced by this Sonoma Valley winery. It is beautifully defined, rich and smooth, layered with ripe, lush black cherry, currant, cedar, toast and spice flavors, all in exquisite balance and finishing with delicacy, complexity and finesse. The tannins are fine and elegant on the finish. Drink 1993-2003. 4,000 cases produced. Release: $30. Current: $30. **94**

1985 KENWOOD VINEYARDS ARTIST SERIES: The 1985 Artist Series is different in style from the rich, opulent 1984 bottling. The 1985 is more elegant and refined, more typical of the vintage, offering plenty of delicious currant, cassis, cedar and spice flavors, fine tannins and good length. Drink 1993-2000. 3,000 cases produced. Release: $30. Current: $30. **91**

1984 KENWOOD VINEYARDS ARTIST SERIES: One of the greatest Artist Series to date, the 1984 is a blockbuster, with deliciously rich, deeply concentrated, very complex flavors of black cherry, spice and plum on a long, full tannic finish. It also shows a lavish overlay of oak that adds complexity to the wine. Drink 1994-2002. 2,700 cases produced. Release: $30. Current: $35. **93**

1983 KENWOOD VINEYARDS ARTIST SERIES: A top-notch 1983, lean and firm, with elegant fruit, fine tannins and a pretty spice and cedar aftertaste. Drink 1993-1998. 2,500 cases produced. Release: $30. Current: $35. **87**

1982 KENWOOD VINEYARDS ARTIST SERIES: Tight, lean and concentrated, the 1982 Artist Series is still quite closed and compact and in need of further cellaring. The spice, cedar and plum flavors are young and undeveloped, and the tannins clamp down on the finish. Drink 1993-1999. 2,200 cases produced. Release: $25. Current: $40. **87**

1981 KENWOOD VINEYARDS ARTIST SERIES: Aging quite gracefully, with ample plum, currant and cassis flavors and pretty floral aromas. It is lean and focused, with a fleshy texture and just the right amount of tannin on the finish, where it picks up cedar and coffee notes. Drink 1991-1996. 1,900 cases produced. Release: $25. Current: $55. **89**

1980 KENWOOD VINEYARDS ARTIST SERIES: Early on this looked like an impressive follow-up to the excellent 1978 and 1979 vintages, but lately it has taken on extreme vegetal and weedy flavors and has much less fruit than it showed previously. The structure is fine, but the flavors don't ring true for Cabernet. Drink 1990-1994. 1,600 cases produced. Release: $20. Current: $55. **80**

1979 KENWOOD VINEYARDS ARTIST SERIES: Another top-notch Artist Series, the 1979 offers a rich array of chocolate, plum, anise and spice flavors that are beautifully balanced, young and focused. My last two tastings indicated this wine has the depth and concentration for another decade of development. Drink 1990-1998. 1,300 cases produced. Release: $20. Current: $70. **91**

1978 KENWOOD VINEYARDS ARTIST SERIES: The most successful of the early Artist Series bottlings, the 1978 continues to amaze with its complexity and durability. While it seemed headed toward an early demise just a few years ago, it has regained its strength and displays rich, concentrated cedar, cinnamon, currant and plum flavors on a long, full finish. The fruit came from the Laurel Glen and Steiner Vineyards, and the wine was aged for the first time in French oak. The wine is ready now, but it appears to have the depth for another five years. Drink 1990-1995. 1,000 cases produced. Release: $20. Current: $100. **90**

1977 KENWOOD VINEYARDS ARTIST SERIES: The first Sonoma Valley bottling, it is fully mature and on the verge of a downward spiral. The fruit is spicy and elegant, with ripe plum, anise and mint flavors that are attractive and enjoyable. Drink 1990-1993. 1,000 cases produced. Release: $15. Current: $120. **82**

1976 KENWOOD VINEYARDS ARTIST SERIES: The 1976 is also fully mature and headed over the hill. It is ripe, with sweet fruit, but the tannins are biting, and the aromas are pungent, overshadowing the spicy cherry flavor. Has value as a collectible. Drink 1990. 1,000 cases produced. Release: $10. Current: $120. **77**

1975 KENWOOD VINEYARDS ARTIST SERIES: Has considerably more value as a collectible than as a bottle to drink. The wine is very mature and well past its prime, with faint cherry and cedar flavors. Bottles with any of the three labels have soared in value from the release price of $6 to more than $200. Drink 1990. 1,000 cases produced. Release: $6.50. Current: $250. **73**

KENWOOD
Sonoma Valley
CABERNET SAUVIGNON
1979
PRODUCED & BOTTLED BY KENWOOD VINEYARDS
KENWOOD, CALIFORNIA

Artist Series   Alc. 12.9% by Vol.

KISTLER VINEYARDS
Kistler Vineyard, Sonoma Valley

CLASSIFICATION: *FIFTH GROWTH*
COLLECTIBILITY RATING: *Not rated*
BEST VINTAGES: *1986, 1985*

A**lthough** currently better known for its Chardonnay and Pinot Noir, Kistler Vineyards in Sonoma County has also been dedicated to mountain-grown Cabernet, particularly from the steep vineyards on Mount Veeder in Napa Valley. With the exception of one of the two bottlings from the 1980 vintage, the 1979 through 1984 vintages came from Mount Veeder grapes. One 1980 Kistler was made from grapes grown in the old Glen Ellen Vineyard in the eastern hills above Sonoma Valley, now the site of Carmenet. The 1985 and 1986 vintages were estate bottled from Kistler's 12-acre vineyard a short distance north of Carmenet, also in the hills. On average, about 1,000 cases of Cabernet are produced each year. The winery is owed by the Kistler family and run by Steve Kistler and Mark Bixler.

Both of the 1980 bottlings are rich, intense and tannic, in need of further cellaring. The 1981 is more concentrated but within the style, while the 1982 is successful for that vintage. The 1983 is the plainest Kistler. Fewer than 100 cases of 1984 were produced, and I have not tasted the wine. The 1985 is by far the finest Kistler, impeccably balanced, rich and deep, followed by another successful 1986 that may with time approach the quality of the superb 1985.

AT A GLANCE

KISTLER VINEYARDS
Nelligan Road
Glen Ellen, CA 95442
(707) 996-5117

Owner: The Kistler family

Winemaker: Stephen Kistler (11 years)

Founded: 1978

First Cabernet vintage: 1979

Cabernet production: 1,000 cases

Cabernet acres owned: 12

Average age of vines: 9 years

Vineyard makeup: Cabernet Sauvignon (100%)

Average wine makeup: Cabernet Sauvignon (100%)

Time in oak: 21 months

Type of oak: French (Nevers)

TASTING NOTES

KISTLER VINEYARDS, Sonoma Valley

1986 KISTLER VINEYARDS KISTLER VINEYARD: The 1986 rivals the 1985 as Kistler's finest, with black pepper, cherry and plum flavors, firm structure and tannins and fine balance that allows the bright fruit flavors to come through. Drink 1995-2002. 521 cases produced. Release: $20. Current: $20. **91**

1985 KISTLER VINEYARDS KISTLER VINEYARD: The greatest Kistler ever produced, this is a remarkably rich and elegant wine, with sharply focused plum, spice and pepper notes that are very enticing. The firm tannins and crisp acidity give it the right balance for midterm to long-term aging. Tempting now but should only get better. Drink 1994-2002. 169 cases produced. Release: $16. Current: $25. **93**

1983 KISTLER VINEYARDS VEEDER HILLS VINEYARD: Spicy and minty, crisp, lean and intense, with peppery fruit of only moderate depth. Drink 1992-1998. 1,010 cases produced. Release: $13.50. Current: $20. **78**

1982 KISTLER VINEYARDS VEEDER HILLS VINEYARD: A very admirable 1982 that is evenhanded, rich, fruity, concentrated and well balanced, with plum and currant flavors. Plenty of oak and tannin add complexity. Shows promise. Drink 1992-1999. 1,010 cases produced. Release: $12. Current: $26. **86**

1981 KISTLER VINEYARDS VEEDER HILLS-VEEDER PEAK: A very successful 1981 that combines rich, intense, concentrated fruit with a measure of elegance and finesse. Well-defined currant, black cherry and spicy oak flavors are lively and persistent. Has enough tannin on the finish to keep it through the decade. Drink 1991-1999. 1,010 cases produced. Release: $12. Current: $32. **87**

1980 KISTLER VINEYARDS VEEDER HILLS-VEEDER PEAK: Thick and dense, still a couple of years from full maturity, with tight herb, currant and tart black cherry flavors and a good dose of oak on the finish. It's well balanced and nicely proportioned, typical of the vintage. Drink 1992-1999. 369 cases produced. Release: $16. Current: $35. **85**

1980 KISTLER VINEYARDS GLEN ELLEN VINEYARD: Similar in style to the Veeder Hills bottling, this is a firm, dense, concentrated wine with intense oak, black cherry and currant flavors. Still hard on the finish, it could use another year or two of cellaring. Drink 1992-1998. 320 cases produced. Release: $18. Current: $35. **84**

CHARLES KRUG WINERY
Vintage Select, Napa Valley

CLASSIFICATION: *FOURTH GROWTH*

COLLECTIBILITY RATING: *Not rated*

BEST VINTAGES: *1986, 1984, 1961, 1958, 1956, 1952, 1946, 1944*

For years Charles Krug Winery in St. Helena was one of the "Big Four" Cabernet producers in Napa Valley, along with Beaulieu Vineyard, Inglenook and Louis M. Martini. The winery was founded in 1861 by Prussian immigrant Charles Krug, and was closed during Prohibition. It was purchased in 1943 by Cesare Mondavi, an Italian immigrant, who rejuvenated the winery with his sons Robert and Peter.

In 1944 Charles Krug Winery produced its first Cabernet Sauvignon, a wine that is still drinking exceptionally well, and with it began a long succession of grand, distinctive, long-lived Cabernets that emphasize ripe, jammy, often raisiny flavors that are broad, rich and full-bodied. Throughout the 1940s, 1950s and into the 1960s, Krug's style was remarkably consistent from vintage to vintage. While lacking the grace and elegance of Beaulieu, the structure or complexity of Inglenook, or the understated elegance and early drinking charm of Martini, the Krug Cabernets aged and endured as well as the others.

Beginning with the 1946 vintage, Krug introduced a Vintage Select bottling as a designation for its best Cabernet lots, which were produced from vineyards in the Oakville and Rutherford areas and aged in used oak and, on occasion, whiskey barrels. Production ranged from 1,000 to 1,500 cases in the early years of the Vintage Select bottlings. The 1952, 1956 and 1958 vintages were all excellent, followed by very fine bottlings in 1961, 1964, 1965 and 1968.

In 1965 Robert Mondavi left Charles Krug Winery, following a number of disputes, to start his own winery. He eventually won a lawsuit that ended in his gaining control of some of the Mondavi family's best vineyards in Oakville. While Robert sought to make Cabernets with greater elegance, finesse and structure, his brother Peter preferred the established Krug style — ripe, bold, 100 percent Cabernet.

In the 1970s, Krug was faced with finding new Cabernet grape sources, having lost some of its best vineyards to the Robert Mondavi Winery. There were some successes, particularly the ripe, rich, opulent 1974 Lot F-1, from Nathan Fay's Stags Leap District vineyard, but overall the wines lacked consistency. In the great 1978 vintage, Krug produced a mediocre bottling, followed by a weak 1979 and bizarre 1980. Moreover, in the 1970s the Krug Cabernets were increasingly out of sync as competition increased and styles changed, moving away from the overripe, 100 percent varietal Cabernets toward wines of greater complexity, refinement, elegance and early drinkability.

Both the 1985 and 1986 vintages, however, indicate that Krug has made the necessary adjustments. Both of those wines show great improvement, with sharply focused flavors, richness and depth without weight, and the judicious use of toasty French oak.

The Charles Krug Winery has 228 acres of Cabernet vineyards in Napa Valley. After a full two decades of decline, and often bland, mediocre wines, the winery has begun to correct its problems by refining its style as a first step toward producing first-rate Cabernets.

TASTING NOTES

CHARLES KRUG WINERY, Vintage Select, Napa Valley

1986 CHARLES KRUG WINERY VINTAGE SELECT: The finest Krug in years, maybe since 1968, the 1986 offers richness and sharply defined fruit, with layers of complexity and elegance. The bright black cherry, cedar, anise and currant flavors are long and lingering. Drink 1994-2002. 7,266 cases produced. Not Released. **87**

1985 CHARLES KRUG WINERY VINTAGE SELECT: Lean and austere for Krug and also closed, the 1985 is fairly oaky with cedar flavors dominating the ripe black cherry and currant flavors, finishing dry and tannic. Has room to grow, and it's well balanced. Drink 1995-2004. 7,266 cases produced. Not Released. **84**

1984 CHARLES KRUG WINERY VINTAGE SELECT: Extremely ripe, with delicious black cherry and raspberry complexities, showing marked improvement in quality. While consistent with the style of overt ripeness, it offers a measure of elegance and refinement missing in previous vintages. Drink 1993-2002. 3,653 cases produced. Not Released. **87**

1983 CHARLES KRUG WINERY VINTAGE SELECT: Oaky and tannic but well balanced, this wine will take time to fully develop. It has the Krug trademark of ripe, jammy fruit with berry, raspberry and cedar notes. Drink 1994-2001. 3,653 cases produced. Not Released. **82**

1981 CHARLES KRUG WINERY VINTAGE SELECT: Earthy, ripe, rich and cedary, a drastic improvement over the 1980, offering plenty of berry, cherry and spice flavors, lean, reined-in tannins and good length, but it's still missing the complexity and depth for greatness. Drink 1992-1998. 4,423 cases produced. Not Released. **82**

1980 CHARLES KRUG WINERY VINTAGE SELECT: Despite pretty, ripe black cherry and raspberry notes, the flavors are tart and sharp but drinkable. In several tastings I have found significant bottle variation, a problem the winery acknowledges. At its best it is good, but

in many cases it was very tart, and it appeared to be going through malolactic in the bottle. Scores ranged from 59 to 79. Drink 1992-1997. 8,858 cases produced. Release: $15. Current: $15. **79**

1979 CHARLES KRUG WINERY VINTAGE SELECT: An improvement over the 1978, the 1979 is one of Krug's better efforts. Because 1979 was a cooler vintage, the fruit is not overripe or overblown. The plum, cherry, anise and prune flavors are livelier and rich in extract. What's missing is complexity and depth. Drink 1990-1995. 2,177 cases produced. Release: $12.50. Current: $20. **82**

1978 CHARLES KRUG WINERY VINTAGE SELECT: The 1978 has always been a major disappointment in view of the vintage in Napa Valley. The Krug is very ripe and earthy, with blunt, direct fruit and very dry tannins; a decent wine from a vintage when many in Napa made great, long-lived wines. Drink 1990-1995. 14,353 cases produced. Release: $11. Current: $22. **78**

1977 CHARLES KRUG WINERY VINTAGE SELECT: The ripe fruit up front dries out quickly, leaving more tannin and less flavor. The anise, plum and prune flavors are decent, but they lack elegance and grace. Drink 1990-1994. 4,029 cases produced. Release: $10. Current: $22. **74**

1974 CHARLES KRUG WINERY VINTAGE SELECT LOT F-1: This wine is from the Fay Vineyard in Stags Leap, and until recently it was drinking exceptionally well, exhibiting the classic Krug style of rich, supple, opulent fruit. Lately it has shown signs of crumbling at the edges. Best to drink it soon unless it has been stored in pristine conditions. Drink 1990-1993. 8,246 cases produced. Release: $9. Current: $50. **88**

1973 CHARLES KRUG WINERY VINTAGE SELECT: The 1973 was good in its prime but nothing more. It is lighter and has less of the fruit extract for which these wines are known. There is a touch of raisin and cherry, but it's tired. Drink 1990. 5,846 cases produced. Release: $9. Current: $40. **73**

1972 CHARLES KRUG WINERY VINTAGE SELECT: The 1972 harvest was a wet, rainy one, yet the Krug, with its ripe and raisiny style, held up well through its first decade of life. It now exhibits a hint of smokiness but lacks depth and complexity. Drink 1990. 3,787 cases produced. Release: $9. Current: $45. **77**

1971 CHARLES KRUG WINERY VINTAGE SELECT: From a fair vintage of early drinking Cabernets, the wine has peaked and is fading. It still offers hints of ripe, mature anise, raisin and prune aromas and a hint of tar, but those flavors do not come through on the palate. Much better 10 years ago. Drink 1990. 7,993 cases produced. Release: $7.50. Current: $35. **79**

1970 CHARLES KRUG WINERY VINTAGE SELECT: Very similar in style and character to the 1968 and 1969 bottlings and showing its age. It's very dry, with prune, anise and spice flavors. Past its best years.

Drink 1990. 11,825 cases produced. Release: $7.50. Current: $60. **75**

1969 CHARLES KRUG WINERY VINTAGE SELECT: In slightly better condition than the 1968 yet with the ripe, spicy anise and prune aromas of an aging wine. There's a touch of fruit peeking through and hints of earth, cherry and cedar on the finish. Drink 1990. 8,262 cases produced. Release: $6.50. Current: $65. **81**

1968 CHARLES KRUG WINERY VINTAGE SELECT: For a long time the 1968 Krug was at the top of the vintage, but it is now in rapid decline. The past few times I have tried it the flavors seemed to be overly mature and fading, showing less of the ripe fruit that characterized the wine five years ago. The nose offers anise, prune and spice aromas, with rather crisp acidity and a touch of cherry on the finish. Its best years are behind it. Drink 1990. 7,668 cases produced. Release: $6.50. Current: $90. **80**

1965 CHARLES KRUG WINERY VINTAGE SELECT: In its prime the 1965 was a fine bottle of Cabernet, but it has begun to lose its fruit. The last vintage made by Robert Mondavi while at Krug, this remains one of the best Krugs of this decade. It's fully mature and displaying subtlety and finesse, with spicy plum and cedar nuances that are complex and intriguing. Has great potential as a collectible. Drink 1990-1993. 8,643 cases produced. Release: $5. Current: $80. **87**

1964 CHARLES KRUG WINERY VINTAGE SELECT: A very pleasant wine from a vintage that peaked years ago, it is still holding on, with spicy, mature fruit and a touch of cherry and plum on the finish. Drink 1990. 5,780 cases produced. Release: $4. Current: $85. **86**

1963 CHARLES KRUG WINERY VINTAGE SELECT: Tasted once in 1985, the 1963 was disjointed and clumsy, with ripe fruit but missing the kind of elegance and finesse you want from an older vintage. Drink 1990. 3,599 cases produced. Release: $3.50. Current: $70. **74**

1962 CHARLES KRUG WINERY VINTAGE SELECT: From another difficult vintage, the 1962 is well past its prime. The last time I tried it, in 1985, it was not showing much fruit or character. Drink 1990. 2,137 cases produced. Release: $3.50. Current: $70. **78**

1961 CHARLES KRUG WINERY VINTAGE SELECT: Despite heavy frosts in this vintage, this Vintage Select stands out as a success. Better years ago, it still displays pretty rose petal and plum flavors and great persistence on the finish. Drink 1990. 1,958 cases produced. Release: $3.50. Current: $135. **89**

1960 CHARLES KRUG WINERY VINTAGE SELECT: The 1960 was a delicious wine for a long time, but it is now in rapid decline, exhibiting light spice, cherry and anise flavors and crisp, mouthwatering acidity on the finish. Best 10 to 15 years ago. Drink 1990. 1,516 cases produced. Release: $2.25. Current: $70. **79**

1959 CHARLES KRUG WINERY VINTAGE SELECT: Another excellent vintage in Napa Valley, the 1959s were best consumed within

the first 10 to 15 years of their lives. The only time I tried the 1959 Krug was in 1985, and it had a very pleasant, smoky, cedary aroma with rich, mature plum flavors. Drink 1990. 7,832 cases produced. Release: $2.25. Current: $150. **85**

1958 CHARLES KRUG WINERY VINTAGE SELECT: The 1958 vintage was a great one in Napa Valley, and the Krug still shows rich, concentrated, ripe plum and currant flavors. It tasted better five years ago but was still holding on the last time I tried it. Remarkably youthful and lively. Drink 1990. 868 cases produced. Release: $2. Current: $465. **88**

1956 CHARLES KRUG WINERY VINTAGE SELECT: The 1956 has been drinking very well now for two decades. It is now in full decline, but the last time I tried it I was amazed to taste how much ripe plum flavor remained in this rich, smooth, elegant wine. Drink 1990. 1,250 cases produced. Release: $1.40. Current: $590. **90**

1952 CHARLES KRUG WINERY VINTAGE SELECT: While only a good vintage in Napa Valley, the 1952 Krug exceeded expectations, producing a very fine wine that is elegant and spicy, with rich, mature plum and prune flavors that are long on the finish. One of the greatest Krugs ever produced. Drink 1990. 1,028 cases produced. Release: $1.26. Current: $750. **92**

1951 CHARLES KRUG WINERY VINTAGE SELECT: The 1951 vintage in Napa was excellent, and the Krug displays very ripe, jammy, sweet fruit flavors of good depth and intensity. Better a decade ago, it is still holding on. Drink 1990. 1,553 cases produced. Release: $1.25. Current: $700. **85**

1950 CHARLES KRUG WINERY VINTAGE SELECT: The fruit is thin and drying out on this wine. Faint hints of cherry and plum. Drink 1990. 1,553 cases produced. Release: $1.25. Current: $500. **79**

1946 CHARLES KRUG WINERY VINTAGE SELECT: This is the first Vintage Select bottling. Like the 1944, it is still holding well despite its age, with very ripe cedar, cassis and plum flavors and a touch of tannin on the finish. Certainly past its peak but holding. Drink 1990. 1,452 cases produced. Release: $1. Current: $750. **88**

1944 CHARLES KRUG WINERY: On the three occasions that I have tried the 1944, I have come away extremely impressed by its longevity. The last time it appeared to be drying out but still exhibiting plenty of ripe fruit, hints of plum, rose petal and anise and good length on the finish. Valuable as a collectible because it is Krug's first Cabernet. Drink 1990. 857 cases produced. Release: $.95. Current: $800. **88**

LA JOTA VINEYARD CO.

Howell Mountain, Napa Valley

CLASSIFICATION: *FIFTH GROWTH*

COLLECTIBILITY RATING: *Not rated*

BEST VINTAGES: *1986, 1985, 1984*

From a rustic stone winery on Howell Mountain, La Jota Vineyard Co. has emerged as one of the promising new wineries in this rejuvenated winegrowing area near Angwin above the Napa Valley floor and northeast of St. Helena. Each of the first four estate-grown La Jota Cabernets has displayed a rich, toasty, oaky character, but there appears to be enough ripe, concentrated currant and black cherry flavors underneath for these wines to develop in eight to 12 years.

Early on, proprietors Bill and Joan Smith employed the services of Randy Dunn to oversee production. Ripe, tannic wines spend a good two years in mostly used oak before getting a flash of toasty vanilla from new oak barrels a few months before bottling. While La Jota wines have been distinct and consistent in style, they have not yet achieved anywhere near the success of Dunn's own Howell Mountain bottlings, which are enormously rich and massively proportioned.

The 1986 shows La Jota at its best. Not only is this a superior vintage, but it demonstrate a refinement in winemaking. Through 1985, production had risen to 1,500 cases. In 1986, production reached 2,700 cases, where the owners predict it will level off.

TASTING NOTES

LA JOTA VINEYARD CO., Howell Mountain, Napa Valley

1986 LA JOTA VINEYARD CO.: La Jota's finest Cabernet to date displays a distinctive style of rich, focused, concentrated, elegant black cherry, currant, cedar and spice flavors. The balance is impeccable, with firm, supple tannins that allow the fruit to carry through on the finish. Drink 1994-2004. 2,700 cases produced. Release: $21. Current: $21. **92**

1985 LA JOTA VINEYARD CO.: An ample overlay of toasty oak introduces this wine; underneath is a well-focused, lean, intense, compact Cabernet with black cherry and oaky vanilla notes. This wine

AT A GLANCE

LA JOTA VINEYARD CO.
1102 Las Posadas Road
Angwin, CA 94508
(707) 965-3020

Owners: Bill and Joan Smith

Winemaker: Bill Smith (7 years)

Founded: 1982

First Cabernet vintage: 1982

Cabernet production: 2,700 cases

Cabernet acres owned: 21

Average age of vines: 11 years

Vineyard makeup: Cabernet Sauvignon (90%), Merlot (5%), Cabernet Franc (5%)

Average wine makeup: Cabernet Sauvignon (94%), Merlot (3%), Cabernet Franc (3%)

Time in oak: 27 months

Type of oak: French (Nevers)

1984
NAPA VALLEY
HOWELL MOUNTAIN

Cabernet Sauvignon

GROWN, PRODUCED AND BOTTLED BY
LA JOTA VINEYARD CO. ANGWIN, NAPA VALLEY, CA
CONTAINS SULFITES
ALCOHOL 13.0% BY VOLUME

will require some aging to soften the oak flavors, but it appears well balanced and has plenty of flavor. Drink 1993-2000. 1,570 cases produced. Release: $18. Current: $18. **88**

1984 LA JOTA VINEYARD CO.: It's lean and tight for a 1984 and showing an abundance of oak, but there are some pretty black currant, spice and cedar flavors that are rich and compact, and it's well balanced. What's required is patience for the ingredients to marry. Drink 1993-1999. 1,206 cases produced. Release: $15. Current: $20. **88**

1983 LA JOTA VINEYARD CO.: Very austere, even for a 1983, this is a tight, lean, hard, fairly tannic wine that will require some cellaring before it's ready to drink. The rich cedar, vanilla and black cherry flavors are tightly wound and in need of time to soften. Drink 1994-2000. 870 cases produced. Release: $15. Current: $20. **84**

1982 LA JOTA VINEYARD CO.: La Jota's first vintage, this is a tough, hard, tannic and oaky wine, with firm, tight black cherry and cedar flavors behind it. It needs more time to come together. Drink 1994-2000. 704 cases produced. Release: $13.50. Current: $25. **84**

LAKESPRING WINERY
Yountville, Napa Valley

CLASSIFICATION: *FIFTH GROWTH*

COLLECTIBILITY RATING: *Not rated*

BEST VINTAGES: *1986, 1985, 1984, 1982*

Without any Cabernet acreage of its own, Lakespring is totally dependent on purchased fruit for its Cabernet. The winery in Yountville has a long-term lease with two key growers in the Yountville-Stags Leap District, Steltzner and the Pelissa vineyard, and in recent vintages the wines have shown tremendous richness, concentration and promise. In seven vintages, all the Cabernets have displayed attractive features, occasionally offering herbal aromas that may appeal to some more than others. The 1980, 1982 and 1984 wines are especially big and rich, loaded with ripe, supple, deeply flavored fruit, particularly the 1984. In 1981 and 1983 the Lakespring Cabernets are less impressive but still very good. The 1985 is more elegant and focused but with good potential for the next decade, while the 1986 is similar in style but needs five years to reach full maturity.

AT A GLANCE
LAKESPRING WINERY
P.O. Box 2036
Yountville, CA 94599
(707) 944-2475

Owner: The Battat family

Winemaker: Randy Mason (9 years)

Founded: 1980

First Cabernet vintage: 1980

Cabernet production: 3,000 cases

Cabernet acres owned: none

Average wine makeup: Cabernet
   Sauvignon (100%)

Time in oak: 18 months

Type of oak: French (Nevers)

TASTING NOTES

LAKESPRING WINERY, Various bottlings

1986 LAKESPRING WINERY: The 1986 has all the elements for greatness but is rather shy and reserved now. It exhibits ripe plum, currant and black cherry flavors that are well focused and concentrated, properly balanced with oak and tannins, similar in style to the excellent 1985. Drink 1994-1999. 1,700 cases produced. Release: $14. Current: $14. **88**

1985 LAKESPRING WINERY: Not quite as dramatic, openly rich or opulent as the 1984, the 1985 nonetheless is a top-notch wine that shows the progress Lakespring has made with Cabernet. It is lean, with well-focused, ripe plum, currant and cherry flavors framed by firm tannins. Drinkable now, it should gain for the next five to seven years and beyond. Drink 1992-1999. 3,300 cases produced. Release: $12. Current: $12. **88**

1984 LAKESPRING WINERY RESERVE SELECTION: The 1984 is

1981

NAPA VALLEY
CABERNET SAUVIGNON

Lakespring

PRODUCED AND BOTTLED BY LAKESPRING WINERY
NAPA, CALIFORNIA U.S.A. 94558
BONDED WINERY #5002
ALCOHOL 12.8% BY VOLUME

full-throttle Cabernet, rich, fat, opulent and supple, with layers of sweet, ripe black currant, cherry, anise and spicy oak flavors. There is plenty of tannin for aging, but this wine is delicious to drink already. Drink 1992-1999. 1,450 cases produced. Release: $15. Current: $20. **92**

1983 LAKESPRING WINERY: Typical of the 1983 vintage with its harsh tannins, this wine nonetheless has ample berry and chocolate aromas and flavors that are appealing, finishing with hints of cherries and currants. Drink 1993-1998. 3,000 cases produced. Release: $11. Current: $13. **85**

1982 LAKESPRING WINERY VINTAGE SELECTION: A very successful 1982 that combines rich, ripe, concentrated black cherry and currant flavors with a touch of anise and oak in a full-bodied, muscular style. While I have had several bottles that seemed overly herbaceous, tannic and lacking fruit, the majority have been as described above. It's mature now but should hold throughout the decade. Drink 1992-1998. 3,600 cases produced. Release: $14. Current: $20. **88**

1981 LAKESPRING WINERY: Another very successful Lakespring, lean and tight, with mint, anise and plum flavors that still need time to develop. Drink 1992-1998. 3,000 cases produced. Release: $11. Current: $18. **86**

1980 LAKESPRING WINERY: Lakespring's first Cabernet is a big, rich, concentrated wine, with ripe plum, anise and chocolate flavors that are framed by dry tannins. The last two times I tasted this wine it seemed to be closing up and taking on a more herbaceous quality, but it still has the extract and richness for further development. Drink 1991-1997. 2,000 cases produced. Release: $10. Current: $21. **88**

LAUREL GLEN VINEYARD

Sonoma Mountain

CLASSIFICATION: *THIRD GROWTH*

COLLECTIBILITY RATING: *AA*

BEST VINTAGES: *1986, 1985, 1984, 1981*

Afte selling Cabernet grapes to the likes of Chateau St. Jean and Kenwood, Laurel Glen owner Patrick Campbell began in 1981 to produce his own commercial wine from this gently sloping vineyard on Sonoma Mountain. With the exception of an "off" vintage in 1983, the results have been superb, making this 4,000-case producer one of the most exciting new names in California Cabernet.

With the 1981 vintage, Laurel Glen established a style of rich, supple, elegant Cabernets that are easy to drink on release yet have the depth of flavor and concentration to carry them for a decade and beyond, as demonstrated by some of Campbell's homemade wines from the 1970s that are still alive and quite pleasant. The 1985, with its great harmony and finesse, is the finest Cabernet ever produced by Laurel Glen, although the 1986 may rival it since it continues to improve with every tasting.

With production up to 4,000 cases and an established vineyard, Laurel Glen is one of the top-quality producers in Sonoma County. As demand and quality have risen, so have prices, but $20 for the 1986 is quite reasonable considering the vintage and the quality. A second label, Counterpoint, is used occasionally for lots of Cabernet not used in the Laurel Glen brand.

AT A GLANCE
LAUREL GLEN VINEYARD
P.O. Box 548
Glen Ellen, CA 95442
(707) 526-3914

Owners: Patrick and Faith Campbell

Winemaker: Patrick Campbell (8 years)

Founded: 1981

First Cabernet vintage: 1981

Cabernet production: 4,000 cases

Cabernet acres owned: 35

Average age of vines: 18 years

Vineyard makeup: Cabernet Sauvignon (84%), Cabernet Franc (11%), Merlot (5%)

Average wine makeup: Cabernet Sauvignon (94%), Cabernet Franc (6%)

Time in oak: 21 months

Type of oak: French (Nevers)

TASTING NOTES

LAUREL GLEN VINEYARD, Sonoma Mountain

1986 LAUREL GLEN VINEYARD: An elegant, delicate 1986 with pretty black cherry and spicy plum flavors but without the richness, depth and complexity of the 1985 and 1981 vintages. Lacks the pure richness and concentration for greatness but offers subtlety, elegance and finesse that promises intriguing drinking in the future. Almost ready, tastes better with each bottle. With time, it may rival the 1985. Drink 1992-1998. 4,000 cases produced. Release: $20. Current: $25. **89**

SONOMA MOUNTAIN
1985 CABERNET SAUVIGNON

1985 LAUREL GLEN VINEYARD: An exquisite 1985, and Laurel Glen's best to date, forward and alluring, with great harmony and finesse and layers of pretty black cherry, currant and spicy oak flavors; it is elegant and refined yet persistent. Tannins are fine and integrated, making it approachable now. Drink 1992-2000. 3,300 cases produced. Release: $18, Current: $35. **93**

1984 LAUREL GLEN VINEYARD: Almost identical in style to the excellent 1981, this is a rich, smooth, forward wine with ripe currant, black cherry and toasty vanilla notes, fleshy enough to begin drinking now but with the concentration and depth to carry it another decade. Drink 1992-2000. 4,000 cases produced. Release: $15. Current: $20. **89**

1983 LAUREL GLEN VINEYARD: This wine has a distinct mossy, musty quality that dominates the flavor and makes it a flawed wine. With hindsight, it should not have been released. Best to avoid. 4,000 cases produced. Release: $11. Current: $11. **59**

1982 LAUREL GLEN VINEYARD: A leaner, tighter wine with a pronounced earth and cedar quality on top of the ripe black cherry flavors. Not quite the depth, richness and complexity of the fine 1981 but nonetheless a very good wine that is still developing. Needs another two years. Drink 1992-1997. 2,800 cases produced. Release: $12.50. Current: $20. **85**

1981 LAUREL GLEN VINEYARD: Laurel Glen's first commercial vintage produced a magnificent wine with beautifully focused, rich, ripe black cherry, currant, plum and cedar flavors that are smooth and supple, fine, integrated tannins and a pretty fruit aftertaste. Lovely now and through the next five years. Drink 1990-1996. 1,500 cases produced. Release: $12.50. Current: $40. **92**

LIVINGSTON VINEYARDS
Moffett Vineyard, Rutherford, Napa Valley

CLASSIFICATION: *FIFTH GROWTH*

COLLECTIBILITY RATING: *Not rated*

BEST VINTAGES: *1986, 1984*

The family-run Livingston winery makes only Cabernet from the small, 8-acre Moffett Vineyard on the west side of Highway 29 near Zinfandel Lane in Rutherford. Winemaker Randy Dunn of Dunn Vineyards acts as consultant. The first vintage, the 1984, tasted lavishly oaky upon release, but lately more fleshy fruit is showing. The 1985 is sleeker and crisper, a notch below the best Napa Valley Cabernets from this great vintage, while the 1986 is impressive for its richness and elegance. Livingston Cabernets are ready to drink on release but appear to have the depth and flavor to continue developing for a decade or more. Prices have risen sharply to $24 a bottle for the 1986, and production is projected to level off at 2,500 cases from the 1986 release of 1,300.

TASTING NOTES

LIVINGSTON VINEYARDS, Moffett Vineyard, Rutherford, Napa Valley

1986 LIVINGSTON VINEYARDS MOFFETT VINEYARD: This is the best Cabernet Livingston produced. It is rich and elegant, firmly structured and rather oaky now, but it exhibits plenty of ripe black cherry and currant flavors, fine tannins and length on the aftertaste. It still needs three to five years before it peaks. Drink 1994-1999. 1,330 cases produced. Release: $24. Current: $24. **90**

1985 LIVINGSTON VINEYARDS MOFFETT VINEYARD: This is a sleeker, leaner, crisper bottling than the 1984 and it too is decidedly oaky, but beneath the wood are pretty cherry, plum and currant flavors. With time it may surpass the excellent 1984. Drink 1993-1999. 1,030 cases produced. Release: $18. Current: $24. **86**

1984 LIVINGSTON VINEYARDS MOFFETT VINEYARD: Although the 1984 Livingston seemed excessively oaky on release, more black cherry and currant flavors are showing through the cedary veneer. Its supple texture and fleshy fruit make it approachable now, but it should continue to improve through the decade. Drink 1991-1996. 936 cases produced. Release: $18. Current: $25. **87**

AT A GLANCE
LIVINGSTON VINEYARDS
1895 Cabernet Lane
St. Helena, CA 94574
(707) 963-2120

Owners: John and Dianne Livingston

Winemaker: Randy Dunn (5 years)

Founded: 1984

First Cabernet vintage: 1984

Cabernet production: 1,300 cases

Cabernet acres owned: 8

Average age of vines: 20 years

Vineyard makeup: Cabernet Sauvignon (75%), Cabernet Franc (12.5%), Merlot (12.5%)

Average wine makeup: Cabernet Sauvignon (100%)

Time in oak: 27 months

Type of oak: French (Nevers, Limousin)

LONG VINEYARDS
Oakville, Napa Valley

CLASSIFICATION: *FOURTH GROWTH*

COLLECTIBILITY RATING: *A*

BEST VINTAGES: *1985, 1984, 1980, 1979*

With an annual production of fewer than 200 cases, Long Vineyards is one of the smallest Cabernet producers in Napa Valley. The winery is owned by Bob and Zelma Long (president of Simi Winery), who are now divorced are but still business partners. The Longs' winery is on Pritchard Hill near Chappellet, but their Cabernet grapes come from a tiny 30-year-old experimental vineyard in Oakville near Robert Mondavi's To-Kalon Vineyard and Martha's Vineyard that is owned and farmed by the University of California at Davis.

The Long Cabernet style is slowly evolving toward wines of great richness, depth and complexity. The first vintage in 1979 was very successful, with sharply focused fruit and great length. The 1980 is bursting with fresh, ripe fruit that is intense and concentrated. No Cabernets were produced in 1981 or 1982, and the 1983 is light and tart, lacking richness and concentration. The 1984 is elegant and ready to drink, while the 1985 is the best bottling to date. The price is high at $36 because the supply is small, and at least a part of the proceeds benefit the UC-Davis department of viticulture and enology.

AT A GLANCE
LONG VINEYARDS
P.O. Box 50
St. Helena, CA 94574
(707) 963-2496

Owners: Bob and Zelma Long

Winemaker: Bob Long (12 years)

Founded: 1977

First Cabernet vintage: 1979

Cabernet production: 200 cases

Cabernet acres owned: none

Average age of vines: 30 years

Vineyard makeup: Cabernet Sauvignon (100%)

Average wine makeup: Cabernet Sauvignon (100%)

Time in oak: 18 months

Type of oak: French (Tarasaund)

TASTING NOTES

LONG VINEYARDS, Oakville, Napa Valley

1986 LONG VINEYARDS: Delicious for its pure black cherry, currant and spice flavors, smooth and elegant, with fine, supple tannins and good length. Impressive for its delicacy and finesse, it is drinking well now and should for the next six to eight years. Drink 1991-1998. 200 cases produced. Not Released. **86**

1985 LONG VINEYARDS: Beautifully defined Cabernet, rich, lush and polished, with layers of complex plum, toasty oak and spicy black cherry flavors that are smooth and satiny on the palate. Well proportioned with firm tannins and crisp acidity. Drink 1995-2005. 200 cases produced. Not Released. **92**

1984 LONG VINEYARDS: Elegant, supple and balanced, with pretty plum, currant and cranberry flavors that are not too tannic nor as fleshy as most 1984s. Ready to drink soon. Drink 1992-2000. 200 cases produced. Release: $32. Current: $35. **88**

1983 LONG VINEYARDS: Light, tart, simple and elegant and not too tannic, sound and correct but unexciting, with a slight sour note on the finish. Could use more richness and fruit. Drink 1991-1995. 200 cases produced. Release: $32. Current: $40. **78**

1980 LONG VINEYARDS: Rich, ripe and complex, bursting with currant, cherry and spice flavors that are deep and rich, intense and powerful yet elegant at the same time. A marvelous wine; one of the top 1980s. Drink 1994-2002. 200 cases produced. Release: $32. Current: $50. **91**

1979 LONG VINEYARDS: Long's first vintage, the 1979 displays ripe, rich cherry, currant, cranberry and spice flavors that are elegant and smooth, finishing with great length and finesse. Near its peak. Drink 1992-1999. 200 cases produced. Release: $32. Current: $50. **90**

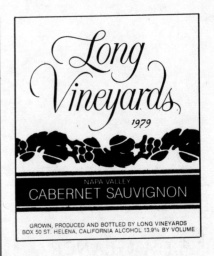

LYETH WINERY
Alexander Valley

CLASSIFICATION: *FIFTH GROWTH*
COLLECTIBILITY RATING: *Not rated*
BEST VINTAGES: *1985, 1984*

AT A GLANCE
LYETH WINERY
24625 Chianti Road
Geyserville, CA 95441
(707) 857-3562

Owner: Lyeth Winery Ltd.
(limited partnership)

Winemaker: Bill Arbios (8 years)

Founded: 1981

First Cabernet vintage: 1981

Cabernet production: 12,000 cases

Cabernet acres owned: 18

Average age of vines: 8 years

Vineyard makeup: Cabernet Sauvignon (75%), Merlot (20%), Cabernet Franc (3%), Malbec (2%)

Average wine makeup: Cabernet Sauvignon (75%), Merlot (20%), Cabernet Franc (3%), Malbec (2%)

Time in oak: 24 months

Type of oak: French

In 1985, Munro "Chip" Lyeth (rhymes with teeth) released his first Cabernet-based proprietary red, a Bordeaux-style blend that included Merlot, Cabernet Franc and a dollop of Malbec. The new wine won widespread acceptance not only for its complexity and finesse, but also because it emphasized the blending of Alexander Valley grapes, as opposed to a 100 percent Cabernet wine.

While the 1981 drank well for its first few years, the last two times I tried it, the bright, spicy cherry flavors had turned overly herbal and oaky, with more vegetal flavors than fruit. The 1982 aged better, although it, too, is rather oaky and herbal, but with more fruit to stand up to those flavors. The 1983 has not evolved as well as one might have hoped, for it now tastes thin and tannic, typical of the vintage. The 1984 and 1985 vintages are clearly the finest, both with more richness, concentration, complexity and depth than earlier editions. If you like these wines now, then I would drink them soon, keeping just a few bottles to see how they age. The disappointing aging curve of the earlier bottlings seems to suggest early consumption. Moreover, the warmer reaches of Alexander Valley tend to yield wines that are rich and fleshy early on, taking on more herb and spice notes as they age. Production has risen to 12,000 cases, but the winery owns only 18 acres of Cabernet and must rely on purchased fruit. Lyeth was sold to an agricultural concern in 1988 after some financial difficulties. Chip Lyeth died later that year.

TASTING NOTES

LYETH WINERY, Alexander Valley

1985 LYETH WINERY: As fine as the 1984 is, the 1985 exceeds it in quality, with beautifully defined fruit, rich and lush, with layers of black cherry, toast, currant and spice flavors, finishing with great length and complexity and just the right amount of tannin to carry it through the decade. Alluring already. Drink 1992-1999. 13,500 cases produced. Release: $22. Current: $22. **92**

1984 LYETH WINERY: A rich, deep, concentrated wine with layers of black cherry, currant, vanilla and toast flavors, it is remarkably elegant and well defined. Offers more richness and depth than previous bottlings, but it is one to keep an eye on after seeing how the earlier vintages aged. Drink 1992-1998. 10,500 cases produced. Release: $18. Current: $25. **90**

1983 LYETH WINERY: An unusually tannic, thin wine, like most of the vintage. Some may call it elegant, but it lacks depth, character and definition. Drink 1992-1995. 8,000 cases produced. Release: $17. Current: $25. **78**

1982 LYETH WINERY: Another Lyeth that strives for understated elegance and succeeds, with lush herb, cherry and cedar flavors that offer a degree of complexity. Not as vegetal as the 1981 but showing more herb and tea nuances, it offers modest cherry and spice flavors, fine tannins and decent length. Drink 1990-1995. 5,000 cases produced. Release: $16. Current: $30. **85**

1981 LYETH WINERY: This elegant, understated 1981 that once featured bright cherry and spicy berry flavors has turned oaky and vegetal with age. It is still elegant, but the flavors are much less satisfying, and there are indications that the vegetal cabbage and oak flavors will continue to dominate the berry fruit. Better three years ago, it's ready now. Drink 1990-1993. 1,200 cases produced. Release: $15. Current: $35. **77**

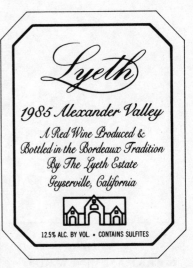

AT A GLANCE

MARKHAM VINEYARDS
2812 North St. Helena
Highway
St. Helena, CA 94574
(707) 963-5292

Owner: Sanraku Inc.

Winemaker: Robert Foley, Jr. (10 years)

Founded: 1978

First Cabernet vintage: 1978

Cabernet production: 3,800 cases

Cabernet acres owned: 160
Markham Vineyard: 100

Average age of vines: 19 years
Markham Vineyard: 25 years

Vineyard makeup: Cabernet Sauvignon (58%), Merlot (32%), Cabernet Franc (10%)
Markham Vineyard: Cabernet Sauvignon (63%), Merlot (21%), Cabernet Franc (16%)

Average wine makeup: Cabernet Sauvignon (86%), Merlot (14%)

Time in oak: 20 months

Type of oak: French (Nevers, Limousin)

MARKHAM VINEYARDS

Markham Vineyard, Yountville, Napa Valley

CLASSIFICATION: *THIRD GROWTH*

COLLECTIBILITY RATING: A

BEST VINTAGES: *1986, 1985, 1984, 1983, 1982, 1980, 1979*

Markham Vineyards Cabernet is one of the most underrated wines and undiscovered values in Napa Valley. From its 100-acre Cabernet holdings in Yountville adjacent to Napanook, home of Dominus, Markham has produced a series of rich, concentrated, tannic and structured Cabernets that have been largely ignored or overlooked by most critics.

Markham Vineyards was founded in 1978 by advertising man Bruce Markham, who hired Bryan del Bondio to run the winery, which is housed in an old stone winery building from 1876. In 1988 Markham sold the winery to Sanraku, Japan's largest winemaker.

The first vintage in 1978 is extremely ripe and somewhat clumsy, but it has all the ingredients to age another 10 years, and with time it may surprise. The 1979 is leaner and richer, followed by a very fine 1980 bottling. Of the next three vintages, the 1982 and 1983 were remarkably successful considering the vintages. The 1984 is rich and lush, and the 1985 is clearly this winery's finest bottling. The 1986, from another excellent vintage, is right on target.

TASTING NOTES

MARKHAM VINEYARDS, Markham Vineyard, Yountville, Napa Valley

1986 MARKHAM VINEYARDS MARKHAM VINEYARD: A big, rich, firmly structured 1986 that with time may rival the 1985 in quality. It has a toasty overlay of oak that marries well with the dense, concentrated black currant and anise flavors. High in extract, well focused and nicely balanced. Drink 1995-2004. 3,850 cases produced. Not Released. **91**

1985 MARKHAM VINEYARDS MARKHAM VINEYARD: Markham's finest Cabernet to date, sleek, supple and elegant with crisp, lively, concentrated cherry and black currant flavors, beautifully integrated tannins and acidity that carries the flavors a long way. Not as open as the 1984, but there's a shade more depth and complexity. Drink 1994-2003. 3,810 cases produced. Not Released. **93**

1984 MARKHAM VINEYARDS MARKHAM VINEYARD: Lush, rich and supple, loaded with fresh, ripe black cherry, plum and currant flavors and chewy tannins. While it appears less tannic, allowing the fruit flavors to come through on the finish, it has the tannins for aging. Drink 1993-2002. 3,855 cases produced. Release: $12. Current: $18. **91**

1983 MARKHAM VINEYARDS MARKHAM VINEYARD: The 1983 is a massively tannic wine that needs time before it can be approached. The black cherry flavors are attractive, and there is plenty of fruit, but the tannins dominate. Extreme patience required. Drink 1995-2000. 4,015 cases produced. Release: $13. Current: $15. **89**

1982 MARKHAM VINEYARDS MARKHAM VINEYARD: This is the best of the early Markhams. Despite a difficult vintage with rain at harvest, it is a richly flavored wine that showcases the sharply focused black cherry and currant flavors. Well focused, and the tannins are supple and integrated. Drink 1994-2002. 6,361 cases produced. Release: $13. Current: $18. **90**

1981 MARKHAM VINEYARDS MARKHAM VINEYARD: It's lean, tannic and more austere than previous vintages, but there's a rich concentration of ripe cherry and currant flavors that should improve with further age. With time this one may surprise. Drink 1992-1998. 3,717 cases produced. Release: $13. Current: $20. **86**

1980 MARKHAM VINEYARDS MARKHAM VINEYARD: The 1980 Markham has beautifully defined supple black cherry, anise and currant flavors. The tannins are less obtrusive than in previous vintages. Drink 1992-1998. 3,920 cases produced. Release: $13. Current: $25. **89**

1979 MARKHAM VINEYARDS MARKHAM VINEYARD: A lean, rich, concentrated 1979 that offers firm tannins and elegant, supple black cherry and currant flavors, with plenty of tannin for further cellaring. Drink 1993-2000. 2,752 cases produced. Release: $13. Current: $28. **88**

1978 MARKHAM VINEYARDS MARKHAM VINEYARD: Markham's first vintage, the 1978 is a ripe, raisiny, somewhat awkward wine with herb and prune flavors that are rich, concentrated and rather blunt, with cedar and currant notes on the finish. With time it may develop grace. Drink 1992-2000. 2,560 cases produced. Release: $13. Current: $35. **85**

1982

Markham Vineyard
YOUNTVILLE

MARKHAM.

NAPA VALLEY

CABERNET
SAUVIGNON

ESTATE GROWN, PRODUCED AND BOTTLED BY
MARKHAM VINEYARDS, ST. HELENA, CALIFORNIA, U.S.A.
RED TABLE WINE

LOUIS M. MARTINI WINERY

Monte Rosso, Sonoma Valley
Special Selection, North Coast

CLASSIFICATION: *THIRD GROWTH*

COLLECTIBILITY RATING: *A*

BEST VINTAGES:

Monte Rosso: 1984

Special Selection: 1970, 1968, 1966, 1959, 1958, 1957, 1955, 1952, 1951, 1947, 1939

AT A GLANCE
LOUIS M. MARTINI WINERY
P.O. Box 112
St. Helena, CA 94574
(707) 963-2736

Owners: The Martini family

Winemaker: Michael Martini (11 years)

Founded: 1922

First Cabernet vintage: 1933
Monte Rosso: 1979
Special Selection: 1944

Cabernet production: 46,000 cases
Monte Rosso: 900 cases
Special Selection: 3,500 cases

Cabernet acres owned: 272
Monte Rosso Vineyard: 40

Average age of vines: 20 years

Vineyard makeup: Cabernet Sauvignon (73%), Merlot (27%)
Monte Rosso Vineyard:
Cabernet
Sauvignon (100%)

Average wine makeup:
Monte Rosso: Cabernet Sauvignon (100%)
Special Selection: Cabernet Sauvignon (97%), Merlot (3%)

Time in oak: 18 months

Type of oak: French, American

Louis M. Martini is one of the great names in California Cabernet. This family-owned and operated winery in St. Helena has for more than 50 years produced some of California's most ageworthy Cabernets as well as some of its finest values. The Martini philosophy simply has been to produce the best bottle of Cabernet possible each year in a fresh, fruity, drinkable style and charge just enough money to cover the costs of grapes and winemaking and make a modest profit. The Martinis have never been wine collectors. If their Cabernets gained nuance and intrigue with age, all the better, but they did not attempt to create wines of great longevity. Perhaps founder Louis M. Martini understood that given the proper treatment, Cabernets with strong varietal personalities would age well on their own with minimal interference from the winemaker.

What has always amazed Cabernet aficionados was not so much that the Martini Cabernets were so delicious and deftly balanced but how exceptionally well they aged. Martini Cabernets often seem light and simple when released, and many people wonder whether they will ever amount to anything. But seasoned Martini drinkers can attest to how well they evolve in the bottle. Only Beaulieu and Inglenook in Napa Valley have track records that rival Martini's, and in five decades of winemaking each of the three has earned its place in the history of California wine.

The Martini winery was founded in 1922 by Italian immigrant Louis M. Martini, who studied winemaking in Italy before opening a winery in Kingsburg, Calif. Martini began making Cabernet in 1933, but after the repeal of Prohibition, he found it difficult to get Cabernet grapes. Still, he managed to produce a Cabernet after repeal and quite likely filled it out with his favorite blending grapes — Zinfandel, Petite Sirah or Barbera — a practice that he continued to his death in 1974.

If Beaulieu was modeled after the classic Bordeaux château, and Inglenook typified the California estate, Martini was the master blender, acquiring grapes from various vineyard locations in California and mixing them to create wines of harmony and grace. The oldest Martini Cabernet I have tasted was the 1939, and while the color looked pale and tea-brown, there was plenty of richness and flavor. It had the mature bottle bouquet of cedar, smoke and anise and faint black cherry flavors enhanced by a smooth, satiny texture. By 1937 Martini recognized that the grape shortage would undermine his efforts to expand production, and he purchased the Monte Rosso (Red Mountain) vineyard in the eastern hills above Glen Ellen in Sonoma Valley. The vineyard was planted to Cabernet around 1941 and began appearing in Martini Cabernets in 1946. Early on the Monte Rosso wine distinguished itself with its richness and sharply focused black cherry and currant aromas. Martini used it as the backbone for the Cabernets, always preferring to add it to the blend rather than keep it separate, a formula that worked quite well. In particular, he liked to mix Monte Rosso fruit with that from his La Loma Vineyard in the Carneros District of Napa Valley, where the fruit was leaner and tarter. He wanted no part of small French (or for that matter American) oak barrels, preferring to ferment and age his wines in 1,500-gallon redwood tanks. André Tchelistcheff is convinced that the combination of Martini's choice, well-manicured vineyards, keen tasting and blending abilities and the absence of small oak barrels guaranteed that Martini Cabernets would age gracefully, and they did.

In the 1940s, the 1947 remains a great vintage for Martini, followed by the fabulous '50s, where the Martini winery hit its stride with a succession of fine bottlings, headed by the 1951, 1952, 1955, 1957, 1958 and 1959. Each of those wines is still holding; in rare instances they are sold at auction. In the 1960s there were also many excellent bottlings, although some drank better early on and have not aged as well. The 1964, 1966 and 1968, however, are still holding on. The 1970 Special Selection is also a superb wine that is fully mature.

Careful reading of the Martini labels over the years reveals Private Reserve and Special Selection bottlings, the two top-of-the-line wines from the early days, and they are usually accompanied by a reference to California Mountain, an appellation that means Monte Rosso. Special Selection is just what the name suggests, the best lots, while Private Reserve refers to wines held for extra bottle age. In recent vintages, the Monte Rosso Cabernets, made entirely from fruit grown in that vineyard, are the ones to focus on.

In the 1970s, the Martini Cabernets took a dip in quality. Louis M.'s son Louis P. Martini, then the winemaker, admits the wines of the 1970s were not as impressive or ageworthy as their predecessors and explains it as simply the nature of the vintages. In his view, for instance, neither 1974 nor 1978 were exceptional years for Martini, even though they were in Napa Valley and throughout the North Coast.

My own theory is that Louis P. is correct, but I also think there

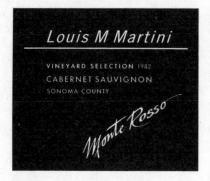

is more to it than that. The Martinis were always experimenters, particularly in the vineyard, growing grapes in different microclimates, as well as concocting different blends. The winery was not a temple of high tech like the Robert Mondavi Winery. In interviews with Louis P., he describes an era, beginning in 1968, when the Martini winery began to undertake a series of experiments using different blends, not only of Cabernet, but also increasingly introducing more Merlot and other varietals into the mix.

That practice resulted in gradually lighter, polished, elegant wines that, while certainly appealing to the Martinis' palate, lacked the richness and concentration of earlier vintages. This stylistic swing is further evidenced in 1968 by the Martinis' production that year of California's first vintage-dated Merlot. Moreover, the winery made at least four different experimental lots of 1968 Cabernet, blends of Napa-Carneros and Monte Rosso fruit, each with varying degrees of Merlot and Malbec in different cooperage, including small American oak barrels. When I tasted the four lots with Louis P. in 1989, the Cabernets with the most Merlot were the most mature and fragile, while the Cabernet from Monte Rosso aged in American oak was the best of the group, capable of another decade of aging. I'm not sure Louis P. agreed, for that was the end of American oak, and the blend increasingly featured more Merlot.

About the same time, the Martini winery began to increase production and needed more grape sources to meet production goals. Once again experimentation played a role in reshaping the style. In 1978, in perhaps the most extreme case, the winery culled fruit from five appellations — Monterey, San Luis Obispo, Carneros and two from Santa Barbara — and bottled a sixth as a blend of those five. The appellation wines revealed their regional characters, but on their own they were not as desirable as the final blend, which featured modest complexity and delicate flavors. Since the 1980s, Martini has moved to North Coast fruit.

As Martini moved toward lighter, more elegant, more forward and fleshier Cabernets, most Napa and Sonoma wineries had begun reaching for high-extract, massively proportioned, 100 percent varietal, lavishly oaked wines. The Martinis recognized this and began putting more richness back in the wines. But they acted slowly and cautiously. Beginning with the 1979 vintage, Monte Rosso fruit was singled out in separate bottlings, in full recognition that this red-soil, mountaintop vineyard is Martini's finest. Under the winemaking of Michael Martini, who took over in the late 1970s, more toasty French oak is showing up in the wines, more as background seasoning than for tannins or structure. The 1984 Monte Rosso is, in my view, the finest Martini Cabernet since the wonderful 1970. The 1987 Monte Rosso is very rich and supple, oozing with sharply focused black cherry and currant flavors and thick, smooth tannins. All of the redwood tanks were torn down in 1989 and replaced with stainless steel, which allows for greater control over fermentation temperatures and ultimately better control over the wines.

Surprisingly, a good many of the great old Louis M. Martini Cabernets can still be found in wine shops, and anyone who has enjoyed the lore of Martini Cabernets but not consumed them should go out of his way to try them. These grand, old wines are well worth the price.

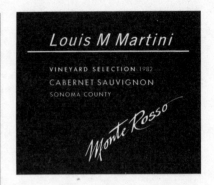

TASTING NOTES
LOUIS M. MARTINI WINERY, Various bottlings

1986 LOUIS M. MARTINI WINERY MONTE ROSSO: Pleasant and attractive in the classic Martini style that makes it drinkable now, rich and supple, with gentle black cherry and currant notes and smooth, supple tannins. A shade richer than the 1985 but a step off the pace from the 1984 Monte Rosso. Drink 1992-1999. 810 cases produced. Not Released. **86**

1985 LOUIS M. MARTINI WINERY MONTE ROSSO: A bit green and mossy but otherwise well made, with plenty of ripe berry flavors to stand behind it. Somewhat disappointing considering the quality of the vintage. Drink 1992-2000. 1,150 cases produced. Release: $22. Current: $22. **80**

1984 LOUIS M. MARTINI WINERY SPECIAL SELECTION: This wine displays open aromas and flavors of ripe black cherry and currant and good intensity, but as usual it's elegant and balanced, ready to drink now or in the next decade. Drink 1991-1997. 2,735 cases produced. Not Released. **85**

1984 LOUIS M. MARTINI WINERY MONTE ROSSO: This wine combines the Martini tradition of understated elegance and ripe, supple, generous fruit. The layers of ripe plum, cherry and spice flavors are soft and gentle, yet there is an underlying intensity that carries them on the finish. Enticing now but should age well for a decade. Best Martini Cabernet since 1970. Drink 1990-1999. 700 cases produced. Release: $22. Current: $22. **89**

1983 LOUIS M. MARTINI WINERY MONTE ROSSO: Uncommonly tannic for a Martini Cabernet, but that's what the vintage provided. This wine is still well balanced, with fresh, ripe flavors that are well defined and built for the cellar. For a Martini wine, that means it should be ready in three to four years. Drink 1993-1999. 1,150 cases produced. Release: $22. Current: $22. **86**

1983 LOUIS M. MARTINI WINERY MONTE ROSSO LOS NINOS: Elegant and supple for a 1983, just what you'd expect from the Martini style, offering plenty of delicate Cabernet flavor. Ready now or in the next five to seven years. Los Niños wines are special bottlings in honor of Michael Martini's children. Drink 1990-1997. 545 cases produced. Release: $25. Current: $25. **83**

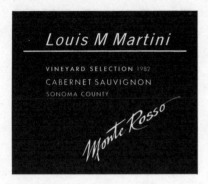

1982 LOUIS M. MARTINI WINERY MONTE ROSSO: From a difficult vintage, this is an evenhanded 1982 that is a touch coarse but backed by ripe cherry and currant-flavored Cabernet fruit and firm tannins. This should be a slow ager. Drink 1993-1999. 2,060 cases produced. Release: $22. Current: $22. **85**

1982 LOUIS M. MARTINI WINERY MONTE ROSSO LOS NINOS: A good, well-made, perfectly enjoyable 1982 that displays pretty black cherry and currant flavors in a supple, elegant style. Simple but pleasant, ready to drink. Drink 1990-1995. 550 cases produced. Release: $25. Current: $25. **82**

1981 LOUIS M. MARTINI WINERY MONTE ROSSO LOS NINOS: Rich and firm for a Martini, with a good concentration of fresh currant and black cherry flavors, finishing with a touch of anise and tannin. It's drinkable now but should hold up well for a decade. Drink 1990-1998. 535 cases produced. Release: $25. Current: $25. **85**

1980 LOUIS M. MARTINI WINERY SPECIAL SELECTION: Fully mature, with spicy anise, olive and elegant black cherry flavors. Most of the tannins have faded, and this wine appears to have the exquisite balance to age for another decade. Drink 1990-1997. 9,350 cases produced. Release: $12. Current: $12. **84**

1979 LOUIS M. MARTINI WINERY MONTE ROSSO LOT 2: Has the characteristic Martini elegance and gentle black cherry and anise flavors that linger on the finish. Just a trace of tannin left but probably enough to carry it another five to seven years. Drink 1991-1996. 2,490 cases produced. Release: $10. Current: $19. **84**

1978 LOUIS M. MARTINI WINERY SPECIAL SELECTION: Mature and complex, with lovely cedar, olive, anise and black cherry flavors that are elegant, smooth and supple. Not a Martini favorite; while it appeared to be fading just a few years ago, it has caught its stride. Ready now, but with its crisp acidity, it should hold up for another six or more years. Drink 1990-1996. 21,388 cases produced. Release: $9. Current: $23. **86**

1977 LOUIS M. MARTINI WINERY SPECIAL SELECTION: Light and faded, never much of a wine for holding, best on release. Drink 1990. 5,464 cases produced. Release: $9. Current: $20. **70**

1976 LOUIS M. MARTINI WINERY SPECIAL SELECTION: Ripe and fairly intense, with black cherry, currant and spicy anise notes and a good dose of tannin on the finish. Good balance for a drought year. Can stand further aging. Drink 1990-1997. 2,693 cases produced. Release: $9. Current: $35. **86**

1974 LOUIS M. MARTINI WINERY SPECIAL SELECTION: Fully mature and fading now after drinking well for its first decade. Most of the fruit and flavor have disappeared, leaving hints of olive and herb on the finish. Never considered a great year for Martini, although the vintage in California was excellent. Drink 1990-1992. 5,411 cases produced. Release: $10. Current: $45. **77**

1972 LOUIS M. MARTINI WINERY SPECIAL SELECTION: Faded and over the hill, from a weak rain-plagued vintage. Drink 1990. 2,055 cases produced. Release: $5. Current: $65. **63**

1970 LOUIS M. MARTINI WINERY SPECIAL SELECTION: One of the modern Martini classics, the 1970 is still holding its own. Though it's lighter and less concentrated than the best 1970s, it is fully mature, with cedar, olive and black cherry flavors and a trace of tannin on the finish. Ready now. Drink 1990-1995. 7,845 cases produced. Release: $8. Current: $90. **88**

1968 LOUIS M. MARTINI WINERY SPECIAL SELECTION: Early on the 1968 was a sensational wine. It is still drinking quite well, but it is at its peak and beginning to shed its rich, supple, black cherry flavors. Drink 1990-1994. 1,926 cases produced. Release: $6. Current: $95. **90**

1966 LOUIS M. MARTINI WINERY SPECIAL SELECTION: Has elegant, complex, mature black cherry and anise flavors that are smooth and delicate on the finish. Past its prime, like most 1966s; should be consumed now. Drink 1990-1992. 2,023 cases produced. Release: $6. Current: $110. **87**

1964 LOUIS M. MARTINI WINERY SPECIAL SELECTION: A shade past its prime but still complete and complex, with cedar, black cherry and anise flavors that are smooth and supple. Drink 1990-1992. 1,582 cases produced. Release: $6. Current: $100. **85**

1962 LOUIS M. MARTINI WINERY PRIVATE RESERVE: Fully mature, with cedar and olive notes to offset the black cherry flavors and evidence of oxidation coming through on the finish. Drink 1990. 1,151 cases produced. Release: $3.50. Current: $80. **73**

1961 LOUIS M. MARTINI WINERY SPECIAL SELECTION: Fully mature, with cedar and spice flavors and a faint hint of Cabernet left. Its best years are behind it, but it's still drinking fine. Drink 1990-1994. 1,092 cases produced. Release: $4. Current: $180. **80**

1959 LOUIS M. MARTINI WINERY SPECIAL SELECTION: Tasted only once in 1987. Typical Martini that had held its own and gained depth and complexity, with great harmony and finesse. I can only imagine it drank exceptionally well a decade earlier. Drink 1990-1992. 1,500 cases produced. Release: $4.50. Current: $140. **87**

1958 LOUIS M. MARTINI WINERY SPECIAL SELECTION: Another in the string of excellent Martinis of the 1950s, the 1958 is also fully mature and on the downward side, but it has provided many moments of sheer pleasure. Plenty of complex, fully developed fruit that is soft and luscious. Drink 1990-1992. 1,750 cases produced. Release: $4.50. Current: $220. **88**

1957 LOUIS M. MARTINI WINERY SPECIAL SELECTION: Long

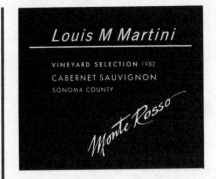

considered a Martini classic, the 1957 is still drinking exceptionally well, though its best years are behind it. The ripe cherry, plum and anise flavors are smooth and refined, elegant and delicious. Drink 1990-1992. 1,994 cases produced. Release: $3.50. Current: $175. **91**

1956 LOUIS M. MARTINI WINERY PRIVATE RESERVE MOUNTAIN: A rich, cedary bouquet with black cherry and anise and traces of oxidation. Drink 1990-1991. 1,500 cases produced. Release: $2.50. Current: $90. **77**

1955 LOUIS M. MARTINI WINERY SPECIAL SELECTION: Until the past few years, the 1955 had aged amazingly well in the finest Martini tradition, exhibiting mature cedar, anise and faint cherry flavors that are elegant and refined, with great length and persistence. Drink 1990-1992. 1,035 cases produced. Release: $2.50. Current: $190. **87**

1952 LOUIS M. MARTINI WINERY SPECIAL SELECTION: The 1952 is considered one of the all-time great Martini Cabernets. I have been fortunate to drink it twice, and both times it was outstanding, showing remarkable complexity, richness, depth and length. A fabulous wine. Drink 1990-1992. About 1,000 cases produced. Release: $2.50. Current: $450. **93**

1951 LOUIS M. MARTINI WINERY SPECIAL SELECTION: From an excellent vintage, the 1951 was holding up fine in 1985, but the last time I tried it the fruit was rapidly deteriorating. Still, it was delicious and would not disappoint anyone who has the opportunity to try it soon. Drink 1990-1992. About 1,000 cases produced. Release: $2. Current: $275. **87**

1947 LOUIS M. MARTINI WINERY SPECIAL SELECTION: I have only had the 1947 once, and it was an amazingly complex and elegant Cabernet that had aged exceptionally well, offering layers of mature anise, cherry and spice nuances. Fully mature. Drink 1990-1992. 1,151 cases produced. Release: $1.50. Current: $750. **90**

1945 LOUIS M. MARTINI WINERY SPECIAL SELECTION: Past its prime, with nut, cedar, pine and coffee flavors where the Cabernet used to be. Tasted in May 1985. Drink 1990. About 1,000 cases produced. Release: $1.50. Current: $400. **75**

1943 LOUIS M. MARTINI WINERY PRIVATE RESERVE VILLA DEL REY: The only time I've tried this wine it tasted very mature and oxidized; a faulty cork was suspected. Tasted in May 1985. Drink 1990. About 1,000 cases produced. Release: $1.50. Current: $400. **70**

1939 LOUIS M. MARTINI WINERY SPECIAL RESERVE: The oldest Martini Cabernet I've tasted, this wine had a very mature, light-garnet color, but on the palate it showed more flavor and richness, with mature, complex cedar and anise flavors that were elegant and lively, remarkably well preserved for a wine this old. Tasted in May 1985. Drink 1990-1992. About 1,000 cases produced. Release: $1.25. Current: $1,000. **90**

MAYACAMAS VINEYARDS

Mount Veeder, Napa Valley

CLASSIFICATION: *FIRST GROWTH*

COLLECTIBILITY RATING: *AAA*

BEST VINTAGES: *1985, 1984, 1983, 1981, 1980, 1979, 1978, 1977, 1974, 1970, 1969, 1968*

Mayacamas Vineyards is legendary for its distinctive, intensely flavored, austere and tannic mountain-grown Cabernets. Its reputation for producing amazingly complex, long-lived wines is well deserved, for Mayacamas Cabernets typically take a decade or longer to mature fully and shed their tannic veneer. In exceptional vintages such as 1970 and 1974, for instance, the wines are still not fully developed and have the potential to age 30 years or longer. Once they do mature, the Mayacamas Cabernets are as rich, complex and structured as any of those produced in California. Because of the great depth, concentration of fruit, firm, hard tannins and slow development, Mayacamas has inspired both a cult following that buys the wine through a winery mailing list and skeptics who question whether the wines will ever evolve, much less into greatness.

Mayacamas, at 2,000 feet of elevation, is high atop Mount Veeder, which is in the rugged Mayacamas Mountain range that forms the western boundary of Napa Valley. The old stone winery dates back to 1889, when it was built and founded by John Henry Fisher, of Stuttgart, Germany, and was known as the Fisher Winery. In 1941, Jack and Mary Taylor bought the winery and began replanting the vineyard and refurbishing the winery. In 1968, Robert Travers, a former stockbroker, led a group of investors who purchased the winery.

The winemaking style at Mayacamas is very deliberate, involving little manipulation or softening of the Cabernets. The wines are typically very ripe, rich, concentrated and tannic, with pretty floral and blueberry flavors early on. After years of tasting these wines on release and then reexamining them as they develop, it is clear that they can be deceptive and unimpressive at first, often not showing very well and enhancing Mayacamas' reputation for being notoriously slow developers.

The oldest Cabernets that I have tasted from Mayacamas date back to 1962, which is believed to be the winery's first vintage. In the vintages from 1962 to 1969, most of the Cabernet fruit was purchased from vineyards on the Napa Valley floor. Of the early wines, the 1964 vintage is still hanging on, but barely, while the best of the 1960s are

AT A GLANCE

MAYACAMAS VINEYARDS
1155 Lokoya Road
Napa, CA 94558
(707) 224-4030

Owner: Mayacamas Vineyards (Robert Travers, president)

Winemaker: Bob Travers (21 years)

Founded: 1889, reestablished: 1941

First Cabernet vintage: 1962

Cabernet production: 2,000 cases

Cabernet acres owned: 14

Average age of vines: 20 years

Vineyard makeup: Cabernet Sauvignon (86%), Merlot (7%), Cabernet Franc (7%)

Average wine makeup: Cabernet Sauvignon (88%), Merlot (6%), Cabernet Franc (6%)

Time in oak: 32 months

Type of oak: French, American

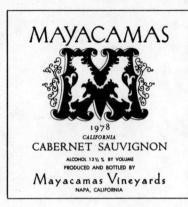

MAYACAMAS
1978
CALIFORNIA
CABERNET SAUVIGNON
ALCOHOL 13½ % BY VOLUME
PRODUCED AND BOTTLED BY
Mayacamas Vineyards
NAPA, CALIFORNIA

clearly the superb 1968 and 1969 vintages, both of which are fully mature and ready to drink. The 1969 in particular is holding up better than most wines from that vintage. Beginning with the 1970 vintage, the Mayacamas Cabernets are 100 percent mountain grown, produced from grapes grown in the Mayacamas Vineyards' 14-acre vineyard and grapes purchased from other mountain vineyards. The 1970 is one of the most magnificent Cabernets ever produced in California, with great depth, intensity of flavor and longevity. The last two tastings left me wondering whether it was still too early to uncork this dramatic wine. It can be consumed now, but it appears to have the character to age 30 years.

The 1971 through 1973 vintages are all holding well but are ready to drink. The 1974 is built much like the 1970, with great intensity, depth and flavor that should easily carry it into the 21st century. The 1975 is a fine example of that vintage, while the 1976 is typical of the drought year, very ripe and tannic. The 1977, 1978 and 1979 vintages are all sensational, ranking among the best Cabernets of those vintages. All are approachable, particularly the 1977, but the 1978 and 1979 both need another five to seven years and can age another 10 to 15 years. In the 1980s, the 1980 and 1981 are both excellent, while the 1982 is damp and disappointing but not atypical for that vintage. The 1983 is an extremely tannic wine from a tannic vintage, and it should age a long, long time. The 1984 is more supple and somewhat lighter for a Mayacamas, while the 1985 is somewhat more elegant and noticeably less tannic.

With their distinctive style, ageability and enormous complexity, Mayacamas Cabernets rank among the top 10 or 15 in California. The Cabernets are among the longest lived and best bets for the cellar. Production rarely reaches 2,000 cases, and even the 1984 at $20 represents great value for consumers and collectors. In future vintages the winery is headed toward estate-bottled Cabernets made exclusively from its vineyard and including small portions of Merlot and Cabernet Franc.

TASTING NOTES

MAYACAMAS VINEYARDS, Mount Veeder, Napa Valley

1986 MAYACAMAS VINEYARDS: Light and simple for a young Mayacamas, which makes me wonder whether I'm missing something. Several notes show the same impression — the berry and pepper notes are clean and attractive, but they are nowhere near as deep, rich and concentrated as the classic Mayacamas style. The tannins are soft enough to drink right now. Drink 1991-1996. 2,150 cases produced. Not Released. **86**

1985 MAYACAMAS VINEYARDS: A gorgeous 1985, brimming with sharply defined ripe currant and plum flavors, with hints of flowers and blueberries that are elegant and supple. Earth and mineral flavors linger on the palate. The crisp acidity and fine, integrated tannins make for impeccable balance and great length. Should be ready in five to eight years and age a long, long time. Drink 1997-2007. 2,025 cases produced. Release: $25. Current: $25. **92**

1984 MAYACAMAS VINEYARDS: Light and fruity for a Mayacamas but typical of the vintage, this wine has bright ripe blueberry and jammy plum notes, but it is not nearly as tannic or structured as most Mayacamas Cabernets. It will be ready sooner but will also age well. Drink 1994-2000. 1,220 cases produced. Release: $20. Current: $20. **90**

1983 MAYACAMAS VINEYARDS: Tannic and intense, this is one of the better balanced 1983s. Promises a long life in the bottle, with enough rich, ripe currant and black cherry flavors to stand up to the dry, hard tannins. Nowhere near ready to drink, this one will require another decade, probably longer, before the tannins subside. Drink 1997-2005. 2,280 cases produced. Release: $20. Current: $25. **90**

1982 MAYACAMAS VINEYARDS: A mediocre wine from a difficult vintage, with herbal, weedy flavors that detract. The structure is fine, but the flavors are off. Drink 1993-1998. 2,700 cases produced. Release: $20. Current: $25. **77**

1981 MAYACAMAS VINEYARDS: A first-rate 1981, firm, tight, lean and concentrated, with bright black cherry, blueberry and raspberry flavors. Not too tannic for a Mayacamas, it is nonetheless well structured and has the intensity and depth for midterm aging. Drinkable now but better in a few years. Drink 1993-1999. 1,830 cases produced. Release: $18. Current: $25. **91**

1980 MAYACAMAS VINEYARDS: Another amazing Mayacamas, the 1980 is a very elegant, supple, spicy and rich wine oozing with the characteristic Mayacamas black cherry, plum and currant flavors and very fine tannins that give it firmness and structure without being too powerful. One of the best from this vintage, a charming Cabernet. Drink 1994-2002. 1,870 cases produced. Release: $18. Current: $30. **92**

1979 MAYACAMAS VINEYARDS: Very intense, packed with ripe, rich fruit, with layers of black cherry, currant, plum and jam notes and very fine, integrated tannins that are well proportioned, leaving a satiny smooth finish. But don't let that fool you; this is still a youngster. Drink 1995-2005. 1,905 cases produced. Release: $18. Current: $35. **95**

1978 MAYACAMAS VINEYARDS: One of the great 1978s, it is deep, rich, ripe and powerful, loaded with intense currant and black cherry flavors, with a touch of earth, pepper and mineral notes that add complexity. A firm, tannic grip on the finish suggests further patience is required. Drink 1994-2004. 1,820 cases produced. Release: $18. Current: $60. **94**

1977 MAYACAMAS VINEYARDS: A beautifully defined 1977, rich,

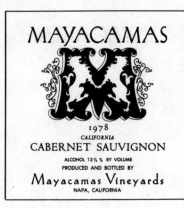

deep and concentrated, with pretty black cherry, mint and currant flavors that are supple and layered on the palate, finishing with complexity, subtlety and elegance. Nearing its peak. Drink 1992-2000. 1,510 cases produced. Release: $15. Current: $60. **92**

1976 MAYACAMAS VINEYARDS: Very ripe and tannic, with supple plum, currant, pepper and mint flavors that are smooth and silky before the tannins kick in, leaving a dry, tannic finish. Very good; it's not quite in balance, but it may have the fruit to outlive the tannin. Drink 1992-1998. 1,380 cases produced. Release: $15. Current: $50. **84**

1975 MAYACAMAS VINEYARDS: A smooth, supple, elegant 1975, with gentle cedar, earth and currant flavors framed by firm tannins. This wine has the long, enduring elegance and flavor that are the trademark of the best Cabernets of this vintage. Very fine balance, with a lingering finish. Drink 1990-1995. 2,315 cases produced. Release: $12. Current: $60. **89**

1974 MAYACAMAS VINEYARDS: A young, intense, beautifully focused 1974, rich and elegant, firm and concentrated, with spicy pepper notes to complement the deep currant and black cherry flavors. This is a complex wine that still has plenty of tannin, but it's nearing its peak. Drink 1992-2004. 2,300 cases produced. Release: $9.50. Current: $115. **95**

1973 MAYACAMAS VINEYARDS: Enticing, with well-focused black cherry flavors and a touch of elegance. This wine is fully developed, smooth and supple but with enough depth and intensity to carry the flavors. The finish offers a sense of delicacy. Drink 1990-1996. 2,050 cases produced. Release: $9. Current: $90. **87**

1972 MAYACAMAS VINEYARDS: A pleasant 1972, with spicy pepper notes and ripe currant and plum flavors. Most of the tannins have been resolved, leaving a silky smooth texture. Drink 1990-1993. 1,620 cases produced. Release: $8. Current: $70. **82**

1971 MAYACAMAS VINEYARDS: A very pretty wine from an underrated vintage, supple and fully mature, with complex plum, cedar, spice and mineral flavors, good depth and richness, moderate tannins and a good follow-through. Ready now. Drink 1990-1995. 1,490 cases produced. Release: $8. Current: $80. **86**

1970 MAYACAMAS VINEYARDS: Along with Heitz Martha's Vineyard, Ridge Monte Bello and Beaulieu Private Reserve, this wine is the cream of the crop from the fabulous 1970 vintage and one of the greatest California Cabernets of the decade. This is a deeply colored wine, rich, bold and dramatic, loaded with fresh, ripe fruit and firm tannins, capable of aging another decade, maybe two. The ripe currant, plum and spicy mint flavors are complex, intense and concentrated, and the finish is long and full. Give it time. Drink 1996-2008. 1,325 cases produced. Release: $8. Current: $130. **96**

1969 MAYACAMAS VINEYARDS: Ready to drink, holding up better than most wines from this vintage, offering sweet, ripe, spicy currant and plum flavors and earth and mineral nuances that are soft and smooth, finishing with delicacy. Most of the tannins have faded. Drink 1990-1995. 1,080 cases produced. Release: $6.50. Current: $100. **89**

1968 MAYACAMAS VINEYARDS: Fully mature and a shade past its peak, this wine has held up remarkably well and has plenty of life, displaying ripe plum and currant flavors along with toasty, earthy notes and a smooth texture. Most of the tannins have been resolved. Drink 1990-1995. 680 cases produced. Release: $4.50. Current: $125. **88**

1967 MAYACAMAS VINEYARDS: A mediocre wine from a vintage that produced elegant, early drinking wines. Never one to keep, this wine is past its peak, decadent and earthy, with harsh, bitter flavors. Best to avoid. 800 cases produced. Release: $4. Current: $125. **65**

1966 MAYACAMAS VINEYARDS: Still plenty of fresh, ripe fruit in this elegant 1966 that is in decline. The spicy black cherry, cedar and currant flavors are smooth and delicate, offering subtlety and complexity on the finish. A slight trace of tannin is still apparent, but this wine is ready. Drink 1990-1993. 530 cases produced. Release: $3.50. Current: $125. **75**

1965 MAYACAMAS VINEYARDS: Swampy and earthy, with faded flavors and not much to like. Better 10 years ago. Best to avoid. 475 cases produced. Release: $2.75. Current: $150. **65**

1963 MAYACAMAS VINEYARDS: From an average vintage in Napa, this 1963 is barely hanging on, with faint black cherry, earth, and cedar flavors that get swampy on the finish. The tannins are gone; better a decade ago. Best to avoid. 420 cases produced. Release: $2. Current: $150. **69**

1962 MAYACAMAS VINEYARDS: From a mediocre vintage, this 1962 still offers black cherry and spice flavors that are very fragile and delicate. It's in decline. Best to avoid. 350 cases produced. Release: $2. Current: $150. **68**

MERRYVALE VINEYARDS
Napa Valley

CLASSIFICATION: *FIFTH GROWTH*
COLLECTIBILITY RATING: *Not rated*
BEST VINTAGES: *1986, 1985, 1983*

Despite only four vintages and no Cabernet acreage of its own, Merryvale, a proprietary red made at Sunny St. Helena Winery in St. Helena, has managed to turn out a consistently complex, austere, richly flavored Cabernet each year. Early on, Ric Forman, of Sterling, Newton and Forman wineries, oversaw winemaking, and the first vintage in 1983 was impressive for its depth and concentration in that tannic year. The 1984 follows that austere style, in contrast to the generally fleshier, more opulent Cabernets from that vintage. The 1985 appears to be the finest, with sharply defined fruit, while the 1986 is slowly evolving along the same course and will need another four to five years to fully develop.

Production remains small at 1,600 cases, and the vineyard sources are solid; Cabernet from Spottswoode and Merlot from Winery Lake have found their way into the Merryvale red. The proprietary blend is named after the Merryvale building in San Francisco and is owned by five partners, including Robin Lail, co-owner of Napanook Vineyard, who is also Christian Moueix's partner in Dominus.

TASTING NOTES
MERRYVALE VINEYARDS, Napa Valley

1986 MERRYVALE VINEYARDS RED TABLE WINE: A firm, structured 1986 with deep black cherry, floral, cedar and anise flavors that are rich, concentrated and well proportioned. This wine is young and elegant, with plenty of tannin to carry it another decade. Drink 1994-2002. 1,604 cases produced. Release: $25. Current: $25. **89**

1985 MERRYVALE VINEYARDS RED TABLE WINE: This one looks like an ager. The fruit is sharply defined, with pretty vanilla, mint, cherry and currant flavors, which are lean and elegant, fine tannins and good length. Should begin drinking well in three to five years and ease through the decade. Drink 1994-2001. 1,662 cases produced. Release: $24. Current: $24. **91**

AT A GLANCE
MERRYVALE VINEYARDS
1000 Main St.
St. Helena, CA 94574
(707) 963-7777

Owners: Bill Harlan, Peter Stocker, John Montgomery, Robin and Jon Lail

Winemaker: Bob Levy (6 years)

Founded: 1983

First Cabernet vintage: 1983

Cabernet production: 1,600 cases

Cabernet acres owned: none

Average age of vines: n/a

Vineyard makeup: n/a

Average wine makeup: Cabernet Sauvignon (74%), Cabernet Franc (13%), Merlot (13%)

Time in oak: 20 months

Type of oak: French (Nevers)

1984 MERRYVALE VINEYARDS RED TABLE WINE: More austere and leaner than most Cabernets from this vintage, with distinct cedar, black cherry and herb flavors that are beginning to develop. Plenty of depth, acidity and tannin for midterm cellaring. Approachable soon. Drink 1993-1998. 1,026 cases produced. Release: $24. Current: $28. **86**

1983 MERRYVALE VINEYARDS RED TABLE WINE: The first vintage from Merryvale produced a very rich and concentrated wine with crisp currant, black cherry, mint and floral notes that are framed by firm tannins. A good candidate for cellaring for five to seven years. Drink 1993-1999. 694 cases produced. Release: $18. Current: $30. **88**

ROBERT MONDAVI WINERY

Reserve, Oakville, Napa Valley

CLASSIFICATION: *FIRST GROWTH*

COLLECTIBILITY RATING: *AA*

BEST VINTAGES: *1986, 1985, 1984, 1979, 1978, 1974, 1971, 1970*

AT A GLANCE

ROBERT MONDAVI WINERY
7801 St. Helena Highway
Oakville, CA 94562
(707) 963-9611

Owners: The Robert Mondavi family

Winemaker: Tim Mondavi (13 years)

Founded: 1966

First Cabernet vintage: 1966
   Reserve: 1971

Cabernet production: 100,000 cases
   (est.)
   Reserve: 14,000 cases

Cabernet acres owned: 374

Average age of vines: 15 years

Vineyard makeup: Cabernet Sauvignon (84%), Merlot (10%), Cabernet Franc (6%)

Average wine makeup: Cabernet Sauvignon (84%), Cabernet Franc (12%), Merlot (4%)

Time in oak: 18 months

Type of oak: French

No one has done more to spread the gospel of Napa Valley Cabernet than Robert Mondavi. Since he persuaded his father, Cesare Mondavi, to purchase the old Charles Krug Winery and move to the valley in the 1940s, he has been on a mission to put California Cabernet on a par with the great Bordeaux, and to a large extent, he has succeeded.

Early in his career, Mondavi developed a particular passion for Cabernet Sauvignon. He identified the best soils and climate in Napa Valley, refined vinification techniques, rewarded growers for providing Cabernet grapes at optimum ripeness levels, aged Cabernet in new French oak barrels and sold the wines to a cautious, but increasingly curious, public. Mondavi realized that, of all California wines, Cabernet Sauvignon and its blending Bordeaux varieties had the greatest potential and could compete internationally.

By the 1960s, Mondavi became disgruntled by the lack of progress and imagination at Charles Krug, both in winemaking and marketing, and he abruptly departed to form his own winery in Oakville in 1966, later winning a lawsuit against his family that resulted in his gaining control of some of the Mondavi family's choicest vineyards.

A man of ideas and vision, Mondavi has been described as a brilliant innovator and tireless experimenter, and through 22 vintages at Krug (see Charles Krug) and 20 at his own winery, those characteristics are readily apparent. A keen student of winemaking, he learned both on his own and from the likes of André Tchelistcheff and John Daniel Jr., in the 1940s and 1950s. Then it was off to Bordeaux, where he meticulously studied the techniques of the Bordelais, touching off a revolution of sorts when he began to age his Cabernets in new French oak. Many vintners followed suit, although not everyone enjoyed the same level of success. In the early 1970s, a good many Cabernets from Napa Valley were lavishly oaked and overoaked, a trend that has recently lessened.

One of the keys to Mondavi's success is that he knows good vineyards. The principal source for the Mondavi Reserve is the historic To-Kalon Vineyard in Oakville, a huge parcel that adjoins Martha's Vineyard (made by Heitz) and yields some of the richest, most concentrated Cabernets produced in Napa Valley. Mondavi's first vintage, in 1966, made in his California mission-style, state-of-the art winery, demonstrated the new direction. While the Charles Krug Cabernets were extremely ripe, coarse, often one-dimensional but nonetheless ageworthy, Mondavi sought refinement, elegance, harmony, balance and finesse in his wines. The 1966 drank extremely well on release, possessing the unmistakable, classic Mondavi flavors of rich mint, currant, berry, cedar and spice, all in harmony and balance. The 1967, 1968 and 1969 vintages were all triumphs, consistent in quality and firmly establishing the Mondavi style. In 1970, Mondavi produced a rich, dramatic Cabernet that is at its peak now, followed in 1971 by the first of his Reserve bottlings, which today remains a classic and the top California wine of that vintage. The 1971 Reserve showed off Mondavi's ability as a blender, for it contains nearly 40 percent Cabernet Franc. No Reserve was produced in 1972, a difficult vintage in Napa Valley, but in 1973, Mondavi was back in stride with a remarkably elegant, rich, savory Reserve that peaked a few years ago but still offers enjoyment.

In 1974, the Mondavi Reserve shows considerable bottle variation. I am told that this is because of a filtration experiment which resulted in some bottles that were mediocre and others that were monumental. I have tried both kinds on numerous occasions, enjoying the great bottle for its massive concentration of ripe, fresh, rich, black cherry and currant flavors and long full finish. The other bottles have turned up frequently as well, and they come across as stripped and dull. Unfortunately the bottles have identical lables. Collectors who buy at auction should be aware of this.

The 1975 vintage that followed returned to elegance and finesse, followed by a successful 1976, a simple but pleasant 1977 that has peaked, and a rich, opulent 1978 that matches the 1974 in quality. The 1979 Reserve is also a sensational wine, just now reaching its pinnacle and showing the ripe flavors found in the 1978.

Beginning with the 1980 Reserve and continuing through the 1983 vintage, however, the wines have not aged nearly as gracefully as their predecessors. Tim Mondavi, the winemaker, is not a fan of any of the vintages, which in part explains why the quality dropped. Perhaps too much manipulation and processing of the wines robbed them of their richness. Surely there were fine wines made in those vintages by wineries nearby. There is also the theory that Mondavi's best grapes and wines were used for the joint-venture wine (see Opus One) that he began producing in 1979 with Baron Philippe de Rothschild of Château Mouton-Rothschild. The Mondavis maintain this isn't the case, insisting that Opus One did not pull fruit from To-Kalon. Nevertheless, the 1980 Reserve is laced with herb and vegetal flavors and is thin and tart, while the Opus One 1980 is much better. The 1981, while looking like a winner early on, lacks depth and complexity; the 1982 has, at times, shown a bark and earth quality that is troublesome. With the 1983 it's the same story. Early on it appeared to have the

1979
Napa Valley
CABERNET SAUVIGNON
ALCOHOL 11% BY VOLUME
PRODUCED AND BOTTLED BY
ROBERT MONDAVI WINERY
OAKVILLE, CALIFORNIA

richness and concentration to stand up to the drying tannins of the 1983 vintage, but in recent tastings, it has been much less inspiring. In the 1984 there is more richness and flavor, with beautiful black cherry fruit that is elegant, seductive and more complex. Both the 1985 and 1986 Reserves show more richness and depth, a signal that Tim Mondavi has readjusted the style, putting more fruit, richness and power back in the wines.

Cabernet Reserve production figures began to creep upward with the huge 1974 and 1978 crops, and in the most recent vintages, they hover around 14,000 cases. In addition, Mondavi produces more than 100,000 cases of the Mondavi regular, which is often a tremendous bottle of wine at a much lower price than the Reserve. Despite its volume, the Reserve ranks high as a collectible.

TASTING NOTES

ROBERT MONDAVI WINERY, Reserve, Oakville, Napa Valley

1986 ROBERT MONDAVI WINERY RESERVE: An amazing wine for its depth and concentration of fruit, it surpasses the superb 1985 Reserve with additional richness, power and pure fruit. With time, the 1986 Reserve may emerge as the finest bottling ever of Mondavi Reserve, a wine with fine aging potential. Defines the elegance Mondavi seeks in his Reserve bottlings. Drink 1996-2004. 14,000 cases produced. Release: $35. Current: $35. **95**

1985 ROBERT MONDAVI WINERY RESERVE: An intense, elegantly proportioned wine, with a rich, deep, concentrated core of currant, cassis and cherry flavors, packaged in a sleek, lean framework. Deep and complex, with long flavors echoing on the finish. Young and undeveloped, this wine has excellent potential. Mondavi's finest since 1978 or 1979. Drink 1993-2002. 15,000 cases produced. Release: $40. Current: $40. **95**

1984 ROBERT MONDAVI WINERY RESERVE: Supple and rich, bursting with ripe fruit in a generous style, with beautifully focused black cherry and currant flavors that are lively and elegant, tannins in the background, very fine texture and flavors that linger long and full on the finish. Great harmony, delicacy and toasty French oak. Drink 1992-2000. 9,000 cases produced. Release: $37. Current: $37. **92**

1983 ROBERT MONDAVI WINERY RESERVE: Tight, lean and firm, with the rich, ripe plum, currant and mint flavors to stand up to the drying tannins and a genteel underlying intensity that gains on the palate. While it is very good, it lacks the supple richness and opulence of Mondavi's greatest. Considering how the 1980, 1981 and 1982 have aged, I would begin to drink this wine up. It's never going to be outstanding. Drink 1991-1999. 15,000 cases produced. Release: $30. Current: $35. **83**

1982 ROBERT MONDAVI WINERY RESERVE: A lean, elegant 1982, with ripe plum, mint and spice flavors that are well proportioned and balanced but not especially rich or generous. The toughest wine in this lineup, with cedar and black cherry flavors coming through on the finish. At times the earthiness has been overbearing. Drink 1992-1998. 14,000 cases produced. Release: $30. Current: $38. **82**

1981 ROBERT MONDAVI WINERY RESERVE: This is a very correct and well-made Reserve that was drinking quite well until the past year, when it began to shed its fruit and richness. It is still a very good wine, with the trademark Mondavi currant and mint nuances, but it lacks depth and complexity and does not appear to have the richness for long-term cellaring. It is drinking about as well as it will. Drink 1990-1995. 12,000 cases produced. Release: $30. Current: $30. **83**

1980 ROBERT MONDAVI WINERY RESERVE: Pronounced herb and vegetal notes override the fruit, and it is tart and unbalanced, greenish and slightly underripe, an odd wine that doesn't fit the Mondavi style. Drink 1992-1998. 13,000 cases produced. Release: $30. Current: $35. **79**

1979 ROBERT MONDAVI WINERY RESERVE: Dense, rich and concentrated, with ripe currant, black cherry and mint flavors that are intense and vibrant, firm tannins and crisp acidity. Develops more flavor and complexity with aeration and shows more muscle than the fleshy 1978. Drink 1991-2000. 11,500 cases produced. Release: $25. Current: $45. **92**

1978 ROBERT MONDAVI WINERY RESERVE: Rich, concentrated and intense, full of currant, cedar, coffee, mint and cherry flavors that are vibrant and complex, with a touch of elegance that gives it delicacy and subtlety without robbing it of its richness and flavor. A beautiful wine with layers of complexity, it gains in the glass. Drink 1990-1998. 11,000 cases produced. Release: $40. Current: $58. **92**

1977 ROBERT MONDAVI WINERY RESERVE: A shade past its peak, the 1977 is still showing plenty of ripe currant, cedar and spice flavors that are elegant and well balanced, ready to drink now. Drink 1990-1993. 9,500 cases produced. Release: $35. Current: $40. **84**

1976 ROBERT MONDAVI WINERY RESERVE: From a drought year that yielded very ripe and somewhat disjointed wines, this wine is rich and concentrated, with layers of cherry, currant and anise flavors that are supported by firm, structured tannins. A big, robust wine much like the 1974. Drink 1990-1994. 8,500 cases produced. Release: $25. Current: $40. **84**

1975 ROBERT MONDAVI WINERY RESERVE: The 1975 was always elegant and delicate compared to the rich opulence of the 1974. In recent tasting it still offers elegance and finesse and is quite enjoyable,

1979
Napa Valley
CABERNET SAUVIGNON
ALCOHOL 13% BY VOLUME
PRODUCED AND BOTTLED BY
ROBERT MONDAVI WINERY
OAKVILLE, CALIFORNIA

but its best days are behind it. Drink 1990-1992. 7,000 cases produced. Release: $30. Current: $75. **86**

1974 ROBERT MONDAVI WINERY RESERVE: A real blockbuster, extremely rich and ripe, jammed with fresh, deep, black cherry and currant flavors, with cedar and anise notes that add complexity. Highlights the character of the vintage with its unusually ripe fruit, powerful concentration and long, full finish. Considerable bottle variation among the different, but identically labeled bottlings, two of which appear to be flawed. Drink 1990-1996. 9,000 cases produced. Release: $30. Current: $95. **92**

1973 ROBERT MONDAVI WINERY RESERVE: The 1973, after drinking exceptionally well for most of its life, is beginning to show the signs of old age. While it's elegant and refined, smooth and supple, with rich tar and cedar notes to complement the currant and spice flavors, it is as good as it will be. Drink 1990-1994. 4,500 cases produced. Release: $12. Current: $80. **82**

1972 ROBERT MONDAVI WINERY: The 1972 vintage was a difficult one, and very few exceptional wines were produced. The 1972 Mondavi was an exception, although it only ripened to 20.6 degrees Brix and 11.4 percent alcohol. It drank very well for the first 12 years of its life. Now it is in full decline, with a touch of brown sugar and mature fruit. Drink 1990. Release: $6. Current: $45. **75**

1971 ROBERT MONDAVI WINERY RESERVE: A monumental wine that is very deep, rich and concentrated, with lively, vibrant fruit that is smooth and supple, yet showing underlying strength. Clearly one of the elite of this vintage. A voluptuous wine, with fruit complexities echoing on finish. Mondavi's first Reserve. Drink 1990-1996. 4,000 cases produced. Release: $12. Current: $130. **93**

1970 ROBERT MONDAVI WINERY UNFINED: The 1970 Mondavi Unfined is still a very rich and dramatic Cabernet, with ripe, complex, cherry, currant and spice flavors that are well proportioned, elegant and supple and a long, full finish. Mature and at its peak, this wine should hold another five to eight years, but it's best to drink it soon. Drink 1990-1996. 4,000 cases produced. Release: $12. Current: $120. **89**

1969 ROBERT MONDAVI WINERY UNFINED: In slightly better condition than the 1968, with a touch more finesse and complexity, the 1969 exhibits rich cherry, currant and anise flavors that are supple and smooth. Most of the tannins have been resolved, and there is a touch of mint on the finish. Best to drink it now, but it should remain healthy another five years. Drink 1990-1995. 3,000 cases produced. Release: $12. Current: $155. **86**

1968 ROBERT MONDAVI WINERY UNFINED: The 1968 vintage was an excellent one in Napa Valley, and the Mondavi Unfined has been drinking well for most of its 20 years. It is now fully mature and in decline, becoming rather fragile, with very ripe, mature currant and cherry flavors. The finish is very dry, slightly coarse and tannic. It's holding on but lacking finesse. Drink 1990-1994. 2,000 cases produced. Release: $8.50. Current: $135. **83**

1967 ROBERT MONDAVI WINERY: Like the 1966, the 1967 drank very well for the first decade after release, but it is now a shadow of its former self. The fruit is fully mature, and there are faint hints of mint, ripe cherry, raisin and spicy cedar. Drink 1990. Release: $5. Current: $100. **84**

1966 ROBERT MONDAVI WINERY: Mondavi's first vintage after departing from Charles Krug, the 1966 reached its peak a decade after the vintage and drank exceptionally well for years. It is now beginning to lose its fruit and charm, though it is still a pleasant wine and an experience to drink. Has good value as a collectible, being Mondavi's first Cabernet. Drink 1990. 1,500 cases produced. Release: $5. Current: $165. **80**

At A Glance

MONTICELLO CELLARS
4242 Big Ranch Road
Napa, CA 94558
(707) 253-2187

Owner: Jay Corley

Winemaker: Alan Phillips (9 years)

Founded: 1980

First Cabernet vintage: 1980
Corley Reserve: 1982

Cabernet production: 10,000 cases
Corley Reserve: 2,000 cases

Cabernet acres owned: 34

Average age of vines: 18 years

Vineyard makeup: Cabernet Sauvignon (77%), Merlot (23%)

Average wine makeup: Cabernet Sauvignon (94%), Merlot (6%)

Time in oak: 24 months

Type of oak: French (Nevers)

MONTICELLO CELLARS

Corley Reserve, Napa Valley

CLASSIFICATION: *FOURTH GROWTH*
COLLECTIBILITY RATING: *Not rated*
BEST VINTAGES: *1986, 1985, 1984, 1983, 1982*

With its Corley Reserve Cabernet, Monticello Cellars, located north of the city of Napa, offers a consistently rich, concentrated, firmly structured Cabernet. The best vintages have been the 1982 and 1984 bottlings, both of which are brimming with fresh, ripe fruit and the kind of intensity, depth and tannins for serious cellaring. The 1983 is firm and hard, a long ager, while the 1985 and 1986 appear a shade lighter and more elegant, showing less fleshy opulence, yet with time they may move up a notch or two. The winery also produces a Jefferson Cuvée from Napa Valley grapes, a very well-made wine that offers good value for the money. Production of the Corley Reserve has climbed to 3,800 cases with the 1986 vintage, but in 1985 the wine was softer than their usual style, so they made a very small amount, only 150 cases.

TASTING NOTES

MONTICELLO CELLARS, Corley Reserve, Napa Valley

1986 MONTICELLO CELLARS CORLEY RESERVE: This is already a charming wine, with pretty black cherry and currant flavors and a supple, lush texture. The elegant style and soft, fine tannins suggest it should be ready in five to seven years. Drink 1993-1999. 3,800 cases produced. Release: $24. Current: $24. **88**

1985 MONTICELLO CELLARS CORLEY RESERVE: A ripe, supple, elegant wine that has generous plum, cherry and spicy currant flavors in a sleek, lean style. Not as dramatic or opulent as many 1985s, this is still a very well-made wine, with fine balance and all the right elements to improve in the next three to five years. Drink 1994-1998. 150 cases produced. Release: $22.50. Current: $22.50. **88**

1984 MONTICELLO CELLARS CORLEY RESERVE: Dense, concentrated and firmer than most 1984s, this is a tight, lean, intense wine that will require a few years' cellaring, but everything is in place for greatness — the rich, thick black currant, plum and cherry flavors, firm, supple tannins and a pretty aftertaste. Drink 1995-2004. 4,000 cases produced. Release: $18.50. Current: $20. **91**

1983 MONTICELLO CELLARS CORLEY RESERVE: Tight, hard, rich and concentrated, better balanced than most 1983s, with generous currant, spice and cedar flavors to stand up to the firm tannins. Closed now but offering ample evidence that it will reward cellaring. Drink 1995-2003. 350 cases produced. Release: $24. Current: $24. **88**

1982 MONTICELLO CELLARS CORLEY RESERVE: Oozing with fresh, ripe, mouth-watering fruit and smooth, supple tannins, this is one of the most charming 1982s, drinking quite well now but with the depth of fruit and concentration to carry it another decade. The rich black currant, cherry, earth and anise flavors are lush and smooth, overriding the intensity of the tannins. Drink 1993-1999. 1,200 cases produced. Release: $15, Current: $30. **90**

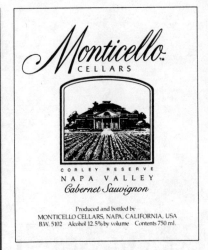

MOUNT EDEN VINEYARDS

Santa Cruz Mountains

CLASSIFICATION: *FOURTH GROWTH*

COLLECTIBILITY RATING: *A*

BEST VINTAGES: *1978, 1977, 1975, 1973*

In the early 1970s, Mount Eden made a string of extraordinarily rich, chewy, complex Cabernets from its tiny 9-acre vineyard in the Santa Cruz Mountains. Founded in 1972, when the old Martin Ray Vineyard was divided, Mount Eden built a cultlike following in its first decade under the winemaking direction of Richard Graff and Phil Woodward of Chalone. The 1973 is enormously intense and concentrated, still a few years from peaking, while the 1974, 1975, 1977 and 1978 are also highly successful vintages. The 1975 is brimming with ripe fruit, while the 1977 is massively proportioned. Both wines are capable of aging 30 years. The 1979 vintage was not very successful at Mount Eden or in the Santa Cruz Mountains.

In the 1980s, the Mount Eden style has shifted away from the high-extract, richly textured, massively proportioned Cabernets to wines of greater elegance, finesse and early drinkability. After a fine 1981, the 1982 and 1983 vintages are less successful. The 1984, 1985 and 1986 Cabernets are complex and flavorful, but considerably leaner and somewhat less interesting. Production is small, about 600 cases. Graff and Woodward left in 1982, and the winery is now owned by a group of investors.

AT A GLANCE

MOUNT EDEN VINEYARDS
22020 Mt. Eden Road
Saratoga, CA 95070
(408) 867-5832

Owner: MEV Corp.

Winemaker: Jeffrey Patterson (8 years)

Founded: 1972

First Cabernet vintage: 1972

Cabernet production: 600 cases

Cabernet acres owned: 9

Average age of vines: 32 years

Vineyard makeup: Cabernet Sauvignon (93%), Merlot (5%), Cabernet Franc (2%)

Average wine makeup: Cabernet Sauvignon (100%)

Time in oak: 22 months

Type of oak: French (Nevers)

TASTING NOTES

MOUNT EDEN VINEYARDS, **Santa Cruz Mountains**

1986 MOUNT EDEN VINEYARDS: A lean, firm wine with pretty fruit, floral notes and bright cherry flavors, but lacking the depth, richness and concentration of earlier vintages. A wine for current drinking rather than long-term cellaring. Drink 1994-2000. 786 cases produced. Not Released. **85**

1985 MOUNT EDEN VINEYARDS: Quite successful, with more complexity and depth, and the best wine since 1978, but still in the leaner, thinner style and not the rich, concentrated style of the early 1970s. A less interesting but still very good Cabernet that should be ready in three to four years. Drink 1994-1998. 622 cases produced. Release: $28. Current: $28. **86**

1984 MOUNT EDEN VINEYARDS: On the lean, firm side for an 1984 and lacking the richness and depth of the best Mount Edens, this is the best wine since 1978, with its ripe black cherry and currant flavors and crisp acidity. It could use a little more body. Drink 1993-1998. 645 cases produced. Release: $22. Current: $26. **84**

1983 MOUNT EDEN VINEYARDS: Much like the 1982 with its leanness, this wine has a touch more ripe fruit and is better balanced. The firm tannins should carry it another three to five years. Drink 1993-1997. 458 cases produced. Release: $20. Current: $20. **79**

1982 MOUNT EDEN VINEYARDS: Not entirely ripe, this is a lean, thin, tannic wine with modest flavor and not much depth. Mediocre as Mount Edens go. Drink 1990-1994. 1,249 cases produced. Release: $18. Current: $20. **70**

1981 MOUNT EDEN VINEYARDS: A tight, lean, compact 1981, with pretty currant and cherry flavors and firm tannins, but lacking the richness and depth of Mount Eden's best. Should mature in the next three years. Drink 1993-1999. 652 cases produced. Release: $18. Current: $25. **86**

1980 MOUNT EDEN VINEYARDS: From an unusually ripe vintage, this 1980 is reaching its peak, offering ripe, spicy fruit that's well defined and elegant, with moderate depth and concentration. A very good wine that is ready now or can age. Drink 1992-1997. 453 cases produced. Release: $30. Current: $35. **85**

1979 MOUNT EDEN VINEYARDS: From a poor vintage in the Santa Cruz Mountains, this wine is laden with earth, bark and cedar flavors that dampen the fruit. An uninspiring vintage and mediocre wine. Drink 1990-1993. 641 cases produced. Release: $25. Current: $30. **69**

1978 MOUNT EDEN VINEYARDS: Not quite as sharply defined as the previous vintages, this 1978 is slightly oaky, with ripe plum and currant flavors and hints of pepper and mint. It's not as tannic or concentrated as the 1977, 1975 or 1973 vintages, but is still built for further cellaring. Drink 1995-2003. 650 cases produced. Release: $25. Current: $45. **88**

1977 MOUNT EDEN VINEYARDS: A massively concentrated wine and one of the best from this vintage, thick and tannic, loaded with black currant, spice, chocolate and cherry flavors that may require another decade before drinking. Underneath the intensity and concentrated fruit is a wine of elegance and complexity. Drink 1995-2005. 200 cases produced. Release: $20. Current: $50. **91**

1976 MOUNT EDEN VINEYARDS: Very ripe and opulent, with rich, almost raisiny fruit, straightforward and blunt. A very good if awkward wine from a difficult vintage. The level of tannins warrants further cellaring. Drink 1993-2000. 175 cases produced. Release: $20. Current: $50. **83**

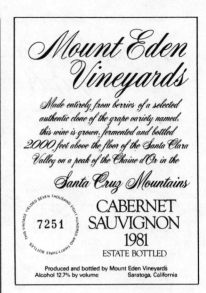

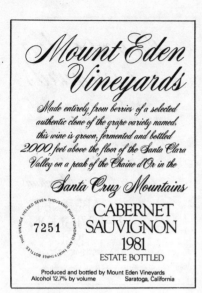

1975 MOUNT EDEN VINEYARDS: A rich, smooth, supple wine with beautifully defined fruit that's ripe and oozing with black cherry, currant, toast and cedar flavors, supported by firm, gritty tannins. This wine is in perfect condition, very complex and deceptively concentrated. It can age another decade with ease. Drink 1994-2004. 255 cases produced. Release: $20. Current: $70. **90**

1974 MOUNT EDEN VINEYARDS: Typical of the 1974 vintage, this is a very ripe and concentrated wine with herb, black cherry and cedar flavors and a good dose of tannin. Not quite as elegant and refined as the excellent 1973, but impressive nonetheless. Still quite tannic. Drink 1994-2002. 437 cases produced. Release: $20. Current: $120. **87**

1973 MOUNT EDEN VINEYARDS: One of the great 1973s and top Mount Edens, this is a rich, massive, chewy, concentrated wine with thick tannins and ripe currant, black cherry and cedar flavors that are youthful and alive. This wine is extremely intense and still quite tannic. It's drinkable but can stand further cellaring. Drink 1995-2005. 391 cases produced. Release: $14. Current: $140. **91**

1972 MOUNT EDEN VINEYARDS: Fully mature and full of life, this 1972 offers spicy, ripe, supple fruit that is enticing and charming. Most of the tannins have faded, and it's in perfect condition now, finishing with very good length and a hint of pepper. Drink 1990-1995. 89 cases produced. Release: $20. Current: $60. **84**

MOUNT VEEDER WINERY
Mount Veeder, Napa Valley

CLASSIFICATION: *FOURTH GROWTH*
COLLECTIBILITY RATING: *A*
BEST VINTAGES:

Proprietary Reserve: 1986

Mount Veeder Vineyards: 1984, 1979, 1973

Since 1973, the tiny Mount Veeder Winery on Mount Veeder has been making some of the richest, most distinctive mountain-grown Cabernets in California. The Mount Veeder Cabernets are not always pretty. On occasion they can be extremely dense and earthy or hard and lean. In the 1980s, the 1981 and 1982 were especially disappointing. But aside from those vintages, there is a strong, uninhibited personality to these high-extract, unfiltered, hugely flavorful and tannic wines. Clearly they are not for the faint of heart.

The Mount Veeder Cabernets, grown on an estate vineyard nearly 2,000 feet above sea level, throw more sediment than any other wines I've ever poured. Even the first vintage, made in 1973 by founders Michael and Arlene Bernstein, has not fully shed its tannins. It is one of the top five or six Cabernets produced that year. The 1974 remains unapproachable, hard, tannic and gamy, while the 1975 is enormously tannic and oaky, in need of further cellaring, followed by an equally tough 1976. In 1977 two Cabernets were produced, one excellent one from Niebaum-Coppola Estate in Rutherford on the valley floor, an exceptional wine that still needs five to six years' cellaring before drinking. The 1977 from the Bernstein Vineyard has pretty fruit but is weighed down by tannins. In 1978 two bottlings were produced, both from mountain grapes, with the Bernstein Vineyard showing a surprisingly smooth and supple texture. The Sidehill Ranch bottling is also attractive. The 1979 is the finest vintage of the decade for Mount Veeder, an elegant, stylish wine that can be enjoyed now.

The 1980 is solid, while the 1983 is hard and tannic. The 1984 is delicious and the 1985 a worthy successor, although it's a long way from drinking. The 1986 Proprietary Reserve is perhaps the finest wine ever produced at Mount Veeder, while the regular estate bottling is impressive for its restraint and elegance.

In 1982 the Bernsteins sold the winery to Henry and Lisille Mathieson, who in 1989 sold it to the partnership of Agustin Huneeus and the Eckes family, owners of Franciscan.

AT A GLANCE
MOUNT VEEDER WINERY
1999 Mount Veeder Road
Napa, CA 94558
(707) 224-4039

Owner: Agustin Huneeus, Eckes Corp., West Germany

Winemaker: Peter Franus (8 years)

Founded: 1973

First Cabernet vintage: 1973

Cabernet production: 2,700 cases
Mount Veeder Vineyards: 2,650 cases
Proprietary Reserve: 50 cases

Cabernet acres owned: 18

Average age of vines: 17 years

Vineyard makeup: Cabernet Sauvignon (85%), Cabernet Franc (5%), Merlot (5%), Petit Verdot (2.5 %), Malbec (2.5%)

Average wine makeup:
Mount Veeder Vineyards: Cabernet Sauvignon (85%), Cabernet Franc (6%), Merlot (4%), Petit Verdot (3%), Malbec (2%) Proprietary Reserve: Cabernet Sauvignon (33%), Cabernet Franc (38%), Merlot (29%)

Time in oak: 22 months

Type of oak: French (Nevers)

TASTING NOTES

MOUNT VEEDER WINERY, **Various bottlings**

1986 MOUNT VEEDER WINERY PROPRIETARY RESERVE: A very impressive wine with elegance, depth and complexity, beautifully focused berry, toast and caramel flavors and a lingering aftertaste that echoes the rich, ripe black cherry and currant notes. Tannins are fine and in balance. Has the potential to be the finest Mount Veeder ever. Drink 1996-2006. 50 cases produced. Not Released. **93**

1986 MOUNT VEEDER WINERY MOUNT VEEDER VINEYARDS: Restrained and elegant for Mount Veeder, this is a rich, supple, well-balanced 1986 with complex vanilla, cherry, cedar and herb flavors supported by smooth yet persistent tannins. Supple enough to approach now but should age well for another decade. Drink 1992-2000. 2,600 cases produced. Not Released. **87**

1985 MOUNT VEEDER WINERY MOUNT VEEDER VINEYARDS: A hard, tight, structured 1985 that will require perseverance. The rich black cherry, blueberry, earth and mineral flavors are raw and coarse and need time to come together. Drink 1997-2004. 2,100 cases produced. Not Released. **87**

1984 MOUNT VEEDER WINERY MOUNT VEEDER VINEYARDS: A delicious 1984, ripe, rich, firm and flavorful, with layers of berry, black cherry and plum flavors and a touch of jam from the ripe fruit. Tannins are lean and firm and in proportion to the supple fruit. Drink 1995-2003. 2,500 cases produced. Release: $14. Current: $14. **88**

1983 MOUNT VEEDER WINERY MOUNT VEEDER VINEYARDS: Firm and tannic, yet there's a core of ripe plum and black cherry flavors underneath that will require another five years to soften. Balance is good, and the flavors are true. Drink 1995-2002. 3,000 cases produced. Release: $14. Current: $15. **84**

1982 MOUNT VEEDER WINERY MOUNT VEEDER VINEYARDS: Weedy, thin and vegetal, an apparent victim of harvest rain, this is the poorest Mount Veeder Cabernet ever produced, lacking ripe fruit, richness and depth. Best to avoid. 4,600 cases produced. Release: $12.50. Current: $13. **68**

1981 MOUNT VEEDER WINERY MOUNT VEEDER VINEYARDS: An off vintage for Mount Veeder, but this is still a good if unexciting wine, a touch earthier and less dramatic than other vintages, the flavors are bland and understated, with earthy, musty mushroom and black cherry flavors. Tannins are softening; ready soon, but not worth waiting. Drink 1992-1997. 2,700 cases produced. Release: $12.50. Current: $20. **77**

1980 MOUNT VEEDER WINERY BERNSTEIN VINEYARDS: Ripe, smooth, supple and elegant for Mount Veeder, loaded with rich black cherry and currant flavors, spice and mineral nuances, fine tannins already. Drink 1992-2000. 2,600 cases produced. Release: $13.50. Current: $30. **87**

1979 MOUNT VEEDER WINERY BERNSTEIN VINEYARDS: The finest Mount Veeder to date, an elegant, stylish, lean and supple wine, with complex cedar, earth, currant, plum and spice flavors. This is a very well-proportioned, beautifully balanced wine that is deep in flavor, long and lingering on the finish. Drink 1990-1997. 2,800 cases produced. Release: $13.50. Current: $35. **92**

1978 MOUNT VEEDER WINERY SIDEHILL RANCH: Elegant, lean and supple, with concentrated currant, mineral, mint and cedar flavors that are silky smooth on the palate, with fine tannins that don't dominate. Attractive now or in the next decade. Drink 1990-2000. 375 cases produced. Release: $13.50. Current: $40. **86**

1977 MOUNT VEEDER WINERY BERNSTEIN VINEYARDS: Ripe, supple and oaky with spicy mint and cherry flavors, as well as some gamy flavors; there's plenty of tannin to shed, but this is a very good 1977 with a pretty core of rich flavor. Simply needs further aging. Drink 1994-2002. 1,350 cases produced. Release: $11. Current: $50. **85**

1977 MOUNT VEEDER WINERY NIEBAUM-COPPOLA: Made in the Mount Veeder style, with great extract, concentration, oak and tannin, this wine from a Rutherford area vineyard has a fleshier texture with beautifully focused plum and cherry flavors before the oak and tannins clamp down. More finesse and elegance underneath the shield of tannins. Drink 1994-2006. 1,225 cases produced. Release: $9.75. Current: $60. **88**

1976 MOUNT VEEDER WINERY BERNSTEIN VINEYARDS: An odd wine because of its juniper, mint and metallic flavors, it's still decent, with ripe plum flavors peeking through, but then it gets oaky and dry. Still tastes awkward. Give it more time. Drink 1995-2000. 775 cases produced. Release: $11. Current: $45. **77**

1975 MOUNT VEEDER WINERY BERNSTEIN VINEYARDS: A fairly typical Mount Veeder, firm and tannic but with pretty ripe cherry and plum flavors and a touch of gamy earthiness that adds complexity. The fruit flavors indicate it's maturing, but the oak and tannins suggest further cellaring. Drink 1995-2004. 850 cases produced. Release: $11. Current: $50. **83**

1974 MOUNT VEEDER WINERY BERNSTEIN VINEYARDS: Lean, and very good length. Remarkably elegant and forward, charming austere and very tannic for a 1974, this is a tough, hard wine that's unusually dry, with ripe cherry, anise and gamy flavors. Not ready to drink, a curious wine that needs time to develop. With further aging it might improve, but for now it's difficult to assess. Drink 1996-2004. 650 cases produced. Release: $8. Current: $65. **80**

1973 MOUNT VEEDER WINERY: A firm, youthful, tannic wine still on its way up, loaded with rich black cherry, raspberry and spicy oak

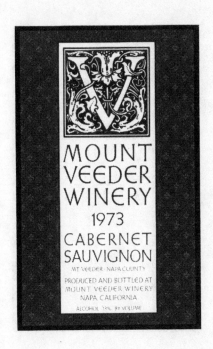

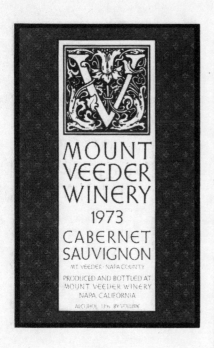

flavors, remarkably vibrant and muscular, still too hard and tannic to drink. A diamond in the rough that is years from its peak. Hard to match for sheer strength. Mount Veeder's first vintage. Drink 1993-2005. 400 cases produced. Release: $8. Current: $80. **90**

NEWTON VINEYARD

Spring Mountain, Napa Valley

CLASSIFICATION: *FOURTH GROWTH*

COLLECTIBILITY RATING: *Not rated*

BEST VINTAGES: **1986, 1985, 1983**

After founding Sterling Vineyards in the late 1960s, Peter and Su Hua Newton sold the winery to the Coca-Cola Bottling Co. and set out with winemaker Ric Forman to launch a new venture, with fruit from a steeply terraced vineyard on Spring Mountain. Originally the brand was to be called Forman, but after a falling out among partners, Forman departed to start his own winery and the Cabernet came out as Newton.

The early Newtons under Forman's direction were markedly inconsistent. The first vintage, the 1979, was fine, distinctive for its mintiness, but the 1980 was seriously flawed by intolerably high levels of volatile acidity. The entire lot of wine was sold off and not released, although I have come across a few people who have bottles in their collections. The 1981 was back on target, simple and pleasant, but the 1982 has taken on an earthy, bitterly tannic quality that is unpleasant. The 1983, made by new winemaker John Kongsgaard, was one of the top wines of the vintage, offering enough rich, concentrated fruit to stand up to the tannins. The 1984 is more elegant and charming, followed by the 1985, which is made in a similar style, emphasizing finesse and subtlety over intensity and power. The 1986 adds more richness and authority and is the best since 1983; with time the 1986 may surpass it.

Although better known for its lush, rich, supple Merlots, Newton produces 5,500 cases of Cabernet that include portions of Cabernet Franc, Merlot and Petit Verdot, all grown in the hillside vineyards adjacent to the winery. Nearly 100 acres are in vines, and despite mountain vineyards' reputation for intensity and tannins, the Newton Cabernets are an expression of refinement, elegance and finesse, ready to drink on release and built for 10 to 15 years of cellaring.

AT A GLANCE

NEWTON VINEYARD
P.O. Box 540
St. Helena, CA 94574
(707) 963-9000

Owners: Peter and Su Hua Newton

Winemaker: John Kongsgaard (6 years)

Founded: 1979

First Cabernet vintage: 1979

Cabernet production: 5,500 cases

Cabernet acres owned: 62

Average age of vines: 10 years

Vineyard makeup: Cabernet Sauvignon, Merlot, Cabernet Franc, Petit Verdot (Percentages unavailable)

Average wine makeup: Cabernet Sauvignon (75%), Cabernet Franc (12%), Merlot (12%), Petit Verdot (1%)

Time in oak: 20 months

Type of oak: French

TASTING NOTES

NEWTON VINEYARD, **Spring Mountain, Napa Valley**

NEWTON

CABERNET
SAUVIGNON

1983
NAPA VALLEY

Grown Produced and Bottled by Newton Vineyard
St Helena Napa Valley California Alc 12.5% by Vol

1986 NEWTON VINEYARD: Defines the Newton Cabernet style of understated and refined elegance, a beautifully crafted wine with a pretty floral and berry bouquet and crisp, sharply focused black cherry and currant flavors. The tannins are in perfect balance, and the flavors echo on the finish. Seductive now but can age. Newton's finest since 1983 and may surpass it in time. Drink 1992-1999. 5,530 cases produced. Release: $16. Current: $17. **91**

1985 NEWTON VINEYARD: Deliciously rich and elegant, with complex black cherry, plum, cedar and spice flavors, bordered by elegant, fine tannins that give it backbone without interfering with the flavors. Some bottle variation noted. Drink 1992-1998. 3,096 cases produced. Release: $15.25. Current: $18. **89**

1984 NEWTON VINEYARD: Spicy and elegant, with layers of delicate cedar, chocolate, plum and vanilla flavors and fine, integrated tannins that make this wine quite enjoyable now. Drink 1991-1996. 3,192 cases produced. Release: $13.50. Current: $19. **87**

1983 NEWTON VINEYARD: A standout 1983 that combines richness, depth, flavor and complexity without being overly tannic. This wine is very approachable for a 1983, with layers of vanilla, chocolate, plum and currant flavors that linger on the palate. A pretty aftertaste echoes those flavors. Drink 1992-1998. 1,824 cases produced. Release: $12.50. Current: $21. **92**

1982 NEWTON VINEYARD: Earthy and bitterly tannic, it seems to be taking a turn for the worse with age, with the fruit being overrun by non-Cabernet flavors. Not much hope for improvement. Best to avoid. 3,096 cases produced. Release: $12.50. Current: $21. **66**

1981 NEWTON VINEYARD: A very good wine, correct and well balanced, with tart, rich fruit the offers hints of cedar, anise and cherry, but it comes across as one-dimensional. With time it may be better. Drink 1992-1997. 2,820 cases produced. Release: $12.50. Current: $21. **83**

1980 NEWTON VINEYARD: A seriously flawed wine marred by volatile acidity. A few cases were released before the entire lot was sold off. Best to avoid. Production not available. Release: $12. **55**

1979 NEWTON VINEYARD: Distinctive for its minty, cedary notes, close to maturity, with supple currant and spice flavors, a smooth texture and fine tannins, finishing with elegance and delicacy. Attractive now. Drink 1990-1995. 742 cases produced. Release: $12. Current: $30. **85**

NIEBAUM-COPPOLA ESTATE

Rubicon, Rutherford, Napa Valley

CLASSIFICATION: *THIRD GROWTH*

COLLECTIBILITY RATING: *AA*

BEST VINTAGES: *1986, 1985, 1982, 1978*

A short distance from the old Inglenook winery is the former residence of its founder Gustave Niebaum. Today it is the home and winery estate of filmmaker Francis Ford Coppola, who purchased the property in the mid-1970s and began making a wine called Rubicon in 1978 under the Niebaum-Coppola label. Coppola is not directly involved in the winemaking, although he is a wine aficionado. He keeps a low profile, relying on André Tchelistcheff to oversee the stylistic development of Rubicon. The 63-acre vineyard, up against the hills west of Rutherford, yields a Cabernet that is deeply concentrated and ageworthy, as evidenced by the old, classic Inglenooks produced from this and the old Inglenook Home vineyard (see Inglenook).

Rubicon is distinctive for its ripe, rich, full-bodied character, a broad assortment of flavors tightly wound together, supported by strong but not abrasive tannins. The 1978 Rubicon has reached maturity but has the stuffings to age another decade, perhaps longer. The 1980, 1981, 1982 and 1984 vintages are consistently excellent, surpassed in quality only by the 1985 and 1986 vintages, which in my view are the finest produced by Coppola. With an aging procedure that includes 30 months in barrel, the Coppola wines are released seven years after harvest. Because of that late release, Rubicon is often overlooked by collectors, but with time this vineyard should continue to prove its excellence. In the long haul, it is one to bank on.

AT A GLANCE

NIEBAUM-COPPOLA ESTATE
P.O. Box 208
Rutherford, CA 94573
(707) 963-9435

Owner: Francis Ford Coppola
Winemaker: Steve Beresini (6 years)
Founded: 1978
First Cabernet vintage: 1978
Cabernet production: 4,800 cases
Cabernet acres owned: 63
Average age of vines: 12 years
Vineyard makeup: Cabernet Sauvignon (70%), Cabernet Franc (23%), Merlot (7%)
Average wine makeup: Cabernet Sauvignon (67%), Cabernet Franc (21%), Merlot (12%)
Time in oak: 30 months
Type of oak: French (Nevers)

TASTING NOTES

NIEBAUM-COPPOLA ESTATE, Rubicon, Rutherford, Napa Valley

1986 NIEBAUM-COPPOLA ESTATE RUBICON: Along with the excellent 1985, the 1986 ranks as one of the finest bottlings of Rubicon. The 1986 is tight, lean and structured, with complex, elegant, sharply defined currant, plum and vanilla flavors that gently unfold on the palate. This wine has the tannic structure for long aging. Flavors echo on the finish. Drink 1996-2004. 4,300 cases produced. Not Released. **92**

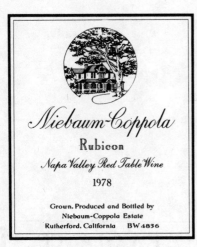

1985 NIEBAUM-COPPOLA ESTATE RUBICON: An elegant, delicately proportioned 1985 that is just opening up, with crisp acidity, firm structure and lively cherry, plum, vanilla and currant flavors that offer intensity and depth. The finish is long and smooth. Should be a beauty. Drink 1995-2003. 4,762 cases produced. Not Released. **91**

1984 NIEBAUM-COPPOLA ESTATE RUBICON: A supple, elegant, comparatively light Rubicon, it is nonetheless very fruity, with cherry and currant flavors of moderate depth and intensity, and it's not too tannic. Like many 1984s, this should be ready soon. Drink 1994-1998. 3,653 cases produced. Not Released. **85**

1982 NIEBAUM-COPPOLA ESTATE RUBICON: Very elegant and stylish, delicately proportioned, with currant and black cherry flavors and crisp acidity. Tannins are fine and softening. Has the balance and proportion for long-term aging, but it's getting close now. Drink 1992-2000. 6,002 cases produced. Release: $40. Current: $40. **89**

1981 NIEBAUM-COPPOLA ESTATE RUBICON: Ripe, forward and supple, a very fruity 1981 with plum, cherry and currant flavors that are tight and concentrated. Needs more time to soften and unfold. Drink 1993-2000. 3,661 cases produced. Release: $35. Current: $35. **87**

1980 NIEBAUM-COPPOLA ESTATE RUBICON: A big, rich, intense 1980 with plenty of ripe fruit that's well balanced and complex, with cedar, plum and black cherry flavors coming through on the finish. Has the depth and balance for midterm to long-term aging. Drink 1992-2002. 3,850 cases produced. Release: $30. Current: $35. **87**

1979 NIEBAUM-COPPOLA ESTATE RUBICON: Not nearly as successful as the 1978, this wine is marred by a mossy bark flavor that inhibits the ripe currant and plum notes from coming through. It's drinkable, but the mossiness may intensify with age. Drink 1990-1994. 3,100 cases produced. Release: $25. Current: $40. **75**

1978 NIEBAUM-COPPOLA ESTATE RUBICON: At its peak and fully mature but still capable of aging, this 1978 fits the mold of the vintage, with its complex ripe currant and cedar flavors and rich, smooth supple texture. Drink 1990-2000. 1,700 cases produced. Release: $25. Current: $45. **88**

OPUS ONE
Oakville, Napa Valley

CLASSIFICATION: *FIRST GROWTH*
COLLECTIBILITY RATING: *AA*
BEST VINTAGES: *1986, 1985, 1984, 1983, 1982, 1980, 1979*

Opus One is the most celebrated wine in California history, and while this Cabernet-based wine has critics of its lofty $50-a-bottle price, is has been superbly made from the first vintage.

A joint-venture partnership between Robert Mondavi Winery in Napa Valley and the late Baron Philippe de Rothschild of Château Mouton-Rothschild in Pauillac, France, Opus One is the marriage of two great winemaking families.

Founded in 1979, Opus One set its style of downplaying the aggressive flavors in Cabernet in favor of understated elegance, emphasizing finesse and restraint over power and tannins, while still maintaining richness and concentration framed by judicious use of new French oak, after the style at Mouton.

When the joint venture was announced in 1980, the partners analyzed different lots of Cabernet in the Mondavi Winery, deciding which blends would become Opus One and which would be used in the Mondavi Reserve. The Opus One grapes come from vineyards primarily in the Oakville area, including portions of Mondavi's vineyard. But it's clear that different stylistic decisions were made in the grape selection for the two wines. Based on how the wines from 1979 to 1983 have aged, Opus One is superior to the Mondavi Reserve. The Mondavi Reserves from 1980 to 1983, in particular, do not have the depth and richness of Opus One, nor do they appear to have the aging capability.

The 1979 Opus One has retained its elegance and finesse and is now drinking exceptionally well. The 1980, which was released at the same time as the 1979, demonstrated vintage differences and stylistic preferences. While the 1979 was 80 percent Cabernet Sauvignon with smaller portions of Merlot and Cabernet Franc, the 1980 was 96 percent Cabernet, a much richer, bolder, dramatic bottling more typical of Napa Valley Cabernet. It, too, has aged amazingly well and is close to its peak. While the Opus Ones from 1981 to 1983 have been exceptional wines, the best Opus' are the 1984, which displays more power and intensity while maintaining elegance and style, the 1985, which is enormously rich and complex with great finesse and delicacy, and the 1986, which is more structured but has all the flavor and intensity

AT A GLANCE
OPUS ONE
P.O. Box 6
Oakville, CA 94562
(707) 963-1979

Owners: Robert Mondavi Winery/ Baron Philippe Rothschild SA

Winemakers: Tim Mondavi/Patrick Leon (10 years)

Founded: 1979

First Cabernet vintage: 1979

Cabernet production: 11,300 cases

Cabernet acres owned: 110

Average age of vines: 5 years

Vineyard makeup: Cabernet Sauvignon (85%), Cabernet Franc (10%), Merlot (5%)

Average wine makeup: Cabernet Sauvignon (89%), Cabernet Franc (8%), Merlot (3%)

Time in oak: 18 months

Type of oak: French

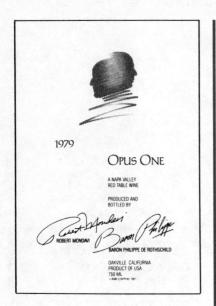

1979

OPUS ONE

A NAPA VALLEY
RED TABLE WINE

PRODUCED AND
BOTTLED BY

ROBERT MONDAVI   BARON PHILIPPE DE ROTHSCHILD

OAKVILLE CALIFORNIA
PRODUCT OF USA
750 ML

of the prior two vintages.

The partnership owns more than 100 acres in Oakville on both sides of Highway 29. A new winery is under construction for the 1990 harvest. At the Opus One vineyard a Bordeaux method of close-spaced planting and vine hedging is being practiced that results in fewer grape clusters per vine in exchange for more vines per acre. Experimental lots of wine from that vineyard were made from the 1988 vintage, but no date or timetable has been set for bottling wines exclusively from that vineyard. Winemaking duties are now shared by Tim Mondavi and Patrick Leon of Mouton.

TASTING NOTES

OPUS ONE, Oakville, Napa Valley

1986 OPUS ONE: A first-rate wine from an excellent vintage, the 1986 displays rich black cherry and currant flavors that are firm, structured and elegant. This wine shows Opus settling in on its style of firm structure and elegance. The 1986 rivals the sensational 1985. Drink 1995-2005. 11,200 cases produced. Not Released. **95**

1985 OPUS ONE: The greatest Opus yet, this is a dramatic, enormously complex wine, rich and concentrated, with beautiful currant, cedar, black cherry and spice nuances that are focused and vibrant on the palate, offering the Opus trademark of finesse and delicacy. Extremely well crafted. Drink 1995-2005. 11,300 cases produced. Release: $55. Current: $55. **95**

1984 OPUS ONE: A ripe, rich, thick and concentrated Opus, true to the vintage, loaded with black cherry, currant, cedar and anise flavors that gently unfold on the palate. Has the richness, depth, tannin and structure for aging. Biggest and thickest Opus yet, but it has an underlying sense of elegance and finesse that further aging should enhance. Drink 1995-2005. 9,000 cases produced. Release: $50. Current: $55. **94**

1983 OPUS ONE: With a gorgeous aroma, this wine is very elegant, crisp and flavorful, the lightest Opus to date but an exceptional wine in a very tough vintage. The spicy currant, cherry and cedar flavors are lively and vibrant up front, and the finish avoids the excessive tannins of most 1983s. Pleasant now but can age another five to seven years. Drink 1992-1997. 8,000 cases produced. Release: $50. Current: $55. **89**

1982 OPUS ONE: One of the finer 1982s, this Opus is elegant and rich, with concentrated, focused currant, herb and cedar flavors that are very well balanced with crisp acidity and firm tannins. Considering the vintage, this wine offers more depth and complexity than most. Drink 1993-2000. 6,000 cases produced. Release: $50. Current: $80. **90**

1981 OPUS ONE: Dense, rich and concentrated, though closed and not as flavorful as 1979 and 1980, this wine offers black currant, cherry, cedar and spice flavors that are all in place with firm, thick tannins and plenty of length. Missing only finesse now; needs more time. Drink 1994-2003. 6,000 cases produced. Release: $50. Current: $90. **88**

1980 OPUS ONE: A much richer, riper, Cabernet-flavored version than the 1979, the 1980 is in step with the vintage, very ripe and concentrated with layers of currant, cedar and cherry flavors that unfold on the palate. Amazingly complex and filled with flavor yet offering a measure of elegance and restraint. Drink 1992-2002. 4,000 cases produced. Release: $50. Current: $130. **93**

1979 OPUS ONE: The debut Opus One has retained its elegance and delicacy, with spicy currant, cedar and cherry flavors that offer richness, depth and complexity without weight. Developing nicely, showing finesse, still a few years away from its peak. Drink 1992-1998. 2,000 cases produced. Release: $50. Current: $190. **90**

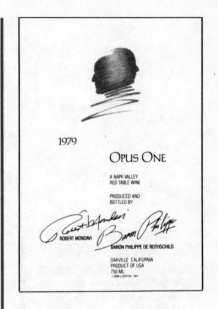

ROBERT PECOTA WINERY

Kara's Vineyard, Calistoga, Napa Valley

CLASSIFICATION: *FIFTH GROWTH*
COLLECTIBILITY RATING: *Not rated*
BEST VINTAGE: <u>1986</u>

Robert Pecota Cabernet comes from an estate vineyard named after Pecota's oldest daughter, Kara. This 10-acre vineyard yields 2,500 cases of Cabernet each year and is in the process of being expanded by another 20 acres. Pecota has been making Cabernet since 1982 and bottling a Kara's Vineyard Cabernet since 1984. The 1982, included here as Pecota's first effort, is a wine that grows on you. It's fully mature and ready to drink. The 1984 Kara's Vineyard is brimming with fresh, ripe fruit, while the 1985 is a rather lean, acidic wine that while correct and pleasant lacks the drama and richness of the best wines from that vintage. The 1986 is the best Kara's to date, with pretty black cherry and currant notes, and should be ready to drink soon. While Pecota's wines are clean, balanced and flavorful, they lack the complexity and richness of Napa Valley's Cabernet gentry.

TASTING NOTES

ROBERT PECOTA WINERY, Kara's Vineyard, Calistoga, Napa Valley

1986 ROBERT PECOTA WINERY KARA'S VINEYARD: Pecota's best effort, this wine has the same pretty black cherry, currant and spice nuances as previous vintages, but the flavors are more voluptuous, and they carry through on the finish, which isn't too acidic. For midterm cellaring. Drink 1993-2000. 1,230 cases produced. Release: $16. Current: $16. **88**

1985 ROBERT PECOTA WINERY KARA'S VINEYARD: A tart, lean, acidic 1985 without the generous fruit of most wines from this vintage. Still plenty of black cherry and currant flavors in a modest, not-too-tannic style. Should be ready to drink soon. Drink 1992-1998. 940 cases produced. Release: $16. Current: $20. **86**

1984 ROBERT PECOTA WINERY KARA'S VINEYARD: This wine is oozing with fresh, ripe, supple black cherry and berry flavors. It's fleshy and smooth until the finish, where it becomes sharp and slightly acidic. Soft tannins make it approachable now. Drink 1990-1996. 540 cases produced. Release: $14. Current: $20. **85**

1982 ROBERT PECOTA WINERY: A very pleasant, elegant, balanced 1982 with simple but correct Cabernet flavors that grow on you. The fresh, ripe berry, cherry and spicy oak flavors are in nice balance, and it's fully mature. Drink 1990-1995. 900 cases produced. Release: $12. Current: $20. **85**

ROBERT PEPI WINERY

Vine Hill Ranch, Oakville, Napa Valley

CLASSIFICATION: *FIFTH GROWTH*

COLLECTIBILITY RATING: *Not rated*

BEST VINTAGES: *1985, 1984, 1982*

AT A GLANCE

ROBERT PEPI WINERY
7585 St. Helena Highway
Oakville, CA 94562
(707) 944-2807

Owners: The Robert Pepi family

Winemaker: Robert Pepi (8 years)

Founded: 1981

First Cabernet vintage: 1981

Cabernet production: 2,700 cases

Cabernet acres owned: none

Average age of vines: n/a

Vineyard makeup: n/a

Average wine makeup: Cabernet Sauvignon (100%)

Time in oak: 36 months

Type of oak: French

Vine Hill Ranch, west of Yountville and near both Napanook (Dominus) and Markham's Cabernet vineyard, is the source of Cabernet Sauvignon for Robert Pepi Winery, which is across the highway. The fruit from independent grower Bob Phillips is typically austere, tight and tannic, with sharply focused currant, black cherry and spicy anise flavors. In five vintages, Robert Pepi has succeeded with a style that emphasizes the firm, concentrated fruit yet keeps the tannins in balance.

Pepi's first vintage, the 1981, is near maturity yet should hold another decade, while the 1982 is highly successful, with its firm structure and layers of flavor. The 1983 is considerably leaner and tannic, followed by the 1984, which is similar in style but with a little more flesh and texture. The 1985 is the best bottling yet, complex and tight, with plenty of flavor. Although it's early to predict how well these Cabernets will age, the Napanook Vineyard nearby has long been the source of ageworthy Cabernets, and Markham's Cabernets also have the depth and intensity for 15 to 20 years' cellaring. The 1985 should sell for about $16.

TASTING NOTES

ROBERT PEPI WINERY, Vine Hill Ranch, Yountville, Napa Valley

1985 ROBERT PEPI WINERY VINE HILL RANCH: Showing early signs of complexity, tight and firm, with lean currant, black cherry and spicy anise flavors that are crisp and focused, finishing with herb and tobacco notes. Needs time. Drink 1996-2002. 2,720 cases produced. Not Released. **90**

1984 ROBERT PEPI WINERY VINE HILL RANCH: A lean, firm 1984 with resolute tannins and well-focused black cherry and cedary oak flavors that need time to come together. Elegantly balanced; has the character of Vine Hill Ranch. Drink 1994-2002. 2,550 cases produced. Release: $16. Current: $16. **87**

1983 ROBERT PEPI WINERY VINE HILL RANCH: Hard, tannic and slightly green, with unripe fruit flavors but also touches of plum and currant that are barely ripe. Not too tannic as 1983s go and balanced overall, with a nice aftertaste. Hard to predict where this one is going, but it may surprise. Drink 1993-1998. 2,700 cases produced. Release: $16. Current: $16. **80**

1982 ROBERT PEPI WINERY VINE HILL RANCH: Gaining complexity, with tight, rich cedar, plum and currant flavors that are firm in structure and delicately balanced. Still shows plenty of oak and tannin, but everything's in place. Very complete and complex as 1982s go. Needs time to soften. Drink 1994-2002. 2,175 cases produced. Release: $14. Current: $17. **88**

1981 ROBERT PEPI WINERY VINE HILL RANCH: A smooth, rich, supple wine with pretty black cherry, plum, anise and currant flavors, fine balance and softening tannins. Nearing maturity but can hold another decade. Drink 1992-2000. 2,000 cases produced. Release: $14. Current: $18. **86**

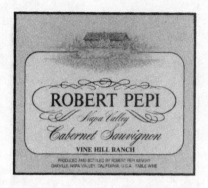

JOSEPH PHELPS VINEYARDS

Eisele Vineyard, Calistoga, Napa Valley
Insignia, Napa Valley
Backus Vineyard, Oakville, Napa Valley

CLASSIFICATION:
    Eisele Vineyard: **FIRST GROWTH**
    Insignia: **FIRST GROWTH**
    Backus Vineyard: **FOURTH GROWTH**

COLLECTIBILITY RATING:
    Eisele Vineyard: **AAA**
    Insignia: **AAA**
    Backus Vineyard: **A**

BEST VINTAGES:
    Eisele Vineyard: 1986, 1979, 1978, 1975

    Insignia: 1986, 1985, 1981, 1980, 1979, 1978, 1977, 1976, 1974

    Backus Vineyard: 1986, 1985, 1981

Joseph Phelps Vineyards' unmistakably massive, bold, dramatic and ageworthy Eisele, Insignia and Backus Cabernets rank among the elite in California. Founded in 1973 by Joseph Phelps, the winery is tucked away in a narrow fold of hills off the Silverado Trail east of St. Helena. While Phelps relied on Napa Valley growers for much of his Cabernet fruit early on, he now owns 105 acres in Napa Valley, including choice parcels in Rutherford on the west side of Highway 29, Oakville, and the Stags Leap District.

The most famous vineyard associated with Phelps' name is the independently owned Eisele Vineyard near Calistoga, which has been legendary for its superb fruit since 1971 when Ridge Vineyards produced a stunning bottle from that vineyard. In 1974 Conn Creek made its greatest vintage from Eisele fruit. Since 1975 Phelps has purchased the grapes from this 40-acre vineyard along the eastern side of the Silverado Trail and has succeeded with a stunning string of magnificent vintages. Grower Milt Eisele sold the vineyard in 1989 to entrepreneur William Farley, of Fruit of the Loom underwear fame, who intends to keep selling at least a portion of the fruit to Phelps' winery.

The Eisele Cabernets age into amazingly rich, smooth and supple wines, but they can be extremely intense and tannic early on. While the Calistoga area is generally regarded as one of the hotter parts of

Napa Valley, a stiff breeze that stirs in the early afternoon cools off the vineyard, according to Eisele. The Cabernets have a distinctive earthy, mineral quality to complement the rich chocolate, currant and black cherry flavors and thick, dense, texture. The 1974 Conn Creek bottling can stand another decade of aging, while Phelps' first bottling in 1975 is one of the classics of that vintage, capable of aging another 10 to 15 years and maybe longer. While the 1977 Eisele lacks the depth of the great vintages, the 1978 is tight and powerful, followed by the thick, dense 1979. The 1981 through 1985 vintages are a notch below the top bottlings, and the 1985 has shown bottle variation. The 1986 promises to be one of the very finest ever from this vineyard.

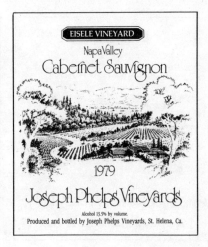

The Phelps Insignia is a classic Bordeaux-style blend that changes with each vintage. It was one of California's first proprietary wines. In most years Insignia relies heavily on Cabernet Sauvignon for its strength and intensity, but in some years the flavors are dominated by the spicy tobacco, mint and herb notes of Merlot. In other vintages, such as 1976, when selection of fruit was more demanding, Insignia was 94 percent Cabernet from Eisele, and no Eisele bottling was produced. Regardless of the composition, it is always a fascinating, complex, rich, tannic and aromatic wine that is challenging for its diversity from one vintage to the next. The top vintages include the 1974, 1976 (from Eisele), 1977, 1978, 1979, 1980, 1981, 1985 and 1986. The last two are as great as it gets.

The 7-acre Backus Vineyard is in the Oakville area along the Silverado Trail. Backus shares the Phelps style of rich, deep, concentrated and tannic fruit, but it is perhaps the least dramatic of the trio. The top vintages are the 1981, 1985 and 1986, the latter two classic examples of Backus' distinctive mint, herb and spice nuances with currant and black cherry notes.

The Eisele and Insignia rank high among California collectibles, and it seems likely that Backus will shortly join that company, based on its uniformly high quality and limited supply. Phelps also makes a Napa Valley Cabernet that can be very good but has nowhere near the stature of the Eisele, Insignia or Backus.

TASTING NOTES

JOSEPH PHELPS VINEYARDS, Eisele Vineyard, Calistoga, Napa Valley

1986 JOSEPH PHELPS VINEYARDS EISELE VINEYARD: Another terrific vintage from Eisele, this is as magnificent as the 1985, a seamless wine with enormous depth and concentration of flavor and the kind of structure and balance that should allow it to age gracefully for 15 to 20 years. It has classic Eisele flavors of rich plum, currant, earth and mineral, along with a toasty oak finish. Drink 1998-2008. 1,500 cases produced. Not Released. **95**

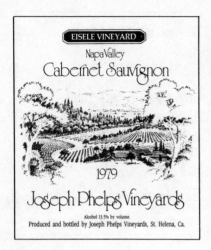

1985 JOSEPH PHELPS VINEYARDS EISELE VINEYARD: Despite some bottle variation, this is a gorgeous Eisele in the style of the fabulous 1975, 1978 and 1979 bottlings, a rich, massive wine with concentrated currant, plum, toast, cinnamon and anise flavors that are deep, intense and lively and backed with firm yet integrated tannins. This appears to be a good candidate for 20 years of aging but should be approachable in five. Drink 1995-2005. 1,500 cases produced. Release: $40. Current: $40. **94**

1984 JOSEPH PHELPS VINEYARDS EISELE VINEYARD: In a vintage where many Cabernets are fat, lush and fleshy, Phelps produced a lean, concentrated, firmly structured wine. This Eisele displays tight, rich currant and spicy mineral flavors and firm, hard tannins that will require another five to eight years' cellaring before they soften. Drink 1995-2000. 1,300 cases produced. Release: $35. Current: $39. **87**

1983 JOSEPH PHELPS VINEYARDS EISELE VINEYARD: A thick, hard, fairly tannic Eisele that will require another five to 10 years before drinking. It's closed, with tightly knit cedar, currant and plum flavors, masked by rough-hewn tannins that are coarse and chewy on the finish. Definitely one for the cellar. Drink 1997-2002. 1,250 cases produced. Release: $25. Current: $35. **86**

1982 JOSEPH PHELPS VINEYARDS EISELE VINEYARD: A lean, elegant wine that is attractive for its subtlety and finesse and pretty if simple fruit flavors, but it lacks the upfront richness, depth, concentration and intensity of most Eiseles. It should reach maturity within the next five to seven years but may surprise and live a longer life because of its crisp acidity and fine balance. Drink 1994-2000. 1,775 cases produced. Release: $30. Current: $33. **85**

1981 JOSEPH PHELPS VINEYARDS EISELE VINEYARD: The earthy mineral flavors stand out from the currant and black cherry fruit in this wine, and it is just beginning to show its full potential. It's leaner and more austere than most Eiseles and most 1981s and quite firm and tannic. There's a supple, silky texture developing, but it's still a long way from maturity. Has the potential to move up a point or two. Drink 1994-2000. 1,050 cases produced. Release: $30. Current: $39. **89**

1979 JOSEPH PHELPS VINEYARDS EISELE VINEYARD: This wine has all the elements of a great Eisele, the rich, concentrated currant, plum, cedar, earth and mineral flavors, along with an understated subtlety and suppleness that makes it approachable now. It's thick, deep, complex and impeccably balanced, with a long, full finish, capable of aging another decade or more. Not quite up to the 1975 or 1978 but outstanding nonetheless. Drink 1993-2000. 1,000 cases produced. Release: $30. Current: $50. **92**

1978 JOSEPH PHELPS VINEYARDS EISELE VINEYARD: In the mold of the fabulous 1975, this wine is amazingly deep and complex, packed with rich, concentrated currant, plum, chocolate, earth and mineral flavors that are tightly knit and just now beginning to open up. The tannins are thick and intense. A great wine that can only become greater. Drink 1995-2010. 755 cases produced. Release: $30. Current: $75. **97**

1977 JOSEPH PHELPS VINEYARDS EISELE VINEYARD: Lacking the depth, concentration and complexity of either the 1975 or 1978, the 1977 is nonetheless an impressive wine. The plum and black cherry flavors are thick, lean and rich but much more direct and ultimately simpler than the standard Eisele. This wine is not yet fully mature, but it's doubtful it will ever reach the high plateau of the great 1975 or 1978. Drink 1991-1998. 1,160 cases produced. Release: $25. Current: $55. **82**

1975 JOSEPH PHELPS VINEYARDS EISELE VINEYARD: This is one of the stars of the 1975 vintage and 1970s decade, a deep, rich, enticingly complex wine with great aging potential that is now just beginning to reach full maturity. The color is very dark and dense, the bouquet is full of cedar, cigar box, black currant and chocolate notes with flavors that unfold on the palate. It's thick, rich and unctuous, backed with firm, fine, integrated tannins. A magnificent wine. Drink 1992-2005. 720 cases produced. Release: $15. Current: $115. **97**

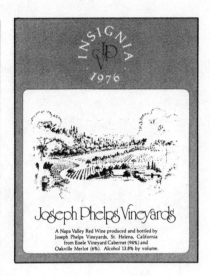

JOSEPH PHELPS VINEYARDS, Insignia, Napa Valley

1986 JOSEPH PHELPS VINEYARDS INSIGNIA: A close companion to the stunning 1985 that with time may even surpass it. This is an enormously deep, rich, supple and complex wine with layers of enticing black currant, mineral, toast and anise flavors that are seductive and long. An amazing wine. Drink 1996-2004. 4,000 cases produced. Not Released. **96**

1985 JOSEPH PHELPS VINEYARDS INSIGNIA: This wine has the potential to be the finest Insignia ever produced, with its incredibly deep, rich, complex flavors and impeccable balance and length. The layers of ripe black currant, cherry and mint flavors are sharply focused, beautifully proportioned and supple and long on the finish. It's distinctive for its elegance and complexity. Drink 1995-2005. 4,700 cases produced. Release: $40. Current: $40. **96**

1984 JOSEPH PHELPS VINEYARDS INSIGNIA: More structured than most 1984s, this is a firm, tight, compact wine with a tough edge that should soften with time. The black currant and mint flavors are well focused and backed with crisp, lean tannins. A long way from its peak, this wine should only get better. Drink 1995-2004. 3,860 cases produced. Release: $30. Current: $35. **89**

1983 JOSEPH PHELPS VINEYARDS INSIGNIA: A real mouthful of Cabernet, very intense, lean and concentrated, packed with rich berry, mint, currant and cedar complexities that are just now beginning to mature. The firm tannins make it a solid candidate for another decade of cellaring. One of the better 1983s, it's 60 percent Cabernet Sauvignon, 20 percent Merlot and 20 percent Cabernet Franc. Drink 1994-2000.

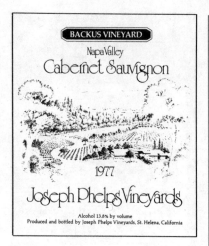

3,480 cases produced. Release: $25. Current: $35. **89**

1982 JOSEPH PHELPS VINEYARDS INSIGNIA: A fairly supple, elegant and forward 1982, this Insignia is 50 percent Cabernet, 30 percent Cabernet Franc and 20 percent Merlot. Showing signs of maturity, with a silky smooth texture and rounded tannins. The earthy, slightly mossy and barklike character detracts from the ripe plum and cherry flavors. There is a touch of bitterness on the finish. Drink 1992-1998. 2,950 cases produced. Release: $25. Current: $32. **85**

1981 JOSEPH PHELPS VINEYARDS INSIGNIA: Sleek and elegant, brimming with fresh, ripe fruit flavors, more forward and approachable than most Insignias. The pretty currant, cherry and plum flavors are bright and lively. It's delicious to drink now but has the tannins for another decade. Drink 1993-2000. 1,480 cases produced. Release: $25. Current: $39. **92**

1980 JOSEPH PHELPS VINEYARDS INSIGNIA: A leaner, more compact Insignia with a shade less richness than the 1979 but with firm concentration and plenty of plum, currant, spice and mineral flavors that are tight and tannic. Nearing its peak but with plenty of life ahead. Drink 1993-1998. 2,585 cases produced. Release: $25. Current: $50. **90**

1979 JOSEPH PHELPS VINEYARDS INSIGNIA: A sleek, seductive, beautifully focused wine that's fully mature now, with rich, ripe, supple black cherry, currant, anise and mint flavors, smooth, soft tannins and crisp, mouthwatering acidity. Ready now but can hold for five to seven years. Drink 1990-1997. 960 cases produced. Release: $25. Current: $55. **90**

1978 JOSEPH PHELPS VINEYARDS INSIGNIA: Not quite in the same league as the previous two vintages, this is lighter in body and depth of flavor, fully mature now, with smooth, satiny tannins and a pretty core of chocolate, mint and currant flavors that linger. Despite its lighter body, many producers would be elated with a wine this seductive. Drink 1990-1997. 1,175 cases produced. Release: $25. Current: $65. **87**

1977 JOSEPH PHELPS VINEYARDS INSIGNIA: A smooth, elegant, beautifully proportioned wine with a touch of earth, herb and cedar complexities that add to the ripe black cherry and plum flavors. Mature now, but the flavors offer depth and complexity, with subtle anise, tar and chocolate on the finish. Ready now but can hold. Drink 1990-1996. 1,900 cases produced. Release: $25. Current: $75. **91**

1976 JOSEPH PHELPS VINEYARDS INSIGNIA: A deep, rich, very ripe wine packed with bold, supple black currant, anise, mint and oak flavors that are concentrated and powerful, with a smooth, satiny texture. The extract, depth of flavor and tannins indicate this wine should age gracefully for the next decade — and then some. This wine is 94 percent Cabernet from the Eisele Vineyard and 6 percent Merlot. Drink 1994-2004. 785 cases produced. Release: $20. Current: $90. **93**

1975 JOSEPH PHELPS VINEYARDS INSIGNIA: A Merlot-dominated Insignia that is decidedly herbal and minty, yet elegant and concentrated and very well balanced. The flavors are less appealing to me than those of the other Insignias. Drink 1990-1995. 473 cases produced. Release: $15. Current: $90. **85**

1974 JOSEPH PHELPS VINEYARDS INSIGNIA: Holding up extremely well and capable of another eight to 10 years of life, still very intense and concentrated, with high extract, complex, rich and deep. It's 94 percent Cabernet. Drink 1990-1998. 670 cases produced. Release: $12. Current: $130. **90**

JOSEPH PHELPS VINEYARDS, Backus Vineyard, Oakville, Napa Valley

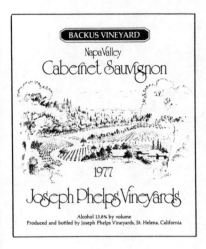

1986 JOSEPH PHELPS VINEYARDS BACKUS VINEYARD: This is the finest Backus ever produced and one of the top 1986s. It's rich, deep, concentrated and intense, with thick currant, plum and spicy mint flavors that are firm and elegant, wrapped in thick tannins. Tight and closed now, this one's for the cellar. Drink 1998-2005. 1,400 cases produced. Not Released. **93**

1985 JOSEPH PHELPS VINEYARDS BACKUS VINEYARD: A rich, sleek, distinctive wine with spice, mint and chocolate flavors and bright cherry and plum notes that can stand up to the firm, integrated tannins. Has the depth of flavor and concentration for midterm cellaring. Drink 1996-2002. 1,980 cases produced. Release: $27.50. Current: $32. **90**

1984 JOSEPH PHELPS VINEYARDS BACKUS VINEYARD: Very ripe and forward, with spicy cherry, plum and mineral flavors that are lean and crisp, unlike most 1984s, which are thick, fleshy and more voluptuous. Still, this wine is well proportioned and elegant, with smooth tannins and a hint of mint on the finish. Close to drinkability. Drink 1992-1997. 1,585 cases produced. Release: $20. Current: $29. **86**

1983 JOSEPH PHELPS VINEYARDS BACKUS VINEYARD: Like most 1983s, it's tight, lean and crisp, but overall well proportioned and better balanced than most, with fresh, ripe cherry, chocolate and mint flavors; not overly tannic. Needs a few years for the tannins to round out, but not for long-term aging. Drink 1994-1998. 800 cases produced. Release: $16.50. Current: $28. **85**

1981 JOSEPH PHELPS VINEYARDS BACKUS VINEYARD: A very supple, generous, fruity wine that's charming to drink now but has the depth of flavor and balance for further aging. Oozing with fresh, ripe, lush cherry, currant, plum and spicy mineral flavors that are very seductive. The tannins are soft and smooth but thick and rich enough for further aging. A style that combines early drinking grace with medium-range aging potential. Drink 1992-2000. 775 cases produced. Release: $15. Current: $44. **91**

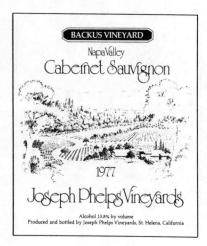

1978 JOSEPH PHELPS VINEYARDS BACKUS VINEYARD: This is a lean, austere Cabernet from a vintage that tended to yield opulent, generous wines. The 1978 Backus offers great richness of flavor and fine structure to carry the currant, earth, mineral and toasty oak flavors. Crisp acidity carries the flavors. Ready now but can still develop. Drink 1991-1997. 1,100 cases produced. Release: $16.50. Current: $55. **89**

1977 JOSEPH PHELPS VINEYARDS BACKUS VINEYARD: Fully mature now, as are most 1977s, with smooth, rich, supple chocolate, plum, spice and toast flavors of medium depth and intensity. The tannins have softened, making it quite enjoyable now, though it can age further. Drink 1990-1995. 530 cases produced. Release: $15. Current: $60. **86**

PINE RIDGE WINERY

Andrus Reserve, Rutherford, Napa Valley
Pine Ridge Stags Leap Vineyard, Stags Leap, Napa Valley
Rutherford Cuvée, Rutherford, Napa Valley
Diamond Mountain, Diamond Mountain, Napa Valley

CLASSIFICATION:

Andrus Reserve: SECOND GROWTH

Pine Ridge Stags Leap Vineyard: THIRD GROWTH

Rutherford Cuvée: THIRD GROWTH

Diamond Mountain: Not rated

COLLECTIBILITY RATING:

Andrus Reserve: AA

Pine Ridge Stags Leap Vineyard: A

Rutherford Cuvée: Not rated

Diamond Mountain: Not rated

BEST VINTAGES:

Andrus Reserve: 1986, 1985, 1984, 1983, 1980

Pine Ridge Stags Leap Vineyard: 1986, 1985, 1984, 1982, 1981

Rutherford Cuvée: 1986, 1985, 1984, 1982, 1980, 1978

Diamond Mountain: 1986

AT A GLANCE

PINE RIDGE WINERY
P.O. Box 2508
Yountville, CA 94599
(707) 253-7500

Owners: The Andrus family

Winemaker: Gary Andrus (11 years)

Founded: 1978

First Cabernet vintage: 1978
  Andrus Reserve: 1980
  Pine Ridge Stags Leap Vineyard: 1981
  Rutherford Cuvée: 1978
  Diamond Mountain: 1986

Cabernet production: 12,000 cases
  Andrus Reserve: 1,000 cases (in some vintages)
  Pine Ridge Stags Leap Vineyard: 1,800 cases
  Rutherford Cuvée: 9,000 cases
  Diamond Mountain: 500 cases

Cabernet acres owned: 107
  Andrus Reserve: 14
  Pine Ridge Stags Leap Vineyard: 17
  Rutherford Cuvée: 66
  Diamond Mountain: 10

Average age of vines: 8 years
  Andrus Reserve: 14 years
  Pine Ridge Stags Leap Vineyard: 9 years
  Rutherford Cuvée: 6 years
  Diamond Mountain: 10 years

continued on next page

With four separate, superb bottlings of Napa Valley Cabernet, Pine Ridge Winery is a study of how winemaking style interacts with the soil and climate. In 1978, winemaker Gary Andrus produced his first Cabernet, bottled under the Rutherford District designation (later renamed Rutherford Cuvée) from Rutherford grapes. This wine has the personality of the Rutherford area — rich, ripe, mature and complex — with a broad array of chocolate, cherry, currant, herb and tea notes, fine, firm tannins and excellent aging potential. The Pine Ridge Rutherford is more polished than Caymus, yet not as intense as Inglenook.

In 1980 Pine Ridge added an Andrus Reserve bottling from Andrus' home property on the west side of Highway 29 in Rutherford near Zinfandel Lane. The wines from this small parcel are clearly richer and more dramatic than the Rutherford Cuvée bottlings, with extremely deep, smooth, explosive fruit. In 1981 Pine Ridge began bottling a Pine Ridge Stags Leap Vineyard Cabernet from the winery's 17-acre vineyard in Stags Leap District, a wine that tends to be more supple and fleshy in texture and less tannic than the Rutherford bottling, with more cedar continued from page 293

Vineyard makeup: Cabernet Sauvignon (53%), Merlot (29%), Cabernet Franc (11%), Petit Verdot (4%), Malbec (3%) Andrus Reserve: Cabernet Sauvignon (71%), Cabernet Franc (21%), Merlot (8%) Pine Ridge Stags Leap Vineyard: Cabernet Sauvignon (100%) Rutherford Cuvée: Cabernet Sauvignon (53%), Merlot (39%), Cabernet Franc (5%), Malbec (3%) Diamond Mountain: Cabernet Sauvignon (100%)

Average wine makeup: Andrus Reserve: Cabernet Sauvignon (84%), Merlot (8%), Cabernet Franc (6%), Malbec (2%) Pine Ridge Stags Leap Vineyard: Cabernet Sauvignon (95%), Cabernet Franc (5%) Rutherford Cuvée: Cabernet Sauvignon (85%), Merlot (8%), Cabernet Franc (7%) Diamond Mountain: Cabernet Sauvignon (100%)

Time in oak: Andrus Reserve: 18 months Pine Ridge Stags Leap Vineyard: 16 months Rutherford Cuvée: 20 months Diamond Mountain: 18 months

Type of oak: Andrus Reserve: French (Nevers) Pine Ridge Stags Leap Vineyard: French (Nevers) Rutherford Cuvée: French (Nevers, Allier) Diamond Mountain: French (Allier)

and cherry flavors and occasionally an earthier quality. Finally in 1986 a Diamond Mountain Cabernet was added to the lineup, and it bears the mountain-grown trademark of austerity, firm tannins and lean, concentrated fruit.

Despite their different locations and microclimates, the Pine Ridge Cabernets share a common thread of understated elegance and rich complexities, which is a tribute to Andrus' winemaking skills. The Pine Ridge wines are never excessive or overdone. Rather they are complex and harmonious, beautifully balanced, emphasizing subtlety and finesse over sheer strength and power. More importantly, the wines are also consistently excellent from year to year. The four Cabernets are made essentially the same way, with small portions of Merlot, Cabernet Franc, Petit Verdot and Malbec added for texture and flavor complexity; Andrus is an unabashed admirer of Bordeaux-style blends and vinification techniques.

Of the four Cabernets, the Andrus Reserve is the most dramatic and collectible, with its bold, intense, concentrated yet supple flavors. It is also the most expensive at $40 a bottle and up and is only produced when Andrus believes the fruit is of superior quality. It is made in limited quantities of no more than 1,000 cases. The best vintages have been the 1980, 1984, 1985 and 1986; no 1981 or 1982 was produced. The Rutherford Cuvée is the largest bottling with 9,000 cases, and it has been excellent in 1978, 1980, 1982, 1984, 1985 and 1986. The best Pine Ridge Stags Leap Vineyard bottlings have been 1981, 1982, 1984, 1985 and 1986. About 1,800 cases are produced annually. The Diamond Mountain vineyard, formerly held by Roddis Vineyard, formerly held by Roddis Vineyard, near Diamond Creek Vineyards, was purchased in 1989 and has the smallest production with 450 cases.

TASTING NOTES

PINE RIDGE WINERY, Andrus Reserve, Rutherford, Napa Valley

1986 PINE RIDGE WINERY ANDRUS RESERVE: A beautifully crafted Andrus Reserve, this wine combines gentle intensity with richness and authority. The supple currant, cassis, toast, anise and mint flavors are framed by toasty oak and firm, structured tannins. Exquisite balance. Drink 1995-2002. 749 cases produced. Release: $40. Current: $40. **92**

1985 PINE RIDGE WINERY ANDRUS RESERVE CUVEE DUET: A silky smooth, elegant and delicate 1985 that has rich, sharply defined cherry, currant, vanilla and anise flavors that are complex, long and fully integrated with the tannins, finishing with hints of herb and tea. Has added value as a collectible; made in conjunction with Château Lynch-Bages. A planned joint-venture wine never materialized, however. This is an orphan. Drink 1994-2002. 1,136 cases produced. Release: $40. Current: $45. **92**

1984 PINE RIDGE WINERY ANDRUS RESERVE: This is an effusively fruity, seductively rich and concentrated wine packed with currant, anise, plum and cherry flavors that are impeccably balanced, finishing with firm, gentle tannins and a long, complex, elegant finish. Drink 1995-2010. 280 cases produced. Release: $37. Current: $40. **93**

1983 PINE RIDGE WINERY ANDRUS RESERVE: Plenty of flavor and concentration for a 1983 with more depth and richness than most. The cranberry, currant and anise flavors are crisp and lean, with tannins in proportion. Drink 1993-2000. 169 cases produced. Release: $35. Current: $45. **88**

1980 PINE RIDGE WINERY ANDRUS RESERVE: Quite possibly the best 1980 produced in Napa Valley, or for that matter California, this wine offers classic cedar and cigar box aromas along with great richness, intensity and depth of flavor. The ripe currant, black cherry and cranberry flavors are firm and concentrated, yet it has a fleshy texture and finishes with firm yet polished tannins. Very elegant, stylish, powerful and complex. Drink 1996-2010. 140 cases produced. Release: $30. Current: $60. **96**

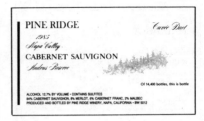

PINE RIDGE WINERY, Pine Ridge Stags Leap Vineyard, Napa Valley

1986 PINE RIDGE WINERY PINE RIDGE STAGS LEAP VINEYARD: Another fine effort from this vineyard, the 1986 falls between the high-extract 1984 bottling and the refined elegance of the 1985. The 1986 is rich and concentrated, with black cherry and currant flavors flanked by toasty oak, elegant and structured, with plenty of flavor on the aftertaste. Should age well. Drink 1995-2005. 1,775 cases produced. Not Released. **91**

1985 PINE RIDGE WINERY PINE RIDGE STAGS LEAP VINEYARD: As excellent as the 1984 is, the 1985 surpasses it in quality. It's sleeker and more elegant, and while lacking the thick extract of the 1984, the flavors are true, pretty Cabernet, with black cherry, currant and spice nuances. It offers a measure of complexity and finesse that makes it the best Stags Leap bottling yet from Pine Ridge. Drink 1994-2010. 1,756 cases produced. Release: $26. Current: $26. **94**

1984 PINE RIDGE WINERY PINE RIDGE STAGS LEAP VINEYARD: This is a thick, massive, effusively fruity 1984, loaded with black cherry, plum, currant, spice and toasty oak flavors, flanked by rich, thick, soft tannins that should ensure very good aging. It's fleshy enough to approach now, but its best years lie ahead. Drink 1995-2008. 1,652 cases produced. Release: $25. Current: $35. **93**

1983 PINE RIDGE WINERY PINE RIDGE STAGS LEAP VINEYARD: Firm, hard and tannic, with smoky truffle aromas and lean, tight black cherry notes on the palate. Unyielding now, but with time this should be a very good wine. Drink 1994-2000. 1,452 cases produced. Release: $20. Current: $26. **85**

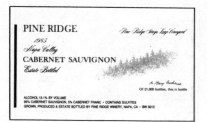

1982 PINE RIDGE WINERY PINE RIDGE STAGS LEAP VINEYARD: A touch earthier than the 1981, this is a rich, gutsy, high-extract wine with plenty of ripe currant and plum flavors. The finish is hard and tannic but in line with the vintage, where the best wines will need time to develop. Drink 1996-2004. 1,116 cases produced. Release: $20. Current: $34. **90**

1981 PINE RIDGE WINERY PINE RIDGE STAGS LEAP VINEYARD: This elegant wine is packed with rich, ripe plum, cherry and currant flavors that are supple, smooth and well proportioned, in line with the character of the Stags Leap District. On the finish there's a touch of smoky oak, and the tannins are soft and refined. Very elegant and fruity. Should age well. Drink 1995-2005. 1,553 cases produced. Release: $20. Current: $50. **92**

PINE RIDGE WINERY, Rutherford Cuvée, Rutherford, Napa Valley

1986 PINE RIDGE WINERY RUTHERFORD CUVEE: This wine continues to improve. From the barrel it was raw and not showing much fruit, but it is beginning to take shape and should be outstanding. It's loaded with rich, ripe plum, spice, tar and floral aromas that are complex and integrated, and the finish is long, full and deep. Drink 1995-2003. 7,437 cases produced. Release: $16. Current: $16. **90**

1985 PINE RIDGE WINERY RUTHERFORD CUVEE: A magnificent 1985 that is as elegant and refined as the 1984 is sumptuous. This wine has beautifully defined, rich black cherry, cassis, plum and oak flavors with a silky, sleek texture and a long, lingering finish. Impeccably well balanced. Drink 1994-2004. 8,668 cases produced. Release: $16. Current: $16. **93**

1984 PINE RIDGE WINERY RUTHERFORD CUVEE: This wine has consistently shown explosive fruit that is rich and concentrated, packed with currant, black cherry, spice, plum, vanilla and oak flavors that gracefully unfold on the palate. The supple texture makes it beguiling now, but the tannins, despite their soft, smooth appearance, are very firm and promise a long life. Drink 1992-2000. 7,128 cases produced. Release: $14. Current: $16. **90**

1983 PINE RIDGE WINERY RUTHERFORD CUVEE: Typical of the vintage, this 1983 is hard, lean, tannic and chewy, with currant and tobacco flavors that are tight and closed and finishing with dry tannins. The flavors are fine, but this wine needs cellaring to soften the tannins. Drink 1993-1998. 4,890 cases produced. Release: $14. Current: $22. **84**

1982 PINE RIDGE WINERY RUTHERFORD CUVEE: A classically proportioned Cabernet and one of the better 1982s, this wine is rich, smooth and supple, with well-focused cherry, currant and chocolate flavors wrapped in firm, rich tannins that promise a long life. Drink 1995-2005. 3,558 cases produced. Release: $13. Current: $24. **90**

1981 PINE RIDGE WINERY RUTHERFORD CUVEE: A narrowly focused wine that offers plenty of ripe fruit flavors and firm, lean tannins that render it one-dimensional. The cherry, currant and anise flavors are full-bodied and assertive, but at this point it lacks complexity and finesse. With time those two elements may develop. Drink 1994-2002. 4,081 cases produced. Release: $13. Current: $28. **88**

1980 PINE RIDGE WINERY RUTHERFORD DISTRICT: A big, rich, bold 1980 with an underlying sense of elegance, this wine is endowed with ripe plum, cherry, olive and cedar flavors that are beautifully defined and luscious. As seductive as it is now, it has the firm tannic structure and youthful personality to carry it another decade. Drink 1993-2000. 2,938 cases produced. Release: $12. Current: $37. **91**

1979 PINE RIDGE WINERY RUTHERFORD DISTRICT: Characteristic of the 1979 vintage, with its understated flavors, this wine is not as ripe as the 1978, and by comparison the cherry, herb and tea flavors are subdued. With time more of the fruit may come forward, but now it's closed and backward. Drink 1990-1995. 3,211 cases produced. Release: $9. Current: $45. **85**

1978 PINE RIDGE WINERY RUTHERFORD DISTRICT: A commendable 1978 that's fully mature, with generous, ripe, complex cherry, currant, tea, tobacco and anise flavors that gently unfold on the palate. Most of the tannins have softened, leaving a long, full, smooth finish. Perfect for drinking now but can handle another five years' cellaring. Drink 1990-1995. 3,950 cases produced. Release: $7.50. Current: $50. **89**

PINE RIDGE WINERY, Diamond Mountain Vineyard, Napa Valley

1986 PINE RIDGE WINERY DIAMOND MOUNTAIN VINEYARD: First Diamond Mountain bottling by Pine Ridge from the former Roddis Vineyard property near Diamond Creek Vineyard. This is a high-extract, firmly tannic wine, more typical of mountain-grown Cabernets than of Pine Ridge's Napa Valley floor bottlings. There's a shade more leanness, concentration and tightly wound fruit that's beautifully focused. A wine that will require patience. Drink 1995-2004. 450 cases produced. Release: $30. Current: $30. **91**

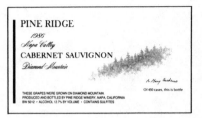

PRESTON VINEYARDS

Dry Creek Valley

CLASSIFICATION: *FIFTH GROWTH*

COLLECTIBILITY RATING: *Not rated*

BEST VINTAGES: *1986, 1985, 1984*

Preston Vineyards in Dry Creek Valley is a family-run operation that switched from grape growing to winemaking. Since the first Cabernet in 1982, the wines have been uniformly well made, displaying elegant, well-defined Cabernet flavors, fine tannins and subtle intensity. These are not wines to cellar for a decade or more but are best enjoyed on release and for six to eight years, longer in some vintages. Of the first five vintages, the wines are nearly equal in quality, with the 1982 and 1983 vintages more successful than many in those years and the 1984, 1985 and 1986 vintages displaying pure Cabernet flavors with plenty of fruit and finesse. At $11 for the 1985 and 1986 vintages, they represent solid values in Cabernet drinking.

TASTING NOTES

PRESTON VINEYARDS, **Dry Creek Valley**

1986 PRESTON VINEYARDS: The 1986 is a shade firmer than the 1984 or 1985 bottlings, with ripe, rich black cherry, currant and anise flavors that are supple and enticing, bordered by fine tannins. The flavors are appealing enough to enjoy now, but two to three years' cellaring will give it greater breadth. Drink 1993-1999. 4,075 cases produced. Release: $11. Current: $11. **88**

1985 PRESTON VINEYARDS: Similar in style to the 1984, 1985 has a gentle underlying feel of intensity that builds on the palate, offering rich cedar, black cherry and currant flavors that are complex and elegant, finishing with firm tannins and hints of anise and cherry. Drink 1993-1999. 3,100 cases produced. Release: $11. Current: $11. **89**

1984 PRESTON VINEYARDS: Rich yet elegant, with well-defined currant, cedar, cassis and raspberry flavors that are smooth and supple and fine tannins. The softness makes it drinkable today, but it has the depth and balance for another five to seven years. Drink 1991-1996. 2,850 cases produced. Release: $11. Current: $14. **87**

AT A GLANCE

PRESTON VINEYARDS
9282 W. Dry Creek Road
Healdsburg, CA 95448
(707) 433-3372

Owner: Lou Preston

Winemaker: Thomas Farella (7 years)

Founded: 1975

First Cabernet vintage: 1982

Cabernet production: 4,000 cases

Cabernet acres owned: 14

Average age of vines: 7 years

Vineyard makeup: Cabernet Sauvignon (92%), Cabernet Franc (5%), Merlot (3%)

Average wine makeup: Cabernet Sauvignon (92%), Cabernet Franc (5%), Merlot (3%)

Time in oak: 14 months

Type of oak: French, American

1983 PRESTON VINEYARDS: The 1983 is firm, lean and tannic, with ample black cherry, anise and plum flavors to stand up to the tannins, but it will require patience. Drink 1993-1998. 2,500 cases produced. Release: $11. Current: $15. **86**

1982 PRESTON VINEYARDS: Fruitier than most 1982s and better balanced, this wine has ripe, supple black cherry and raspberry flavors that are bright and lively, with good concentration, delicacy and length. Not too tannic, it's drinking well already. Drink 1990-1996. 1,700 cases produced. Release: $11. Current: $18. **87**

RAVENSWOOD

Pickberry Vineyard, Sonoma County

CLASSIFICATION: *FIFTH GROWTH*
COLLECTIBILITY RATING: *Not rated*
BEST VINTAGES: *Pickberry Vineyard: 1986*

AT A GLANCE

RAVENSWOOD
21415 Broadway
Sonoma, CA 95476
(707) 938-1960

Owners: W. Reed Foster, John R. Kemble Jr., Joel Peterson

Winemaker: Joel Peterson (12 years)

Founded: 1977

First Cabernet vintage: 1977

Cabernet production: 3,500 cases
   Sonoma County: 3,000 cases
   Pickberry Vineyard: 500 cases

Cabernet acres owned: none

Average age of vines: n/a

Vineyard makeup: n/a

Average wine makeup:
   Sonoma County: Cabernet Sauvignon (88%), Merlot (7%), Cabernet Franc (5%)
   Pickberry Vineyard: Cabernet Sauvignon (50%), Cabernet Franc (40%), Merlot (10%)

Time in oak: 20 months

Type of oak: French (Nevers)

avenswood is a prime example of what a winery has to endure when it doesn't own any Cabernet vineyards. This small Sonoma winery has succeeded in creating some intensely flavored, evenly balanced Cabernets with fruit purchased from such faraway sources as El Dorado County. Most of the time Alexander Valley and Sonoma Valley are the sources of fruit, and most of the recent — and best — bottlings bear the Sonoma County appellation, reflecting a blend of those diverse grape sources.

Perhaps Ravenswood's finest Cabernet-style wine is a new one called Pickberry, a proprietary blend that includes Merlot and Cabernet Franc, grown on Sonoma Mountain. The 1986 is very rich, concentrated and tannic in the truest Ravenswood style. Notes on the older vintages, dating back to 1977, show some good, often exotic, sometimes uneven wines. With the Pickberry Vineyard under an extended agreement to sell to Ravenswood's Joel Peterson, the future looks brighter and more secure.

TASTING NOTES

RAVENSWOOD, Various bottlings

1986 RAVENSWOOD PICKBERRY VINEYARD: Despite the mouth-drying tannins, there are pretty anise, plum and currant flavors that are concentrated and well focused. The tannic style may be excessive for some; needs five years. Drink 1994-1997. 550 cases produced. Release: $25. Current: $25. **89**

1986 RAVENSWOOD SONOMA COUNTY: One of the best Ravenswood Cabernets to date, the 1986 Sonoma County is firmly structured, with well-defined fruit framed by oak and tannin and pretty currant and cherry flavors that linger on the palate. Drink 1995-2002. 3,000 cases produced. Release: $12. Current: $14. **86**

1985 RAVENSWOOD SONOMA COUNTY: This is a big, muscular, tannic and concentrated wine that will require another five years before it is fully mature and ready to drink. All the elements are there for a very fine wine. The mint and cherry flavors are tight and closed now. Drink 1995-2001. 1,540 cases produced. Release: $12. Current: $14. **85**

1984 RAVENSWOOD SONOMA COUNTY: A chili and pickle flavor detracts from the fruit flavor in this one. Not for everyone. Otherwise it's well balanced and attractive. The flavors grow on you. Drink 1992-1997. 1,400 cases produced. Release: $12. Current: $14. **80**

1983 RAVENSWOOD SONOMA COUNTY: Light and simple, a decent wine that is disproportionately tannic and dry. Drink 1991-1995. 1,350 cases produced. Release: $9.50. Current: $14. **76**

1982 RAVENSWOOD SONOMA COUNTY: This wine, while quite showy early on, has closed up and is now quite tannic. The plum and cherry flavors have taken on an earthy quality. Probably drinking as well as it will. Drink 1990-1995. 1,500 cases produced. Release: $11. Current: $18. **84**

1980 RAVENSWOOD SONOMA COUNTY: Tart and ripe, with berry and cherry flavors accented by a juniper berry quality. The 1980 is fully mature and perfectly drinkable, but it comes across as raw and slightly out of focus. Drink 1990-1997. 640 cases produced. Release: $10.50. Current: $16. **79**

1979 RAVENSWOOD CALIFORNIA: This wine is flawed by "off" cabbage and chemical flavors. Best to avoid. 875 cases produced. Release: $8. Current: $10. **59**

1978 RAVENSWOOD CALIFORNIA: Without quite the character of the 1978 Sonoma Valley, the California bottling is heavily oaked and tannic without the bright fruit peeking through. It is still on the youthful side, however, and has the depth and concentration for further development. Drink 1991-1998. 536 cases produced. Release: $10.50. Current: $20. **81**

1978 RAVENSWOOD SONOMA VALLEY: A top-notch 1978 that is developing quite nicely, retaining its ripe, tart fruitiness and supported by firm, rich tannins. Plum, spice, pepper and cherry notes echo on the finish. Drink 1990-1998. 530 cases produced. Release: $11.25. Current: $28. **83**

1977 RAVENSWOOD EL DORADO COUNTY: Fully mature and at its peak, with spicy berry and oak flavors that are not classically Cabernet, but it is nonetheless very well made. Plenty of depth and richness on the finish, picking up traces of anise. Drink 1990-1995. 800 cases produced. Release: $8.50. Current: $22. **82**

RAVENS

WOOD
CABERNET
SAUVIGNON
EL DORADO COUNTY
1 9 7 7
CELLARED BY RAVENSWOOD
FORESTVILLE. CALIFORNIA
ALCOHOL 13.9 PER CENT

RAYMOND VINEYARD AND CELLAR

Private Reserve, Rutherford, Napa Valley

CLASSIFICATION: *FIFTH GROWTH*

COLLECTIBILITY RATING: *Not rated*

BEST VINTAGES: *1985, 1984*

AT A GLANCE

RAYMOND VINEYARD AND CELLAR
849 Zinfandel Lane
St. Helena, CA 94574
(707) 963-3141

Owner: Kirin Brewery, Japan

Winemaker: Walt Raymond (15 years)

Founded: 1974

First Cabernet vintage: 1974
Private Reserve: 1980

Cabernet production: 17,500 cases
Private Reserve: 3,000 cases

Cabernet acres owned: 32

Average age of vines: 18 years

Vineyard makeup: Cabernet Sauvignon (86%), Merlot (14%)

Average wine makeup: Cabernet Sauvignon (100%)

Time in oak: 30 months

Type of oak: French

The Raymond family is one of the oldest winemaking families in Napa Valley. The Raymonds owned Beringer Vineyards until 1971, when they sold it to Nestlé and the Labryuère family of France. With money from the winery sale, Roy Raymond Sr. bought a 90-acre parcel on Zinfandel Lane, where he and his sons Roy Jr. and Walt founded the winery in 1974. The Raymonds farm 32 acres of Cabernet and Merlot and produce 17,500 cases, from which they choose a few thousand cases for their Private Reserve designation. In 1988 part-interest in the winery was sold to the Japanese brewer Kirin; Roy Jr. still manages the vineyards, and Walt oversees winemaking.

The Raymond Private Reserve Cabernets are very ripe, rich, lush, smooth and supple wines, with layers of herb, chocolate, plum and cherry flavors and round, polished tannins. Drinkable on release, they age well for up to 10 years, but because they are so smooth and delicious, drinking them early is advisable. In the notes that follow, I have tracked the vineyard since the 1974 vintage; the first Private Reserve bottling is the 1980, but it was sold only at the winery, as the Raymonds felt it was too herbaceous and not in the right style for the introduction of the series. The 1974 is fully mature and in decline, with the telltale chocolate and herb notes and a touch of cedar. The 1976 is well balanced and ready to drink. The 1977 drank exceptionally well for the first five years after release and is best consumed soon. The 1978 was a lighter vintage for Raymond, and it, too, is fully mature. The 1979 showed a shade more richness and depth, while both of the 1980s are somewhat more herbaceous than usual. The 1981 is sumptuous now, with a full bouquet of flowers and herbs, followed by an elegant, delicate 1982. The 1983 is intense and not overly tannic, while the 1984 Private Reserve is classic Raymond, with richness and intensity. The 1985 and 1986 Reserves are equally successful.

TASTING NOTES

RAYMOND VINEYARD AND CELLAR, **Various bottlings**

1986 RAYMOND VINEYARD AND CELLAR PRIVATE RESERVE:
Firm, rich and structured, tightly wound, with currant, herb, cedar and
vanilla notes. Not quite the complexity and finesse of the 1985 but
perhaps more structured. Drinkable already, but should age well for
five to 10 years. Drink 1993-1999. 3,000 cases produced. Not Released. **86**

1985 RAYMOND VINEYARD AND CELLAR PRIVATE RESERVE:
Another winner, the 1985 is smooth and elegant, with well-defined
currant, plum, herb, cedar and smoky oak flavors that are balanced
with crisp acidity and fine tannins. Supple enough to drink now, but
probably better in two to three years. Drink 1992-1998. 4,000 cases produced. Not Released. **88**

1984 RAYMOND VINEYARD AND CELLAR PRIVATE RESERVE:
Classic Raymond style, rich, intense, supple and drinkable on release,
the 1984 has the characteristic herb, chocolate, currant and spice flavors
deftly balanced so that no one element dominates. Complex and enticing. From an excellent vintage, a first-rate wine. Drink 1992-1999.
2,800 cases produced. Release: $20. Current: $20. **89**

1983 RAYMOND VINEYARD AND CELLAR PRIVATE RESERVE:
Intense, lean and concentrated, the 1983 will need time for its tannins
to soften enough to allow the herb, currant and plum flavors to emerge.
Drink 1993-2000. 2,200 cases produced. Release: $18. Current: $25. **84**

1982 RAYMOND VINEYARD AND CELLAR PRIVATE RESERVE:
While many 1982s have taken on a wet, earthy quality, the Raymond
remains correct and well balanced, with a touch of cedar and bark
but plenty of currant, herb and plum flavors to offset it. Intense and
elegant. Drink 1990-1996. 1,800 cases produced. Release: $16. Current:
$27. **85**

1981 RAYMOND VINEYARD AND CELLAR PRIVATE RESERVE:
At its peak, with a bottle bouquet of fresh herbs, currants and anise
and flavors to match. Plenty of intensity and concentration to carry
it another five years and beyond, but it is drinking exceptionally well.
Drink 1990-1995. 1,200 cases produced. Release: $16. Current: $35. **87**

1981 RAYMOND VINEYARD AND CELLAR: Smooth and polished,
an early charmer, drinking very well now, with characteristic herb, cedar,
chocolate and currant flavors in harmony. Drink 1990-1993. 10,000 cases
produced. Release: $11. Current: $16.50. **85**

1980 RAYMOND VINEYARD AND CELLAR PRIVATE RESERVE:
Fully mature and, like the 1980 regular, more herbaceous than usual,
the herb, tea, spice and cherry flavors are elegant and graceful, with
enough tannin to carry it another five years. Ready now. Was not released commercially but has been sold at the winery. Drink 1990-1996.
1,200 cases produced. Release: $16. Current: $34. **85**

1980 RAYMOND VINEYARD AND CELLAR: From a ripe year that
accentuated the herbaceousness of the fruit, the 1980 Raymond lacks
the grace and elegance of prior vintages but offers all the ripeness and

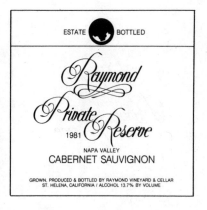

tannins of the 1980 vintage. Drink 1990-1993. 10,000 cases produced. Release: $12. Current: $17. **82**

1979 RAYMOND VINEYARD AND CELLAR: Impressive for its richness and suppleness early on and drinking well into the 1980s, fully mature and perhaps a shade past its prime but quite enjoyable nonetheless. Drink 1990-1992. 9,300 cases produced. Release: $12. Current: $20. **85**

1978 RAYMOND VINEYARD AND CELLAR: Ripe and herbal early on, mellow and supple now, with cedar, chocolate and berry flavors. Most of the tannins have faded. Drink 1990-1993. 5,300 cases produced. Release: $10. Current: $21. **82**

1977 RAYMOND VINEYARD AND CELLAR: A lovely wine on release and today as well, best consumed now as it is beginning to lose its fruit and intensity. The cedar, herb and currant flavors still ring true. Drink 1990-1992. 4,300 cases produced. Release: $8.50. Current: $27. **84**

1976 RAYMOND VINEYARD AND CELLAR: The Raymonds succeeded with a well-balanced, easy-to-drink wine from a difficult vintage. This wine was best in the mid-1980s and is fading. Drink 1990. 3,000 cases produced. Release: $6. Current: $27. **78**

1974 RAYMOND VINEYARD AND CELLAR: Raymond's first Cabernet set the style in a very ripe vintage. The herb, currant and spicy cedar flavors were in harmony on release and drank well for a full decade. Drink 1990. 800 cases produced. Release: $5.50. Current: $40. **78**

RIDGE VINEYARDS

Monte Bello, Santa Cruz Mountains
York Creek, Spring Mountain, Napa Valley

CLASSIFICATION:
   Monte Bello: *FIRST GROWTH*
   York Creek: *FOURTH GROWTH*

COLLECTIBILITY RATING:
   Monte Bello: *AAA*
   York Creek: *Not rated*

BEST VINTAGES:
   Monte Bello: 1985, 1984, 1981, 1977, 1978, 1974, 1970, 1969, 1964

   York Creek: 1986, 1985, 1984, 1980, 1979, 1977

AT A GLANCE

RIDGE VINEYARDS
17100 Monte Bello Road
Cupertino, CA 95014
(408) 867-3233

Owner: Akihito Otsuka
   (Otsuka Pharmaceutical), Japan

Winemaker: Paul Draper (20 years)

Founded: 1959

First Cabernet vintage: 1962
   Monte Bello: 1962
   York Creek: 1974

Cabernet production: 12,000 cases
   Monte Bello: 2,400 cases
   York Creek: 5,600 cases

Cabernet acres owned: 50
   Monte Bello Vineyard: 50
   York Creek Vineyard: 30

Average age of vines: 25 years
   Monte Bello: 25 years
   York Creek: 18 years

Vineyard makeup:
   Monte Bello: Cabernet
   Sauvignon (82%), Merlot
   (10%), Petit Verdot (5%),
   Cabernet Franc (3%)
   York Creek: Cabernet
   Sauvignon (80%), Merlot
   (15%), Cabernet Franc (5%)

Average wine makeup:
   Monte Bello: Cabernet
   Sauvignon (93%), Merlot (7%)
   York Creek: Cabernet
   Sauvignon (89%), Merlot (8%),
   Cabernet Franc (3%)

Time in oak: 18 months

Type of oak:
   Monte Bello: French,
   American
   York Creek: American

For nearly three decades Ridge Vineyards, high atop the steep Santa Cruz Mountains above Cupertino, has been making one of California's most complex, distinctive and ageworthy Cabernets from its 50-acre Monte Bello Vineyard. This vineyard, elevation 2,300 feet, was first planted in the 1880s but later was abandoned along with the carved-stone winery during Prohibition.

In 1959, a group of Stanford Research Institute scientists headed by Dave Bennion purchased the vineyard and winery and began tending the vines on weekends. The early Cabernets and Zinfandels, made from grapes purchased throughout California, were so good, however, that the owners began to spend more time building the winery business. By 1969 Ridge needed a full-time winemaker, and the partners hired Paul Draper, who is still in charge. In 1986 Ridge was acquired by Akihito Otsuka of Otsuka Pharmaceutical Co. of Japan.

With its rich soils and cool climate, Monte Bello is considered an ideal location for Cabernet Sauvignon. Its proximity to the Pacific Ocean, less than 20 miles away, provides for many damp, foggy mornings and brisk, breezy afternoons, which allow the grapes to ripen slowly and evenly. Often, however, it is too cold and the Monte Bello grapes fail to reach full maturity. In those years Ridge does not release a Monte Bello bottling, the two most recent examples being 1983 and 1979.

Draper has the Château Latour style in mind when he makes Monte Bello's deep, rich, intense, concentrated yet elegant and refined Cabernets. Draper credits the vineyard's maturity (most of the vines are 25 years old or older), the wild, natural yeasts in the vineyard, and the vinification process itself. Ridge does little to manipulate its wines. The grapes are fermented on their own yeasts; are not fined, filtered

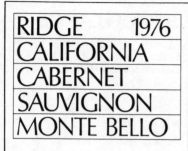

ESTATE GROWN, 100% CABERNET SAUVIGNON
SANTA CRUZ MTNS   ALCOHOL 12.7% BY VOLUME
PRODUCED AND BOTTLED BY RIDGE VINEYARDS
17100 MONTE BELLO RD, CUPERTINO, CALIFORNIA

or acidified; are aged in French oak barrels; and are rarely overly alcoholic, often between 11.5 percent and 12.4 percent alcohol.

Few wineries can point to a record of excellence that rivals Monte Bello. Since 1962 Ridge has produced a succession of monumental Cabernets, including the 1964, 1969, 1970, 1974, 1977, 1978, 1981, 1984 and 1985. These sensational wines are amazingly concentrated, deep and ageworthy. The 1964 is a beautifully proportioned wine with classic cigar box and spice flavors that are smooth and rich. It is only now fully mature and ready to drink. Both the 1970 and 1974 are years away from reaching their zenith. They are extremely rich, intense and concentrated, endowed with enough tannin to sustain them for 30 years. The 1968 and 1971 have been spectacular, but in recent tastings they were somewhat less showy but nonetheless fine. The 1984 and 1985 are stunning wines, deep, rich, supple and complex, built on the same aging curve as the 1970 and 1974. They are treasures for collectors who appreciate their durability and exquisite complexities. In a good year only 2,000 to 2,500 cases are produced, but in 1984, quite possibly Monte Bello's greatest vintage, more than 3,000 cases were made. Grapes or wine from Monte Bello not used in the blend turn up in Ridge's Santa Cruz Mountain bottling.

Ridge also produces a second mountain-grown Cabernet from the York Creek Vineyard on Spring Mountain in Napa Valley, and while this is also a very fine, elegant, often outstanding Cabernet, it is not nearly as rich, complex or awesome as Monte Bello. The York Creek connection stems from the friendship of Draper and York Creek owner Fritz Maytag of the Maytag appliance family, who also owns the Anchor Steam Brewery in San Francisco.

The York Creek Cabernets tend to be very ripe, bordering on jammy, and compared with mountain-grown Cabernets from Napa Valley, they are fleshier and more supple and less austere and tannic. In the 1970s, the 1974, 1975, 1977, 1978 and 1979 vintages were all very successful, evidence of the consistently high quality of the vineyard. In the 1980s, the 1980 is excellent, but the 1981 through 1983 vintages are less inspiring. With the 1984, 1985 and 1986 vintages, York Creek is once again showing elegance, ripe, rich fruit and plenty of depth. The 1985 is the finest Cabernet I've tasted from this vineyard. It should drink well for 10 to 15 years, but does not have the great aging potential of Monte Bello.

Ridge's two other regular Cabernet bottlings, the Santa Cruz Mountain and Jimsomare, can be very good but typically are not nearly as impressive as either Monte Bello or York Creek.

TASTING NOTES

RIDGE VINEYARDS, Monte Bello, Santa Cruz Mountains

1986 RIDGE VINEYARDS MONTE BELLO: At first, the 1986 showed a heavy dose of oak and toasty cedar, but now after six tastings I find more black cherry and currant flavors developing. This wine lacks the richness and opulence of the great Monte Bellos, and I have found great bottle variation, but it offers elegance and structure that warrants watching. Drink 1994-1999. 2,079 cases produced. Release: $35. Current: $35. **85**

1985 RIDGE VINEYARDS MONTE BELLO: A magnificent 1985 and one of the great Monte Bellos, with beautifully defined, richly flavored layers of cedar, plum, black cherry and vanilla supported by firm, lean tannins and a great aftertaste of fruit and minerals. This wine is very close in quality to the colossal 1984 and should be cellared another five to seven years. Drink 1995-2005. 2,220 cases produced. Release: $40. Current: $50. **95**

1984 RIDGE VINEYARDS MONTE BELLO: Another stunning Monte Bello, this is a monumental wine — big, rich, massively proportioned, intensely flavored, packed with fresh, ripe, supple currant, black cherry, vanilla and spice flavors. This wine has the tannin and depth for midterm to long-term aging. Drink 1995-2005. 3,125 cases produced. Release: $35. Current: $60. **97**

1983 RIDGE VINEYARDS, SANTA CRUZ MOUNTAINS (MONTE BELLO): The 1983 Monte Bello was declassified because it didn't meet quality standards, but it is a very decent bottle of wine. Hard and tight as 1983s go, it is nonetheless balanced and has decent fruit. It will never be a great wine, but the black currant and cherry flavors that echo on the finish promise it should be pleasant drinking in five years. Drink 1994-2000. 2,677 cases produced. Release: $12. Current: $15. **84**

1982 RIDGE VINEYARDS MONTE BELLO: Disappointing like the 1980 with its hard, tannic veneer. Hard rains hit Monte Bello just before and during harvest, leaving a wine without the typical richness and concentration of fruit. But it's a decent wine, a curiosity because of its hardness and woody damp earth aromas. Drink 1992-1998. 4,350 cases produced. Release: $18. Current: $25. **75**

1981 RIDGE VINEYARDS MONTE BELLO: An elegant, complex, concentrated Monte Bello with firm, deep, compact black currant, plum and cherry aromas and flavors that are beautifully proportioned, gently unfolding on the palate. Firm tannins and plenty of ripe, rich fruit on the finish. This one still needs time to develop fully. Drink 1996-2004. 2,648 cases produced. Release: $25. Current: $45. **92**

1980 RIDGE VINEYARDS MONTE BELLO: This has always been an unusual Monte Bello, for despite its apparent ripeness it lacks concentration and depth of flavor, and it is extremely hard and oaky. It smells and tastes like a Bordeaux, so perhaps with further aging it will blossom like one. Drink 1995-2005. 4,125 cases produced. Release: $30. Current: $36. **80**

RIDGE 1976
CALIFORNIA
CABERNET
SAUVIGNON
MONTE BELLO

ESTATE GROWN, 100% CABERNET SAUVIGNON
SANTA CRUZ MTNS   ALCOHOL 12.7% BY VOLUME
PRODUCED AND BOTTLED BY RIDGE VINEYARDS
17100 MONTE BELLO RD, CUPERTINO, CALIFORNIA

RIDGE 1976
CALIFORNIA
CABERNET
SAUVIGNON
MONTE BELLO

ESTATE GROWN, 100% CABERNET SAUVIGNON
SANTA CRUZ MTNS   ALCOHOL 12.7% BY VOLUME
PRODUCED AND BOTTLED BY RIDGE VINEYARDS
17100 MONTE BELLO RD, CUPERTINO, CALIFORNIA

1978 RIDGE VINEYARDS MONTE BELLO: From another warm vintage, this is a ripe, supple, complex and generous Monte Bello, loaded with ripe black currant, spice, mineral and anise flavors that lavishly cover the palate. It has the richness, concentration and depth for another decade, since it's still displaying a fair amount of tannin. Drink 1993-2003. 1,820 cases produced. Release: $30. Current: $60. **91**

1977 RIDGE VINEYARDS MONTE BELLO: One of the greatest four or five Monte Bellos. It is very deep and concentrated, just beginning to open up, with cedar, black currant and cherry flavors that are very deep and complex, and it's still quite tannic and firm. Needs more time but promises greatness. Drink 1995-2005. 840 cases produced. Release: $40. Current: $80. **94**

1976 RIDGE VINEYARDS MONTE BELLO: From a very hot, dry vintage, this Monte Bello is extremely ripe, with sweet raisin and prune flavors that are deep and concentrated, finishing with a burst of heat and fruit. There is still a trace of tannin and the alcohol stands out, but it's a perfectly good bottle of wine. Try with a wedge of Stilton. Drink 1990-1998. 1,577 cases produced. Release: $15. Current: $65. **83**

1975 RIDGE VINEYARDS MONTE BELLO: A very successful and charming 1975, this Monte Bello has plenty of rich, supple, lively fruit that is complex and long on the finish. Not too tannic, it is a very harmonious wine that can be enjoyed now and for another eight to 10 years. Drink 1990-1999. 1,850 cases produced. Release: $10. Current: $85. **88**

1974 RIDGE VINEYARDS MONTE BELLO: One of the great 1974s, rich, ripe and opulent, overflowing with sweet plum and currant flavors that are youthful and concentrated, framed by thick, gutsy tannins. Despite its strength, it has an underlying sense of elegance and finesse, with great length. It's drinking well now, but if you're down to your final bottles, hold on another five to seven years. Drink 1990-1998. 1,260 cases produced. Release: $12. Current: $140. **93**

1973 RIDGE VINEYARDS MONTE BELLO: Lively, elegant and complex, with mint, cedar, sweet black cherry and anise flavors that are lean and well focused with firm tannins and fine balance. Has matured gracefully and is ready to drink. Drink 1990-1994. 1,094 cases produced. Release: $10. Current: $110. **87**

1972 RIDGE VINEYARDS MONTE BELLO: This was a wet, rainy vintage throughout most of California; Monte Bello produced a surprisingly good wine that is still drinking well but is a shade past its prime. It displays earthy mushroom aromas, but pretty fruit and a touch of bell pepper on the finish. Drink 1990-1992. 740 cases produced. Release: $10. Current: $100. **84**

1971 RIDGE VINEYARDS MONTE BELLO: Fully mature and at its peak, this is a rich, smooth and lively wine from a mediocre vintage that offers hints of prune, plum, cedar and tobacco. There's still a trace of tannin on the finish but the fruit is drying up. Drink 1990-1993. 630 cases produced. Release: $10. Current: $145. **85**

1970 RIDGE VINEYARDS MONTE BELLO: The greatest Monte Bello of the 1970s, just a notch ahead of the 1977, and along with 1984 and 1985 among the top three wines ever produced from this great vineyard. This is a magnificently rich and complex Cabernet with great depth of flavor and concentration of fruit and tannins. A sensational wine that will last another decade and quite possibly two. A masterpiece. Drink 1994-2005. 540 cases produced. Release: $10. Current: $190. **96**

1969 RIDGE VINEYARDS MONTE BELLO: This vintage surpasses the 1968 in quality and ranks among the top five Monte Bellos for its sheer elegance, youthful vigor, bright, complex fruit and great length. The spicy plum, black cherry and floral flavors echo on the finish. Can stand another decade. Drink 1990-2000. 300 cases produced. Release: $7.50. Current: $200. **92**

1968 RIDGE VINEYARDS MONTE BELLO: A very successful Monte Bello from a great vintage, it has reached maturity and can age further, but it's probably drinking about as well as it will. Its rich, concentrated fruit is still fresh and ripe, with hints of chocolate and oak, but the finish is still quite dry and tannic. With proper storage it can age another five to seven years. Drink 1990-1997. 200 cases produced. Release: $7.50. Current: $190. **87**

1965 RIDGE VINEYARDS MONTE BELLO: A remarkably complex and elegant wine that has held up well, displaying classic cigar box aromas and mature cherry and bell pepper flavors. Firm structure and good length on the finish. Drink 1990-1993. 90 cases produced. Release: $6.50. Current: $275. **86**

1964 RIDGE VINEYARDS MONTE BELLO: A classic Monte Bello that's rich, smooth and mellow, with complex, well-focused Cabernet flavors, cigar box aromas and fine length. At its peak now but showing no signs of faltering. Drink 1990-1995. 70 cases produced. Release: $6.50. Current: $310. **90**

1963 RIDGE VINEYARDS MONTE BELLO: The 1963 is well into decline but still drinkable, with mature, slightly vegetal flavors. What's amazing about this wine is that the grapes never fully ripened, leaving a wine of 10.5 percent alcohol. Not much to look forward to, but may have more value as a collectible because of its age and rarity. Drink 1990. 100 cases produced. Release: $5.00. Current: $130. **70**

RIDGE VINEYARDS, York Creek, Spring Mountain, Napa Valley

1986 RIDGE VINEYARDS YORK CREEK: An impressive York Creek for its lean concentration of rich, ripe black currant, cedar and spicy cherry flavors. Not as supple and complex as the 1984 or 1985 bottlings, but close, with its enticing fruit and subtle nuances. The struc-

RIDGE
CALIFORNIA
CABERNET
SAUVIGNON
1963

MONTE BELLO GRAPES 2300' ESTATE GROWN AND BOTTLED JAN 1968 ALCOHOL 10.7% BY VOLUME PRODUCED AND BOTTLED BY RIDGE VINEYARDS 17100 MONTE BELLO RD, CUPERTINO, CALIFORNIA

```
RIDGE    1980
CALIFORNIA
CABERNET
SAUVIGNON
YORK CREEK
```

GRAPES, 85% CABERNET SAUVIGNON, 15% MERLOT
SPRING MTN, NAPA COUNTY   ALCOHOL 14.1% BY VOLUME
PRODUCED AND BOTTLED BY RIDGE VINEYARDS, BW 4488
17100 MONTE BELLO RD, BOX AI, CUPERTINO, CALIFORNIA

ture now is firm, and it's showing a pretty kiss of oak on the finish. Needs time to soften. Drink 1993-2000. 5,333 cases produced. Not Released. **88**

1985 RIDGE VINEYARDS YORK CREEK: The greatest York Creek ever produced, this is a highly complex and enticing Cabernet with layers of ripe black cherry, currant and spicy cedar flavors that marry well on the palate and finish with great length. Elegant, deep and tasty. Charming now but should age well for another decade. Drink 1990-2000. 4,087 cases produced. Release: $16. Current: $16. **92**

1984 RIDGE VINEYARDS YORK CREEK: A top-notch 1984, this is a deliciously rich and fruity wine with tiers of ripe, supple black cherry, currant, floral and spice flavors that turn to anise and cedar on the finish. Very complex and seductive, approachable now because of the soft tannins. One to stock up on for sheer drinking pleasure. Drink 1990-1998. 6,900 cases produced. Release: $14. Current: $16. **88**

1983 RIDGE VINEYARDS YORK CREEK: A lean, crisp, tannic 1983 that is nearing maturity but will probably always be on the tannic side. Drink 1992-1996. 6,390 cases produced. Release: $12. Current: $15. **73**

1982 RIDGE VINEYARDS YORK CREEK: Except for the 1976 and 1983, this is the least impressive York Creek bottling. It's a lean, hard, oaky, tannic wine without the charming ripe fruit usually found in York Creek Cabernets. It's closed and thin on the finish, but may show modest improvement with age. Drink 1994-2000. 6,909 cases produced. Release: $12. Current: $15. **73**

1981 RIDGE VINEYARDS YORK CREEK: A disappointing 1981 that is decent but not in the typical fruity York Creek style. It's lean, hard and overly oaky, without the rich, ripe, concentrated fruit to stand up to it. With time it will soften and perhaps show better. Drink 1994-2000. 4,925 cases produced. Release: $12. Current: $20. **76**

1980 RIDGE VINEYARDS YORK CREEK: Very ripe, bordering on jammy, packed with rich currant, black cherry and plum flavors are supported by firm tannins and spicy oak. A big, full-bodied wine that should continue to improve for five to seven years. Alcoholic on the finish. Drink 1992-1999. 3,516 cases produced. Release: $12. Current: $22. **88**

1979 RIDGE VINEYARDS YORK CREEK: Extremely ripe, almost raisiny, with plenty of depth and concentration, this is a fresh, youthful wine on its way up, filled with fruit and supported by firm tannins. It's drinkable now, but should continue to improve for another decade. Drink 1990-1998. 3,100 cases produced. Release: $12. Current: $30. **88**

1978 RIDGE VINEYARDS YORK CREEK: From a very ripe vintage, the 1978 is teeming with supple black cherry, currant and plum flavors with hints of pepper and oak. Fully mature now but with the depth and tannins for another seven to 10 years. Drink 1990-1998. 5,983 cases produced. Release: $12. Current: $35. **87**

1977 RIDGE VINEYARDS YORK CREEK: A very pleasant 1977 with plenty of ripe, generous plum, cherry and spicy currant flavors that are mature, offering a wine with a silky smooth texture and lots of flavor. Most of the tannins have softened. Drink 1990-1996. 1,780 cases produced. Release: $12. Current: $35. **88**

1976 RIDGE VINEYARDS YORK CREEK: From an extremely ripe vintage, this is a pruney, earthy wine that is disjointed and unpleasant, quite uncharacteristic of this vineyard. Best to avoid. 1,150 cases produced. Release: $10. Current: $30. **68**

1975 RIDGE VINEYARDS YORK CREEK: Extremely ripe and fruity for a 1975 with layers of plum, currant and black cherry flavors that explode on the palate, leaving a warm, supple, generous feeling. The enormous fruit and concentration in this wine make you think it could go on and on, but it's near its peak now. Drink 1992-2000. 800 cases produced. Release: $10. Current: $45. **87**

1974 RIDGE VINEYARDS YORK CREEK: A smooth, spicy, elegant 1974 that's mature and ready to drink, offering ripe, supple black currant, cherry and spicy oak flavors that are fresh, lively, complex and delicate, finishing with good length. First York Creek bottling. Drink 1990-1997. 536 cases produced. Release: $6.75. Current: $50. **87**

RIDGE   1980
CALIFORNIA
CABERNET
SAUVIGNON
YORK CREEK

GRAPES, 85% CABERNET SAUVIGNON, 15% MERLOT
SPRING MTN, NAPA COUNTY   ALCOHOL 14.1% BY VOLUME
PRODUCED AND BOTTLED BY RIDGE VINEYARDS, BW 4488
17100 MONTE BELLO RD, BOX AI, CUPERTINO, CALIFORNIA

ROMBAUER VINEYARDS
La Meilleur du Chai, Napa Valley

CLASSIFICATION:
  La Meilleur du Chai: FOURTH GROWTH
  Napa Valley: FIFTH GROWTH
COLLECTIBILITY RATING: *Not rated*
BEST VINTAGES: *La Meilleur du Chai: 1986, 1985, 1984, 1983*

Through its first six vintages, Rombauer Vineyards has often produced very good, solid, correct Cabernets that display thick, rich, concentrated fruit and lack only complexity, with an occasional lean and unexciting vintage. In 1983 the winery introduced a limited bottling called Le Meilleur du Chai, a Bordeaux-style blend that varies each year, and it is truly a fine wine — deep, complex and ageworthy. Of the Cabernets, the 1980, 1985 and 1986 are the best, while all four vintages of La Meilleur du Chai, from 1983 to 1986, are impressive and worth a try, with deep, rich, supple fruit that is complex and ageworthy. All of the fruit is purchased in Napa Valley; proprietors Koerner and Joan Rombauer own 10 acres of Merlot and a winery on the Silverado Trail north of St. Helena where a number of wineries custom-crush and barrel-age their wines.

TASTING NOTES

ROMBAUER VINEYARDS, Various bottlings

1986 ROMBAUER VINEYARDS LE MEILLEUR DU CHAI: Packed with fresh, ripe fruit, tight and lean, with well-defined currant, cherry and spicy oak flavors that are elegant and complex, fine tannins and excellent length. Young and just beginning to develop, this wine should age gracefully for a decade or more. Drink 1994-2002. 500 cases produced. Not Released. **89**

1986 ROMBAUER VINEYARDS: The 1986 appears to be the best regular bottling of Rombauer to date, a well-balanced wine with ample plum and currant flavors and just the right amount of tannin. Drink 1992-1997. 3,000 cases produced. Release: $15. Current: $15. **86**

1985 ROMBAUER VINEYARDS LE MEILLEUR DU CHAI: Leaner and more austere with a distinctive minty component, this is a firm,

---

AT A GLANCE
ROMBAUER VINEYARDS
3522 Silverado Trail
St. Helena, CA 94574
(707) 963-5170

Owners: Koerner and Joan Rombauer

Winemaker: Greg Grahan (1 year)

Founded: 1982

First Cabernet vintage: 1980
  La Meilleur du Chai: 1983

Cabernet production: 3,000 cases
  La Meilleur du Chai: 500 cases
  Napa Valley: 2,500 cases

Cabernet acres owned: 10 (Merlot)

Average age of vines: 11 years

Vineyard makeup: Merlot (100%)

Average wine makeup:
  La Meilleur du Chai: Cabernet Sauvignon (60%), Cabernet Franc (31%), Merlot (9%)
  Napa Valley: Cabernet Sauvignon (85%), Cabernet Franc (9%), Merlot (6%)

Time in oak: 21 months

Type of oak: French (Nevers)

tight, elegant wine with cedar, black cherry and mint flavors that are crisp and lively. There are ample tannins for aging that are integrated into the wine. Drink 1993-2002. 425 cases produced. Release: $35. Current: $37.50. **90**

1985 ROMBAUER VINEYARDS: The 1985 fits the Rombauer style of lean, crisp, balanced wines, but it lacks drama and richness. There is plenty to like in the well-proportioned, bright black cherry, currant and mint flavors and balanced tannins. Drink 1991-1997. 2,000 cases produced. Release: $14.75. Current: $17. **85**

1984 ROMBAUER VINEYARDS LE MEILLEUR DU CHAI: Distinctive for its richness and elegance, with rich, supple cedar, black cherry, spice and anise flavors that are fresh and lively, medium-bodied, long and delicate on the finish. Drink 1992-2000. 450 cases produced. Release: $32.50. Current: $35. **90**

1984 ROMBAUER VINEYARDS: This is a very likable Cabernet, but given the vintage, when many rich, opulent, concentrated wines were produced, this one comes across as fruity and elegant but lacking richness and depth. The currant and plum flavors ring true, and it's well balanced; technically correct, but not inspired. Drink 1991-1995. 1,500 cases produced. Release: $13.50. Current: $21. **84**

1983 ROMBAUER VINEYARDS LE MEILLEUR DU CHAI: The 1983 is a big, thick, rich, muscular wine with layers of cedar, currant, mint and chocolate flavors that are supple and smooth and bordered by firm tannins. Drink 1993-2001. 415 cases produced. Release: $30. Current: $40. **90**

1983 ROMBAUER VINEYARDS: A mediocre wine from a poor vintage, very lean and tannic, lacking richness and charm. It's drinkable but, like most 1983s, uninspiring. Drink 1990-1994. 1,500 cases produced. Release: $13.50. Current: $19. **73**

1982 ROMBAUER VINEYARDS: A modest success given the vintage, the 1982 has reached its peak and offers ripe cherry and plum flavors with a touch of anise on the finish. There's plenty of tannin left for aging, but it's best now while it still has its fruit. Drink 1990-1994. 1,000 cases produced. Release: $12. Current: $23. **83**

1981 ROMBAUER VINEYARDS: Lean, tight and well balanced for a 1981 with decent fruit of moderate depth and intensity, but lacking the richness and complexity of the best wines from the vintage. The cherry and plum flavors are straightforward and tannic, in need of further cellaring. Drink 1993-1998. 1,000 cases produced. Release: $12. Current: $24. **82**

1980 ROMBAUER VINEYARDS: Rombauer's first vintage is a big, thick, rich Cabernet with plenty of power and lots of flavor and tannin. The tobacco, currant, herb and cedar flavors are firm and concentrated, still youthful and undeveloped. Plenty of tannin yet to lose. Drink 1993-2000. 500 cases produced. Release: $10. Current: $25. **86**

RUTHERFORD HILL WINERY

XVS, St. Helena, Napa Valley

CLASSIFICATION: *FIFTH GROWTH*
COLLECTIBILITY RATING: *Not rated*
BEST VINTAGES:
  XVS: *1986, 1985*

  Napa Valley: *1984, 1980 (Lot 2)*

Considering its excellent vineyards and the success of its sister winery, Freemark Abbey, with Cabernet, Rutherford Hill Winery has never fully lived up to expectations. A partnership, headed by Bill Jaeger and Chuck Carpy owns select Cabernet and Merlot vines in the heart of Rutherford, yet the Rutherford Hill Cabernets have been simple, easy drinking wines more suited for restaurant sales than for laying away in the cellar.

The 1984, 1985 and 1986 vintages, however, show more concentration, structure and depth of flavor. They also appear to be more ageworthy. With the exception of the 1979 and 1980 Cask 2 Limited Edition bottlings, the early Cabernets have faded and are poor examples of wines from some superb vintages. Jerry Luper joined the winery as winemaker after the 1986 vintage, and his experience with Cabernet at Freemark Abbey and Château Montelena (along with J.E. Luper Private Reserve and Diamond Creek) should come in handy at Rutherford Hill. The top-of-the-line XVS bottlings, for Exceptional Vineyard Selection, are made in 2,000-case lots. Another 17,000 cases of Rutherford Hill Cabernet are also produced, and these wines are best consumed soon after release.

TASTING NOTES

RUTHERFORD HILL WINERY, Various bottlings

1986 RUTHERFORD HILL WINERY XVS: The second XVS bottling is ripe, sleek and elegant, with plenty of ripe black cherry and currant flavors and deceptively firm tannins. While it is sharply focused and complex, this wine has the depth and structure for medium- to long-term aging. Drink 1994-2000. 2,000 cases produced. Not Released. **88**

1985 RUTHERFORD HILL WINERY XVS: Rutherford Hill's finest effort to date, a rich, intense, concentrated wine that is tight, closed and in need of five to seven years' cellaring. The currant, black cherry and chocolate flavors are complex and rich, and there is a good dose of tannin on the finish. Drink 1995-2001. 2,000 cases produced. Release: $25. Current: $25. **89**

1984 RUTHERFORD HILL WINERY: Rich, concentrated and flavorful, displaying ripe black cherry and currant flavors along with a curtain of tannins. The flavors linger on the finish. Best Rutherford Hill Cabernet in a while. Drink 1994-2000. 14,834 cases produced. Release: $12.50. Current: $15. **88**

1983 RUTHERFORD HILL WINERY: Fairly typical of the 1983 vintage, lean and austere, but with rich cherry and plum flavors to stand up to the tannins. At its peak and ready to drink now and through the next five years. Drink 1990-1995. 16,439 cases produced. Release: $12.50. Current: $16. **83**

1982 RUTHERFORD HILL WINERY: From a difficult vintage, a decent wine with tart black cherry and herb notes that are straightforward and pleasant but not especially complex. Drink 1990-1994. 17,878 cases produced. Release: $12.50. Current: $17. **83**

1981 RUTHERFORD HILL WINERY: Supple and more elegant, fully mature, with cedar, herb, cherry and chocolate flavors of moderate depth and complexity. Still tannic, it can be enjoyed now or in the next five years. Drink 1990-1995. 9,851 cases produced. Release: $11.50. Current: $18. **85**

1980 RUTHERFORD HILL WINERY: A big, bold, ripe Cabernet, though not especially complex, that has all the ingredients in balance but has not developed into anything special. Drink 1990-1994. 9,574 cases produced. Release: $11.50. Current: $19. **82**

1980 RUTHERFORD HILL WINERY CASK LOT 2 LIMITED EDITION: A bigger, richer, more complex version of the regular bottling, the Cask Lot 2 has complex fruit and cedar flavors and good depth and tannins to give it firmness and structure. Drink 1990-1996. 2,000 cases produced. Release: $15. Current: $20. **88**

1979 RUTHERFORD HILL WINERY: Always a superior wine to the 1978, with mature herb and chocolate flavors that are well focused and long on the finish. Has been drinking well for several years. Drink 1990-1995. 9,971 cases produced. Release: $11.50. Current: $22. **87**

1978 RUTHERFORD HILL WINERY: At times this has been a rich, dense, overripe and somewhat clumsy wine, yet it has remained in balance and aged well, although it is not at the top of its class for this superb vintage. The plum and cedar flavors border on overripe. My last few tastings have indicated it is declining. Drink 1990-1993. 16,471 cases produced. Release: $12. Current: $22. **82**

1977 RUTHERFORD HILL WINERY: Fully mature and in decline,

the 1977 is a simple, one-dimensional wine that never developed any complexities. It drank about as well as it ever did the year it was released. Drink 1990. 11,337 cases produced. Release: $10. Current: $18. **72**

1976 RUTHERFORD HILL WINERY: From a drought year when most Cabernets were overripe, this wine is typical with overripe fruit and harsh tannins. Most 1976s have not developed very well. This wine is no exception. Drink 1990. 5,505 cases produced. Release: $9. Current: $17. **73**

1975 RUTHERFORD HILL WINERY: Old and tired, well past its peak with very mature Cabernet flavors that are coarse and simple. Best to avoid. 4,984 cases produced. Release: $9. Current: $18. **69**

SANTA CRUZ MOUNTAIN VINEYARD

Bates Ranch, Santa Cruz Mountains

CLASSIFICATION: *FOURTH GROWTH*

COLLECTIBILITY RATING: *A*

BEST VINTAGES: *1986, 1985, 1978*

F ew California Cabernets can match the sheer concentration and tannic intensity of those produced by Santa Cruz Mountain Vineyard. Proprietor and winemaker Ken Burnap, a former restaurateur from Los Angeles, has won a cult following for his Cabernets, but they are not for everyone. They are typically very ripe, bordering on raisiny, with concentrated, complex, earthy fruit flavors and the kind of firm, dry tannins that require a full decade to begin softening. Since 1978 the Bates Ranch in the Santa Cruz Mountains has been the source of Cabernet fruit for Burnap. The 1978 is now ready to drink, amply endowed with lavish fruit. The 1979 is successful for a difficult vintage, followed by an extremely ripe 1980 and a good but somewhat oaky 1981. The 1982 vintage was another tough one in the Santa Cruz Mountains, and it shows in this bottling. The 1983 is typically hard and austere, while the 1984 is well balanced and should be drinkable earlier than the 1983. Both the 1985 and 1986 Cabernets show Santa Cruz Mountain Vineyard at the top of its form, with rich, deep, dramatic fruit wrapped in firm tannins. Both wines will need another five years' cellaring before the tannins begin to soften.

AT A GLANCE

SANTA CRUZ MOUNTAIN VINEYARD
2300 Jarvis Road
Santa Cruz, CA 95065
(408) 426-6209

Owner: Ken Burnap

Winemaker: Ken Burnap (15 years)

Founded: 1974

First Cabernet vintage: 1977

Cabernet production: 1,300 cases

Cabernet acres owned: none

Average age of vines: n/a

Vineyard makeup: n/a

Average wine makeup: Cabernet Sauvignon (97%), Merlot (3%)

Time in oak: 21 months

Type of oak: French, American

TASTING NOTES

SANTA CRUZ MOUNTAIN VINEYARD, Bates Ranch, Santa Cruz Mountains

1986 SANTA CRUZ MOUNTAIN VINEYARD BATES RANCH: A worthy successor to the stellar 1985, this is another rich, dramatic, very concentrated wine loaded with ripe currant, black cherry, mineral and herb flavors that are young and tight with austere tannins on the finish. It should surpass the 1985 as Santa Cruz Mountain Vineyard's finest. These wines are built to age, so lay this one away another 10 to 12 years. Drink 1996-2006. 1,200 cases produced. Not Released. **93**

1985 SANTA CRUZ MOUNTAIN VINEYARD BATES RANCH: One of the finest wines produced by Santa Cruz Mountain Vineyard, it

is firm, tight and austere, with layers of rich, ripe, lean fruit accented by black cherry, herb, spice and cedar nuances and extremely dry tannins on the finish. This wine should age two decades or more and be ready to sip in five to eight years at the earliest. Drink 1995-2005. 1,125 cases produced. Not Released. **92**

1984 SANTA CRUZ MOUNTAIN VINEYARD BATES RANCH: A ripe, lean, focused 1984 that offers attractive black cherry, currant, spice and cedar notes and crisp, firm tannins. Not as opulent as most 1984s, but it's well balanced and starting to drink well. Built for midterm cellaring. Drink 1992-1998. 1,100 cases produced. Not Released. **87**

1983 SANTA CRUZ MOUNTAIN VINEYARD BATES RANCH: This was a tough vintage throughout California, producing crisp, lean, hard and austere wines that were disproportionately tannic, but beneath the tannins this wine has a rich core of fruit that will require another eight to 10 years before it's ready to drink. Even then it may be tannic. Drink 1996-2004. 1,800 cases produced. Release: $12. Current: $12. **84**

1982 SANTA CRUZ MOUNTAIN VINEYARD BATES RANCH: From a rainy vintage, this wine shows the ill effects of too much water at harvest. It is earthy and woody, with decent but barely ripe fruit that gets thin and remains very tannic. Still needs time to soften. Drink 1994-1998. 1,800 cases produced. Release: $12. Current: $14. **72**

1981 SANTA CRUZ MOUNTAIN VINEYARD BATES RANCH: A respectable 1981 with ample, rich berry flavors, but it is also quite heavily oaked, which imparts a dry, oaky flavor that currently dominates the wine. With time the oak may be less of a factor, but now it's too strong a presence and detracts from the overall quality. Drink 1994-1999. 1,600 cases produced. Release: $12. Current: $20. **79**

1980 SANTA CRUZ MOUNTAIN VINEYARD BATES RANCH: Extremely ripe, harvested at 25 degrees Brix, with delicious black cherry and currant flavors that are supple and concentrated, supported by firm tannins and excellent depth. The overripe style may not appeal to everyone, but this wine is balanced and loaded with fruit. Approachable now or can age. Drink 1990-1997. 840 cases produced. Release: $12. Current: $18. **86**

1979 SANTA CRUZ MOUNTAIN VINEYARD BATES RANCH: From a difficult vintage, this is a tough, dry, earthy wine that will need more time to mature. The austere fruit is tight and lean, with hints of cedar, earth and black currant. Lacks the depth and richness of the 1978. Drink 1993-2000. 1,225 cases produced. Release: $12. Current: $35. **79**

1978 SANTA CRUZ MOUNTAIN VINEYARD BATES RANCH: An impressive, complex, delicious 1978, with layers of ripe black cherry, currant, anise, mineral and toasty oak flavors that provide an intriguing bouquet. The texture is smooth, and the tannins are supple. Drink 1990-1998. 750 cases produced. Release: $12. Current: $35. **90**

V. SATTUI WINERY

Preston Vineyard, Rutherford, Napa Valley

CLASSIFICATION: *FIFTH GROWTH*
COLLECTIBILITY RATING: *Not rated*
BEST VINTAGES: *1986, 1985, 1984*

F ew people outside of tourists or Napa Valley residents ever taste the Sattui Cabernets because they are sold almost exclusively through the winery in St. Helena and its mailing list. Sattui's best Cabernet comes from Preston Vineyard in Rutherford, where the grapes have yielded consistently fine, elegant, complex and well-balanced Cabernets. Although the wines have medium body and delicate flavors, Sattui manages to extract enough richness from the fruit to make wines of great appeal. The most recent vintages — 1984, 1985 and 1986 — show the Sattui style at its best. The 1986 shows more toasty oak than previous vintages and should develop for up to 10 years.

TASTING NOTES

V. SATTUI WINERY, **Preston Vineyard, Rutherford, Napa Valley**

1986 V. SATTUI WINERY PRESTON VINEYARD: The best Sattui Cabernet, this is a rich, sharply focused 1986 that shows more toasty oak than previous vintages, but all the ripe, elegant, delicate Cabernet fruit. The cherry and currant flavors echo on the finish. Ready now and capable of aging another eight to 10 years. Drink 1991-1998. 2,487 cases produced. Release: $16.75. Current: $16.75. **88**

1985 V. SATTUI WINERY PRESTON VINEYARD: A typical Sattui Cabernet, elegant, refined, delicate and balanced, with pretty black cherry and currant flavors, a subtle dose of toasty oak and fine, light tannins. Very drinkable now. Drink 1990-1996. 3,143 cases produced. Release: $15.75. Current: $15.75. **87**

1984 V. SATTUI WINERY PRESTON VINEYARD: Impressive for its delicate and elegant structure, the 1984 is much like the previous Sattui wines, with well-focused cedar, currant, plum and cherry flavors and light tannins. Drink 1990-1996. 2,850 cases produced. Release: $13.75. Current: $19.75. **86**

AT A GLANCE

V. SATTUI WINERY
1111 White Lane
St. Helena, CA 95474
(707) 963-7774
Owner: Darryl Sattui
Winemaker: Darryl Sattui (14 years)
Founded: 1885, reestablished: 1975
First Cabernet vintage: 1973
Cabernet production: 6,000 cases
  Preston Vineyard: 2,800 cases
Cabernet acres owned: 18
  Preston Vineyard: 12
Average age of vines: 16 years
Vineyard makeup: Cabernet
  Sauvignon (100%)
Average wine makeup: Cabernet
  Sauvignon (100%)
Time in oak: 22 months
Type of oak: French (Nevers)

1983 V. SATTUI WINERY PRESTON VINEYARD: A rich yet elegant 1983 that has layers of cedar, plum, currant and spice yet avoids being too tannic. Delicately balanced. Drink 1990-1995. 1,613 cases produced. Release: $13.75. Current: $19.75. **81**

1982 V. SATTUI WINERY PRESTON VINEYARD RESERVE: A correct Cabernet with unusual herb and plum flavors that are not bad but not what you'd expect from Cabernet. The fruit is ripe and elegant, and most of the tannins have softened. Drink 1990-1994. 385 cases produced. Release: $22.50. Current: $30. **78**

1980 V. SATTUI WINERY PRESTON VINEYARD RESERVE: Elegant, refined and ready to drink, the 1980 has spice, currant and cherry flavors bordered by light, cedary oak that adds complexity. Delicately balanced with fine tannins. Drink 1990-1995. 372 cases produced. Release: $30. Current: $45. **85**

SEQUOIA GROVE VINEYARDS
Estate, Rutherford, Napa Valley

CLASSIFICATION: *FIFTH GROWTH*
COLLECTIBILITY RATING: *Not rated*
BEST VINTAGES: *Estate: 1986, 1985*

I have long been a fan of the Allen family's Sequoia Grove Cabernets, for they have been consistently rich, concentrated, opulent and firmly tannic, built for cellaring. Unfortunately not all of their Cabernets have aged as gracefully as I had hoped; but the Rutherford estate vineyard has produced two superb bottlings in 1985 and 1986, and these are the wines to focus on.

Before they planted their own 6-acre Cabernet vineyard, the Allens purchased Cabernet from Napa Valley and Alexander Valley vineyards. The first Sequoia Grove Cabernets, both from Napa Valley, were the 1980 Cask One and Cask Two. Both of these wines have developed nicely and are nearing full maturity. The 1981 Napa Valley is oakier and drier than when released, and the 1981 Alexander Valley is also fairly tannic. In 1982 the Napa Valley-Alexander Valley bottling has an overriding earthy quality, while the Napa Valley Rutherford Estate is much leaner and harder than it showed earlier. The 1983 is lean and thin, and the 1984 is strong and sturdy but not up to the vintage's best. With the 1985 Estate, Sequoia Grove has produced its finest Cabernet to date, followed by an excellent 1986 Estate. The 1985 and 1986 Napa County bottlings are also very good, but they're not as deep and concentrated. They should be drunk sooner.

TASTING NOTES

SEQUOIA GROVE VINEYARDS, **Various bottlings**

1986 SEQUOIA GROVE VINEYARDS ESTATE: After the 1985 Estate, the finest Sequoia Grove Cabernet, from the estate vineyard in Rutherford. The beautifully defined cassis and currant flavors are rich in extract and depth, developing complexity and nuance, finishing with plum and oak flavors. Drink 1994-2000. 1,986 cases produced. Release: $22. Current: $22. **90**

1986 SEQUOIA GROVE VINEYARDS NAPA COUNTY: Impressive for its ripe currant, spice and berry flavors, this appears to be a wine

---

AT A GLANCE

SEQUOIA GROVE VINEYARDS
P.O. Box 449
Rutherford, CA 94573
(707) 944-2945

Owner: Sequoia Grove Vineyards

Winemaker: Jim Allen (9 years)

Founded: 1980

First Cabernet vintage: 1980
   Estate: 1982

Cabernet production:
   Estate: 2,000 cases
   Napa County: 6,000 cases

Cabernet acres owned: 6

Average age of vines: 9 years

Vineyard makeup: Cabernet Sauvignon (89%), Cabernet Franc (7%), Merlot (3%), Petit Verdot (1%)

Average wine makeup: Cabernet Sauvignon (96%), Cabernet Franc (3%), Merlot (1%)

Time in oak: 18 months

Type of oak: French (Tronçais, Nevers)

that will drink well within the next five years. The tannins are in the background, but it lacks the richness and concentration for long-term cellaring. Drink 1993-1998. 6,776 cases produced. Release: $16. Current: $16. **88**

1985 SEQUOIA GROVE VINEYARDS ESTATE: Elegant and delicious, with ripe, intense black currant, vanilla and cherry flavors, a smooth, rich texture and a long, fruity finish. The moderate tannins are approachable now, but it's sure to improve in the cellar. The best yet from Sequoia Grove. Drink 1992-2005. 2,064 cases produced. Release: $28. Current: $32. **92**

1985 SEQUOIA GROVE VINEYARDS NAPA COUNTY: This is a rich, supple, forward wine that is fairly typical of the vintage with its generous, supple, ripe fruit, refined, integrated tannins and elegant structure. Ready soon but missing the depth for long-term cellaring. Drink 1992-1997. 4,101 cases produced. Release: $16. Current: $16. **86**

1984 SEQUOIA GROVE VINEYARDS NAPA VALLEY: A strong, sturdy wine with thick, ripe plum, anise, cherry and olive flavors and plenty of oak and tannin on the finish. It's a mouthful with a fleshy feel up front. Needs time to come around. Drink 1992-2002. 4,502 cases produced. Release: $12. Current: $18. **85**

1983 SEQUOIA GROVE VINEYARDS NAPA-ALEXANDER VALLEYS: A lean, thin, straightforward wine with ripe cherry and mint flavors of medium depth. Like most 1983s it lacks the richness and concentration of fruit for aging. Drink 1991-1994. 2,144 cases produced. Release: $12.50. Current: $18. **77**

1982 SEQUOIA GROVE VINEYARDS ESTATE: This 1982 has turned into a lean, hard, tannic wine that is best left alone for another five years. There is not much ripe fruit showing now, and a cedar-bark flavor overshadows the lean, crisp cherry and plum flavors. Overall it's balanced but a bit hard now. Give it time. Drink 1995-2003. 406 cases produced. Release: $14. Current: $22. **82**

1982 SEQUOIA GROVE VINEYARDS NAPA-ALEXANDER VALLEYS: Disjointed and awkward, with an earthy flavor that detracts from the ripe, spicy fruit underneath leaving a dry, almost moldy aftertaste. This wine has shown better but has been disappointing in the most recent tastings. Drink 1990-1998. 2,068 cases produced. Release: $12. Current: $20. **78**

1981 SEQUOIA GROVE VINEYARDS ALEXANDER VALLEY: The herbaceousness of Alexander Valley Cabernet comes through in this wine, yet it is not overpowering but rather pleasant, adding complexity to the ripe currant and cedar flavors. This is a fairly tannic wine, structured for cellaring. Needs more time. Drink 1993-1999. 854 cases produced. Release: $12. Current: $35. **84**

1981 SEQUOIA GROVE VINEYARDS NAPA VALLEY: This wine has noticeably more oak, and it's much drier than the Alexander Valley bottling, so it also appears more tannic. The fruit is ripe and supple, but it's overshadowed by the drying oak. With further aging the fruit may show better. Drink 1994-1999. 1,169 cases produced. Release: $12. Current: $25. **80**

1980 SEQUOIA GROVE VINEYARDS CASK ONE: Earthier and more tannic than Cask Two, this wine is also a shade leaner, with bright black cherry flavors that are ripe and attractive. Overall they are very close in quality. Drink 1992-2000. 444 cases produced. Release: $12. Current: $30. **85**

1980 SEQUOIA GROVE VINEYARDS CASK TWO: A mild-mannered 1980 that is rich and concentrated, displaying very ripe, almost jammy fruit with hints of cherries, plums and anise in the background. The ripeness of the fruit makes it forward and supple, yet the fine tannins guarantee another decade of life. Drinking well now. Drink 1992-1999. 440 cases produced. Release: $12. Current: $45. **87**

SHAFER VINEYARDS

Hillside Select, Stags Leap District, Napa Valley
Estate, Stags Leap District, Napa Valley

CLASSIFICATION: *THIRD GROWTH*
COLLECTIBILITY RATING: *A*
BEST VINTAGES:

Hillside Select (Reserve): 1986, 1985, 1984, 1983, 1982

Estate: 1986, 1985, 1984, 1982, 1979

With a string of exceptionally well-made Cabernets beginning with the 1982 vintage, Shafer Vineyards has emerged as one of the promising new producers in the Stags Leap District of Napa Valley. This family-owned and operated winery began when John Shafer became a grape grower in the early 1970s and started bottling Cabernet with the 1978 vintage. While the wines from 1978 to 1980 were solid and well made, they lacked the refinement and rich, supple elegance of the wines from 1982 to 1986. Both the 1978 and 1979 vintages are sturdy, tannic wines that have not fully matured. The 1980 vintage proved a weaker bottling, lacking the fruit and concentration of earlier efforts. No 1981 was produced, but the 1982 displayed a tighter structure and prettier flavors. In 1982 the winery also began producing a Reserve wine, now known as Hillside Select, from grapes grown along the hillsides near the winery.

In 1983 Doug Shafer took over winemaking, and there was a noticeable improvement. Both of the 1983 bottlings were successful, displaying richness and intensity without weight. The Hillside Select is riper and richer, with deeper fruit than the regular bottling, and it shows a touch more herbaceousness. From 1984 to 1986, both bottlings from each vintage have been excellent, displaying the Stags Leap District character of richness, bright cherry and currant flavors and supple tannins that make the wines rich and approachable early on and capable of aging 10 to 15 years.

The Shafers farm 42 acres of Cabernet Sauvignon, Merlot and Cabernet Franc at the foot of the Stags Leap rock outcropping and has also purchased grapes to augment its supply. Despite inconsistencies early on, Shafer has settled on a style that distinguishes its regular and Hillside Select Cabernets, making it the most improved and perhaps underrated Cabernet producer in Stags Leap.

AT A GLANCE

SHAFER VINEYARDS
6154 Silverado Trail
Napa, CA 94558
(707) 944-2877

Owners: John and Elizabeth Shafer

Winemaker: Doug Shafer (6 years)

Founded: 1979

First Cabernet vintage: 1978
Hillside Select: 1983

Cabernet production: 7,000 cases
Hillside Select: 2,000 cases
Estate: 5,000 cases

Cabernet acres owned: 42

Average age of vines: 10 years

Vineyard makeup: Cabernet Sauvignon (72%), Cabernet Franc (14%), Merlot (14%)

Average wine makeup:
Hillside Select: Cabernet Sauvignon (100%)
Estate: Cabernet Sauvignon (90%), Cabernet Franc (5%), Merlot (5%)

Time in oak:
Hillside Select: 23 months
Estate: 18 months

Type of oak:
Hillside Select: French (Nevers)
Estate: French (Nevers), American

Tasting Notes

Shafer Vineyards, Hillside Select, Stags Leap District, Napa Valley

1986 Shafer Vineyards Hillside Select: An excellent 1986, with deliciously rich, elegant, concentrated fruit and layers of berry, cherry, cedar and spice flavors that are narrowly focused and long on the finish. Not too tannic. Drink 1994-2002. 2,000 cases produced. Not Released. **92**

1985 Shafer Vineyards Hillside Select: Deeper and richer in flavor than the 1985 regular bottling, but with similar ripe cherry, currant, cassis, chocolate, and mint flavors on the finish. The tannins are also more evident, but this is still a beautifully balanced wine that should drink well throughout the decade. Drink 1993-2000. 2,000 cases produced. Not Released. **93**

1984 Shafer Vineyards Hillside Select: A wine with great finesse and delicacy, more subtle and elegant than the 1984 Estate. It lacks some of the exuberant flavor of the regular 1984, but it has an underlying intensity and depth and the flavors are more reined in. Still, there's plenty of cassis, currant, cherry and mint flavors. Drink 1992-2000. 1,800 cases produced. Release: $24.50. Current: $24.50. **92**

1983 Shafer Vineyards Hillside Select: Riper and richer than the 1983 Estate bottling, the Hillside Select has greater depth and concentration of berry, currant and chocolate flavors. Overall it's fruitier and very generous on the palate, with a persistent finish. Both are excellent wines but quite different in style. Drink 1992-1999. 900 cases produced. Release: $22. Current: $22. **89**

1982 Shafer Vineyards Reserve: Big, thick, rich and concentrated, the 1982 Reserve offers mint and herb aromas along with a touch of cola and sassafras. It's beginning to develop fruit complexity and suppleness on the palate, but the tannins are still quite firm. Showing much better now than it has in the past. Drink 1992-1998. 1,200 cases produced. Release: $18. Current: $25. **89**

Shafer Vineyards, Estate, Stags Leap District, Napa Valley

1986 Shafer Vineyards Estate: With beautifully focused, rich black cherry and currant flavors, this is a sleek, elegant, well-defined Cabernet that ranks as Shafer's best effort to date. The delicate balance allows the fruit to show, yet it's bordered by just the right amount of tannin. Drink 1994-2002. 5,000 cases produced. Release: $16. Current: $16. **93**

Shafer
1986
Napa Valley
Stags Leap District

CABERNET
SAUVIGNON

84% Cabernet Sauvignon 8% Merlot 8% Cabernet Franc
Produced & Bottled by Shafer Vineyards, Napa, CA
Alcohol 13.2% by Volume Contains Sulfites

1985 SHAFER VINEYARDS ESTATE: A classically structured Stags Leap District wine with sharply defined ripe cherry, cassis, currant and spice flavors that have a gentle underlying intensity. The most supple Shafer Cabernet to date. Drink 1992-1998. 5,000 cases produced. Release: $15.50. Current: $15.50. **91**

1984 SHAFER VINEYARDS ESTATE: Another top-notch vintage for Shafer, the 1984 has great harmony and finesse, beautifully integrated fruit, layers of smooth, ripe, fleshy, cherry, currant, vanilla and spice flavors and supple tannins that allow the flavors to echo on the finish. A remarkable achievement. Drink 1990-1998. 4,000 cases produced. Release: $14. Current: $16. **91**

1983 SHAFER VINEYARDS ESTATE: Lean, concentrated, elegant and well focused, with rich, ripe black cherry, currant, herb and mint flavors that hang together very well, finishing with finesse. One of the prettiest wines from the difficult 1983 vintage. Drink 1992-1997. 3,700 cases produced. Release: $13. Current: $13. **87**

1982 SHAFER VINEYARDS ESTATE: Tight and concentrated, with firm structure and plenty of flavor, the 1982 was very successful for Shafer. Its herb, cherry and cassis flavors are firm and focused, and the tannins are firm and in the right proportion. Ready soon but should age well, too. Drink 1992-2000. 3,500 cases produced. Release: $13. Current: $18. **88**

1980 SHAFER VINEYARDS ESTATE: Green bell pepper and weedy herbal aromas dominate the fruit. What's missing is the ripe, concentrated, sharply focused Cabernet fruit. The tannins are dry, and the fruit fades on the finish. Not much hope for improvement. Drink 1990-1992. 2,000 cases produced. Release: $12. Current: $25. **77**

1979 SHAFER VINEYARDS ESTATE: Deep in color and well focused, with mature cedar, vanilla, anise and black cherry flavors that are fresh and lively, still quite concentrated and tannic, but better balanced and livelier than the 1978. The finish offers mint and chocolate nuances. Drink 1992-2000. 1,000 cases produced. Release: $12. Current: $35. **89**

1978 SHAFER VINEYARDS ESTATE: The 1978 Shafer has a wonderful, complex aroma of tobacco, cherries and cedar, but it's still very dry and tannic and comes across as one-dimensional on the palate. The flavors are mature and attractive, but the tannins haven't dropped out, robbing it of complexity. With time the tannins will subside, but will the fruit still be there? Drink 1992-2000. 1,000 cases produced. Release: $11. Current: $50. **85**

SILVER OAK CELLARS

Alexander Valley
Napa Valley
Bonny's Vineyard, Oakville, Napa Valley

CLASSIFICATION:
  Alexander Valley: *THIRD GROWTH*
  Napa Valley: *FOURTH GROWTH*
  Bonny's Vineyard: *FIFTH GROWTH*

COLLECTIBILITY RATING:
  Alexander Valley: *AA*
  Napa Valley: *Not rated*
  Bonny's Vineyard: *Not rated*

BEST VINTAGES:
  Alexander Valley: 1985, 1982, 1980, 1978, 1977, 1975, 1974

  Napa Valley: 1985, 1982

A Cabernet specialist, Silver Oak Cellars bottles three separate wines each vintage. By far the most impressive is the Alexander Valley bottling, which winemaker and part-owner Justin Meyer has been producing since 1972. Since 1979 Silver Oak has bottled a Napa Valley Cabernet from purchased grapes grown in Calistoga, and a Bonny's Vineyard Cabernet, named after Meyer's wife, from their vineyard in Oakville, where their handsome stone winery is located. The Napa Valley bottling has been consistently very good, while the Bonny's Vineyard tends to polarize critics and consumers with its dense, weedy black currant and vegetal flavors, and on occasion it has displayed a pickle barrel quality that I do not find attractive, but many people do.

The strength of the Silver Oak Cabernets is clearly the Alexander Valley bottling, produced from 100 percent estate-grown Cabernet in the southernmost area of Alexander Valley (called North Coast before the appellation was approved) and aged entirely in American oak barrels, half of which are new each year. The Justin Meyer-Silver Oak style features ripe, fleshy, complex fruit that offers anise, olive, black cherry, spice and vanilla notes and a rich, smooth, polished texture, making the wines drinkable on release. My notes reflect wines that are complete and harmonious, where fruit is forward and fleshy, oak just a seasoning and the tannins soft yet thick enough to ensure 10 to 15 years' development.

The 1972, from a poor vintage, is still holding up well and remains one of the top wines from this vintage. The 1973 is fairly oaky

AT A GLANCE

SILVER OAK CELLARS
915 Oakville Crossroad
Oakville, CA 94562
(707) 944-8808

Owners: Justin R. Meyer and Raymond T. Duncan

Winemaker: Justin Meyer (17 years)

Founded: 1972

First Cabernet vintage: 1972
  Alexander Valley: 1972
  Napa Valley: 1979
  Bonny's Vineyard: 1979

Cabernet production: 22,000 cases
  Alexander Valley: 17,500 cases
  Napa Valley: 3,500 cases
  Bonny's Vineyard: 1,000 cases

Cabernet acres owned: 200

Average age of vines: 14 years

Vineyard makeup: Cabernet Sauvignon (100%)

Average wine makeup: Cabernet Sauvignon (100%)

Time in oak: 26 months

Type of oak: American

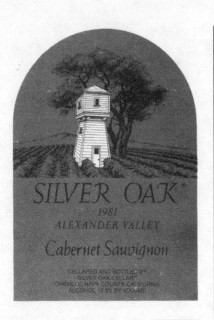

but still drinking well, while the 1974 marks the first great Silver Oak. It is an exceptional Cabernet for its rich, explosive fruit. The 1975, 1976 and 1977 vintages are also very fine, indicative of the winery's consistency in style and quality. The 1978 is another stunning bottling, incredibly rich and smooth and capable of aging into the 21st century. In 1979 Silver Oak produced an elegant, delicious wine, followed by a very ripe, concentrated 1980, a supple, complex 1981 and a very successful 1982 that has long aging potential. The 1983 is another very promising vintage, while the 1984 is ripe and forward, typical with the vintage. The 1985 is by far the most dramatic, complex and ageworthy Cabernet ever produced by Silver Oak. Production has climbed to roughly 20,000 cases.

For my taste, the Napa Valley bottlings have been consistent, if somewhat less showy and awe-inspiring than the Alexander Valley vintages, particularly in 1980, 1981 and 1983. In 1982, 1984 and 1985 they are much more complex and appealing. About 3,500 cases are produced. Bonny's Vineyard is close to the Napa River, where vines tend to get more water and produce large crops. Those factors may account for the weedy, herbaceous quality I find in these wines. Meyer is trying new techniques of pruning and thinning, an indication that he too is not totally pleased with the results and believes he can make a better wine. The 1984 and 1985 are the best so far, with better balance and more richness, but at $45 the 1984 is very pricey, even though fewer than 1,000 cases were produced.

TASTING NOTES

SILVER OAK CELLARS, Alexander Valley (North Coast)

1985 SILVER OAK CELLARS ALEXANDER VALLEY: Silver Oak's finest Cabernet to date, surpassing the 1974 bottling, this is an enormously rich, complex and concentrated wine with layers of ripe, fleshy, intense plum, currant, cedar and anise flavors that are lively and elegant. Absolutely delicious. Alluring now but best in five years. Drink 1995-2005. 19,900 cases produced. Release: $24. Current: $24. **93**

1984 SILVER OAK CELLARS ALEXANDER VALLEY: Another very ripe, supple Silver Oak, more forward, with complex cedar, vanilla, cherry and plum flavors that are fresh and lively. Despite its supple charm, this wine has excellent depth along with the intensity and tannins to carry it another decade. Drink 1992-1999. 14,000 cases produced. Release: $22. Current: $28. **89**

1983 SILVER OAK CELLARS ALEXANDER VALLEY: A rich, supple yet tannic 1983 that has more depth and richness than most wines from this tannic vintage. With another five years' cellaring, the hard tannins on the finish should be more palatable and the generous fruit should make it more interesting. Drink 1995-2002. 14,000 cases produced. Release: $20. Current: $30. **86**

1982 SILVER OAK CELLARS ALEXANDER VALLEY: This wine needs time to soften and develop, but it should be outstanding. Now it's a lean, tannic, cedary wine with firm concentration of plum, currant and cedar flavors. It's tannic on the finish. Drink 1994-2002. 12,500 cases produced. Release: $19. Current: $40. **90**

1981 SILVER OAK CELLARS ALEXANDER VALLEY: A ripe, supple, complex 1981 with distinct green olive and ripe plum flavors that are coarse and tannic for Silver Oak. Once the tannins soften in three or four years it should be fine. Drink 1994-2000. 11,200 cases produced. Release: $19. Current: $35. **86**

1980 SILVER OAK CELLARS ALEXANDER VALLEY: Very ripe, almost jammy and Port-like in aroma, this is a deeply concentrated wine packed with ripe plum, currant and spicy jam notes that are full-bodied and long on the finish. Drinkable now because of its supple, fleshy texture and soft tannins, but it has the concentration for further cellaring. Drink 1990-2000. 12,000 cases produced. Release: $18. Current: $45. **88**

1979 SILVER OAK CELLARS ALEXANDER VALLEY: An elegant, complex, well-structured 1979 with tart black cherry, currant and cedar flavors that are backed by fine, firm tannins. Not as complex as other Silver Oak Cabernets, but this wine has plenty of room to grow. Drink 1992-1999. 12,500 cases produced. Release: $16. Current: $65. **85**

1978 SILVER OAK CELLARS ALEXANDER VALLEY: Beautifully defined black cherry and currant flavors that are rich and ripe, with a trace of dusty oak and firm tannins on the finish. Lovely now for its voluptuous fruit, but it has the intensity and concentration for another decade. One of the best Alexander Valley bottlings, along with 1974 and 1985. Drink 1992-2002. 8,500 cases produced. Release: $16. Current: $100. **93**

1977 SILVER OAK CELLARS ALEXANDER VALLEY: A rich, ripe and supple 1977 with complex plum, currant and cedary oak flavors that are bright and lively. Charming now but has the depth and concentration for another decade. Drink 1990-1997. 7,350 cases produced. Release: $14. Current: $85. **88**

1976 SILVER OAK CELLARS ALEXANDER VALLEY: A highly successful 1976 from a very hot and dry vintage, this wine is deep, rich and concentrated, with seductive black cherry, chocolate and violet aromas. The richness and concentration come through on the palate with a measure of delicacy. Drinkable now but has the intensity, fruit and tannins for another decade. Drink 1992-2002. 6,600 cases produced. Release: $12. Current: $70. **86**

1975 SILVER OAK CELLARS ALEXANDER VALLEY: An elegant, complex and supple 1975 with spicy cherry and plum flavors and a

touch of cedar on the finish. Most of the tannins have been resolved, but the fruit is young and vibrant. Delicious now but can still age. Drink 1990-1996. 6,000 cases produced. Release: $10. Current: $95. **88**

1974 SILVER OAK CELLARS NORTH COAST: Amazingly rich and complex in the finest 1974 fashion, this wine has explosive fruit on the palate with plum, cherry and oak flavors that turn smoky and toasty on the finish. Beautiful now, but it can age another decade. Drink 1990-2000. 4,000 cases produced. Release: $8. Current: $135. **93**

1973 SILVER OAK CELLARS NORTH COAST: A shade oakier than the '72 but with pretty, ripe plum, cedar and currant flavors that taper off on the finish. Still in good condition for a 1973, but it's probably best to drink now. Drink 1990-1994. 1,800 cases produced. Release: $7. Current: $130. **81**

1972 SILVER OAK CELLARS NORTH COAST: Impressive for a 1972, this wine is holding up very well. It's fully mature, elegant and supple, with spicy cherry, cedar and smoky anise flavors that are crisp and lively on the finish. Drink 1990-1995. 1,100 cases produced. Release: $6. Current: $160. **86**

SILVER OAK CELLARS, Calistoga Napa Valley

1985 SILVER OAK CELLARS NAPA VALLEY: Unlike most 1985s, which are showy and beautifully defined, this is a very tight, closed and concentrated wine with firm, hard tannins that will probably need a decade to develop fully. The potential is there for a very good, possibly outstanding Cabernet, but for now it's difficult to determine how good a wine this one will eventually be. Drink 1996-2006. 3,550 cases produced. Release: $24. Current: $24. **85**

1984 SILVER OAK CELLARS NAPA VALLEY: This is a very attractive 1984 with generous fruit and firm, hard tannins that will require a decade to mature fully. The flavors are complex — tea, flowers, plum and anise — but still very tight and closed. Drink 1996-2004. 2,500 cases produced. Release: $22. Current: $28. **86**

1983 SILVER OAK CELLARS NAPA VALLEY: A lighter, leaner and more tannic Silver Oak that's typical of the vintage. The 1985 has spicy fruit and some vegetal notes, finishing on the tannic side. This wine does not appear to have the richness and concentration to stand up to the tannins, but time will tell. Drink 1993-1996. 3,000 cases produced. Release: $20. Current: $30. **74**

1982 SILVER OAK CELLARS NAPA VALLEY: The best of the Silver Oak Napa Valley bottlings, this 1982 offers generous, ripe cherry and currant flavors accented by spicy oak notes that are rich, concentrated and tannic. Young and on its way up. Drink 1995-2005. 3,500 cases produced. Release: $19. Current: $32. **88**

1981 SILVER OAK CELLARS NAPA VALLEY: A tight, young, dense

1981 that's quite oaky. The fruit is ripe but one-dimensional now. With time this wine may have more to show, but for now it's rather closed and unexciting. Drink 1994-2000. 4,100 cases produced. Release: $19. Current: $42. **79**

1980 SILVER OAK CELLARS NAPA VALLEY: A decent Cabernet that is dominated by a pronounced tar and vegetal character that is not overly appealing. Otherwise it's well balanced and drinkable, but one of Silver Oak's weakest bottlings. Drink 1992-1997. 4,000 cases produced. Release: $18. Current: $50. **73**

1979 SILVER OAK CELLARS NAPA VALLEY: Silver Oak's first Napa Valley bottling, this is a tough, youthful 1979 that offers ripe, hard, cherry and plum flavors supported by firm, coarse tannins. Still needs time to soften. Drink 1995-2005. 4,400 cases produced. Release: $18. Current: $55. **82**

SILVER OAK CELLARS, Bonny's Vineyard, Oakville, Napa Valley

1985 SILVER OAK CELLARS BONNY'S VINEYARD: An attractive 1985 for its ripe fruit and olive, mint, plum and tar notes, this is a big, full-bodied wine with ample tannins for aging. It's fairly dense and concentrated and will require patience to reach full maturity. Drink 1995-2004. 970 cases produced. Not Released. **85**

1984 SILVER OAK CELLARS BONNY'S VINEYARD: A supple, complex 1984 with distinct green olive, plum and spicy tobacco notes along with bell pepper flavors that are deep and long on the palate. If those flavors and this style appeal to you, you'll love this wine. Drink 1994-2000. 950 cases produced. Release: $45. Current: $45. **84**

1983 SILVER OAK CELLARS BONNY'S VINEYARD: Stylistically lighter and more elegant than most from this vineyard and the most appealing to me of the early bottlings. It's leaner and not nearly as dense, but because of that it's more palatable and the flavors are truer to Cabernet. Drink 1990-1993. 1,250 cases produced. Release: $40. Current: $40. **82**

1982 SILVER OAK CELLARS BONNY'S VINEYARD: Another good but wildly herbaceous Bonny's, this is a rich, concentrated, fairly tannic wine with ample oak flavors. Still quite closed and compact, this wine's best years are still ahead. Drink 1994-2002. 900 cases produced. Release: $35. Current: $40. **78**

1981 SILVER OAK CELLARS BONNY'S VINEYARD: A major improvement over the previous two bottlings, displaying berry, cherry and spicy oak flavors that are well balanced and in harmony. Firm tannins need more time. Drink 1994-2000. 970 cases produced. Release: $35. Current: $50. **77**

1980 SILVER OAK CELLARS BONNY'S VINEYARD: Very ripe and

vegetal, with the same pickle barrel and green chile pepper flavors as in the 1979. This wine has a shade more fruit, but it's definitely tilted toward the vegetal side of Cabernet. Drink 1993-1998. 1,000 cases produced. Release: $30. Current: $50. **70**

1979 SILVER OAK CELLARS BONNY'S VINEYARD: An extreme style that may appeal more to others, this wine has pickle barrel, chili pepper and vegetable flavors and not much in the way of fruit. Not my style but still drinkable. First Bonny's Vineyard bottling. Drink 1992-1998. 1,200 cases produced. Release: $30. Current: $55. **72**

SILVERADO VINEYARDS

Stags Leap District, Napa Valley

CLASSIFICATION: *SECOND GROWTH*

COLLECTIBILITY RATING: *A*

BEST VINTAGES: *1986, 1985, 1984, 1983, 1982, 1981*

One of the fastest-rising stars in Napa Valley is Silverado Vineyards, owned by the family of the late Walt Disney, the cartoonist and founder of Disneyland. This Stags Leap District winery since 1981 has produced a string of magnificent Cabernets from its 65-acre vineyard on the west side of the Silverado Trail across from the Stags Leap rock outcropping.

For years fruit from this excellent vineyard was sold to Napa Valley wineries, but beginning in 1981 the winery made its own Cabernets under the winemaking direction of Jack Stuart. With each vintage, the wines have improved in quality; overall they have been consistently outstanding. The Silverado style emphasizes layers of rich, concentrated fruit and firm, fine tannins, in part displaying the softness of tannins characteristic of the Stags Leap District. The 1981, after appearing supple and forward early on, has recently shown more richness and backbone and appears to have the intensity and depth to last throughout the century. The 1982 is highly successful for the vintage, as is the 1983, which manages to tone down the vintage's harsh tannins. The 1984 combines a supple texture with firm intensity, while the 1985 and 1986 exceed it in quality, the latter displaying explosive fruit and great concentration, with a sense of elegance and finesse. At $13.50, the 1986 is one of the greatest Cabernet buys available, for Silverado Cabernets typically drink well on release and show the potential to age for 10 to 20 years. As the wines age and display their complexity, they will likely move to the forefront of Napa Valley Cabernets. Production hovers around 10,000 cases.

AT A GLANCE

SILVERADO VINEYARDS
6121 Silverado Trail
Napa, CA 94558
(707) 257-1770

Owners: Lillian Disney, Diane Disney Miller, Ron Miller

Winemaker: Jack Stuart (8 years)

Founded: 1981

First Cabernet vintage: 1981

Cabernet production: 10,000 cases

Cabernet acres owned: 65

Average age of vines: 15 years

Vineyard makeup: Cabernet Sauvignon (93%), Merlot (7%)

Average wine makeup: Cabernet Sauvignon (93%), Merlot (7%)

Time in oak: 15 months

Type of oak: French

TASTING NOTES

SILVERADO VINEYARDS, Stags Leap District, Napa Valley

1986 SILVERADO VINEYARDS: Openly fruity, with firm tannins and ample oak, this is a lean, elegant and supple wine, packed with rich

black cherry, cassis, currant, raspberry and toasty French oak flavors. Not quite as concentrated as the 1984 and 1985, it is nonetheless built for aging. Best in five to seven years, but could go 15. Drink 1995-2005. 9,800 cases produced. Release: $13.50, Current: $13.50. **94**

1985 SILVERADO VINEYARDS: One of the finest Silverados, a beautifully styled, elegant, supple, textured wine oozing with rich currant, black cherry, raspberry and vanilla flavors and buttery nuances on the finish. Complex and intriguing, deep and structured, this is a seductive wine that ranks among the finest of the vintage. Drink 1995-2002. 11,000 cases produced. Release: $12.50, Current: $16. **92**

1984 SILVERADO VINEYARDS: Deceptively supple and more generous than previous bottlings, showing ripe currant, plum and cherry flavors before the tannins clamp down. Despite its charm, it is a thick, massively concentrated wine with elegant, textured fruit and gutsy tannins. It's approachable now, but its best years are ahead. Drink 1996-2002. 7,800 cases produced. Release: $11.50, Current: $20. **91**

1983 SILVERADO VINEYARDS: Rich, vibrant and concentrated, with rough, firm tannins and a solid core of delicious cassis, currant and black cherry flavors. It has the balance and intensity to carry it a decade or more. Needs five years to reach its peak. Drink 1995-2000. 8,000 cases produced. Release: $11, Current: $20. **88**

1982 SILVERADO VINEYARDS: Deep in color, with rich black cherry, earth, oak, chocolate and mint flavors that are deep and concentrated. Not as tannic as the 1981 but perhaps better balanced, especially considering the generally mediocre quality of this vintage. Finishes with a burst of cherry and chocolate flavors. Drink 1993-2000. 8,000 cases produced. Release: $11, Current: $22. **88**

1981 SILVERADO VINEYARDS: Silverado's first vintage is rich and tannic, with a firm structure and pretty tobacco, plum, cherry, currant and cedar flavors that are deep and concentrated. Beautifully balanced, with intensity and length, it is nearing maturity but is capable of aging another decade. Slightly more closed than in previous tastings. Drink 1992-2000. 3,500 cases produced. Release: $11, Current: $25. **90**

SIMI WINERY
Reserve, Alexander Valley

CLASSIFICATION: *THIRD GROWTH*

COLLECTIBILITY RATING: A

BEST VINTAGES: *1986, 1985, 1984, 1982*

Since the arrival of winemaker Zelma Long in 1979, Simi Winery has gradually regained its stature as one of Sonoma County's finest Cabernet producers. Simi has a long, proud history of winemaking dating back to 1876, when it was known as Montepulciano, and some of its Zinfandels and Cabernets of the 1930s and 1940s are legendary in California. In 1971 Russell Green revived the old Simi Winery near Healdsburg, which had fallen into disrepair, and hired Michael Dixon as president. Dixon in turn hired Mary Ann Graf as winemaker and André Tchelistcheff as consultant before luring Long away from Robert Mondavi Winery. Meanwhile, Simi changed hands, going from Green to Scottish & Newcastle, to Schieffelin and then Moët-Hennessy, which is part of Louis Vuitton.

Under Long the Simi Reserve Cabernets, made from estate-grown Alexander Valley fruit, represent the winery's finest bottlings. While they are the best wines to concentrate on, the Sonoma County bottlings are often excellent and worthy of cellaring.

The notes that follow cover Cabernets dating back to 1970, so collectors who have these old wines can see how well they age. The 1972, for instance, is holding very well, despite the generally mediocre reputation of the vintage. In 1974 two wines of reserve quality were produced, a Reserve Vintage bottling, which is still excellent, and a Special Reserve bottling, which is not as rich or complex and is beginning to fade. The 1975 is fully mature and ready to drink. The 1978 Reserve has not aged particularly well, and although it drank well on release it is not a keeper. The 1979 Reserve is extremely intense and fairly oaky, built for the long haul and still a few years away from full development. The 1980 is similar in style, very intense and concentrated, in need of further cellaring. No Reserve was produced in 1981, but the 1982, made from Napa and Sonoma grapes, is rich and flavorful, improving with every tasting and now showing better than ever. No 1983 Reserve was produced, but the 1984 Reserve is absolutely delicious, rich and supple, brimming with ripe fruit, followed by equally sensational 1985 and 1986 vintages.

AT A GLANCE
SIMI WINERY
16275 Healdsburg Ave.
Healdsburg, CA 95448
(707) 433-6981

Owner: Moët-Hennessy-Louis Vuitton, France

Winemaker: Zelma Long (10 years)

Founded: 1876

First Cabernet vintage: Unknown

Cabernet production: 35,000 cases Reserve: 2,000 cases

Cabernet acres owned: 127

Average age of vines: 6 years

Vineyard makeup: Cabernet Sauvignon (78%), Cabernet Franc (14%), Merlot (6%), Petit Verdot (2%)

Average wine makeup: Cabernet Sauvignon (94%), Merlot (4%), Petit Verdot (2%)

Time in oak: 18 months

Type of oak: French

TASTING NOTES

SIMI WINERY, Reserve, Alexander Valley

1986 SIMI WINERY RESERVE: One of the great Simi Reserves, displaying rich, elegant, beautifully defined black cherry, currant and anise flavors that are framed by toasty oak. This wine succeeds with its understated elegance and refinement, and the tannins are in perfect proportion, soft enough to tempt you now. Drink 1993-2002. 1,700 cases produced. Not Released. **92**

1985 SIMI WINERY RESERVE: Dense, rich and concentrated, the 1985 Reserve is the finest Cabernet ever produced at Simi. It is packed with well-focused plum, black cherry and currant flavors that are deep and complex and linger on the palate. Young and closed but very elegant. Drink 1994-2003. 2,300 cases produced. Not Released. **94**

1984 SIMI WINERY RESERVE: Simply delicious, brimming with fresh, ripe raspberry, currant, plum and spice flavors, an excellent wine that is already lovely to drink. It has a smooth, rich, supple character, with fine tannins and the depth and intensity to carry it another decade. Drink 1993-2000. 800 cases produced. Release: $22.50. Current: $22.50. **92**

1982 SIMI WINERY RESERVE SONOMA-NAPA COUNTIES: Lean and concentrated, with fresh, berry, currant, anise and plum flavors that are showing a satiny texture but are backed with firm, chunky tannins. A tight, firm, youthful wine that can age a decade or more. With time it may develop more complexity. Drink 1996-2004. 3,400 cases produced. Release: $20. Current: $20. **88**

1980 SIMI WINERY RESERVE: Similar in style to the oaky, tannic, thick 1979, very tight, concentrated and backward, a long way from maturity. With time it may evolve into an elegant, complex wine, but it is difficult to assess at this stage. Drink 1994-2000. 2,400 cases produced. Release: $20. Current: $30. **84**

1979 SIMI WINERY RESERVE: Similar in style to the 1978 with its lavish oak and tannins, the 1979 has more richness, concentration and flavor, with berry, plum and spice components that are backed with lively acidity and firm, balanced tannins. The fruit echoes on the palate. Drink 1992-1999. 1,700 cases produced. Release: $20. Current: $36. **87**

1978 SIMI WINERY RESERVE: Big, ripe and somewhat clumsy with oak and tannins dominating the ripe currant and cherry flavors. While the flavors are attractive, they do not have the richness and concentration to stand up to the oak and tannins. Drink 1990. 2,700 cases produced. Release: $17. Current: $26. **72**

1977 SIMI WINERY SPECIAL SELECTION: Well past its prime now, with very ripe, mature cherry flavors of moderate depth and character. Drink 1990. 1,700 cases produced. Release: $20. Current: $23. **70**

1975 SIMI WINERY: Smooth, refined and elegant, fully mature, with delicate black cherry, currant, spice and mint flavors. Very harmonious and complete, developing tobacco complexities on the finish. Drink 1990. 11,000 cases produced. Release: $6. Current: $32. **85**

1974 SIMI WINERY RESERVE VINTAGE: For the first decade of its life, the Reserve Vintage drank exceptionally well and ranked among the top 1974s produced in California. Very deep color, rich and supple, it still exhibits pretty black cherry, mint and currant flavors, smooth, rounded tannins and a pleasant black cherry aftertaste. Ready now but has the depth and concentration for further development. Drink 1990-1996. 14,000 cases produced. Release: $20. Current: $45. **87**

1974 SIMI WINERY SPECIAL RESERVE: A more supple, elegant bottling than the 1974 Reserve Vintage, with crisper acidity and good length, but the flavors are not as deep, rich or concentrated. Released in 1984. Drink 1990. 2,000 cases produced. Release: $25. Current: $65. **83**

1973 SIMI WINERY: A lean, austere wine that lacks richness and depth of flavor and has not developed complexity. It's simple and drinkable but not exciting. Drink 1990. 10,000 cases produced. Release: $6. Current: $25. **72**

1972 SIMI WINERY: Holding on remarkably well considering the generally poor vintage. Offers spicy, supple cherry and anise flavors that are fully developed. Lively acidity carries the finish. Drink 1990. 10,000 cases produced. Release: $5. Current: $25. **80**

1971 SIMI WINERY: Fuller and more flavorful than the 1970, with ripe plum and spicy cherry flavors that are supple and mature and beginning to fade on the finish. A notch above the '70 in quality, but past its prime. Drink 1990. 8,000 cases produced. Release: $5. Current: $30. **75**

1970 SIMI WINERY: Fully developed and in decline, with mature color and flavors, fading on the palate, with spicy, ripe cherry flavors. Drink 1990. 5,000 cases produced. Release: $4.50. Current: $50. **73**

SMITH-MADRONE VINEYARD

Spring Mountain, Napa Valley

CLASSIFICATION: *FIFTH GROWTH*

COLLECTIBILITY RATING: *Not rated*

BEST VINTAGES: *1985, 1984*

Through eight vintages, Smith-Madrone on Spring Mountain has been inconsistent in both style and quality. At times these mountain-grown Cabernets from the Smith family's 11-acre Cabernet vineyard are rich and flavorful, with firmness, depth and complexity. The best two vintages are the most recent offerings, the 1984 and 1985, both of which display deeply concentrated fruit and excellent aging potential. The first two Cabernets, from the 1978 and 1979 vintages, were also very good, but have paled in comparison to the most recent bottlings. The 1980 is light and simple, followed by a thin 1981 and a 1982 that is decent but unexciting. The 1983 is hard and tannic, in need of five more years' cellaring. In 1986, an excellent year in Napa Valley, Smith-Madrone produced a mediocre wine that was sold in bulk.

TASTING NOTES

SMITH-MADRONE VINEYARD, Spring Mountain, Napa Valley

1985 SMITH-MADRONE VINEYARD: Elegant and refined for Smith-Madrone, the 1985 is packed with ripe, concentrated fruit, currant, black cherry and anise flavors, framed with firm tannins. Has a touch more finesse and elegance than the 1984, with hints of cherry and mint on the aftertaste. Drink 1994-2002. 1,500 cases produced. Release: $14. Current: $14. **90**

1984 SMITH-MADRONE VINEYARD: By far the best Smith-Madrone to date, the 1984 is rich and concentrated, with thick black currant, cherry and plum flavors that are ripe and well balanced, with the tannins for long-term aging. Could use a little finesse, but with time that may come. Drink 1994-2004. 1,100 cases produced. Release: $14. Current: $14. **91**

1983 SMITH-MADRONE VINEYARD: The 1983 presents a massive dose of hard tannins and concentrated fruit, and like most wines from this vintage it has a tough streak to it. Hard and chewy; needs time to develop but may not be worth the wait. Drink 1995-2005. 700 cases produced. Release: $12.50. Current: $15. **84**

1982 SMITH-MADRONE VINEYARD: Offers a shade more body and flavor than the 1981, with clean currant and black cherry flavors, but overall it's a simple, decent wine, nothing more. Drink 1990-1993. 800 cases produced. Release: $12.50. Current: $15. **79**

1981 SMITH-MADRONE VINEYARD: Thin and medium-bodied with light black cherry and raspberry flavors, this is a light, delicate wine that is flavorful, but considering the vintage, unexciting. Drink 1990-1993. 600 cases produced. Release: $12.50. Current: $15. **78**

1980 SMITH-MADRONE VINEYARD: Light, green and cedary, with tobacco and Merlot flavors, a much different style, lacking the richness and concentration of the best 1980s, but still a decent wine. Drink 1990. 600 cases produced. Release: $12.50. Current: $18. **79**

1979 SMITH-MADRONE VINEYARD: Denser and more concentrated than the 1978, still closed and tannic with a deep color and ripe berry, spice, currant and black cherry flavors. Finishes with a dry, tannic bite. Still needs a long time to come around. Drink 1993-2000. 350 cases produced. Release: $14. Current: $25. **86**

1978 SMITH-MADRONE VINEYARD: Smith-Madrone's first vintage, the 1978 is deep in color, with ripe raspberry, currant and berry flavors, delicately balanced but shallow in the middle and very oaky. Fully mature; it should be consumed soon. Drink 1990-1995. 200 cases produced. Release: $14. Current: $25. **84**

ESTATE BOTTLED

SMITH·MADRONE

NAPA VALLEY
CABERNET SAUVIGNON

GROWN, PRODUCED AND BOTTLED BY SMITH·MADRONE
4022 SPRING MOUNTAIN ROAD, ST. HELENA, CALIFORNIA
ALCOHOL 12.8% BY VOLUME

SPOTTSWOODE WINERY
St. Helena, Napa Valley

CLASSIFICATION: *SECOND GROWTH*
COLLECTIBILITY RATING: *AA*
BEST VINTAGES: *1986, 1985, 1984, 1983, 1982*

Few Napa Valley Cabernets have made as dramatic a debut as those produced by Spottswoode in St. Helena. Spottswoode's excellent, mature, carefully nurtured vineyard produces rich, concentrated, effusively fruity Cabernet berries. The fruit is vinified to achieve a structured wine offering uncommon depth and complexity along with the promise of longevity. In five vintages, these sharply focused, beautifully defined Cabernets have risen to the top echelon of Napa Valley producers, and they are increasingly being sought by collectors.

This scenic 40-acre vineyard along the western outskirts of St. Helena is owned by Mary Novak, who planted the vineyard in the early 1970s and sold Cabernet, Merlot and Cabernet Franc to distinguished Cabernet producers such as Duckhorn and St. Clement. Beginning with the 1982 vintage, Spottswoode has produced a series of excellent Cabernets. The climate and soil allow the grapes to mature fully without overripening and taking on jammy flavors, and the grapes are naturally high in acidity, which adds to their structure and ageability. Tony Soter is winemaker, who also owns the Etude brand of Cabernet and Pinot Noir. The typical Spottswoode Cabernet includes 5 percent Cabernet Franc, and the wine is aged in French oak barrels.

Now seven years old, the 1982 Spottswoode is still a tightly wound, richly complex wine that offers hints of elegance and finesse but is years away from its peak. The 1983 is firm and tannic yet intensely flavored. The 1984 is more forward and supple, yet still intense and rigid, and will be ready to drink before either the 1982 or 1983 vintages. The 1985 and 1986 vintages are simply sensational, surpassing the previous three vintages. The 1985 is beautifully proportioned, a sensational wine from a great vintage, while the 1986 is a dramatic Cabernet, deep, rich and graceful.

With their success, Spottswoode's Cabernets have risen in price from $18 for the 1982 to $30 for the 1986. Production has climbed from 1,200 cases in 1982 to 2,400 in 1986.

TASTING NOTES

SPOTTSWOODE WINERY, St. Helena, Napa Valley

1986 SPOTTSWOODE WINERY: The fabulous 1985 was a difficult act to follow, but this is a dramatic wine with rich, beautifully defined currant, black cherry, cassis, anise and toasty oak flavors that unfold gracefully. Without a doubt, one of the stars of a very fine vintage. Has the tannin and firm structure for long-term cellaring. Drink 1996-2006. 2,400 cases produced. Release: $30. Current: $30. **96**

1985 SPOTTSWOODE WINERY: A stunning 1985, beautifully proportioned and elegantly styled, with a massive concentration of rich, ripe currant, cherry and cassis flavors, floral and herb aromas and black cherry on the finish. Its sleek, lean framework is deceiving, and the fine tannins promise a long life ahead. Drink 1995-2005. 2,000 cases produced. Release: $25. Current: $35. **95**

1984 SPOTTSWOODE WINERY: Not as focused or structured as the 1982 or 1983, typical of the vintage, a ripe, supple, fleshy wine with pretty toasty oak, ripe plum, cassis and currant flavors that are rich and generous. Forward and enticing to drink now. Drink 1992-1998. 1,450 cases produced. Release: $25. Current: $45. **90**

1983 SPOTTSWOODE WINERY: In a year of hard, lean, thin Cabernets, this is a richly textured, intensely flavored wine with ample cassis, currant, plum and mint flavors to stand up to the strong tannins. The depth and concentration of fruit promise a long life. Drink 1995-2005. 1,400 cases produced. Release: $25. Current: $45. **89**

1982 SPOTTSWOODE WINERY: Spottswoode's first wine from its own vineyard is one of the top wines of the vintage, a rich, deeply concentrated Cabernet with floral, perfumed aromas and tight, thick tannins wrapped around an abundance of ripe plum, cherry and cassis flavors that finish with a touch of elegance and finesse. A stunning debut that should age well. Drink 1995-2003. 1,200 cases produced. Release: $18. Current: $60. **90**

SPRING MOUNTAIN VINEYARDS

Napa Valley

CLASSIFICATION: *FIFTH GROWTH*

COLLECTIBILITY RATING: *Not rated*

BEST VINTAGES: *1986, 1985, 1984, 1979*

I n the late 1960s and early 1970s, Spring Mountain Vineyards was one of the bright new stars of the Napa Valley wine scene. A 1969 Cabernet was legendary in the valley for its richness and distinctive mint-chocolate character, yet few people realized that this magnificent wine was a portion of the Heitz Martha's Vineyard Cabernet that year. Joe Heitz sold it to Spring Mountain in order to generate cash flow for his winery. Proprietor Michael Robbins also owned the Wildwood Ranch, a Cabernet vineyard near Caymus Vineyards along the eastern boundary of Rutherford, before selling it to Sterling in the mid-1980s. That vineyard produced a number of excellent vintages for Spring Mountain, and until the wine boom of the mid-1970s, Spring Mountain had a cult following for its Cabernets.

I have not tried any of the older Spring Mountain Cabernets recently, although my memories of the ones from the early 1970s are positive.

In the early 1980s Robbins lost interest in winemaking and put Spring Mountain up for sale. He never sold it, but instead he lent the beautiful Victorian mansion as part of the set for the television wine country soap opera "Falcon Crest."

My notes on Spring Mountain go back to 1977, a wine that has aged gracefully. That wine was followed by a fairly hard, tannic 1978 that may never shed its tannic veneer. The 1979 is similar, in the Spring Mountain style of intense, hard, tannic Cabernet, but with a richer core of fruit to match the tannins. The 1980 follows that style, yet is maturing faster. The 1981 is simple and uninspired, while the 1982 is weedy and vegetal, a wine to avoid. The 1983 is overly lean and acidic with modest flavor. The 1984 is an excellent wine, with deep, rich fruit and layers of flavor, followed by a tightly wound 1985 that may need 10 years to peak. The 1986 is the best Spring Mountain in my memory, adding a suppleness and warmth that is missing in other bottlings.

AT A GLANCE

SPRING MOUNTAIN VINEYARDS
2805 Spring Mountain Road
St. Helena, CA 94574
(707) 963-5233

Owner: Michael Robbins

Winemaker: Greg Vita (4 years)

Founded: 1968

First Cabernet vintage: 1968-1969

Cabernet production: 3,400 cases

Cabernet acres owned: 13

Average age of vines: 9 years

Vineyard makeup: Cabernet Sauvignon (93%), Merlot (7%)

Average wine makeup: Cabernet Sauvignon (87%), Merlot (9%), Cabernet Franc (4%)

Time in oak: 24 months

Type of oak: French (Nevers)

TASTING NOTES

SPRING MOUNTAIN VINEYARDS, Napa Valley

1986 SPRING MOUNTAIN VINEYARDS: This appears to be the finest Spring Mountain Cabernet in a long, long time. Loaded with rich, ripe, enticing black cherry and currant flavors that are sharply defined and elegant, finishing with toasty oak notes that add complexity. Has a suppleness that other recent Spring Mountain Cabernets are missing. Drink 1996-2004. 3,684 cases produced. Not Released. **90**

1985 SPRING MOUNTAIN VINEYARDS: Not quite on par with the best 1985s, this is still an impressive wine, with a very firm, tannic structure and tight cherry, currant and spice flavors that are closed. Has plenty of potential but needs time to develop. Rough and tannic, may need 15 years. Drink 1997-2005. 3,396 cases produced. Release: $20. Current: $20. **88**

1984 SPRING MOUNTAIN VINEYARDS: An excellent 1984 and one of Spring Mountain's finest, with beautifully focused black cherry, currant, anise and plum flavors that are rich, supple, fleshy and elegant. Has the depth and structure for midterm aging. Coarse on the finish. Drink 1994-2000. 2,363 cases produced. Release: $15. Current: $22. **89**

1983 SPRING MOUNTAIN VINEYARDS: While decent to drink, the 1983 has a modest ripe cherry flavor that lacks the richness and concentration to stand up to the mouth-drying tannins. Drink 1993-1998. 4,221 cases produced. Release: $15. Current: $18. **79**

1982 SPRING MOUNTAIN VINEYARDS: Stinky, weedy and vegetal with overriding tar flavors and overbearing tannins. Best to avoid. 5,739 cases produced. Release: $15. Current: $15. **66**

1981 SPRING MOUNTAIN VINEYARDS: Firm and structured but ultimately simple, with tart black cherry, herb and oak flavors that are evenly balanced but unexciting. A good wine that lacks pizzazz now. Drink 1992-1996. 11,390 cases produced. Release: $14. Current: $16. **78**

1980 SPRING MOUNTAIN VINEYARDS: A big, rich, concentrated wine, high in extract, tannic and full-bodied, with ripe plum, black cherry, cedar and spice flavors. While it lacks elegance and finesse now, it has all the ingredients to gain with cellaring. Drink 1990-1994. 11,162 cases produced. Release: $13. Current: $24. **86**

1979 SPRING MOUNTAIN VINEYARDS: Tight, lean, hard and rich, with tart black cherry, currant, cedar, leather and anise flavors, fine balance, supple tannins and good length. Straightforward, but with an element of elegance and finesse. Flavors linger on the palate. Drink 1992-1998. 9,987 cases produced. Release: $13. Current: $32. **87**

1978 SPRING MOUNTAIN VINEYARDS: Very ripe, hard and tannic with ripe plum, anise and currant flavors, but it is still rather tannic on the finish. Drink 1990-1996. 10,236 cases produced. Release: $12.

SPRING MOUNTAIN
1982
Napa Valley
CABERNET SAUVIGNON
PRODUCED AND BOTTLED BY
Spring Mountain Vineyards, St. Helena, Ca. U.S.A. • B.W. 4521
ALCOHOL 13 1% BY VOLUME

Current: $25. **83**

1977 SPRING MOUNTAIN VINEYARDS: Fully mature and aging gracefully, with complex, ripe plum flavors and gamy, truffle nuances that are deep and concentrated. It's drinkable now but can age another five years. Drink 1990-1995. 5,986 cases produced. Release: $9.50. Current: $20. **85**

St. Clement Vineyards
St. Helena, Napa Valley

CLASSIFICATION: *THIRD GROWTH*
COLLECTIBILITY RATING: *A*
BEST VINTAGES: *1986, 1985, 1984, 1983, 1982, 1979, 1978, 1977*

In a decade of Cabernet vintages, tiny St. Clement has put together an exceptional collection of wines. Founded in 1975 by William Casey, was purchased in 1987 by Japanese brewer Sapporo USA. St. Clement owns only 1.5 acres, buying its grapes from vineyards such as Spottswoode. Its excellent sources produce wines that are often extremely rich and concentrated.

The first release combined the 1975-1976 vintages, and the 1977 proved remarkably profound, with layers of smooth, polished fruit and good intensity. The 1978 was very successful, with generous flavors and fine balance. The 1979 is similar to the 1977, with its smooth, supple texture and layers of rich fruit. The 1980 was thin and hard, out of character for St. Clement, and it was followed by a tough 1981. The 1982 is beautifully balanced, one of the best Cabernets of the vintage. The 1983 also succeeded in a tannic, hard vintage, while the 1984 is more fruity and approachable. The 1985 appears to be the finest St. Clement bottling to date, with great depth, intensity, flavor and aging potential over the next decade. The 1986 is a shade less intense and concentrated but still very fine. Winemaker Dennis Johns manages to blend together key vineyards for St. Clement Cabernet, but the absence of a consistent, reliable source of fruit is the winery's key weakness.

At a Glance
ST. CLEMENT VINEYARDS
P.O. Box 261
St. Helena, CA 94574
(707) 963-7221

Owner: Sapporo USA, Japan
Winemaker: Dennis Johns (12 years)
Founded: 1975
First Cabernet vintage: 1975-1976
Cabernet production: 2,500 cases
Cabernet acres owned: 1.5
Average age of vines: 20 years
Vineyard makeup: Cabernet Sauvignon (100%)
Average wine makeup: Cabernet Sauvignon (95%), Merlot (5%)
Time in oak: 15 months
Type of oak: French (Tronçais, Allier, Nevers)

Tasting Notes

ST. CLEMENT VINEYARDS, St. Helena, Napa Valley

1986 ST. CLEMENT VINEYARDS: Distinctive for its toasty French oak aromas and layers of ripe cherry and currant flavors, this wine is elegant and balanced, with sharply focused flavors and just the right amount of tannin to sustain it for another 12 to 15 years. Tempting already with its pretty fruit, this wine should begin to peak at five to six years. Drink 1993-2001. 2,000 cases produced. Not Released. **87**

1985 ST. CLEMENT VINEYARDS: The best St. Clement to date, a remarkably complex and elegant wine with layers of fruit and spicy

1981
ST. CLEMENT

✛ NAPA VALLEY ✛

CABERNET SAUVIGNON
Alcohol 13.0% by Volume
Produced and Bottled by St. Clement Vineyards
St. Helena, California, U.S.A.

mineral notes that highlight the beautifully focused black cherry, plum and berry flavors. Like the best 1985s, the tannins are fine and integrated, finishing with a burst of fruit. Alluring now but a good bet for midterm aging. Drink 1994-2002. 2,665 cases produced. Release: $17. Current: $17. **93**

1984 ST. CLEMENT VINEYARDS: The explosive black cherry flavors are rich, ripe and supple, with a silky smooth texture, firm yet fine tannins and plenty of spicy anise, currant and plum notes. Forward and fruity yet concentrated and complex. Fleshy enough to start drinking now. Drink 1992-1998. 2,300 cases produced. Release: $15. Current: $15. **89**

1983 ST. CLEMENT VINEYARDS: An amazingly rich, supple, fleshy 1983 with layers of ripe currant, black cherry, spice and toasty mineral flavors that offer depth, complexity and richness. The finish is long and fruity, with plenty of tannins for aging. Drink 1995-2005. 2,256 cases produced. Release: $14.50. Current: $18. **91**

1982 ST. CLEMENT VINEYARDS: A beautifully knit, rich and elegant 1982, clearly one of the vintage's stars, supple and satiny, with pretty black cherry and currant flavors, finishing with spicy anise and mineral notes. Alluring now but with the balance and fruit to age. Drink 1992-2000. 3,024 cases produced. Release: $13.50. Current: $20. **91**

1981 ST. CLEMENT VINEYARDS: A lean, austere 1981 with ripe cedar and currant flavors that are hard and tannic without offering much fruit or depth. Very closed with some currant and plum peeking through on the finish. Hard to tell where this one is going. Drink 1994-1999. 2,565 cases produced. Release: $12.50. Current: $24. **85**

1980 ST. CLEMENT VINEYARDS: A thin, lean wine without much fruit or depth. The currant and plum flavors are ripe but not especially rich or complex. The finish offers some cedar flavors but lacks intensity and follow-through. Ultimately simple. Drink 1990-1994. 650 cases produced. Release: $12.50. Current: $24. **82**

1979 ST. CLEMENT VINEYARDS: Rich, smooth and deep, with supple, thick, ripe currant, black cherry and anise flavors that are sharply focused. Nearing maturity now but with tannins for aging. Offers more richness, concentration, depth and complexity than the 1978. Drink 1992-2001. 1,500 cases produced. Release: $11. Current: $35. **90**

1978 ST. CLEMENT VINEYARDS: A smooth, ripe, supple wine that's nearing its peak, with generous, rich cherry, currant, mineral and plum flavors that are elegant and balanced, finishing with a burst of fruit and tannin. Has the concentration and depth for further aging. Drink 1990-1997. 400 cases produced. Release: $10. Current: $40. **88**

1977 ST. CLEMENT VINEYARDS: Ripe, smooth and supple, with herb and mineral notes to complement the ripe currant and plummy flavors. Good balance and depth, plenty of flavor, richness and intensity and a pretty follow-through. Has the depth and extract for further aging. Drink 1990-1999. 650 cases produced. Release: $10. Current: $45. **90**

1975-1976 ST. CLEMENT VINEYARDS: This first St. Clement Cabernet is a blend of two vintages; this wine leans toward the 1976 in character with its rich, generous, ripe black cherry, anise and currant flavors, but there's also a sense of elegance and suppleness from the 1975. Plenty of color, extract and depth for further aging. Drink 1993-2000. 650 cases produced. Release: $8. Current: $50. **87**

STAG'S LEAP WINE CELLARS

Cask 23, Stags Leap District, Napa Valley
SLV, Stags Leap District, Napa Valley

CLASSIFICATION:
 Cask 23: FIRST GROWTH
 SLV: THIRD GROWTH

COLLECTIBILITY RATING:
 Cask 23: AAA
 SLV: A

BEST VINTAGES:
 Cask 23: 1986, 1985, 1979, 1978, 1977, 1974

 SLV: 1986, 1985, 1984, 1981

 Lot 2: 1977

AT A GLANCE

STAG'S LEAP WINE CELLARS
5766 Silverado Trail
Napa, CA 94558
(707) 944-2020

Owners: Barbara and Warren Winiarski

Winemaker: Warren Winiarski (17 years)

Founded: 1972

First Cabernet vintage: 1972
 Cask 23: 1974
 SLV: 1972

Cabernet production: 18,000 cases
 Cask 23: 1,000 cases
 SLV: 7,000 cases

Cabernet acres owned: 75

Average age of vines: 10 years

Vineyard makeup: Cabernet Sauvignon (90%), Merlot (10%)

Average wine makeup:
 Cask 23: Cabernet Sauvignon (94%), Merlot (6%)
 SLV: Cabernet Sauvignon (98%), Merlot (2%)

Time in oak: 16 months

Type of oak: French

Stag's Leap Wine Cellars is one of California's most famous Cabernet producers. Founded in 1972 by Barbara and Warren Winiarski, Stag's Leap Wine Cellars owes much of its international renown to the famous Paris Tasting of 1976, when the Winiarskis' second vintage, a 1973 Cabernet, won a blind tasting with French critics as judges that featured first-growth Bordeaux, including châteaux Mouton Rothschild, Haut-Brion, Montrose and Léoville-Las Cases. More important than vanquishing the Bordeaux, this tasting catapulted Stag's Leap Wine Cellars into the international limelight as the tasting generated an enormous amount of publicity both in the United States, which was celebrating its bicentennial, and in Europe.

Stag's Leap Wine Cellars' reputation for distinctive, beautifully sculpted Cabernet is well deserved. In the early 1970s in Napa Valley, Warren Winiarski developed a style of Cabernet from his own Stag's Leap Vineyard (now known on the label as SLV) that he once described as putting the "iron fist in a velvet glove." He creates wines of great harmony, richness, intensity and suppleness, extremely seductive and luscious early on yet supported by firm, smooth, unobtrusive tannins that allow the wines to age gracefully for 10 to 15 years and sometimes even longer.

A former lecturer in Greek classics at the University of Chicago, Winiarski abandoned a career in academics for winemaking in the 1960s. On his arrival in Napa Valley he worked for Lee Stewart at the old Souverain Winery and later joined Robert Mondavi before starting his own winery in 1972. In the 1970s, when massive, high-extract, heavily oaked, richly tannic and varietally expressive Cabernets were the rage,

Winiarski's wines stood out for their harmony, complexity, delicacy and subtlety, yet in most instances they have aged just as well as or better than their counterparts while being considerably more enjoyable in the interim. As Winiarski once observed of the 1970s style of Cabernet, "It was a time when California winemakers were asking what Cabernet Sauvignon grapes *could* give, as opposed to what they *should* give."

Stag's Leap Wine Cellars Cabernets, softened by Merlot and the polished tannins that are characteristic of the Stags Leap District, are typically more moderate than aggressive, more supple than structured, and rarely excessive. Among the many brilliant Cabernets produced by Stag's Leap Wine Cellars, there have been inconsistencies, particularly in the late 1970s and early 1980s. But, the three most recent vintages, 1984, 1985 and 1986, are the finest ever and indicate that Stag's Leap Wine Cellars is back on track.

The 1972 vintage is frail and faded but may have value as a collectible because it is Stag's Leap's first Cabernet. The 1973 Paris champion remains supple and attractive, although a shade past its apogee. The 1974 is fully mature and at its peak, while the 1974 Cask 23, a proprietary wine that is primarily Cabernet, offers a shade more richness and depth but is best consumed now. With the 1976 vintage, the Lot 2 is superior in quality. The 1977s are all drinking well, although the Cask 23 bottling stands out for its depth, complexity and endurance. It has been slow to evolve and remains one of the top wines of the vintage.

Again in 1978 both the Stag's Leap Vineyard and Cask 23 are superb wines, with the nod going to the Cask 23, which has another five to 10 years of life remaining. In 1979, the Cask 23 is clearly the finer bottling, as the regular SLV has an off, mossy quality. The 1980 vintage was also unsuccessful, but the 1981 is a wonderful Cabernet that is smooth and supple. In 1982 and 1983, the Stag's Leap Vineyard bottlings are excessively vegetal and weedy; however, the 1983 Cask 23 is quite impressive for its balance and depth in a difficult vintage.

Beginning with the 1984 vintage and carrying through the 1986 wines, the Stag's Leap Cabernets have been the best ever produced by Winiarski. The 1984 bottlings offer rich, ripe, fleshy fruit, with the Cask 23 bottling needing more time to blossom. The 1985 Cask 23 is one of the greatest Cabernets ever produced in California, offering uncommon richness, intensity, depth and complexity. The 1985 SLV is also an exceptional wine for its effusive fruitiness and grace. In 1986 the Cask 23 is sensational, combining richness and power with elegance and finesse.

While Stag's Leap Cabernets are expensive, they are also in high demand among consumers and connoisseurs, particularly the Cask 23, of which there are only 1,000 cases made each year. The 1973 bottling and the 1985 Cask 23 are among the highlights for collectors. The regular Napa Valley bottling, not from the Stag's Leap Vineyard, is often very good but not up to the quality of the SLV and Cask 23.

TASTING NOTES

STAG'S LEAP WINE CELLARS, Cask 23, Stags Leap District, Napa Valley

1986 STAG'S LEAP WINE CELLARS CASK 23: A remarkable Cask 23 that combines power and concentration with elegance and finesse. The cherry, currant, cedar and spice flavors are beautifully orchestrated with firm, gentle tannins and understated elegance. One of the finest from Stag's Leap Wine Cellars. Drink 1994-2003. 605 cases produced. Not Released. **92**

1985 STAG'S LEAP WINE CELLARS CASK 23: Clearly the finest Cabernet Sauvignon ever produced by Warren Winiarski and one of the greatest ever made in California, this is an astonishingly rich, concentrated and elegant wine that harnesses the ripe, sharply focused black cherry, currant and cedar flavors and renders a magnificent wine of great distinction. Defines the "iron fist in a velvet glove." The persistence of flavor and impeccable balance are stunning. Drink 1994-2005. 1,018 cases produced. Release: $75. Current: $75. **98**

1984 STAG'S LEAP WINE CELLARS CASK 23: Firm, more austere and tannic than the 1984 SLV bottling, but more lush and expansive. This is a tightly wound wine brimming with fresh ripe currant and cherry flavors. There's plenty of flavor, harmony and finesse. Generous and warm on the palate. Drink 1994-2000. 800 cases produced. Release: $40. Current: $40. **93**

1983 STAG'S LEAP WINE CELLARS CASK 23: Remarkably well balanced and concentrated for a 1983, with intense spicy cherry flavors stand up to the firm tannins. Needs more time to soften but there's plenty to like in this complex wine. Drink 1993-1999. 1,077 cases produced. Release: $35. Current: $55. **88**

1979 STAG'S LEAP WINE CELLARS CASK 23: A very successful 1979, with soft, supple, harmonious black cherry and herb flavors that are rich and complex and persistent on the finish. Most of the tannins have been resolved. Drink 1990-1992. 1,204 cases produced. Release: $35. Current: $55. **88**

1978 STAG'S LEAP WINE CELLARS CASK 23: A delicious mouthful of Cabernet, deep in color, with wonderfully rich, concentrated flavors, great depth and layers of fruit complexity bordered by thick tannins. The ripe cherry, currant and cedar flavors are well focused and lively. Still improving. Drink 1990-1995. 1,000 cases produced. Release: $35. Current: $90. **92**

1977 STAG'S LEAP WINE CELLARS CASK 23: Slow to evolve, drinking better now than it has in years. Fully mature, with complex cedar, herb, cherry and spice notes. Most of the tannins have mellowed, leaving a rich, full-bodied wine with fine length and balance. Drink 1990-1993. 1,000 cases produced. Release: $30. Current: $75. **91**

1974 STAG'S LEAP WINE CELLARS CASK 23: Although this wine has more richness and depth than the regular bottling, it too has reached its plateau and is in perfect drinking condition. The rich cedar, chocolate, herb and cherry flavors are smooth and satiny. Drink 1990-1993. 100 cases produced. Release: $12. Current: $135. **88**

STAG'S LEAP WINE CELLARS, SLV, Stags Leap District, Napa Valley

1986 STAG'S LEAP WINE CELLARS SLV: Distinctively rich and elegant, with firm acidity and delicate tannins, with layers of cedar, currant and black cherry flavors that are crisp and lively. Because of its suppleness and elegance, this wine is already drinkable but should improve for a decade or more. Drink 1992-1999. 6,248 cases produced. Release: $28. Current: $28. **89**

1985 STAG'S LEAP WINE CELLARS SLV: The 1985 is simply delicious, fresh and ripe, very lean and concentrated, bursting with currant, cherry, spice and cedar flavors, supple, well-integrated flavors and tannins. Beautifully balanced, displaying richness, elegance and finesse. Alluring already. Drink 1993-1999. 8,810 cases produced. Release: $26. Current: $26. **94**

1984 STAG'S LEAP WINE CELLARS SLV: Very ripe and flavorful, loaded with supple cherry, cedar, currant and anise flavors that are broad and lush, smooth supple tannins and mouth-watering acidity. Beautifully defined, with understated elegance, suppleness and intensity. Drink 1994-2000. 6,000 cases produced. Release: $21. Current: $30. **92**

1983 STAG'S LEAP WINE CELLARS STAG'S LEAP VINEYARDS: An earthy flavor dominates the currant and cedar flavors, and it's extremely tannic and drying on the palate. I have never had much luck with this wine and consider it a mediocre offering from Stag's Leap. Drink 1990-1995. 6,668 cases produced. Release: $18. Current: $25. **73**

1982 STAG'S LEAP WINE CELLARS STAG'S LEAP VINEYARDS: Weedy, vegetal notes overshadow the ripe currant and cherry flavors. Not one of Stag's Leap Wine Cellars' better efforts, it is still perfectly drinkable, and the style may appeal more to others. Drink 1990-1993. 9,865 cases produced. Release: $16.50. Current: $25. **75**

1981 STAG'S LEAP WINE CELLARS STAG'S LEAP VINEYARDS: Very attractive, plenty of ripe currant, cedar and cherry flavors, with a nice touch of toasty vanilla oak, fine balance, supple texture, elegant structure and rather firm tannins. Gentle, supple finesse. A sleeper. Drink 1992-1998. 7,534 cases produced. Release: $15. Current: $32. **91**

1979 STAG'S LEAP WINE CELLARS STAG'S LEAP VINEYARDS: This wine has never appealed to me — it tastes extremely dry and tannic without much in the way of fruit or charm. Drink 1990. 6,000 cases produced. Release: $15. Current: $32. **68**

1978 STAG'S LEAP WINE CELLARS STAG'S LEAP VINEYARDS: Rich, smooth and concentrated, delicately balanced, with spice, cedar and cherry flavors that are sharply focused and still quite youthful and tannic. Drink 1990-1995. 3,000 cases produced. Release: $13.50. Current: $45. **89**

1977 STAG'S LEAP WINE CELLARS STAG'S LEAP VINEYARDS: Ripe and earthy yet elegant and harmonious, with complex cherry, cedar and currant flavors that hang together nicely. Supple and balanced, it finishes with a good dose of tannin, maybe a grain more than it needs. Drink 1990-1992. 2,000 cases produced. Release: $9. Current: $35. **85**

1976 STAG'S LEAP WINE CELLARS LOT 2: Better than the regular 1976, the Lot 2 is still rather dry and austere, with some cedary richness and hints of tobacco, chocolate and plum coming through. Drink 1990-1992. 1,000 cases produced. Release: $11. Current: $60. **80**

1976 STAG'S LEAP WINE CELLARS STAG'S LEAP VINEYARDS: A decent but simple 1976 with spicy cherry flavors that are drying out, excessively tannic. Drink 1990. 2,000 cases produced. Release: $10. Current: $40. **73**

1975 STAG'S LEAP WINE CELLARS STAG'S LEAP VINEYARDS: Fully mature and a shade past its prime, the 1975 has mature herb, cedar and spicy Cabernet flavors that are rather frail. Drink 1990. 2,300 cases produced. Release: $8.50. Current: $50. **74**

1974 STAG'S LEAP WINE CELLARS STAG'S LEAP VINEYARDS: Plenty of fruit, harmony, elegance and grace. At its peak now; should be consumed while the fruit is still fresh, concentrated and lively on the palate. Drink 1990-1992. 450 cases produced. Release: $8. Current: $110. **87**

1973 STAG'S LEAP WINE CELLARS STAG'S LEAP VINEYARDS: The 1973 vintage put Stag's Leap Wine Cellars on the international wine map. Although its best years are behind it, there is still plenty to like in this wine. The aromas are pure and attractive, and the spicy cherry, cedar, toast and chocolate flavors are complex and enticing. It has value as a collectible. Drink 1990. 400 cases produced. Release: $6. Current: $135. **86**

1972 STAG'S LEAP WINE CELLARS STAG'S LEAP VINEYARDS: The first vintage from Stag's Leap Wine Cellars is now old and fading. There's a touch of fruit left, but it's extremely dry on the finish. While there is not much to look forward to for drinking, this wine has value as a collectible. Drink 1990. 100 cases produced. Release: $5.50. Current: $80. **70**

STAGS' LEAP WINERY

Stags Leap District, Napa Valley

CLASSIFICATION: *FIFTH GROWTH*
COLLECTIBILITY RATING: *Not rated*
BEST VINTAGES: *1986, 1985, 1984*

Despite the renown of its neighbor, Stag's Leap Wine Cellars, and of the newly formed Stags Leap District, Carl Doumani's Stags' Leap Winery Cabernets are virtually unknown to most wine consumers. Doumani has specialized in less popular varietals such as Petite Sirah and Chenin Blanc, but his Cabernet, while clearly not in the same class as any of the top Stags Leap District producers, is very good, consistent and pleasant. Doumani's Cabernets are almost the antithesis of his rich, bold, tannic Petite Sirahs, for they tend to be leaner and less opulent, though nonetheless well proportioned and flavorful.

The first vintage in 1981 is aging well, offering pretty black cherry aromas and flavors. The 1982 is weedy and vegetal, a poor vintage, followed by a clean, decent 1983. The 1984 is the best of the lot, displaying more fruit and fleshiness than is typical of the winery, but without the opulence of the 1984s in general. Both 1985 and 1986 stay the course of restrained, reined-in Cabernet but don't measure up to the best from these two sensational vintages. A touch more richness would make these wines eminently more exciting. With 68 acres planted to Cabernet, Stags' Leap Winery has the vineyards to upgrade its Cabernets to higher levels of quality.

AT A GLANCE

STAGS' LEAP WINERY
6150 Silverado Trail
Napa, CA 94558
(707) 944-1303

Owner: Carl Doumani
Winemaker: Robert Brittan (1 year)
Founded: 1970
First Cabernet vintage: 1981
Cabernet production: 7,800 cases
Cabernet acres owned: 68
Average age of vines: 15 years
Vineyard makeup: Cabernet Sauvignon (59%), Merlot (36%), Cabernet Franc (5%)
Average wine makeup: Cabernet Sauvignon (94%), Cabernet Franc (6%)
Time in oak: 18 months
Type of oak: French

TASTING NOTES

STAGS' LEAP WINERY, Stags Leap District, Napa Valley

1986 STAGS' LEAP WINERY: The lean, well-defined fruit is totally consistent with Stags' Leap Winery's style. This wine has pretty black currant, cherry and peppery oak flavors before the fine tannins kick in. Fine structure makes it approachable now and for the next five to seven years. Drink 1992-1997. 7,860 cases produced. Not Released. **86**

1985 STAGS' LEAP WINERY: Restrained but nicely proportioned, lacking the richness and opulence of the best 1985s, but it is well balanced with peppery berry flavors and lean, firm tannins. Stays within the winery's style of restraint and balance, but could be more daring.

Drink 1992-1997. 7,672 cases produced. Release: $15. Current: $16. **85**

1984 STAGS' LEAP WINERY: A lean, well-proportioned wine that lacks the richness and fleshy texture of most Cabernets from this vintage. Well-balanced black cherry and spice flavors stand up to the tannins. A graceful, elegant wine that should be ready to drink soon. Drink 1992-1997. 5,187 cases produced. Release: $13.50. Current: $18. **87**

1983 STAGS' LEAP WINERY: Correct and supple, with ripe black cherry and spice flavors that turn dry and tannic on the palate and on the finish. Well balanced as 1983s go. Drink 1993-1997. 3,425 cases produced. Release: $12.75. Current: $20. **80**

1982 STAGS' LEAP WINERY: Weedy, vegetal and tannic, not as charming as the 1981 but still a decent wine. Many of the Stags Leap District wines were vegetal in 1982, perhaps victims of rain and unripened grapes. This one simply lacks ripe fruit. Drink 1992-1996. 3,034 cases produced. Release: $12. Current: $20. **71**

1981 STAGS' LEAP WINERY: The first Cabernet from Stags' Leap is well mannered and deftly balanced between ripe, supple black cherry flavors and a touch of cedar with firm tannins on the finish. Aging gracefully. Drink 1991-1997. 2,712 cases produced. Release: $11. Current: $25. **85**

STELTZNER VINEYARDS

Stags Leap District, Napa Valley

CLASSIFICATION: *THIRD GROWTH*

COLLECTIBILITY RATING: *A*

BEST VINTAGES: *1986, 1985, 1984, 1983, 1982, 1981, 1980, 1979*

F or years Steltzner Vineyards in the Stags Leap District was a prime source of Cabernet grapes for Napa Valley wineries without vineyards of their own. One memorable bottling was the Conn Creek 1973, which is drinking exceptionally well and still has years of life ahead. Grower Richard Steltzner still sells grapes to a few wineries, but since the 1977 vintage he has been bottling Cabernet under his own name with remarkable success. The Steltzner Cabernets bear the Stags Leap District trademark of fine, supple tannins, and they are typically very ripe, with cherry, currant and plum flavors. The Cabernets start off with some rough edges, but with five to seven years' age they begin to show more silk and polish without losing their flavor appeal.

All of the Steltzner Cabernets are holding up. The 1977 is at its peak, showing the aromas of the Yugoslavian oak in which it was aged. The 1978 is young and flavorful, lacking the complexity of the best wines from this vintage, but still with time to gain it. In 1979 grape concentrate was added to the fermenting musts when the grape sugars stalled at 19 degrees Brix, but the result is very successful, as are the 1980 and 1981 vintages. In 1982 Steltzner produced a rich, elegant wine in a difficult vintage, followed by similarly fine bottlings in 1983, 1984, 1985 and 1986. The 1985, with its tremendous depth of character and layers of fruit, remains the best bottling so far, displaying the thick, chunky character that needs time to round out.

AT A GLANCE

STELTZNER VINEYARDS
5998 Silverado Trail
Napa, CA 94558
(707) 252-7272

Owners: Christine and Richard Steltzner

Winemaker: Dick Steltzner (12 years)

Founded: 1965

First Cabernet vintage: 1977

Cabernet production: 5,000 cases

Cabernet acres owned: 41

Average age of vines: 18 years

Vineyard makeup: Cabernet Sauvignon (94%), Merlot (3%), Cabernet Franc (3%)

Average wine makeup: Cabernet Sauvignon (97%), Cabernet Franc (3%)

Time in oak: 26 months

Type of oak: French (Allier)

TASTING NOTES

STELTZNER VINEYARDS, Stags Leap District, Napa Valley

1986 STELTZNER VINEYARDS: An exceptional effort, the 1986 is a deep, rich, full-bodied wine, packed with ripe currant, cassis, black cherry and cedary oak flavors that with time may rival the 1985 as Steltzner's finest effort. Right now it comes up just short of the dramatic flavors and complexity of the 1985. Drink 1993-2000. 5,000 cases pro-

duced. Release: $16. Current: $16. **90**

1985 STELTZNER VINEYARDS: With its amazing array of fruit flavors and rich, tannic structure, the 1985 is the finest Cabernet ever produced by this Stags Leap District vintner. The rich black cherry, raspberry, currant and plum flavors are thick and chunky but very concentrated, deep and long. Steltzner's Cabernets typically need two to three years' cellaring to round out the edges. The 1985 will be best in five to seven years, but it's delicious now. Drink 1993-2000. 5,000 cases produced. Release: $16. Current: $19. **93**

1984 STELTZNER VINEYARDS: Ripe, fleshy, supple and complex, typifying the rich, opulent style of the vintage. The fruit is ripe and forward, with layers of cherry, currant, herb and anise, framed by toasty French oak. Young and intense, it is attractive to drink now because the tannins are soft and rich, yet it has the stuffings to age through the decade. Drink 1992-2000. 3,000 cases produced. Release: $15. Current: $19. **91**

1983 STELTZNER VINEYARDS: Another top-flight bottling from a difficult vintage, it succeeds with more richness and fleshy fruit to stand up to the firm, dry tannins. It is also quite flavorful, with complex earth, cedar, black cherry and raspberry flavors that are crisp and concentrated. Drink 1991-1996. 3,000 cases produced. Release: $14. Current: $18. **90**

1982 STELTZNER VINEYARDS: From a difficult vintage, the 1982 Stelztner manages to capture ripe fruit in an elegant framework. It's sharply focused, with ripe black cherry and currant flavors that still are youthful and compact. Drink 1990-1996. 3,000 cases produced. Release: $14. Current: $28. **90**

1981 STELTZNER VINEYARDS: This has always been a delicious, open wine, and it continues to drink very well. It's loaded with rich, concentrated black cherry and anise flavors that are complex and elegant, bordered by firm tannins and an oaky aftertaste. Still gaining. Drink 1990-1996. 1,500 cases produced. Release: $14. Current: $38. **89**

1980 STELTZNER VINEYARDS: A youthful, tart, concentrated wine that still needs aging, with Steltzner's characteristic cherry and spicy plum flavors and firm, rich tannins that make this wine approachable now or in the next five to seven years. Aging quite well. Drink 1991-1997. 200 cases produced. Release: $14. Current: $38. **88**

1979 STELTZNER VINEYARDS: Grape concentrate was added to the fermenting musts in 1979, after the sugars stalled on the vine at 19 degrees Brix. The result is a rich, smooth, elegant, flavorful wine that exhibits supple black cherry and currant flavors. Ready now. Drink 1990-1995. 1,000 cases produced. Release: $14. Current: $42. **89**

1978 STELTZNER VINEYARDS: A very successful 1978 that is very ripe and fruity with currant, plum and cherry flavors that are deep and framed by firm tannins. While this wine shows no signs of fading, it has not developed as much complexity or finesse as the best wines of the vintage, although it still has time to develop. Drink 1990-1996. 500 cases produced. Release: $14. Current: $50. **87**

1977 STELTZNER VINEYARDS: Steltzner's first vintage has evolved into an elegant, supple, pleasing Cabernet that has been drinking well for several years. The use of Yugoslavian oak is quite apparent and overshadows the ripe fruit, but overall it's a nice bottle. Drink 1990-1995. 500 cases produced. Release: $14. Current: $45. **85**

STERLING VINEYARDS

Reserve, Napa Valley
Diamond Mountain Ranch, Diamond Mountain, Napa Valley

CLASSIFICATION:
Reserve: SECOND GROWTH
Diamond Mountain Ranch: FOURTH GROWTH
COLLECTIBILITY RATING:
Reserve: AA
Diamond Mountain Ranch: Not rated
BEST VINTAGES:
Reserve: 1986, 1985, 1984, 1980, 1978, 1977, 1974, 1973

Diamond Mountain Ranch: 1986, 1985, 1982

Sterling Vineyards has long been one of the big names in Napa Valley Cabernet, dating back to the late 1960s and early 1970s when Ric Forman was the winemaker. Under his direction, Sterling Reserve reached lofty plateaus, with sensational 1973, 1974, 1977 and 1978 bottlings that are still developing. As fine as those wines were, Sterling is making its greatest Reserve wines today, with the 1984, 1985 and 1986 vintages. A new Diamond Mountain Ranch bottling adds a distinctive, austere, richly flavored, mountain-grown Cabernet to its lineup.

Founded in 1969 by Peter and Su Hua Newton and a group of investors and owned by Coca-Cola before its sale to the current owner, Seagram Classics Wine Co., Sterling Vineyards set out to make serious, ageworthy Cabernets at its hilltop château that were modeled after the great Bordeaux. Early vintages included Merlot for softness and complexity, and in recent bottlings there is also a small percentage of Cabernet Franc and Petit Verdot.

Not all Sterling Cabernets were smashing successes. The 1970 was seriously flawed by excessive oak and varnish flavors, and in 1975, 1976 and 1982 the Reserves were not up to the usual standards. In 1979, 1981 and 1983 the wines are merely very good. In the 1970s, the 1977 stands out as one of the great wines of the vintage, while in the 1980s, under the direction of Theo Rosenbrand and Bill Dyer, the 1985 Reserve is simply amazing for its richness, concentration and depth. The 1984 and 1986 bottlings are close companions in quality.

The first Diamond Mountain Ranch Cabernet was produced in 1982 and was impressive for its austerity, concentration and structure. The 1983 and 1984 vintages showed improvement, but the 1985 is the finest bottling to date. The 1986 is a worthy successor. Production hovers between 5,500 and 6,000 cases, nearly twice as much as the Reserve.

Sterling owns some of the finest Cabernet vineyards in the Napa Valley, with 261 acres planted to Bordeaux varieties. The Reserve and Diamond Mountain Cabernets are both superbly made, ageworthy Cabernets. A regular Sterling Cabernet is equally well made but not as complex or rich as the two top-of-the-line bottlings.

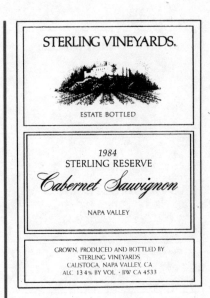

TASTING NOTES

STERLING VINEYARDS, Reserve, Napa Valley

1986 STERLING VINEYARDS RESERVE: This is the third in a string of sensational Sterling Reserves, and it is one of the best ever produced, a very rich, deep, elegant wine with great concentration of flavor, supple texture, integrated tannins and length. The spicy currant, berry, cherry and plum flavors are accented by toasty oak and anise notes that echo on the finish. Drink 1996-2006. 3,432 cases produced. Not Released. **94**

1985 STERLING VINEYARDS RESERVE: As superb as the 1986 is, the 1985 Reserve surpasses it in quality, with an added dimension of richness, depth, intensity and concentration that should carry it 15 to 20 years. The thick, deep, currant, black cherry, anise and spice flavors are supple and layered, finishing with crisp acidity, firm tannins and great length. A masterpiece that ranks as the finest Sterling Reserve ever produced. Drink 1996-2008. 2,492 cases produced. Release: $30. Current: $38. **96**

1984 STERLING VINEYARDS RESERVE: Bursting with flavor, this wine has the richness, complexity and balance to become one of the finest Sterling Reserves ever produced. The bright, ripe fruit is fresh and lively, fleshy and supple with plum, cherry and currant flavors that are crisp and delicate, and there's enough tannin for midterm aging. Drink 1994-2002. 2,268 cases produced. Release: $25. Current: $38. **92**

1983 STERLING VINEYARDS RESERVE: Extremely dry and tannic, very austere and concentrated, with tight, lean mint, currant and berry flavors that dry out on the finish. A wine that requires great patience but with room to improve. Drink 1995-2000. 3,360 cases produced. Release: $22.50. Current: $30. **82**

1982 STERLING VINEYARDS RESERVE: The weakest Reserve ever produced, the 1982 is actually showing better now than when released, but the herb, mulch and earth flavors dominate the crisp black cherry flavor, particularly on the finish. It's drinkable but not memorable. There is some bottle variation. Drink 1992-1996. 4,807 cases produced. Release: $22.50. Current: $25. **75**

1981 STERLING VINEYARDS RESERVE: Very austere, hard and tan-

nic, with tight currant, cherry and oak flavors that lack charm and richness. This is a firmly structured wine that will require patience for its full development. Drink 1994-1998. 6,237 cases produced. Release: $22.50. Current: $28. **85**

1980 STERLING VINEYARDS RESERVE: Rich, smooth and elegant, with layers of ripe plum, black currant, cherry and smoky oak, this is a very fine 1980 with supple tannins, delicate balance and a gentle intensity that makes it approachable now or capable of another five to eight years' cellaring. Drink 1992-1998. 4,848 cases produced. Release: $27.50. Current: $37. **91**

1979 STERLING VINEYARDS RESERVE: Lighter and simpler than most Reserves, still a very attractive wine, with an elegant framework, pretty cherry, spice, and herb flavors and soft, gentle tannins. Drinkable now or over the next five to seven years. Drink 1990-1995. 6,538 cases produced. Release: $27.50. Current: $32. **85**

1978 STERLING VINEYARDS RESERVE: A very young and attractive wine with crisp currant, black cherry and smoky oak flavors and a very pretty aftertaste, supplanted by plenty of tannin. Falls short of the richness and suppleness of the magnificent 1977, but has the structure and flavor for further development. Drink 1992-1998. 5,016 cases produced. Release: $27.50. Current: $35. **90**

1977 STERLING VINEYARDS RESERVE: This is a gorgeous 1977, rich, smooth and elegant, and one of the great wines from this vintage. The opulent black cherry, currant and cedar flavors are complemented by a minty anise note that adds complexity. There are still tannins for aging, the balance is impeccable and the finish is long and full. Drink 1992-2000. 3,500 cases produced. Release: $27.50. Current: $32. **93**

1976 STERLING VINEYARDS RESERVE: A big, rich, ripe, high-extract wine with a heavy oak flavor and dryness that detracts from the overall quality. Too much new oak overwhelms the fruit, leaving the wine out of balance. Time may soften the oak. Drink 1994-1998. 3,690 cases produced. Release: $25. Current: $40. **76**

1975 STERLING VINEYARDS RESERVE: A dry, dusty oakiness overrides the rich, ripe currant and spice flavors. An awkward, harsh, woody wine that dries the palate. Under all the wood lies some fruit, but it's questionable whether this wine will ever come into balance. Drink 1994-2000. 3,800 cases produced. Release: $20. Current: $55. **78**

1974 STERLING VINEYARDS RESERVE: A rich, bold, dramatic 1974 with generous layers of black currant, berry, spice and cedar flavors that are thick and supple, wrapped in firm tannins and a thick veneer of dusty oak. Fruit echoes on the finish. Approaching maturity but can hold another decade. Drink 1992-2002. 3,600 cases produced. Release: $20. Current: $80. **90**

1973 STERLING VINEYARDS RESERVE: This is a hearty, robust wine still on its way up, with plenty of ripe plum, currant, cedar and spice flavors and a lively personality. The firm tannins need time to soften. Holding up quite well; may gain a point or two. Drink 1992-1998. 3,850 cases produced. Release: $10. Current: $70. **89**

STERLING VINEYARDS, Diamond Mountain Ranch, Diamond Mountain, Napa Valley

1986 STERLING VINEYARDS DIAMOND MOUNTAIN RANCH: Austere, with firm, dry tannins and aromatic plum and cherry notes, deeply concentrated and built for six to eight years' cellaring. Has the potential for greatness, but patience is required. Drink 1996-2003. 6,000 cases produced. Not Released. **88**

1985 STERLING VINEYARDS DIAMOND MOUNTAIN RANCH: Has the potential to be an outstanding wine, with its amazing concentration and intensity, but not a wine for the faint of heart. It's extremely hard and tannic, with sharply focused, tart black cherry and currant flavors, finishing with a wallop of tannin. Best cellared for a decade — or more. Drink 1995-2003. 5,700 cases produced. Release: $16. Current: $16. **90**

1984 STERLING VINEYARDS DIAMOND MOUNTAIN RANCH: Curious because it lacks the opulence of most Cabernets from this excellent vintage, but it is true to the austere style of the Diamond Mountain Ranch Cabernets. This wine has ripe plum and cherry flavors but does not appear to have the concentration and intensity to stand up to the tannins. Still, it's a pretty good wine that needs three more years' cellaring. Drink 1993-1997. 5,500 cases produced. Release: $15. Current: $18. **85**

1983 STERLING VINEYARDS DIAMOND MOUNTAIN RANCH: This wine has improved dramatically with age. Early on it was extremely hard and tannic, with unyielding fruit, but in the last two tastings it has shown pretty floral aromas and more cherry and plum flavors than before. It's still tannic as 1983s go, but is beginning to shed some of its austerity. Drink 1994-2002. 4,100 cases produced. Release: $15. Current: $18. **87**

1982 STERLING VINEYARDS DIAMOND MOUNTAIN RANCH: The 1982 marked the first bottling of Sterling's Diamond Mountain Ranch Cabernet. Typical of the vintage and appellation, it is a firm, tight, austere, ageworthy wine that will need another six to eight years before it's fully mature. The black cherry, cedar and earth flavors are tightly concentrated and framed by tough tannins. Drink 1995-2003. 3,100 cases produced. Release: $15. Current: $20. **88**

AT A GLANCE
STONEGATE WINERY
1183 Dunaweal Lane
Calistoga, CA 94515
(707) 942-6500

Owners: Barbara and James Spaulding

Winemaker: David Spaulding (15 years)

Founded: 1973

First Cabernet vintage: 1973
Estate: 1984

Cabernet production: 4,400 cases

Cabernet acres owned: 18

Average age of vines: 19 years

Vineyard makeup: Cabernet Sauvignon (74%), Merlot (26%)

Average wine makeup: Cabernet Sauvignon (91%), Merlot (9%)

Time in oak: 24 months

Type of oak: French (Nevers)

STONEGATE WINERY
Estate, Calistoga, Napa Valley

CLASSIFICATION: *FIFTH GROWTH*
COLLECTIBILITY RATING: *Not rated*
BEST VINTAGES: *1985, 1984, 1978*

Stonegate, a small winery near Calistoga, is owned and operated by the Spaulding family. David Spaulding is the winemaker, and he relies on mountain-grown Cabernet Sauvignon from the hills west of Calistoga. The early Stonegate wines were inconsistent in quality and style, but recently the winery has moved away from the overly oaked wines of the 1970s to some exceptionally well-made, rich, chunky, concentrated wines in the 1980s.

My notes go back to the 1977, a chewy, oaky Cabernet that is still developing, followed by an exceptional 1978 and a likable 1979. The 1980 is ripe and jammy, while the 1981 and 1982 are the least impressive. No 1983 was released under the Stonegate label, as the quality of the wines did not meet winery standards. The 1984 and 1985 vintages both show Stonegate at its best since 1978, and one hopes it will stay on this track, for both of these estate-grown wines are well made and balanced, loaded with ripe, flavorful fruit and just the right amount of tannin for both current drinking and 10 years' cellaring.

TASTING NOTES

STONEGATE WINERY, Estate, Calistoga, Napa Valley

1986 STONEGATE WINERY ESTATE: Spicy and peppery, with a distinct peppermint note, rather lean and tight, lacking the breadth of flavor and richness of the 1984 or 1985 bottlings. Lacks the flavor and depth one would expect from the fine 1986 vintage. Drink 1990-1995. 3,000 cases produced. Not Released. **79**

1985 STONEGATE WINERY ESTATE: A sleek, rich, elegant 1985 with generous black cherry, spice, mineral and currant flavors and firm tannins and oak. This wine has potential to be one of the finest Stonegates produced, but it is a step behind the best 1985s. Drink 1993-1998. 4,403 cases produced. Release: $16. Current: $16. **87**

1984 STONEGATE WINERY ESTATE: A ripe, concentrated, chunky 1984 that has all the ingredients for greatness but needs time to smooth out. There are plenty of rich, ripe currant, plum and black cherry flavors backed by firm tannins. With time this could be outstanding, surpassing the quality of the excellent 1978. Drink 1993-1998. 4,580 cases produced. Release: $14. Current: $14. **88**

1982 STONEGATE WINERY: A well-made wine from a very spotty vintage, offering decent, understated plum and currant flavors and firm, dry tannins that may take another five years to soften. With the ripe fruit it's nearly ready to drink, and time may not appreciably improve the quality. Drink 1991-1996. 5,497 cases produced. Release: $12. Current: $18. **80**

1981 STONEGATE WINERY: The oak is dry and overshadows the bright, supple fruit. With time the dry oakiness may subside, but now it dominates the flavor and texture. Drink 1992-1996. 4,005 cases produced. Release: $12. Current: $17. **79**

1980 STONEGATE WINERY: Very ripe, with jammy plum and black cherry flavors that are smooth and supple up front and firm and dry on the finish. Close to maturity, this is a very good, fairly typical 1980, oozing with fruit and charm. Drink 1991-1997. 2,258 cases produced. Release: $12. Current: $22. **86**

1979 STONEGATE WINERY: More like the 1977 than the 1978, with a heavy dose of dry, spicy oak, this wine still offers plenty of ripe, supple fruit and has a decent balance, but it's going to need more time. Drink 1993-1997. 2,757 cases produced. Release: $12. Current: $24. **84**

1978 STONEGATE WINERY: A forward 1978 with rich, supple, concentrated, sumptuous plum, black cherry, currant and spice flavors and soft, smooth tannins that make it perfectly drinkable now. With its concentration and depth, this wine can last another decade. Still the best Stonegate every produced. Drink 1991-2000. 1,797 cases produced. Release: $12. Current: $30. **91**

1977 STONEGATE WINERY: A big, robust, oaky wine, offering rich, ripe, chewy fruit and plenty of dry, spicy oak flavors that are still young and undeveloped. This wine needs further aging for the fruit and oak to mellow. Drink 1993-1999. 1,060 cases produced. Release: $10. Current: $25. **81**

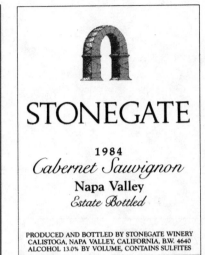

PHILIP TOGNI VINEYARD

Spring Mountain, Napa Valley

CLASSIFICATION: *FIFTH GROWTH*
COLLECTIBILITY RATING: A
BEST VINTAGES: *1986, 1985*

Philip Togni has enjoyed a distinguished career as a winemaker in California that spans a quarter century. Togni, a graduate of the University of Bordeaux, where he studied under Emile Peynaud, began making wine in 1954, including a stint at Château Lascombes in Margaux. Beginning in 1958 he worked at Mayacamas, followed by Chalone (where he was the first winemaker), Chappellet and Cuvaison. In 1985 he founded his own estate winery on Spring Mountain. He is also winemaking consultant for Chimney Rock.

Togni has long been a fan of mountain-grown Cabernet. The early Cabernets he made at Chappellet, particularly the 1968 through 1970 vintages, were especially memorable. Some of his Cuvaison Cabernets of the late 1970s and 1980s have not aged as well. He began producing Philip Togni Spring Mountain Cabernets in 1983 with a successful vintage that is still hard and tight. The 1984 is more open, with pretty flavors but not quite the concentration of the 1983. The 1985 is lean, concentrated and fairly oaky, while the 1986 is by far the finest, a deeply perfumed and richly flavored wine that will need three to five years to fully mature. Togni's fruit comes from a 7-acre vineyard that includes Merlot and Cabernet Franc.

TASTING NOTES

PHILIP TOGNI VINEYARD, Spring Mountain, Napa Valley

1986 PHILIP TOGNI VINEYARD: By far the most impressive Togni Cabernet, a big, rich, opulent, concentrated wine with sharply defined black currant flavors that are thick and powerful, yet showing a measure of elegance and restraint. With several hours' aeration, this wine blossoms into a magnificent Cabernet with celestial aromas and flavors. Drink 1993-2005. 386 cases produced. Release: $22. Current: $22. **93**

1985 PHILIP TOGNI VINEYARD: Lavishly oaked with a spicy cedar note overriding the thick, austere, concentrated black currant, plum and cherry flavors. Will need time to smooth out, but has the depth and flavor for greatness. Drink 1995-2004. 125 cases produced. Release: $20. Current: $25. **89**

1984 PHILIP TOGNI VINEYARD: Not quite as showy or opulent as most 1984s, dominated by cedary oak that overshadows the ripe plum and currant flavors. While a very good wine, it lacks the depth and pure Cabernet flavors of the 1983 or 1986 bottlings, but has plenty of tannin and flavor for cellaring. Drink 1994-2003. 180 cases produced. Release: $18. Current: $35. **86**

1983 PHILIP TOGNI VINEYARD: Togni's first vintage is hard, tight, lean and chunky, with firm tannins and a rich core of weedy black currant flavors framed by spicy cedar oak. Impressive for its concentration and balance, but it needs five to seven years' cellaring to reach its peak. Drink 1995-2005. 90 cases produced. Release: $18. Current: $50. **87**

PHILIP TOGNI
Vineyard

TELEPHONE (707) 963-3731

1986
Napa Valley
CABERNET SAUVIGNON   *Estate Bottled*

■ THIS TABLE WINE WAS GROWN & ESTATE BOTTLED BY PHILIP TOGNI VINEYARD, SPRING MOUNTAIN, ST. HELENA, NAPA VALLEY, CALIFORNIA, USA. CONTAINS SULFITES.

TREFETHEN VINEYARDS

Reserve, Yountville, Napa Valley
Estate, Yountville, Napa Valley

CLASSIFICATION: *FIFTH GROWTH*
COLLECTIBILITY RATING: *Not Rated*
BEST VINTAGES: *Reserve: 1986, 1985*

AT A GLANCE

TREFETHEN VINEYARDS
P.O. Box 2460
Napa, CA 94558
(707) 255-7700

Owners: John and Janet Trefethen

Winemakers: David Whitehouse (14
    years)/Peter Luthi (6 years)

Founded: 1968

First Cabernet vintage: 1974
    Reserve: 1985

Cabernet production: 11,000 cases
    Reserve: 1,000 cases
    Estate: 10,000 cases

Cabernet acres owned: 115

Average age of vines: 17 years

Vineyard makeup: Cabernet
    Sauvignon (85%), Merlot (15%)

Average wine makeup: Cabernet
    Sauvignon (85%), Merlot (15%)

Time in oak:
    Reserve: 24 months
    Estate: 12 months

Type of oak: French (Nevers),
    American

Few consumers associate Trefethen with fine Cabernet, but this winery, in a cool part of Napa Valley between Napa and Yountville, has made some surprisingly good Cabernets since 1974. Trefethen's Cabernets are nowhere near the upper echelon of Napa Valley producers, yet the two most recent Reserve bottlings, from 1985 and 1986, are dramatic improvements from earlier vintages and should help establish Trefethen's Cabernet credentials, as both are excellent wines that offer depth and aging potential, clear evidence that the winery is taking Cabernet more seriously these days. The winery, owned and operated by the Trefethen family, has been making Cabernet since 1974 from grapes grown on their huge 550-acre estate. The early vintages, 1974 through 1979, have aged gracefully with the exception of the 1976, which is a tough and tannic wine from a drought year. All the other wines are smooth and elegant, with distinctive herb, anise, spice, cherry and tar notes.

In the 1980s, both the 1980 and 1982 were major disappointments, while the 1981 has evolved into a rich, complex wine. Both the 1983 and 1984 vintages are good, yet not up to the best efforts from those vintages, and the 1985 vintage is surprisingly light, with green, vegetal flavors. In contrast, the 1985 Reserve is rich and flavorful, followed by an excellent 1986 Reserve that is similar to the 1985 Reserve in depth and concentration.

TASTING NOTES

TREFETHEN VINEYARDS, Reserve, Yountville, Napa Valley

1986 TREFETHEN VINEYARDS RESERVE: The 1986 Reserve will surpass the excellent 1985 Reserve as Trefethen's finest bottling ever. Richer and more concentrated than the regular 1986 Estate or 1985 Reserve bottlings, it is packed with juicy plum, black cherry and spice flavors and firm tannins. Drink 1995-2005. 1,000 cases produced. Not Released. **90**

1985 TREFETHEN VINEYARDS RESERVE: Remarkably elegant and refined, this is a richly flavored, lean and delicate Cabernet with layers of cedar, tobacco, plum and mint flavors backed by lean tannins. Should begin drinking well within three age and age a decade or more. Drink 1993-2000. 969 cases produced. Not Released. **90**

TREFETHEN VINEYARDS, Estate, Yountville, Napa Valley

1986 TREFETHEN VINEYARDS ESTATE: Very generous with ripe plum, anise and black cherry flavors and fine, supple tannins. Very nicely balanced and a worthy successor to the fine 1985 bottling. Drink 1996-2002. 10,400 cases produced. Release: $15.25. Current: $15.25. **87**

1985 TREFETHEN VINEYARDS ESTATE: Considering how many magnificent 1985 were produced, the 1985 Trefethen is disappointing. While it's a decent, enjoyable wine, it lacks the richness and complexity of the vintage's top wines and offers a vegetal, green bean note that detracts from the true Cabernet flavor. Drink 1992-1997. 9,501 cases produced. Not Released. **80**

1984 TREFETHEN VINEYARDS ESTATE: A rich, supple, concentrated wine with plenty of herb, mineral, chocolate and berry flavors. This wine is already drinkable but has the tannins for another five to seven years' development. Drink 1991-1995. 9,500 cases produced. Release: $14. Current: $16. **84**

1983 TREFETHEN VINEYARDS ESTATE: Lean and austere with firm, gritty tannins, but just enough fruit to back it up. The ripe plum, currant and chocolate flavors are well focused and evenhanded. Should age well. Drink 1994-2000. 9,653 cases produced. Release: $11.75. Current: $22. **84**

1982 TREFETHEN VINEYARDS ESTATE: Extremely weedy and vegetal. The winery removed the wine from the market after discovering how poorly it was showing after release. Best to avoid. **58**

1981 TREFETHEN VINEYARDS ESTATE: The 1981 Trefethen has evolved into a rich, supple, complex wine with tiers of vanilla, chocolate and currant flavors that spread out on the palate. It's firmly tannic on the finish. Drink 1990-1995. 8,842 cases produced. Release: $11. Current: $28. **87**

1980 TREFETHEN VINEYARDS ESTATE: A weak 1980 that exhibits vegetal, tarry flavors that detract from the quality. A mediocre wine in a vintage that proved difficult for many producers. Best to avoid. 6,980 cases produced. Release: $11. Current: $20. **68**

1979 TREFETHEN VINEYARDS ESTATE: Ripe, supple and concentrated, with firm tannins and cedar and black currant flavors, the 1979 is full-bodied and fairly dry on the finish, but it has the depth and concentration to carry it another five years. At its peak now. Drink 1990-1996. 6,192 cases produced. Release: $11. Current: $35. **86**

1978 TREFETHEN VINEYARDS ESTATE: Similar in style to the 1977 but with less depth and flavor, this is a well-made wine with supple cedar, herb, anise, and currant flavors and firm tannins, but it's wanting in complexity and richness. Drink 1991-1995. 3,764 cases produced. Release: $10. Current: $45. **81**

1977 TREFETHEN VINEYARDS ESTATE: Elegant and supple, fully mature with well-balanced, polished, delicate spice, cedar, tar and plum flavors that are ripe, sweet and full. A very pleasant 1977 that is aging gracefully. Drink 1990-1995. 3,687 cases produced. Release: $8.50. Current: $45. **86**

1976 TREFETHEN VINEYARDS ESTATE: Sharp and biting with raw tannins and cedar and herb flavors, the 1976 has depth and character but is awkward on the palate, like many wines from this vintage. Drink 1990-1996. 2,098 cases produced. Release: $7.50. Current: $45. **76**

1975 TREFETHEN VINEYARDS ESTATE: Sleeker and more refined than the 1974, the 1975 is an elegant wine with mature cedar and herb flavors. It has reached its peak and is in decline. Drink 1990-1994. 783 cases produced. Release: $7.50. Current: $55. **83**

1974 TREFETHEN VINEYARDS ESTATE: Ripe and concentrated, this wine has held up well, with mature spice, tar, herb, anise, vegetal and chocolate flavors that are rich and full, developing a silky texture. Drink 1990-1997. 835 cases produced. Release: $8. Current: $65. **84**

TUDAL WINERY
St. Helena, Napa Valley

CLASSIFICATION: *FIFTH GROWTH*

COLLECTIBILITY RATING: *Not rated*

BEST VINTAGES: *1986, 1985, 1984, 1979*

Tudal is a small vineyard and winery operation north of St. Helena that was founded in 1979 by Arnold Tudal. Tudal removed an old walnut orchard to plant his 7-acre Cabernet vineyard and now produces up to 2,000 cases a year. While the Tudal Cabernets are consistently very well made and occasionally exceptional in quality, they are not especially well known, even in Napa Valley, as the proprietor keeps a low profile. Aside from a poor 1982 vintage, all of the Tudal Cabernets are worth seeking out, for they drink well early on and age quite well.

The first vintage, the 1979, proved highly successful, with showy fruit and good depth. The 1980 borders on jammy, but the 1981 is smooth and supple. The 1983 succeeds by not being overly tannic, while the 1984 combines richness and loads of fresh, ripe fruit. The 1985 is a shade leaner but well balanced, followed by another impressive bottling from the 1986 vintage. Tudal's Cabernets are 100 percent varietal and age up to 36 months in oak. Despite that, they typically display little in the way of oak flavor, but offer plenty of delicious fruit.

AT A GLANCE
TUDAL WINERY
1015 Big Tree Road
St. Helena, CA 94574
(707) 963-3947

Owner: The Tudal family

Winemaker: Arnold Tudal (10 years)

Founded: 1979

First Cabernet vintage: 1979

Cabernet production: 2,000 cases

Cabernet acres owned: 7

Average age of vines: 15 years

Vineyard makeup: Cabernet Sauvignon (100%)

Average wine makeup: Cabernet Sauvignon (100%)

Time in oak: 36 months

Type of oak: French (Nevers)

TASTING NOTES

TUDAL WINERY, St. Helena, Napa Valley

1986 TUDAL WINERY: Impressive for its elegance and sharply focused, fresh, ripe, rich black cherry and currant flavors. The tannins are lean but ample for midterm to long-range cellaring, and the finish is long and fruity. Best in three to five years. Drink 1994-2002. 1,800 cases produced. Release: $14.50. Current: $14.50. **89**

1985 TUDAL WINERY: A lean, elegant, well-proportioned 1985 that offers layers of ripe, focused fruit, hints of cherry, currant and cedar and fine tannins that make it appealing now and also a good candidate for midterm cellaring. It should be near its peak in two or three years. Drink 1993-1999. 1,400 cases produced. Release: $14.50. Current: $14.50. **89**

1984 TUDAL WINERY: An exceptional 1984 that combines richness

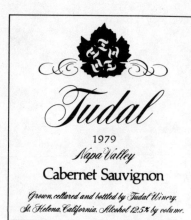

with elegance and grace. The fruit is sharply focused, with ripe black cherry and currant flavors and a touch of spicy oak. The tannins are firm and lean, yet there's enough depth to carry this wine a decade with ease. Drink 1993-2001. 1,000 cases produced. Release: $12.50. Current: $15. **91**

1983 TUDAL WINERY: A very successful and supple 1983 that avoids being overly tannic and manages to offer ripe, smooth black cherry and currant flavors with good concentration. The tannins are there for aging, and they don't bite on the finish. Already drinkable but better in three years. Drink 1992-1998. 1,500 cases produced. Release: $12.50. Current: $19. **86**

1982 TUDAL WINERY: Earthy and herbal, with diluted flavors, an apparent victim of the harvest rains that resulted in variable wines. Not up to par for Tudal but still drinkable. On the palate it's supple and balanced, missing the sharply focused, ripe fruit. Drink 1990-1993. 2,100 cases produced. Release: $12. Current: $25. **72**

1981 TUDAL WINERY: Charming for its rich, smooth, supple texture and well-defined cedar, tobacco and currant flavors, this wine is close to its peak. Like most 1981s, its appeal lies in its drinkability now and in the next five to seven years. Drink 1991-1997. 1,000 cases produced. Release: $12. Current: $25. **88**

1980 TUDAL WINERY: Extremely ripe, bordering on jammy, with intense and concentrated currant, spice and cedar flavors that can stand up to the 14 percent alcohol. It may be overpowering for many. Best suited for a cheese course. Tannins still dominate on the finish. Drink 1992-1996. 1,250 cases produced. Release: $11.50. Current: $25. **85**

1979 TUDAL WINERY: A ripe, supple, forward 1979 with very intense cherry, spice and anise flavors that are complex and well focused. Close to maturity now but with the depth of flavor and tannins to carry it another decade. Drink 1992-2000. 630 cases produced. Release: $10.75. Current: $25. **90**

VICHON WINERY

SLD, Stags Leap District, Napa Valley

CLASSIFICATION: *FIFTH GROWTH*

COLLECTIBILITY RATING: *Not rated*

BEST VINTAGES:

SLD: 1986, 1985

Napa Valley: 1985, 1984

Vichon Winery was founded in 1980 by a general partnership that included some of the leading restaurateurs and hoteliers in the United States. The name "Vichon" came from the three general partners — George Vierra, Peter Brucher and Doug Watson. Vierra (now at Merlion in Napa Valley) coined the term "food wines" to refer to the crisper acidity, lower alcohol and delicate balance of his wines. The early Vichon Cabernets were clean, balanced and flavorful, but they lacked richness and complexity.

In 1980 the winery, on Oakville Grade, produced two Cabernets, one from the celebrated Fay Vineyard in the Stags Leap District (now owned by Warren Winiarski of Stag's Leap Wine Cellars) and a second from Volker Eisele Vineyard in Chiles Valley, an offshoot of Napa Valley. The 1980 Fay is fully mature, displaying the soft, smooth tannins of the area with pretty black cherry flavors. The 1980 Volker Eisele is much leaner. In 1981 only one bottling was produced, and it is lean and firm but ready to drink. In 1982 three bottlings were produced, under the Fay, Eisele and Napa Valley designations, and all three are decent but unexciting. The 1983 is fairly tannic, with crisp acidity and just enough fruit to stand up to the tannins. The 1984 is the best of the early bottling, noticeably richer and more concentrated, while the 1985 SLD (Stags Leap District) is by far the finest offering to date. A Napa Valley 1985 is also very good but missing the elegance and finesse of the SLD bottling. The 1986 SLD is also superb.

In 1984 Vichon faced a power struggle among its partners and as a result, was acquired by the Robert Mondavi Winery. Tim Mondavi is now president of Vichon. Vichon doesn't own any vineyards, but the Mondavis do, including good Cabernet acreage in Stags Leap. The SLD bottling is clearly the best and is the wine to concentrate on.

AT A GLANCE

VICHON WINERY
P.O. Box 363
Oakville, CA 94562
(707) 944-2811

Owner: The Robert Mondavi family

Winemaker: Karen Culler (1 year)

Founded: 1980

First Cabernet vintage: 1980
SLD: 1985

Cabernet production: 10,000 cases
SLD: 3,500 cases
Napa Valley: 6,500 cases

Cabernet acres owned: 5

Average age of vines: 6 years

Vineyard makeup: Cabernet Sauvignon (97%), Malbec (3%)

Average wine makeup: Cabernet Sauvignon (97%), Cabernet Franc (3%)

Time in oak: 18 months

Type of oak: French (Nevers)

VICHON

1985 Napa Valley
CABERNET SAUVIGNON

SLD

Alcohol 12.5% by Volume
Produced and Bottled by Vichon Winery
Oakville, California 94562 · BW-4989

TASTING NOTES

VICHON WINERY, Various bottlings

1986 VICHON WINERY SLD: An excellent 1986 that is elegant and sophisticated, offering rich, well-defined fruit and firm structure, with complex herb, cherry, currant and anise flavors that are supported by supple yet firm tannins. The finish is long and fruity and it is already a pleasure to drink. Drink 1991-1997. 2,540 cases produced. Release: $21. Current: $21. **90**

1985 VICHON WINERY SLD: By far the finest Vichon Cabernet, this 1985 has gorgeous, rich, ripe, supple layers of black cherry, currant and spice flavors, with just the right dose of tannin to give it backbone and support. Delicious now but should drink well throughout the decade. Drink 1992-2000. 4,000 cases produced. Release: $18. Current: $20. **92**

1985 VICHON WINERY NAPA VALLEY: Doesn't quite have the elegance and finesse of the SLD bottling, but this is still a very attractive Cabernet with plenty of flavor and fine balance. Drink it before the SLD. Drink 1992-1997. 7,500 cases produced. Release: $13. Current: $14. **88**

1984 VICHON WINERY NAPA VALLEY: Fairly rich and concentrated, with more intensity and stuffing than previous efforts. It's loaded with fresh, ripe plum, cherry and mint flavors and backed with firm, crisp tannins. Like most '84s it can be enjoyed now, but it has the depth for another five to seven years in the cellar. Drink 1992-1997. 600 cases produced. Release: $11.25. Current: $13. **88**

1984 VICHON WINERY FAY VINEYARD: Charming, with pretty black cherry and currant flavors that are fresh, lively and supple and a fruity aftertaste. Not very tannic nor structured for aging. Drink this one while it's fresh and fruity. Drink 1990-1994. 1,935 cases produced. Release: $14. Current: $18. **85**

1983 VICHON WINERY NAPA VALLEY: Pleasant for an 1983 because it's not too tannic, but the flavors are simple, with shades of plum and cherry, finishing with crisp acidity and a touch of tannin. Approachable now. Drink 1990-1995. 10,000 cases produced. Release: $10. Current: $14. **80**

1982 VICHON WINERY NAPA VALLEY: Like the other 1982 bottlings, light and simple, with decent fresh, ripe fruit flavors that lack depth and complexity. A restaurant-style wine that should be consumed. Drink 1990-1993. 5,400 cases produced. Release: $13. Current: $15. **76**

1982 VICHON WINERY VOLKER EISELE: A lean, ripe, simple Cabernet with pleasant spice and cherry flavors, soft tannins and modest depth. Drink 1990-1994. 2,000 cases produced. Release: $16. Current: $19. **78**

1982 VICHON WINERY FAY VINEYARD: A decent but uninspiring 1982 marked by dense, herbal green olive and plum flavors that are a bit murky and lack focus. It's drinkable and may improve with further bottle age, but it's the weakest vintage in the Vichon lineup. Drink 1990-1995. 2,500 cases produced. Release: $14. Current: $23. **79**

1981 VICHON WINERY NAPA VALLEY: A lean and simple 1981 with pretty cherry and spice flavors but not much depth or complexity, finishing with herb and tobacco notes. Drink 1990-1994. 4,600 cases produced. Release: $13. Current: $20. **80**

1980 VICHON WINERY VOLKER EISELE VINEYARD: A shade leaner and less fruity than the Napa Valley bottling, this wine has spicy cherry and plum flavors that are ripe and smooth. Drink 1990-1995. 800 cases produced. Release: $16. Current: $25. **83**

1980 VICHON WINERY FAY VINEYARD: Vichon's first Cabernet, this is a ripe, smooth, supple 1980 with bright black cherry, spice and currant flavors that are very well focused. Most of the tannins have softened, making it quite drinkable now or in the next five years. Drink 1990-1995. 1,400 cases produced. Release: $16. Current: $25. **85**

Villa Mt. Eden Winery

Reserve, Oakville, Napa Valley
Estate, Oakville, Napa Valley

CLASSIFICATION: *FIFTH GROWTH*

COLLECTIBILITY RATING: *Not rated*

BEST VINTAGES:

Reserve: 1978

Estate: 1977, 1975, 1974

I n the 1970s, Villa Mt. Eden was one of the bright new stars in Napa Valley, with two rich, opulent, blockbuster Cabernets in 1974 and 1978, made from 100 percent estate-grown fruit under the direction of Nils Venge. The winery in Oakville was originally founded in 1881 and rejuvenated in 1970 by James and Anne McWilliams, the latter the granddaughter of A.P. Giannini, founder of Bank of America. In 1982, Venge departed to join Dennis Groth at Groth Vineyards, and in 1986 the McWilliams sold the winery to Stimson Lane/Château Ste. Michelle, which is owned by U.S. Tobacco Co.

The early Villa Mt. Eden Cabernets are clearly the finest. The 1974 has just reached its peak and has another seven to 10 years' development, while the 1978 Reserve still needs three or four years to develop fully. The 1975 was another wonderful wine, with its generous fruit and deft balance, but not all the wines were as magnificent. The 1976 is overly earthy, and the 1978 Estate pales in comparison with the deeply fruity Reserve. Both bottlings in 1979 are a notch below Napa Valley's best in that vintage. The 1980 is a bizarre wine, sour and harsh, while the 1980 Reserve is only marginally better. The 1981, 1982, 1984, 1985 and 1986 have all been very good wines, but the style has shifted from the rich, high-extract, fleshy Cabernets toward a simpler, easy-to-drink, restaurant style that renders good, sound, clean and pleasant wines, but none that are memorable.

At a Glance

VILLA MT. EDEN WINERY
620 Oakville Crossroad
Oakville, CA 95462
(707) 944-2414

Owner: Stimson Lane/Château Ste. Michelle (U.S. Tobacco Co.)

Winemaker: Mike McGrath (6 years)

Founded: 1881, reestablished: 1970

First Cabernet vintage: 1974

Cabernet production: 8,000 cases Reserve: 1,100 (in some vintages)

Cabernet acres owned: 23

Average age of vines: 20 years

Vineyard makeup: Cabernet Sauvignon (100%)

Average wine makeup: Cabernet Sauvignon (100%)

Time in oak: 18 months

Type of oak: French (Nevers)

TASTING NOTES

Villa Mt. Eden Winery, Reserve, Oakville, Napa Valley

1982 VILLA MT. EDEN WINERY RESERVE: Has more fruit and substance than the regular 1982, offering ripe fruit without the vegetal notes. This is a simple, easy-to-drink wine that represents the best Villa Mt. Eden produced that vintage, but it is not a wine of Reserve quality. Drink 1992-1997. 1,254 cases produced. Release: $16.70. Current: $16.70. **84**

1981 VILLA MT. EDEN WINERY RESERVE: A very pleasant, likable 1981 with fresh, ripe, rich black cherry aromas and flavors and a pretty touch of toasty oak. Lacks the richness and concentration for greatness but is in step with the vintage, which produced very fruity, easy-to-drink wines for midterm aging. Drink 1990-1996. 1,144 cases produced. Release: $16.70. Current: $20. **85**

1980 VILLA MT. EDEN WINERY RESERVE: This is a modest but ultimately insignificant improvement over the 1980 Estate bottling. It is weedy, thin and vegetal, and it tastes stripped, as if overfiltered. The currant and black cherry flavors come through on the finish, but overall it's an awkward, clumsy effort. Drink 1992-1996. 1,143 cases produced. Release: $20. Current: $24. **70**

1979 VILLA MT. EDEN WINERY RESERVE: A notch richer and more concentrated that the 1979 Estate, this wine is also much more tannic. There's a slight wet earth and bark aroma that overrides the fruit and leaves a very dry, slightly bitter, tannic finish. With time this wine may improve, but for now its liabilities offset its assets. Drink 1994-2000. 500 cases produced. Release: $20. Current: $30. **75**

1978 VILLA MT. EDEN WINERY RESERVE: This Reserve is richer, more concentrated and more tannic than the regular Estate bottling. It's fairly thick and tannic with rich, ripe black cherry and currant flavors, coarse, chewy tannins and a slightly bitter aftertaste. Fits the reserve definition well; a wine built for aging. Drink 1994-2004. 761 cases produced. Release: $20. Current: $42. **88**

VILLA MT. EDEN WINERY, Estate, Oakville, Napa Valley

1986 VILLA MT. EDEN WINERY ESTATE: The best Estate wine since the very fine 1975 and 1977 bottlings, this wine is nonetheless much like the 1984 and 1985 vintages. It displays ripe, well-defined fruit and toasty oak but lacks the richness and intensity for long-term cellaring. Drink 1990-1996. 9,700 cases produced. Not Released. **84**

1985 VILLA MT. EDEN WINERY ESTATE: This wine has plenty of ripe Cabernet flavor, but for a 1985 it is light and simple, straightforward, not too tannic or rich. It appears to be an early drinking wine with charming black cherry and berry flavors. Drink 1990-1994. 8,095 cases produced. Not Released. **82**

1984 VILLA MT. EDEN WINERY ESTATE: This is a rather light and fruity wine that's pleasant to drink already and does not appear to have the stuffings for even midterm aging. The flavors are true Cabernet, spicy berry and cherry, but ultimately simple and uninspiring. Drink 1990-1994. 1,004 cases produced. Not Released. **80**

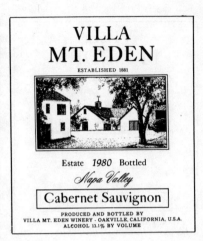

1983 VILLA MT. EDEN WINERY ESTATE: Lean and simple, this 1983 offers decent Cabernet flavor, but it's light and thin and does not provide much flavor or interest. One bright note: It's not tannic. Drink 1990-1993. 7,588 cases produced. Release: $10. Current: $10. **72**

1982 VILLA MT. EDEN WINERY ESTATE: A decent but unexciting 1982 with light vegetal and earthy aromas interspersed with weedy fruit flavors that turn tannic and watery on the finish. Lacks balance and depth. Drink 1990-1993. 8,143 cases produced. Release: $9. Current: $9. **70**

1980 VILLA MT. EDEN WINERY ESTATE: This has always been a bizarre, flawed wine that tastes like chemicals and is very harsh and tannic. The finish is sour and earthy. Best to avoid. 3,922 cases produced. Release: $11.70. Current: $14. **62**

1979 VILLA MT. EDEN WINERY ESTATE: A lighter wine as 1979s go, fully mature, has been ready to drink for the past five years. The fruit is ripe and elegant, with cedar notes in the background, but it is not a deep, intense, concentrated wine. Drink 1990-1993. 2,773 cases produced. Release: $12. Current: $23. **78**

1978 VILLA MT. EDEN WINERY ESTATE: This is a good 1978, with generous, ripe, supple yet ultimately simple fruit. It's not quite up to Villa Mt. Eden's standards nor does it rank among the best of this excellent vintage. Despite the flavor it does not have the richness or concentration typical of this estate's wines. Drink 1990-1994. 2,421 cases produced. Release: $8. Current: $27. **78**

1977 VILLA MT. EDEN WINERY ESTATE: A beautifully preserved 1977 that is youthful and full of rich, ripe, sumptuous black cherry, vanilla, anise and spice flavors that coat the palate. This wine is delicious now, but with its firm tannins and ample fruit it still has a long life ahead. Drink 1991-2002. 2,383 cases produced. Release: $8. Current: $36. **89**

1976 VILLA MT. EDEN WINERY ESTATE: A decent 1976, but one of Villa Mt. Eden's poorer efforts, this wine has ample ripe fruit but also an "off" tar and earth quality that interferes with the flavor of the wine. Drink 1990-1994. 860 cases produced. Release: $7. Current: $38. **70**

1975 VILLA MT. EDEN WINERY ESTATE: A rich, smooth, supple and elegant 1975 that is fully mature, with generous black currant, cedar, anise and cherry flavors that are rich and luscious. Despite its allure now, this wine has the delicate balance and richness of flavor for another decade. Drink 1990-2000. 616 cases produced. Release: $7. Current: $50. **89**

1974 VILLA MT. EDEN WINERY ESTATE: This has always been an extraordinary 1974, with its rich, ripe, opulent fruit, layers of flavor complexity and concentration, with herb, chocolate, plum and cherry notes and firm tannins. It continues to age with grace and character. Drink 1990-1997. 219 cases produced. Release: $7. Current: $60. **90**

APPENDICES

APPENDICES

APPENDIX I
All Wines Tasted, Listed Alphabetically by Winery

Score	Vintage	Appellation/Vineyard	Case Prod.	Release Price	Current Price	Drink
ALEXANDER VALLEY VINEYARDS						
88	1986	Alexander Valley	13,522	$11.50	$11.50	1992-1998
88	1985	Alexander Valley	15,745	$11.00	$12.00	1991-1997
92	1984	Alexander Valley	5,600	$10.50	$13.50	1992-2000
90	1983	Alexander Valley	3,792	$10.50	$14.50	1992-1998
90	1982	Alexander Valley	3,987	$10.00	$16.00	1990-1996
87	1981	Alexander Valley	3,625	$9.00	$16.00	1990-1994
83	1980	Alexander Valley	2,552	$9.00	$16.00	1990-1994
86	1979	Alexander Valley	2,819	$7.00	$18.00	1990-1996
80	1978	Alexander Valley	3,734	$6.50	$20.00	1990-1993
60	1976	Alexander Valley	2,080	$5.50	$18.00	Avoid
75	1975	Alexander Valley	3,416	$5.50	$20.00	1990-1992
BEAULIEU VINEYARD						
93	1986	Napa Valley Rutherford Georges de Latour Private Reserve	15,000*	NR		1995-2005
95	1985	Napa Valley Rutherford Georges de Latour Private Reserve	15,000	NR		1995-2003
91	1984	Napa Valley Rutherford Georges de Latour Private Reserve	15,000	$25.00	$28.00	1994-2002
82	1983	Napa Valley Rutherford Georges de Latour Private Reserve	15,000	$24.00	$28.00	1992-1997
88	1982	Napa Valley Rutherford Georges de Latour Private Reserve	15,000	$24.00	$32.00	1995-2005
87	1981	Napa Valley Rutherford Georges de Latour Private Reserve	15,000	$24.00	$30.00	1993-2000
93	1980	Napa Valley Rutherford Georges de Latour Private Reserve	15,000	$24.00	$35.00	1995-2005
90	1979	Napa Valley Rutherford Georges de Latour Private Reserve	15,000	$21.00	$43.00	1993-2000
91	1978	Napa Valley Rutherford Georges de Latour Private Reserve	15,000	$19.00	$45.00	1990-2000
79	1977	Napa Valley Rutherford Georges de Latour Private Reserve	15,000	$16.00	$46.00	1990-1991
86	1976	Napa Valley Rutherford Georges de Latour Private Reserve	15,000	$19.00	$60.00	1990-1996
79	1975	Napa Valley Rutherford Georges de Latour Private Reserve	15,000	$16.00	$50.00	1990-1992
79	1974	Napa Valley Rutherford Georges de Latour Private Reserve	15,000	$12.00	$70.00	1990-1991
79	1973	Napa Valley Rutherford Georges de Latour Private Reserve	15,000	$9.00	$50.00	1990
73	1972	Napa Valley Rutherford Georges de Latour Private Reserve	15,000	$6.00	$40.00	1990
67	1971	Napa Valley Rutherford Georges de Latour Private Reserve	15,000	$8.00	$60.00	Avoid
95	1970	Napa Valley Rutherford Georges de Latour Private Reserve	15,000	$8.00	$130.00	1990-1995
90	1969	Napa Valley Rutherford Georges de Latour Private Reserve	15,000	$6.50	$120.00	1990-1995
91	1968	Napa Valley Rutherford Georges de Latour Private Reserve	15,000	$6.00	$150.00	1990-1996
85	1967	Napa Valley Rutherford Georges de Latour Private Reserve	15,000	$5.25	$120.00	1990-1993
87	1966	Napa Valley Rutherford Georges de Latour Private Reserve	15,000	$5.25	$140.00	1990-1994
85	1965	Napa Valley Rutherford Georges de Latour Private Reserve	15,000	$5.25	$120.00	1990-1993
84	1964	Napa Valley Rutherford Georges de Latour Private Reserve	24,000	$4.25	$145.00	1990-1994
70	1963	Napa Valley Rutherford Georges de Latour Private Reserve	15,000	$3.50	$145.00	1990
73	1962	Napa Valley Rutherford Georges de Latour Private Reserve	15,000	$3.50	$140.00	1990
78	1961	Napa Valley Rutherford Georges de Latour Private Reserve	15,000	$3.50	$200.00	1990-1992
89	1959	Napa Valley Rutherford Georges de Latour Private Reserve	15,000	$3.50	$350.00	1990-1992
96	1958	Napa Valley Rutherford Georges de Latour Private Reserve	15,000	$3.00	$400.00	1990-1994
88	1956	Napa Valley Rutherford Georges de Latour Private Reserve	15,000	$2.50	$600.00	1990-1991
90	1951	Napa Valley Rutherford Georges de Latour Private Reserve	15,000	$1.82	$950.00	1990-1992
85	1948	Napa Valley Rutherford Georges de Latour Private Reserve	15,000	$1.82	$800.00	1990-1992
93	1947	Napa Valley Rutherford Georges de Latour Private Reserve	15,000	$1.82	$1000.00	1990-1995
88	1946	Napa Valley Rutherford Georges de Latour Private Reserve	15,000	$1.47	$1000.00	1990-1994
87	1944	Napa Valley Rutherford Georges de Latour Private Reserve	15,000	$1.47	$1100.00	1990-1992
87	1942	Napa Valley Rutherford Georges de Latour Private Reserve	15,000	$1.45	$1200.00	1990-1992
85	1941	Napa Valley Rutherford Georges de Latour Private Reserve	15,000	$1.45	$1200.00	1990-1992
82	1939	Napa Valley Rutherford Georges de Latour Private Reserve	15,000	$1.45	$1500.00	1990
BERINGER VINEYARDS						
96	1986	Napa Valley Private Reserve	4,000	NR		1995-2003
96	1985	Napa Valley Private Reserve	8,000	NR		1994-2004
94	1984	Napa Valley Private Reserve	8,000	$25.00	$31.00	1993-2001
89	1983	Napa Valley Private Reserve	8,000	$19.00	$30.00	1994-2000

NA — not available. NR — not released. * — Beaulieu production figures are estimates.

Score	Vintage	Appellation/Vineyard	Case Prod.	Release Price	Current Price	Drink
92	1982	Napa Valley Private Reserve	4,000	$19.00	$35.00	1992-1999
91	1981	Napa Valley Private Reserve	3,000	$18.00	$40.00	1990-1997
85	1980	Napa Valley Yountville Private Reserve State Lane Vineyard	2.000	$15.00	$40.00	1991-1997
89	1980	Napa Valley St. Helena Private Reserve Lemmon-Chabot Vineyard	2,000	$20.00	$42.00	1990-1997
89	1979	Napa Valley Yountville Private Reserve State Lane Vineyard	2,000	$15.00	$42.00	1990-1996
92	1978	Napa Valley St. Helena Private Reserve Lemmon Ranch Vineyard	3,000	$15.00	$44.00	1990-1998
88	1977	Napa Valley St. Helena Private Reserve Lemmon Ranch Vineyard	2,500	$12.00	$50.00	1990-1995
93	1986	Napa Valley St. Helena Chabot Vineyard	1,000	NR		1994-2002
91	1985	Napa Valley St. Helena Chabot Vineyard	1,000	NR		1992-2000
87	1984	Napa Valley St. Helena Chabot Vineyard	750	NR		1991-1997
85	1983	Napa Valley St. Helena Chabot Vineyard	1,000	$27.00	$27.00	1992-1998
89	1982	Napa Valley St. Helena Chabot Vineyard	1,200	$25.00	$38.00	1993-2000
87	1981	Napa Valley St. Helena Chabot Vineyard	1,000	$23.00	$42.00	1990-1996

BUEHLER VINEYARDS

Score	Vintage	Appellation/Vineyard	Case Prod.	Release Price	Current Price	Drink
91	1986	Napa Valley	3,829	$15.00	$15.00	1996-2005
93	1985	Napa Valley	3,060	$14.00	$16.00	1995-2004
87	1984	Napa Valley	2,639	$13.00	$16.00	1995-2003
91	1983	Napa Valley	2,292	$12.00	$20.00	1993-2001
88	1982	Napa Valley	2,953	$12.00	$30.00	1994-2004
85	1981	Napa Valley	2,214	$11.00	$20.00	1994-2000
82	1980	Napa Valley	794	$10.00	$25.00	1994-2002
87	1978	Napa Valley	224	$10.00	$35.00	1990-1998

BUENA VISTA WINERY

Score	Vintage	Appellation/Vineyard	Case Prod.	Release Price	Current Price	Drink
93	1986	Sonoma Valley Carneros Private Reserve	3,150	NR		1995-2005
93	1985	Sonoma Valley Carneros Private Reserve	2,900	$18.00	$18.00	1993-2000
90	1984	Sonoma Valley Carneros Private Reserve	2,700	$18.00	$18.00	1990-1996
87	1983	Sonoma Valley Carneros Private Reserve	3,500	$18.00	$18.00	1990-1999
85	1982	Sonoma Valley Carneros Private Reserve	3,700	$18.00	$30.00	1991-1996
86	1981	Sonoma Valley Carneros Private Reserve (Special Selection)	2,730	$18.00	$32.00	1990-1995
84	1980	Sonoma Valley Carneros Special Selection	2,141	$18.00	$35.00	1990-1996
92	1979	Sonoma Valley Carneros Special Selection	2,595	$18.00	$50.00	1991-1996
90	1978	Sonoma Valley Carneros Special Selection	2,020	$18.00	$60.00	1990-1996
72	1977	Sonoma Valley Carneros Cask 34	2,146	$12.00	$40.00	1990
66	1976	Sonoma Valley Carneros	994	$12.00	$40.00	Avoid
64	1975	Sonoma Valley Carneros	3,864	$12.00	$30.00	Avoid
68	1974	Sonoma Valley Carneros Cask 25	3,046	$12.00	$40.00	Avoid

BURGESS CELLARS

Score	Vintage	Appellation/Vineyard	Case Prod.	Release Price	Current Price	Drink
91	1986	Napa Valley Vintage Selection	6,600	NR		1995-2004
93	1985	Napa Valley Vintage Selection	6,600	$18.00	$18.00	1992-2002
93	1984	Napa Valley Vintage Selection	7,200	$17.00	$19.00	1996-2006
87	1983	Napa Valley Vintage Selection	6,500	$17.00	$21.00	1994-2002
88	1982	Napa Valley Vintage Selection	8,300	$16.00	$23.00	1994-2002
88	1981	Napa Valley Vintage Selection	6,900	$16.00	$25.00	1993-2002
88	1980	Napa Valley Vintage Selection	5,800	$16.00	$28.00	1994-2002
87	1979	Napa Valley Vintage Selection	2,800	$16.00	$30.00	1993-1999
93	1978	Napa Valley Vintage Selection	2,800	$14.00	$34.00	1992-2000
92	1977	Napa Valley Vintage Selection	3,000	$12.00	$45.00	1992-2000
87	1976	Napa Valley Vintage Selection	2,200	$12.00	$41.00	1991-1997
88	1975	Napa Valley Vintage Selection	1,800	$9.00	$45.00	1990-2000
86	1974	Napa Valley Vintage Selection	1,100	$9.00	$50.00	1990-1996

CAKEBREAD CELLARS

Score	Vintage	Appellation/Vineyard	Case Prod.	Release Price	Current Price	Drink
89	1986	Napa Valley	5,000	$18.00	$18.00	1992-1998
84	1985	Napa Valley	5,000	$17.00	$17.00	1992-1996
85	1985	Napa Valley Rutherford Rutherford Reserve	700	NR		1993-1998
89	1984	Napa Valley	5,000	$16.00	$25.00	1992-2000
77	1983	Napa Valley	4,000	$16.00	$25.00	1992-1995
88	1983	Napa Valley Rutherford Rutherford Reserve	300	$35.00	$35.00	1993-2000
86	1982	Napa Valley	5,000	$16.00	$35.00	1994-2000
88	1981	Napa Valley	4,000	$16.00	$50.00	1990-1995

NA — not available.   NR — not released.   * — Beaulieu production figures are estimates.

Score	Vintage	Appellation/Vineyard	Case Prod.	Release Price	Current Price	Drink
84	1980	Napa Valley	4,000	$14.00	$45.00	1993-2000
82	1979	Napa Valley	3,300	$13.00	$45.00	1990-1995
85	1978	Napa Valley	900	$12.00	$60.00	1992-2000
86	1978	Napa Valley Rutherford Lot 2	80	$12.00	$100.00	1991-2000

CARMENET VINEYARD

Score	Vintage	Appellation/Vineyard	Case Prod.	Release Price	Current Price	Drink
93	1986	Sonoma Valley	9,469	$20.00	$20.00	1994-2005
91	1985	Sonoma Valley	6,040	$18.50	$22.00	1994-2004
92	1984	Sonoma Valley	6,641	$16.00	$30.00	1992-2004
85	1983	Sonoma Valley	6,175	$17.50	$25.00	1994-2004
87	1982	Sonoma Valley	5,348	$16.00	$30.00	1993-2003

CAYMUS VINEYARDS

Score	Vintage	Appellation/Vineyard	Case Prod.	Release Price	Current Price	Drink
98	1986	Napa Valley Rutherford Special Selection	1,000	NR		1995-2005
99	1985	Napa Valley Rutherford Special Selection	1,000	NR		1995-2005
98	1984	Napa Valley Rutherford Special Selection	1,000	$35.00	$50.00	1995-2008
91	1983	Napa Valley Rutherford Special Selection	1,100	$35.00	$50.00	1993-2006
92	1982	Napa Valley Rutherford Special Selection	750	$35.00	$65.00	1995-2006
93	1981	Napa Valley Rutherford Special Selection	1,250	$35.00	$60.00	1995-2006
92	1980	Napa Valley Rutherford Special Selection	750	$30.00	$80.00	1993-2000
97	1979	Napa Valley Rutherford Special Selection	600	$30.00	$85.00	1994-2006
97	1978	Napa Valley Rutherford Special Selection	600	$30.00	$90.00	1994-2005
90	1976	Napa Valley Rutherford Special Selection	270	$35.00	$150.00	1993-1998
92	1975	Napa Valley Rutherford Special Selection	180	$22.00	$175.00	1992-2000
92	1986	Napa Valley Rutherford Estate	4,000	$22.00	$22.00	1995-2005
92	1985	Napa Valley Rutherford Estate	3,500	$18.00	$28.00	1994-2003
91	1984	Napa Valley Rutherford Estate	3,200	$16.00	$30.00	1993-2002
87	1983	Napa Valley Rutherford Estate	3,000	$15.00	$30.00	1994-2002
90	1982	Napa Valley Rutherford Estate	4,200	$14.00	$33.00	1993-2000
88	1981	Napa Valley Rutherford Estate	3,200	$14.00	$35.00	1990-1998
90	1980	Napa Valley Rutherford Estate	4,300	$12.50	$35.00	1993-2000
92	1979	Napa Valley Rutherford Estate	2,700	$12.00	$35.00	1992-1998
87	1978	Napa Valley Rutherford Estate	2,600	$12.00	$60.00	1990-1996
77	1977	Napa Valley Rutherford Estate	1,700	$10.00	$40.00	1990-1994
85	1976	Napa Valley Rutherford Estate	1,600	$10.00	$60.00	1990-1995
89	1975	Napa Valley Rutherford Estate	1,300	$8.50	$80.00	1990-1998
87	1974	Napa Valley Rutherford Estate	950	$7.00	$110.00	1990-1996
93	1973	Napa Valley Rutherford Estate	850	$6.00	$120.00	1990-2000
86	1972	Napa Valley Rutherford Estate	230	$4.50	$110.00	1990-1993

CHAPPELLET VINEYARD

Score	Vintage	Appellation/Vineyard	Case Prod.	Release Price	Current Price	Drink
92	1986	Napa Valley Reserve	6,000	NR		1994-2003
88	1985	Napa Valley Reserve	6,000	$20.00	$20.00	1994-2000
87	1984	Napa Valley Reserve	8,000	$18.00	$23.00	1992-1996
77	1983	Napa Valley	8,700	$12.00	$15.00	1990-1995
80	1982	Napa Valley	11,800	$9.25	$14.00	1990-1993
79	1981	Napa Valley	8,000	$11.00	$18.00	1990-1995
91	1980	Napa Valley	7,000	$18.00	$28.00	1993-1998
79	1979	Napa Valley	6,400	$13.00	$26.00	1990-1995
88	1978	Napa Valley	7,000	$13.00	$40.00	1992-1998
82	1977	Napa Valley	4,500	$12.00	$33.00	1990-1994
76	1976	Napa Valley	4,500	$12.00	$37.00	1990
78	1975	Napa Valley	5,000	$10.00	$45.00	1990
70	1974	Napa Valley	3,500	$7.50	$45.00	1990
69	1973	Napa Valley	2,500	$7.50	$65.00	Avoid
67	1972	Napa Valley	1,500	$6.50	$40.00	Avoid
65	1971	Napa Valley	1,000	$7.50	$80.00	Avoid
93	1970	Napa Valley	700	$7.50	$160.00	1990-1995
87	1969	Napa Valley	400	$10.00	$150.00	1990-1995
88	1968	Napa Valley	200	$5.50	$100.00	1990-1996

CHATEAU MONTELENA WINERY

Score	Vintage	Appellation/Vineyard	Case Prod.	Release Price	Current Price	Drink
93	1986	Napa Valley Calistoga Estate	12,900	NR		1995-2004

NA — not available. NR — not released. * — Beaulieu production figures are estimates.

Score	Vintage	Appellation/Vineyard	Case Prod.	Release Price	Current Price	Drink
95	1985	Napa Valley Calistoga Estate	9,723	$25.00	$25.00	1996-2006
94	1984	Napa Valley Calistoga Estate	11,439	$20.00	$25.00	1998-2006
92	1983	Napa Valley Calistoga Estate	8,517	$18.00	$26.00	1994-2002
92	1982	Napa Valley Calistoga Estate	11,425	$16.00	$33.00	1992-2002
80	1981	Napa Valley Calistoga Estate	7,144	$16.00	$25.00	1990-1994
86	1980	Napa Valley Calistoga Estate	10,000	$16.00	$40.00	1991-1997
88	1979	Alexander Valley Sonoma	1,164	$14.00	$45.00	1991-1998
87	1979	Napa Valley Calistoga Estate	5,776	$16.00	$45.00	1992-1998
87	1978	Alexander Valley Sonoma	1,560	$12.00	$50.00	1990-1996
93	1978	Napa Valley Calistoga Estate	7,500	$16.00	$60.00	1993-2005
91	1977	Alexander Valley Sonoma	3,298	$12.00	$65.00	1992-1999
94	1977	Napa Valley Calistoga	3,800	$12.00	$65.00	1995-2005
90	1976	North Coast	5,769	$10.00	$75.00	1990-1995
86	1975	North Coast	6,675	$9.00	$100.00	1993-2000
87	1974	Alexander Valley Sonoma	6,000	$9.00	$100.00	1992-2000
90	1974	Napa Valley Calistoga	1,100	$9.00	$100.00	1993-2003
87	1973	Alexander Valley Sonoma	3,000	$8.50	$100.00	1990-2001

CHIMNEY ROCK WINE CELLARS

Score	Vintage	Appellation/Vineyard	Case Prod.	Release Price	Current Price	Drink
86	1986	Napa Valley Stags Leap District	5,700	$15.00	$15.00	1990-1996
87	1985	Napa Valley Stags Leap District	2,900	$15.00	$15.00	1990-1997
82	1984	Napa Valley Stags Leap District	2,800	$15.00	$15.00	1990-1996

CLOS DU BOIS WINERY

Score	Vintage	Appellation/Vineyard	Case Prod.	Release Price	Current Price	Drink
82	1985	Alexander Valley Briarcrest Vineyard	3,721	$16.00	$16.00	1993-1998
87	1984	Alexander Valley Briarcrest Vineyard	1,711	$16.00	$24.00	1993-2000
74	1983	Alexander Valley Briarcrest Vineyard	1,122	$12.00	$20.00	1990-1994
66	1982	Alexander Valley Briarcrest Vineyard	2,075	$12.00	$25.00	Avoid
88	1981	Alexander Valley Briarcrest Vineyard	2,095	$12.00	$32.00	1991-1998
80	1980	Alexander Valley Briarcrest Vineyard	1,227	$12.00	$32.00	1990-1995
88	1985	Alexander Valley Marlstone Vineyard	5,917	$19.50	$19.50	1992-1998
89	1984	Alexander Valley Marlstone Vineyard	3,957	$19.50	$24.00	1992-1997
70	1983	Alexander Valley Marlstone Vineyard	1,600	$19.50	$20.00	1990-1993
79	1982	Alexander Valley Marlstone Vineyard	2,496	$16.00	$16.00	1990-1994
85	1981	Alexander Valley Marlstone Vineyard	1,005	$15.00	$32.00	1990-1995
77	1980	Alexander Valley Marlstone Vineyard	3,833	$15.00	$32.00	1991-1998
75	1979	Alexander Valley Marlstone Vineyard	3,395	$16.00	$30.00	1990-1994
72	1978	Alexander Valley Marlstone Vineyard	3,129	$16.00	$30.00	1990

CLOS DU VAL WINE CO.

Score	Vintage	Appellation/Vineyard	Case Prod.	Release Price	Current Price	Drink
94	1985	Napa Valley Stags Leap District Reserve	750	NR		1995-2006
90	1982	Napa Valley Stags Leap District Reserve	2,600	$28.00	$37.00	1997-2005
92	1979	Napa Valley Stags Leap District Reserve	1,200	$25.00	$55.00	1996-2008
94	1978	Napa Valley Stags Leap District Reserve	2,400	$30.00	$55.00	1993-2010
87	1977	Napa Valley Stags Leap District Reserve	2,900	$20.00	$53.00	1990-2001
90	1973	Napa Valley Stags Leap District Reserve	100	$10.00	$100.00	1990-2000
91	1986	Napa Valley Stags Leap District Estate	21,000	NR		1994-2002
93	1985	Napa Valley Stags Leap District Estate	25,000	$16.00	$16.00	1993-2005
92	1984	Napa Valley Stags Leap District Estate	20,500	$15.00	$16.50	1992-2004
86	1983	Napa Valley Stags Leap District Estate	23,500	$15.00	$17.50	1994-2002
88	1982	Napa Valley Stags Leap District Estate	21,000	$13.25	$24.00	1992-2000
82	1981	Napa Valley Stags Leap District Estate	21,500	$12.50	$25.00	1990-1996
88	1980	Napa Valley Stags Leap District Estate	17,400	$12.50	$28.00	1990-1995
90	1979	Napa Valley Stags Leap District Estate	15,400	$12.50	$45.00	1990-2002
92	1978	Napa Valley Stags Leap District Estate	14,000	$12.00	$40.00	1990-2000
89	1977	Napa Valley Stags Leap District Estate	14,700	$10.00	$40.00	1990-2000
82	1976	Napa Valley	6,800	$9.00	$55.00	1990-1995
89	1975	Napa Valley Stags Leap District Estate	9,300	$9.00	$65.00	1990-2000
91	1974	Napa Valley Stags Leap District Estate	7,600	$7.50	$75.00	1990-2000
86	1973	Napa Valley Stags Leap District Estate	2,760	$6.00	$70.00	1990-1995
90	1972	Napa Valley Stags Leap District Estate	3,500	$6.00	$100.00	1990-1998
92	1986	Napa Valley Joli Val	5,000	$12.50	$12.50	1994-2004

NA — not available.   NR — not released.   * — Beaulieu production figures are estimates.

Score	Vintage	Appellation/Vineyard	Case Prod.	Release Price	Current Price	Drink
B.R. COHN						
94	1986	Sonoma Valley Olive Hill Vineyard	2,400	$18.00	$20.00	1993-2001
94	1985	Sonoma Valley Olive Hill Vineyard	2,000	$16.00	$22.00	1993-2000
93	1984	Sonoma Valley Olive Hill Vineyard	900	$15.00	$22.00	1991-1998
CONN CREEK WINERY						
87	1986	Napa Valley Barrel Select	6,550	NR		1994-2000
85	1985	Napa Valley Barrel Select	6,000	NR		1991-1995
87	1985	Napa Valley St. Helena Barrel Select Private Reserve	1,100	NR		1992-1997
86	1984	Napa Valley Barrel Select Lot 79	4,450	$13.00	$13.00	1991-1996
88	1984	Napa Valley St. Helena Collins Vineyard Private Reserve	1,100	$23.00	$23.00	1994-2002
82	1983	Napa Valley Barrel Select	5,000	$13.00	$15.00	1992-1996
87	1983	Napa Valley St. Helena Collins Vineyard Proprietor's Special Selection	40	$0.00	$70.00	1991-1997
85	1982	Napa Valley Barrel Select	7,100	$12.00	$16.00	1992-1997
85	1982	Napa Valley St. Helena Collins Vineyard Proprietor's Special Selection	40	$0.00	$70.00	1995-2004
85	1981	Napa Valley	5,700	$14.00	$18.00	1990-1995
86	1981	Napa Valley St. Helena Collins Vineyard Proprietor's Special Selection	40	$0.00	$70.00	1994-2002
88	1980	Napa Valley	5,700	$13.00	$28.00	1993-2000
93	1980	Napa Valley St. Helena Collins Vineyard Proprietor's Special Selection	40	$0.00	$70.00	1995-2004
77	1979	Napa Valley	6,270	$13.00	$25.00	1993-1998
86	1978	Napa Valley Lot 1	3,000	$12.00	$30.00	1990-2000
92	1978	Napa Valley Lot 2	2,500	$13.00	$35.00	1990-2000
90	1977	Napa Valley	2,000	$12.00	$40.00	1991-1998
86	1976	Napa Valley	2,000	$12.00	$45.00	1990-1995
94	1974	Napa Valley Calistoga	900	$9.00	$70.00	1990-1998
92	1973	Napa Valley Stags Leap District	400	$9.00	$70.00	1990-2000
CUVAISON WINERY						
93	1986	Napa Valley	5,000	$15.00	$15.00	1993-2001
90	1985	Napa Valley	3,000	$14.00	$14.00	1992-1999
89	1984	Napa Valley	3,000	$14.00	$14.00	1991-1996
75	1983	Napa Valley	2,000	$12.00	$15.00	1990-1992
82	1982	Napa Valley	2,000	$11.00	$15.00	1994-2000
74	1981	Napa Valley	6,000	$11.00	$15.00	1993-1999
77	1980	Napa Valley	5,000	$11.00	$18.00	1994-2001
75	1979	Napa Valley	5,000	$11.00	$20.00	1993-2000
72	1978	Napa Valley	5,000	$10.00	$20.00	1995-2002
79	1977	Napa Valley	6,000	$10.00	$35.00	1992-1998
79	1976	Napa Valley	6,000	$10.00	$35.00	1992-1996
79	1975	Napa Valley	5,000	$10.00	$40.00	1990-1995
88	1975	Napa Valley Spring Mountain Philip Togni Signature	400	$40.00	$60.00	1992-1998
DE MOOR WINERY						
79	1985	Napa Valley	1,800	$14.00	$14.00	1991-1996
88	1984	Napa Valley	2,400	$14.00	$16.00	1992-2002
86	1983	Napa Valley	2,400	$12.00	$16.00	1995-2003
88	1982	Napa Valley Owners' Selection	2,000	$12.00	$19.00	1995-2003
86	1982	Napa Valley	1,000	$12.00	$18.00	1994-2001
86	1981	Napa Valley Napa Cellars	1,800	$12.00	$25.00	1990-1997
80	1980	Napa Valley Napa Cellars	1,600	$12.00	$20.00	1990-1996
85	1979	Napa Valley Napa Cellars	1,600	$10.00	$25.00	1990-1998
89	1978	Napa Valley Napa Cellars	1,700	$10.00	$28.00	1990-2000
DIAMOND CREEK VINEYARD						
94	1986	Napa Valley Diamond Mountain Gravelly Meadow	795	$30.00	$30.00	1997-2010
92	1985	Napa Valley Diamond Mountain Gravelly Meadow	736	$30.00	$40.00	1995-2007
94	1984	Napa Valley Diamond Mountain Gravelly Meadow	470	$25.00	$40.00	1994-2007
89	1983	Napa Valley Diamond Mountain Gravelly Meadow	520	$20.00	$25.00	1994-2004
89	1982	Napa Valley Diamond Mountain Gravelly Meadow	404	$20.00	$35.00	1995-2005
84	1982	Napa Valley Diamond Mountain Gravelly Meadow Special Selection	140	$20.00	$35.00	1994-2000
89	1981	Napa Valley Diamond Mountain Gravelly Meadow	656	$20.00	$35.00	1995-2004
92	1980	Napa Valley Diamond Mountain Gravelly Meadow	460	$20.00	$40.00	1996-2006
91	1979	Napa Valley Diamond Mountain Gravelly Meadow	194	$15.00	$60.00	1995-2005

NA — not available.   NR — not released.   * — Beaulieu production figures are estimates.

Score	Vintage	Appellation/Vineyard	Case Prod.	Release Price	Current Price	Drink
93	1978	Napa Valley Diamond Mountain Gravelly Meadow	315	$12.50	$75.00	1995-2005
89	1977	Napa Valley Diamond Mountain Gravelly Meadow	422	$10.00	$55.00	1994-2000
85	1976	Napa Valley Diamond Mountain Gravelly Meadow	96	$9.00	$90.00	1990-1999
85	1975	Napa Valley Diamond Mountain Gravelly Meadow	95	$7.50	$55.00	1991-2000
88	1974	Napa Valley Diamond Mountain Gravelly Meadow	105	$7.50	$135.00	1990-1997
96	1986	Napa Valley Diamond Mountain Red Rock Terrace	970	$30.00	$30.00	1996-2010
93	1985	Napa Valley Diamond Mountain Red Rock Terrace	643	$30.00	$40.00	1996-2009
96	1984	Napa Valley Diamond Mountain Red Rock Terrace	620	$25.00	$40.00	1994-2006
88	1983	Napa Valley Diamond Mountain Red Rock Terrace	651	$20.00	$25.00	1996-2005
87	1982	Napa Valley Diamond Mountain Red Rock Terrace	753	$20.00	$35.00	1995-2004
80	1982	Napa Valley Diamond Mountain Red Rock Terrace Special Selection	192	$20.00	$35.00	1993-1999
91	1981	Napa Valley Diamond Mountain Red Rock Terrace	497	$20.00	$35.00	1993-2002
86	1980	Napa Valley Diamond Mountain Red Rock Terrace	591	$20.00	$40.00	1994-2004
92	1979	Napa Valley Diamond Mountain Red Rock Terrace	263	$15.00	$60.00	1993-2000
92	1978	Napa Valley Diamond Mountain Red Rock Terrace	468	$12.50	$75.00	1992-2004
88	1977	Napa Valley Diamond Mountain Red Rock Terrace First Pick	238	$10.00	$50.00	1994-2003
75	1977	Napa Valley Diamond Mountain Red Rock Terrace Second Pick	60	$10.00	$40.00	1993-1996
85	1976	Napa Valley Diamond Mountain Red Rock Terrace	283	$9.00	$90.00	1990-1999
88	1975	Napa Valley Diamond Mountain Red Rock Terrace	286	$7.50	$75.00	1992-1997
74	1972	Napa Valley Diamond Mountain Red Rock Terrace	25	$7.50	$200.00	1990-1992
96	1986	Napa Valley Diamond Mountain Volcanic Hill	1,035	$30.00	$30.00	1996-2012
93	1985	Napa Valley Diamond Mountain Volcanic Hill	1,100	$30.00	$40.00	1996-2010
94	1984	Napa Valley Diamond Mountain Volcanic Hill	1,224	$25.00	$40.00	1997-2007
89	1983	Napa Valley Diamond Mountain Volcanic Hill	1,442	$20.00	$25.00	1996-2007
89	1982	Napa Valley Diamond Mountain Volcanic Hill	1,420	$20.00	$35.00	1997-2007
79	1982	Napa Valley Diamond Mountain Volcanic Hill Special Selection	258	$20.00	$35.00	1993-1999
92	1981	Napa Valley Diamond Mountain Volcanic Hill	1,026	$20.00	$35.00	1996-2006
90	1980	Napa Valley Diamond Mountain Volcanic Hill	883	$20.00	$40.00	1998-2008
95	1979	Napa Valley Diamond Mountain Volcanic Hill First Pick	50	$15.00	$60.00	1994-2006
82	1979	Napa Valley Diamond Mountain Volcanic Hill Second Pick	415	$15.00	$40.00	1993-1999
95	1978	Napa Valley Diamond Mountain Volcanic Hill	503	$12.50	$75.00	1993-2006
84	1977	Napa Valley Diamond Mountain Volcanic Hill	591	$10.00	$45.00	1990-1992
87	1976	Napa Valley Diamond Mountain Volcanic Hill	428	$9.00	$90.00	1991-1999
93	1975	Napa Valley Diamond Mountain Volcanic Hill	571	$7.50	$80.00	1993-2000
87	1974	Napa Valley Diamond Mountain Volcanic Hill	485	$7.50	$135.00	1992-2000
80	1973	Napa Valley Diamond Mountain Volcanic Hill	150	$7.50	$200.00	1990-1996
85	1972	Napa Valley Diamond Mountain Volcanic Hill	40	$7.50	$200.00	1990-1995
92	1984	Napa Valley Diamond Mountain Lake	130	$50.00	$120.00	1995-2004
99	1978	Napa Valley Diamond Mountain Lake	25	$25.00	$250.00	1994-2002
89	1985	Napa Valley Diamond Mountain Three Vineyard Blend	10	$50.00	$50.00	1998-2004
89	1984	Napa Valley Diamond Mountain Three Vineyard Blend	50	$50.00	$50.00	1995-2000
90	1981	Napa Valley Diamond Mountain Three Vineyard Blend	15	$20.00	$50.00	1995-2005

DOMINUS ESTATE

Score	Vintage	Appellation/Vineyard	Case Prod.	Release Price	Current Price	Drink
93	1986	Napa Valley Yountville Napanook	6,300	NR		1995-2004
95	1985	Napa Valley Yountville Napanook	4,000	$45.00	$45.00	1995-2005
90	1984	Napa Valley Yountville Napanook	4,200	$40.00	$45.00	1994-2002
87	1983	Napa Valley Yountville Napanook	2,100	$43.00	$43.00	1994-2002

DUCKHORN VINEYARDS

Score	Vintage	Appellation/Vineyard	Case Prod.	Release Price	Current Price	Drink
94	1986	Napa Valley	4,000	$18.00	$18.00	1995-2003
92	1985	Napa Valley	2,800	$17.50	$26.00	1996-2010
92	1984	Napa Valley	2,000	$17.00	$30.00	1994-2004
88	1983	Napa Valley	3,000	$16.00	$30.00	1994-2000
90	1982	Napa Valley	3,800	$15.00	$38.00	1992-1998
87	1981	Napa Valley	950	$15.00	$45.00	1993-2000
91	1980	Napa Valley	1,600	$14.00	$50.00	1992-2002
92	1978	Napa Valley	800	$10.50	$85.00	1990-1998

DUNN VINEYARDS

Score	Vintage	Appellation/Vineyard	Case Prod.	Release Price	Current Price	Drink
94	1986	Napa Valley Howell Mountain	2,000	$30.00	$30.00	1993-2000
89	1985	Napa Valley Howell Mountain	1,800	$30.00	$55.00	1995-2002
97	1984	Napa Valley Howell Mountain	1,800	$25.00	$85.00	1996-2002

NA — not available.　　NR — not released.　　* — Beaulieu production figures are estimates.

Score	Vintage	Appellation/Vineyard	Case Prod.	Release Price	Current Price	Drink
92	1983	Napa Valley Howell Mountain	1,600	$18.00	$90.00	1995-2005
95	1982	Napa Valley Howell Mountain	1,800	$15.00	$130.00	1992-2000
90	1981	Napa Valley Howell Mountain	940	$14.00	$150.00	1991-1996
92	1980	Napa Valley Howell Mountain	825	$13.00	$170.00	1993-2000
91	1979	Napa Valley Howell Mountain	660	$12.50	$160.00	1990-1997
93	1986	Napa Valley	2,000	$27.00	$27.00	1993-2000
94	1985	Napa Valley	2,000	$20.00	$45.00	1992-2000
93	1984	Napa Valley	2,100	$18.00	$55.00	1994-2004
95	1983	Napa Valley	1,500	$15.00	$60.00	1994-2004
94	1982	Napa Valley	1,250	$13.00	$85.00	1992-2000

EBERLE WINERY

85	1986	Paso Robles	4,196	$12.00	$12.00	1993-1997
89	1985	Paso Robles	2,814	$12.00	$14.00	1992-1998
86	1984	Paso Robles	3,013	$12.00	$17.00	1992-1996
84	1983	Paso Robles	2,800	$10.00	$18.00	1991-1994
72	1982	Paso Robles	2,500	$10.00	$24.00	1990-1994
71	1982	Paso Robles Reserve	76	$25.00	$30.00	1991-1996
85	1981	Paso Robles	2,500	$10.00	$24.00	1990-1994
80	1981	Paso Robles Reserve	191	$25.00	$35.00	1991-1995
78	1980	Paso Robles	2,000	$10.00	$24.00	1990-1994
82	1979	San Luis Obispo	1,000	$10.00	$25.00	1990-1995

FAR NIENTE WINERY

91	1986	Napa Valley Oakville	12,000	$30.00	$30.00	1995-2003
92	1985	Napa Valley Oakville	10,000	$28.00	$28.00	1994-2002
92	1984	Napa Valley Oakville	8,500	$25.00	$30.00	1994-2002
87	1983	Napa Valley Oakville	5,500	$25.00	$32.00	1993-2000
82	1982	Napa Valley Oakville	3,000	$25.00	$35.00	1993-1999

FISHER VINEYARDS

90	1986	Sonoma County Coach Insignia	1,500	$20.00	$20.00	1993-2000
90	1985	Sonoma County Coach Insignia	1,200	$18.00	$20.00	1993-2000
89	1984	Sonoma County Coach Insignia	1,200	$18.00	$25.00	1992-1999

FLORA SPRINGS WINE CO.

85	1986	Napa Valley Rutherford Trilogy	1,400	$33.00	$33.00	1993-1998
88	1985	Napa Valley Rutherford Trilogy	1,200	$30.00	$30.00	1992-1998
84	1984	Napa Valley Rutherford Trilogy	700	$30.00	$35.00	1992-1998
77	1986	Napa Valley	3,500	$15.00	$15.00	1990-1994
88	1985	Napa Valley	4,000	$15.00	$15.00	1991-1999
85	1934	Napa Valley	3,000	$13.00	$18.00	1990-1996
85	1980	Napa Valley	1,200	$12.00	$20.00	1990-1996

FORMAN VINEYARD

93	1986	Napa Valley	1,800	$20.00	$20.00	1995-2004
93	1985	Napa Valley	1,600	$18.00	$30.00	1994-2002
92	1984	Napa Valley	1,000	$18.00	$35.00	1992-2000
90	1983	Napa Valley	600	$15.50	$45.00	1994-2001

FRANCISCAN VINEYARDS

88	1985	Napa Valley Oakville Library Selection	2,000	$17.50	$17.50	1990-1996
89	1985	Napa Valley Oakville Meritage	450	$20.00	$20.00	1993-2000
87	1985	Napa Valley Oakville Reserve	1,800	$18.00	$18.00	1991-1997
87	1984	Napa Valley Oakville Private Reserve	5,400	$9.00	$12.00	1990-1996
85	1983	Napa Valley Oakville Private Reserve	3,000	$8.50	$14.00	1993-1998
79	1979	Napa Valley Oakville	9,000	$8.50	$18.00	1990
78	1978	Napa Valley Oakville Reserve	4,000	$15.00	$20.00	1990-1992
82	1975	Napa Valley Oakville Reserve	3,000	$12.00	$32.00	1990

FREEMARK ABBEY WINERY

90	1986	Napa Valley Rutherford Bosche	4,000	NR		1994-2002
93	1985	Napa Valley Rutherford Bosche	3,500	$24.00	$24.00	1995-2005
88	1984	Napa Valley Rutherford Bosche	3,076	$20.00	$20.00	1995-2003

NA — not available.   NR — not released.   ∗ — Beaulieu production figures are estimates.

Score	Vintage	Appellation/Vineyard	Case Prod.	Release Price	Current Price	Drink
86	1983	Napa Valley Rutherford Bosche	2,860	$18.00	$18.00	1995-2003
88	1982	Napa Valley Rutherford Bosche	3,592	$15.00	$26.00	1996-2002
86	1981	Napa Valley Rutherford Bosche	2,704	$14.00	$24.00	1994-2000
88	1980	Napa Valley Rutherford Bosche	2,740	$14.50	$36.00	1990-1996
93	1979	Napa Valley Rutherford Bosche	2,982	$12.00	$30.00	1990-1997
93	1978	Napa Valley Rutherford Bosche	3,908	$12.50	$35.00	1990-1995
88	1977	Napa Valley Rutherford Bosche	3,532	$12.50	$25.00	1990-1994
85	1976	Napa Valley Rutherford Bosche	3,109	$12.50	$45.00	1990-1994
90	1975	Napa Valley Rutherford Bosche	2,632	$10.00	$48.00	1990-1995
91	1974	Napa Valley Rutherford Bosche	4,127	$7.75	$75.00	1990-1998
88	1973	Napa Valley Rutherford Bosche	3,495	$8.00	$70.00	1990-1993
80	1972	Napa Valley Rutherford Bosche	3,183	$6.00	$30.00	1990-1992
86	1971	Napa Valley Rutherford Bosche	1,015	$6.75	$40.00	1990
91	1970	Napa Valley Rutherford Bosche	424	$8.75	$100.00	1990

FROG'S LEAP WINERY

Score	Vintage	Appellation/Vineyard	Case Prod.	Release Price	Current Price	Drink
94	1986	Napa Valley	2,600	$14.00	$14.00	1993-1999
85	1985	Napa Valley	2,300	$12.00	$12.00	1992-1998
92	1984	Napa Valley	1,900	$10.00	$25.00	1991-1997
80	1983	Napa Valley	1,100	$10.00	$20.00	1990-1994
87	1982	Napa Valley	900	$9.00	$25.00	1990-1996

GIRARD WINERY

Score	Vintage	Appellation/Vineyard	Case Prod.	Release Price	Current Price	Drink
91	1986	Napa Valley Oakville Reserve	584	NR		1994-2002
89	1985	Napa Valley Oakville Reserve	480	$25.00	$25.00	1993-2000
92	1984	Napa Valley Oakville Reserve	684	$25.00	$25.00	1994-2004
87	1983	Napa Valley Oakville Reserve	548	$18.00	$20.00	1994-2000
87	1982	Napa Valley Oakville	2,107	$12.50	$30.00	1994-2004
86	1981	Napa Valley Oakville	1,595	$12.50	$20.00	1993-2000
92	1980	Napa Valley Oakville	1,480	$11.00	$25.00	1991-2000

GRACE FAMILY VINEYARD

Score	Vintage	Appellation/Vineyard	Case Prod.	Release Price	Current Price	Drink
93	1986	Napa Valley St. Helena Estate	150	$40.00	$40.00	1994-2003
95	1985	Napa Valley St. Helena Estate	126	$50.00	$90.00	1993-2004
92	1984	Napa Valley St. Helena Estate	150	$38.00	$125.00	1994-2004
91	1983	Napa Valley St. Helena Estate	175	$38.00	$130.00	1994-2002
89	1982	Napa Valley St. Helena Estate	225	$31.00	$155.00	1993-1999
88	1981	Napa Valley St. Helena Estate	185	$28.00	$150.00	1992-1998
92	1980	Napa Valley St. Helena Estate	183	$25.00	$275.00	1993-2002
92	1979	Napa Valley St. Helena Estate	56	$20.00	$150.00	1991-2000
86	1978	Napa Valley St. Helena Estate	48	$20.00	$275.00	1990-1995

GRGICH HILLS CELLAR

Score	Vintage	Appellation/Vineyard	Case Prod.	Release Price	Current Price	Drink
91	1986	Napa Valley Yountville	10,000	NR		1994-2002
92	1985	Napa Valley Yountville	10,000	NR		1994-2005
94	1984	Napa Valley Yountville	10,000	$17.00	$17.00	1993-2005
88	1983	Napa Valley Yountville	10,000	$17.00	$23.00	1994-2003
87	1982	Napa Valley Yountville	3,000	$17.00	$28.00	1992-1998
86	1981	Napa Valley Yountville	2,000	$17.00	$28.00	1991-1997
90	1980	Napa County-Sonoma County	2,000	$16.00	$32.00	1991-2000

GROTH VINEYARDS & WINERY

Score	Vintage	Appellation/Vineyard	Case Prod.	Release Price	Current Price	Drink
93	1986	Napa Valley Oakville Reserve	475	NR		1993-2003
93	1985	Napa Valley Oakville Reserve	500	NR		1996-2004
94	1984	Napa Valley Oakville Reserve	500	$25.00	$25.00	1992-2000
92	1983	Napa Valley Oakville Reserve	200	$25.00	$30.00	1996-2004
92	1986	Napa Valley Oakville Estate	6,400	$18.00	$18.00	1994-2001
91	1985	Napa Valley Oakville Estate	7,800	$16.00	$16.00	1994-2002
92	1984	Napa Valley Oakville Estate	6,500	$14.00	$18.00	1993-2000
88	1983	Napa Valley Oakville Estate	10,000	$13.00	$21.00	1994-2000
88	1982	Napa Valley Oakville Estate	7,000	$13.00	$24.00	1992-1998

GUNDLACH BUNDSCHU WINERY

Score	Vintage	Appellation/Vineyard	Case Prod.	Release Price	Current Price	Drink
89	1986	Sonoma Valley Rhinefarm	5,000	$12.00	$12.00	1993-1998

NA — not available.   NR — not released.   ∗ — Beaulieu production figures are estimates.

Score	Vintage	Appellation/Vineyard	Case Prod.	Release Price	Current Price	Drink
91	1985	Sonoma Valley Rhinefarm	5,000	$9.00	$10.00	1992-2000
85	1984	Sonoma Valley Rhinefarm	5,000	$9.00	$12.00	1992-1997
73	1983	Sonoma Valley Rhinefarm	4,500	$9.00	$14.00	1991-1994
65	1982	Sonoma Valley Rhinefarm	4,500	$9.00	$13.00	Avoid
90	1981	Sonoma Valley Rhinefarm Vintage Reserve	800	$20.00	$26.00	1994-2002
84	1981	Sonoma Valley	4,000	$7.00	$20.00	1994-1999
79	1984	Sonoma Valley Batto Ranch	800	$14.00	$16.00	1990-1991
77	1983	Sonoma Valley Batto Ranch	1,000	$10.00	$15.00	1990-1993
70	1982	Sonoma Valley Batto Ranch	1,000	$10.00	$18.00	1990-1992
88	1981	Sonoma Valley Batto Ranch	950	$10.00	$18.00	1990-1993
80	1980	Sonoma Valley Batto Ranch	950	$8.00	$20.00	1990-1993
80	1979	Sonoma Valley Batto Ranch	900	$8.00	$22.00	1990-1993
89	1977	Sonoma Valley Batto Ranch	900	$8.00	$24.00	1990-1995

HAYWOOD WINERY

Score	Vintage	Appellation/Vineyard	Case Prod.	Release Price	Current Price	Drink
91	1986	Sonoma Valley	2,612	$16.00	$16.00	1994-2003
89	1985	Sonoma Valley	2,141	$14.50	$14.50	1996-2004
88	1984	Sonoma Valley	856	$12.50	$20.00	1995-2002
77	1983	Sonoma Valley	711	$12.50	$20.00	1995-2003
79	1982	Sonoma Valley	608	$11.00	$20.00	1994-2000
85	1981	Sonoma Valley	1,081	$11.00	$20.00	1994-2001
86	1980	Sonoma Valley	570	$9.75	$12.00	1992-1999

HEITZ WINE CELLARS

Score	Vintage	Appellation/Vineyard	Case Prod.	Release Price	Current Price	Drink
98	1985	Napa Valley Oakville Martha's Vineyard	4,848	NR		1995-2010
97	1984	Napa Valley Oakville Martha's Vineyard	4,421	$40.00	$40.00	1997-2007
89	1983	Napa Valley Oakville Martha's Vineyard	4,356	$32.50	$42.00	1997-2005
88	1982	Napa Valley Oakville Martha's Vineyard	5,100	$30.00	$45.00	1996-2003
89	1981	Napa Valley Oakville Martha's Vineyard	3,113	$30.00	$50.00	1997-2004
89	1980	Napa Valley Oakville Martha's Vineyard	2,966	$30.00	$55.00	1996-2006
93	1979	Napa Valley Oakville Martha's Vineyard	5,469	$25.00	$60.00	1994-2004
91	1978	Napa Valley Oakville Martha's Vineyard	5,000	$22.00	$75.00	1994-2002
90	1977	Napa Valley Oakville Martha's Vineyard	2,800	$30.00	$75.00	1991-2000
85	1976	Napa Valley Oakville Martha's Vineyard	1,664	$30.00	$75.00	1995-2004
92	1975	Napa Valley Oakville Martha's Vineyard	4,895	$25.00	$100.00	1993-2003
99	1974	Napa Valley Oakville Martha's Vineyard	4,543	$25.00	$200.00	1994-2008
92	1973	Napa Valley Oakville Martha's Vineyard	2,329	$11.00	$120.00	1991-2000
79	1972	Napa Valley Oakville Martha's Vineyard	1,445	$12.75	$100.00	1990-1994
98	1970	Napa Valley Oakville Martha's Vineyard	866	$12.75	$275.00	1993-2005
93	1969	Napa Valley Oakville Martha's Vineyard	1,016	$12.75	$275.00	1990-1995
99	1968	Napa Valley Oakville Martha's Vineyard	749	$9.50	$375.00	1990-1995
86	1967	Napa Valley Oakville Martha's Vineyard	2,208	$7.50	$300.00	1990-1996
92	1966	Napa Valley Oakville Martha's Vineyard	392	$8.00	$425.00	1990-1997
92	1985	Napa Valley Rutherford Bella Oaks Vineyard	4,037	NR		1994-2003
86	1984	Napa Valley Rutherford Bella Oaks Vineyard	2,944	$25.00	$25.00	1994-2002
86	1983	Napa Valley Rutherford Bella Oaks Vineyard	2,944	$15.00	$25.00	1994-2001
85	1982	Napa Valley Rutherford Bella Oaks Vineyard	2,944	$16.00	$30.00	1993-2000
90	1981	Napa Valley Rutherford Bella Oaks Vineyard	3,225	$16.00	$38.00	1992-1999
93	1980	Napa Valley Rutherford Bella Oaks Vineyard	2,280	$20.00	$45.00	1994-2004
89	1978	Napa Valley Rutherford Bella Oaks Vineyard	4,837	$15.00	$40.00	1990-1998
91	1977	Napa Valley Rutherford Bella Oaks Vineyard	4,185	$30.00	$57.00	1991-1997
85	1976	Napa Valley Rutherford Bella Oaks Vineyard	895	$30.00	$62.00	1991-1996

HESS COLLECTION WINERY

Score	Vintage	Appellation/Vineyard	Case Prod.	Release Price	Current Price	Drink
93	1986	Napa Valley Mount Veeder Reserve	2,000	NR		1995-2003
91	1986	Napa Valley Mount Veeder Estate	10,000	$14.00	$14.00	1994-2000
96	1985	Napa Valley Mount Veeder Estate	5,000	$13.00	$13.00	1994-2002
93	1984	Napa Valley Mount Veeder Reserve	250	$22.00	$30.00	1992-2000
88	1983	Napa Valley Mount Veeder Reserve	250	$22.00	$30.00	1990-1997
84	1983	Napa Valley Mount Veeder Estate	900	$13.00	$18.00	1990-1995

WILLIAM HILL WINERY

Score	Vintage	Appellation/Vineyard	Case Prod.	Release Price	Current Price	Drink
95	1986	Napa Valley Gold Label Reserve	13,595	$24.50	$24.50	1996-2006

NA — not available.   NR — not released.   * — Beaulieu production figures are estimates.

Score	Vintage	Appellation/Vineyard	Case Prod.	Release Price	Current Price	Drink
94	1985	Napa Valley Gold Label Reserve	10,204	$22.50	$22.50	1995-2005
91	1984	Napa Valley Gold Label Reserve	7,752	$18.25	$26.00	1994-2002
85	1983	Napa Valley Mount Veeder Gold Label	8,405	$18.25	$25.00	1994-1999
90	1982	Napa Valley Mount Veeder Gold Label	11,907	$18.00	$32.00	1994-2002
85	1981	Napa Valley Mount Veeder Gold Label	5,772	$16.25	$34.00	1990-1995
87	1980	Napa Valley Mount Veeder Gold Label	4,961	$18.25	$36.00	1990-1996
93	1979	Napa Valley Mount Veeder Gold Label	4,412	$18.00	$45.00	1990-2000
95	1978	Napa Valley Mount Veeder Gold Label	4,451	$16.25	$60.00	1991-1997

INGLENOOK-NAPA VALLEY

Score	Vintage	Appellation/Vineyard	Case Prod.	Release Price	Current Price	Drink
92	1986	Napa Valley Rutherford Reserve Cask	6,000	NR		1996-2004
95	1985	Napa Valley Rutherford Reserve Cask	10,388	NR		1994-2002
92	1984	Napa Valley Rutherford Reserve Cask	5,237	NR		1992-2002
89	1983	Napa Valley Rutherford Reserve Cask	11,188	$15.50	$19.00	1994-2000
91	1982	Napa Valley Rutherford Reserve Cask	4,631	$22.00	$28.00	1994-2001
93	1981	Napa Valley Rutherford Reserve Cask	12,115	$15.50	$20.00	1992-2000
88	1980	Napa Valley Rutherford Cask	9,305	$15.50	$22.00	1991-1996
77	1979	Napa Valley Rutherford Cask	2,672	$10.75	$23.00	1990
86	1978	Napa Valley Rutherford Cask	11,969	$9.25	$26.00	1990-1994
84	1977	Napa Valley Rutherford Cask	6,291	$8.75	$23.00	1990-1994
72	1976	Napa Valley Rutherford Cask	4,147	$8.75	$19.00	1990
86	1974	Napa Valley Rutherford Cask	11,864	$9.00	$45.00	1990-1995
67	1973	Napa Valley Rutherford Cask	6,494	$8.00	$39.00	Avoid
67	1972	Napa Valley Rutherford Cask	7,278	$7.00	$44.00	Avoid
73	1971	Napa Valley Rutherford Cask	2,978	$6.50	$50.00	1990-1991
85	1970	Napa Valley Rutherford Cask	8,109	$6.50	$75.00	1990-1995
80	1969	Napa Valley Rutherford Cask	12,508	$6.50	$80.00	1990-1992
85	1968	Napa Valley Rutherford Cask	5,218	$6.00	$90.00	1990-1995
73	1967	Napa Valley Rutherford Cask	4,194	$6.00	$60.00	1990
73	1966	Napa Valley Rutherford Cask	3,190	$5.75	$95.00	1990
80	1960	Napa Valley Rutherford Cask	2,500	$2.75	$140.00	1990
94	1958	Napa Valley Rutherford Cask	2,500	$2.50	$300.00	1990
93	1955	Napa Valley Rutherford Cask	2,500	$1.85	$375.00	1990
92	1949	Napa Valley Rutherford Cask	2,000	$1.49	$750.00	1990-1993
87	1946	Napa Valley Rutherford	8,000	$1.49	$1100.00	1990-1995
91	1943	Napa Valley Rutherford	7,000	$1.49	$1000.00	1990-1995
100	1941	Napa Valley Rutherford	5,000	$1.49	$1400.00	1990-2005
95	1933	Napa Valley Rutherford	5,000	$1.30	$1600.00	1990
87	1897	California Claret-Medoc Type	2,000	NA		1990-1995
92	1986	Napa Valley Rutherford Reunion	4,251	NR		1996-2006
94	1985	Napa Valley Rutherford Reunion	3,602	$35.00	$35.00	1993-2000
92	1984	Napa Valley Rutherford Reunion	2,932	$35.00	$35.00	1993-2000
93	1983	Napa Valley Rutherford Reunion	1,991	$33.00	$40.00	1993-2001

IRON HORSE VINEYARDS

Score	Vintage	Appellation/Vineyard	Case Prod.	Release Price	Current Price	Drink
88	1986	Alexander Valley Cabernets	3,500	$17.50	$17.50	1993-2000
87	1985	Alexander Valley Cabernets	3,000	$16.00	$16.50	1992-1999
86	1984	Alexander Valley	1,900	$14.00	$16.00	1992-1998
82	1983	Alexander Valley	2,000	$12.00	$15.50	1992-1997
83	1982	Alexander Valley	2,500	$12.00	$18.00	1994-1999
79	1981	Alexander Valley	1,700	$12.00	$15.50	1992-1998
86	1980	Alexander Valley	1,000	$12.00	$20.00	1992-1998
91	1979	Alexander Valley	1,000	$12.00	$25.00	1992-1998
80	1978	Alexander Valley	1,250	$12.00	$25.00	1990-1994

JOHNSON TURNBULL VINEYARDS

Score	Vintage	Appellation/Vineyard	Case Prod.	Release Price	Current Price	Drink
87	1986	Napa Valley Oakville Vineyard Selection 67	1,280	$20.00	$20.00	1995-2005
95	1986	Napa Valley Oakville Vineyard Selection 82	1,540	$14.50	$14.50	1992-2000
83	1985	Napa Valley Oakville	2,350	$14.50	$17.50	1994-2000
90	1984	Napa Valley Oakville	1,825	$14.50	$18.00	1993-1999
88	1983	Napa Valley Oakville	1,300	$12.50	$18.00	1993-1998
82	1982	Napa Valley Oakville	2,275	$12.50	$18.00	1994-1998
87	1981	Napa Valley Oakville	1,250	$12.00	$20.00	1995-2000

NA — not available.　　NR — not released.　　* — Beaulieu production figures are estimates.

Score	Vintage	Appellation/Vineyard	Case Prod.	Release Price	Current Price	Drink
87	1980	Napa Valley Oakville	1,100	$12.00	$26.00	1994-2000
85	1979	Napa Valley Oakville	450	$10.50	$26.00	1993-1998

JORDAN VINEYARD AND WINERY

Score	Vintage	Appellation/Vineyard	Case Prod.	Release Price	Current Price	Drink
88	1986	Alexander Valley Estate	58,000	NR		1990-1995
85	1985	Alexander Valley Estate	53,698	$19.50	$19.50	1990-1994
86	1984	Alexander Valley Estate	50,500	$19.00	$25.00	1990-1993
78	1983	Alexander Valley Estate	51,400	$18.00	$30.00	1990-1992
73	1982	Alexander Valley Estate	50,800	$18.00	$36.00	1990-1991
84	1981	Alexander Valley Estate	47,000	$17.00	$40.00	1990-1994
80	1980	Alexander Valley Estate	56,400	$17.00	$45.00	1990-1992
79	1979	Alexander Valley Estate	47,000	$16.00	$50.00	1990-1992
81	1978	Alexander Valley Estate	58,000	$16.00	$70.00	1990-1993
77	1977	Alexander Valley	35,000	$14.00	$70.00	1990-1992
79	1976	Alexander Valley	35,000	$10.00	$70.00	1990-1992

ROBERT KEENAN WINERY

Score	Vintage	Appellation/Vineyard	Case Prod.	Release Price	Current Price	Drink
94	1986	Napa Valley	3,395	$16.50	$16.50	1992-2000
86	1985	Napa Valley	2,400	$15.00	$15.00	1993-1998
92	1984	Napa Valley	3,500	$13.50	$30.00	1994-2002
87	1983	Napa Valley	3,400	$11.00	$18.00	1995-2000
88	1982	Napa Valley	2,900	$10.00	$20.00	1993-2000
84	1981	Napa Valley	3,298	$13.50	$22.00	1993-1999
80	1980	Napa Valley	3,272	$13.50	$23.00	1993-2000
74	1979	Napa Valley	2,460	$12.00	$30.00	1994-2000
74	1978	Napa Valley	2,044	$12.00	$40.00	1994-2000
69	1977	Napa Valley	843	$12.00	$50.00	Avoid

KENWOOD VINEYARDS

Score	Vintage	Appellation/Vineyard	Case Prod.	Release Price	Current Price	Drink
94	1986	Sonoma Valley Artist Series	4,000	$30.00	$30.00	1993-2003
91	1985	Sonoma Valley Artist Series	3,000	$30.00	$30.00	1993-2000
93	1984	Sonoma Valley Artist Series	2,700	$30.00	$35.00	1994-2002
87	1983	Sonoma Valley Artist Series	2,500	$30.00	$35.00	1993-1998
87	1982	Sonoma Valley Artist Series	2,200	$25.00	$40.00	1993-1999
89	1981	Sonoma Valley Artist Series	1,900	$25.00	$55.00	1991-1996
80	1980	Sonoma Valley Artist Series	1,600	$20.00	$55.00	1990-1994
91	1979	Sonoma Valley Artist Series	1,300	$20.00	$70.00	1990-1998
90	1978	Sonoma Valley Artist Series	1,000	$20.00	$100.00	1990-1995
82	1977	Sonoma Valley Artist Series	1,000	$15.00	$120.00	1990-1993
77	1976	Sonoma Valley Artist Series	1,000	$10.00	$120.00	1990
73	1975	Sonoma Valley Artist Series	1,000	$6.50	$250.00	1990

KISTLER VINEYARDS

Score	Vintage	Appellation/Vineyard	Case Prod.	Release Price	Current Price	Drink
91	1986	Sonoma Valley Kistler Vineyard	521	$20.00	$20.00	1995-2002
93	1985	Sonoma Valley Kistler Vineyard	169	$16.00	$25.00	1994-2002
78	1983	Napa Valley Mount Veeder Veeder Hills Vineyard	1,010	$13.50	$20.00	1992-1998
86	1982	Napa Valley Mount Veeder Veeder Hills Vineyard	1,010	$12.00	$26.00	1992-1999
87	1981	Napa Valley Mount Veeder Veeder Hills-Veeder Peak	1,010	$12.00	$32.00	1991-1999
85	1980	Napa Valley Mount Veeder Veeder Hills-Veeder Peak	369	$16.00	$35.00	1992-1999
84	1980	Sonoma Valley Glen Ellen Vineyard	320	$18.00	$35.00	1992-1998

CHARLES KRUG WINERY

Score	Vintage	Appellation/Vineyard	Case Prod.	Release Price	Current Price	Drink
87	1986	Napa Valley Vintage Select	7,266	NR		1994-2002
84	1985	Napa Valley Vintage Select	7,266	NR		1995-2004
87	1984	Napa Valley Vintage Select	3,653	NR		1993-2002
82	1983	Napa Valley Vintage Select	3,653	NR		1994-2001
82	1981	Napa Valley Vintage Select	4,423	NR		1992-1998
79	1980	Napa Valley Vintage Select	8,858	$15.00	$15.00	1992-1997
82	1979	Napa Valley Vintage Select	2,177	$12.50	$20.00	1990-1995
78	1978	Napa Valley Vintage Select	14,353	$11.00	$22.00	1990-1995
74	1977	Napa Valley Vintage Select	4,029	$10.00	$22.00	1990-1994
88	1974	Napa Valley Vintage Select Lot F-1	8,246	$9.00	$50.00	1990-1993
73	1973	Napa Valley Vintage Select	5,846	$9.00	$40.00	1990
77	1972	Napa Valley Vintage Select	3,787	$9.00	$45.00	1990

NA — not available.   NR — not released.   ∗ — Beaulieu production figures are estimates.

Score	Vintage	Appellation/Vineyard	Case Prod.	Release Price	Current Price	Drink
79	1971	Napa Valley Vintage Select	7,993	$7.50	$35.00	1990
75	1970	Napa Valley Vintage Select	11,825	$7.50	$60.00	1990
81	1969	Napa Valley Vintage Select	8,262	$6.50	$65.00	1990
80	1968	Napa Valley Vintage Select	7,668	$6.50	$90.00	1990
87	1965	Napa Valley Vintage Select	8,643	$5.00	$80.00	1990-1993
86	1964	Napa Valley Vintage Select	5,780	$4.00	$85.00	1990
74	1963	Napa Valley Vintage Select	3,599	$3.50	$70.00	1990
78	1962	Napa Valley Vintage Select	2,137	$3.50	$70.00	1990
89	1961	Napa Valley Vintage Select	1,958	$3.50	$135.00	1990
79	1960	Napa Valley Vintage Select	1,516	$2.25	$70.00	1990
85	1959	Napa Valley Vintage Select	7,832	$2.25	$150.00	1990
88	1958	Napa Valley Vintage Select	868	$2.00	$465.00	1990
90	1956	Napa Valley Vintage Select	1,250	$1.40	$590.00	1990
92	1952	Napa Valley Vintage Select	1,028	$1.26	$750.00	1990
85	1951	Napa Valley Vintage Select	1,553	$1.25	$700.00	1990
79	1950	Napa Valley Vintage Select	1,553	$1.25	$500.00	1990
88	1946	Napa Valley Vintage Select	1,452	$1.00	$750.00	1990
88	1944	Napa Valley	857	$0.95	$800.00	1990

LA JOTA VINEYARD COMPANY

Score	Vintage	Appellation/Vineyard	Case Prod.	Release Price	Current Price	Drink
92	1986	Napa Valley Howell Mountain	2,700	$21.00	$21.00	1994-2004
88	1985	Napa Valley Howell Mountain	1,570	$18.00	$18.00	1993-2000
88	1984	Napa Valley Howell Mountain	1,206	$15.00	$20.00	1993-1999
84	1983	Napa Valley Howell Mountain	870	$15.00	$20.00	1994-2000
84	1982	Napa Valley Howell Mountain	704	$13.50	$25.00	1994-2000

LAKESPRING WINERY

Score	Vintage	Appellation/Vineyard	Case Prod.	Release Price	Current Price	Drink
88	1986	Napa Valley Yountville	1,700	$14.00	$14.00	1994-1999
88	1985	Napa Valley Yountville	3,300	$12.00	$12.00	1992-1999
92	1984	Napa Valley Yountville Reserve Selection	1,450	$15.00	$20.00	1992-1999
85	1983	Napa Valley Yountville	3,000	$11.00	$13.00	1993-1998
88	1982	Napa Valley Yountville Vintage Selection	3,600	$14.00	$20.00	1992-1998
86	1981	Napa Valley Yountville	3,000	$11.00	$18.00	1992-1998
88	1980	Napa Valley	2,000	$10.00	$21.00	1991-1997

LAUREL GLEN VINEYARD

Score	Vintage	Appellation/Vineyard	Case Prod.	Release Price	Current Price	Drink
89	1986	Sonoma Mountain	4,000	$20.00	$25.00	1992-1998
93	1985	Sonoma Mountain	3,300	$18.00	$35.00	1992-2000
89	1984	Sonoma Mountain	4,000	$15.00	$20.00	1992-2000
59	1983	Sonoma Mountain	4,000	$11.00	$11.00	Avoid
85	1982	Sonoma Mountain	2,800	$12.50	$20.00	1992-1997
92	1981	Sonoma Mountain	1,500	$12.50	$40.00	1990-1996

LIVINGSTON VINEYARDS

Score	Vintage	Appellation/Vineyard	Case Prod.	Release Price	Current Price	Drink
90	1986	Napa Valley Rutherford Moffett Vineyard	1,330	$24.00	$24.00	1994-1999
86	1985	Napa Valley Rutherford Moffett Vineyard	1,030	$18.00	$24.00	1993-1999
87	1984	Napa Valley Rutherford Moffett Vineyard	936	$18.00	$25.00	1991-1996

LONG VINEYARDS

Score	Vintage	Appellation/Vineyard	Case Prod.	Release Price	Current Price	Drink
86	1986	Napa Valley Oakville	200	NR		1991-1998
92	1985	Napa Valley Oakville	200	$36.00	$36.00	1995-2005
88	1984	Napa Valley Oakville	200	$32.00	$35.00	1992-2000
78	1983	Napa Valley Oakville	200	$32.00	$40.00	1991-1995
91	1980	Napa Valley Oakville	200	$32.00	$50.00	1994-2002
90	1979	Napa Valley Oakville	200	$32.00	$50.00	1992-1999

LYETH WINERY

Score	Vintage	Appellation/Vineyard	Case Prod.	Release Price	Current Price	Drink
92	1985	Alexander Valley	13,500	$22.00	$22.00	1992-1999
90	1984	Alexander Valley	10,500	$18.00	$25.00	1992-1998
78	1983	Alexander Valley	8,000	$17.00	$25.00	1992-1995
85	1982	Alexander Valley	5,000	$16.00	$30.00	1990-1995
77	1981	Alexander Valley	1,200	$15.00	$35.00	1990-1993

MARKHAM VINEYARDS

Score	Vintage	Appellation/Vineyard	Case Prod.	Release Price	Current Price	Drink
91	1986	Napa Valley Yountville Markham Vineyard	3,850	NR		1995-2004

NA — not available.   NR — not released.   * — Beaulieu production figures are estimates.

Score	Vintage	Appellation/Vineyard	Case Prod.	Release Price	Current Price	Drink
93	1985	Napa Valley Yountville Markham Vineyard	3,810	NR		1994-2003
91	1984	Napa Valley Yountville Markham Vineyard	3,855	$12.00	$18.00	1993-2002
89	1983	Napa Valley Yountville Markham Vineyard	4,015	$13.00	$15.00	1995-2000
90	1982	Napa Valley Yountville Markham Vineyard	6,361	$13.00	$18.00	1994-2002
86	1981	Napa Valley Yountville Markham Vineyard	3,717	$13.00	$20.00	1992-1998
89	1980	Napa Valley Yountville Markham Vineyard	3,920	$13.00	$25.00	1992-1998
88	1979	Napa Valley Yountville Markham Vineyard	2,752	$13.00	$28.00	1993-2000
85	1978	Napa Valley Yountville Markham Vineyard	2,560	$13.00	$35.00	1992-2000

LOUIS M. MARTINI WINERY

Score	Vintage	Appellation/Vineyard	Case Prod.	Release Price	Current Price	Drink
86	1986	Sonoma Valley Monte Rosso	810	NR		1992-1999
80	1985	Sonoma Valley Monte Rosso	1,150	$22.00	$22.00	1992-2000
85	1984	North Coast Special Selection	2,735	NR		1991-1997
89	1984	Sonoma Valley Monte Rosso	700	$22.00	$22.00	1990-1999
86	1983	Sonoma Valley Monte Rosso	1,150	$22.00	$22.00	1993-1999
83	1983	Sonoma Valley Monte Rosso Los Ninos	545	$25.00	$25.00	1990-1997
85	1982	Sonoma Valley Monte Rosso	2,060	$22.00	$22.00	1993-1999
82	1982	Sonoma Valley Monte Rosso Los Ninos	550	$25.00	$25.00	1990-1995
85	1981	Sonoma Valley Monte Rosso Los Ninos	535	$25.00	$25.00	1990-1998
84	1980	North Coast Special Selection	9,350	$12.00	$12.00	1990-1997
84	1979	Sonoma Valley Monte Rosso Lot 2	2,490	$10.00	$19.00	1991-1996
86	1978	California Special Selection	21,388	$9.00	$23.00	1990-1996
70	1977	California Special Selection	5,464	$9.00	$20.00	1990
86	1976	California Special Selection	2,693	$9.00	$35.00	1990-1997
77	1974	California Special Selection	5,411	$10.00	$45.00	1990-1992
63	1972	California Special Selection	2,055	$5.00	$65.00	Avoid
88	1970	California Special Selection	7,845	$8.00	$90.00	1990-1995
90	1968	California Special Selection	1,926	$6.00	$95.00	1990-1994
87	1966	California Special Selection	2,023	$6.00	$110.00	1990-1992
85	1964	California Special Selection	1,582	$6.00	$100.00	1990-1992
73	1962	California Private Reserve	1,151	$3.50	$80.00	1990
80	1961	California Special Selection	1,092	$4.00	$180.00	1990-1994
87	1959	California Special Selection	1,500	$4.50	$140.00	1990-1992
88	1958	California Special Selection	1,750	$4.50	$220.00	1990-1992
91	1957	California Special Selection	1,994	$3.50	$175.00	1990-1992
77	1956	California Private Reserve	1,500	$2.50	$90.00	1990-1991
87	1955	California Special Selection	1,035	$2.50	$190.00	1990-1992
93	1952	California Special Selection	1,000	$2.50	$450.00	1990-1992
87	1951	California Special Selection	1,000	$2.00	$275.00	1990-1992
90	1947	California Special Selection	1,151	$1.50	$750.00	1990-1992
75	1945	California Special Selection	1,000	$1.50	$400.00	1990
70	1943	California Private Reserve Villa del Rey	1,000	$1.50	$400.00	1990
90	1939	California Special Reserve	1,000	$1.25	$1000.00	1990-1992

MAYACAMAS VINEYARDS

Score	Vintage	Appellation/Vineyard	Case Prod.	Release Price	Current Price	Drink
86	1986	Napa Valley Mount Veeder	2,150	NR		1991-1996
92	1985	Napa Valley Mount Veeder	2,025	NR		1997-2007
90	1984	Napa Valley Mount Veeder	1,220	$20.00	$20.00	1994-2000
90	1983	Napa Valley Mount Veeder	2,280	$20.00	$25.00	1997-2005
77	1982	Napa Valley Mount Veeder	2,700	$20.00	$25.00	1993-1998
91	1981	Napa Valley Mount Veeder	1,830	$18.00	$25.00	1993-1999
92	1980	Napa Valley Mount Veeder	1,870	$18.00	$30.00	1994-2002
95	1979	Napa Valley Mount Veeder	1,905	$18.00	$35.00	1995-2005
94	1978	Napa Valley Mount Veeder	1,820	$18.00	$60.00	1994-2004
92	1977	Napa Valley Mount Veeder	1,510	$15.00	$60.00	1992-2000
84	1976	Napa Valley Mount Veeder	1,380	$15.00	$50.00	1992-1998
89	1975	Napa Valley Mount Veeder	2,315	$12.00	$60.00	1990-1995
95	1974	Napa Valley Mount Veeder	2,300	$9.50	$115.00	1992-2004
87	1973	Napa Valley Mount Veeder	2,050	$9.00	$90.00	1990-1996
82	1972	Napa Valley Mount Veeder	1,620	$8.00	$70.00	1990-1993
86	1971	Napa Valley Mount Veeder	1,490	$8.00	$80.00	1990-1995
96	1970	Napa Valley Mount Veeder	1,325	$8.00	$130.00	1996-2008

NA — not available.   NR — not released.   * — Beaulieu production figures are estimates.

Score	Vintage	Appellation/Vineyard	Case Prod.	Release Price	Current Price	Drink
89	1969	California	1,080	$6.50	$100.00	1990-1995
88	1968	California	680	$4.50	$125.00	1990-1995
65	1967	California	800	$4.00	$125.00	Avoid
75	1966	California	530	$3.50	$125.00	1990-1993
65	1965	California	475	$2.75	$150.00	Avoid
69	1963	California	420	$2.00	$150.00	Avoid
68	1962	California	350	$2.00	$150.00	Avoid

MERRYVALE VINEYARDS

Score	Vintage	Appellation/Vineyard	Case Prod.	Release Price	Current Price	Drink
89	1986	Napa Valley Red Table Wine	1,604	$25.00	$25.00	1994-2002
91	1985	Napa Valley Red Table Wine	1,662	$24.00	$24.00	1994-2001
86	1984	Napa Valley Red Table Wine	1,026	$24.00	$28.00	1993-1998
88	1983	Napa Valley Red Table Wine	694	$18.00	$30.00	1993-1999

ROBERT MONDAVI WINERY

Score	Vintage	Appellation/Vineyard	Case Prod.	Release Price	Current Price	Drink
95	1986	Napa Valley Oakville Reserve	14,000	$35.00	$35.00	1993-2000
95	1985	Napa Valley Oakville Reserve	15,000	$40.00	$40.00	1993-2002
92	1984	Napa Valley Oakville Reserve	9,000	$37.00	$37.00	1992-2000
83	1983	Napa Valley Oakville Reserve	15,000	$30.00	$35.00	1991-1999
82	1982	Napa Valley Oakville Reserve	14,000	$30.00	$38.00	1992-1998
83	1981	Napa Valley Oakville Reserve	12,000	$30.00	$30.00	1990-1995
79	1980	Napa Valley Oakville Reserve	13,000	$30.00	$35.00	1992-1998
92	1979	Napa Valley Oakville Reserve	11,500	$25.00	$45.00	1991-2000
92	1978	Napa Valley Oakville Reserve	11,000	$40.00	$58.00	1990-1998
84	1977	Napa Valley Oakville Reserve	9,500	$35.00	$40.00	1990-1993
84	1976	Napa Valley Oakville Reserve	8,500	$25.00	$40.00	1990-1994
86	1975	Napa Valley Oakville Reserve	7,000	$30.00	$75.00	1990-1992
92	1974	Napa Valley Oakville Reserve	9,000	$30.00	$95.00	1990-1996
82	1973	Napa Valley Oakville Reserve	4,500	$12.00	$80.00	1990-1994
75	1972	Napa Valley Oakville	NA	$6.00	$45.00	1990
93	1971	Napa Valley Oakville Reserve	4,000	$12.00	$130.00	1990-1996
89	1970	Napa Valley Oakville Unfined	4,000	$12.00	$120.00	1990-1996
86	1969	Napa Valley Oakville Unfined	3,000	$12.00	$155.00	1990-1995
83	1968	Napa Valley Oakville Unfined	2,000	$8.50	$135.00	1990-1994
84	1967	Napa Valley Oakville	NA	$5.00	$100.00	1990
80	1966	Napa Valley Oakville	1,500	$5.00	$165.00	1990

MONTICELLO CELLARS

Score	Vintage	Appellation/Vineyard	Case Prod.	Release Price	Current Price	Drink
88	1986	Napa Valley Corley Reserve	3,800	$24.00	$24.00	1993-1999
88	1985	Napa Valley Corley Reserve	150	$22.50	$22.50	1994-1998
91	1984	Napa Valley Corley Reserve	4,000	$18.50	$20.00	1995-2004
88	1983	Napa Valley Corley Reserve	350	$24.00	$24.00	1995-2003
90	1982	Napa Valley Corley Reserve	1,200	$15.00	$30.00	1993-1999

MOUNT EDEN VINEYARDS

Score	Vintage	Appellation/Vineyard	Case Prod.	Release Price	Current Price	Drink
85	1986	Santa Cruz Mountains	786	NR		1994-2000
86	1985	Santa Cruz Mountains	622	$28.00	$28.00	1994-1998
84	1984	Santa Cruz Mountains	645	$22.00	$26.00	1993-1998
79	1983	Santa Cruz Mountains	458	$20.00	$20.00	1993-1997
70	1982	Santa Cruz Mountains	1,249	$18.00	$20.00	1990-1994
86	1981	Santa Cruz Mountains	652	$18.00	$25.00	1993-1999
85	1980	Santa Cruz Mountains	453	$30.00	$35.00	1992-1997
69	1979	Santa Cruz Mountains	641	$25.00	$30.00	Avoid
88	1978	Santa Cruz Mountains	650	$25.00	$45.00	1995-2003
91	1977	Santa Cruz Mountains	200	$20.00	$50.00	1995-2005
83	1976	Santa Cruz Mountains	175	$20.00	$50.00	1993-2000
90	1975	Santa Cruz Mountains	255	$20.00	$70.00	1994-2004
87	1974	Santa Cruz Mountains	437	$20.00	$120.00	1994-2002
91	1973	Santa Cruz Mountains	391	$14.00	$140.00	1995-2005
84	1972	Santa Cruz Mountains	89	$20.00	$60.00	1990-1995

MOUNT VEEDER WINERY

Score	Vintage	Appellation/Vineyard	Case Prod.	Release Price	Current Price	Drink
87	1986	Napa Valley Mount Veeder Mt. Veeder Vineyards	2,600	NR		1992-2000
93	1986	Napa Valley Mount Veeder Proprietary Reserve	50	NR		1996-2006

NA — not available.   NR — not released.   * — Beaulieu production figures are estimates.

Score	Vintage	Appellation/Vineyard	Case Prod.	Release Price	Current Price	Drink
87	1985	Napa Valley Mount Veeder Mt. Veeder Vineyards	2,100	NR	$14.00	1997-2004
88	1984	Napa Valley Mount Veeder Mt. Veeder Vineyards	2,500	$14.00	$14.00	1995-2003
84	1983	Napa Valley Mount Veeder Mt. Veeder Vineyards	3,000	$14.00	$15.00	1995-2002
68	1982	Napa Valley Mount Veeder Mt. Veeder Vineyards	4,600	$12.50	$13.00	Avoid
77	1981	Napa Valley Mount Veeder Mt. Veeder Vineyards	2,700	$12.50	$20.00	1992-1997
87	1980	Napa Valley Mount Veeder Bernstein Vineyards	2,600	$13.50	$30.00	1992-2000
92	1979	Napa Valley Mount Veeder Bernstein Vineyards	2,800	$13.50	$35.00	1990-1997
89	1978	Napa Valley Mount Veeder Bernstein Vineyards	3,500	$12.75	$40.00	1992-2002
86	1978	Napa Valley Mount Veeder Sidehill Ranch	375	$13.50	$40.00	1990-2000
85	1977	Napa Valley Mount Veeder Bernstein Vineyards	1,350	$11.00	$50.00	1994-2002
88	1977	Napa Valley Rutherford Niebaum-Coppola	1,225	$9.75	$60.00	1996-2006
77	1976	Napa Valley Mount Veeder Bernstein Vineyards	775	$11.00	$45.00	1994-2000
83	1975	Napa Valley Mount Veeder Bernstein Vineyards	850	$11.00	$50.00	1995-2004
80	1974	Napa Valley Mount Veeder	650	$8.00	$50.00	1996-2004
90	1973	Napa Valley Mount Veeder	400	$8.00	$80.00	1993-2005

NEWTON VINEYARD

Score	Vintage	Appellation/Vineyard	Case Prod.	Release Price	Current Price	Drink
91	1986	Napa Valley Spring Mountain	5,530	$16.00	$16.00	1992-1999
89	1985	Napa Valley Spring Mountain	3,096	$15.25	$18.00	1992-1998
87	1984	Napa Valley Spring Mountain	3,192	$13.50	$19.00	1991-1996
92	1983	Napa Valley Spring Mountain	1,824	$12.50	$21.00	1992-1998
66	1982	Napa Valley Spring Mountain	3,096	$12.50	$21.00	Avoid
83	1981	Napa Valley Spring Mountain	2,820	$12.50	$21.00	1992-1997
55	1980	Napa Valley Spring Mountain	NA	$12.00	NA	Avoid
85	1979	Napa Valley Spring Mountain	742	$12.00	$30.00	1990-1995

NIEBAUM-COPPOLA ESTATE

Score	Vintage	Appellation/Vineyard	Case Prod.	Release Price	Current Price	Drink
92	1986	Napa Valley Rutherford Rubicon	4,300	NR		1996-2004
91	1985	Napa Valley Rutherford Rubicon	4,762	NR		1995-2003
85	1984	Napa Valley Rutherford Rubicon	3,653	NR		1994-1998
89	1982	Napa Valley Rutherford Rubicon	6,002	$40.00	$40.00	1992-2000
87	1981	Napa Valley Rutherford Rubicon	3,661	$35.00	$35.00	1993-2000
87	1980	Napa Valley Rutherford Rubicon	3,850	$30.00	$35.00	1992-2002
75	1979	Napa Valley Rutherford Rubicon	3,100	$25.00	$40.00	1990-1994
88	1978	Napa Valley Rutherford Rubicon	1,700	$25.00	$45.00	1990-2000

OPUS ONE

Score	Vintage	Appellation/Vineyard	Case Prod.	Release Price	Current Price	Drink
95	1986	Napa Valley Oakville	11,200	NR		1995-2005
95	1985	Napa Valley Oakville	11,300	$55.00	$55.00	1995-2005
94	1984	Napa Valley Oakville	9,000	$50.00	$55.00	1995-2005
89	1983	Napa Valley Oakville	8,000	$50.00	$55.00	1992-1997
90	1982	Napa Valley Oakville	6,000	$50.00	$80.00	1993-2000
88	1981	Napa Valley Oakville	6,000	$50.00	$90.00	1994-2003
93	1980	Napa Valley Oakville	4,000	$50.00	$130.00	1992-2002
90	1979	Napa Valley Oakville	2,000	$50.00	$190.00	1992-1998

ROBERT PECOTA WINERY

Score	Vintage	Appellation/Vineyard	Case Prod.	Release Price	Current Price	Drink
88	1986	Napa Valley Calistoga Kara's Vineyard	1,230	$16.00	$16.00	1993-2000
86	1985	Napa Valley Calistoga Kara's Vineyard	940	$16.00	$20.00	1992-1998
85	1984	Napa Valley Calistoga Kara's Vineyard	540	$14.00	$20.00	1990-1996
85	1982	Napa Valley	900	$12.00	$20.00	1990-1995

ROBERT PEPI WINERY

Score	Vintage	Appellation/Vineyard	Case Prod.	Release Price	Current Price	Drink
90	1985	Napa Valley Yountville Vine Hill Ranch	2,720	NR		1996-2002
87	1984	Napa Valley Yountville Vine Hill Ranch	2,550	$16.00	$16.00	1994-2002
80	1983	Napa Valley Yountville Vine Hill Ranch	2,700	$16.00	$16.00	1993-1998
88	1982	Napa Valley Yountville Vine Hill Ranch	2,175	$14.00	$17.00	1994-2002
86	1981	Napa Valley Yountville Vine Hill Ranch	2,000	$14.00	$18.00	1992-2000

JOSEPH PHELPS VINEYARDS

Score	Vintage	Appellation/Vineyard	Case Prod.	Release Price	Current Price	Drink
95	1986	Napa Valley Calistoga Eisele Vineyard	1,500	NR		1998-2008
94	1985	Napa Valley Calistoga Eisele Vineyard	1,500	$40.00	$40.00	1995-2005
87	1984	Napa Valley Calistoga Eisele Vineyard	1,300	$35.00	$39.00	1995-2000
86	1983	Napa Valley Calistoga Eisele Vineyard	1,250	$25.00	$35.00	1997-2002

NA — not available.   NR — not released.   * — Beaulieu production figures are estimates.

Score	Vintage	Appellation/Vineyard	Case Prod.	Release Price	Current Price	Drink
85	1982	Napa Valley Calistoga Eisele Vineyard	1,775	$30.00	$33.00	1994-2000
89	1981	Napa Valley Calistoga Eisele Vineyard	1,050	$30.00	$39.00	1994-2000
92	1979	Napa Valley Calistoga Eisele Vineyard	1,000	$30.00	$50.00	1993-2000
97	1978	Napa Valley Calistoga Eisele Vineyard	755	$30.00	$75.00	1995-2010
82	1977	Napa Valley Calistoga Eisele Vineyard	1,160	$25.00	$55.00	1991-1998
97	1975	Napa Valley Calistoga Eisele Vineyard	720	$15.00	$115.00	1992-2005
96	1986	Napa Valley Insignia	4,000	NR		1996-2004
96	1985	Napa Valley Insignia	4,700	$40.00	$40.00	1995-2005
89	1984	Napa Valley Insignia	3,860	$30.00	$35.00	1995-2004
89	1983	Napa Valley Insignia	3,480	$25.00	$35.00	1994-2000
85	1982	Napa Valley Insignia	2,950	$25.00	$32.00	1992-1998
92	1981	Napa Valley Insignia	1,480	$25.00	$39.00	1993-2000
90	1980	Napa Valley Insignia	2,585	$25.00	$50.00	1993-1998
90	1979	Napa Valley Insignia	960	$25.00	$55.00	1990-1997
87	1978	Napa Valley Insignia	1,175	$25.00	$65.00	1990-1997
91	1977	Napa Valley Insignia	1,900	$25.00	$75.00	1990-1996
93	1976	Napa Valley Insignia (Eisele Vineyard)	785	$20.00	$90.00	1994-2004
85	1975	Napa Valley Insignia	473	$15.00	$90.00	1990-1995
90	1974	Napa Valley Insignia	670	$12.00	$130.00	1990-1998
93	1986	Napa Valley Oakville Backus Vineyard	1,400	NR		1998-2005
90	1985	Napa Valley Oakville Backus Vineyard	1,980	$27.50	$32.00	1996-2002
86	1984	Napa Valley Oakville Backus Vineyard	1,585	$20.00	$29.00	1992-1997
85	1983	Napa Valley Oakville Backus Vineyard	800	$16.50	$28.00	1994-1998
91	1981	Napa Valley Oakville Backus Vineyard	775	$15.00	$44.00	1992-2000
89	1978	Napa Valley Oakville Backus Vineyard	1,100	$16.50	$55.00	1991-1997
86	1977	Napa Valley Oakville Backus Vineyard	530	$15.00	$60.00	1990-1995

PINE RIDGE WINERY

Score	Vintage	Appellation/Vineyard	Case Prod.	Release Price	Current Price	Drink
92	1986	Napa Valley Rutherford Andrus Reserve	749	$40.00	$40.00	1995-2002
92	1985	Napa Valley Rutherford Andrus Reserve Cuveé Duet	1,136	$40.00	$45.00	1994-2002
93	1984	Napa Valley Rutherford Andrus Reserve	280	$37.00	$40.00	1993-2010
88	1983	Napa Valley Rutherford Andrus Reserve	169	$35.00	$45.00	1993-2000
96	1980	Napa Valley Rutherford Andrus Reserve	140	$30.00	$60.00	1996-2010
91	1986	Napa Valley Stags Leap District Pine Ridge Stags Leap Vineyard	1,775	NR		1995-2005
94	1985	Napa Valley Stags Leap District Pine Ridge Stags Leap Vineyard	1,756	$26.00	$26.00	1994-2010
93	1984	Napa Valley Stags Leap District Pine Ridge Stags Leap Vineyard	1,652	$25.00	$35.00	1995-2008
85	1983	Napa Valley Stags Leap District Pine Ridge Stags Leap Vineyard	1,452	$20.00	$26.00	1994-2000
90	1982	Napa Valley Stags Leap District Pine Ridge Stags Leap Vineyard	1,116	$20.00	$34.00	1996-2004
92	1981	Napa Valley Stags Leap District Pine Ridge Stags Leap Vineyard	1,553	$20.00	$50.00	1995-2005
91	1986	Napa Valley Diamond Mountain Diamond Mountain Vineyard	450	$30.00	$30.00	1995-2004
90	1986	Napa Valley Rutherford Rutherford Cuveé	7,437	$16.00	$16.00	1995-2003
93	1985	Napa Valley Rutherford Rutherford Cuveé	8,668	$16.00	$16.00	1994-2004
90	1984	Napa Valley Rutherford Rutherford Cuveé	7,128	$14.00	$16.00	1992-2000
84	1983	Napa Valley Rutherford Rutherford Cuveé	4,890	$14.00	$22.00	1993-1998
90	1982	Napa Valley Rutherford Rutherford Cuveé	3,558	$13.00	$24.00	1995-2005
88	1981	Napa Valley Rutherford Rutherford Cuveé	4,081	$13.00	$28.00	1994-2002
91	1980	Napa Valley Rutherford Rutherford District	2,938	$12.00	$37.00	1993-2000
85	1979	Napa Valley Rutherford Rutherford District	3,211	$9.00	$45.00	1990-1995
89	1978	Napa Valley Rutherford Rutherford District	3,950	$7.50	$50.00	1990-1995

PRESTON VINEYARDS

Score	Vintage	Appellation/Vineyard	Case Prod.	Release Price	Current Price	Drink
88	1986	Dry Creek Valley	4,075	$11.00	$11.00	1993-1999
89	1985	Dry Creek Valley	3,100	$11.00	$11.00	1993-1999
87	1984	Dry Creek Valley	2,850	$11.00	$14.00	1991-1996
86	1983	Dry Creek Valley	2,500	$11.00	$15.00	1993-1998
87	1982	Dry Creek Valley	1,700	$11.00	$18.00	1990-1996

RAVENSWOOD

Score	Vintage	Appellation/Vineyard	Case Prod.	Release Price	Current Price	Drink
89	1986	Sonoma Mountain Pickberry Vineyard	550	$25.00	$25.00	1994-1997
86	1986	Sonoma County	3,000	$12.00	$14.00	1995-2002
85	1985	Sonoma County	1,540	$12.00	$14.00	1995-2001
80	1984	Sonoma County	1,400	$12.00	$14.00	1992-1997
76	1983	Sonoma County	1,350	$9.50	$14.00	1991-1995

NA — not available.   NR — not released.   * — Beaulieu production figures are estimates.

Score	Vintage	Appellation/Vineyard	Case Prod.	Release Price	Current Price	Drink
84	1982	Sonoma County	1,500	$11.00	$18.00	1990-1995
79	1930	Sonoma County	640	$10.50	$16.00	1990-1997
59	1979	California	875	$8.00	$10.00	Avoid
81	1978	California	536	$10.50	$20.00	1991-1998
83	1978	Sonoma Valley Olive Hill	530	$11.25	$28.00	1990-1998
82	1977	El Dorado County Madrona Vineyards	800	$8.50	$22.00	1990-1995

RAYMOND VINEYARD AND CELLAR

Score	Vintage	Appellation/Vineyard	Case Prod.	Release Price	Current Price	Drink
86	1986	Napa Valley Rutherford Private Reserve	3,000	NR		1993-1999
88	1985	Napa Valley Rutherford Private Reserve	4,000	NR		1992-1998
89	1984	Napa Valley Rutherford Private Reserve	2,800	$20.00	$20.00	1992-1999
84	1983	Napa Valley Rutherford Private Reserve	2,200	$18.00	$25.00	1993-2000
85	1982	Napa Valley Rutherford Private Reserve	1,800	$16.00	$27.00	1990-1996
85	1981	Napa Valley Rutherford	10,000	$11.00	$16.50	1990-1993
87	1981	Napa Valley Rutherford Private Reserve	1,200	$16.00	$35.00	1990-1995
82	1980	Napa Valley Rutherford	10,000	$12.00	$17.00	1990-1993
85	1980	Napa Valley Rutherford Private Reserve	1,200	$0.00	$34.00	1990-1996
85	1979	Napa Valley Rutherford	9,300	$12.00	$20.00	1990-1992
82	1978	Napa Valley Rutherford	5,300	$10.00	$21.00	1990-1993
84	1977	Napa Valley Rutherford	4,300	$8.50	$27.00	1990-1992
78	1976	Napa Valley Rutherford	3,000	$6.00	$27.00	1990
78	1974	Napa Valley Rutherford	800	$5.50	$40.00	1990

RIDGE VINEYARDS

Score	Vintage	Appellation/Vineyard	Case Prod.	Release Price	Current Price	Drink
85	1986	Santa Cruz Mountains Monte Bello	2,079	$35.00	$35.00	1994-1999
95	1985	Santa Cruz Mountains Monte Bello	2,220	$40.00	$50.00	1995-2005
97	1984	Santa Cruz Mountains Monte Bello	3,125	$35.00	$60.00	1995-2005
84	1983	Santa Cruz Mountains Monte Bello	2,677	$12.00	$15.00	1994-2000
75	1982	Santa Cruz Mountains Monte Bello	4,350	$18.00	$25.00	1992-1998
92	1981	Santa Cruz Mountains Monte Bello	2,648	$25.00	$45.00	1996-2004
80	1980	Santa Cruz Mountains Monte Bello	4,125	$30.00	$36.00	1995-2005
91	1978	Santa Cruz Mountains Monte Bello	1,820	$30.00	$60.00	1993-2003
94	1977	Santa Cruz Mountains Monte Bello	840	$40.00	$80.00	1995-2005
83	1976	Santa Cruz Mountains Monte Bello	1,577	$15.00	$65.00	1990-1998
88	1975	Santa Cruz Mountains Monte Bello	1,850	$10.00	$85.00	1990-1999
93	1974	Santa Cruz Mountains Monte Bello	1,260	$12.00	$140.00	1990-1998
87	1973	Santa Cruz Mountains Monte Bello	1,094	$10.00	$110.00	1990-1994
84	1972	Santa Cruz Mountains Monte Bello	740	$10.00	$100.00	1990-1992
85	1971	Santa Cruz Mountains Monte Bello	630	$10.00	$145.00	1990-1993
96	1970	Santa Cruz Mountains Monte Bello	540	$10.00	$190.00	1994-2005
92	1969	Santa Cruz Mountains Monte Bello	300	$7.50	$200.00	1990-2000
87	1968	Santa Cruz Mountains Monte Bello	200	$7.50	$190.00	1990-1997
86	1965	Santa Cruz Mountains Monte Bello	90	$6.50	$275.00	1990-1993
90	1964	Santa Cruz Mountains Monte Bello	70	$6.50	$310.00	1990-1995
70	1963	Santa Cruz Mountains Monte Bello	100	$5.00	$130.00	1990
88	1986	Napa Valley Spring Mountain York Creek	5,333	NR		1993-2000
92	1985	Napa Valley Spring Mountain York Creek	4,087	$16.00	$16.00	1990-2000
88	1984	Napa Valley Spring Mountain York Creek	6,900	$14.00	$16.00	1990-1998
73	1983	Napa Valley Spring Mountain York Creek	6,390	$12.00	$15.00	1992-1996
73	1982	Napa Valley Spring Mountain York Creek	6,909	$12.00	$15.00	1994-2000
76	1981	Napa Valley Spring Mountain York Creek	4,925	$12.00	$20.00	1994-2000
88	1980	Napa Valley Spring Mountain York Creek	3,516	$12.00	$22.00	1992-1999
88	1979	Napa Valley Spring Mountain York Creek	3,100	$12.00	$30.00	1990-1998
87	1978	Napa Valley Spring Mountain York Creek	5,983	$12.00	$35.00	1990-1998
88	1977	Napa Valley Spring Mountain York Creek	1,780	$12.00	$35.00	1990-1996
68	1976	Napa Valley Spring Mountain York Creek	1,150	$10.00	$30.00	Avoid
87	1975	Napa Valley Spring Mountain York Creek	800	$10.00	$45.00	1992-2000
87	1974	Napa Valley Spring Mountain York Creek	536	$6.75	$50.00	1990-1997

ROMBAUER VINEYARDS

Score	Vintage	Appellation/Vineyard	Case Prod.	Release Price	Current Price	Drink
86	1986	Napa Valley	3,000	$15.00	$15.00	1992-1997
89	1986	Napa Valley Le Meilleur Du Chai	500	NR		1994-2002
85	1985	Napa Valley	2,000	$14.75	$17.00	1991-1997

NA — not available.   NR — not released.   * — Beaulieu production figures are estimates.

Score	Vintage	Appellation/Vineyard	Case Prod.	Release Price	Current Price	Drink
90	1985	Napa Valley Le Meilleur Du Chai	425	$37.50	$37.50	1993-2002
84	1984	Napa Valley	1,500	$13.50	$21.00	1991-1995
90	1984	Napa Valley Le Meilleur Du Chai	450	$32.50	$35.00	1992-2000
73	1983	Napa Valley	1,500	$13.50	$19.00	1990-1994
90	1983	Napa Valley Le Meilleur Du Chai	415	$30.00	$40.00	1993-2001
83	1982	Napa Valley	1,000	$12.00	$23.00	1990-1994
82	1981	Napa Valley	1,000	$12.00	$24.00	1993-1998
86	1980	Napa Valley	500	$10.00	$25.00	1993-2000

RUTHERFORD HILL WINERY

Score	Vintage	Appellation/Vineyard	Case Prod.	Release Price	Current Price	Drink
88	1986	Napa Valley XVS	2,000	NR		1994-2000
89	1985	Napa Valley XVS	2,000	$25.00	$25.00	1995-2001
88	1984	Napa Valley	14,834	$12.50	$15.00	1994-2000
83	1983	Napa Valley	16,439	$12.50	$16.00	1990-1995
83	1982	Napa Valley	17,878	$12.50	$17.00	1990-1994
85	1981	Napa Valley	9,851	$11.50	$18.00	1990-1995
82	1980	Napa Valley	9,574	$11.50	$19.00	1990-1994
88	1980	Napa Valley Cask Lot 2 Limited Edition	2,000	$15.00	$20.00	1990-1996
87	1979	Napa Valley	9,971	$11.50	$22.00	1990-1995
82	1978	Napa Valley	16,471	$12.00	$22.00	1990-1993
72	1977	Napa Valley	11,337	$10.00	$18.00	1990
73	1976	Napa Valley	5,505	$9.00	$17.00	1990
69	1975	Napa Valley	4,984	$9.00	$18.00	Avoid

SANTA CRUZ MOUNTAIN VINEYARD

Score	Vintage	Appellation/Vineyard	Case Prod.	Release Price	Current Price	Drink
93	1986	Santa Cruz Mountains Bates Ranch	1,200	NR		1996-2006
92	1985	Santa Cruz Mountains Bates Ranch	1,125	NR		1995-2005
87	1984	Santa Cruz Mountains Bates Ranch	1,100	NR		1992-1998
84	1983	Santa Cruz Mountains Bates Ranch	1,800	$12.00	$12.00	1996-2004
72	1982	Santa Cruz Mountains Bates Ranch	1,800	$12.00	$14.00	1994-1998
79	1981	Santa Cruz Mountains Bates Ranch	1,600	$12.00	$20.00	1994-1994
86	1980	Santa Cruz Mountains Bates Ranch	840	$12.00	$18.00	1990-1997
79	1979	Santa Cruz Mountains Bates Ranch	1,225	$12.00	$35.00	1993-2000
90	1978	Santa Cruz Mountains Bates Ranch	750	$12.00	$35.00	1990-1998

V. SATTUI WINERY

Score	Vintage	Appellation/Vineyard	Case Prod.	Release Price	Current Price	Drink
88	1986	Napa Valley Rutherford Preston Vineyard	2,487	$16.75	$16.75	1991-1998
87	1985	Napa Valley Rutherford Preston Vineyard	3,143	$15.75	$15.75	1990-1996
86	1984	Napa Valley Rutherford Preston Vineyard	2,850	$13.75	$19.75	1990-1996
81	1983	Napa Valley Rutherford Preston Vineyard	1,613	$13.75	$19.75	1990-1995
78	1982	Napa Valley Rutherford Preston Vineyard Reserve	385	$22.50	$30.00	1990-1994
85	1980	Napa Valley Rutherford Preston Vineyard Reserve	372	$30.00	$45.00	1990-1995

SEQUOIA GROVE VINEYARDS

Score	Vintage	Appellation/Vineyard	Case Prod.	Release Price	Current Price	Drink
88	1986	Napa County	6,776	$16.00	$16.00	1993-1998
90	1986	Napa Valley Rutherford Estate	1,986	$22.00	$22.00	1994-2000
86	1985	Napa County	4,101	$16.00	$16.00	1992-1997
92	1985	Napa Valley Rutherford Estate	2,064	$28.00	$32.00	1992-2005
85	1984	Napa Valley	4,502	$12.00	$18.00	1992-2002
77	1983	Napa-Alexander Valleys	2,144	$12.50	$18.00	1991-1994
82	1982	Napa Valley Rutherford Estate	406	$14.00	$22.00	1995-2003
78	1982	Napa-Alexander Valleys	2,068	$12.00	$20.00	1990-1998
84	1981	Alexander Valley	854	$12.00	$35.00	1993-1999
80	1981	Napa Valley	1,169	$12.00	$25.00	1994-1999
85	1980	Napa Valley Cask One	444	$12.00	$30.00	1992-2000
87	1980	Napa Valley Cask Two	440	$12.00	$45.00	1992-1999

SHAFER VINEYARDS

Score	Vintage	Appellation/Vineyard	Case Prod.	Release Price	Current Price	Drink
92	1986	Napa Valley Stags Leap District Hillside Select	2,000	NR		1994-2002
93	1985	Napa Valley Stags Leap District Hillside Select	2,000	NR		1993-2000
92	1984	Napa Valley Stags Leap District Hillside Select	1,800	$24.50	$24.50	1992-2000
89	1983	Napa Valley Stags Leap District Hillside Select	900	$22.00	$22.00	1992-1999
89	1982	Napa Valley Stags Leap District Reserve	1,200	$18.00	$25.00	1992-1998
93	1986	Napa Valley Stags Leap District	5,000	$16.00	$16.00	1994-2002

NA — not available.   NR — not released.   * — Beaulieu production figures are estimates.

Score	Vintage	Appellation/Vineyard	Case Prod.	Release Price	Current Price	Drink
91	1985	Napa Valley Stags Leap District	5,000	$15.50	$15.50	1992-1998
91	1984	Napa Valley Stags Leap District	4,000	$14.00	$16.00	1990-1998
87	1983	Napa Valley Stags Leap District	3,700	$13.00	$13.00	1992-1997
88	1982	Napa Valley Stags Leap District	3,500	$13.00	$18.00	1992-2000
77	1980	Napa Valley Stags Leap District	2,000	$12.00	$25.00	1990-1992
89	1979	Napa Valley Stags Leap District	1,000	$12.00	$35.00	1992-2000
85	1978	Napa Valley Stags Leap District	1,000	$11.00	$50.00	1992-2000

SILVER OAK CELLARS

Score	Vintage	Appellation/Vineyard	Case Prod.	Release Price	Current Price	Drink
93	1985	Alexander Valley	19,900	$24.00	$24.00	1995-2005
89	1984	Alexander Valley	14,000	$22.00	$28.00	1992-1999
86	1983	Alexander Valley	14,000	$20.00	$30.00	1995-2002
90	1982	Alexander Valley	12,500	$19.00	$40.00	1994-2002
86	1981	Alexander Valley	11,200	$19.00	$35.00	1994-2000
88	1980	Alexander Valley	12,000	$18.00	$45.00	1990-2000
85	1979	Alexander Valley	12,500	$16.00	$65.00	1992-1999
93	1978	Alexander Valley	8,500	$16.00	$100.00	1992-2002
88	1977	Alexander Valley	7,350	$14.00	$85.00	1990-1997
86	1976	Alexander Valley	6,600	$12.00	$70.00	1992-2002
88	1975	Alexander Valley	6,000	$10.00	$95.00	1990-1996
93	1974	North Coast	4,000	$8.00	$135.00	1990-2000
81	1973	North Coast	1,800	$7.00	$130.00	1990-1994
86	1972	North Coast	1,100	$6.00	$160.00	1990-1995
85	1985	Napa Valley Calistoga	3,550	$24.00	$24.00	1996-2006
86	1984	Napa Valley Calistoga	2,500	$22.00	$28.00	1996-2004
74	1983	Napa Valley Calistoga	3,000	$20.00	$30.00	1993-1996
88	1982	Napa Valley Calistoga	3,500	$19.00	$32.00	1995-2005
79	1981	Napa Valley Calistoga	4,100	$19.00	$40.00	1994-2000
73	1980	Napa Valley Calistoga	4,000	$18.00	$45.00	1992-1997
82	1979	Napa Valley Calistoga	4,400	$18.00	$55.00	1995-2005
85	1985	Napa Valley Oakville Bonny's Vineyard	970	NR		1995-2004
84	1984	Napa Valley Oakville Bonny's Vineyard	950	$45.00	$45.00	1994-2000
82	1983	Napa Valley Oakville Bonny's Vineyard	1,250	$40.00	$40.00	1990-1993
78	1982	Napa Valley Oakville Bonny's Vineyard	900	$35.00	$42.00	1994-2002
77	1981	Napa Valley Oakville Bonny's Vineyard	970	$35.00	$50.00	1994-2000
70	1980	Napa Valley Oakville Bonny's Vineyard	1,000	$30.00	$50.00	1993-1998
72	1979	Napa Valley Oakville Bonny's Vineyard	1,200	$30.00	$55.00	1992-1998

SILVERADO VINEYARDS

Score	Vintage	Appellation/Vineyard	Case Prod.	Release Price	Current Price	Drink
94	1986	Napa Valley Stags Leap District	9,800	$13.50	$13.50	1995-2005
92	1985	Napa Valley Stags Leap District	11,000	$12.50	$16.00	1995-2002
91	1984	Napa Valley Stags Leap District	7,800	$11.50	$20.00	1996-2002
88	1983	Napa Valley Stags Leap District	8,000	$11.00	$20.00	1995-2000
88	1982	Napa Valley Stags Leap District	8,000	$11.00	$22.00	1993-2000
90	1981	Napa Valley Stags Leap District	3,500	$11.00	$25.00	1992-2000

SIMI WINERY

Score	Vintage	Appellation/Vineyard	Case Prod.	Release Price	Current Price	Drink
92	1986	Alexander Valley Reserve	1,700	NR		1993-2002
94	1985	Alexander Valley Reserve	2,300	NR		1994-2003
92	1984	Alexander Valley Reserve	800	$22.50	$22.50	1993-2000
88	1982	Sonoma-Napa Counties Reserve	3,400	$20.00	$20.00	1996-2004
84	1980	Alexander Valley Reserve	2,400	$20.00	$30.00	1994-2000
87	1979	Alexander Valley Reserve	1,700	$20.00	$36.00	1992-1999
72	1978	Alexander Valley Reserve	2,700	$17.00	$26.00	1990
70	1977	Alexander Valley Special Selection	1,700	$20.00	$23.00	1990
85	1975	Alexander Valley	11,000	$6.00	$32.00	1990
87	1974	Alexander Valley Reserve Vintage	14,000	$20.00	$45.00	1990-1996
83	1974	Alexander Valley Special Reserve	2,000	$25.00	$65.00	1990
72	1973	Alexander Valley	10,000	$6.00	$25.00	1990
80	1972	Alexander Valley	10,000	$5.00	$25.00	1990
75	1971	Alexander Valley	8,000	$5.00	$30.00	1990
73	1970	Alexander Valley	5,000	$4.50	$50.00	1990

NA — not available.   NR — not released.   ∗ — Beaulieu production figures are estimates.

Score	Vintage	Appellation/Vineyard	Case Prod.	Release Price	Current Price	Drink
SMITH-MADRONE VINEYARD						
90	1985	Napa Valley Spring Mountain	1,500	$14.00	$14.00	1994-2002
91	1984	Napa Valley Spring Mountain	1,100	$14.00	$14.00	1994-2004
84	1983	Napa Valley Spring Mountain	700	$12.50	$15.00	1995-2005
79	1982	Napa Valley Spring Mountain	800	$12.50	$15.00	1990-1993
78	1981	Napa Valley Spring Mountain	600	$12.50	$15.00	1990-1993
79	1980	Napa Valley Spring Mountain	600	$12.50	$18.00	1990
86	1979	Napa Valley Spring Mountain	350	$14.00	$25.00	1993-2000
84	1978	Napa Valley Spring Mountain	200	$14.00	$25.00	1990-1995
SPOTTSWOODE WINERY						
95	1986	Napa Valley St. Helena	2,400	$30.00	$30.00	1996-2006
95	1985	Napa Valley St. Helena	2,000	$25.00	$35.00	1995-2005
90	1984	Napa Valley St. Helena	1,450	$25.00	$45.00	1992-1998
89	1983	Napa Valley St. Helena	1,400	$25.00	$45.00	1995-2005
90	1982	Napa Valley St. Helena	1,200	$18.00	$60.00	1995-2003
SPRING MOUNTAIN VINEYARDS						
90	1986	Napa Valley	3,684	NR		1996-2004
88	1985	Napa Valley	3,396	$20.00	$20.00	1997-2005
89	1984	Napa Valley	2,363	$15.00	$22.00	1994-2000
79	1983	Napa Valley	4,221	$15.00	$18.00	1993-1998
66	1982	Napa Valley	5,739	$15.00	$15.00	Avoid
78	1981	Napa Valley	11,390	$14.00	$16.00	1992-1996
86	1980	Napa Valley	11,162	$13.00	$24.00	1990-1994
87	1979	Napa Valley	9,987	$13.00	$32.00	1992-1998
83	1978	Napa Valley	10,236	$12.00	$25.00	1990-1996
85	1977	Napa Valley	5,986	$9.50	$20.00	1990-1995
ST. CLEMENT VINEYARDS						
87	1986	Napa Valley	2,000	NR		1993-2001
93	1985	Napa Valley	2,665	$17.00	$17.00	1994-2002
89	1984	Napa Valley	2,300	$15.00	$15.00	1992-1998
91	1983	Napa Valley	2,256	$14.50	$18.00	1995-2005
91	1982	Napa Valley	3,024	$13.50	$20.00	1992-2000
85	1981	Napa Valley	2,565	$12.50	$24.00	1994-1999
82	1980	Napa Valley	650	$12.50	$24.00	1990-1994
90	1979	Napa Valley	1,500	$11.00	$35.00	1992-2001
88	1978	Napa Valley	400	$10.00	$40.00	1990-1997
90	1977	Napa Valley	650	$10.00	$45.00	1990-1999
87	1975-76	Napa Valley	650	$8.00	$50.00	1993-2000
STAG'S LEAP WINE CELLARS						
92	1986	Napa Valley Stags Leap District Cask 23	605	NR		1994-2003
98	1985	Napa Valley Stags Leap District Cask 23	1,018	$75.00	$75.00	1994-2005
93	1984	Napa Valley Stags Leap District Cask 23	800	$40.00	$40.00	1994-2000
88	1983	Napa Valley Stags Leap District Cask 23	1,077	$35.00	$55.00	1993-1999
88	1979	Napa Valley Stags Leap District Cask 23	1,204	$35.00	$55.00	1990-1992
92	1978	Napa Valley Stags Leap District Cask 23	1,000	$35.00	$90.00	1990-1995
91	1977	Napa Valley Stags Leap District Cask 23	1,000	$30.00	$75.00	1990-1993
88	1974	Napa Valley Stags Leap District Cask 23	100	$12.00	$135.00	1990-1993
89	1986	Napa Valley Stags Leap District SLV	6,248	$28.00	$28.00	1992-1999
94	1985	Napa Valley Stags Leap District SLV	8,810	$26.00	$26.00	1993-1999
92	1984	Napa Valley Stags Leap District SLV	6,000	$21.00	$30.00	1994-2000
73	1983	Napa Valley Stags Leap District Stag's Leap Vineyards	6,668	$18.00	$25.00	1990-1995
75	1982	Napa Valley Stags Leap District Stag's Leap Vineyards	9,865	$16.50	$25.00	1990-1993
91	1981	Napa Valley Stags Leap District Stag's Leap Vineyards	7,534	$15.00	$32.00	1992-1998
68	1979	Napa Valley Stags Leap District Stag's Leap Vineyards	6,000	$15.00	$32.00	Avoid
89	1978	Napa Valley Stags Leap District Stag's Leap Vineyards	3,000	$13.50	$45.00	1990-1995
85	1977	Napa Valley Stags Leap District Stag's Leap Vineyards	2,000	$9.00	$35.00	1990-1992
90	1977	Napa Valley Stags Leap District Lot 2	2,000	$10.00	$50.00	1990-1996
73	1976	Napa Valley Stags Leap District Stag's Leap Vineyards	2,000	$10.00	$40.00	1990
80	1976	Napa Valley Stags Leap District Lot 2	1,000	$11.00	$60.00	1990-1992

NA — not available.　　NR — not released.　　∗ — Beaulieu production figures are estimates.

Score	Vintage	Appellation/Vineyard	Case Prod.	Release Price	Current Price	Drink
74	1975	Napa Valley Stags Leap District Stag's Leap Vineyards	2,300	$8.50	$50.00	1990
87	1974	Napa Valley Stags Leap District Stag's Leap Vineyards	450	$8.00	$110.00	1990-1992
86	1973	Napa Valley Stags Leap District Stag's Leap Vineyards	400	$6.00	$135.00	1990
70	1972	Napa Valley Stags Leap District Stag's Leap Vineyards	100	$5.50	$80.00	1990

STAGS' LEAP WINERY

Score	Vintage	Appellation/Vineyard	Case Prod.	Release Price	Current Price	Drink
86	1986	Napa Valley Stags Leap District	7,860	NR		1992-1997
85	1985	Napa Valley Stags Leap District	7,672	$15.00	$16.00	1992-1997
87	1984	Napa Valley Stags Leap District	5,187	$13.50	$18.00	1992-1997
80	1983	Napa Valley Stags Leap District	3,425	$12.75	$20.00	1993-1997
71	1982	Napa Valley Stags Leap District	3,034	$12.00	$20.00	1992-1996
85	1981	Napa Valley Stags Leap District	2,712	$11.00	$25.00	1991-1997

STELTZNER VINEYARDS

Score	Vintage	Appellation/Vineyard	Case Prod.	Release Price	Current Price	Drink
90	1986	Napa Valley Stags Leap District	5,000	$16.00	$16.00	1993-2000
93	1985	Napa Valley Stags Leap District	5,000	$16.00	$19.00	1993-2000
91	1984	Napa Valley Stags Leap District	3,000	$15.00	$19.00	1992-2000
90	1983	Napa Valley Stags Leap District	3,000	$14.00	$18.00	1991-1996
90	1982	Napa Valley Stags Leap District	3,000	$14.00	$28.00	1990-1996
89	1981	Napa Valley Stags Leap District	1,500	$14.00	$38.00	1990-1996
88	1980	Napa Valley Stags Leap District	200	$14.00	$38.00	1991-1997
89	1979	Napa Valley Stags Leap District	1,000	$14.00	$42.00	1990-1995
87	1978	Napa Valley Stags Leap District	500	$14.00	$50.00	1990-1996
85	1977	Napa Valley Stags Leap District	500	$14.00	$45.00	1990-1995

STERLING VINEYARDS

Score	Vintage	Appellation/Vineyard	Case Prod.	Release Price	Current Price	Drink
94	1986	Napa Valley Reserve	3,432	NR		1996-2006
96	1985	Napa Valley Reserve	2,492	$30.00	$38.00	1996-2008
92	1984	Napa Valley Reserve	2,268	$25.00	$38.00	1994-2002
82	1983	Napa Valley Reserve	3,360	$22.50	$30.00	1995-2000
75	1982	Napa Valley Reserve	4,807	$22.50	$25.00	1992-1996
85	1981	Napa Valley Reserve	6,237	$22.50	$28.00	1994-1998
91	1980	Napa Valley Reserve	4,848	$27.50	$37.00	1992-1998
85	1979	Napa Valley Reserve	6,538	$27.50	$32.00	1990-1995
90	1978	Napa Valley Reserve	5,016	$27.50	$35.00	1992-1998
93	1977	Napa Valley Reserve	3,500	$27.50	$32.00	1992-2000
76	1976	Napa Valley Reserve	3,690	$25.00	$40.00	1994-1998
78	1975	Napa Valley Reserve	3,800	$20.00	$55.00	1994-2000
90	1974	Napa Valley Reserve	3,600	$20.00	$80.00	1992-2002
89	1973	Napa Valley Reserve	3,850	$10.00	$70.00	1992-1998
88	1986	Napa Valley Diamond Mountain Diamond Mountain Ranch	6,000	NR		1996-2003
90	1985	Napa Valley Diamond Mountain Diamond Mountain Ranch	5,700	$16.00	$16.00	1995-2003
85	1984	Napa Valley Diamond Mountain Diamond Mountain Ranch	5,500	$15.00	$18.00	1993-1997
87	1983	Napa Valley Diamond Mountain Diamond Mountain Ranch	4,100	$15.00	$18.00	1994-2002
88	1982	Napa Valley Diamond Mountain Diamond Mountain Ranch	3,100	$15.00	$20.00	1995-2003

STONEGATE WINERY

Score	Vintage	Appellation/Vineyard	Case Prod.	Release Price	Current Price	Drink
79	1986	Napa Valley Estate	3,000	NR		1990-1995
87	1985	Napa Valley Estate	4,403	$16.00	$16.00	1993-1998
88	1984	Napa Valley Estate	4,580	$14.00	$14.00	1993-1998
80	1982	Napa Valley	5,497	$12.00	$18.00	1991-1996
79	1981	Napa Valley	4,005	$12.00	$17.00	1992-1996
86	1980	Napa Valley	2,258	$12.00	$22.00	1991-1997
84	1979	Napa Valley	2,757	$12.00	$24.00	1993-1997
91	1978	Napa Valley	1,797	$12.00	$30.00	1991-2000
81	1977	Napa Valley	1,060	$10.00	$25.00	1993-1999

PHILIP TOGNI VINEYARD

Score	Vintage	Appellation/Vineyard	Case Prod.	Release Price	Current Price	Drink
93	1986	Napa Valley Spring Mountain	386	$22.00	$22.00	1993-2005
89	1985	Napa Valley Spring Mountain	125	$20.00	$25.00	1995-2004
86	1984	Napa Valley Spring Mountain	180	$18.00	$35.00	1994-2003
87	1983	Napa Valley Spring Mountain	90	$18.00	$50.00	1995-2005

NA — not available.   NR — not released.   ∗ — Beaulieu production figures are estimates.

Score	Vintage	Appellation/Vineyard	Case Prod.	Release Price	Current Price	Drink
TREFETHEN VINEYARDS						
90	1986	Napa Valley Yountville Reserve	1,000	NR		1995-2005
90	1985	Napa Valley Yountville Reserve	969	NR		1993-2000
87	1986	Napa Valley Yountville	10,400	$15.25	$15.25	1996-2002
80	1985	Napa Valley Yountville	9,501	NR		1992-1997
84	1984	Napa Valley Yountville	9,500	$14.00	$16.00	1991-1995
84	1983	Napa Valley Yountville	9,653	$11.75	$22.00	1994-2000
58	1982	Napa Valley Yountville	NA	$11.00	NA	Avoid
87	1981	Napa Valley Yountville	8,842	$11.00	$28.00	1990-1995
68	1980	Napa Valley Yountville	6,980	$11.00	$20.00	Avoid
86	1979	Napa Valley Yountville	6,192	$11.00	$35.00	1990-1996
81	1978	Napa Valley Yountville	3,764	$10.00	$45.00	1991-1995
86	1977	Napa Valley Yountville	3,687	$8.50	$45.00	1990-1995
76	1976	Napa Valley Yountville	2,098	$7.50	$45.00	1990-1996
83	1975	Napa Valley Yountville	783	$7.50	$55.00	1990-1994
84	1974	Napa Valley Yountville	835	$8.00	$65.00	1990-1997
TUDAL WINERY						
89	1986	Napa Valley St. Helena	1,800	$14.50	$14.50	1994-2002
89	1985	Napa Valley St. Helena	1,400	$14.50	$14.50	1993-1999
91	1984	Napa Valley St. Helena	1,000	$12.50	$15.00	1993-2001
86	1983	Napa Valley St. Helena	1,500	$12.50	$19.00	1992-1998
72	1982	Napa Valley St. Helena	2,100	$12.00	$25.00	1990-1993
88	1981	Napa Valley St. Helena	1,000	$12.00	$25.00	1991-1997
85	1980	Napa Valley St. Helena	1,250	$11.50	$25.00	1992-1996
90	1979	Napa Valley St. Helena	630	$10.75	$25.00	1992-2000
VICHON WINERY						
90	1986	Napa Valley Stags Leap District SLD	2,540	$21.00	$21.00	1991-1997
92	1985	Napa Valley Stags Leap District SLD	4,000	$18.00	$20.00	1992-2000
88	1985	Napa Valley	7,500	$13.00	$14.00	1992-1997
88	1984	Napa Valley	600	$11.25	$13.00	1992-1997
85	1984	Napa Valley Stags Leap District Fay Vineyard	1,935	$14.00	$18.00	1990-1994
80	1983	Napa Valley	10,000	$10.00	$14.00	1990-1995
76	1982	Napa Valley	5,400	$13.00	$15.00	1990-1993
78	1982	Napa Valley Volker Eisele	2,000	$16.00	$19.00	1990-1994
79	1982	Napa Valley Stags Leap District Fay Vineyard	2,500	$14.00	$23.00	1990-1995
80	1981	Napa Valley	4,600	$13.00	$20.00	1990-1994
83	1980	Napa Valley Volker Eisele Vineyard	800	$16.00	$25.00	1990-1995
85	1980	Napa Valley Stags Leap District Fay Vineyard	1,400	$16.00	$25.00	1990-1995
VILLA MT. EDEN WINERY						
84	1982	Napa Valley Oakville Reserve	1,254	$16.70	$16.70	1992-1997
85	1981	Napa Valley Oakville Reserve	1,144	$16.70	$20.00	1990-1996
70	1980	Napa Valley Oakville Reserve	1,143	$20.00	$20.00	1992-1996
75	1979	Napa Valley Oakville Reserve	500	$20.00	$30.00	1994-2000
88	1978	Napa Valley Oakville Reserve	761	$20.00	$42.00	1994-2004
84	1986	Napa Valley Oakville Estate	9,700	NR		1990-1996
82	1985	Napa Valley Oakville Estate	8,095	NR		1990-1994
80	1984	Napa Valley Oakville Estate	1,004	NR		1990-1994
72	1983	Napa Valley Oakville Estate	7,588	$10.00	$10.00	1990-1993
70	1982	Napa Valley Oakville Estate	8,143	$9.00	$9.00	1990-1993
62	1980	Napa Valley Oakville Estate	3,922	$11.70	$14.00	Avoid
78	1979	Napa Valley Oakville Estate	2,773	$12.00	$21.00	1990-1993
78	1978	Napa Valley Oakville Estate	2,421	$8.00	$25.00	1990-1994
86	1977	Napa Valley Oakville Estate	2,383	$8.00	$36.00	1991-2002
70	1976	Napa Valley Oakville Estate	860	$7.00	$38.00	1990-1994
89	1975	Napa Valley Oakville Estate	616	$7.00	$50.00	1990-2000
90	1974	Napa Valley Oakville Estate	219	$7.00	$60.00	1990-1997

NA — not available.   NR — not released.   * — Beaulieu production figures are estimates.

APPENDIX 2
All Wines Tasted, Listed by Score

Vintage	Winery	Appellation/Vineyard	Case Prod.	Release Price	Current Price	Drink
SCORE: 100						
1941	INGLENOOK-NAPA VALLEY	Napa Valley Rutherford	5,000	$1.49	$1400.00	1990-2005
SCORE: 99						
1985	CAYMUS VINEYARDS	Napa Valley Rutherford Special Selection	1,000	NR		1995-2005
1978	DIAMOND CREEK VINEYARD	Napa Valley Diamond Mountain Lake	25	$25.00	$250.00	1994-2002
1974	HEITZ WINE CELLARS	Napa Valley Oakville Martha's Vineyard	4,543	$25.00	$200.00	1994-2008
1968	HEITZ WINE CELLARS	Napa Valley Oakville Martha's Vineyard	749	$9.50	$375.00	1990-1995
SCORE: 98						
1986	CAYMUS VINEYARDS	Napa Valley Rutherford Special Selection	1,000	NR		1995-2005
1984	CAYMUS VINEYARDS	Napa Valley Rutherford Special Selection	1,000	$35.00	$50.00	1995-2008
1985	HEITZ WINE CELLARS	Napa Valley Oakville Martha's Vineyard	4,848	NR		1995-2010
1970	HEITZ WINE CELLARS	Napa Valley Oakville Martha's Vineyard	866	$12.75	$275.00	1993-2005
1985	STAG'S LEAP WINE CELLARS	Napa Valley Stags Leap District Cask 23	1,018	$75.00	$75.00	1994-2005
SCORE: 97						
1979	CAYMUS VINEYARDS	Napa Valley Rutherford Special Selection	600	$30.00	$85.00	1994-2006
1978	CAYMUS VINEYARDS	Napa Valley Rutherford Special Selection	600	$30.00	$90.00	1994-2005
1984	DUNN VINEYARDS	Napa Valley Howell Mountain	1,800	$25.00	$85.00	1996-2002
1984	HEITZ WINE CELLARS	Napa Valley Oakville Martha's Vineyard	4,421	$40.00	$40.00	1997-2007
1978	JOSEPH PHELPS VINEYARDS	Napa Valley Calistoga Eisele Vineyard	755	$30.00	$75.00	1995-2010
1975	JOSEPH PHELPS VINEYARDS	Napa Valley Calistoga Eisele Vineyard	720	$15.00	$115.00	1992-2005
1984	RIDGE VINEYARDS	Santa Cruz Mountains Monte Bello	3,125	$35.00	$60.00	1995-2005
SCORE :96						
1958	BEAULIEU VINEYARD	Napa Valley Rutherford Georges de Latour Private Reserve	15,000	$3.00	$400.00	1990-1994
1986	BERINGER VINEYARDS	Napa Valley Private Reserve	4,000	NR		1995-2003
1985	BERINGER VINEYARDS	Napa Valley Private Reserve	8,000	NR		1994-2004
1986	DIAMOND CREEK VINEYARD	Napa Valley Diamond Mountain Red Rock Terrace	970	$30.00	$30.00	1996-2010
1986	DIAMOND CREEK VINEYARD	Napa Valley Diamond Mountain Volcanic Hill	1,035	$30.00	$30.00	1996-2012
1984	DIAMOND CREEK VINEYARD	Napa Valley Diamond Mountain Red Rock Terrace	620	$25.00	$40.00	1994-2006
1985	HESS COLLECTION WINERY	Napa Valley Mount Veeder	5,000	$13.00	$13.00	1994-2002
1970	MAYACAMAS VINEYARDS	Napa Valley Mount Veeder	1,325	$8.00	$130.00	1996-2008
1986	JOSEPH PHELPS VINEYARDS	Napa Valley Insignia	4,000	NR		1996-2004
1985	JOSEPH PHELPS VINEYARDS	Napa Valley Insignia	4,700	$40.00	$40.00	1995-2005
1980	PINE RIDGE WINERY	Napa Valley Rutherford Andrus Reserve	140	$30.00	$60.00	1996-2010
1970	RIDGE VINEYARDS	Santa Cruz Mountains Monte Bello	540	$10.00	$190.00	1994-2005
1985	STERLING VINEYARDS	Napa Valley Reserve	2,492	$30.00	$38.00	1996-2008
SCORE: 95						
1985	BEAULIEU VINEYARD	Napa Valley Rutherford Georges de Latour Private Reserve	15,000	NR		1995-2003
1970	BEAULIEU VINEYARD	Napa Valley Rutherford Georges de Latour Private Reserve	15,000	$8.00	$130.00	1990-1995
1985	CHATEAU MONTELENA WINERY	Napa Valley Calistoga Estate	9,723	$25.00	$25.00	1996-2006
1979	DIAMOND CREEK VINEYARD	Napa Valley Diamond Mountain Volcanic Hill, First Pick	50	$15.00	$60.00	1994-2006
1978	DIAMOND CREEK VINEYARD	Napa Valley Diamond Mountain Volcanic Hill	503	$12.50	$75.00	1993-2006
1985	DOMINUS ESTATE	Napa Valley Yountville Napanook	4,000	$45.00	$45.00	1995-2005
1983	DUNN VINEYARDS	Napa Valley	1,500	$15.00	$60.00	1994-2004
1982	DUNN VINEYARDS	Napa Valley Howell Mountain	1,800	$15.00	$130.00	1992-2000
1985	GRACE FAMILY VINEYARD	Napa Valley St. Helena Estate	126	$50.00	$90.00	1993-2004
1986	WILLIAM HILL WINERY	Napa Valley Reserve	13,595	$24.50	$24.50	1996-2006

NA — not available.   NR — not released.   * — Beaulieu production figures are estimates.

Vintage	Winery	Appellation/Vineyard	Case Prod.	Release Price	Current Price	Drink
1978	WILLIAM HILL WINERY	Napa Valley Gold Label	4,451	$16.25	$60.00	1991-1997
1985	INGLENOOK-NAPA VALLEY	Napa Valley Rutherford Reserve Cask	10,388	NR		1994-2002
1933	INGLENOOK-NAPA VALLEY	Napa Valley Rutherford	5,000	$1.30	$1600.00	1990
1986	JOHNSON TURNBULL VINEYARDS	Napa Valley Oakville Vineyard Selection 82	1,540	$14.50	$14.50	1992-2000
1979	MAYACAMAS VINEYARDS	Napa Valley Mount Veeder	1,905	$18.00	$35.00	1995-2005
1974	MAYACAMAS VINEYARDS	Napa Valley Mount Veeder	2,300	$9.50	$115.00	1992-2004
1986	ROBERT MONDAVI WINERY	Napa Valley Oakville Reserve	14,000	$35.00	$35.00	1993-2000
1985	ROBERT MONDAVI WINERY	Napa Valley Oakville Reserve	15,000	$40.00	$40.00	1993-2002
1986	OPUS ONE	Napa Valley Oakville	11,200	NR		1995-2005
1985	OPUS ONE	Napa Valley Oakville	11,300	$55.00	$55.00	1995-2005
1986	JOSEPH PHELPS VINEYARDS	Napa Valley Calistoga Eisele Vineyard	1,500	NR		1998-2008
1985	RIDGE VINEYARDS	Santa-Cruz Mountains Monte Bello	2,220	$40.00	$50.00	1995-2005
1986	SPOTTSWOODE WINERY	Napa Valley St. Helena	2,400	$30.00	$30.00	1996-2006
1985	SPOTTSWOODE WINERY	Napa Valley St. Helena	2,000	$25.00	$35.00	1995-2005

SCORE: 94

Vintage	Winery	Appellation/Vineyard	Case Prod.	Release Price	Current Price	Drink
1984	BERINGER VINEYARDS	Napa Valley Private Reserve	8,000	$25.00	$31.00	1993-2001
1984	CHATEAU MONTELENA WINERY	Napa Valley Calistoga Estate	11,439	$20.00	$25.00	1998-2006
1977	CHATEAU MONTELENA WINERY	Napa Valley Calistoga	3,800	$12.00	$65.00	1995-2005
1985	CLOS DU VAL WINE CO.	Napa Valley Stags Leap District Reserve	750	NR		1995-2006
1978	CLOS DU VAL WINE CO.	Napa Valley Stags Leap District Reserve	2,400	$30.00	$55.00	1993-2010
1986	B.R. COHN	Sonoma Valley Olive Hill Vineyard	2,400	$18.00	$20.00	1993-2001
1985	B.R. COHN	Sonoma Valley Olive Hill Vineyard	2,000	$16.00	$22.00	1993-2000
1974	CONN CREEK WINERY	Napa Valley Calistoga	900	$9.00	$70.00	1990-1998
1986	DIAMOND CREEK VINEYARD	Napa Valley Diamond Mountain Gravelly Meadow	795	$30.00	$30.00	1997-2010
1984	DIAMOND CREEK VINEYARD	Napa Valley Diamond Mountain Gravelly Meadow	470	$25.00	$40.00	1994-2007
1984	DIAMOND CREEK VINEYARD	Napa Valley Diamond Mountain Volcanic Hill	1,224	$25.00	$40.00	1997-2007
1986	DUCKHORN VINEYARDS	Napa Valley	4,000	$18.00	$18.00	1995-2003
1986	DUNN VINEYARDS	Napa Valley Howell Mountain	2,000	$30.00	$30.00	1993-2000
1985	DUNN VINEYARDS	Napa Valley	2,000	$20.00	$45.00	1992-2000
1982	DUNN VINEYARDS	Napa Valley	1,250	$13.00	$85.00	1992-2000
1986	FROG'S LEAP WINERY	Napa Valley	2,600	$14.00	$14.00	1993-1999
1984	GRGICH HILLS CELLAR	Napa Valley Yountville	10,000	$17.00	$17.00	1993-2005
1984	GROTH VINEYARDS AND WINERY	Napa Valley Oakville Reserve	500	$25.00	$25.00	1992-2000
1985	WILLIAM HILL WINERY	Napa Valley Reserve	10,204	$22.50	$22.50	1995-2005
1985	INGLENOOK-NAPA VALLEY	Napa Valley Rutherford Reunion	3,602	$35.00	$35.00	1993-2000
1958	INGLENOOK-NAPA VALLEY	Napa Valley Rutherford Cask	2,500	$2.50	$300.00	1990
1986	ROBERT KEENAN WINERY	Napa Valley	3,395	$16.50	$16.50	1992-2000
1986	KENWOOD VINEYARDS	Sonoma Valley Artist Series	4,000	$30.00	$30.00	1993-2003
1978	MAYACAMAS VINEYARDS	Napa Valley Mount Veeder	1,820	$18.00	$60.00	1994-2004
1984	OPUS ONE	Napa Valley Oakville	9,000	$50.00	$55.00	1995-2005
1985	JOSEPH PHELPS VINEYARDS	Napa Valley Calistoga Eisele Vineyard	1,500	$40.00	$40.00	1995-2005
1985	PINE RIDGE WINERY	Napa Valley Stags Leap District Pine Ridge Stags Leap Vineyard	1,756	$26.00	$26.00	1994-2010
1977	RIDGE VINEYARDS	Santa Cruz Mountains Monte Bello	840	$40.00	$80.00	1995-2005
1986	SILVERADO VINEYARDS	Napa Valley Stags Leap District	9,800	$13.50	$13.50	1995-2005
1985	SIMI WINERY	Alexander Valley Reserve	2,300	NR		1994-2003
1985	STAG'S LEAP WINE CELLARS	Napa Valley Stags Leap District SLV	8,810	$26.00	$26.00	1993-1999
1986	STERLING VINEYARDS	Napa Valley Reserve	3,432	NR		1996-2006

SCORE: 93

Vintage	Winery	Appellation/Vineyard	Case Prod.	Release Price	Current Price	Drink
1986	BEAULIEU VINEYARD	Napa Valley Rutherford Georges de Latour Private Reserve	15,000	NR		1995-2005
1980	BEAULIEU VINEYARD	Napa Valley Rutherford Georges de Latour Private Reserve	15,000	$24.00	$35.00	1995-2005
1947	BEAULIEU VINEYARD	Napa Valley Rutherford Georges de Latour Private Reserve	15,000	$1.82	$1000.00	1990-1995
1986	BERINGER VINEYARDS	Napa Valley St. Helena Chabot Vineyard	1,000	NR		1994-2002
1985	BUEHLER VINEYARDS	Napa Valley	3,060	$14.00	$16.00	1995-2004

NA — not available.   NR — not released.   ∗ — Beaulieu production figures are estimates.

Vintage	Winery	Appellation/Vineyard	Case Prod.	Release Price	Current Price	Drink
1986	BUENA VISTA WINERY	Sonoma Valley Carneros Private Reserve	3,150	$18.00	$18.00	1995-2005
1985	BUENA VISTA WINERY	Sonoma Valley Carneros Private Reserve	2,900	$18.00	$18.00	1993-2000
1985	BURGESS CELLARS	Napa Valley Vintage Selection	6,600	$18.00	$18.00	1992-2002
1984	BURGESS CELLARS	Napa Valley Vintage Selection	7,200	$17.00	$19.00	1996-2006
1978	BURGESS CELLARS	Napa Valley Vintage Selection	2,800	$14.00	$34.00	1992-2000
1986	CARMENET VINEYARD	Sonoma Valley	9,469	$20.00	$20.00	1994-2005
1981	CAYMUS VINEYARDS	Napa Valley Rutherford Special Selection	1,250	$35.00	$60.00	1995-2006
1973	CAYMUS VINEYARDS	Napa Valley Rutherford Estate	850	$6.00	$120.00	1990-2000
1970	CHAPPELLET VINEYARD	Napa Valley	700	$7.50	$160.00	1990-1995
1986	CHATEAU MONTELENA WINERY	Napa Valley Calistoga Estate	12,900	NR		1995-2004
1978	CHATEAU MONTELENA WINERY	Napa Valley Calistoga Estate	7,500	$16.00	$60.00	1993-2005
1985	CLOS DU VAL WINE CO.	Napa Valley Stags Leap District Estate	25,000	$16.00	$16.00	1993-2005
1984	B.R. COHN	Sonoma Valley Olive Hill Vineyard	900	$15.00	$22.00	1991-1998
1980	CONN CREEK WINERY	Napa Valley St. Helena Collins Vineyard Proprietor's Special Selection	40	NA	$70.00	1995-2004
1986	CUVAISON WINERY	Napa Valley	5,000	$15.00	$15.00	1993-2001
1985	DIAMOND CREEK VINEYARD	Napa Valley Diamond Mountain Red Rock Terrace	643	$30.00	$40.00	1996-2009
1985	DIAMOND CREEK VINEYARD	Napa Valley Diamond Mountain Volcanic Hill	1,100	$30.00	$40.00	1996-2010
1978	DIAMOND CREEK VINEYARD	Napa Valley Diamond Mountain Gravelly Meadow	315	$12.50	$75.00	1995-2005
1975	DIAMOND CREEK VINEYARD	Napa Valley Diamond Mountain Volcanic Hill	571	$7.50	$80.00	1993-2005
1986	DOMINUS ESTATE	Napa Valley Yountville Napanook	6,300	NR		1995-2004
1986	DUNN VINEYARDS	Napa Valley	2,000	$27.00	$27.00	1993-2000
1984	DUNN VINEYARDS	Napa Valley	2,100	$18.00	$55.00	1994-2004
1986	FORMAN VINEYARD	Napa Valley	1,800	$20.00	$20.00	1995-2004
1985	FORMAN VINEYARD	Napa Valley	1,600	$18.00	$30.00	1994-2002
1985	FREEMARK ABBEY WINERY	Napa Valley Rutherford Bosche	3,500	$24.00	$24.00	1995-2005
1979	FREEMARK ABBEY WINERY	Napa Valley Rutherford Bosche	2,982	$12.00	$30.00	1990-1997
1978	FREEMARK ABBEY WINERY	Napa Valley Rutherford Bosche	3,908	$12.50	$35.00	1990-1995
1986	GRACE FAMILY VINEYARD	Napa Valley St. Helena Estate	150	$40.00	$40.00	1994-2003
1986	GROTH VINEYARDS AND WINERY	Napa Valley Oakville Reserve	475	NR		1993-2003
1985	GROTH VINEYARDS AND WINERY	Napa Valley Oakville Reserve	500	NR		1996-2004
1980	HEITZ WINE CELLARS	Napa Valley Rutherford Bella Oaks Vyd	2,280	$20.00	$45.00	1994-2004
1979	HEITZ WINE CELLARS	Napa Valley Oakville Martha's Vineyard	5,469	$25.00	$60.00	1994-2004
1969	HEITZ WINE CELLARS	Napa Valley Oakville Martha's Vineyard	1,016	$12.75	$275.00	1990-1995
1986	HESS COLLECTION WINERY	Napa Valley Mount Veeder Reserve	2,000	NR		1995-2003
1984	HESS COLLECTION WINERY	Napa Valley Mount Veeder Reserve	250	$22.00	$30.00	1992-2000
1979	WILLIAM HILL WINERY	Napa Valley Mount Veeder Gold Label	4,412	$18.00	$45.00	1990-2000
1983	INGLENOOK-NAPA VALLEY	Napa Valley Rutherford Reunion	1,991	$33.00	$40.00	1993-2001
1981	INGLENOOK-NAPA VALLEY	Napa Valley Rutherford Reserve Cask	12,115	$15.50	$20.00	1992-2000
1955	INGLENOOK-NAPA VALLEY	Napa Valley RutherfordCask	2,500	$1.85	$375.00	1990
1984	KENWOOD VINEYARDS	Sonoma Valley Artist Series	2,700	$30.00	$35.00	1994-2002
1985	KISTLER VINEYARDS	Sonoma Valley Kistler Vineyard	169	$16.00	$25.00	1994-2002
1985	LAUREL GLEN VINEYARD	Sonoma Mountain	3,300	$18.00	$35.00	1992-2000
1985	MARKHAM VINEYARDS	Napa Valley Yountville Markham Vineyard	3,810	NR		1994-2003
1952	LOUIS M. MARTINI WINERY	California Special Selection	1,000	$2.50	$450.00	1990-1992
1971	ROBERT MONDAVI WINERY	Napa Valley Oakville Reserve	4,000	$12.00	$130.00	1990-1996
1986	MOUNT VEEDER WINERY	Napa Valley Mount Veeder Proprietary Reserve	50	NR		1996-2006
1980	OPUS ONE	Napa Valley Oakville	4,000	$50.00	$130.00	1992-2002
1986	JOSEPH PHELPS VINEYARDS	Napa Valley Oakville Backus Vineyard	1,400	NR		1998-2005
1976	JOSEPH PHELPS VINEYARDS	Napa Valley Insignia	785	$20.00	$90.00	1994-2004
1985	PINE RIDGE WINERY	Napa Valley Rutherford Rutherford Cuveé	8,668	$16.00	$16.00	1994-2004
1984	PINE RIDGE WINERY	Napa Valley Stags Leap District Pine Ridge Stags Leap Vineyard	1,652	$25.00	$35.00	1995-2008
1984	PINE RIDGE WINERY	Napa Valley Rutherford Andrus Reserve	280	$37.00	$40.00	1993-2010
1974	RIDGE VINEYARDS	Santa Cruz Mountains Monte Bello	1,260	$12.00	$140.00	1990-1998

NA — not available.   NR — not released.   * — Beaulieu production figures are estimates.

Vintage	Winery	Appellation/Vineyard	Case Prod.	Release Price	Current Price	Drink
1986	SANTA CRUZ MOUNTAIN VYD	Santa Cruz Mountains Bates Ranch	1,200	NR		1996-2006
1986	SHAFER VINEYARDS	Napa Valley Stags Leap District	5,000	$16.00	$16.00	1994-2002
1985	SHAFER VINEYARDS	Napa Valley Stags Leap District Hillside Select	2,000	NR		1993-2000
1985	SILVER OAK CELLARS	Alexander Valley	19,900	$24.00	$24.00	1995-2005
1978	SILVER OAK CELLARS	Alexander Valley	8,500	$16.00	$100.00	1992-2002
1974	SILVER OAK CELLARS	North Coast	4,000	$8.00	$135.00	1990-2000
1985	ST. CLEMENT VINEYARDS	Napa Valley	2,665	$17.00	$17.00	1994-2002
1984	STAG'S LEAP WINE CELLARS	Napa Valley Stags Leap District Cask 23	800	$40.00	$40.00	1994-2000
1985	STELTZNER VINEYARDS	Napa Valley Stags Leap District	5,000	$16.00	$19.00	1993-2000
1977	STERLING VINEYARDS	Napa Valley Reserve	3,500	$27.50	$32.00	1992-2000
1986	PHILIP TOGNI VINEYARD	Napa Valley Spring Mountain	386	$22.00	$22.00	1993-2005

SCORE: 92

Vintage	Winery	Appellation/Vineyard	Case Prod.	Release Price	Current Price	Drink
1984	ALEXANDER VALLEY VINEYARDS	Alexander Valley	5,600	$10.50	$13.50	1992-2000
1982	BERINGER VINEYARDS	Napa Valley Private Reserve	4,000	$19.00	$35.00	1992-1999
1978	BERINGER VINEYARDS	Napa Valley St. Helena Private Reserve Lemmon Ranch Vineyard	3,000	$15.00	$44.00	1990-1998
1979	BUENA VISTA WINERY	Sonoma Valley Carneros Special Selection	2,595	$18.00	$50.00	1991-1996
1977	BURGESS CELLARS	Napa Valley Vintage Selection	3,000	$12.00	$45.00	1992-2000
1984	CARMENET VINEYARD	Sonoma Valley	6,641	$16.00	$30.00	1992-2004
1986	CAYMUS VINEYARDS	Napa Valley Rutherford Estate	4,000	$22.00	$22.00	1995-2005
1985	CAYMUS VINEYARDS	Napa Valley Rutherford Estate	3,500	$18.00	$28.00	1994-2003
1982	CAYMUS VINEYARDS	Napa Valley Rutherford Special Selection	750	$35.00	$65.00	1995-2006
1980	CAYMUS VINEYARDS	Napa Valley Rutherford Special Selection	750	$30.00	$80.00	1993-2000
1979	CAYMUS VINEYARDS	Napa Valley Rutherford Estate	2,700	$12.00	$35.00	1992-1998
1975	CAYMUS VINEYARDS	Napa Valley Rutherford Special Selection	180	$22.00	$175.00	1992-2000
1986	CHAPPELLET VINEYARD	Napa Valley Reserve	6,000	NR		1994-2003
1983	CHATEAU MONTELENA WINERY	Napa Valley Calistoga Estate	8,517	$18.00	$26.00	1994-2002
1982	CHATEAU MONTELENA WINERY	Napa Valley Calistoga Estate	11,425	$16.00	$33.00	1992-2002
1986	CLOS DU VAL WINE CO.	Napa Valley Joli Val	5,000	NR		1994-2004
1984	CLOS DU VAL WINE CO.	Napa Valley Stags Leap District Estate	20,500	$15.00	$16.50	1992-2004
1979	CLOS DU VAL WINE CO.	Napa Valley Stags Leap District Reserve	1,200	$25.00	$55.00	1996-2008
1978	CLOS DU VAL WINE CO.	Napa Valley Stags Leap District Estate	14,000	$12.00	$40.00	1990-2000
1978	CONN CREEK WINERY	Napa Valley Lot 2	2,500	$13.00	$35.00	1990-2000
1973	CONN CREEK WINERY	Napa Valley Stags Leap District	400	$9.00	$70.00	1990-2000
1985	DIAMOND CREEK VINEYARD	Napa Valley Diamond Mountain Gravelly Meadow	736	$30.00	$40.00	1995-2007
1984	DIAMOND CREEK VINEYARD	Napa Valley Diamond Mountain Lake	130	$50.00	$120.00	1995-2004
1981	DIAMOND CREEK VINEYARD	Napa Valley Diamond Mountain Volcanic Hill	1,026	$20.00	$35.00	1996-2006
1980	DIAMOND CREEK VINEYARD	Napa Valley Diamond Mountain Gravelly Meadow	460	$20.00	$40.00	1996-2006
1979	DIAMOND CREEK VINEYARD	Napa Valley Diamond Mountain Red Rock Terrace	263	$15.00	$60.00	1993-2000
1978	DIAMOND CREEK VINEYARD	Napa Valley Diamond Mountain Red Rock Terrace	468	$12.50	$75.00	1992-2004
1985	DUCKHORN VINEYARDS	Napa Valley	2,800	$17.50	$26.00	1996-2010
1984	DUCKHORN VINEYARDS	Napa Valley	2,000	$17.00	$30.00	1994-2004
1978	DUCKHORN VINEYARDS	Napa Valley	800	$10.50	$85.00	1990-1998
1983	DUNN VINEYARDS	Napa Valley Howell Mountain	1,600	$18.00	$90.00	1995-2005
1980	DUNN VINEYARDS	Napa Valley Howell Mountain	825	$13.00	$170.00	1993-2000
1985	FAR NIENTE WINERY	Napa Valley Oakville	10,000	$28.00	$28.00	1994-2002
1984	FAR NIENTE WINERY	Napa Valley Oakville	8,500	$25.00	$30.00	1994-2002
1984	FORMAN VINEYARD	Napa Valley	1,000	$18.00	$35.00	1992-2000
1984	FROG'S LEAP WINERY	Napa Valley	1,900	$10.00	$25.00	1991-1997
1984	GIRARD WINERY	Napa Valley Oakville Reserve	684	$25.00	$25.00	1994-2004
1980	GIRARD WINERY	Napa Valley Oakville	1,480	$11.00	$25.00	1991-2000
1984	GRACE FAMILY VINEYARD	Napa Valley St. Helena Estate	150	$38.00	$125.00	1994-2004
1980	GRACE FAMILY VINEYARD	Napa Valley St. Helena Estate	183	$25.00	$275.00	1993-2002
1979	GRACE FAMILY VINEYARD	Napa Valley St. Helena Estate	56	$20.00	$150.00	1991-2000

NA — not available.   NR — not released.   * — Beaulieu production figures are estimates.

Vintage	Winery	Appellation/Vineyard	Case Prod.	Release Price	Current Price	Drink
1985	GRGICH HILLS CELLAR	Napa Valley Yountville	10,000	NR		1994-2005
1986	GROTH VINEYARDS AND WINERY	Napa Valley Oakville Estate	6,400	$18.00	$18.00	1994-2001
1984	GROTH VINEYARDS AND WINERY	Napa Valley Oakville Estate	6,500	$14.00	$18.00	1993-2000
1983	GROTH VINEYARDS & WINERY	Napa Valley Oakville Reserve	200	$25.00	$30.00	1996-2004
1985	HEITZ WINE CELLARS	Napa Valley Rutherford Bella Oaks Vyd	4,037	NR		1994-2003
1975	HEITZ WINE CELLARS	Napa Valley Oakville Martha's Vineyard	4,895	$25.00	$100.00	1993-2003
1973	HEITZ WINE CELLARS	Napa Valley Oakville Martha's Vineyard	2,329	$11.00	$120.00	1991-2000
1966	HEITZ WINE CELLARS	Napa Valley Oakville Martha's Vineyard	392	$8.00	$425.00	1990-1997
1986	INGLENOOK-NAPA VALLEY	Napa Valley Rutherford Reunion	4,251	NR		1996-2006
1986	INGLENOOK-NAPA VALLEY	Napa Valley Rutherford Reserve Cask	6,000	NR		1996-2004
1984	INGLENOOK-NAPA VALLEY	Napa Valley Rutherford Reunion	2,932	$35.00	$35.00	1993-2000
1984	INGLENOOK-NAPA VALLEY	Napa Valley Rutherford Reserve Cask	5,237	NR		1992-2002
1949	INGLENOOK-NAPA VALLEY	Napa Valley Rutherford Cask	2,000	$1.49	$750.00	1990-1993
1984	ROBERT KEENAN WINERY	Napa Valley	3,500	$13.50	$30.00	1994-2002
1952	CHARLES KRUG WINERY	Napa Valley Vintage Select	1,028	$1.26	$750.00	1990
1986	LA JOTA VINEYARD COMPANY	Napa Valley Howell Mountain	2,700	$21.00	$21.00	1994-2004
1984	LAKESPRING WINERY	Napa Valley Yountville Reserve Selection	1,450	$15.00	$20.00	1992-1999
1981	LAUREL GLEN VINEYARD	Sonoma Mountain	1,500	$12.50	$40.00	1990-1996
1985	LONG VINEYARDS	Napa Valley Oakville	200	$36.00	$36.00	1995-2005
1985	LYETH WINERY	Alexander Valley	13,500	$22.00	$22.00	1992-1999
1985	MAYACAMAS VINEYARDS	Napa Valley Mount Veeder	2,025	NR		1997-2007
1980	MAYACAMAS VINEYARDS	Napa Valley Mount Veeder	1,870	$18.00	$30.00	1994-2002
1977	MAYACAMAS VINEYARDS	Napa Valley Mount Veeder	1,510	$15.00	$60.00	1992-2000
1984	ROBERT MONDAVI WINERY	Napa Valley Oakville Reserve	9,000	$37.00	$37.00	1992-2000
1979	ROBERT MONDAVI WINERY	Napa Valley Oakville Reserve	11,500	$25.00	$45.00	1991-2000
1978	ROBERT MONDAVI WINERY	Napa Valley Oakville Reserve	11,000	$40.00	$58.00	1990-1998
1974	ROBERT MONDAVI WINERY	Napa Valley Oakville Reserve	9,000	$30.00	$95.00	1990-1996
1979	MOUNT VEEDER WINERY	Napa Valley Mount Veeder Bernstein Vyds	2,800	$13.50	$35.00	1990-1997
1983	NEWTON VINEYARD	Napa Valley Estate	1,824	$12.50	$21.00	1992-1998
1986	NIEBAUM-COPPOLA ESTATE	Napa Valley Rutherford Rubicon	4,300	NR		1996-2004
1981	JOSEPH PHELPS VINEYARDS	Napa Valley Insignia	1,480	$25.00	$39.00	1993-2000
1979	JOSEPH PHELPS VINEYARDS	Napa Valley Calistoga Eisele Vineyard	1,000	$30.00	$50.00	1993-2000
1986	PINE RIDGE WINERY	Napa Valley Rutherford Andrus Reserve	749	$40.00	$40.00	1995-2002
1985	PINE RIDGE WINERY	Napa Valley Rutherford Andrus Reserve Cuveé Duet	1,136	$40.00	$45.00	1994-2002
1981	PINE RIDGE WINERY	Napa Valley Stags Leap District Pine Ridge Stags Leap Vineyard	1,553	$20.00	$50.00	1995-2005
1985	RIDGE VINEYARDS	Napa County Spring Mountain York Creek	4,087	$16.00	$16.00	1990-2000
1981	RIDGE VINEYARDS	Santa Cruz Mountains Monte Bello	2,648	$25.00	$45.00	1996-2004
1969	RIDGE VINEYARDS	Santa Cruz Mountains Monte Bello	300	$7.50	$200.00	1990-2000
1985	SANTA CRUZ MOUNTAIN VYD	Santa Cruz Mountains Bates Ranch	1,125	NR		1995-2005
1985	SEQUOIA GROVE VINEYARDS	Napa Valley Rutherford Estate	2,064	$28.00	$32.00	1992-2005
1986	SHAFER VINEYARDS	Napa Valley Stags Leap District Hillside Select	2,000	NR		1994-2002
1984	SHAFER VINEYARDS	Napa Valley Stags Leap District Hillside Select	1,800	$24.50	$24.50	1992-2000
1985	SILVERADO VINEYARDS	Napa Valley Stags Leap District	11,000	$12.50	$16.00	1995-2002
1986	SIMI WINERY	Alexander Valley Reserve	1,700	NR		1993-2002
1984	SIMI WINERY	Alexander Valley Reserve	800	$22.50	$22.50	1993-2000
1986	STAG'S LEAP WINE CELLARS	Napa Valley Stags Leap District Cask 23	605	NR		1994-2003
1984	STAG'S LEAP WINE CELLARS	Napa Valley Stags Leap District SLV	6,000	$21.00	$30.00	1994-2000
1978	STAG'S LEAP WINE CELLARS	Napa Valley Stags Leap District Cask 23	1,000	$35.00	$90.00	1990-1995
1984	STERLING VINEYARDS	Napa Valley Reserve	2,268	$25.00	$38.00	1994-2002
1985	VICHON WINERY	Napa Valley Stags Leap District SLD	4,000	$18.00	$20.00	1992-2000

SCORE: 91

Vintage	Winery	Appellation/Vineyard	Case Prod.	Release Price	Current Price	Drink
1984	BEAULIEU VINEYARD	Napa Valley Rutherford Georges de Latour Private Reserve	15,000	$25.00	$28.00	1994-2002
1978	BEAULIEU VINEYARD	Napa Valley Rutherford Georges de Latour Private Reserve	15,000	$19.00	$45.00	1990-2000

NA — not available.   NR — not released.   * — Beaulieu production figures are estimates.

Vintage	Winery	Appellation/Vineyard	Case Prod.	Release Price	Current Price	Drink
1968	BEAULIEU VINEYARD	Napa Valley Rutherford Georges de Latour Private Reserve	15,000	$6.00	$150.00	1990-1996
1985	BERINGER VINEYARDS	Napa Valley St. Helena Chabot Vineyard	1,000	NR		1992-2000
1981	BERINGER VINEYARDS	Napa Valley Private Reserve	3,000	$18.00	$40.00	1990-1997
1986	BUEHLER VINEYARDS	Napa Valley	3,829	$15.00	$15.00	1996-2005
1983	BUEHLER VINEYARDS	Napa Valley	2,292	$12.00	$20.00	1993-2001
1986	BURGESS CELLARS	Napa Valley Vintage Selection	6,600	NR		1995-2004
1985	CARMENET VINEYARD	Sonoma Valley	6,040	$18.50	$22.00	1994-2004
1984	CAYMUS VINEYARDS	Napa Valley Rutherford Estate	3,200	$16.00	$30.00	1993-2002
1983	CAYMUS VINEYARDS	Napa Valley Rutherford Special Selection	1,100	$35.00	$50.00	1993-2006
1980	CHAPPELLET VINEYARD	Napa Valley	7,000	$18.00	$28.00	1993-1998
1977	CHATEAU MONTELENA WINERY	Alexander Valley Sonoma	3,298	$12.00	$65.00	1992-1999
1986	CLOS DU VAL WINE CO.	Napa Valley Stags Leap District Estate	21,000	NR		1994-2002
1974	CLOS DU VAL WINE CO.	Napa Valley Stags Leap District Estate	7,600	$7.50	$75.00	1990-2000
1981	DIAMOND CREEK VINEYARD	Napa Valley Diamond Mountain Red Rock Terrace	497	$20.00	$35.00	1993-2002
1979	DIAMOND CREEK VINEYARD	Napa Valley Diamond Mountain Gravelly Meadow	194	$15.00	$60.00	1995-2005
1980	DUCKHORN VINEYARDS	Napa Valley	1,600	$14.00	$50.00	1992-2002
1979	DUNN VINEYARDS	Napa Valley Howell Mountain	660	$12.50	$160.00	1990-1997
1986	FAR NIENTE WINERY	Napa Valley Oakville	12,000	$30.00	$30.00	1995-2003
1974	FREEMARK ABBEY WINERY	Napa Valley Rutherford Bosche	4,127	$7.75	$75.00	1990-1998
1970	FREEMARK ABBEY WINERY	Napa Valley Rutherford Bosche	424	$8.75	$100.00	1990
1986	GIRARD WINERY	Napa Valley Oakville Reserve	584	NR		1994-2002
1983	GRACE FAMILY VINEYARD	Napa Valley St. Helena Estate	175	$38.00	$130.00	1994-2002
1986	GRGICH HILLS CELLAR	Napa Valley Yountville	10,000	NR		1994-2002
1985	GROTH VINEYARDS & WINERY	Napa Valley Oakville Estate	7,800	$16.00	$16.00	1994-2002
1985	GUNDLACH BUNDSCHU WINERY	Sonoma Valley Rhinefarm	5,000	$9.00	$10.00	1992-2000
1986	HAYWOOD WINERY	Sonoma Valley	2,612	$16.00	$16.00	1994-2003
1978	HEITZ WINE CELLARS	Napa Valley Oakville Martha's Vineyard	5,000	$22.00	$75.00	1994-2002
1977	HEITZ WINE CELLARS	Napa Valley Rutherford Bella Oaks Vyd	4,185	$30.00	$57.00	1991-1997
1986	HESS COLLECTION WINERY	Napa Valley Mount Veeder	10,000	$14.00	$14.00	1994-2000
1984	WILLIAM HILL WINERY	Napa Valley Reserve	7,752	$18.25	$26.00	1994-2002
1982	INGLENOOK-NAPA VALLEY	Napa Valley Rutherford Reserve Cask	4,631	$22.00	$28.00	1994-2001
1943	INGLENOOK-NAPA VALLEY	Napa Valley Rutherford	7,000	$1.49	$1000.00	1990-1995
1979	IRON HORSE VINEYARDS	Alexander Valley	1,000	$12.00	$25.00	1992-1998
1985	KENWOOD VINEYARDS	Sonoma Valley Artist Series	3,000	$30.00	$30.00	1993-2000
1979	KENWOOD VINEYARDS	Sonoma Valley Artist Series	1,300	$20.00	$70.00	1990-1998
1986	KISTLER VINEYARDS	Sonoma Valley Kistler Vineyard	521	$20.00	$20.00	1995-2002
1980	LONG VINEYARDS	Napa Valley Oakville	200	$32.00	$50.00	1994-2002
1986	MARKHAM VINEYARDS	Napa Valley Yountville Markham Vineyard	3,850	NR		1995-2004
1984	MARKHAM VINEYARDS	Napa Valley Yountville Markham Vineyard	3,855	$12.00	$18.00	1993-2002
1957	LOUIS M. MARTINI WINERY	California Special Selection	1,994	$3.50	$175.00	1990-1992
1981	MAYACAMAS VINEYARDS	Napa Valley Mount Veeder	1,830	$18.00	$25.00	1993-1999
1985	MERRYVALE VINEYARDS	Napa Valley Red Table Wine	1,662	$24.00	$24.00	1994-2001
1984	MONTICELLO CELLARS	Napa Valley Corley Reserve	4,000	$18.50	$20.00	1995-2004
1977	MOUNT EDEN VINEYARDS	Santa Cruz Mountains	200	$20.00	$50.00	1995-2005
1973	MOUNT EDEN VINEYARDS	Santa Cruz Mountains	391	$14.00	$140.00	1995-2005
1986	NEWTON VINEYARD	Napa Valley Spring Mountain Estate	5,530	$16.00	$16.00	1992-1999
1985	NIEBAUM-COPPOLA ESTATE	Napa Valley Rutherford Rubicon	4,762	NR		1995-2003
1981	JOSEPH PHELPS VINEYARDS	Napa Valley Oakville Backus Vineyard	775	$15.00	$44.00	1992-2000
1977	JOSEPH PHELPS VINEYARDS	Napa Valley Insignia	1,900	$25.00	$75.00	1990-1996
1986	PINE RIDGE WINERY	Napa Valley Stags Leap District Pine Ridge Stags Leap Vineyard	1,775	NR		1995-2005
1986	PINE RIDGE WINERY	Napa Valley Diamond Mountain Diamond Mountain Vineyard	450	$30.00	$30.00	1995-2004
1980	PINE RIDGE WINERY	Napa Valley Rutherford Rutherford District	2,938	$12.00	$37.00	1993-2000
1978	RIDGE VINEYARDS	Santa Cruz Mountains Monte Bello	1,820	$30.00	$60.00	1993-2003
1985	SHAFER VINEYARDS	Napa Valley Stags Leap District	5,000	$15.50	$15.50	1992-1998
1984	SHAFER VINEYARDS	Napa Valley Stags Leap District	4,000	$14.00	$16.00	1990-1998
1984	SILVERADO VINEYARDS	Napa Valley Stags Leap District	7,800	$11.50	$20.00	1996-2002

NA — not available.   NR — not released.   * — Beaulieu production figures are estimates.

Vintage	Winery	Appellation/Vineyard	Case Prod.	Release Price	Current Price	Drink
1984	SMITH-MADRONE VINEYARD	Napa Valley Spring Mountain	1,100	$14.00	$14.00	1994-2004
1983	ST. CLEMENT VINEYARDS	Napa Valley	2,256	$14.50	$18.00	1995-2005
1982	ST. CLEMENT VINEYARDS	Napa Valley	3,024	$13.50	$20.00	1992-2000
1981	STAG'S LEAP WINE CELLARS	Napa Valley Stags Leap District Stag's Leap Vineyards	7,534	$15.00	$32.00	1992-1998
1977	STAG'S LEAP WINE CELLARS	Napa Valley Stags Leap District Cask 23	1,000	$30.00	$75.00	1990-1993
1984	STELTZNER VINEYARDS	Napa Valley Stags Leap District	3,000	$15.00	$19.00	1992-2000
1980	STERLING VINEYARDS	Napa Valley Reserve	4,848	$27.50	$37.00	1992-1998
1978	STONEGATE WINERY	Napa Valley	1,797	$12.00	$30.00	1991-2000
1984	TUDAL WINERY	Napa Valley St. Helena	1,000	$12.50	$15.00	1993-2001

SCORE: 90

Vintage	Winery	Appellation/Vineyard	Case Prod.	Release Price	Current Price	Drink
1983	ALEXANDER VALLEY VINEYARDS	Alexander Valley	3,792	$10.50	$14.50	1992-1998
1982	ALEXANDER VALLEY VINEYARDS	Alexander Valley	3,987	$10.00	$16.00	1990-1996
1979	BEAULIEU VINEYARD	Napa Valley Rutherford Georges de Latour Private Reserve	15,000	$21.00	$43.00	1993-2000
1969	BEAULIEU VINEYARD	Napa Valley Rutherford Georges de Latour Private Reserve	15,000	$6.50	$120.00	1990-1995
1951	BEAULIEU VINEYARD	Napa Valley Rutherford Georges de Latour Private Reserve	15,000	$1.82	$950.00	1990-1992
1984	BUENA VISTA WINERY	Sonoma Valley Carneros Private Reserve	2,700	$18.00	$18.00	1990-1996
1978	BUENA VISTA WINERY	Sonoma Valley Carneros Special Selection	2,020	$18.00	$60.00	1990-1996
1982	CAYMUS VINEYARDS	Napa Valley Rutherford Estate	4,200	$14.00	$33.00	1993-2000
1980	CAYMUS VINEYARDS	Napa Valley Rutherford Estate	4,300	$12.50	$35.00	1993-2000
1976	CAYMUS VINEYARDS	Napa Valley Rutherford Special Selection	270	$35.00	$150.00	1993-1998
1976	CHATEAU MONTELENA WINERY	North Coast	5,769	$10.00	$75.00	1990-1995
1974	CHATEAU MONTELENA WINERY	Napa Valley Calistoga	1,100	$9.00	$100.00	1993-2003
1982	CLOS DU VAL WINE CO.	Napa Valley Stags Leap District Reserve	2,600	$28.00	$37.00	1997-2005
1979	CLOS DU VAL WINE CO.	Napa Valley Stags Leap District Estate	15,400	$12.50	$45.00	1990-2002
1973	CLOS DU VAL WINE CO.	Napa Valley Stags Leap District Reserve	100	$10.00	$100.00	1990-2000
1972	CLOS DU VAL WINE CO.	Napa Valley Stags Leap District Estate	3,500	$6.00	$100.00	1990-1998
1977	CONN CREEK WINERY	Napa Valley	2,000	$12.00	$40.00	1991-1998
1985	CUVAISON WINERY	Napa Valley	3,000	$14.00	$14.00	1992-1999
1981	DIAMOND CREEK VINEYARD	Napa Valley Diamond Mountain Three Vineyard Blend	15	$20.00	$50.00	1995-2005
1980	DIAMOND CREEK VINEYARD	Napa Valley Diamond Mountain Volcanic Hill	883	$20.00	$40.00	1998-2008
1984	DOMINUS ESTATE	Napa Valley Yountville Napanook	4,200	$40.00	$45.00	1994-2002
1982	DUCKHORN VINEYARDS	Napa Valley	3,800	$15.00	$38.00	1992-1998
1981	DUNN VINEYARDS	Napa Valley Howell Mountain	940	$14.00	$150.00	1991-1996
1986	FISHER VINEYARDS	Sonoma County Coach Insignia	1,500	$20.00	$20.00	1993-2000
1985	FISHER VINEYARDS	Sonoma County Coach Insignia	1,200	$18.00	$20.00	1993-2000
1983	FORMAN VINEYARD	Napa Valley	600	$15.50	$45.00	1994-2001
1986	FREEMARK ABBEY WINERY	Napa Valley Rutherford Bosche	4,000	NR		1994-2002
1975	FREEMARK ABBEY WINERY	Napa Valley Rutherford Bosche	2,632	$10.00	$48.00	1990-1995
1980	GRGICH HILLS CELLAR	Napa County-Sonoma County	2,000	$16.00	$32.00	1991-2000
1981	GUNDLACH BUNDSCHU WINERY	Sonoma Valley Rhinefarm Vintage Reserve	800	$20.00	$26.00	1994-2002
1981	HEITZ WINE CELLARS	Napa Valley Rutherford Bella Oaks Vineyard	3,225	$16.00	$38.00	1992-1999
1977	HEITZ WINE CELLARS	Napa Valley Oakville Martha's Vineyard	2,800	$30.00	$75.00	1991-2000
1982	WILLIAM HILL WINERY	Napa Valley Mount Veeder Gold Label	11,907	$18.00	$32.00	1994-2002
1984	JOHNSON TURNBULL VINEYARDS	Napa Valley Oakville	1,825	$14.50	$18.00	1993-1999
1978	KENWOOD VINEYARDS	Sonoma Valley Artist Series	1,000	$20.00	$100.00	1990-1995
1956	CHARLES KRUG WINERY	Napa Valley Vintage Select	1,250	$1.40	$590.00	1990
1986	LIVINGSTON VINEYARDS	Napa Valley Rutherford Moffett Vineyard	1,330	$24.00	$24.00	1994-1999
1979	LONG VINEYARDS	Napa Valley Oakville	200	$32.00	$50.00	1992-1999
1984	LYETH WINERY	Alexander Valley	10,500	$18.00	$25.00	1992-1998
1982	MARKHAM VINEYARDS	Napa Valley Yountville Markham Vineyard	6,361	$13.00	$18.00	1994-2002
1968	LOUIS M. MARTINI WINERY	California Special Selection	1,926	$6.00	$95.00	1990-1994
1947	LOUIS M. MARTINI WINERY	California Special Selection	1,151	$1.50	$750.00	1990-1992
1939	LOUIS M. MARTINI WINERY	California Special Reserve	1,000	$1.25	$1000.00	1990-1992

NA — not available.   NR — not released.   * — Beaulieu production figures are estimates.

Vintage	Winery	Appellation/Vineyard	Case Prod.	Release Price	Current Price	Drink
1984	MAYACAMAS VINEYARDS	Napa Valley Mount Veeder	1,220	$20.00	$20.00	1994-2000
1983	MAYACAMAS VINEYARDS	Napa Valley Mount Veeder	2,280	$20.00	$25.00	1997-2005
1982	MONTICELLO CELLARS	Napa Valley Corley Reserve	1,200	$15.00	$30.00	1993-1999
1975	MOUNT EDEN VINEYARDS	Santa Cruz Mountains	255	$20.00	$70.00	1994-2004
1973	MOUNT VEEDER WINERY	Napa Valley Mount Veeder	400	$8.00	$80.00	1993-2005
1982	OPUS ONE	Napa Valley Oakville	6,000	$50.00	$80.00	1993-2000
1979	OPUS ONE	Napa Valley Oakville	2,000	$50.00	$190.00	1992-1998
1985	ROBERT PEPI WINERY	Napa Valley Yountville Vine Hill Ranch	2,720	NR		1996-2002
1985	JOSEPH PHELPS VINEYARDS	Napa Valley Oakville Backus Vineyard	1,980	$27.50	$32.00	1996-2002
1980	JOSEPH PHELPS VINEYARDS	Napa Valley Insignia	2,585	$25.00	$50.00	1993-1998
1979	JOSEPH PHELPS VINEYARDS	Napa Valley Insignia	960	$25.00	$55.00	1990-1997
1974	JOSEPH PHELPS VINEYARDS	Napa Valley Insignia	670	$12.00	$130.00	1990-1998
1986	PINE RIDGE WINERY	Napa Valley Rutherford Rutherford Cuveé	7,437	$16.00	$16.00	1995-2003
1984	PINE RIDGE WINERY	Napa Valley Rutherford Rutherford Cuveé	7,128	$14.00	$16.00	1992-2000
1982	PINE RIDGE WINERY	Napa Valley Rutherford Rutherford Cuveé	3,558	$13.00	$24.00	1995-2005
1982	PINE RIDGE WINERY	Napa Valley Stags Leap District Pine Ridge Stags Leap Vineyard	1,116	$20.00	$34.00	1996-2004
1964	RIDGE VINEYARDS	Santa Cruz Mountains Monte Bello	70	$6.50	$310.00	1990-1995
1985	ROMBAUER VINEYARDS	Napa Valley Le Meilleur Du Chai	425	$37.50	$37.50	1993-2002
1984	ROMBAUER VINEYARDS	Napa Valley Le Meilleur Du Chai	450	$32.50	$35.00	1992-2000
1983	ROMBAUER VINEYARDS	Napa Valley Le Meilleur Du Chai	415	$30.00	$40.00	1993-2001
1978	SANTA CRUZ MOUNTAIN VYD	Santa Cruz Mountains Bates Ranch	750	$12.00	$35.00	1990-1998
1986	SEQUOIA GROVE VINEYARDS	Napa Valley Rutherford Estate	1,986	$22.00	$22.00	1994-2000
1982	SILVER OAK CELLARS	Alexander Valley	12,500	$19.00	$40.00	1994-2002
1981	SILVERADO VINEYARDS	Napa Valley Stags Leap District	3,500	$11.00	$25.00	1992-2000
1985	SMITH-MADRONE VINEYARD	Napa Valley Spring Mountain	1,500	$14.00	$14.00	1994-2002
1984	SPOTTSWOODE WINERY	Napa Valley St. Helena	1,450	$25.00	$45.00	1992-1998
1982	SPOTTSWOODE WINERY	Napa Valley St. Helena	1,200	$18.00	$60.00	1995-2003
1986	SPRING MOUNTAIN VINEYARDS	Napa Valley Spring Mountain	3,684	NR		1996-2004
1979	ST. CLEMENT VINEYARDS	Napa Valley	1,500	$11.00	$35.00	1992-2001
1977	ST. CLEMENT VINEYARDS	Napa Valley	650	$10.00	$45.00	1990-1999
1977	STAG'S LEAP WINE CELLARS	Napa Valley Stags Leap District Lot 2	2,000	$10.00	$50.00	1990-1996
1986	STELTZNER VINEYARDS	Napa Valley Stags Leap District	5,000	$16.00	$16.00	1993-2000
1983	STELTZNER VINEYARDS	Napa Valley Stags Leap District	3,000	$14.00	$18.00	1991-1996
1982	STELTZNER VINEYARDS	Napa Valley Stags Leap District	3,000	$14.00	$28.00	1990-1996
1985	STERLING VINEYARDS	Napa Valley Diamond Mountain Diamond Mountain Ranch	5,700	$16.00	$16.00	1995-2003
1978	STERLING VINEYARDS	Napa Valley Reserve	5,016	$27.50	$35.00	1992-1998
1974	STERLING VINEYARDS	Napa Valley Reserve	3,600	$20.00	$80.00	1992-2002
1986	TREFETHEN VINEYARDS	Napa Valley Yountville Reserve	1,000	NR		1995-2005
1985	TREFETHEN VINEYARDS	Napa Valley Yountville Reserve	969	NR		1993-2000
1979	TUDAL WINERY	Napa Valley St. Helena	630	$10.75	$25.00	1992-2000
1986	VICHON WINERY	Napa Valley Stags Leap District SLD	2,540	$21.00	$21.00	1991-1997
1974	VILLA MT. EDEN WINERY	Napa Valley Oakville Estate	219	$7.00	$60.00	1990-1997

SCORE: 89

Vintage	Winery	Appellation/Vineyard	Case Prod.	Release Price	Current Price	Drink
1959	BEAULIEU VINEYARD	Napa Valley Rutherford Georges de Latour Private Reserve	15,000	$3.50	$350.00	1990-1992
1983	BERINGER VINEYARDS	Napa Valley Private Reserve	8,000	$19.00	$30.00	1994-2000
1982	BERINGER VINEYARDS	Napa Valley St. Helena Chabot Vineyard	1,200	$25.00	$38.00	1993-2000
1980	BERINGER VINEYARDS	Napa Valley St. Helena Private Reserve Lemmon-Chabot Vineyard	2,000	$20.00	$42.00	1990-1997
1979	BERINGER VINEYARDS	Napa Valley Yountville Private Reserve State Lane Vineyard	2,000	$15.00	$42.00	1990-1996
1986	CAKEBREAD CELLARS	Napa Valley	5,000	$18.00	$18.00	1992-1998
1984	CAKEBREAD CELLARS	Napa Valley	5,000	$16.00	$25.00	1992-2000
1975	CAYMUS VINEYARDS	Napa Valley Rutherford Estate	1,300	$8.50	$80.00	1990-1998
1984	CLOS DU BOIS WINERY	Alexander Valley Marlstone Vineyard	3,957	$19.50	$24.00	1992-1997
1977	CLOS DU VAL WINE CO.	Napa Valley Stags Leap District Estate	14,700	$10.00	$40.00	1990-2000
1975	CLOS DU VAL WINE CO.	Napa Valley Stags Leap District Estate	9,300	$9.00	$65.00	1990-2000
1984	CUVAISON WINERY	Napa Valley	3,000	$14.00	$14.00	1991-1996

NA — not available.   NR — not released.   * — Beaulieu production figures are estimates.

Vintage	Winery	Appellation/Vineyard	Case Prod.	Release Price	Current Price	Drink
1978	DE MOOR WINERY	Napa Valley (Napa Cellars)	1,700	$10.00	$28.00	1990-2000
1985	DIAMOND CREEK VINEYARD	Napa Valley Diamond Mountain Three Vineyard Blend	10	$50.00	$50.00	1998-2004
1984	DIAMOND CREEK VINEYARD	Napa Valley Diamond Mountain Three Vineyard Blend	50	$50.00	$50.00	1995-2000
1983	DIAMOND CREEK VINEYARD	Napa Valley Diamond Mountain Gravelly Meadow	520	$20.00	$25.00	1994-2004
1983	DIAMOND CREEK VINEYARD	Napa Valley Diamond Mountain Volcanic Hill	1,442	$20.00	$25.00	1996-2007
1982	DIAMOND CREEK VINEYARD	Napa Valley Diamond Mountain Gravelly Meadow	404	$20.00	$35.00	1995-2005
1982	DIAMOND CREEK VINEYARD	Napa Valley Diamond Mountain Volcanic Hill	1,420	$20.00	$35.00	1997-2007
1981	DIAMOND CREEK VINEYARD	Napa Valley Diamond Mountain Gravelly Meadow	656	$20.00	$35.00	1995-2004
1977	DIAMOND CREEK VINEYARD	Napa Valley Diamond Mountain Gravelly Meadow	422	$10.00	$55.00	1994-2000
1985	DUNN VINEYARDS	Napa Valley Howell Mountain	1,800	$30.00	$55.00	1995-2002
1985	EBERLE WINERY	Paso Robles	2,814	$12.00	$14.00	1992-1998
1984	FISHER VINEYARDS	Sonoma County Coach Insignia	1,200	$18.00	$25.00	1992-1999
1985	FRANCISCAN VINEYARDS	Napa Valley Oakville Meritage	450	$20.00	$20.00	1993-2000
1985	GIRARD WINERY	Napa Valley Oakville Reserve	480	$25.00	$25.00	1993-2000
1982	GRACE FAMILY VINEYARD	Napa Valley St. Helena Estate	225	$31.00	$155.00	1993-1999
1986	GUNDLACH BUNDSCHU WINERY	Sonoma Valley Rhinefarm	5,000	$12.00	$12.00	1993-1998
1977	GUNDLACH BUNDSCHU WINERY	Sonoma Valley Batto Ranch	900	$8.00	$24.00	1990-1995
1985	HAYWOOD WINERY	Sonoma Valley	2,141	$14.50	$14.50	1996-2004
1983	HEITZ WINE CELLARS	Napa Valley Oakville Martha's Vineyard	4,356	$32.50	$42.00	1997-2005
1981	HEITZ WINE CELLARS	Napa Valley Oakville Martha's Vineyard	3,113	$30.00	$50.00	1997-2004
1980	HEITZ WINE CELLARS	Napa Valley Oakville Martha's Vineyard	2,966	$30.00	$55.00	1996-2006
1978	HEITZ WINE CELLARS	Napa Valley Rutherford Bella Oaks Vyd	4,837	$15.00	$40.00	1990-1998
1983	INGLENOOK-NAPA VALLEY	Napa Valley Rutherford Reserve Cask	11,188	$15.50	$19.00	1994-2000
1981	KENWOOD VINEYARDS	Sonoma Valley Artist Series	1,900	$25.00	$55.00	1991-1996
1961	CHARLES KRUG WINERY	Napa Valley Vintage Select	1,958	$3.50	$135.00	1990
1986	LAUREL GLEN VINEYARD	Sonoma Mountain	4,000	$20.00	$25.00	1992-1998
1984	LAUREL GLEN VINEYARD	Sonoma Mountain	4,000	$15.00	$20.00	1992-2000
1983	MARKHAM VINEYARDS	Napa Valley Yountville Markham Vineyard	4,015	$13.00	$15.00	1995-2000
1980	MARKHAM VINEYARDS	Napa Valley Yountville Markham Vineyard	3,920	$13.00	$25.00	1992-1998
1984	LOUIS M. MARTINI WINERY	Sonoma Valley Monte Rosso	700	$22.00	$22.00	1990-1999
1975	MAYACAMAS VINEYARDS	Napa Valley Mount Veeder	2,315	$12.00	$60.00	1990-1995
1969	MAYACAMAS VINEYARDS	California	1,080	$6.50	$100.00	1990-1995
1986	MERRYVALE VINEYARDS	Napa Valley Red Table Wine	1,604	$25.00	$25.00	1994-2002
1970	ROBERT MONDAVI WINERY	Napa Valley Oakville Unfined	4,000	$12.00	$120.00	1990-1996
1978	MOUNT VEEDER WINERY	Napa Valley Mount VeederBernstein Vyds	3,500	$12.75	$40.00	1992-2002
1985	NEWTON VINEYARD	Napa Valley Spring Mountain Estate	3,096	$15.25	$18.00	1992-1998
1982	NIEBAUM-COPPOLA ESTATE	Napa Valley Rutherford Rubicon	6,002	$40.00	$40.00	1992-2000
1983	OPUS ONE	Napa Valley Oakville	8,000	$50.00	$55.00	1992-1997
1984	JOSEPH PHELPS VINEYARDS	Napa Valley Insignia	3,860	$30.00	$35.00	1995-2004
1983	JOSEPH PHELPS VINEYARDS	Napa Valley Insignia	3,480	$25.00	$35.00	1994-2000
1981	JOSEPH PHELPS VINEYARDS	Napa Valley Calistoga Eisele Vineyard	1,050	$30.00	$39.00	1994-2000
1978	JOSEPH PHELPS VINEYARDS	Napa Valley Oakville Backus Vineyard	1,100	$16.50	$55.00	1991-1997
1978	PINE RIDGE WINERY	Napa Valley Rutherford Rutherford District	3,950	$7.50	$50.00	1990-1995
1985	PRESTON VINEYARDS	Dry Creek Valley	3,100	$11.00	$11.00	1993-1999
1986	RAVENSWOOD	Sonoma Mountain Pickberry Vineyard	550	$25.00	$25.00	1994-1997
1984	RAYMOND VINEYARD & CELLAR	Napa Valley Rutherford Private Reserve	2,800	$20.00	$20.00	1992-1999
1986	ROMBAUER VINEYARDS	Napa Valley Le Meilleur Du Chai	500	NR		1994-2002
1985	RUTHERFORD HILL WINERY	Napa Valley St. Helena XVS	2,000	$25.00	$25.00	1995-2001
1983	SHAFER VINEYARDS	Napa Valley Stags Leap District Hillside Select	900	$22.00	$22.00	1992-1999

NA — not available.   NR — not released.   * — Beaulieu production figures are estimates.

Vintage	Winery	Appellation/Vineyard	Case Prod.	Release Price	Current Price	Drink
1982	SHAFER VINEYARDS	Napa Valley Stags Leap District Reserve	1,200	$18.00	$25.00	1992-1998
1979	SHAFER VINEYARDS	Napa Valley Stags Leap District	1,000	$12.00	$35.00	1992-2000
1984	SILVER OAK CELLARS	Alexander Valley	14,000	$22.00	$28.00	1992-1999
1983	SPOTTSWOODE WINERY	Napa Valley St. Helena	1,400	$25.00	$45.00	1995-2005
1984	SPRING MOUNTAIN VINEYARDS	Napa Valley Spring Mountain	2,363	$15.00	$22.00	1994-2000
1984	ST. CLEMENT VINEYARDS	Napa Valley	2,300	$15.00	$15.00	1992-1998
1986	STAG'S LEAP WINE CELLARS	Napa Valley Stags Leap District SLV	6,248	$28.00	$28.00	1992-1999
1978	STAG'S LEAP WINE CELLARS	Napa Valley Stags Leap District Stag's Leap Vineyards	3,000	$13.50	$45.00	1990-1995
1981	STELTZNER VINEYARDS	Napa Valley Stags Leap District	1,500	$14.00	$38.00	1990-1996
1979	STELTZNER VINEYARDS	Napa Valley Stags Leap District	1,000	$14.00	$42.00	1990-1995
1973	STERLING VINEYARDS	Napa Valley Reserve	3,850	$10.00	$70.00	1992-1998
1985	PHILIP TOGNI VINEYARD	Napa Valley Spring Mountain	125	$20.00	$25.00	1995-2004
1986	TUDAL WINERY	Napa Valley St. Helena	1,800	$14.50	$14.50	1994-2002
1985	TUDAL WINERY	Napa Valley St. Helena	1,400	$14.50	$14.50	1993-1999
1975	VILLA MT. EDEN WINERY	Napa Valley Oakville Estate	616	$7.00	$50.00	1990-2000

SCORE: 88

Vintage	Winery	Appellation/Vineyard	Case Prod.	Release Price	Current Price	Drink
1986	ALEXANDER VALLEY VINEYARDS	Alexander Valley	13,522	$11.50	$11.50	1992-1998
1985	ALEXANDER VALLEY VINEYARDS	Alexander Valley	15,745	$11.00	$12.00	1991-1997
1982	BEAULIEU VINEYARD	Napa Valley Rutherford Georges de Latour Private Reserve	15,000	$24.00	$32.00	1995-2005
1956	BEAULIEU VINEYARD	Napa Valley Rutherford Georges de Latour Private Reserve	15,000	$2.50	$600.00	1990-1991
1946	BEAULIEU VINEYARD	Napa Valley Rutherford Georges de Latour Private Reserve	15,000	$1.47	$1000.00	1990-1994
1977	BERINGER VINEYARDS	Napa Valley St. Helena Private Reserve Lemmon Ranch Vineyard	2,500	$12.00	$50.00	1990-1995
1982	BUEHLER VINEYARDS	Napa Valley	2,953	$12.00	$30.00	1994-2004
1982	BURGESS CELLARS	Napa Valley Vintage Selection	8,300	$16.00	$23.00	1994-2002
1981	BURGESS CELLARS	Napa Valley Vintage Selection	6,900	$16.00	$25.00	1993-2002
1980	BURGESS CELLARS	Napa Valley Vintage Selection	5,800	$16.00	$28.00	1994-2002
1975	BURGESS CELLARS	Napa Valley Vintage Selection	1,800	$9.00	$45.00	1990-2000
1983	CAKEBREAD CELLARS	Napa Valley Rutherford Rutherford Reserve	300	$35.00	$35.00	1993-2000
1981	CAKEBREAD CELLARS	Napa Valley	4,000	$16.00	$50.00	1990-1995
1981	CAYMUS VINEYARDS	Napa Valley Rutherford Estate	3,200	$14.00	$35.00	1990-1998
1985	CHAPPELLET VINEYARD	Napa Valley Reserve	6,000	$20.00	$20.00	1994-2000
1978	CHAPPELLET VINEYARD	Napa Valley	7,000	$13.00	$40.00	1992-1998
1968	CHAPPELLET VINEYARD	Napa Valley	200	$5.50	$100.00	1990-1996
1979	CHATEAU MONTELENA WINERY	Alexander Valley Sonoma	1,164	$14.00	$45.00	1991-1998
1985	CLOS DU BOIS WINERY	Alexander Valley Marlstone Vineyard	5,917	$19.50	$19.50	1992-1998
1981	CLOS DU BOIS WINERY	Alexander Valley Briarcrest Vineyard	2,095	$12.00	$32.00	1991-1998
1982	CLOS DU VAL WINE CO.	Napa Valley Stags Leap District Estate	21,000	$13.25	$24.00	1992-2000
1980	CLOS DU VAL WINE CO.	Napa Valley Stags Leap District Estate	17,400	$12.50	$28.00	1990-1995
1984	CONN CREEK WINERY	Napa Valley St. Helena Collins Vineyard Private Reserve	1,100	$23.00	$23.00	1994-2002
1980	CONN CREEK WINERY	Napa Valley	5,700	$13.00	$28.00	1993-2000
1975	CUVAISON WINERY	Napa Valley Spring Mountain Philip Togni Signature	400	$40.00	$60.00	1992-1998
1984	DE MOOR WINERY	Napa Valley	2,400	$14.00	$16.00	1992-2002
1982	DE MOOR WINERY	Napa Valley Owners' Selection	2,000	$12.00	$19.00	1995-2003
1983	DIAMOND CREEK VINEYARD	Napa Valley Diamond Mountain Red Rock Terrace	651	$20.00	$25.00	1996-2005
1977	DIAMOND CREEK VINEYARD	Napa Valley Diamond Mountain Red Rock Terrace, First Pick	238	$10.00	$50.00	1994-2003
1975	DIAMOND CREEK VINEYARD	Napa Valley Diamond Mountain Red Rock Terrace	286	$7.50	$75.00	1992-1997
1974	DIAMOND CREEK VINEYARD	Napa Valley Diamond Mountain Gravelly Meadow	105	$7.50	$135.00	1990-1997
1983	DUCKHORN VINEYARDS	Napa Valley	3,000	$16.00	$30.00	1994-2000

NA — not available.   NR — not released.   * — Beaulieu production figures are estimates.

Vintage	Winery	Appellation/Vineyard	Case Prod.	Release Price	Current Price	Drink
1985	FLORA SPRINGS WINE CO.	Napa Valley	4,000	$15.00	$15.00	1991-1999
1985	FLORA SPRINGS WINE CO.	Napa Valley Rutherford Trilogy	1,200	$30.00	$30.00	1992-1998
1985	FRANCISCAN VINEYARDS	Napa Valley Oakville Library Selection	2,000	$17.50	$17.50	1990-1996
1984	FREEMARK ABBEY WINERY	Napa Valley Rutherford Bosche	3,076	$20.00	$20.00	1995-2003
1982	FREEMARK ABBEY WINERY	Napa Valley Rutherford Bosche	3,592	$15.00	$26.00	1996-2002
1980	FREEMARK ABBEY WINERY	Napa Valley Rutherford Bosche	2,740	$14.50	$36.00	1990-1996
1977	FREEMARK ABBEY WINERY	Napa Valley Rutherford Bosche	3,532	$12.50	$25.00	1990-1994
1973	FREEMARK ABBEY WINERY	Napa Valley Rutherford Bosche	3,495	$8.00	$70.00	1990-1993
1981	GRACE FAMILY VINEYARD	Napa Valley St. Helena Estate	185	$28.00	$150.00	1992-1998
1983	GRGICH HILLS CELLAR	Napa Valley Yountville	10,000	$17.00	$23.00	1994-2003
1983	GROTH VINEYARDS & WINERY	Napa Valley Oakville Estate	10,000	$13.00	$21.00	1994-2000
1982	GROTH VINEYARDS & WINERY	Napa Valley Oakville Estate	7,000	$13.00	$24.00	1992-1998
1981	GUNDLACH BUNDSCHU WINERY	Sonoma Valley Batto Ranch	950	$10.00	$18.00	1990-1993
1984	HAYWOOD WINERY	Sonoma Valley	856	$12.50	$20.00	1995-2002
1982	HEITZ WINE CELLARS	Napa Valley Oakville Martha's Vineyard	5,100	$30.00	$45.00	1996-2003
1983	HESS COLLECTION WINERY	Napa Valley Mount Veeder Reserve	250	$22.00	$30.00	1990-1997
1980	INGLENOOK-NAPA VALLEY	Napa Valley Rutherford Cask	9,305	$15.50	$22.00	1991-1996
1986	IRON HORSE VINEYARDS	Alexander Valley Cabernets	3,500	$17.50	$17.50	1993-2000
1983	JOHNSON TURNBULL VINEYARDS	Napa Valley Oakville	1,300	$12.50	$18.00	1993-1998
1986	JORDAN VINEYARD AND WINERY	Alexander Valley Estate	58,000	NR		1990-1995
1982	ROBERT KEENAN WINERY	Napa Valley	2,900	$10.00	$20.00	1993-2000
1974	CHARLES KRUG WINERY	Napa Valley Stags Leap District Lot F-1 Vintage Select	8,246	$9.00	$50.00	1990-1993
1958	CHARLES KRUG WINERY	Napa Valley Vintage Select	868	$2.00	$465.00	1990
1946	CHARLES KRUG WINERY	Napa Valley Vintage Select	1,452	$1.00	$750.00	1990
1944	CHARLES KRUG WINERY	Napa Valley	857	$0.95	$800.00	1990
1985	LA JOTA VINEYARD COMPANY	Napa Valley Howell Mountain	1,570	$18.00	$18.00	1993-2000
1984	LA JOTA VINEYARD COMPANY	Napa Valley Howell Mountain	1,206	$15.00	$20.00	1993-1999
1986	LAKESPRING WINERY	Napa Valley Yountville	1,700	$14.00	$14.00	1994-1999
1985	LAKESPRING WINERY	Napa Valley Yountville	3,300	$12.00	$12.00	1992-1999
1982	LAKESPRING WINERY	Napa Valley Yountville Vintage Selection	3,600	$14.00	$20.00	1992-1998
1980	LAKESPRING WINERY	Napa Valley	2,000	$10.00	$21.00	1991-1997
1984	LONG VINEYARDS	Napa Valley Oakville	200	$32.00	$35.00	1992-2000
1979	MARKHAM VINEYARDS	Napa Valley Yountville Markham Vineyard	2,752	$13.00	$28.00	1993-2000
1970	LOUIS M. MARTINI WINERY	California Special Selection	7,845	$8.00	$90.00	1990-1995
1958	LOUIS M. MARTINI WINERY	California Special Selection	1,750	$4.50	$220.00	1990-1992
1968	MAYACAMAS VINEYARDS	California	680	$4.50	$125.00	1990-1995
1983	MERRYVALE VINEYARDS	Napa Valley Red Table Wine	694	$18.00	$30.00	1993-1999
1986	MONTICELLO CELLARS	Napa Valley Corley Reserve	3,800	$24.00	$24.00	1993-1999
1985	MONTICELLO CELLARS	Napa Valley Corley Reserve	150	$22.50	$22.50	1994-1998
1983	MONTICELLO CELLARS	Napa Valley Corley Reserve	350	$24.00	$24.00	1995-2003
1978	MOUNT EDEN VINEYARDS	Santa Cruz Mountains	650	$25.00	$45.00	1995-2003
1984	MOUNT VEEDER WINERY	Napa Valley Mount Veeder Mt. Veeder Vineyards	2,500	$14.00	$14.00	1995-2003
1977	MOUNT VEEDER WINERY	Napa Valley Rutherford Niebaum-Coppola	1,225	$9.75	$60.00	1996-2006
1978	NIEBAUM-COPPOLA ESTATE	Napa Valley Rutherford Rubicon	1,700	$25.00	$45.00	1990-2000
1981	OPUS ONE	Napa Valley Oakville	6,000	$50.00	$90.00	1994-2003
1986	ROBERT PECOTA WINERY	Napa Valley Calistoga Kara's Vineyard	1,230	$16.00	$16.00	1993-2000
1982	ROBERT PEPI WINERY	Napa Valley Yountville Vine Hill Ranch	2,175	$14.00	$17.00	1994-2002
1983	PINE RIDGE WINERY	Napa Valley Rutherford Andrus Reserve	169	$35.00	$45.00	1993-2000
1981	PINE RIDGE WINERY	Napa Valley Rutherford Rutherford Cuveé	4,081	$13.00	$28.00	1994-2002
1986	PRESTON VINEYARDS	Dry Creek Valley	4,075	$11.00	$11.00	1993-1999
1985	RAYMOND VINEYARD & CELLAR	Napa Valley Rutherford Private Reserve	4,000	NR		1992-1998
1986	RIDGE VINEYARDS	Napa Valley York Creek	5,333	NR		1993-2000
1984	RIDGE VINEYARDS	Napa County Spring Mountain York Creek	6,900	$14.00	$16.00	1990-1998
1980	RIDGE VINEYARDS	Napa County Spring Mountain York Creek	3,516	$12.00	$22.00	1992-1999
1979	RIDGE VINEYARDS	Napa County Spring Mountain York Creek	3,100	$12.00	$30.00	1990-1998
1977	RIDGE VINEYARDS	Napa County Spring Mountain York Creek	1,780	$12.00	$35.00	1990-1996
1975	RIDGE VINEYARDS	Santa Cruz Mountains Monte Bello	1,850	$10.00	$85.00	1990-1999
1986	RUTHERFORD HILL WINERY	Napa Valley St. Helena XVS	2,000	NR		1994-2000

NA — not available.   NR — not released.   * — Beaulieu production figures are estimates.

Vintage	Winery	Appellation/Vineyard	Case Prod.	Release Price	Current Price	Drink
1984	RUTHERFORD HILL WINERY	Napa Valley	14,834	$12.50	$15.00	1994-2000
1980	RUTHERFORD HILL WINERY	Napa Valley Cask Lot 2 Limited Edition	2,000	$15.00	$20.00	1990-1996
1986	V. SATTUI WINERY	Napa Valley Rutherford Preston Vineyard	2,487	$16.75	$16.75	1991-1998
1986	SEQUOIA GROVE VINEYARDS	Napa County	6,776	$16.00	$16.00	1993-1998
1982	SHAFER VINEYARDS	Napa Valley Stags Leap District	3,500	$13.00	$18.00	1992-2000
1982	SILVER OAK CELLARS	Napa Valley Calistoga	3,500	$19.00	$32.00	1995-2005
1980	SILVER OAK CELLARS	Alexander Valley	12,000	$18.00	$45.00	1990-2000
1977	SILVER OAK CELLARS	Alexander Valley	7,350	$14.00	$85.00	1990-1997
1975	SILVER OAK CELLARS	Alexander Valley	6,000	$10.00	$95.00	1990-1996
1983	SILVERADO VINEYARDS	Napa Valley Stags Leap District	8,000	$11.00	$20.00	1995-2000
1982	SILVERADO VINEYARDS	Napa Valley Stags Leap District	8,000	$11.00	$22.00	1993-2000
1982	SIMI WINERY	Sonoma-Napa Counties Reserve	3,400	$20.00	$20.00	1996-2004
1985	SPRING MOUNTAIN VINEYARDS	Napa Valley Spring Mountain	3,396	$20.00	$20.00	1997-2005
1978	ST. CLEMENT VINEYARDS	Napa Valley	400	$10.00	$40.00	1990-1997
1983	STAG'S LEAP WINE CELLARS	Napa Valley Stags Leap District Cask 23	1,077	$35.00	$55.00	1993-1999
1979	STAG'S LEAP WINE CELLARS	Napa Valley Stags Leap District Cask 23	1,204	$35.00	$55.00	1990-1992
1974	STAG'S LEAP WINE CELLARS	Napa Valley Stags Leap District Cask 23	100	$12.00	$135.00	1990-1993
1980	STELTZNER VINEYARDS	Napa Valley Stags Leap District	200	$14.00	$38.00	1991-1997
1986	STERLING VINEYARDS	Napa Valley Diamond Mountain Diamond Mountain Ranch	6,000	NR		1996-2003
1982	STERLING VINEYARDS	Napa Valley Diamond Mountain Diamond Mountain Ranch	3,100	$15.00	$20.00	1995-2003
1984	STONEGATE WINERY	Napa Valley Calistoga Estate	4,580	$14.00	$14.00	1993-1998
1981	TUDAL WINERY	Napa Valley St. Helena	1,000	$12.00	$25.00	1991-1997
1985	VICHON WINERY	Napa Valley	7,500	$13.00	$14.00	1992-1997
1984	VICHON WINERY	Napa Valley	600	$11.25	$13.00	1992-1997
1978	VILLA MT. EDEN WINERY	Napa Valley Oakville Reserve	761	$20.00	$42.00	1994-2004

SCORE: 87

Vintage	Winery	Appellation/Vineyard	Case Prod.	Release Price	Current Price	Drink
1981	ALEXANDER VALLEY VINEYARDS	Alexander Valley	3,625	$9.00	$16.00	1990-1994
1981	BEAULIEU VINEYARD	Napa Valley Rutherford Georges de Latour Private Reserve	15,000	$24.00	$30.00	1993-2000
1966	BEAULIEU VINEYARD	Napa Valley Rutherford Georges de Latour Private Reserve	15,000	$5.25	$140.00	1990-1994
1944	BEAULIEU VINEYARD	Napa Valley Rutherford Georges de Latour Private Reserve	15,000	$1.47	$1100.00	1990-1992
1942	BEAULIEU VINEYARD	Napa Valley Rutherford Georges de Latour Private Reserve	15,000	$1.45	$1200.00	1990-1992
1984	BERINGER VINEYARDS	Napa Valley St. Helena Chabot Vineyard	750	NR		1991-1997
1981	BERINGER VINEYARDS	Napa Valley St. Helena Chabot Vineyard	1,000	$23.00	$42.00	1990-1996
1984	BUEHLER VINEYARDS	Napa Valley	2,639	$13.00	$16.00	1995-2003
1978	BUEHLER VINEYARDS	Napa Valley	224	$10.00	$35.00	1990-1998
1983	BUENA VISTA WINERY	Sonoma Valley Carneros Private Reserve	3,500	$18.00	$18.00	1990-1999
1983	BURGESS CELLARS	Napa Valley Vintage Selection	6,500	$17.00	$21.00	1994-2002
1979	BURGESS CELLARS	Napa Valley Vintage Selection	2,800	$16.00	$30.00	1993-1999
1976	BURGESS CELLARS	Napa Valley Vintage Selection	2,200	$12.00	$41.00	1991-1997
1982	CARMENET VINEYARD	Sonoma Valley	5,348	$16.00	$30.00	1993-2003
1983	CAYMUS VINEYARDS	Napa Valley Rutherford Estate	3,000	$15.00	$30.00	1994-2002
1978	CAYMUS VINEYARDS	Napa Valley Rutherford Estate	2,600	$12.00	$60.00	1990-1996
1974	CAYMUS VINEYARDS	Napa Valley Rutherford Estate	950	$7.00	$110.00	1990-1996
1984	CHAPPELLET VINEYARD	Napa Valley Reserve	8,000	$18.00	$23.00	1992-1996
1969	CHAPPELLET VINEYARD	Napa Valley	400	$10.00	$150.00	1990-1995
1979	CHATEAU MONTELENA WINERY	Napa Valley Calistoga Estate	5,776	$16.00	$45.00	1992-1998
1978	CHATEAU MONTELENA WINERY	Alexander Valley Sonoma	1,560	$12.00	$50.00	1990-1996
1974	CHATEAU MONTELENA WINERY	Alexander Valley Sonoma	6,000	$9.00	$100.00	1992-2000
1973	CHATEAU MONTELENA WINERY	Alexander Valley Sonoma	3,000	$8.50	$100.00	1990-2001
1985	CHIMNEY ROCK WINE CELLARS	Napa Valley Stags Leap District	2,900	$15.00	$15.00	1990-1997
1984	CLOS DU BOIS WINERY	Alexander Valley Briarcrest Vineyard	1,711	$16.00	$24.00	1993-2000
1977	CLOS DU VAL WINE CO.	Napa Valley Stags Leap District Reserve	2,900	$20.00	$53.00	1990-2001
1986	CONN CREEK WINERY	Napa Valley Barrel Select	6,550	NR		1994-2000
1985	CONN CREEK WINERY	Napa Valley St. Helena Barrel Select Private Reserve	1,100	NR		1992-1997

NA — not available.   NR — not released.   * — Beaulieu production figures are estimates.

Vintage	Winery	Appellation/Vineyard	Case Prod.	Release Price	Current Price	Drink
1983	CONN CREEK WINERY	Napa Valley St. Helena Collins Vineyard Proprietor's Special Selection	40		$70.00	1991-1997
1982	DIAMOND CREEK VINEYARD	Napa Valley Diamond Mountain Red Rock Terrace	753	$20.00	$35.00	1995-2004
1976	DIAMOND CREEK VINEYARD	Napa Valley Diamond Mountain Volcanic Hill	428	$9.00	$90.00	1991-1999
1974	DIAMOND CREEK VINEYARD	Napa Valley Diamond Mountain Volcanic Hill	485	$7.50	$135.00	1992-2000
1983	DOMINUS ESTATE	Napa Valley Yountville Napanook	2,100	$43.00	$43.00	1994-2002
1981	DUCKHORN VINEYARDS	Napa Valley	950	$15.00	$45.00	1993-2000
1983	FAR NIENTE WINERY	Napa Valley Oakville	5,500	$25.00	$32.00	1993-2000
1985	FRANCISCAN VINEYARDS	Napa Valley Oakville Reserve	1,800	$18.00	$18.00	1991-1997
1984	FRANCISCAN VINEYARDS	Napa Valley Oakville Private Reserve	5,400	$9.00	$12.00	1990-1996
1982	FROG'S LEAP WINERY	Napa Valley	900	$9.00	$25.00	1990-1996
1983	GIRARD WINERY	Napa Valley Oakville Reserve	548	$18.00	$20.00	1994-2000
1982	GIRARD WINERY	Napa Valley Oakville	2,107	$12.50	$30.00	1994-2004
1982	GRGICH HILLS CELLAR	Napa Valley Yountville	3,000	$17.00	$28.00	1992-1998
1980	WILLIAM HILL WINERY	Napa Valley Mount Veeder Gold Label	4,961	$18.25	$36.00	1990-1996
1946	INGLENOOK-NAPA VALLEY	Napa Valley Rutherford	8,000	$1.49	$1100.00	1990-1995
1897	INGLENOOK-NAPA VALLEY	California Claret-Medoc Type	2,000	NR		1990-1995
1985	IRON HORSE VINEYARDS	Alexander Valley Cabernets	3,000	$16.00	$16.50	1992-1999
1986	JOHNSON TURNBULL VINEYARDS	Napa Valley Oakville Vineyard Selection 67	1,280	$20.00	$20.00	1995-2005
1981	JOHNSON TURNBULL VINEYARDS	Napa Valley Oakville	1,250	$12.00	$20.00	1995-2000
1980	JOHNSON TURNBULL VINEYARDS	Napa Valley Oakville	1,100	$12.00	$26.00	1994-2000
1983	ROBERT KEENAN WINERY	Napa Valley	3,400	$11.00	$18.00	1995-2000
1983	KENWOOD VINEYARDS	Sonoma Valley Artist Series	2,500	$30.00	$35.00	1993-1998
1982	KENWOOD VINEYARDS	Sonoma Valley Artist Series	2,200	$25.00	$40.00	1993-1999
1981	KISTLER VINEYARDS	Napa Valley Mount Veeder Veeder Hills-Veeder Peak	1,010	$12.00	$32.00	1991-1999
1986	CHARLES KRUG WINERY	Napa Valley Vintage Select	7,266	NR		1994-2002
1984	CHARLES KRUG WINERY	Napa Valley Vintage Select	3,653	NR		1993-2002
1965	CHARLES KRUG WINERY	Napa Valley Vintage Select	8,643	$5.00	$80.00	1990-1993
1984	LIVINGSTON VINEYARDS	Napa Valley Rutherford Moffett Vineyard	936	$18.00	$25.00	1991-1996
1966	LOUIS M. MARTINI WINERY	California Special Selection	2,023	$6.00	$110.00	1990-1992
1959	LOUIS M. MARTINI WINERY	California Special Selection	1,500	$4.50	$140.00	1990-1992
1955	LOUIS M. MARTINI WINERY	California Special Selection	1,035	$2.50	$190.00	1990-1992
1951	LOUIS M. MARTINI WINERY	California Special Selection	1,000	$2.00	$275.00	1990-1992
1973	MAYACAMAS VINEYARDS	Napa Valley Mount Veeder	2,050	$9.00	$90.00	1990-1996
1974	MOUNT EDEN VINEYARDS	Santa Cruz Mountains	437	$20.00	$120.00	1994-2002
1986	MOUNT VEEDER WINERY	Napa Valley Mount Veeder Mt. Veeder Vds	2,600	NR		1992-2000
1985	MOUNT VEEDER WINERY	Napa Valley Mount Veeder Mt. Veeder Vds	2,100	NR		1997-2004
1980	MOUNT VEEDER WINERY	Napa Valley Mount Veeder Bernstein Vyds	2,600	$13.50	$30.00	1992-2000
1984	NEWTON VINEYARD	Napa Valley Estate	3,192	$13.50	$19.00	1991-1996
1981	NIEBAUM-COPPOLA ESTATE	Napa Valley Rutherford Rubicon	3,661	$35.00	$35.00	1993-2000
1980	NIEBAUM-COPPOLA ESTATE	Napa Valley Rutherford Rubicon	3,850	$30.00	$35.00	1992-2002
1984	ROBERT PEPI WINERY	Napa Valley Yountville Vine Hill Ranch	2,550	$16.00	$16.00	1994-2002
1984	JOSEPH PHELPS VINEYARDS	Napa Valley Calistoga Eisele Vineyard	1,300	$35.00	$39.00	1995-2000
1978	JOSEPH PHELPS VINEYARDS	Napa Valley Insignia	1,175	$25.00	$65.00	1990-1997
1984	PRESTON VINEYARDS	Dry Creek Valley	2,850	$11.00	$14.00	1991-1996
1982	PRESTON VINEYARDS	Dry Creek Valley	1,700	$11.00	$18.00	1990-1996
1981	RAYMOND VINEYARD & CELLAR	Napa Valley Rutherford Private Reserve	1,200	$16.00	$35.00	1990-1995
1978	RIDGE VINEYARDS	Napa County Spring Mountain York Creek	5,983	$12.00	$35.00	1990-1998
1975	RIDGE VINEYARDS	Napa County Spring Mountain York Creek	800	$10.00	$45.00	1992-2000
1974	RIDGE VINEYARDS	Napa County Spring Mountain York Creek	536	$6.75	$50.00	1990-1997
1973	RIDGE VINEYARDS	Santa Cruz Mountains Monte Bello	1,094	$10.00	$110.00	1990-1994
1968	RIDGE VINEYARDS	Santa Cruz Mountains Monte Bello	200	$7.50	$190.00	1990-1997
1979	RUTHERFORD HILL WINERY	Napa Valley	9,971	$11.50	$22.00	1990-1995
1984	SANTA CRUZ MOUNTAIN VYD	Santa Cruz Mountains Bates Ranch	1,100	NR		1992-1998
1985	V. SATTUI WINERY	Napa Valley Rutherford Preston Vineyard	3,143	$15.75	$15.75	1990-1996
1980	SEQUOIA GROVE VINEYARDS	Napa Valley Cask Two	440	$12.00	$45.00	1992-1999
1983	SHAFER VINEYARDS	Napa Valley Stags Leap District	3,700	$13.00	$13.00	1992-1997

NA — not available.   NR — not released.   * — Beaulieu production figures are estimates.

Vintage	Winery	Appellation/Vineyard	Case Prod.	Release Price	Current Price	Drink
1979	SIMI WINERY	Alexander Valley Reserve	1,700	$20.00	$36.00	1992-1999
1974	SIMI WINERY	Alexander Valley Reserve Vintage	14,000	$20.00	$45.00	1990-1996
1979	SPRING MOUNTAIN VINEYARDS	Napa Valley Rutherford	9,987	$13.00	$32.00	1992-1998
1986	ST. CLEMENT VINEYARDS	Napa Valley	2,000		NR	1993-2001
1975-76	ST. CLEMENT VINEYARDS	Napa Valley NV	650	$8.00	$50.00	1993-2000
1974	STAG'S LEAP WINE CELLARS	Napa Valley Stags Leap District Stag's Leap Vineyards	450	$8.00	$110.00	1990-1992
1984	STAGS' LEAP WINERY	Napa Valley Stags Leap District	5,187	$13.50	$18.00	1992-1997
1978	STELTZNER VINEYARDS	Napa Valley Stags Leap District	500	$14.00	$50.00	1990-1996
1983	STERLING VINEYARDS	Napa Valley Diamond Mountain Diamond Mountain Ranch	4,100	$15.00	$18.00	1994-2002
1985	STONEGATE WINERY	Napa Valley Calistoga Estate	4,403	$16.00	$16.00	1993-1998
1983	PHILIP TOGNI VINEYARD	Napa Valley Spring Mountain	90	$18.00	$50.00	1995-2005
1986	TREFETHEN VINEYARDS	Napa Valley Yountville	10,400	$15.25	$15.25	1996-2002
1981	TREFETHEN VINEYARDS	Napa Valley Yountville	8,842	$11.00	$28.00	1990-1995

SCORE: 86

Vintage	Winery	Appellation/Vineyard	Case Prod.	Release Price	Current Price	Drink
1979	ALEXANDER VALLEY VINEYARDS	Alexander Valley	2,819	$7.00	$18.00	1990-1996
1976	BEAULIEU VINEYARD	Napa Valley Rutherford Georges de Latour Private Reserve	15,000	$19.00	$60.00	1990-1996
1981	BUENA VISTA WINERY	Sonoma Valley Carneros Private Reserve (Special Selection)	2,730	$18.00	$32.00	1990-1995
1974	BURGESS CELLARS	Napa Valley Vintage Selection	1,100	$9.00	$50.00	1990-1996
1982	CAKEBREAD CELLARS	Napa Valley	5,000	$16.00	$35.00	1994-2000
1978	CAKEBREAD CELLARS	Napa Valley Rutherford Lot 2	80	$12.00	$100.00	1991-2000
1972	CAYMUS VINEYARDS	Napa Valley Rutherford Estate	230	$4.50	$110.00	1990-1993
1980	CHATEAU MONTELENA WINERY	Napa Valley Calistoga Estate	10,000	$16.00	$40.00	1991-1997
1975	CHATEAU MONTELENA WINERY	North Coast	6,675	$9.00	$100.00	1993-2000
1986	CHIMNEY ROCK WINE CELLARS	Napa Valley Stags Leap District	5,700	$15.00	$15.00	1990-1996
1983	CLOS DU VAL WINE CO.	Napa Valley Stags Leap District Estate	23,500	$15.00	$17.50	1994-2002
1973	CLOS DU VAL WINE CO.	Napa Valley Stags Leap District Estate	2,760	$6.00	$70.00	1990-1995
1984	CONN CREEK WINERY	Napa Valley Barrel Select Lot 79	4,450	$13.00	$13.00	1991-1996
1981	CONN CREEK WINERY	Napa Valley St. Helena Collins Vineyard Proprietor's Special Selection	40		$70.00	1994-2002
1978	CONN CREEK WINERY	Napa Valley Lot 1	3,000	$12.00	$30.00	1990-2000
1976	CONN CREEK WINERY	Napa Valley	2,000	$12.00	$45.00	1990-1995
1983	DE MOOR WINERY	Napa Valley	2,400	$12.00	$16.00	1995-2003
1982	DE MOOR WINERY	Napa Valley	1,000	$12.00	$18.00	1994-2001
1981	DE MOOR WINERY	Napa Valley (Napa Cellars)	1,800	$12.00	$25.00	1990-1997
1980	DIAMOND CREEK VINEYARD	Napa Valley Diamond Mountain Red Rock Terrace	591	$20.00	$40.00	1994-2004
1984	EBERLE WINERY	Paso Robles	3,013	$12.00	$17.00	1992-1996
1983	FREEMARK ABBEY WINERY	Napa Valley Rutherford Bosche	2,860	$18.00	$18.00	1995-2003
1981	FREEMARK ABBEY WINERY	Napa Valley Rutherford Bosche	2,704	$14.00	$24.00	1994-2000
1971	FREEMARK ABBEY WINERY	Napa Valley Rutherford Bosche	1,015	$6.75	$40.00	1990
1981	GIRARD WINERY	Napa Valley Oakville	1,595	$12.50	$20.00	1993-2000
1978	GRACE FAMILY VINEYARD	Napa Valley St. Helena Estate	48	$20.00	$275.00	1990-1995
1981	GRGICH HILLS CELLAR	Napa Valley Yountville	2,000	$17.00	$28.00	1991-1997
1980	HAYWOOD WINERY	Sonoma Valley	570	$9.75	$12.00	1992-1999
1984	HEITZ WINE CELLARS	Napa Valley Rutherford Bella Oaks Vyd	2,944	$25.00	$25.00	1994-2002
1983	HEITZ WINE CELLARS	Napa Valley Rutherford Bella Oaks Vyd	2,944	$15.00	$25.00	1994-2001
1967	HEITZ WINE CELLARS	Napa Valley Oakville Martha's Vineyard	2,208	$7.50	$300.00	1990-1996
1978	INGLENOOK-NAPA VALLEY	Napa Valley Rutherford Cask	11,969	$9.25	$26.00	1990-1994
1974	INGLENOOK-NAPA VALLEY	Napa Valley Rutherford Cask	11,864	$9.00	$45.00	1990-1995
1984	IRON HORSE VINEYARDS	Alexander Valley	1,900	$14.00	$16.00	1992-1998
1980	IRON HORSE VINEYARDS	Alexander Valley	1,000	$12.00	$20.00	1992-1998
1984	JORDAN VINEYARD AND WINERY	Alexander Valley Estate	50,500	$19.00	$25.00	1990-1993
1985	ROBERT KEENAN WINERY	Napa Valley	2,400	$15.00	$15.00	1993-1998
1982	KISTLER VINEYARDS	Napa Valley Mount Veeder Veeder Hills Vineyard	1,010	$12.00	$26.00	1992-1999
1964	CHARLES KRUG WINERY	Napa Valley Vintage Select	5,780	$4.00	$85.00	1990

NA — not available.   NR — not released.   ∗ — Beaulieu production figures are estimates.

Vintage	Winery	Appellation/Vineyard	Case Prod.	Release Price	Current Price	Drink
1981	LAKESPRING WINERY	Napa Valley Yountville	3,000	$11.00	$18.00	1992-1998
1985	LIVINGSTON VINEYARDS	Napa Valley Rutherford Moffett Vineyard	1,030	$18.00	$24.00	1993-1999
1986	LONG VINEYARDS	Napa Valley Oakville	200	NR		1991-1998
1981	MARKHAM VINEYARDS	Napa Valley Yountville Markham Vyd	3,717	$13.00	$20.00	1992-1998
1986	LOUIS M. MARTINI WINERY	Sonoma Valley Monte Rosso	810	NR		1992-1999
1983	LOUIS M. MARTINI WINERY	Sonoma Valley Monte Rosso	1,150	$22.00	$22.00	1993-1999
1978	LOUIS M. MARTINI WINERY	California Special Selection	21,388	$9.00	$23.00	1990-1996
1976	LOUIS M. MARTINI WINERY	California Special Selection	2,693	$9.00	$35.00	1990-1997
1986	MAYACAMAS VINEYARDS	Napa Valley Mount Veeder	2,150	NR		1991-1996
1971	MAYACAMAS VINEYARDS	Napa Valley Mount Veeder	1,490	$8.00	$80.00	1990-1995
1984	MERRYVALE VINEYARDS	Napa Valley Red Table Wine	1,026	$24.00	$28.00	1993-1998
1975	ROBERT MONDAVI WINERY	Napa Valley Oakville Reserve	7,000	$30.00	$75.00	1990-1992
1969	ROBERT MONDAVI WINERY	Napa Valley Oakville Unfined	3,000	$12.00	$155.00	1990-1995
1985	MOUNT EDEN VINEYARDS	Santa Cruz Mountains	622	$28.00	$28.00	1994-1998
1981	MOUNT EDEN VINEYARDS	Santa Cruz Mountains	652	$18.00	$25.00	1993-1999
1978	MOUNT VEEDER WINERY	Napa Valley Mount Veeder Sidehill Ranch	375	$13.50	$40.00	1990-2000
1985	ROBERT PECOTA WINERY	Napa Valley Calistoga Kara's Vineyard	940	$16.00	$20.00	1992-1998
1981	ROBERT PEPI WINERY	Napa Valley Yountville Vine Hill Ranch	2,000	$14.00	$18.00	1992-2000
1984	JOSEPH PHELPS VINEYARDS	Napa Valley Oakville Backus Vineyard	1,585	$20.00	$29.00	1992-1997
1983	JOSEPH PHELPS VINEYARDS	Napa Valley Calistoga Eisele Vineyard	1,250	$25.00	$35.00	1997-2002
1977	JOSEPH PHELPS VINEYARDS	Napa Valley Oakville Backus Vineyard	530	$15.00	$60.00	1990-1995
1983	PRESTON VINEYARDS	Dry Creek Valley	2,500	$11.00	$15.00	1993-1998
1986	RAVENSWOOD	Sonoma County	3,000	$12.00	$14.00	1995-2002
1986	RAYMOND VINEYARD & CELLAR	Napa Valley Rutherford Private Reserve	3,000	NR		1993-1999
1965	RIDGE VINEYARDS	Santa Cruz Mountains Monte Bello	90	$6.50	$275.00	1990-1993
1986	ROMBAUER VINEYARDS	Napa Valley	3,000	$15.00	$15.00	1992-1997
1980	ROMBAUER VINEYARDS	Napa Valley	500	$10.00	$25.00	1993-2000
1980	SANTA CRUZ MOUNTAIN VYD	Santa Cruz Mountains Bates Ranch	840	$12.00	$18.00	1990-1997
1984	V. SATTUI WINERY	Napa Valley Rutherford Preston Vineyard	2,850	$13.75	$19.75	1990-1996
1985	SEQUOIA GROVE VINEYARDS	Napa County	4,101	$16.00	$16.00	1992-1997
1984	SILVER OAK CELLARS	Napa Valley Calistoga	2,500	$22.00	$28.00	1996-2004
1983	SILVER OAK CELLARS	Alexander Valley	14,000	$20.00	$30.00	1995-2002
1981	SILVER OAK CELLARS	Alexander Valley	11,200	$19.00	$35.00	1994-2000
1976	SILVER OAK CELLARS	Alexander Valley	6,600	$12.00	$70.00	1992-2002
1972	SILVER OAK CELLARS	North Coast	1,100	$6.00	$160.00	1990-1995
1979	SMITH-MADRONE VINEYARD	Napa Valley Spring Mountain	350	$14.00	$25.00	1993-2000
1980	SPRING MOUNTAIN VINEYARDS	Napa Valley Rutherford	11,162	$13.00	$24.00	1990-1994
1973	STAG'S LEAP WINE CELLARS	Napa Valley Stags Leap District Stag's Leap Vineyards	400	$6.00	$135.00	1990
1986	STAGS' LEAP WINERY	Napa Valley Stags Leap District	7,860	NR		1992-1997
1980	STONEGATE WINERY	Napa Valley	2,258	$12.00	$22.00	1991-1997
1984	PHILIP TOGNI VINEYARD	Napa Valley Spring Mountain	180	$18.00	$35.00	1994-2003
1979	TREFETHEN VINEYARDS	Napa Valley Yountville	6,192	$11.00	$35.00	1990-1996
1977	TREFETHEN VINEYARDS	Napa Valley Yountville	3,687	$8.50	$45.00	1990-1995
1983	TUDAL WINERY	Napa Valley St. Helena	1,500	$12.50	$19.00	1992-1998
1977	VILLA MT. EDEN WINERY	Napa Valley Oakville Estate	2,383	$8.00	$36.00	1991-2002

SCORE: 85

Vintage	Winery	Appellation/Vineyard	Case Prod.	Release Price	Current Price	Drink
1967	BEAULIEU VINEYARD	Napa Valley Rutherford Georges de Latour Private Reserve	15,000	$5.25	$120.00	1990-1993
1965	BEAULIEU VINEYARD	Napa Valley Rutherford Georges de Latour Private Reserve	15,000	$5.25	$120.00	1990-1993
1948	BEAULIEU VINEYARD	Napa Valley Rutherford Georges de Latour Private Reserve	15,000	$1.82	$800.00	1990-1992
1941	BEAULIEU VINEYARD	Napa Valley Rutherford Georges de Latour Private Reserve	15,000	$1.45	$1200.00	1990-1992
1983	BERINGER VINEYARDS	Napa Valley St. Helena Chabot Vineyard	1,000	$27.00	$27.00	1992-1998
1980	BERINGER VINEYARDS	Napa Valley Yountville Private Reserve State Lane Vineyard	2,000	$15.00	$40.00	1991-1997
1981	BUEHLER VINEYARDS	Napa Valley	2,214	$11.00	$20.00	1994-2000
1982	BUENA VISTA WINERY	Sonoma Valley Carneros Private Reserve	3,700	$18.00	$30.00	1991-1996

NA — not available.　　NR — not released.　　∗ — Beaulieu production figures are estimates.

Vintage	Winery	Appellation/Vineyard	Case Prod.	Release Price	Current Price	Drink
1985	CAKEBREAD CELLARS	Napa Valley Rutherford Rutherford Reserve	700	NR		1993-1998
1978	CAKEBREAD CELLARS	Napa Valley	900	$12.00	$60.00	1992-2000
1983	CARMENET VINEYARD	Sonoma Valley	6,175	$17.50	$25.00	1994-2004
1976	CAYMUS VINEYARDS	Napa Valley Rutherford Estate	1,600	$10.00	$60.00	1990-1995
1981	CLOS DU BOIS WINERY	Alexander Valley Marlstone Vineyard	1,005	$15.00	$32.00	1990-1995
1985	CONN CREEK WINERY	Napa Valley Barrel Select	6,000	NR		1991-1995
1982	CONN CREEK WINERY	Napa Valley St. Helena Collins Vineyard Proprietor's Special Selection	40		$70.00	1995-2004
1982	CONN CREEK WINERY	Napa Valley Barrel Select	7,100	$12.00	$16.00	1992-1997
1981	CONN CREEK WINERY	Napa Valley	5,700	$14.00	$18.00	1990-1995
1979	DE MOOR WINERY	Napa Valley (Napa Cellars)	1,600	$10.00	$25.00	1990-1998
1976	DIAMOND CREEK VINEYARD	Napa Valley Diamond Mountain Red Rock Terrace	283	$9.00	$90.00	1990-1999
1976	DIAMOND CREEK VINEYARD	Napa Valley Diamond Mountain Gravelly Meadow	96	$9.00	$90.00	1990-1999
1975	DIAMOND CREEK VINEYARD	Napa Valley Diamond Mountain Gravelly Meadow	95	$7.50	$55.00	1991-2000
1972	DIAMOND CREEK VINEYARD	Napa Valley Diamond Mountain Volcanic Hill	40	$7.50	$200.00	1990-1995
1986	EBERLE WINERY	Paso Robles	4,196	$12.00	$12.00	1993-1997
1981	EBERLE WINERY	Paso Robles	2,500	$10.00	$24.00	1990-1994
1986	FLORA SPRINGS WINE CO.	Napa Valley Rutherford Trilogy	1,400	$33.00	$33.00	1993-1998
1984	FLORA SPRINGS WINE CO.	Napa Valley	3,000	$13.00	$18.00	1990-1996
1980	FLORA SPRINGS WINE CO.	Napa Valley	1,200	$12.00	$20.00	1990-1996
1983	FRANCISCAN VINEYARDS	Napa Valley Oakville Private Reserve	3,000	$8.50	$14.00	1993-1998
1976	FREEMARK ABBEY WINERY	Napa Valley Rutherford Bosche	3,109	$12.50	$45.00	1990-1994
1985	FROG'S LEAP WINERY	Napa Valley	2,300	$12.00	$12.00	1992-1998
1984	GUNDLACH BUNDSCHU WINERY	Sonoma Valley Rhinefarm	5,000	$9.00	$12.00	1992-1997
1981	HAYWOOD WINERY	Sonoma Valley	1,081	$11.00	$20.00	1994-2001
1982	HEITZ WINE CELLARS	Napa Valley Rutherford Bella Oaks Vineyard	2,944	$16.00	$30.00	1993-2000
1976	HEITZ WINE CELLARS	Napa Valley Rutherford Bella Oaks Vineyard	895	$30.00	$62.00	1991-1996
1976	HEITZ WINE CELLARS	Napa Valley Oakville Martha's Vineyard	1,664	$30.00	$75.00	1995-2004
1983	WILLIAM HILL WINERY	Napa Valley Mount Veeder Gold Label	8,405	$18.25	$25.00	1994-1999
1981	WILLIAM HILL WINERY	Napa Valley Mount Veeder Gold Label	5,772	$16.25	$34.00	1990-1995
1970	INGLENOOK-NAPA VALLEY	Napa Valley Rutherford Cask	8,109	$6.50	$75.00	1990-1995
1968	INGLENOOK-NAPA VALLEY	Napa Valley Rutherford Cask	5,218	$6.00	$90.00	1990-1995
1979	JOHNSON TURNBULL VINEYARDS	Napa Valley Oakville	450	$10.50	$26.00	1993-1998
1985	JORDAN VINEYARD AND WINERY	Alexander Valley Estate	53,698	$19.50	$19.50	1990-1994
1980	KISTLER VINEYARDS	Napa Valley Mount Veeder Veeder Hills-Veeder Peak	369	$16.00	$35.00	1992-1999
1959	CHARLES KRUG WINERY	Napa Valley Vintage Select	7,832	$2.25	$150.00	1990
1951	CHARLES KRUG WINERY	Napa Valley Vintage Select	1,553	$1.25	$700.00	1990
1983	LAKESPRING WINERY	Napa Valley Yountville	3,000	$11.00	$13.00	1993-1998
1982	LAUREL GLEN VINEYARD	Sonoma Mountain	2,800	$12.50	$20.00	1992-1997
1982	LYETH WINERY	Alexander Valley	5,000	$16.00	$30.00	1990-1995
1978	MARKHAM VINEYARDS	Napa Valley Yountville Markham Vineyard	2,560	$13.00	$35.00	1992-2000
1984	LOUIS M. MARTINI WINERY	North Coast Special Selection	2,735	NR		1991-1997
1982	LOUIS M. MARTINI WINERY	Sonoma Valley Monte Rosso	2,060	$22.00	$22.00	1993-1999
1981	LOUIS M. MARTINI WINERY	Sonoma Valley Monte Rosso Los Ninos	535	$25.00	$25.00	1990-1998
1964	LOUIS M. MARTINI WINERY	California Special Selection	1,582	$6.00	$100.00	1990-1992
1986	MOUNT EDEN VINEYARDS	Santa Cruz Mountains	786	NR		1994-2000
1980	MOUNT EDEN VINEYARDS	Santa Cruz Mountains	453	$30.00	$35.00	1992-1997
1977	MOUNT VEEDER WINERY	Napa Valley Mount Veeder Bernstein Vineyards	1,350	$11.00	$50.00	1994-2002
1979	NEWTON VINEYARD	Napa Valley	742	$12.00	$30.00	1990-1995
1984	NIEBAUM-COPPOLA ESTATE	Napa Valley Rutherford Rubicon	3,653	NR		1994-1998
1984	ROBERT PECOTA WINERY	Napa Valley Calistoga Kara's Vineyard	540	$14.00	$20.00	1990-1996
1982	ROBERT PECOTA WINERY	Napa Valley	900	$12.00	$20.00	1990-1995
1983	JOSEPH PHELPS VINEYARDS	Napa Valley Oakville Backus Vineyard	800	$16.50	$28.00	1994-1998
1982	JOSEPH PHELPS VINEYARDS	Napa Valley Calistoga Eisele Vineyard	1,775	$30.00	$33.00	1994-2000
1982	JOSEPH PHELPS VINEYARDS	Napa Valley Insignia	2,950	$25.00	$32.00	1992-1998

NA — not available.   NR — not released.   * — Beaulieu production figures are estimates.

Vintage	Winery	Appellation/Vineyard	Case Prod.	Release Price	Current Price	Drink
1975	JOSEPH PHELPS VINEYARDS	Napa Valley Insignia	473	$15.00	$90.00	1990-1995
1983	PINE RIDGE WINERY	Napa Valley Stags Leap District Pine Ridge Stags Leap Vineyard	1,452	$20.00	$26.00	1994-2000
1979	PINE RIDGE WINERY	Napa Valley Rutherford Rutherford District	3,211	$9.00	$45.00	1990-1995
1985	RAVENSWOOD	Sonoma County	1,540	$12.00	$14.00	1995-2001
1982	RAYMOND VINEYARD & CELLAR	Napa Valley Rutherford Private Reserve	1,800	$16.00	$27.00	1990-1996
1981	RAYMOND VINEYARD & CELLAR	Napa Valley Rutherford	10,000	$11.00	$16.50	1990-1993
1980	RAYMOND VINEYARD & CELLAR	Napa Valley Rutherford Private Reserve	1,200		$34.00	1990-1996
1979	RAYMOND VINEYARD & CELLAR	Napa Valley Rutherford	9,300	$12.00	$20.00	1990-1992
1986	RIDGE VINEYARDS	Santa Cruz Mountains Monte Bello	2,079	$35.00	$35.00	1994-1999
1971	RIDGE VINEYARDS	Santa Cruz Mountains Monte Bello	630	$10.00	$145.00	1990-1993
1985	ROMBAUER VINEYARDS	Napa Valley	2,000	$14.75	$17.00	1991-1997
1981	RUTHERFORD HILL WINERY	Napa Valley	9,851	$11.50	$18.00	1990-1995
1980	V. SATTUI WINERY	Napa Valley Rutherford Preston Vineyard Reserve	372	$30.00	$45.00	1990-1995
1984	SEQUOIA GROVE VINEYARDS	Napa Valley	4,502	$12.00	$18.00	1992-2002
1980	SEQUOIA GROVE VINEYARDS	Napa Valley Cask One	444	$12.00	$30.00	1992-2000
1978	SHAFER VINEYARDS	Napa Valley Stags Leap District	1,000	$11.00	$50.00	1992-2000
1985	SILVER OAK CELLARS	Napa Valley Calistoga	3,550	$24.00	$24.00	1996-2006
1985	SILVER OAK CELLARS	Napa Valley Oakville Bonny's Vineyard	970	NR		1995-2004
1979	SILVER OAK CELLARS	Alexander Valley	12,500	$16.00	$65.00	1992-1999
1975	SIMI WINERY	Alexander Valley	11,000	$6.00	$32.00	1990
1977	SPRING MOUNTAIN VINEYARDS	Napa Valley Rutherford	5,986	$9.50	$20.00	1990-1995
1981	ST. CLEMENT VINEYARDS	Napa Valley	2,565	$12.50	$24.00	1994-1999
1977	STAG'S LEAP WINE CELLARS	Napa Valley Stags Leap District Stag's Leap Vineyards	2,000	$9.00	$35.00	1990-1992
1985	STAGS' LEAP WINERY	Napa Valley Stags Leap District	7,672	$15.00	$16.00	1992-1997
1981	STAGS' LEAP WINERY	Napa Valley Stags Leap District	2,712	$11.00	$25.00	1991-1997
1977	STELTZNER VINEYARDS	Napa Valley Stags Leap District	500	$14.00	$45.00	1990-1995
1984	STERLING VINEYARDS	Napa Valley Diamond Mountain Diamond Mountain Ranch	5,500	$15.00	$18.00	1993-1997
1981	STERLING VINEYARDS	Napa Valley Reserve	6,237	$22.50	$28.00	1994-1998
1979	STERLING VINEYARDS	Napa Valley Reserve	6,538	$27.50	$32.00	1990-1995
1980	TUDAL WINERY	Napa Valley St. Helena	1,250	$11.50	$25.00	1992-1996
1984	VICHON WINERY	Napa Valley Stags Leap District Fay Vineyard	1,935	$14.00	$18.00	1990-1994
1980	VICHON WINERY	Napa Valley Stags Leap District Fay Vineyard	1,400	$16.00	$25.00	1990-1995
1981	VILLA MT. EDEN WINERY	Napa Valley Oakville Reserve	1,144	$16.70	$20.00	1990-1996

SCORE: 84

Vintage	Winery	Appellation/Vineyard	Case Prod.	Release Price	Current Price	Drink
1964	BEAULIEU VINEYARD	Napa Valley Rutherford Georges de Latour Private Reserve	15,000	$4.25	$145.00	1990-1994
1980	BUENA VISTA WINERY	Sonoma Valley Carneros Special Selection	2,141	$18.00	$35.00	1990-1996
1985	CAKEBREAD CELLARS	Napa Valley	5,000	$17.00	$17.00	1992-1996
1980	CAKEBREAD CELLARS	Napa Valley	4,000	$14.00	$45.00	1993-2000
1982	DIAMOND CREEK VINEYARD	Napa Valley Diamond Mountain Gravelly Meadow, Special Selection	140	$20.00	$35.00	1994-2000
1977	DIAMOND CREEK VINEYARD	Napa Valley Diamond Mountain Volcanic Hill	591	$10.00	$45.00	1990-1992
1983	EBERLE WINERY	Paso Robles	2,800	$10.00	$18.00	1991-1994
1984	FLORA SPRINGS WINE CO.	Napa Valley Rutherford Trilogy	700	$30.00	$35.00	1992-1998
1981	GUNDLACH BUNDSCHU WINERY	Sonoma Valley	4,000	$7.00	$20.00	1994-1999
1983	HESS COLLECTION WINERY	Napa Valley Mount Veeder	900	$13.00	$18.00	1990-1995
1977	INGLENOOK-NAPA VALLEY	Napa Valley Rutherford Cask	6,291	$8.75	$23.00	1990-1994
1981	JORDAN VINEYARD AND WINERY	Alexander Valley Estate	47,000	$17.00	$40.00	1990-1994
1981	ROBERT KEENAN WINERY	Napa Valley	3,298	$13.50	$22.00	1993-1999
1980	KISTLER VINEYARDS	Sonoma Valley Glen Ellen Vineyard	320	$18.00	$35.00	1992-1998
1985	CHARLES KRUG WINERY	Napa Valley Vintage Select	7,266	NR		1995-2004
1983	LA JOTA VINEYARD CO.	Napa Valley Howell Mountain	870	$15.00	$20.00	1994-2000
1982	LA JOTA VINEYARD CO.	Napa Valley	704	$13.50	$25.00	1994-2000

NA — not available.   NR — not released.   * — Beaulieu production figures are estimates.

Vintage	Winery	Appellation/Vineyard	Case Prod.	Release Price	Current Price	Drink
1985	CHARLES KRUG WINERY	Napa Valley Vintage Select	7,266	NR		1995-2004
1983	LA JOTA VINEYARD CO.	Napa Valley Howell Mountain	870	$15.00	$20.00	1994-2000
1982	LA JOTA VINEYARD CO.	Napa Valley Howell Mountain	704	$13.50	$25.00	1994-2000
1980	LOUIS M. MARTINI WINERY	North Coast Special Selection	9,350	$12.00	$12.00	1990-1997
1979	LOUIS M. MARTINI WINERY	Sonoma Valley Monte Rosso Lot 2	2,490	$10.00	$19.00	1991-1996
1976	MAYACAMAS VINEYARDS	Napa Valley Mount Veeder	1,380	$15.00	$50.00	1992-1998
1977	ROBERT MONDAVI WINERY	Napa Valley Oakville Reserve	9,500	$35.00	$40.00	1990-1993
1976	ROBERT MONDAVI WINERY	Napa Valley Oakville Reserve	8,500	$25.00	$40.00	1990-1994
1967	ROBERT MONDAVI WINERY	Napa Valley Oakville	NA	$5.00	$100.00	1990
1984	MOUNT EDEN VINEYARDS	Santa Cruz Mountains	645	$22.00	$26.00	1993-1998
1972	MOUNT EDEN VINEYARDS	Santa Cruz Mountains	89	$20.00	$60.00	1990-1995
1983	MOUNT VEEDER WINERY	Napa Valley Mount Veeder Mt. Veeder Vineyards	3,000	$14.00	$15.00	1995-2002
1983	PINE RIDGE WINERY	Napa Valley Rutherford Rutherford Cuveé	4,890	$14.00	$22.00	1993-1998
1982	RAVENSWOOD	Sonoma County	1,500	$11.00	$18.00	1990-1995
1983	RAYMOND VINEYARD & CELLAR	Napa Valley Rutherford Private Reserve	2,200	$18.00	$25.00	1993-2000
1977	RAYMOND VINEYARD & CELLAR	Napa Valley Rutherford	4,300	$8.50	$27.00	1990-1992
1983	RIDGE VINEYARDS	Santa Cruz Mountains Monte Bello	2,677	$12.00	$15.00	1994-2000
1972	RIDGE VINEYARDS	Santa Cruz Mountains Monte Bello	740	$10.00	$100.00	1990-1992
1984	ROMBAUER VINEYARDS	Napa Valley	1,500	$13.50	$21.00	1991-1995
1983	SANTA CRUZ MOUNTAIN VINEYARD	Santa Cruz Mountains Bates Ranch	1,800	$12.00	$12.00	1996-2004
1981	SEQUOIA GROVE VINEYARDS	Alexander Valley	854	$12.00	$35.00	1993-1999
1984	SILVER OAK CELLARS	Napa Valley Oakville Bonny's Vineyard	950	$45.00	$45.00	1994-2000
1980	SIMI WINERY	Alexander Valley Reserve	2,400	$20.00	$30.00	1994-2000
1983	SMITH-MADRONE VINEYARD	Napa Valley Spring Mountain	700	$12.50	$15.00	1995-2005
1978	SMITH-MADRONE VINEYARD	Napa Valley Spring Mountain	200	$14.00	$25.00	1990-1995
1979	STONEGATE WINERY	Napa Valley	2,757	$12.00	$24.00	1993-1997
1984	TREFETHEN VINEYARDS	Napa Valley Yountville	9,500	$14.00	$16.00	1991-1995
1983	TREFETHEN VINEYARDS	Napa Valley Yountville	9,653	$11.75	$22.00	1994-2000
1974	TREFETHEN VINEYARDS	Napa Valley Yountville	835	$8.00	$65.00	1990-1997
1986	VILLA MT. EDEN WINERY	Napa Valley Oakville Estate	9,700	NR		1990-1996
1982	VILLA MT. EDEN WINERY	Napa Valley Oakville Reserve	1,254	$16.70	$16.70	1992-1997

SCORE: 83

Vintage	Winery	Appellation/Vineyard	Case Prod.	Release Price	Current Price	Drink
1980	ALEXANDER VALLEY VINEYARDS	Alexander Valley	2,552	$9.00	$16.00	1990-1994
1982	IRON HORSE VINEYARDS	Alexander Valley	2,500	$12.00	$18.00	1994-1999
1985	JOHNSON TURNBULL VINEYARDS	Napa Valley Oakville	2,350	$14.50	$17.50	1994-2000
1983	LOUIS M. MARTINI WINERY	Sonoma Valley Monte Rosso Los Ninos	545	$25.00	$25.00	1990-1997
1983	ROBERT MONDAVI WINERY	Napa Valley Oakville Reserve	15,000	$30.00	$35.00	1991-1999
1981	ROBERT MONDAVI WINERY	Napa Valley Oakville Reserve	12,000	$30.00	$30.00	1990-1995
1968	ROBERT MONDAVI WINERY	Napa Valley Oakville Unfined	2,000	$8.50	$135.00	1990-1994
1976	MOUNT EDEN VINEYARDS	Santa Cruz Mountains	175	$20.00	$50.00	1993-2000
1975	MOUNT VEEDER WINERY	Napa Valley Mount Veeder Bernstein Vineyards	850	$11.00	$50.00	1995-2004
1981	NEWTON VINEYARD	Napa Valley	2,820	$12.50	$21.00	1992-1997
1978	RAVENSWOOD	Sonoma Valley Olive Hill	530	$11.25	$28.00	1990-1998
1976	RIDGE VINEYARDS	Santa Cruz Mountains Monte Bello	1,577	$15.00	$65.00	1990-1998
1982	ROMBAUER VINEYARDS	Napa Valley	1,000	$12.00	$23.00	1990-1994
1983	RUTHERFORD HILL WINERY	Napa Valley	16,439	$12.50	$16.00	1990-1995
1982	RUTHERFORD HILL WINERY	Napa Valley	17,878	$12.50	$17.00	1990-1994
1974	SIMI WINERY	Alexander Valley Special Reserve	2,000	$25.00	$65.00	1990
1978	SPRING MOUNTAIN VINEYARDS	Napa Valley Rutherford	10,236	$12.00	$25.00	1990-1996
1975	TREFETHEN VINEYARDS	Napa Valley Yountville	783	$7.50	$55.00	1990-1994
1980	VICHON WINERY	Napa Valley Volker Eisele Vineyard	800	$16.00	$25.00	1990-1995

SCORE: 82

Vintage	Winery	Appellation/Vineyard	Case Prod.	Release Price	Current Price	Drink
1983	BEAULIEU VINEYARD	Napa Valley Rutherford Georges de Latour Private Reserve	15,000	$24.00	$28.00	1992-1997
1939	BEAULIEU VINEYARD	Napa Valley Rutherford Georges de Latour Private Reserve	15,000	$1.45	$1500.00	1990
1980	BUEHLER VINEYARDS	Napa Valley	794	$10.00	$25.00	1994-2002

NA — not available.   NR — not released.   ∗ — Beaulieu production figures are estimates.

Vintage	Winery	Appellation/Vineyard	Case Prod.	Release Price	Current Price	Drink
1979	CAKEBREAD CELLARS	Napa Valley	3,300	$13.00	$45.00	1990-1995
1977	CHAPPELLET VINEYARD	Napa Valley	4,500	$12.00	$33.00	1990-1994
1984	CHIMNEY ROCK WINE CELLARS	Napa Valley Stags Leap District	2,800	$15.00	$15.00	1990-1996
1985	CLOS DU BOIS WINERY	Alexander Valley Briarcrest Vineyard	3,721	$16.00	$16.00	1993-1998
1981	CLOS DU VAL WINE CO.	Napa Valley Stags Leap District Estate	21,500	$12.50	$25.00	1990-1996
1976	CLOS DU VAL WINE CO.	Napa Valley	6,800	$9.00	$55.00	1990-1995
1983	CONN CREEK WINERY	Napa Valley Barrel Select	5,000	$13.00	$15.00	1992-1996
1982	CUVAISON WINERY	Napa Valley	2,000	$11.00	$15.00	1994-2000
1979	DIAMOND CREEK VINEYARD	Napa Valley Diamond Mountain Volcanic Hill, Second Pick	415	$15.00	$40.00	1993-1999
1979	EBERLE WINERY	San Luis Obispo	1,000	$10.00	$25.00	1990-1995
1982	FAR NIENTE WINERY	Napa Valley Oakville	3,000	$25.00	$35.00	1993-1999
1975	FRANCISCAN VINEYARDS	Napa Valley Oakville Reserve	3,000	$12.00	$32.00	1990
1983	IRON HORSE VINEYARDS	Alexander Valley	2,000	$12.00	$15.50	1992-1997
1982	JOHNSON TURNBULL VINEYARDS	Napa Valley Oakville	2,275	$12.50	$18.00	1994-1998
1977	KENWOOD VINEYARDS	Sonoma Valley Artist Series	1,000	$15.00	$120.00	1990-1993
1983	CHARLES KRUG WINERY	Napa Valley Vintage Select	3,653	NR		1994-2001
1981	CHARLES KRUG WINERY	Napa Valley Vintage Select	4,423	NR		1992-1998
1979	CHARLES KRUG WINERY	Napa Valley Vintage Select	2,177	$12.50	$20.00	1990-1995
1982	LOUIS M. MARTINI WINERY	Sonoma Valley Monte Rosso Los Ninos	550	$25.00	$25.00	1990-1995
1972	MAYACAMAS VINEYARDS	Napa Valley Mount Veeder	1,620	$8.00	$70.00	1990-1993
1982	ROBERT MONDAVI WINERY	Napa Valley Oakville Reserve	14,000	$30.00	$38.00	1992-1998
1973	ROBERT MONDAVI WINERY	Napa Valley Oakville Reserve	4,500	$12.00	$80.00	1990-1994
1977	JOSEPH PHELPS VINEYARDS	Napa Valley Calistoga Eisele Vineyard	1,160	$25.00	$55.00	1991-1998
1977	RAVENSWOOD	El Dorado County Madrona Vineyards	800	$8.50	$22.00	1990-1995
1980	RAYMOND VINEYARD & CELLAR	Napa Valley Rutherford	10,000	$12.00	$17.00	1990-1993
1978	RAYMOND VINEYARD & CELLAR	Napa Valley Rutherford	5,300	$10.00	$21.00	1990-1993
1981	ROMBAUER VINEYARDS	Napa Valley	1,000	$12.00	$24.00	1993-1998
1980	RUTHERFORD HILL WINERY	Napa Valley	9,574	$11.50	$19.00	1990-1994
1978	RUTHERFORD HILL WINERY	Napa Valley	16,471	$12.00	$22.00	1990-1993
1982	SEQUOIA GROVE VINEYARDS	Napa Valley Rutherford Estate	406	$14.00	$22.00	1995-2003
1983	SILVER OAK CELLARS	Napa Valley Oakville Bonny's Vineyard	1,250	$40.00	$40.00	1990-1993
1979	SILVER OAK CELLARS	Napa Valley Calistoga	4,400	$18.00	$55.00	1995-2005
1980	ST. CLEMENT VINEYARDS	Napa Valley	650	$12.50	$24.00	1990-1994
1983	STERLING VINEYARDS	Napa Valley Reserve	3,360	$22.50	$30.00	1995-2000
1985	VILLA MT. EDEN WINERY	Napa Valley Oakville Estate	8,095	NR		1990-1994

SCORE: 81

Vintage	Winery	Appellation/Vineyard	Case Prod.	Release Price	Current Price	Drink
1978	JORDAN VINEYARD AND WINERY	Alexander Valley Estate	58,000	$16.00	$70.00	1990-1993
1969	CHARLES KRUG WINERY	Napa Valley Vintage Select	8,262	$6.50	$65.00	1990
1978	RAVENSWOOD	California	536	$10.50	$20.00	1991-1998
1983	V. SATTUI WINERY	Napa Valley Rutherford Preston Vineyard	1,613	$13.75	$19.75	1990-1995
1973	SILVER OAK CELLARS	North Coast	1,800	$7.00	$130.00	1990-1994
1977	STONEGATE WINERY	Napa Valley	1,060	$10.00	$25.00	1993-1999
1978	TREFETHEN VINEYARDS	Napa Valley Yountville	3,764	$10.00	$45.00	1991-1995

SCORE: 80

Vintage	Winery	Appellation/Vineyard	Case Prod.	Release Price	Current Price	Drink
1978	ALEXANDER VALLEY VINEYARDS	Alexander Valley	3,734	$6.50	$20.00	1990-1993
1982	CHAPPELLET VINEYARD	Napa Valley	11,800	$9.25	$14.00	1990-1993
1981	CHATEAU MONTELENA WINERY	Napa Valley Calistoga Estate	7,144	$16.00	$25.00	1990-1994
1980	CLOS DU BOIS WINERY	Alexander Valley Briarcrest Vineyard	1,227	$12.00	$32.00	1990-1995
1980	DE MOOR WINERY	Napa Valley (Napa Cellars)	1,600	$12.00	$20.00	1990-1996
1982	DIAMOND CREEK VINEYARD	Napa Valley Diamond Mountain Red Rock Terrace, Special Selection	192	$20.00	$35.00	1993-1999
1973	DIAMOND CREEK VINEYARD	Napa Valley Diamond Mountain Volcanic Hill	150	$7.50	$200.00	1990-1996
1981	EBERLE WINERY	Paso Robles Reserve	191	$25.00	$35.00	1991-1995
1972	FREEMARK ABBEY WINERY	Napa Valley Rutherford Bosche	3,183	$6.00	$30.00	1990-1992
1983	FROG'S LEAP WINERY	Napa Valley	1,100	$10.00	$20.00	1990-1994
1980	GUNDLACH BUNDSCHU WINERY	Sonoma Valley Batto Ranch	950	$8.00	$20.00	1990-1993
1979	GUNDLACH BUNDSCHU WINERY	Sonoma Valley Batto Ranch	900	$8.00	$22.00	1990-1993
1969	INGLENOOK-NAPA VALLEY	Napa Valley Rutherford Cask	12,508	$6.50	$80.00	1990-1992

NA — not available.   NR — not released.   * — Beaulieu production figures are estimates.

420

Vintage	Winery	Appellation/Vineyard	Case Prod.	Release Price	Current Price	Drink
1960	INGLENOOK-NAPA VALLEY	Napa Valley Rutherford Cask	2,500	$2.75	$140.00	1990
1978	IRON HORSE VINEYARDS	Alexander Valley	1,250	$12.00	$25.00	1990-1994
1980	JORDAN VINEYARD AND WINERY	Alexander Valley Estate	56,400	$17.00	$45.00	1990-1992
1980	ROBERT KEENAN WINERY	Napa Valley	3,272	$13.50	$23.00	1993-2000
1980	KENWOOD VINEYARDS	Sonoma Valley Artist Series	1,600	$20.00	$55.00	1990-1994
1968	CHARLES KRUG WINERY	Napa Valley Vintage Select	7,668	$6.50	$90.00	1990
1985	LOUIS M. MARTINI WINERY	Sonoma Valley Monte Rosso	1,150	$22.00	$22.00	1992-2000
1961	LOUIS M. MARTINI WINERY	California Special Selection	1,092	$4.00	$180.00	1990-1994
1966	ROBERT MONDAVI WINERY	Napa Valley Oakville	1,500	$5.00	$165.00	1990
1974	MOUNT VEEDER WINERY	Napa Valley Mount Veeder	650	$8.00	$50.00	1996-2004
1983	ROBERT PEPI WINERY	Napa Valley Yountville Vine Hill Ranch	2,700	$16.00	$16.00	1993-1998
1984	RAVENSWOOD	Sonoma County	1,400	$12.00	$14.00	1992-1997
1980	RIDGE VINEYARDS	Santa Cruz Mountains Monte Bello	4,125	$30.00	$36.00	1995-2005
1981	SEQUOIA GROVE VINEYARDS	Napa Valley	1,169	$12.00	$25.00	1994-1999
1972	SIMI WINERY	Alexander Valley	10,000	$5.00	$25.00	1990
1976	STAG'S LEAP WINE CELLARS	Napa Valley Stags Leap District Lot 2	1,000	$11.00	$60.00	1990-1992
1983	STAGS' LEAP WINERY	Napa Valley Stags Leap District	3,425	$12.75	$20.00	1993-1997
1982	STONEGATE WINERY	Napa Valley	5,497	$12.00	$18.00	1991-1996
1985	TREFETHEN VINEYARDS	Napa Valley Yountville	9,501	NR		1992-1997
1983	VICHON WINERY	Napa Valley	10,000	$10.00	$14.00	1990-1995
1981	VICHON WINERY	Napa Valley	4,600	$13.00	$20.00	1990-1994
1984	VILLA MT. EDEN WINERY	Napa Valley Oakville Estate	1,004	NR		1990-1994

SCORE: 79

Vintage	Winery	Appellation/Vineyard	Case Prod.	Release Price	Current Price	Drink
1977	BEAULIEU VINEYARD	Napa Valley Rutherford Georges de Latour Private Reserve	15,000	$16.00	$46.00	1990-1991
1975	BEAULIEU VINEYARD	Napa Valley Rutherford Georges de Latour Private Reserve	15,000	$16.00	$50.00	1990-1992
1974	BEAULIEU VINEYARD	Napa Valley Rutherford Georges de Latour Private Reserve	15,000	$12.00	$70.00	1990-1991
1973	BEAULIEU VINEYARD	Napa Valley Rutherford Georges de Latour Private Reserve	15,000	$9.00	$50.00	1990
1981	CHAPPELLET VINEYARD	Napa Valley	8,000	$11.00	$18.00	1990-1995
1979	CHAPPELLET VINEYARD	Napa Valley	6,400	$13.00	$26.00	1990-1995
1982	CLOS DU BOIS WINERY	Alexander Valley Marlstone Vineyard	2,496	$16.00	$16.00	1990-1994
1977	CUVAISON WINERY	Napa Valley	6,000	$10.00	$35.00	1992-1998
1976	CUVAISON WINERY	Napa Valley	6,000	$10.00	$35.00	1992-1996
1975	CUVAISON WINERY	Napa Valley	5,000	$10.00	$40.00	1990-1995
1985	DE MOOR WINERY	Napa Valley	1,800	$14.00	$14.00	1991-1996
1982	DIAMOND CREEK VINEYARD	Napa Valley Diamond Mountain Volcanic Hill, Special Selection	258	$20.00	$35.00	1993-1999
1979	FRANCISCAN VINEYARDS	Napa Valley Oakville	9,000	$8.50	$18.00	1990
1984	GUNDLACH BUNDSCHU WINERY	Sonoma Valley Batto Ranch	800	$14.00	$16.00	1990-1991
1982	HAYWOOD WINERY	Sonoma Valley	608	$11.00	$20.00	1994-2000
1972	HEITZ WINE CELLARS	Napa Valley Oakville Martha's Vineyard	1,445	$12.75	$100.00	1990-1994
1981	IRON HORSE VINEYARDS	Alexander Valley	1,700	$12.00	$15.50	1992-1998
1979	JORDAN VINEYARD AND WINERY	Alexander Valley Estate	47,000	$16.00	$50.00	1990-1992
1976	JORDAN VINEYARD AND WINERY	Alexander Valley	35,000	$10.00	$70.00	1990-1992
1980	CHARLES KRUG WINERY	Napa Valley Vintage Select	8,858	$15.00	$15.00	1992-1997
1971	CHARLES KRUG WINERY	Napa Valley Vintage Select	7,993	$7.50	$35.00	1990
1960	CHARLES KRUG WINERY	Napa Valley Vintage Select	1,516	$2.25	$70.00	1990
1950	CHARLES KRUG WINERY	Napa Valley Vintage Select	1,553	$1.25	$500.00	1990
1980	ROBERT MONDAVI WINERY	Napa Valley Oakville Reserve	13,000	$30.00	$35.00	1992-1998
1983	MOUNT EDEN VINEYARDS	Santa Cruz Mountains	458	$20.00	$20.00	1993-1997
1980	RAVENSWOOD	Sonoma County	640	$10.50	$16.00	1990-1997
1981	SANTA CRUZ MOUNTAIN VYD	Santa Cruz Mountains Bates Ranch	1,600	$12.00	$20.00	1994-1999
1979	SANTA CRUZ MOUNTAIN VYD	Santa Cruz Mountains Bates Ranch	1,225	$12.00	$35.00	1993-2000
1981	SILVER OAK CELLARS	Napa Valley Calistoga	4,100	$19.00	$40.00	1994-2000
1982	SMITH-MADRONE VINEYARD	Napa Valley Spring Mountain	800	$12.50	$15.00	1990-1993
1980	SMITH-MADRONE VINEYARD	Napa Valley Spring Mountain	600	$12.50	$18.00	1990
1983	SPRING MOUNTAIN VINEYARDS	Napa Valley Spring Mountain	4,221	$15.00	$18.00	1993-1998

NA — not available.　　NR — not released.　　∗ — Beaulieu production figures are estimates.

Vintage	Winery	Appellation/Vineyard	Case Prod.	Release Price	Current Price	Drink
1986	STONEGATE WINERY	Napa Valley Calistoga Estate	3,000	NR		1990-1995
1981	STONEGATE WINERY	Napa Valley	4,005	$12.00	$17.00	1992-1996
1982	VICHON WINERY	Napa Valley Stags Leap District Fay Vineyard	2,500	$14.00	$23.00	1990-1995

SCORE: 78

Vintage	Winery	Appellation/Vineyard	Case Prod.	Release Price	Current Price	Drink
1961	BEAULIEU VINEYARD	Napa Valley Rutherford Georges de Latour Private Reserve	15,000	$3.50	$200.00	1990-1992
1975	CHAPPELLET VINEYARD	Napa Valley	5,000	$10.00	$45.00	1990
1980	EBERLE WINERY	Paso Robles	2,000	$10.00	$24.00	1990-1994
1978	FRANCISCAN VINEYARDS	Napa Valley Oakville Reserve	4,000	$15.00	$20.00	1990-1992
1983	JORDAN VINEYARD AND WINERY	Alexander Valley Estate	51,400	$18.00	$30.00	1990-1992
1983	KISTLER VINEYARDS	Napa Valley Mount Veeder Veeder Hills Vineyard	1,010	$13.50	$20.00	1992-1998
1978	CHARLES KRUG WINERY	Napa Valley Vintage Select	14,353	$11.00	$22.00	1990-1995
1962	CHARLES KRUG WINERY	Napa Valley Vintage Select	2,137	$3.50	$70.00	1990
1983	LONG VINEYARDS	Napa Valley Oakville	200	$32.00	$40.00	1991-1995
1983	LYETH WINERY	Alexander Valley	8,000	$17.00	$25.00	1992-1995
1976	RAYMOND VINEYARD & CELLAR	Napa Valley Rutherford	3,000	$6.00	$27.00	1990
1974	RAYMOND VINEYARD & CELLAR	Napa Valley Rutherford	800	$5.50	$40.00	1990
1982	V. SATTUI WINERY	Napa Valley Rutherford Preston Vineyard Reserve	385	$22.50	$30.00	1990-1994
1982	SEQUOIA GROVE VINEYARDS	Napa-Alexander Valleys	2,068	$12.00	$20.00	1990-1998
1982	SILVER OAK CELLARS	Napa Valley Oakville Bonny's Vineyard	900	$35.00	$42.00	1994-2002
1981	SMITH-MADRONE VINEYARD	Napa Valley Spring Mountain	600	$12.50	$15.00	1990-1993
1981	SPRING MOUNTAIN VINEYARDS	Napa Valley Rutherford	11,390	$14.00	$16.00	1992-1996
1975	STERLING VINEYARDS	Napa Valley Reserve	3,800	$20.00	$55.00	1994-2000
1982	VICHON WINERY	Napa Valley Volker Eisele	2,000	$16.00	$19.00	1990-1994
1979	VILLA MT. EDEN WINERY	Napa Valley Oakville Estate	2,773	$12.00	$21.00	1990-1993
1978	VILLA MT. EDEN WINERY	Napa Valley Oakville Estate	2,421	$8.00	$25.00	1990-1994

SCORE: 77

Vintage	Winery	Appellation/Vineyard	Case Prod.	Release Price	Current Price	Drink
1983	CAKEBREAD CELLARS	Napa Valley	4,000	$16.00	$25.00	1992-1995
1977	CAYMUS VINEYARDS	Napa Valley Rutherford Estate	1,700	$10.00	$40.00	1990-1994
1983	CHAPPELLET VINEYARD	Napa Valley	8,700	$12.00	$15.00	1990-1995
1980	CLOS DU BOIS WINERY	Alexander Valley Marlstone Vineyard	3,833	$15.00	$32.00	1991-1998
1979	CONN CREEK WINERY	Napa Valley	6,270	$13.00	$25.00	1993-1998
1980	CUVAISON WINERY	Napa Valley	5,000	$11.00	$18.00	1994-2001
1986	FLORA SPRINGS WINE CO.	Napa Valley	3,500	$15.00	$15.00	1990-1994
1983	GUNDLACH BUNDSCHU WINERY	Sonoma Valley Batto Ranch	1,000	$10.00	$15.00	1990-1993
1983	HAYWOOD WINERY	Sonoma Valley	711	$12.50	$20.00	1995-2003
1979	INGLENOOK-NAPA VALLEY	Napa Valley Rutherford Cask	2,672	$10.75	$23.00	1990
1977	JORDAN VINEYARD AND WINERY	Alexander Valley	35,000	$14.00	$70.00	1990-1992
1976	KENWOOD VINEYARDS	Sonoma Valley Artist Series	1,000	$10.00	$120.00	1990
1972	CHARLES KRUG WINERY	Napa Valley Vintage Select	3,787	$9.00	$45.00	1990
1981	LYETH WINERY	Alexander Valley	1,200	$15.00	$35.00	1990-1993
1974	LOUIS M. MARTINI WINERY	California Special Selection	5,411	$10.00	$45.00	1990-1992
1956	LOUIS M. MARTINI WINERY	California Private Reserve Mountain	1,500	$2.50	$90.00	1990-1991
1982	MAYACAMAS VINEYARDS	Napa Valley Mount Veeder	2,700	$20.00	$25.00	1993-1998
1981	MOUNT VEEDER WINERY	Napa Valley Mount Veeder Mt. Veeder Vineyards	2,700	$12.50	$20.00	1992-1997
1976	MOUNT VEEDER WINERY	Napa Valley Mount Veeder Bernstein Vineyards	775	$11.00	$45.00	1994-2000
1983	SEQUOIA GROVE VINEYARDS	Napa-Alexander Valleys	2,144	$12.50	$18.00	1991-1994
1980	SHAFER VINEYARDS	Napa Valley Stags Leap District	2,000	$12.00	$25.00	1990-1992
1981	SILVER OAK CELLARS	Napa Valley Oakville Bonny's Vineyard	970	$35.00	$50.00	1994-2000

SCORE: 76

Vintage	Winery	Appellation/Vineyard	Case Prod.	Release Price	Current Price	Drink
1976	CHAPPELLET VINEYARD	Napa Valley	4,500	$12.00	$37.00	1990
1983	RAVENSWOOD	Sonoma County	1,350	$9.50	$14.00	1991-1995
1981	RIDGE VINEYARDS	Napa County Spring Mountain York Creek	4,925	$12.00	$20.00	1994-2000
1976	STERLING VINEYARDS	Napa Valley Reserve	3,690	$25.00	$40.00	1994-1998

NA — not available.   NR — not released.   * — Beaulieu production figures are estimates.

Vintage	Winery	Appellation/Vineyard	Case Prod.	Release Price	Current Price	Drink
1976	TREFETHEN VINEYARDS	Napa Valley Yountville	2,098	$7.50	$45.00	1990-1996
1982	VICHON WINERY	Napa Valley	5,400	$13.00	$15.00	1990-1993

SCORE: 75

Vintage	Winery	Appellation/Vineyard	Case Prod.	Release Price	Current Price	Drink
1975	ALEXANDER VALLEY VINEYARDS	Alexander Valley	3,416	$5.50	$20.00	1990-1992
1979	CLOS DU BOIS WINERY	Alexander Valley Marlstone Vineyard	3,395	$16.00	$30.00	1990-1994
1983	CUVAISON WINERY	Napa Valley	2,000	$12.00	$15.00	1990-1992
1979	CUVAISON WINERY	Napa Valley	5,000	$11.00	$20.00	1993-2000
1977	DIAMOND CREEK VINEYARD	Napa Valley Diamond Mountain Red Rock Terrace, Second Pick	60	$10.00	$40.00	1993-1996
1970	CHARLES KRUG WINERY	Napa Valley Vintage Select	11,825	$7.50	$60.00	1990
1945	LOUIS M. MARTINI WINERY	California Special Selection	1,000	$1.50	$400.00	1990
1966	MAYACAMAS VINEYARDS	California	530	$3.50	$125.00	1990-1993
1972	ROBERT MONDAVI WINERY	Napa Valley Oakville	NA	$6.00	$45.00	1990
1979	NIEBAUM-COPPOLA ESTATE	Napa Valley Rutherford Rubicon	3,100	$25.00	$40.00	1990-1994
1982	RIDGE VINEYARDS	Santa Cruz Mountains Monte Bello	4,350	$18.00	$25.00	1992-1998
1971	SIMI WINERY	Alexander Valley	8,000	$5.00	$30.00	1990
1982	STAG'S LEAP WINE CELLARS	Napa Valley Stags Leap District Stag's Leap Vineyards	9,865	$16.50	$25.00	1990-1993
1982	STERLING VINEYARDS	Napa Valley Reserve	4,807	$22.50	$25.00	1992-1996
1979	VILLA MT. EDEN WINERY	Napa Valley Oakville Reserve	500	$20.00	$30.00	1994-2000

SCORE: 74

Vintage	Winery	Appellation/Vineyard	Case Prod.	Release Price	Current Price	Drink
1983	CLOS DU BOIS WINERY	Alexander Valley Briarcrest Vineyard	1,122	$12.00	$20.00	1990-1994
1981	CUVAISON WINERY	Napa Valley	6,000	$11.00	$15.00	1993-1999
1972	DIAMOND CREEK VINEYARD	Napa Valley Diamond Mountain Red Rock Terrace	25	$7.50	$200.00	1990-1992
1979	ROBERT KEENAN WINERY	Napa Valley	2,460	$12.00	$30.00	1994-2000
1978	ROBERT KEENAN WINERY	Napa Valley	2,044	$12.00	$40.00	1994-2000
1977	CHARLES KRUG WINERY	Napa Valley Vintage Select	4,029	$10.00	$22.00	1990-1994
1963	CHARLES KRUG WINERY	Napa Valley Vintage Select	3,599	$3.50	$70.00	1990
1983	SILVER OAK CELLARS	Napa Valley Calistoga	3,000	$20.00	$30.00	1993-1996
1975	STAG'S LEAP WINE CELLARS	Napa Valley Stags Leap District Stag's Leap Vineyards	2,300	$8.50	$50.00	1990

SCORE: 73

Vintage	Winery	Appellation/Vineyard	Case Prod.	Release Price	Current Price	Drink
1972	BEAULIEU VINEYARD	Napa Valley Rutherford Georges de Latour Private Reserve	15,000	$6.00	$40.00	1990
1962	BEAULIEU VINEYARD	Napa Valley Rutherford Georges de Latour Private Reserve	15,000	$3.50	$140.00	1990
1983	GUNDLACH BUNDSCHU WINERY	Sonoma Valley Rhinefarm	4,500	$9.00	$14.00	1991-1994
1971	INGLENOOK-NAPA VALLEY	Napa Valley Rutherford Cask	2,978	$6.50	$50.00	1990-1991
1967	INGLENOOK-NAPA VALLEY	Napa Valley Rutherford Cask	4,194	$6.00	$60.00	1990
1966	INGLENOOK-NAPA VALLEY	Napa Valley Rutherford Cask	3,190	$5.75	$95.00	1990
1982	JORDAN VINEYARD AND WINERY	Alexander Valley Estate	50,800	$18.00	$36.00	1990-1991
1975	KENWOOD VINEYARDS	Sonoma Valley Artist Series	1,000	$6.50	$250.00	1990
1973	CHARLES KRUG WINERY	Napa Valley Vintage Select	5,846	$9.00	$40.00	1990
1962	LOUIS M. MARTINI WINERY	California Private Reserve	1,151	$3.50	$80.00	1990
1983	RIDGE VINEYARDS	Napa County Spring Mountain York Creek	6,390	$12.00	$15.00	1992-1996
1982	RIDGE VINEYARDS	Napa County Spring Mountain York Creek	6,909	$12.00	$15.00	1994-2000
1983	ROMBAUER VINEYARDS	Napa Valley	1,500	$13.50	$19.00	1990-1994
1976	RUTHERFORD HILL WINERY	Napa Valley	5,505	$9.00	$17.00	1990
1980	SILVER OAK CELLARS	Napa Valley Calistoga	4,000	$18.00	$45.00	1992-1997
1970	SIMI WINERY	Alexander Valley	5,000	$4.50	$50.00	1990
1983	STAG'S LEAP WINE CELLARS	Napa Valley Stags Leap District Stag's Leap Vineyards	6,668	$18.00	$25.00	1990-1995
1976	STAG'S LEAP WINE CELLARS	Napa Valley Stags Leap District Stag's Leap Vineyards	2,000	$10.00	$40.00	1990

SCORE: 72

Vintage	Winery	Appellation/Vineyard	Case Prod.	Release Price	Current Price	Drink
1977	BUENA VISTA WINERY	Sonoma Valley Carneros Cask 34	2,146	$12.00	$40.00	1990
1978	CLOS DU BOIS WINERY	Alexander Valley Marlstone Vineyard	3,129	$16.00	$30.00	1990
1978	CUVAISON WINERY	Napa Valley	5,000	$10.00	$20.00	1995-2002

NA — not available.   NR — not released.   * — Beaulieu production figures are estimates.

Vintage	Winery	Appellation/Vineyard	Case Prod.	Release Price	Current Price	Drink
1982	EBERLE WINERY	Paso Robles	2,500	$10.00	$24.00	1990-1994
1976	INGLENOOK-NAPA VALLEY	Napa Valley Rutherford Cask	4,147	$8.75	$19.00	1990
1977	RUTHERFORD HILL WINERY	Napa Valley	11,337	$10.00	$18.00	1990
1982	SANTA CRUZ MOUNTAIN VYD.	Santa Cruz Mountains Bates Ranch	1,800	$12.00	$14.00	1994-1998
1979	SILVER OAK CELLARS	Napa Valley Oakville Bonny's Vineyard	1,200	$30.00	$55.00	1992-1998
1978	SIMI WINERY	Alexander Valley Reserve	2,700	$17.00	$26.00	1990
1973	SIMI WINERY	Alexander Valley	10,000	$6.00	$25.00	1990
1982	TUDAL WINERY	Napa Valley St. Helena	2,100	$12.00	$25.00	1990-1993
1983	VILLA MT. EDEN WINERY	Napa Valley Oakville Estate	7,588	$10.00	$10.00	1990-1993

SCORE: 71

Vintage	Winery	Appellation/Vineyard	Case Prod.	Release Price	Current Price	Drink
1982	EBERLE WINERY	Paso Robles Reserve	76	$25.00	$30.00	1991-1996
1982	STAGS' LEAP WINERY	Napa Valley Stags Leap District	3,034	$12.00	$20.00	1992-1996

SCORE: 70

Vintage	Winery	Appellation/Vineyard	Case Prod.	Release Price	Current Price	Drink
1963	BEAULIEU VINEYARD	Napa Valley Rutherford Georges de Latour Private Reserve	15,000	$3.50	$145.00	1990
1974	CHAPPELLET VINEYARD	Napa Valley	3,500	$7.50	$45.00	1990
1983	CLOS DU BOIS WINERY	Alexander Valley Marlstone Vineyard	1,600	$19.50	$20.00	1990-1993
1982	GUNDLACH BUNDSCHU WINERY	Sonoma Valley Batto Ranch	1,000	$10.00	$18.00	1990-1992
1977	LOUIS M. MARTINI WINERY	California Special Selection	5,464	$9.00	$20.00	1990
1943	LOUIS M. MARTINI WINERY	California Private Reserve Villa del Rey	1,000	$1.50	$400.00	1990
1982	MOUNT EDEN VINEYARDS	Santa Cruz Mountains	1,249	$18.00	$20.00	1990-1994
1963	RIDGE VINEYARDS	Santa Cruz Mountains Monte Bello	100	$5.00	$130.00	1990
1980	SILVER OAK CELLARS	Napa Valley Oakville Bonny's Vineyard	1,000	$30.00	$50.00	1993-1998
1977	SIMI WINERY	Alexander Valley Special Selection	1,700	$20.00	$23.00	1990
1972	STAG'S LEAP WINE CELLARS	Napa Valley Stags Leap District Stag's Leap Vineyards	100	$5.50	$80.00	1990
1982	VILLA MT. EDEN WINERY	Napa Valley Oakville Estate	8,143	$9.00	$9.00	1990-1993
1980	VILLA MT. EDEN WINERY	Napa Valley Oakville Reserve	1,143	$20.00	$20.00	1992-1996
1976	VILLA MT. EDEN WINERY	Napa Valley Oakville Estate	860	$7.00	$38.00	1990-1994

SCORE: 69

Vintage	Winery	Appellation/Vineyard	Case Prod.	Release Price	Current Price	Drink
1973	CHAPPELLET VINEYARD	Napa Valley	2,500	$7.50	$65.00	Avoid
1977	ROBERT KEENAN WINERY	Napa Valley	843	$12.00	$50.00	Avoid
1963	MAYACAMAS VINEYARDS	California	420	$2.00	$150.00	Avoid
1979	MOUNT EDEN VINEYARDS	Santa Cruz Mountains	641	$25.00	$30.00	Avoid
1975	RUTHERFORD HILL WINERY	Napa Valley	4,984	$9.00	$18.00	Avoid

SCORE: 68

Vintage	Winery	Appellation/Vineyard	Case Prod.	Release Price	Current Price	Drink
1974	BUENA VISTA WINERY	Sonoma Valley Carneros Cask 25	3,046	$12.00	$40.00	Avoid
1962	MAYACAMAS VINEYARDS	California	350	$2.00	$150.00	Avoid
1982	MOUNT VEEDER WINERY	Napa Valley Mount Veeder Mt. Veeder Vineyards	4,600	$12.50	$13.00	Avoid
1976	RIDGE VINEYARDS	Napa County Spring Mountain York Creek	1,150	$10.00	$30.00	Avoid
1979	STAG'S LEAP WINE CELLARS	Napa Valley Stags Leap District Stag's Leap Vineyards	6,000	$15.00	$32.00	Avoid
1980	TREFETHEN VINEYARDS	Napa Valley Yountville	6,980	$11.00	$20.00	Avoid

SCORE: 67

Vintage	Winery	Appellation/Vineyard	Case Prod.	Release Price	Current Price	Drink
1971	BEAULIEU VINEYARD	Napa Valley Rutherford Georges de Latour Private Reserve	15,000	$8.00	$60.00	Avoid
1972	CHAPPELLET VINEYARD	Napa Valley	1,500	$6.50	$40.00	Avoid
1973	INGLENOOK-NAPA VALLEY	Napa Valley Rutherford Cask	6,494	$8.00	$39.00	Avoid
1972	INGLENOOK-NAPA VALLEY	Napa Valley Rutherford Cask	7,278	$7.00	$44.00	Avoid

SCORE: 66

Vintage	Winery	Appellation/Vineyard	Case Prod.	Release Price	Current Price	Drink
1976	BUENA VISTA WINERY	Sonoma Valley Carneros	994	$12.00	$40.00	Avoid
1982	CLOS DU BOIS WINERY	Alexander Valley Briarcrest Vineyard	2,075	$12.00	$25.00	Avoid
1982	NEWTON VINEYARD	Napa Valley	3,096	$12.50	$21.00	Avoid
1982	SPRING MOUNTAIN VINEYARDS	Napa Valley	5,739	$15.00	$15.00	Avoid

SCORE: 65

Vintage	Winery	Appellation/Vineyard	Case Prod.	Release Price	Current Price	Drink
1971	CHAPPELLET VINEYARD	Napa Valley	1,000	$7.50	$80.00	Avoid

NA — not available.   NR — not released.   * — Beaulieu production figures are estimates.

Vintage	Winery	Appellation/Vineyard	Case Prod.	Release Price	Current Price	Drink
1982	GUNDLACH BUNDSCHU WINERY	Sonoma Valley Rhinefarm	4,500	$9.00	$13.00	Avoid
1967	MAYACAMAS VINEYARDS	California	800	$4.00	$125.00	Avoid
1965	MAYACAMAS VINEYARDS	California	475	$2.75	$150.00	Avoid

SCORE: 64

| 1975 | BUENA VISTA WINERY | Sonoma Valley Carneros | 3,864 | $12.00 | $30.00 | Avoid |

SCORE: 63

| 1972 | LOUIS M. MARTINI WINERY | California Special Selection | 2,055 | $5.00 | $65.00 | Avoid |

SCORE: 62

| 1980 | VILLA MT. EDEN WINERY | Napa Valley Oakville Estate | 3,922 | $11.70 | $14.00 | Avoid |

SCORE: 60

| 1976 | ALEXANDER VALLEY VINEYARDS | Alexander Valley | 2,080 | $5.50 | $18.00 | Avoid |

SCORE: 59

| 1983 | LAUREL GLEN VINEYARD | Sonoma Mountain | 4,000 | $11.00 | $11.00 | Avoid |
| 1979 | RAVENSWOOD | California | 875 | $8.00 | $10.00 | Avoid |

SCORE: 58

| 1982 | TREFETHEN VINEYARDS | Napa Valley Yountville | NA | $11.00 | NA | Avoid |

SCORE: 55

| 1980 | NEWTON VINEYARD | Napa Valley | NA | $12.00 | NA | Avoid |

NA — not available.   NR — not released.   * — Beaulieu production figures are estimates.

APPENDIX 3
All Wines Tasted, Listed by Vintage, Score and Winery

Score	Winery	Appellation/Vineyard	Case Prod.	Release Price	Current Price	Drink
VINTAGE: 1987						
95-100	BERINGER VINEYARDS	Napa Valley Private Reserve		NR		NA
95-100	GRACE FAMILY VINEYARD	Napa Valley St.Helena	126	NR		NA
95-100	GRGICH HILLS CELLARS	Napa Valley Yountville	10,000	NR		NA
95-100	ROBERT KEENAN WINERY	Napa Valley Spring Mountain		NR		NA
95-100	SPOTTSWOODE WINERY	Napa Valley St.Helena		NR		NA
95-100	STERLING VINEYARDS	Napa Valley Reserve		NR		NA
90-94	BERINGER VINEYARDS	Napa Valley St. Helena Chabot Vineyard		NR		NA
90-94	BEAULIEU VINEYARD	Napa Valley Rutherford Private Reserve		NR		NA
90-94	BUEHLER VINEYARDS	Napa Valley		NR		NA
90-94	CARMENET VINEYARD	Sonoma Valley		NR		NA
90-94	CAYMUS VINEYARDS	Napa Valley Rutherford Estate		NR		NA
90-94	CHATEAU MONTELENA WINERY	Napa Valley Calistoga	7,000	NR		NA
90-94	CONN CREEK WINERY	Napa Valley		NR		NA
90-94	CONN CREEK WINERY	Napa Valley St. Helena Private Reserve		NR		NA
90-94	DIAMOND CREEK VINEYARDS	Napa Valley Diamond Mountain Gravelly Meadow	287	NR		NA
90-94	DIAMOND CREEK VINEYARDS	Napa Valley Diamond Mountain Red Rock Terrace	570	NR		NA
90-94	DOMINUS ESTATE	Napa Valley Yountville	6,500	NR		NA
90-94	DUNN VINEYARDS	Napa Valley Howell Mountain		NR		NA
90-94	DUNN VINEYARDS	Napa Valley		NR		NA
90-94	FAR NIENTE WINERY	Napa Valley Oakville		NR		NA
90-94	FLORA SPRINGS WINE CO.	Napa Valley		NR		NA
90-94	GIRARD WINERY	Napa Valley Oakville Reserve	800	NR		NA
90-94	GROTH VINEYARDS AND WINERY	Napa Valley Oakville		NR		NA
90-94	HESS COLLECTION WINERY	Napa Valley Mount Veeder (Estate)		NR		NA
90-94	WILLIAM HILL WINERY	Napa Valley Reserve		NR		NA
90-94	INGLENOOK-NAPA VALLEY	Napa Valley Rutherford Reserve Cask		NR		NA
90-94	IRON HORSE VINEYARDS	Alexander Valley Cabernets		NR		NA
90-94	JOHNSON TURNBULL VINEYARDS	Napa Valley Oakville Vineyard Selection 67		NR		NA
90-94	LA JOTA VINEYARD CO.	Napa Valley Howell Mountain		NR		NA
90-94	LAUREL GLEN VINEYARD	Sonoma Mountain		NR		NA
90-94	LIVINGSTON VINEYARDS	Napa Valley Rutherford		NR		NA
90-94	LOUIS M. MARTINI WINERY	Sonoma Valley Monte Rosso		NR		NA
90-94	ROBERT MONDAVI WINERY	Napa Valley Oakville Reserve		NR		NA
90-94	NEWTON VINEYARD	Napa Valley Spring Mountain		NR		NA
90-94	PINE RIDGE WINERY	Napa Valley Rutherford Rutherford Cuvée		NR		NA
90-94	RAVENSWOOD	Sonoma County		NR		NA
90-94	SANTA CRUZ MOUNTAIN VYD	Santa Cruz Mountains Bates Ranch		NR		NA
90-94	SILVERADO VINEYARDS	Napa Valley Stags Leap District		NR		NA
90-94	SIMI WINERY	Alexander Valley Reserve		NR		NA
90-94	STAG'S LEAP WINE CELLARS	Napa Valley Stags Leap District Cask 23		NR		NA
90-94	TREFETHEN VINEYARDS	Napa Valley Yountville Reserve		NR		NA
90-94	VICHON WINERY	Napa Valley Stags Leap District SLD		NR		NA
90-94	VILLA MT. EDEN WINERY	Napa Valley Oakville		NR		NA
80-89	CHAPPELLET VINEYARD	Napa Valley		NR		NA
80-89	CHIMNEY ROCK WINE CELLARS	Napa Valley Stags Leap District		NR		NA
80-89	CLOS DU VAL WINERY	Napa Valley Stags Leap District Estate		NR		NA
80-89	DIAMOND CREEK VINEYARDS	Napa Valley Diamond Mountain Volcanic Hill	726	NR		NA
80-89	DUCKHORN VINEYARDS	Napa Valley		NR		NA
80-89	FISHER VINEYARDS	Sonoma Valley Coach Insignia		NR		NA
80-89	FRANCISCAN VINEYARDS	Napa Valley Oakville Meritage	1,200	NR		NA
80-89	GUNDLACH BUNDSCHU WINERY	Sonoma Valley Rhinefarm		NR		NA
80-89	HAYWOOD WINERY	Sonoma Valley	2,000	NR		NA

NA — not available.   NR — not released.   ∗ — Beaulieu production figures are estimates.

Score	Winery	Appellation/Vineyard	Case Prod.	Release Price	Current Price	Drink
80-89	JOHNSON TURNBULL VINEYARDS	Napa Valley Oakville		NR		NA
80-89	LAKESPRING WINERY	Napa Valley Yountville		NR		NA
80-89	MONTICELLO CELLARS	Napa Valley Corley Reserve	3,200	NR		NA
80-89	MOUNT EDEN VINEYARDS	Santa Cruz Mountains	730	NR		NA
80-89	ROBERT PECOTA WINERY	Napa Valley Calistoga Kara's Vineyard	1,300	NR		NA
80-89	JOSEPH PHELPS VINEYARDS	Napa Valley Oakville Backus Vineyard		NR		NA
80-89	JOSEPH PHELPS VINEYARDS	Napa Valley Calistoga Eisele Vineyard		NR		NA
80-89	PINE RIDGE WINERY	Napa Valley Diamond Mountain Diamond Mountain		NR		NA
80-89	PINE RIDGE WINERY	Napa Valley Rutherford Andrus Reserve		NR		NA
80-89	PINE RIDGE WINERY	Napa Valley Stags Leap District Pine Ridge Stags Leap Vineyard		NR		NA
80-89	RIDGE VINEYARDS	Santa Cruz Mountains Monte Bello	800-1000	NR		NA
80-89	SHAFER VINEYARDS	Napa Valley Stags Leap Hillside Select		NR		NA
80-89	STAG'S LEAP WINE CELLARS	Napa Valley Stags Leap District SLV		NR		NA
80-89	STELTZNER VINEYARDS	Napa Valley Stags Leap District	5,000	NR		NA
80-89	STERLING VINEYARDS	Napa Valley Diamond Mountain Diamond Mountain Ranch		NR		NA

VINTAGE: 1986

Score	Winery	Appellation/Vineyard	Case Prod.	Release Price	Current Price	Drink
98	CAYMUS VINEYARDS	Napa Valley Rutherford Special Selection	1,000	NR		1995-2005
96	BERINGER VINEYARDS	Napa Valley Private Reserve	4,000	NR		1995-2003
96	DIAMOND CREEK VINEYARD	Napa Valley Diamond Mountain Red Rock Terrace	970	$30.00	$30.00	1996-2010
96	DIAMOND CREEK VINEYARD	Napa Valley Diamond Mountain Volcanic Hill	1,035	$30.00	$30.00	1996-2012
96	JOSEPH PHELPS VINEYARDS	Napa Valley Insignia	4,000	NR		1996-2004
95	WILLIAM HILL WINERY	Napa Valley Gold Label Reserve	13,595	$24.50	$24.50	1996-2006
95	JOHNSON TURNBULL VINEYARDS	Napa Valley Oakville Vineyard Selection 82	1,540	$14.50	$14.50	1992-2000
95	ROBERT MONDAVI WINERY	Napa Valley Oakville Reserve	14,000	$35.00	$35.00	1993-2000
95	OPUS ONE	Napa Valley Oakville	11,200	NR		1995-2005
95	JOSEPH PHELPS VINEYARDS	Napa Valley Calistoga Eisele Vineyard	1,500	NR		1998-2008
95	SPOTTSWOODE WINERY	Napa Valley St. Helena	2,400	$30.00	$30.00	1996-2006
94	B.R. COHN	Sonoma Valley Olive Hill Vineyard	2,400	$18.00	$20.00	1993-2001
94	DIAMOND CREEK VINEYARD	Napa Valley Diamond Mountain Gravelly Meadow	795	$30.00	$30.00	1997-2010
94	DUCKHORN VINEYARDS	Napa Valley	4,000	$18.00	$18.00	1995-2003
94	DUNN VINEYARDS	Napa Valley Howell Mountain	2,000	$30.00	$30.00	1993-2000
94	FROG'S LEAP WINERY	Napa Valley	2,600	$14.00	$14.00	1993-1999
94	ROBERT KEENAN WINERY	Napa Valley Spring Mountain	3,395	$16.50	$16.50	1992-2000
94	KENWOOD VINEYARDS	Sonoma Valley Artist Series	4,000	$30.00	$30.00	1993-2003
94	SILVERADO VINEYARDS	Napa Valley Stags Leap District	9,800	$13.50	$13.50	1995-2005
94	STERLING VINEYARDS	Napa Valley Reserve	3,432	NR		1996-2006
93	BEAULIEU VINEYARD	Napa Valley Rutherford Georges de Latour Private Reserve	15,000	NR		1995-2005
93	BERINGER VINEYARDS	Napa Valley St. Helena Chabot Vineyard	1,000	NR		1994-2002
93	BUENA VISTA WINERY	Sonoma Valley Carneros Private Reserve	3,150	$18	$18	1995-2005
93	CARMENET VINEYARD	Sonoma Valley	9,469	$20.00	$20.00	1994-2005
93	CHATEAU MONTELENA WINERY	Napa Valley Calistoga Estate	12,900	NR		1995-2004
93	CUVAISON WINERY	Napa Valley	5,000	$15.00	$15.00	1993-2001
93	DOMINUS ESTATE	Napa Valley Yountville Napanook	6,300	NR		1995-2004
93	DUNN VINEYARDS	Napa Valley	2,000	$27.00	$27.00	1993-2000
93	FORMAN VINEYARD	Napa Valley	1,800	$20.00	$20.00	1995-2004
93	GRACE FAMILY VINEYARD	Napa Valley St. Helena Estate	150	$40.00	$40.00	1994-2003
93	GROTH VINEYARDS & WINERY	Napa Valley Oakville Reserve	475	NR		1993-2003
93	HESS COLLECTION WINERY	Napa Valley Mount Veeder Reserve	2,000	NR		1995-2003
93	MOUNT VEEDER WINERY	Napa Valley Mount Veeder Proprietary Reserve	50	NR		1996-2006
93	JOSEPH PHELPS VINEYARDS	Napa Valley Oakville Backus Vineyard	1,400	NR		1998-2005
93	SANTA CRUZ MOUNTAIN VYD	Santa Cruz Mountains Bates Ranch	1,200	NR		1996-2006
93	SHAFER VINEYARDS	Napa Valley Stags Leap District	5,000	$16.00	$16.00	1994-2002

NA — not available.   NR — not released.   * — Beaulieu production figures are estimates.

Score	Winery	Appellation/Vineyard	Case Prod.	Release Price	Current Price	Drink
93	PHILIP TOGNI VINEYARD	Napa Valley Spring Mountain	386	$22.00	$22.00	1993-2005
92	CAYMUS VINEYARDS	Napa Valley Rutherford Estate	4,000	$22.00	$22.00	1995-2005
92	CHAPPELLET VINEYARD	Napa Valley Reserve	6,000	NR		1994-2003
92	CLOS DU VAL WINE CO.	Napa Valley Joli Val	5,000	NR		1994-2004
92	GROTH VINEYARDS & WINERY	Napa Valley Oakville Estate	6,400	$18.00	$18.00	1994-2001
92	INGLENOOK-NAPA VALLEY	Napa Valley Rutherford Reserve Cask	6,000	NR		1996-2004
92	INGLENOOK-NAPA VALLEY	Napa Valley Rutherford Reunion	4,251	NR		1996-2006
92	LA JOTA VINEYARD CO.	Napa Valley Howell Mountain	2,700	$21.00	$21.00	1994-2004
92	NIEBAUM-COPPOLA ESTATE	Napa Valley Rutherford Rubicon	4,300	NR		1996-2004
92	PINE RIDGE WINERY	Napa Valley Rutherford Andrus Reserve	749	$40.00	$40.00	1995-2002
92	SHAFER VINEYARDS	Napa Valley Stags Leap District Hillside Select	2,000	NR		1994-2002
92	SIMI WINERY	Alexander Valley Reserve	1,700	NR		1993-2002
92	STAG'S LEAP WINE CELLARS	Napa Valley Stags Leap District Cask 23	605	NR		1994-2003
91	BUEHLER VINEYARDS	Napa Valley	3,829	$15.00	$15.00	1996-2005
91	BURGESS CELLARS	Napa Valley Vintage Selection	6,600	NR		1995-2004
91	CLOS DU VAL WINE CO.	Napa Valley Stags Leap District Estate	21,000	NR		1994-2004
91	FAR NIENTE WINERY	Napa Valley Oakville	12,000	$30.00	$30.00	1995-2003
91	GIRARD WINERY	Napa Valley Oakville Reserve	584	NR		1994-2002
91	GRGICH HILLS CELLAR	Napa Valley Yountville	10,000	NR		1994-2002
91	HAYWOOD WINERY	Sonoma Valley	2,612	$16.00	$16.00	1994-2003
91	HESS COLLECTION WINERY	Napa Valley Mount Veeder	10,000	$14.00	$14.00	1994-2000
91	KISTLER VINEYARDS	Sonoma Valley Kistler Vineyard	521	$20.00	$20.00	1995-2002
91	MARKHAM VINEYARDS	Napa Valley Yountville Markham Vineyard	3,850	NR		1995-2004
91	NEWTON VINEYARD	Napa Valley Spring Mountain Estate	5,530	$16.00	$16.00	1992-1999
91	PINE RIDGE WINERY	Napa Valley Diamond Mountain Diamond Mountain Vineyard	450	$30.00	$30.00	1995-2004
91	PINE RIDGE WINERY	Napa Valley Stags Leap District Pine Ridge Stags Leap Vineyard	1,775	NR		1995-2005
90	FISHER VINEYARDS	Sonoma County Coach Insignia	1,500	$20.00	$20.00	1993-2000
90	FREEMARK ABBEY WINERY	Napa Valley Rutherford Bosche	4,000	NR		1994-2002
90	LIVINGSTON VINEYARDS	Napa Valley Rutherford Moffett Vineyard	1,330	$24.00	$24.00	1994-1999
90	PINE RIDGE WINERY	Napa Valley Rutherford Rutherford Cuveé	7,437	$16.00	$16.00	1995-2003
90	SEQUOIA GROVE VINEYARDS	Napa Valley Rutherford Estate	1,986	$22.00	$22.00	1994-2000
90	SPRING MOUNTAIN VINEYARDS	Napa Valley Spring Mountain	3,684	NR		1996-2004
90	STELTZNER VINEYARDS	Napa Valley Stags Leap District	5,000	$16.00	$16.00	1993-2000
90	TREFETHEN VINEYARDS	Napa Valley Yountville Reserve	1,000	NR		1995-2005
90	VICHON WINERY	Napa Valley Stags Leap District SLD	2,540	$21.00	$21.00	1991-1997
89	CAKEBREAD CELLARS	Napa Valley	5,000	$18.00	$18.00	1992-1998
89	GUNDLACH BUNDSCHU WINERY	Sonoma Valley Rhinefarm	5,000	$12.00	$12.00	1993-1998
89	LAUREL GLEN VINEYARD	Sonoma Mountain	4,000	$20.00	$25.00	1992-1998
89	MERRYVALE VINEYARDS	Napa Valley Red Table Wine	1,604	$25.00	$25.00	1994-2002
89	RAVENSWOOD	Sonoma Mountain Pickberry Vineyard	550	$25.00	$25.00	1994-1997
89	ROMBAUER VINEYARDS	Napa Valley Le Meilleur Du Chai	500	NR		1994-2002
89	STAG'S LEAP WINE CELLARS	Napa Valley Stags Leap District SLV	6,248	$28.00	$28.00	1992-1999
89	TUDAL WINERY	Napa Valley St. Helena	1,800	$14.50	$14.50	1994-2002
88	ALEXANDER VALLEY VINEYARDS	Alexander Valley	13,522	$11.50	$11.50	1992-1998
88	IRON HORSE VINEYARDS	Alexander Valley Cabernets	3,500	$17.50	$17.50	1993-2000
88	JORDAN VINEYARD AND WINERY	Alexander Valley Estate	58,000	NR		1990-1995
88	LAKESPRING WINERY	Napa Valley Yountville	1,700	$14.00	$14.00	1994-1999
88	MONTICELLO CELLARS	Napa Valley Oakville Corley Reserve	3,800	$24.00	$24.00	1993-1999
88	ROBERT PECOTA WINERY	Napa Valley Calistoga Kara's Vineyard	1,230	$16.00	$16.00	1993-2000
88	PRESTON VINEYARDS	Dry Creek Valley	4,075	$11.00	$11.00	1993-1999
88	RIDGE VINEYARDS	Napa Valley York Creek	5,333	NR		1993-2000
88	RUTHERFORD HILL WINERY	Napa Valley St. Helena XVS	2,000	NR		1994-2000
88	V. SATTUI WINERY	Napa Valley Rutherford Preston Vineyard	2,487	$16.75	$16.75	1991-1998
88	SEQUOIA GROVE VINEYARDS	Napa County	6,776	$16.00	$16.00	1993-1998
88	STERLING VINEYARDS	Napa Valley Diamond Mountain Diamond Mountain Ranch	6,000	NR		1996-2003
87	CONN CREEK WINERY	Napa Valley Barrel Select	• 6,550	NR		1994-2000
87	JOHNSON TURNBULL VINEYARDS	Napa Valley Oakville Vineyard Selection 67	1,280	$20.00	$20.00	1995-2005

NA — not available.   NR — not released.   ∗ — Beaulieu production figures are estimates.

Score	Winery	Appellation/Vineyard	Case Prod.	Release Price	Current Price	Drink
87	CHARLES KRUG WINERY	Napa Valley Vintage Select	7,266	NR		1994-2002
87	MOUNT VEEDER WINERY	Napa Valley Mount Veeder Mt. Veeder Vineyards	2,600	NR		1992-2000
87	ST. CLEMENT VINEYARDS	Napa Valley	2,000	NR		1993-2001
87	TREFETHEN VINEYARDS	Napa Valley Yountville	10,400	$15.25	$15.25	1996-2002
86	CHIMNEY ROCK WINE CELLARS	Napa Valley Stags Leap District	5,700	$15.00	$15.00	1990-1996
86	LONG VINEYARDS	Napa Valley Oakville	200	NR		1991-1998
86	LOUIS M. MARTINI WINERY	Sonoma Valley Monte Rosso	810	NR		1992-1999
86	MAYACAMAS VINEYARDS	Napa Valley Mount Veeder	2,150	NR		1991-1996
86	ROMBAUER VINEYARDS	Napa Valley	3,000	$15.00	$15.00	1992-1997
86	RAVENSWOOD	Sonoma County	3,000	$12.00	$14.00	1995-2002
86	RAYMOND VINEYARD AND CELLAR	Napa Valley Rutherford Private Reserve	3,000	NR		1993-1999
86	STAGS' LEAP WINERY	Napa Valley Stags Leap District	7,860	NR		1992-1997
85	EBERLE WINERY	Paso Robles	4,196	$12.00	$12.00	1993-1997
85	FLORA SPRINGS WINE CO.	Napa Valley Rutherford Trilogy	1,400	$33.00	$33.00	1993-1998
85	MOUNT EDEN VINEYARDS	Santa Cruz Mountains	786	NR		1994-2000
85	RIDGE VINEYARDS	Santa Cruz Mountains Monte Bello	2,079	$35.00	$35.00	1994-1999
84	VILLA MT. EDEN WINERY	Napa Valley Oakville Estate	9,700	NR		1990-1996
79	STONEGATE WINERY	Napa Valley Calistoga Estate	3,000	NR		1990-1995
77	FLORA SPRINGS WINE CO.	Napa Valley	3,500	$15.00	$15.00	1990-1994

VINTAGE: 1985

Score	Winery	Appellation/Vineyard	Case Prod.	Release Price	Current Price	Drink
99	CAYMUS VINEYARDS	Napa Valley Rutherford Special Selection	1,000	NR		1995-2005
98	HEITZ WINE CELLARS	Napa Valley Oakville Martha's Vineyard	4,848	NR		1995-2010
98	STAG'S LEAP WINE CELLARS	Napa Valley Stags Leap District Cask 23	1,018	$75	$75	1994-2005
96	BERINGER VINEYARDS	Napa Valley Private Reserve	8,000	NR		1994-2004
96	HESS COLLECTION WINERY	Napa Valley Mount Veeder	5,000	$13.00	$13.00	1994-2002
96	JOSEPH PHELPS VINEYARDS	Napa Valley Insignia	4,700	$40.00	$40.00	1995-2005
96	STERLING VINEYARDS	Napa Valley Reserve	2,492	$30.00	$38.00	1996-2008
95	BEAULIEU VINEYARD	Napa Valley Rutherford Georges de Latour Private Reserve	15,000	NR		1995-2003
95	CHATEAU MONTELENA WINERY	Napa Valley Calistoga Estate	9,723	$25.00	$25.00	1996-2006
95	DOMINUS ESTATE	Napa Valley Yountville Napanook	4,000	$45.00	$45.00	1995-2005
95	GRACE FAMILY VINEYARD	Napa Valley St. Helena Estate	126	$50.00	$90.00	1993-2004
95	INGLENOOK-NAPA VALLEY	Napa Valley Rutherford Reserve Cask	10,388	NR		1994-2002
95	ROBERT MONDAVI WINERY	Napa Valley Oakville Reserve	15,000	$40.00	$40.00	1993-2002
95	OPUS ONE	Napa Valley Oakville	11,300	$55.00	$55.00	1995-2005
95	RIDGE VINEYARDS	Santa Cruz Mountains Monte Bello	2,220	$40.00	$50.00	1995-2005
95	SPOTTSWOODE WINERY	Napa Valley St. Helena	2,000	$25.00	$35.00	1995-2005
94	CLOS DU VAL WINE CO.	Napa Valley Stags Leap District Reserve	750	NR		1995-2006
94	B.R. COHN	Sonoma Valley Olive Hill Vineyard	2,000	$16.00	$22.00	1993-2000
94	DUNN VINEYARDS	Napa Valley	2,000	$20.00	$45.00	1992-2000
94	WILLIAM HILL WINERY	Napa Valley Gold Label Reserve	10,204	$22.50	$22.50	1995-2005
94	INGLENOOK-NAPA VALLEY	Napa Valley Rutherford Reunion	3,602	$35.00	$35.00	1993-2000
94	JOSEPH PHELPS VINEYARDS	Napa Valley Calistoga Eisele Vineyard	1,500	$40.00	$40.00	1995-2005
94	PINE RIDGE WINERY	Napa Valley Stags Leap District Pine Ridge Stags Leap Vineyard	1,756	$26.00	$26.00	1994-2010
94	SIMI WINERY	Alexander Valley Reserve	2,300	NR		1994-2003
94	STAG'S LEAP WINE CELLARS	Napa Valley Stags Leap District SLV	8,810	$26.00	$26.00	1993-1999
93	BUEHLER VINEYARDS	Napa Valley	3,060	$14.00	$16.00	1995-2004
93	BUENA VISTA WINERY	Sonoma Valley Carneros Private Reserve	2,900	$18.00	$18.00	1993-2000
93	BURGESS CELLARS	Napa Valley Vintage Selection	6,600	$18.00	$18.00	1992-2002
93	CLOS DU VAL WINE CO.	Napa Valley Stags Leap District Estate	25,000	$16.00	$16.00	1993-2005
93	DIAMOND CREEK VINEYARD	Napa Valley Diamond Mountain Red Rock Terrace	643	$30.00	$40.00	1996-2009
93	DIAMOND CREEK VINEYARD	Napa Valley Diamond Mountain Volcanic Hill	1,100	$30.00	$40.00	1996-2010
93	FORMAN VINEYARD	Napa Valley	1,600	$18.00	$30.00	1994-2002
93	FREEMARK ABBEY WINERY	Napa Valley Rutherford Bosche	3,500	$24.00	$24.00	1995-2005
93	GROTH VINEYARDS & WINERY	Napa Valley Oakville Reserve	500	NR		1996-2004

NA — not available.   NR — not released.   * — Beaulieu production figures are estimates.

Score	Winery	Appellation/Vineyard	Case Prod.	Release Price	Current Price	Drink
93	KISTLER VINEYARDS	Sonoma Valley Kistler Vineyard	169	$16.00	$25.00	1994-2002
93	LAUREL GLEN VINEYARD	Sonoma Mountain	3,300	$18.00	$35.00	1992-2000
93	MARKHAM VINEYARDS	Napa Valley Yountville Markham Vineyard	3,810	NR		1994-2003
93	PINE RIDGE WINERY	Napa Valley Rutherford Rutherford Cuveé	8,668	$16.00	$16.00	1994-2004
93	SHAFER VINEYARDS	Napa Valley Stags Leap District Hillside Select	2,000	NR		1993-2000
93	SILVER OAK CELLARS	Alexander Valley	19,900	$24.00	$24.00	1995-2005
93	ST. CLEMENT VINEYARDS	Napa Valley	2,665	$17.00	$17.00	1994-2002
93	STELTZNER VINEYARDS	Napa Valley Stags Leap District	5,000	$16.00	$19.00	1993-2000
92	CAYMUS VINEYARDS	Napa Valley Rutherford Estate	3,500	$18.00	$28.00	1994-2003
92	DIAMOND CREEK VINEYARD	Napa Valley Diamond Mountain Gravelly Meadow	736	$30.00	$40.00	1995-2007
92	DUCKHORN VINEYARDS	Napa Valley	2,800	$17.50	$26.00	1996-2010
92	FAR NIENTE WINERY	Napa Valley Oakville	10,000	$28.00	$28.00	1994-2002
92	GRGICH HILLS CELLAR	Napa Valley Yountville	10,000	NR		1994-2005
92	HEITZ WINE CELLARS	Napa Valley Rutherford Bella Oaks Vineyard	4,037	NR		1994-2003
92	LONG VINEYARDS	Napa Valley Oakville	200	$36.00	$36.00	1995-2005
92	LYETH WINERY	Alexander Valley	13,500	$22.00	$22.00	1992-1999
92	MAYACAMAS VINEYARDS	Napa Valley Mount Veeder	2,025	$25.00	$25.00	1997-2007
92	PINE RIDGE WINERY	Napa Valley Rutherford Andrus Reserve Cuveé Duet	1,136	$40.00	$45.00	1994-2002
92	RIDGE VINEYARDS	Napa County Spring Mountain York Creek	4,087	$16.00	$16.00	1990-2000
92	SANTA CRUZ MOUNTAIN VYD	Santa Cruz Mountains Bates Ranch	1,125	NR		1995-2005
92	SEQUOIA GROVE VINEYARDS	Napa Valley Rutherford Estate	2,064	$28.00	$32.00	1992-2005
92	SILVERADO VINEYARDS	Napa Valley Stags Leap District	11,000	$12.50	$16.00	1995-2002
92	VICHON WINERY	Napa Valley Stags Leap District SLD	4,000	$18.00	$20.00	1992-2000
91	BERINGER VINEYARDS	Napa Valley St. Helena Chabot Vineyard	1,000	NR		1992-2000
91	CARMENET VINEYARD	Sonoma Valley	6,040	$18.50	$22.00	1994-2004
91	GROTH VINEYARDS & WINERY	Napa Valley Oakville Estate	7,800	$16.00	$16.00	1994-2002
91	GUNDLACH BUNDSCHU WINERY	Sonoma Valley Rhinefarm	5,000	$9.00	$10.00	1992-2000
91	KENWOOD VINEYARDS	Sonoma Valley Artist Series	3,000	$30.00	$30.00	1993-2000
91	MERRYVALE VINEYARDS	Napa Valley Red Table Wine	1,662	$24.00	$24.00	1994-2001
91	NIEBAUM-COPPOLA ESTATE	Napa Valley Rutherford Rubicon	4,762	NR		1995-2003
90	ROBERT PEPI WINERY	Napa Valley Yountville Vine Hill Ranch	2,720	NR		1996-2002
91	SHAFER VINEYARDS	Napa Valley Stags Leap District	5,000	$15.50	$15.50	1992-1998
90	CUVAISON WINERY	Napa Valley	3,000	$14.00	$14.00	1992-1999
90	FISHER VINEYARDS	Sonoma County Coach Insignia	1,200	$18.00	$20.00	1993-2000
90	JOSEPH PHELPS VINEYARDS	Napa Valley Oakville Backus Vineyard	1,980	$27.50	$32.00	1996-2002
90	ROMBAUER VINEYARDS	Napa Valley Le Meilleur Du Chai	425	$37.50	$37.50	1993-2002
90	SMITH-MADRONE VINEYARD	Napa Valley Spring Mountain	1,500	$14.00	$14.00	1994-2002
90	STERLING VINEYARDS	Napa Valley Diamond Mountain Diamond Mountain Ranch	5,700	$16.00	$16.00	1995-2003
90	TREFETHEN VINEYARDS	Napa Valley Yountville Reserve	969	NR		1993-2000
89	DIAMOND CREEK VINEYARD	Napa Valley Diamond Mountain Three Vineyard Blend	10	$50.00	$50.00	1998-2004
89	DUNN VINEYARDS	Napa Valley Howell Mountain	1,800	$30.00	$55.00	1995-2002
89	EBERLE WINERY	Paso Robles	2,814	$12.00	$14.00	1992-1998
89	FRANCISCAN VINEYARDS	Napa Valley Oakville Meritage	450	$20.00	$20.00	1993-2000
89	GIRARD WINERY	Napa Valley Oakville Reserve	480	$25.00	$25.00	1993-2000
89	HAYWOOD WINERY	Sonoma Valley	2,141	$14.50	$14.50	1996-2004
89	NEWTON VINEYARD	Napa Valley Spring Mountain Estate	3,096	$15.25	$18.00	1992-1998
89	PRESTON VINEYARDS	Dry Creek Valley	3,100	$11.00	$11.00	1993-1999
89	RUTHERFORD HILL WINERY	Napa Valley St. Helena XVS	2,000	$25.00	$25.00	1995-2001
89	PHILIP TOGNI VINEYARD	Napa Valley Spring Mountain	125	$20.00	$25.00	1995-2004
89	TUDAL WINERY	Napa Valley St. Helena	1,400	$14.50	$14.50	1993-1999
88	ALEXANDER VALLEY VINEYARDS	Alexander Valley	15,745	$11.00	$12.00	1991-1997
88	CHAPPELLET VINEYARD	Napa Valley Reserve	6,000	$20.00	$20.00	1994-2000
88	CLOS DU BOIS WINERY	Alexander Valley Marlstone Vineyard	5,917	$19.50	$19.50	1992-1998
88	FLORA SPRINGS WINE CO.	Napa Valley	4,000	$15.00	$15.00	1991-1999
88	FLORA SPRINGS WINE CO.	Napa Valley Rutherford Trilogy	1,200	$30.00	$30.00	1992-1998

NA — not available.   NR — not released.   * — Beaulieu production figures are estimates.

Score	Winery	Appellation/Vineyard	Case Prod.	Release Price	Current Price	Drink
88	FRANCISCAN VINEYARDS	Napa Valley Oakville Library Selection	2,000	$17.50	$17.50	1990-1996
88	LA JOTA VINEYARD CO.	Napa Valley Howell Mountain	1,570	$18.00	$18.00	1993-2000
88	LAKESPRING WINERY	Napa Valley Yountville	3,300	$12.00	$12.00	1992-1999
88	MONTICELLO CELLARS	Napa Valley Oakville Corley Reserve	150	$22.50	$22.50	1994-1998
88	RAYMOND VINEYARD AND CELLAR	Napa Valley Rutherford Private Reserve	4,000	NR		1992-1998
88	SPRING MOUNTAIN VINEYARDS	Napa Valley Spring Mountain	3,396	$20.00	$20.00	1997-2005
88	VICHON WINERY	Napa Valley	7,500	$13.00	$14.00	1992-1997
87	CHIMNEY ROCK WINE CELLARS	Napa Valley Stags Leap District	2,900	$15.00	$15.00	1990-1997
87	CONN CREEK WINERY	Napa Valley St. Helena Barrel Select Private Reserve	1,100	NR		1992-1997
87	FRANCISCAN VINEYARDS	Napa Valley Oakville Reserve	1,800	$18.00	$18.00	1991-1997
87	IRON HORSE VINEYARDS	Alexander Valley Cabernets	3,000	$16.00	$16.50	1992-1999
87	MOUNT VEEDER WINERY	Napa Valley Mount Veeder Mt. Veeder Vineyards	2,100	NR		1997-2004
87	V. SATTUI WINERY	Napa Valley Rutherford Preston Vineyard	3,143	$15.75	$15.75	1990-1996
87	STONEGATE WINERY	Napa Valley Calistoga Estate	4,403	$16.00	$16.00	1993-1998
86	ROBERT KEENAN WINERY	Napa Valley Spring Mountain	2,400	$15.00	$15.00	1993-1998
86	LIVINGSTON VINEYARDS	Napa Valley Rutherford Moffett Vineyard	1,030	$18.00	$24.00	1993-1999
86	MOUNT EDEN VINEYARDS	Santa Cruz Mountains	622	$28.00	$28.00	1994-1998
86	ROBERT PECOTA WINERY	Napa Valley Calistoga Kara's Vineyard	940	$16.00	$20.00	1992-1998
86	SEQUOIA GROVE VINEYARDS	Napa County	4,101	$16.00	$16.00	1992-1997
85	CAKEBREAD CELLARS	Napa Valley Rutherford Rutherford Reserve	700	NR		1993-1998
85	CONN CREEK WINERY	Napa Valley Barrel Select	6,000	NR		1991-1995
85	FROG'S LEAP WINERY	Napa Valley	2,300	$12.00	$12.00	1992-1998
85	JORDAN VINEYARD AND WINERY	Alexander Valley Estate	53,698	$19.50	$19.50	1990-1994
85	RAVENSWOOD	Sonoma County	1,540	$12.00	$14.00	1995-2001
85	ROMBAUER VINEYARDS	Napa Valley	2,000	$14.75	$17.00	1991-1997
85	SILVER OAK CELLARS	Napa Valley Calistoga	3,550	$24.00	$24.00	1996-2006
85	SILVER OAK CELLARS	Napa Valley Oakville Bonny's Vineyard	970	NR		1995-2004
85	STAGS' LEAP WINERY	Napa Valley Stags Leap District	7,672	$15.00	$16.00	1992-1997
84	CAKEBREAD CELLARS	Napa Valley	5,000	$17.00	$17.00	1992-1996
84	CHARLES KRUG WINERY	Napa Valley Vintage Select	7,266	NR		1995-2004
83	JOHNSON TURNBULL VINEYARDS	Napa Valley Oakville	2,350	$14.50	$17.50	1994-2000
82	CLOS DU BOIS WINERY	Alexander Valley Briarcrest Vineyard	3,721	$16.00	$16.00	1993-1998
82	VILLA MT. EDEN WINERY	Napa Valley Oakville Estate	8,095	NR		1990-1994
80	LOUIS M. MARTINI WINERY	Sonoma Valley Monte Rosso	1,150	$22.00	$22.00	1992-2000
80	TREFETHEN VINEYARDS	Napa Valley Yountville	9,501	NR		1992-1997
79	DE MOOR WINERY	Napa Valley	1,800	$14.00	$14.00	1991-1996

VINTAGE: 1984

Score	Winery	Appellation/Vineyard	Case Prod.	Release Price	Current Price	Drink
98	CAYMUS VINEYARDS	Napa Valley Rutherford Special Selection	1,000	$35.00	$50.00	1995-2008
97	DUNN VINEYARDS	Napa Valley Howell Mountain	1,800	$25.00	$85.00	1996-2002
97	HEITZ WINE CELLARS	Napa Valley Oakville Martha's Vineyard	4,421	$40.00	$40.00	1997-2007
97	RIDGE VINEYARDS	Santa Cruz Mountains Monte Bello	3,125	$35.00	$60.00	1995-2005
96	DIAMOND CREEK VINEYARD	Napa Valley Diamond Mountain Red Rock Terrace	620	$25.00	$40.00	1994-2006
94	BERINGER VINEYARDS	Napa Valley Private Reserve	8,000	$25.00	$31.00	1993-2001
94	CHATEAU MONTELENA WINERY	Napa Valley Calistoga Estate	11,439	$20.00	$25.00	1998-2006
94	DIAMOND CREEK VINEYARD	Napa Valley Diamond Mountain Gravelly Meadow	470	$25.00	$40.00	1994-2007
94	DIAMOND CREEK VINEYARD	Napa Valley Diamond Mountain Volcanic Hill	1,224	$25.00	$40.00	1997-2007
94	GRGICH HILLS CELLAR	Napa Valley Yountville	10,000	$17.00	$17.00	1993-2005
94	GROTH VINEYARDS & WINERY	Napa Valley Oakville Reserve	500	$25.00	$25.00	1992-2000
94	OPUS ONE	Napa Valley Oakville	9,000	$50.00	$55.00	1995-2005
93	BURGESS CELLARS	Napa Valley Vintage Selection	7,200	$17.00	$19.00	1996-2006
93	B.R. COHN	Sonoma Valley Olive Hill Vineyard	900	$15.00	$22.00	1991-1998
93	DUNN VINEYARDS	Napa Valley	2,100	$18.00	$55.00	1994-2004
93	HESS COLLECTION WINERY	Napa Valley Mount Veeder Reserve	250	$22.00	$30.00	1992-2000
93	KENWOOD VINEYARDS	Sonoma Valley Artist Series	2,700	$30.00	$35.00	1994-2002
93	PINE RIDGE WINERY	Napa Valley Rutherford Andrus Reserve	280	$37.00	$40.00	1993-2010

NA — not available.   NR — not released.   * — Beaulieu production figures are estimates.

Score	Winery	Appellation/Vineyard	Case Prod.	Release Price	Current Price	Drink
93	PINE RIDGE WINERY	Napa Valley Stags Leap District Pine Ridge Stags Leap Vineyard	1,652	$25.00	$35.00	1995-2008
93	STAG'S LEAP WINE CELLARS	Napa Valley Stags Leap District Cask 23	800	$40.00	$40.00	1994-2000
92	ALEXANDER VALLEY VINEYARDS	Alexander Valley	5,600	$10.50	$13.50	1992-2000
92	CARMENET VINEYARD	Sonoma Valley	6,641	$16.00	$30.00	1992-2004
92	CLOS DU VAL WINE CO.	Napa Valley Stags Leap District Estate	20,500	$15.00	$16.50	1992-2004
92	DIAMOND CREEK VINEYARD	Napa Valley Diamond Mountain Lake	130	$50.00	$120.00	1995-2004
92	DUCKHORN VINEYARDS	Napa Valley	2,000	$17.00	$30.00	1994-2004
92	FAR NIENTE WINERY	Napa Valley Oakville	8,500	$25.00	$30.00	1994-2002
92	FORMAN VINEYARD	Napa Valley	1,000	$18.00	$35.00	1992-2000
92	FROG'S LEAP WINERY	Napa Valley Rutherford	1,900	$10.00	$25.00	1991-1997
92	GIRARD WINERY	Napa Valley Oakville Reserve	684	$25.00	$25.00	1994-2004
92	GRACE FAMILY VINEYARD	Napa Valley St. Helena Estate	150	$38.00	$125.00	1994-2004
92	GROTH VINEYARDS & WINERY	Napa Valley Oakville Estate	6,500	$14.00	$18.00	1993-2000
92	INGLENOOK-NAPA VALLEY	Napa Valley Rutherford Reserve Cask	5,237	NR		1992-2002
92	INGLENOOK-NAPA VALLEY	Napa Valley Rutherford Reunion	2,932	$35.00	$35.00	1993-2000
92	ROBERT KEENAN WINERY	Napa Valley Spring Mountain	3,500	$13.50	$30.00	1994-2002
92	LAKESPRING WINERY	Napa Valley Yountville Reserve Selection	1,450	$15.00	$20.00	1992-1999
92	ROBERT MONDAVI WINERY	Napa Valley Oakville Reserve	9,000	$37.00	$37.00	1992-2000
92	SHAFER VINEYARDS	Napa Valley Stags Leap District Hillside Select	1,800	$24.50	$24.50	1992-2000
92	SIMI WINERY	Alexander Valley Reserve	800	$22.50	$22.50	1993-2000
92	STAG'S LEAP WINE CELLARS	Napa Valley Stags Leap District SLV	6,000	$21.00	$30.00	1994-2000
92	STERLING VINEYARDS	Napa Valley Reserve	2,268	$25.00	$38.00	1994-2002
91	BEAULIEU VINEYARD	Napa Valley Rutherford Georges de Latour Private Reserve	15,000	$25.00	$28.00	1994-2002
91	CAYMUS VINEYARDS	Napa Valley Rutherford Estate	3,200	$16.00	$30.00	1993-2002
91	WILLIAM HILL WINERY	Napa Valley Reserve	7,752	$18.25	$26.00	1994-2002
91	MARKHAM VINEYARDS	Napa Valley Yountville Markham Vineyard	3,855	$12.00	$18.00	1993-2002
91	MONTICELLO CELLARS	Napa Valley Oakville Corley Reserve	4,000	$18.50	$20.00	1995-2004
91	SHAFER VINEYARDS	Napa Valley Stags Leap District	4,000	$14.00	$16.00	1990-1998
91	SILVERADO VINEYARDS	Napa Valley Stags Leap District	7,800	$11.50	$20.00	1996-2002
91	SMITH-MADRONE VINEYARD	Napa Valley Spring Mountain	1,100	$14.00	$14.00	1994-2004
91	STELTZNER VINEYARDS	Napa Valley Stags Leap District	3,000	$15.00	$19.00	1992-2000
91	TUDAL WINERY	Napa Valley St. Helena	1,000	$12.50	$15.00	1993-2001
90	BUENA VISTA WINERY	Sonoma Valley Carneros Private Reserve	2,700	$18.00	$18.00	1990-1996
90	DOMINUS ESTATE	Napa Valley Yountville Napanook	4,200	$40.00	$45.00	1994-2002
90	JOHNSON TURNBULL VINEYARDS	Napa Valley Oakville	1,825	$14.50	$18.00	1993-1999
90	LYETH WINERY	Alexander Valley	10,500	$18.00	$25.00	1992-1998
90	MAYACAMAS VINEYARDS	Napa Valley Mount Veeder	1,220	$20.00	$20.00	1994-2000
90	PINE RIDGE WINERY	Napa Valley Rutherford Rutherford Cuveé	7,128	$14.00	$16.00	1992-2000
90	ROMBAUER VINEYARDS	Napa Valley Le Meilleur Du Chai	450	$32.50	$35.00	1992-2000
90	SPOTTSWOODE WINERY	Napa Valley St. Helena	1,450	$25.00	$45.00	1992-1998
89	CAKEBREAD CELLARS	Napa Valley	5,000	$16.00	$25.00	1992-2000
89	CLOS DU BOIS WINERY	Alexander Valley Marlstone Vineyard	3,957	$19.50	$24.00	1992-1997
89	CUVAISON WINERY	Napa Valley	3,000	$14.00	$14.00	1991-1996
89	DIAMOND CREEK VINEYARD	Napa Valley Diamond Mountain Three Vineyard Blend	50	$50.00	$50.00	1995-2000
89	FISHER VINEYARDS	Sonoma County Coach Insignia	1,200	$18.00	$25.00	1992-1999
89	LAUREL GLEN VINEYARD	Sonoma Mountain	4,000	$15.00	$20.00	1992-2000
89	LOUIS M. MARTINI WINERY	Sonoma Valley Monte Rosso	700	$22.00	$22.00	1990-1999
89	JOSEPH PHELPS VINEYARDS	Napa Valley Insignia	3,860	$30.00	$35.00	1995-2004
89	RAYMOND VINEYARD AND CELLAR	Napa Valley Rutherford Private Reserve	2,800	$20.00	$20.00	1992-1999
89	SILVER OAK CELLARS	Alexander Valley	14,000	$22.00	$28.00	1992-1999
89	SPRING MOUNTAIN VINEYARDS	Napa Valley Spring Mountain	2,363	$15.00	$22.00	1994-2000
89	ST. CLEMENT VINEYARDS	Napa Valley	2,300	$15.00	$15.00	1992-1998
88	CONN CREEK WINERY	Napa Valley St. Helena Collins Vineyard Private Reserve	1,100	$23.00	$23.00	1994-2002
88	DE MOOR WINERY	Napa Valley	2,400	$14.00	$16.00	1992-2002
88	FREEMARK ABBEY WINERY	Napa Valley Rutherford Bosche	3,076	$20.00	$20.00	1995-2003

NA — not available.   NR — not released.   * — Beaulieu production figures are estimates.

Score	Winery	Appellation/Vineyard	Case Prod.	Release Price	Current Price	Drink
88	HAYWOOD WINERY	Sonoma Valley	856	$12.50	$20.00	1995-2002
88	LA JOTA VINEYARD CO.	Napa Valley Howell Mountain	1,206	$15.00	$20.00	1993-1999
88	LONG VINEYARDS	Napa Valley Oakville	200	$32.00	$35.00	1992-2000
88	MOUNT VEEDER WINERY	Napa Valley Mount Veeder Mt. Veeder Vineyards	2,500	$14.00	$14.00	1995-2003
88	RIDGE VINEYARDS	Napa County Spring Mountain York Creek	6,900	$14.00	$16.00	1990-1998
88	RUTHERFORD HILL WINERY	Napa Valley	14,834	$12.50	$15.00	1994-2000
88	STONEGATE WINERY	Napa Valley Calistoga Estate	4,580	$14.00	$14.00	1993-1998
88	VICHON WINERY	Napa Valley	600	$11.25	$13.00	1992-1997
87	BERINGER VINEYARDS	Napa Valley St. Helena Chabot Vineyard	750	NR		1991-1997
87	BUEHLER VINEYARDS	Napa Valley	2,639	$13.00	$16.00	1995-2003
87	CLOS DU BOIS WINERY	Alexander Valley Briarcrest Vineyard	1,711	$16.00	$24.00	1993-2000
87	CHAPPELLET VINEYARD	Napa Valley Reserve	8,000	$18.00	$23.00	1992-1996
87	FRANCISCAN VINEYARDS	Napa Valley Oakville Private Reserve	5,400	$9.00	$12.00	1990-1996
87	CHARLES KRUG WINERY	Napa Valley Vintage Select	3,653	NR		1993-2002
87	LIVINGSTON VINEYARDS	Napa Valley Rutherford Moffett Vineyard	936	$18.00	$25.00	1991-1996
87	NEWTON VINEYARD	Napa Valley Estate	3,192	$13.50	$19.00	1991-1996
87	ROBERT PEPI WINERY	Napa Valley Yountville Vine Hill Ranch	2,550	$16.00	$16.00	1994-2002
87	JOSEPH PHELPS VINEYARDS	Napa Valley Calistoga Eisele Vineyard	1,300	$35.00	$39.00	1995-2000
87	PRESTON VINEYARDS	Dry Creek Valley	2,850	$11.00	$14.00	1991-1996
87	SANTA CRUZ MOUNTAIN VYD	Santa Cruz Mountains Bates Ranch	1,100	NR		1992-1998
87	STAGS' LEAP WINERY	Napa Valley Stags Leap District	5,187	$13.50	$18.00	1992-1997
86	CONN CREEK WINERY	Napa Valley Barrel Select Lot 79	4,450	$13.00	$13.00	1991-1996
86	EBERLE WINERY	Paso Robles	3,013	$12.00	$17.00	1992-1996
86	HEITZ WINE CELLARS	Napa Valley Rutherford Bella Oaks Vineyard	2,944	$25.00	$25.00	1994-2002
86	IRON HORSE VINEYARDS	Alexander Valley	1,900	$14.00	$16.00	1992-1998
86	JORDAN VINEYARD AND WINERY	Alexander Valley Estate	50,500	$19.00	$25.00	1990-1993
86	MERRYVALE VINEYARDS	Napa Valley Red Table Wine	1,026	$24.00	$28.00	1993-1998
86	JOSEPH PHELPS VINEYARDS	Napa Valley Oakville Backus Vineyard	1,585	$20.00	$29.00	1992-1997
86	V. SATTUI WINERY	Napa Valley Rutherford Preston Vineyard	2,850	$13.75	$19.75	1990-1996
86	SILVER OAK CELLARS	Napa Valley Calistoga	2,500	$22.00	$28.00	1996-2004
86	PHILIP TOGNI VINEYARD	Napa Valley Spring Mountain	180	$18.00	$35.00	1994-2003
85	FLORA SPRINGS WINE CO.	Napa Valley	3,000	$13.00	$18.00	1990-1996
85	GUNDLACH BUNDSCHU WINERY	Sonoma Valley Rhinefarm	5,000	$9.00	$12.00	1992-1997
85	LOUIS M. MARTINI WINERY	North Coast Special Selection	2,735	NR		1991-1997
85	NIEBAUM-COPPOLA ESTATE	Napa Valley Rutherford Rubicon	3,653	NR		1994-1998
85	ROBERT PECOTA WINERY	Napa Valley Calistoga Kara's Vineyard	540	$14.00	$20.00	1990-1996
85	SEQUOIA GROVE VINEYARDS	Napa Valley	4,502	$12.00	$18.00	1992-2002
85	STERLING VINEYARDS	Napa Valley Diamond Mountain Diamond Mountain Ranch	5,500	$15.00	$18.00	1993-1997
85	VICHON WINERY	Napa Valley Stags Leap District Fay Vineyard	1,935	$14.00	$18.00	1990-1994
84	FLORA SPRINGS WINE CO.	Napa Valley Rutherford Trilogy	700	$30.00	$35.00	1992-1998
84	MOUNT EDEN VINEYARDS	Santa Cruz Mountains	645	$22.00	$26.00	1993-1998
84	ROMBAUER VINEYARDS	Napa Valley	1,500	$13.50	$21.00	1991-1995
84	SILVER OAK CELLARS	Napa Valley Oakville Bonny's Vineyard	950	$45.00	$45.00	1994-2000
84	TREFETHEN VINEYARDS	Napa Valley Yountville	9,500	$14.00	$16.00	1991-1995
82	CHIMNEY ROCK WINE CELLARS	Napa Valley Stags Leap District	2,800	$15.00	$15.00	1990-1996
80	VILLA MT. EDEN WINERY	Napa Valley Oakville Estate	1,004	NR		1990-1994
80	RAVENSWOOD	Sonoma County	1,400	$12.00	$14.00	1992-1997
79	GUNDLACH BUNDSCHU WINERY	Sonoma Valley Batto Ranch	800	$14.00	$16.00	1990-1991

VINTAGE: 1983

Score	Winery	Appellation/Vineyard	Case Prod.	Release Price	Current Price	Drink
95	DUNN VINEYARDS	Napa Valley	1,500	$15.00	$60.00	1994-2004
93	INGLENOOK-NAPA VALLEY	Napa Valley Rutherford Reunion	1,991	$33.00	$40.00	1993-2001
92	CHATEAU MONTELENA WINERY	Napa Valley Calistoga Estate	8,517	$18.00	$26.00	1994-2002
92	DUNN VINEYARDS	Napa Valley Howell Mountain	1,600	$18.00	$90.00	1995-2005
92	GROTH VINEYARDS & WINERY	Napa Valley Oakville Reserve	200	$25.00	$30.00	1996-2004
92	NEWTON VINEYARD	Napa Valley Estate	1,824	$12.50	$21.00	1992-1998
91	CAYMUS VINEYARDS	Napa Valley Rutherford Special Selection	1,100	$35.00	$50.00	1993-2006
91	BUEHLER VINEYARDS	Napa Valley	2,292	$12.00	$20.00	1993-2001

NA — not available.   NR — not released.   * — Beaulieu production figures are estimates.

Score	Winery	Appellation/Vineyard	Case Prod.	Release Price	Current Price	Drink
91	GRACE FAMILY VINEYARD	Napa Valley St. Helena Estate	175	$38.00	$130.00	1994-2002
91	ST. CLEMENT VINEYARDS	Napa Valley	2,256	$14.50	$18.00	1995-2005
90	ALEXANDER VALLEY VINEYARDS	Alexander Valley	3,792	$10.50	$14.50	1992-1998
90	FORMAN VINEYARD	Napa Valley	600	$15.50	$45.00	1994-2001
90	MAYACAMAS VINEYARDS	Napa Valley Mount Veeder	2,280	$20.00	$25.00	1997-2005
90	ROMBAUER VINEYARDS	Napa Valley Le Meilleur Du Chai	415	$30.00	$40.00	1993-2001
90	STELTZNER VINEYARDS	Napa Valley Stags Leap District	3,000	$14.00	$18.00	1991-1996
89	BERINGER VINEYARDS	Napa Valley Private Reserve	8,000	$19.00	$30.00	1994-2000
89	DIAMOND CREEK VINEYARD	Napa Valley Diamond Mountain Gravelly Meadow	520	$20.00	$25.00	1994-2004
89	DIAMOND CREEK VINEYARD	Napa Valley Diamond Mountain Volcanic Hill	1,442	$20.00	$25.00	1996-2007
89	HEITZ WINE CELLARS	Napa Valley Oakville Martha's Vineyard	4,356	$32.50	$42.00	1997-2005
89	INGLENOOK-NAPA VALLEY	Napa Valley Rutherford Reserve Cask	11,188	$15.50	$19.00	1994-2000
89	OPUS ONE	Napa Valley Oakville	8,000	$50.00	$55.00	1992-1997
89	MARKHAM VINEYARDS	Napa Valley Yountville Markham Vineyard	4,015	$13.00	$15.00	1995-2000
89	JOSEPH PHELPS VINEYARDS	Napa Valley Insignia	3,480	$25.00	$35.00	1994-2000
89	SHAFER VINEYARDS	Napa Valley Stags Leap District Hillside Select	900	$22.00	$22.00	1992-1999
89	SPOTTSWOODE WINERY	Napa Valley St. Helena	1,400	$25.00	$45.00	1995-2005
88	CAKEBREAD CELLARS	Napa Valley Rutherford Rutherford Reserve	300	$35.00	$35.00	1993-2000
88	DIAMOND CREEK VINEYARD	Napa Valley Diamond Mountain Red Rock Terrace	651	$20.00	$25.00	1996-2005
88	DUCKHORN VINEYARDS	Napa Valley	3,000	$16.00	$30.00	1994-2000
88	GRGICH HILLS CELLAR	Napa Valley Yountville	10,000	$17.00	$23.00	1994-2003
88	GROTH VINEYARDS & WINERY	Napa Valley Oakville Estate	10,000	$13.00	$21.00	1994-2000
88	HESS COLLECTION WINERY	Napa Valley Mount Veeder Reserve	250	$22.00	$30.00	1990-1997
88	JOHNSON TURNBULL VINEYARDS	Napa Valley Oakville	1,300	$12.50	$18.00	1993-1998
88	MERRYVALE VINEYARDS	Napa Valley Red Table Wine	694	$18.00	$30.00	1993-1999
88	MONTICELLO CELLARS	Napa Valley Oakville Corley Reserve	350	$24.00	$24.00	1995-2003
88	PINE RIDGE WINERY	Napa Valley Rutherford Andrus Reserve	169	$35.00	$45.00	1993-2000
88	SILVERADO VINEYARDS	Napa Valley Stags Leap District	8,000	$11.00	$20.00	1995-2000
88	STAG'S LEAP WINE CELLARS	Napa Valley Stags Leap District Cask 23	1,077	$35.00	$55.00	1993-1999
87	BUENA VISTA WINERY	Sonoma Valley Carneros Private Reserve	3,500	$18.00	$18.00	1990-1999
87	BURGESS CELLARS	Napa Valley Vintage Selection	6,500	$17.00	$21.00	1994-2002
87	CAYMUS VINEYARDS	Napa Valley Rutherford Estate	3,000	$15.00	$30.00	1994-2002
87	CONN CREEK WINERY	Napa Valley St. Helena Collins Vineyard Proprietor's Special Selection	40		$70.00	1991-1997
87	DOMINUS ESTATE	Napa Valley Yountville Napanook	2,100	$43.00	$43.00	1994-2002
87	FAR NIENTE WINERY	Napa Valley Oakville	5,500	$25.00	$32.00	1993-2000
87	GIRARD WINERY	Napa Valley Oakville Reserve	548	$18.00	$20.00	1994-2000
87	ROBERT KEENAN WINERY	Napa Valley Spring Mountain	3,400	$11.00	$18.00	1995-2000
87	KENWOOD VINEYARDS	Sonoma Valley Artist Series	2,500	$30.00	$35.00	1993-1998
87	SHAFER VINEYARDS	Napa Valley Stags Leap District	3,700	$13.00	$13.00	1992-1997
87	STERLING VINEYARDS	Napa Valley Diamond Mountain Diamond Mountain Ranch	4,100	$15.00	$18.00	1994-2002
87	PHILIP TOGNI VINEYARD	Napa Valley Spring Mountain	90	$18.00	$50.00	1995-2005
86	CLOS DU VAL WINE CO.	Napa Valley Stags Leap District Estate	23,500	$15.00	$17.50	1994-2002
86	DE MOOR WINERY	Napa Valley	2,400	$12.00	$16.00	1995-2003
86	FREEMARK ABBEY WINERY	Napa Valley Rutherford Bosche	2,860	$18.00	$18.00	1995-2003
86	HEITZ WINE CELLARS	Napa Valley Rutherford Bella Oaks Vineyard	2,944	$15.00	$25.00	1994-2001
86	LOUIS M. MARTINI WINERY	Sonoma Valley Monte Rosso	1,150	$22.00	$22.00	1993-1999
86	JOSEPH PHELPS VINEYARDS	Napa Valley Calistoga Eisele Vineyard	1,250	$25.00	$35.00	1997-2002
86	PRESTON VINEYARDS	Dry Creek Valley	2,500	$11.00	$15.00	1993-1998
86	SILVER OAK CELLARS	Alexander Valley	14,000	$20.00	$30.00	1995-2002
86	TUDAL WINERY	Napa Valley St. Helena	1,500	$12.50	$19.00	1992-1998
85	BERINGER VINEYARDS	Napa Valley St. Helena Chabot Vineyard	1,000	$27.00	$27.00	1992-1998
85	CARMENET VINEYARD	Sonoma Valley	6,175	$17.50	$25.00	1994-2004
85	FRANCISCAN VINEYARDS	Napa Valley Oakville Private Reserve	3,000	$8.50	$14.00	1993-1998

NA — not available.   NR — not released.   * — Beaulieu production figures are estimates.

Score	Winery	Appellation/Vineyard	Case Prod.	Release Price	Current Price	Drink
85	WILLIAM HILL WINERY	Napa Valley Mount Veeder Gold Label	8,405	$18.25	$25.00	1994-1999
85	LAKESPRING WINERY	Napa Valley Yountville	3,000	$11.00	$13.00	1993-1998
85	JOSEPH PHELPS VINEYARDS	Napa Valley Oakville Backus Vineyard	800	$16.50	$28.00	1994-1998
85	PINE RIDGE WINERY	Napa Valley Stags Leap District Pine Ridge Stags Leap Vineyard	1,452	$20.00	$26.00	1994-2000
84	EBERLE WINERY	Paso Robles	2,800	$10.00	$18.00	1991-1994
84	HESS COLLECTION WINERY	Napa Valley Mount Veeder	900	$13.00	$18.00	1990-1995
84	LA JOTA VINEYARD CO.	Napa Valley Howell Mountain	870	$15.00	$20.00	1994-2000
84	MOUNT VEEDER WINERY	Napa Valley Mount Veeder Mt. Veeder Vineyards	3,000	$14.00	$15.00	1995-2002
84	PINE RIDGE WINERY	Napa Valley Rutherford Rutherford Cuveé	4,890	$14.00	$22.00	1993-1998
84	RAYMOND VINEYARD AND CELLAR	Napa Valley Rutherford Private Reserve	2,200	$18.00	$25.00	1993-2000
84	RIDGE VINEYARDS	Santa Cruz Mountains (Monte Bello)	2,677	$12.00	$15.00	1994-2000
84	SANTA CRUZ MOUNTAIN VYD	Santa Cruz Mountains Bates Ranch	1,800	$12.00	$12.00	1996-2004
84	SMITH-MADRONE VINEYARD	Napa Valley Spring Mountain	700	$12.50	$15.00	1995-2005
84	TREFETHEN VINEYARDS	Napa Valley Yountville	9,653	$11.75	$22.00	1994-2000
83	LOUIS M. MARTINI WINERY	Sonoma Valley Monte Rosso Los Ninos	545	$25.00	$25.00	1990-1997
83	ROBERT MONDAVI WINERY	Napa Valley Oakville Reserve	15,000	$30.00	$35.00	1991-1999
83	RUTHERFORD HILL WINERY	Napa Valley	16,439	$12.50	$16.00	1990-1995
82	BEAULIEU VINEYARD	Napa Valley Rutherford Georges de Latour Private Reserve	15,000	$24.00	$28.00	1992-1997
82	CONN CREEK WINERY	Napa Valley Barrel Select	5,000	$13.00	$15.00	1992-1996
82	IRON HORSE VINEYARDS	Alexander Valley	2,000	$12.00	$15.50	1992-1997
82	CHARLES KRUG WINERY	Napa Valley Vintage Select	3,653	NR		1994-2001
82	SILVER OAK CELLARS	Napa Valley Oakville Bonny's Vineyard	1,250	$40.00	$40.00	1990-1993
82	STERLING VINEYARDS	Napa Valley Reserve	3,360	$22.50	$30.00	1995-2000
81	V. SATTUI WINERY	Napa Valley Rutherford Preston Vineyard	1,613	$13.75	$19.75	1990-1995
80	FROG'S LEAP WINERY	Napa Valley	1,100	$10.00	$20.00	1990-1994
80	ROBERT PEPI WINERY	Napa Valley Yountville Vine Hill Ranch	2,700	$16.00	$16.00	1993-1998
80	STAGS' LEAP WINERY	Napa Valley Stags Leap District	3,425	$12.75	$20.00	1993-1997
80	VICHON WINERY	Napa Valley	10,000	$10.00	$14.00	1990-1995
79	MOUNT EDEN VINEYARDS	Santa Cruz Mountains	458	$20.00	$20.00	1993-1997
79	SPRING MOUNTAIN VINEYARDS	Napa Valley Spring Mountain	4,221	$15.00	$18.00	1993-1998
78	JORDAN VINEYARD AND WINERY	Alexander Valley Estate	51,400	$18.00	$30.00	1990-1992
78	KISTLER VINEYARDS	Napa Valley Mount Veeder Veeder Hills Vineyard	1,010	$13.50	$20.00	1992-1998
78	LONG VINEYARDS	Napa Valley Oakville	200	$32.00	$40.00	1991-1995
78	LYETH WINERY	Alexander Valley	8,000	$17.00	$25.00	1992-1995
77	CAKEBREAD CELLARS	Napa Valley	4,000	$16.00	$25.00	1992-1995
77	CHAPPELLET VINEYARD	Napa Valley	8,700	$12.00	$15.00	1990-1995
77	GUNDLACH BUNDSCHU WINERY	Sonoma Valley Batto Ranch	1,000	$10.00	$15.00	1990-1993
77	HAYWOOD WINERY	Sonoma Valley	711	$12.50	$20.00	1995-2003
77	SEQUOIA GROVE VINEYARDS	Napa-Alexander Valleys	2,144	$12.50	$18.00	1991-1994
76	RAVENSWOOD	Sonoma County	1,350	$9.50	$14.00	1991-1995
75	CUVAISON WINERY	Napa Valley	2,000	$12.00	$15.00	1990-1992
74	CLOS DU BOIS WINERY	Alexander Valley Briarcrest Vineyard	1,122	$12.00	$20.00	1990-1994
74	SILVER OAK CELLARS	Napa Valley Calistoga	3,000	$20.00	$30.00	1993-1996
73	GUNDLACH BUNDSCHU WINERY	Sonoma Valley Rhinefarm	4,500	$9.00	$14.00	1991-1994
73	RIDGE VINEYARDS	Napa County Spring Mountain York Creek	6,390	$12.00	$15.00	1992-1996
73	ROMBAUER VINEYARDS	Napa Valley	1,500	$13.50	$19.00	1990-1994
73	STAG'S LEAP WINE CELLARS	Napa Valley Stags Leap District Stag's Leap Vineyards	6,668	$18.00	$25.00	1990-1995
72	VILLA MT. EDEN WINERY	Napa Valley Oakville Estate	7,588	$10.00	$10.00	1990-1993
70	CLOS DU BOIS WINERY	Alexander Valley Marlstone Vineyard	1,600	$19.50	$20.00	1990-1993
59	LAUREL GLEN VINEYARD	Sonoma Mountain	4,000	$11.00	$11.00	Avoid

VINTAGE: 1982

95	DUNN VINEYARDS	Napa Valley Howell Mountain	1,800	$15.00	$130.00	1992-2000
94	DUNN VINEYARDS	Napa Valley	1,250	$13.00	$85.00	1992-2000
92	BERINGER VINEYARDS	Napa Valley Private Reserve	4,000	$19.00	$35.00	1992-1999

NA — not available.   NR — not released.   * — Beaulieu production figures are estimates.

Score	Winery	Appellation/Vineyard	Case Prod.	Release Price	Current Price	Drink
92	CAYMUS VINEYARDS	Napa Valley Rutherford Special Selection	750	$35.00	$65.00	1995-2006
92	CHATEAU MONTELENA WINERY	Napa Valley Calistoga Estate	11,425	$16.00	$33.00	1992-2002
91	INGLENOOK-NAPA VALLEY	Napa Valley Rutherford Reserve Cask	4,631	$22.00	$28.00	1994-2001
91	ST. CLEMENT VINEYARDS	Napa Valley	3,024	$13.50	$20.00	1992-2000
90	ALEXANDER VALLEY VINEYARDS	Alexander Valley	3,987	$10.00	$16.00	1990-1996
90	CAYMUS VINEYARDS	Napa Valley Rutherford Estate	4,200	$14.00	$33.00	1993-2000
90	CLOS DU VAL WINE CO.	Napa Valley Stags Leap District Reserve	2,600	$28.00	$37.00	1997-2005
90	DUCKHORN VINEYARDS	Napa Valley	3,800	$15.00	$38.00	1992-1998
90	WILLIAM HILL WINERY	Napa Valley Mount Veeder Gold Label	11,907	$18.00	$32.00	1994-2002
90	MARKHAM VINEYARDS	Napa Valley Yountville Markham Vineyard	6,361	$13.00	$18.00	1994-2002
90	MONTICELLO CELLARS	Napa Valley Corley Reserve	1,200	$15.00	$30.00	1993-1999
90	OPUS ONE	Napa Valley Oakville	6,000	$50.00	$80.00	1993-2000
90	PINE RIDGE WINERY	Napa Valley Rutherford Rutherford Cuveé	3,558	$13.00	$24.00	1995-2005
90	PINE RIDGE WINERY	Napa Valley Stags Leap District Pine Ridge Stags Leap Vineyard	1,116	$20.00	$34.00	1996-2004
90	SILVER OAK CELLARS	Alexander Valley	12,500	$19.00	$40.00	1994-2002
90	SPOTTSWOODE WINERY	Napa Valley St. Helena	1,200	$18.00	$60.00	1995-2003
90	STELTZNER VINEYARDS	Napa Valley Stags Leap District	3,000	$14.00	$28.00	1990-1996
89	BERINGER VINEYARDS	Napa Valley St. Helena Chabot Vineyard	1,200	$25.00	$38.00	1993-2000
89	DIAMOND CREEK VINEYARD	Napa Valley Diamond Mountain Gravelly Meadow	404	$20.00	$35.00	1995-2005
89	DIAMOND CREEK VINEYARD	Napa Valley Diamond Mountain Volcanic Hill	1,420	$20.00	$35.00	1997-2007
89	GRACE FAMILY VINEYARD	Napa Valley St. Helena Estate	225	$31.00	$155.00	1993-1999
89	NIEBAUM-COPPOLA ESTATE	Napa Valley Rutherford Rubicon	6,002	$40.00	$40.00	1992-2000
89	SHAFER VINEYARDS	Napa Valley Stags Leap District Reserve	1,200	$18.00	$25.00	1992-1998
88	BEAULIEU VINEYARD	Napa Valley Rutherford Georges de Latour Private Reserve	15,000	$24.00	$32.00	1995-2005
88	BUEHLER VINEYARDS	Napa Valley	2,953	$12.00	$30.00	1994-2004
88	BURGESS CELLARS	Napa Valley Vintage Selection	8,300	$16.00	$23.00	1994-2002
88	CLOS DU VAL WINE CO.	Napa Valley Stags Leap District Estate	21,000	$13.25	$24.00	1992-2000
88	DE MOOR WINERY	Napa Valley Owners' Selection	2,000	$12.00	$19.00	1995-2003
88	FREEMARK ABBEY WINERY	Napa Valley Rutherford Bosche	3,592	$15.00	$26.00	1996-2002
88	GROTH VINEYARDS & WINERY	Napa Valley Oakville Estate	7,000	$13.00	$24.00	1992-1998
88	HEITZ WINE CELLARS	Napa Valley Oakville Martha's Vineyard	5,100	$30.00	$45.00	1996-2003
88	LAKESPRING WINERY	Napa Valley Yountville Vintage Selection	3,600	$14.00	$20.00	1992-1998
88	ROBERT KEENAN WINERY	Napa Valley Spring Mountain	2,900	$10.00	$20.00	1993-2000
88	ROBERT PEPI WINERY	Napa Valley Yountville Vine Hill Ranch	2,175	$14.00	$17.00	1994-2002
88	SHAFER VINEYARDS	Napa Valley Stags Leap District	3,500	$13.00	$18.00	1992-2000
88	SILVER OAK CELLARS	Napa Valley Calistoga	3,500	$19.00	$32.00	1995-2005
88	SILVERADO VINEYARDS	Napa Valley Stags Leap District	8,000	$11.00	$22.00	1993-2000
88	SIMI WINERY	Sonoma-Napa Counties Reserve	3,400	$20.00	$20.00	1996-2004
88	STERLING VINEYARDS	Napa Valley Diamond Mountain Diamond Mountain Ranch	3,100	$15.00	$20.00	1995-2003
87	CARMENET VINEYARD	Sonoma Valley	5,348	$16.00	$30.00	1993-2003
87	DIAMOND CREEK VINEYARD	Napa Valley Diamond Mountain Red Rock Terrace	753	$20.00	$35.00	1995-2004
87	FROG'S LEAP WINERY	Napa Valley	900	$9.00	$25.00	1990-1996
87	GIRARD WINERY	Napa Valley Oakville	2,107	$12.50	$30.00	1994-2004
87	GRGICH HILLS CELLAR	Napa Valley Yountville	3,000	$17.00	$28.00	1992-1998
87	PRESTON VINEYARDS	Dry Creek Valley	1,700	$11.00	$18.00	1990-1996
87	KENWOOD VINEYARDS	Sonoma Valley Artist Series	2,200	$25.00	$40.00	1993-1999
86	CAKEBREAD CELLARS	Napa Valley	5,000	$16.00	$35.00	1994-2000
86	DE MOOR WINERY	Napa Valley	1,000	$12.00	$18.00	1994-2001
86	KISTLER VINEYARDS	Napa Valley Mount Veeder Veeder Hills Vineyard	1,010	$12.00	$26.00	1992-1999
85	BUENA VISTA WINERY	Sonoma Valley Carneros Private Reserve	3,700	$18.00	$30.00	1991-1996
85	CONN CREEK WINERY	Napa Valley Barrel Select	7,100	$12.00	$16.00	1992-1997
85	CONN CREEK WINERY	Napa Valley St. Helena Collins Vineyard Proprietor's Special Selection	40		$70.00	1995-2004

NA — not available.   NR — not released.   * — Beaulieu production figures are estimates.

Score	Winery	Appellation/Vineyard	Case Prod.	Release Price	Current Price	Drink
85	HEITZ WINE CELLARS	Napa Valley Rutherford Bella Oaks Vineyard	2,944	$16.00	$30.00	1993-2000
85	LAUREL GLEN VINEYARD	Sonoma Mountain	2,800	$12.50	$20.00	1992-1997
85	LYETH WINERY	Alexander Valley	5,000	$16.00	$30.00	1990-1995
85	LOUIS M. MARTINI WINERY	Sonoma Valley Monte Rosso	2,060	$22.00	$22.00	1993-1999
85	ROBERT PECOTA WINERY	Napa Valley	900	$12.00	$20.00	1990-1995
85	JOSEPH PHELPS VINEYARDS	Napa Valley Calistoga Eisele Vineyard	1,775	$30.00	$33.00	1994-2000
85	JOSEPH PHELPS VINEYARDS	Napa Valley Insignia	2,950	$25.00	$32.00	1992-1998
85	RAYMOND VINEYARD AND CELLAR	Napa Valley Rutherford Private Reserve	1,800	$16.00	$27.00	1990-1996
84	DIAMOND CREEK VINEYARD	Napa Valley Diamond Mountain Gravelly Meadow, Special Selection	140	$20.00	$35.00	1994-2000
84	LA JOTA VINEYARD CO.	Napa Valley	704	$13.50	$25.00	1994-2000
84	RAVENSWOOD	Sonoma County	1,500	$11.00	$18.00	1990-1995
84	VILLA MT. EDEN WINERY	Napa Valley Oakville Reserve	1,254	$16.70	$16.70	1992-1997
83	IRON HORSE VINEYARDS	Alexander Valley	2,500	$12.00	$18.00	1994-1999
83	ROMBAUER VINEYARDS	Napa Valley	1,000	$12.00	$23.00	1990-1994
83	RUTHERFORD HILL WINERY	Napa Valley	17,878	$12.50	$17.00	1990-1994
82	CUVAISON WINERY	Napa Valley	2,000	$11.00	$15.00	1994-2000
82	FAR NIENTE WINERY	Napa Valley Oakville	3,000	$25.00	$35.00	1993-1999
82	JOHNSON TURNBULL VINEYARDS	Napa Valley Oakville	2,275	$12.50	$18.00	1994-1998
82	LOUIS M. MARTINI WINERY	Sonoma Valley Monte Rosso Los Ninos	550	$25.00	$25.00	1990-1995
82	ROBERT MONDAVI WINERY	Napa Valley Oakville Reserve	14,000	$30.00	$38.00	1992-1998
82	SEQUOIA GROVE VINEYARDS	Napa Valley Rutherford Estate	406	$14.00	$22.00	1995-2003
80	CHAPPELLET VINEYARD	Napa Valley	11,800	$9.25	$14.00	1990-1993
80	DIAMOND CREEK VINEYARD	Napa Valley Diamond Mountain Red Rock Terrace, Special Selection	192	$20.00	$35.00	1993-1999
80	STONEGATE WINERY	Napa Valley	5,497	$12.00	$18.00	1991-1996
79	CLOS DU BOIS WINERY	Alexander Valley Marlstone Vineyard	2,496	$16.00	$16.00	1990-1994
79	DIAMOND CREEK VINEYARD	Napa Valley Diamond Mountain Volcanic Hill, Special Selection	258	$20.00	$35.00	1993-1999
79	HAYWOOD WINERY	Sonoma Valley	608	$11.00	$20.00	1994-2000
79	SMITH-MADRONE VINEYARD	Napa Valley Spring Mountain	800	$12.50	$15.00	1990-1993
79	VICHON WINERY	Napa Valley Stags Leap District Fay Vineyard	2,500	$14.00	$23.00	1990-1995
78	V. SATTUI WINERY	Napa Valley Rutherford Preston Vineyard Reserve	385	$22.50	$30.00	1990-1994
78	SEQUOIA GROVE VINEYARDS	Napa-Alexander Valleys	2,068	$12.00	$20.00	1990-1998
78	SILVER OAK CELLARS	Napa Valley Oakville Bonny's Vineyard	900	$35.00	$42.00	1994-2002
78	VICHON WINERY	Napa Valley Volker Eisele	2,000	$16.00	$19.00	1990-1994
77	MAYACAMAS VINEYARDS	Napa Valley Mount Veeder	2,700	$20.00	$25.00	1993-1998
76	VICHON WINERY	Napa Valley	5,400	$13.00	$15.00	1990-1993
75	RIDGE VINEYARDS	Santa Cruz Mountains Monte Bello	4,350	$18.00	$25.00	1992-1998
75	STAG'S LEAP WINE CELLARS	Napa Valley Stags Leap District Stag's Leap Vineyards	9,865	$16.50	$25.00	1990-1993
75	STERLING VINEYARDS	Napa Valley Reserve	4,807	$22.50	$25.00	1992-1996
73	JORDAN VINEYARD AND WINERY	Alexander Valley Estate	50,800	$18.00	$36.00	1990-1991
73	RIDGE VINEYARDS	Napa County Spring Mountain York Creek	6,909	$12.00	$15.00	1994-2000
72	EBERLE WINERY	Paso Robles	2,500	$10.00	$24.00	1990-1994
72	SANTA CRUZ MOUNTAIN VYD	Santa Cruz Mountains Bates Ranch	1,800	$12.00	$14.00	1994-1998
72	TUDAL WINERY	Napa Valley St. Helena	2,100	$12.00	$25.00	1990-1993
71	EBERLE WINERY	Paso Robles Reserve	76	$25.00	$30.00	1991-1996
71	STAGS' LEAP WINERY	Napa Valley Stags Leap District	3,034	$12.00	$20.00	1992-1996
70	GUNDLACH BUNDSCHU WINERY	Sonoma Valley Batto Ranch	1,000	$10.00	$18.00	1990-1992
70	MOUNT EDEN VINEYARDS	Santa Cruz Mountains	1,249	$18.00	$20.00	1990-1994
70	VILLA MT. EDEN WINERY	Napa Valley Oakville Estate	8,143	$9.00	$9.00	1990-1993
68	MOUNT VEEDER WINERY	Napa Valley Mount Veeder Mt. Veeder Vineyards	4,600	$12.50	$13.00	Avoid
66	CLOS DU BOIS WINERY	Alexander Valley Briarcrest Vineyard	2,075	$12.00	$25.00	Avoid
66	NEWTON VINEYARD	Napa Valley	3,096	$12.50	$21.00	Avoid
66	SPRING MOUNTAIN VINEYARDS	Napa Valley	5,739	$15.00	$15.00	Avoid
65	GUNDLACH BUNDSCHU WINERY	Sonoma Valley Rhinefarm	4,500	$9.00	$13.00	Avoid

NA — not available.   NR — not released.   * — Beaulieu production figures are estimates.

Score	Winery	Appellation/Vineyard	Case Prod.	Release Price	Current Price	Drink
58	TREFETHEN VINEYARDS	Napa Valley Yountville	NA	$11.00	NA	Avoid

VINTAGE: 1981

Score	Winery	Appellation/Vineyard	Case Prod.	Release Price	Current Price	Drink
93	CAYMUS VINEYARDS	Napa Valley Rutherford Special Selection	1,250	$35.00	$60.00	1995-2006
93	INGLENOOK-NAPA VALLEY	Napa Valley Rutherford Reserve Cask	12,115	$15.50	$20.00	1992-2000
92	DIAMOND CREEK VINEYARD	Napa Valley Diamond Mountain Volcanic Hill	1,026	$20.00	$35.00	1996-2006
92	LAUREL GLEN VINEYARD	Sonoma Mountain	1,500	$12.50	$40.00	1990-1996
92	JOSEPH PHELPS VINEYARDS	Napa Valley Insignia	1,480	$25.00	$39.00	1993-2000
92	PINE RIDGE WINERY	Napa Valley Stags Leap District Pine Ridge Stags Leap Vineyard	1,553	$20.00	$50.00	1995-2005
92	RIDGE VINEYARDS	Santa Cruz Mountains Monte Bello	2,648	$25.00	$45.00	1996-2004
91	BERINGER VINEYARDS	Napa Valley Private Reserve	3,000	$18.00	$40.00	1990-1997
91	DIAMOND CREEK VINEYARD	Napa Valley Diamond Mountain Red Rock Terrace	497	$20.00	$35.00	1993-2002
91	MAYACAMAS VINEYARDS	Napa Valley Mount Veeder	1,830	$18.00	$25.00	1993-1999
91	JOSEPH PHELPS VINEYARDS	Napa Valley Oakville Backus Vineyard	775	$15.00	$44.00	1992-2000
91	STAG'S LEAP WINE CELLARS	Napa Valley Stags Leap District Stag's Leap Vineyards	7,534	$15.00	$32.00	1992-1998
90	DIAMOND CREEK VINEYARD	Napa Valley Diamond Mountain Three Vineyard Blend	15	$20.00	$50.00	1995-2005
90	DUNN VINEYARDS	Napa Valley Howell Mountain	940	$14.00	$150.00	1991-1996
90	GUNDLACH BUNDSCHU WINERY	Sonoma Valley Rhinefarm Vineyards Vintage Reserve	800	$20.00	$26.00	1994-2002
90	HEITZ WINE CELLARS	Napa Valley Rutherford Bella Oaks Vineyard	3,225	$16.00	$38.00	1992-1999
90	SILVERADO VINEYARDS	Napa Valley Stags Leap District	3,500	$11.00	$25.00	1992-2000
89	DIAMOND CREEK VINEYARD	Napa Valley Diamond Mountain Gravelly Meadow	656	$20.00	$35.00	1995-2004
89	HEITZ WINE CELLARS	Napa Valley Oakville Martha's Vineyard	3,113	$30.00	$50.00	1997-2004
89	KENWOOD VINEYARDS	Sonoma Valley Artist Series	1,900	$25.00	$55.00	1991-1996
89	JOSEPH PHELPS VINEYARDS	Napa Valley Calistoga Eisele Vineyard	1,050	$30.00	$39.00	1994-2000
89	STELTZNER VINEYARDS	Napa Valley Stags Leap District	1,500	$14.00	$38.00	1990-1996
88	BURGESS CELLARS	Napa Valley Vintage Selection	6,900	$16.00	$25.00	1993-2002
88	CAKEBREAD CELLARS	Napa Valley	4,000	$16.00	$50.00	1990-1995
88	CAYMUS VINEYARDS	Napa Valley Rutherford Estate	3,200	$14.00	$35.00	1990-1998
88	CLOS DU BOIS WINERY	Alexander Valley Briarcrest Vineyard	2,095	$12.00	$32.00	1991-1998
88	GRACE FAMILY VINEYARD	Napa Valley St. Helena Estate	185	$28.00	$150.00	1992-1998
88	GUNDLACH BUNDSCHU WINERY	Sonoma Valley Batto Ranch	950	$10.00	$18.00	1990-1993
88	OPUS ONE	Napa Valley Oakville	6,000	$50.00	$90.00	1994-2003
88	PINE RIDGE WINERY	Napa Valley Rutherford Rutherford Cuveé	4,081	$13.00	$28.00	1994-2002
88	TUDAL WINERY	Napa Valley St. Helena	1,000	$12.00	$25.00	1991-1997
87	ALEXANDER VALLEY VINEYARDS	Alexander Valley	3,625	$9.00	$16.00	1990-1994
87	BEAULIEU VINEYARD	Napa Valley Rutherford Georges de Latour Private Reserve	15,000	$24.00	$30.00	1993-2000
87	BERINGER VINEYARDS	Napa Valley St. Helena Chabot Vineyard	1,000	$23.00	$42.00	1990-1996
87	DUCKHORN VINEYARDS	Napa Valley	950	$15.00	$45.00	1993-2000
87	JOHNSON TURNBULL VINEYARDS	Napa Valley Oakville	1,250	$12.00	$20.00	1995-2000
87	KISTLER VINEYARDS	Napa Valley Mount Veeder Veeder Hills-Veeder Peak	1,010	$12.00	$32.00	1991-1999
87	NIEBAUM-COPPOLA ESTATE	Napa Valley Rutherford Rubicon	3,661	$35.00	$35.00	1993-2000
87	RAYMOND VINEYARD AND CELLAR	Napa Valley Rutherford Private Reserve	1,200	$16.00	$35.00	1990-1995
87	TREFETHEN VINEYARDS	Napa Valley Yountville	8,842	$11.00	$28.00	1990-1995
86	BUENA VISTA WINERY	Sonoma Valley Carneros Private Reserve (Special Selection)	2,730	$18.00	$32.00	1990
86	CONN CREEK WINERY	Napa Valley St. Helena Collins Vineyard Proprietor's Special Selection	40		$70.00	1994-2002
86	DE MOOR WINERY	Napa Valley (Napa Cellars)	1,800	$12.00	$25.00	1990-1997
86	FREEMARK ABBEY WINERY	Napa Valley Rutherford Bosche	2,704	$14.00	$24.00	1994-2000
86	GIRARD WINERY	Napa Valley Oakville	1,595	$12.50	$20.00	1993-2000
86	GRGICH HILLS CELLAR	Napa Valley Yountville	2,000	$17.00	$28.00	1991-1997

NA — not available.   NR — not released.   * — Beaulieu production figures are estimates.

Score	Winery	Appellation/Vineyard	Case Prod.	Release Price	Current Price	Drink
86	LAKESPRING WINERY	Napa Valley Yountville	3,000	$11.00	$18.00	1992-1998
86	MARKHAM VINEYARDS	Napa Valley Yountville Markham Vineyard	3,717	$13.00	$20.00	1992-1998
86	MOUNT EDEN VINEYARDS	Santa Cruz Mountains	652	$18.00	$25.00	1993-1999
86	ROBERT PEPI WINERY	Napa Valley Yountville Vine Hill Ranch	2,000	$14.00	$18.00	1992-2000
86	SILVER OAK CELLARS	Alexander Valley	11,200	$19.00	$35.00	1994-2000
85	BUEHLER VINEYARDS	Napa Valley	2,214	$11.00	$20.00	1994-2000
85	CLOS DU BOIS WINERY	Alexander Valley Marlstone Vineyard	1,005	$15.00	$32.00	1990-1995
85	CONN CREEK WINERY	Napa Valley	5,700	$14.00	$18.00	1990-1995
85	EBERLE WINERY	Paso Robles	2,500	$10.00	$24.00	1990-1994
85	HAYWOOD WINERY	Sonoma Valley	1,081	$11.00	$20.00	1994-2001
85	WILLIAM HILL WINERY	Napa Valley Mount Veeder Gold Label	5,772	$16.25	$34.00	1990-1995
85	LOUIS M. MARTINI WINERY	Sonoma Valley Monte Rosso Los Ninos	535	$25.00	$25.00	1990-1998
85	RAYMOND VINEYARD AND CELLAR	Napa Valley Rutherford	10,000	$11.00	$16.50	1990-1993
85	RUTHERFORD HILL WINERY	Napa Valley	9,851	$11.50	$18.00	1990-1995
85	STAGS' LEAP WINERY	Napa Valley Stags Leap District	2,712	$11.00	$25.00	1991-1997
85	ST. CLEMENT VINEYARDS	Napa Valley	2,565	$12.50	$24.00	1994-1999
85	STERLING VINEYARDS	Napa Valley Reserve	6,237	$22.50	$28.00	1994-1998
85	VILLA MT. EDEN WINERY	Napa Valley Oakville Reserve	1,144	$16.70	$20.00	1990-1996
84	GUNDLACH BUNDSCHU WINERY	Sonoma Valley	4,000	$7.00	$20.00	1994-1999
84	JORDAN VINEYARD AND WINERY	Alexander Valley Estate	47,000	$17.00	$40.00	1990-1994
84	ROBERT KEENAN WINERY	Napa Valley	3,298	$13.50	$22.00	1993-1999
84	SEQUOIA GROVE VINEYARDS	Alexander Valley	854	$12.00	$35.00	1993-1999
83	ROBERT MONDAVI WINERY	Napa Valley Oakville Reserve	12,000	$30.00	$30.00	1990-1995
83	NEWTON VINEYARD	Napa Valley	2,820	$12.50	$21.00	1992-1997
82	CLOS DU VAL WINE CO.	Napa Valley Stags Leap District Estate	21,500	$12.50	$25.00	1990-1996
82	CHARLES KRUG WINERY	Napa Valley Vintage Select	4,423	NR		1992-1998
82	ROMBAUER VINEYARDS	Napa Valley	1,000	$12.00	$24.00	1993-1998
80	CHATEAU MONTELENA WINERY	Napa Valley Calistoga Estate	7,144	$16.00	$25.00	1990-1994
80	EBERLE WINERY	Paso Robles Reserve	191	$25.00	$35.00	1991-1995
80	SEQUOIA GROVE VINEYARDS	Napa Valley	1,169	$12.00	$25.00	1994-1999
80	VICHON WINERY	Napa Valley	4,600	$13.00	$20.00	1990-1994
79	CHAPPELLET VINEYARD	Napa Valley	8,000	$11.00	$18.00	1990-1995
79	IRON HORSE VINEYARDS	Alexander Valley	1,700	$12.00	$15.50	1992-1998
79	SANTA CRUZ MOUNTAIN VYD	Santa Cruz Mountains Bates Ranch	1,600	$12.00	$20.00	1994-1999
79	SILVER OAK CELLARS	Napa Valley Calistoga	4,100	$19.00	$40.00	1994-2000
79	STONEGATE WINERY	Napa Valley	4,005	$12.00	$17.00	1992-1996
78	SMITH-MADRONE VINEYARD	Napa Valley Spring Mountain	600	$12.50	$15.00	1990-1993
78	SPRING MOUNTAIN VINEYARDS	Napa Valley Rutherford	11,390	$14.00	$16.00	1992-1996
77	LYETH WINERY	Alexander Valley	1,200	$15.00	$35.00	1990-1993
77	MOUNT VEEDER WINERY	Napa Valley Mount Veeder Mt. Veeder Vineyards	2,700	$12.50	$20.00	1992-1997
77	SILVER OAK CELLARS	Napa Valley Oakville Bonny's Vineyard	970	$35.00	$50.00	1994-2000
76	RIDGE VINEYARDS	Napa County Spring Mountain York Creek	4,925	$12.00	$20.00	1994-2000
74	CUVAISON WINERY	Napa Valley	6,000	$11.00	$15.00	1993-1999

VINTAGE: 1980

Score	Winery	Appellation/Vineyard	Case Prod.	Release Price	Current Price	Drink
96	PINE RIDGE WINERY	Napa Valley Rutherford Andrus Reserve	140	$30.00	$60.00	1996-2010
93	BEAULIEU VINEYARD	Napa Valley Rutherford Georges de Latour Private Reserve	15,000	$24.00	$35.00	1995-2005
93	CONN CREEK WINERY	Napa Valley St. Helena Collins Vineyard Proprietor's Special Selection	40		$70.00	1995-2004
93	HEITZ WINE CELLARS	Napa Valley Rutherford Bella Oaks Vineyard	2,280	$20.00	$45.00	1994-2004
93	OPUS ONE	Napa Valley Oakville	4,000	$50.00	$130.00	1992-2002
92	DIAMOND CREEK VINEYARD	Napa Valley Diamond Mountain Gravelly Meadow	460	$20.00	$40.00	1996-2006
92	CAYMUS VINEYARDS	Napa Valley Rutherford Special Selection	750	$30.00	$80.00	1993-2000
92	DUNN VINEYARDS	Napa Valley Howell Mountain	825	$13.00	$170.00	1993-2000
92	GIRARD WINERY	Napa Valley Oakville	1,480	$11.00	$25.00	1991-2000
92	GRACE FAMILY VINEYARD	Napa Valley St. Helena Estate	183	$25.00	$275.00	1993-2002

NA — not available.   NR — not released.   * — Beaulieu production figures are estimates.

Score	Winery	Appellation/Vineyard	Case Prod.	Release Price	Current Price	Drink
92	MAYACAMAS VINEYARDS	Napa Valley Mount Veeder	1,870	$18.00	$30.00	1994-2002
91	CHAPPELLET VINEYARD	Napa Valley	7,000	$18.00	$28.00	1993-1998
91	DUCKHORN VINEYARDS	Napa Valley	1,600	$14.00	$50.00	1992-2002
91	LONG VINEYARDS	Napa Valley Oakville	200	$32.00	$50.00	1994-2002
91	PINE RIDGE WINERY	Napa Valley Rutherford Rutherford District	2,938	$12.00	$37.00	1993-2000
91	STERLING VINEYARDS	Napa Valley Reserve	4,848	$27.50	$37.00	1992-1998
90	CAYMUS VINEYARDS	Napa Valley Rutherford Estate	4,300	$12.50	$35.00	1993-2000
90	DIAMOND CREEK VINEYARD	Napa Valley Diamond Mountain Volcanic Hill	883	$20.00	$40.00	1998-2008
90	GRGICH HILLS CELLAR	Napa County-Sonoma County	2,000	$16.00	$32.00	1991-2000
90	JOSEPH PHELPS VINEYARDS	Napa Valley Insignia	2,585	$25.00	$50.00	1993-1998
89	BERINGER VINEYARDS	Napa Valley St. Helena Private Reserve Lemmon-Chabot Vineyard	2,000	$20.00	$42.00	1990-1997
89	HEITZ WINE CELLARS	Napa Valley Oakville Martha's Vineyard	2,966	$30.00	$55.00	1996-2006
89	MARKHAM VINEYARDS	Napa Valley Yountville Markham Vineyard	3,920	$13.00	$25.00	1992-1998
88	BURGESS CELLARS	Napa Valley Vintage Selection	5,800	$16.00	$28.00	1994-2002
88	CLOS DU VAL WINE CO.	Napa Valley Stags Leap District Estate	17,400	$12.50	$28.00	1990-1995
88	CONN CREEK WINERY	Napa Valley	5,700	$13.00	$28.00	1993-2000
88	FREEMARK ABBEY WINERY	Napa Valley Rutherford Bosche	2,740	$14.50	$36.00	1990-1996
88	INGLENOOK-NAPA VALLEY	Napa Valley Rutherford Cask	9,305	$15.50	$22.00	1991-1996
88	LAKESPRING WINERY	Napa Valley	2,000	$10.00	$21.00	1991-1997
88	RIDGE VINEYARDS	Napa County Spring Mountain York Creek	3,516	$12.00	$22.00	1992-1999
88	RUTHERFORD HILL WINERY	Napa Valley Cask Lot 2 Limited Edition	2,000	$15.00	$20.00	1990-1996
88	SILVER OAK CELLARS	Alexander Valley	12,000	$18.00	$45.00	1990-2000
88	STELTZNER VINEYARDS	Napa Valley Stags Leap District	200	$14.00	$38.00	1991-1997
87	WILLIAM HILL WINERY	Napa Valley Mount Veeder Gold Label	4,961	$18.25	$36.00	1990-1996
87	JOHNSON TURNBULL VINEYARDS	Napa Valley Oakville	1,100	$12.00	$26.00	1994-2000
87	MOUNT VEEDER WINERY	Napa Valley Mount Veeder Bernstein Vineyards	2,600	$13.50	$30.00	1992-2000
87	NIEBAUM-COPPOLA ESTATE	Napa Valley Rutherford Rubicon	3,850	$30.00	$35.00	1992-2002
87	SEQUOIA GROVE VINEYARDS	Napa Valley Cask Two	440	$12.00	$45.00	1992-1999
86	CHATEAU MONTELENA WINERY	Napa Valley Calistoga Estate	10,000	$16.00	$40.00	1991-1997
86	DIAMOND CREEK VINEYARD	Napa Valley Diamond Mountain Red Rock Terrace	591	$20.00	$40.00	1994-2004
86	HAYWOOD WINERY	Sonoma Valley	570	$9.75	$12.00	1992-1999
86	IRON HORSE VINEYARDS	Alexander Valley	1,000	$12.00	$20.00	1992-1998
86	ROMBAUER VINEYARDS	Napa Valley	500	$10.00	$25.00	1993-2000
86	SANTA CRUZ MOUNTAIN VYD	Santa Cruz Mountains Bates Ranch	840	$12.00	$18.00	1990-1997
86	SPRING MOUNTAIN VINEYARDS	Napa Valley Rutherford	11,162	$13.00	$24.00	1990-1994
86	STONEGATE WINERY	Napa Valley	2,258	$12.00	$22.00	1991-1997
85	BERINGER VINEYARDS	Napa Valley Yountville Private Reserve State Lane Vineyard	2,000	$15.00	$40.00	1991-1997
85	FLORA SPRINGS WINE CO.	Napa Valley	1,200	$12.00	$20.00	1990-1996
85	KISTLER VINEYARDS	Napa Valley Mount Veeder Veeder Hills-Veeder Peak	369	$16.00	$35.00	1992-1999
85	MOUNT EDEN VINEYARDS	Santa Cruz Mountains	453	$30.00	$35.00	1992-1997
85	RAYMOND VINEYARD AND CELLAR	Napa Valley Rutherford Private Reserve	1,200		$34.00	1990-1996
85	V. SATTUI WINERY	Napa Valley Rutherford Preston Vineyard Reserve	372	$30.00	$45.00	1990-1995
85	SEQUOIA GROVE VINEYARDS	Napa Valley Cask One	444	$12.00	$30.00	1992-2000
85	TUDAL WINERY	Napa Valley St. Helena	1,250	$11.50	$25.00	1992-1996
85	VICHON WINERY	Napa Valley Stags Leap District Fay Vineyard	1,400	$16.00	$25.00	1990-1995
84	BUENA VISTA WINERY	Sonoma Valley Carneros Special Selection	2,141	$18.00	$35.00	1990
84	CAKEBREAD CELLARS	Napa Valley	4,000	$14.00	$45.00	1993-2000
84	KISTLER VINEYARDS	Sonoma Valley Glen Ellen Vineyard	320	$18.00	$35.00	1992-1998
84	LOUIS M. MARTINI WINERY	North Coast Special Selection	9,350	$12.00	$12.00	1990-1997
84	SIMI WINERY	Alexander Valley Reserve	2,400	$20.00	$30.00	1994-2000
83	ALEXANDER VALLEY VINEYARDS	Alexander Valley	2,552	$9.00	$16.00	1990-1994

NA — not available.   NR — not released.   ∗ — Beaulieu production figures are estimates.

Score	Winery	Appellation/Vineyard	Case Prod.	Release Price	Current Price	Drink
83	VICHON WINERY	Napa Valley Volker Eisele Vineyard	800	$16.00	$25.00	1990-1995
82	BUEHLER VINEYARDS	Napa Valley	794	$10.00	$25.00	1994-2002
82	RAYMOND VINEYARD AND CELLAR	Napa Valley Rutherford	10,000	$12.00	$17.00	1990-1993
82	RUTHERFORD HILL WINERY	Napa Valley	9,574	$11.50	$19.00	1990-1994
82	ST. CLEMENT VINEYARDS	Napa Valley	650	$12.50	$24.00	1990-1994
80	CLOS DU BOIS WINERY	Alexander Valley Briarcrest Vineyard	1,227	$12.00	$32.00	1990-1995
80	DE MOOR WINERY	Napa Valley (Napa Cellars)	1,600	$12.00	$20.00	1990-1996
80	GUNDLACH BUNDSCHU WINERY	Sonoma Valley Batto Ranch	950	$8.00	$20.00	1990-1993
80	JORDAN VINEYARD AND WINERY	Alexander Valley Estate	56,400	$17.00	$45.00	1990-1992
80	ROBERT KEENAN WINERY	Napa Valley	3,272	$13.50	$23.00	1993-2000
80	KENWOOD VINEYARDS	Sonoma Valley Artist Series	1,600	$20.00	$55.00	1990-1994
80	RIDGE VINEYARDS	Santa Cruz Mountains Monte Bello	4,125	$30.00	$36.00	1995-2005
79	CHARLES KRUG WINERY	Napa Valley Vintage Select	8,858	$15.00	$15.00	1992-1997
79	ROBERT MONDAVI WINERY	Napa Valley Oakville Reserve	13,000	$30.00	$35.00	1992-1998
79	RAVENSWOOD	Sonoma County	640	$10.50	$16.00	1990-1997
79	SMITH-MADRONE VINEYARD	Napa Valley Spring Mountain	600	$12.50	$18.00	1990
78	EBERLE WINERY	Paso Robles	2,000	$10.00	$24.00	1990-1994
77	CLOS DU BOIS WINERY	Alexander Valley Marlstone Vineyard	3,833	$15.00	$32.00	1991-1998
77	CUVAISON WINERY	Napa Valley	5,000	$11.00	$18.00	1994-2001
77	SHAFER VINEYARDS	Napa Valley Stags Leap District	2,000	$12.00	$25.00	1990-1992
73	SILVER OAK CELLARS	Napa Valley Calistoga	4,000	$18.00	$45.00	1992-1997
70	SILVER OAK CELLARS	Napa Valley Oakville Bonny's Vineyard	1,000	$30.00	$50.00	1993-1998
70	VILLA MT. EDEN WINERY	Napa Valley Oakville Reserve	1,143	$20.00	$20.00	1992-1996
68	TREFETHEN VINEYARDS	Napa Valley Yountville	6,980	$11.00	$20.00	Avoid
62	VILLA MT. EDEN WINERY	Napa Valley Oakville Estate	3,922	$11.70	$14.00	Avoid
55	NEWTON VINEYARD	Napa Valley	NA	$12.00	NA	Avoid

VINTAGE: 1979

Score	Winery	Appellation/Vineyard	Case Prod.	Release Price	Current Price	Drink
97	CAYMUS VINEYARDS	Napa Valley Rutherford Special Selection	600	$30.00	$85.00	1994-2006
95	DIAMOND CREEK VINEYARD	Napa Valley Diamond Mountain Volcanic Hill, First Pick	50	$15.00	$60.00	1994-2006
95	MAYACAMAS VINEYARDS	Napa Valley Mount Veeder	1,905	$18.00	$35.00	1995-2005
93	FREEMARK ABBEY WINERY	Napa Valley Rutherford Bosche	2,982	$12.00	$30.00	1990-1997
93	HEITZ WINE CELLARS	Napa Valley Oakville Martha's Vineyard	5,469	$25.00	$60.00	1994-2004
93	WILLIAM HILL WINERY	Napa Valley Mount Veeder Gold Label	4,412	$18.00	$45.00	1990-2000
92	BUENA VISTA WINERY	Sonoma Valley Carneros Special Selection	2,595	$18.00	$50.00	1991
92	CAYMUS VINEYARDS	Napa Valley Rutherford Estate	2,700	$12.00	$35.00	1992-1998
92	CLOS DU VAL WINE CO.	Napa Valley Stags Leap District Reserve	1,200	$25.00	$55.00	1996-2008
92	DIAMOND CREEK VINEYARD	Napa Valley Diamond Mountain Red Rock Terrace	263	$15.00	$60.00	1993-2000
92	GRACE FAMILY VINEYARD	Napa Valley St. Helena Estate	56	$20.00	$150.00	1991-2000
92	ROBERT MONDAVI WINERY	Napa Valley Oakville Reserve	11,500	$25.00	$45.00	1991-2000
92	MOUNT VEEDER WINERY	Napa Valley Mount Veeder Bernstein Vineyards	2,800	$13.50	$35.00	1990-1997
92	JOSEPH PHELPS VINEYARDS	Napa Valley Calistoga Eisele Vineyard	1,000	$30.00	$50.00	1993-2000
91	DIAMOND CREEK VINEYARD	Napa Valley Diamond Mountain Gravelly Meadow	194	$15.00	$60.00	1995-2005
91	DUNN VINEYARDS	Napa Valley Howell Mountain	660	$12.50	$160.00	1990-1997
91	IRON HORSE VINEYARDS	Alexander Valley	1,000	$12.00	$25.00	1992-1998
91	KENWOOD VINEYARDS	Sonoma Valley Artist Series	1,300	$20.00	$70.00	1990-1998
90	BEAULIEU VINEYARD	Napa Valley Rutherford Georges de Latour Private Reserve	15,000	$21.00	$43.00	1993-2000
90	CLOS DU VAL WINE CO.	Napa Valley Stags Leap District Estate	15,400	$12.50	$45.00	1990-2002
90	LONG VINEYARDS	Napa Valley Oakville	200	$32.00	$50.00	1992-1999
90	OPUS ONE	Napa Valley Oakville	2,000	$50.00	$190.00	1992-1998
90	JOSEPH PHELPS VINEYARDS	Napa Valley Insignia	960	$25.00	$55.00	1990-1997
90	ST. CLEMENT VINEYARDS	Napa Valley	1,500	$11.00	$35.00	1992-2001
90	TUDAL WINERY	Napa Valley St. Helena	630	$10.75	$25.00	1992-2000
89	BERINGER VINEYARDS	Napa Valley Yountville Private Reserve State Lane Vineyard	2,000	$15.00	$42.00	1990-1996

NA — not available.   NR — not released.   * — Beaulieu production figures are estimates.

Score	Winery	Appellation/Vineyard	Case Prod.	Release Price	Current Price	Drink
89	SHAFER VINEYARDS	Napa Valley Stags Leap District	1,000	$12.00	$35.00	1992-2000
89	STELTZNER VINEYARDS	Napa Valley Stags Leap District	1,000	$14.00	$42.00	1990-1995
88	CHATEAU MONTELENA WINERY	Alexander Valley Sonoma	1,164	$14.00	$45.00	1991-1998
88	MARKHAM VINEYARDS	Napa Valley Yountville Markham Vineyard	2,752	$13.00	$28.00	1993-2000
88	RIDGE VINEYARDS	Napa County Spring Mountain York Creek	3,100	$12.00	$30.00	1990-1998
88	STAG'S LEAP WINE CELLARS	Napa Valley Stags Leap District Cask 23	1,204	$35.00	$55.00	1990-1992
87	BURGESS CELLARS	Napa Valley Vintage Selection	2,800	$16.00	$30.00	1993-1999
87	CHATEAU MONTELENA WINERY	Napa Valley Calistoga Estate	5,776	$16.00	$45.00	1992-1998
87	RUTHERFORD HILL WINERY	Napa Valley	9,971	$11.50	$22.00	1990-1995
87	SIMI WINERY	Alexander Valley Reserve	1,700	$20.00	$36.00	1992-1999
87	SPRING MOUNTAIN VINEYARDS	Napa Valley Rutherford	9,987	$13.00	$32.00	1992-1998
86	ALEXANDER VALLEY VINEYARDS	Alexander Valley	2,819	$7.00	$18.00	1990-1996
86	SMITH-MADRONE VINEYARD	Napa Valley Spring Mountain	350	$14.00	$25.00	1993-2000
86	TREFETHEN VINEYARDS	Napa Valley Yountville	6,192	$11.00	$35.00	1990-1996
85	DE MOOR WINERY	Napa Valley (Napa Cellars)	1,600	$10.00	$25.00	1990-1998
85	JOHNSON TURNBULL VINEYARDS	Napa Valley Oakville	450	$10.50	$26.00	1993-1998
85	NEWTON VINEYARD	Napa Valley	742	$12.00	$30.00	1990-1995
85	PINE RIDGE WINERY	Napa Valley Rutherford Rutherford District	3,211	$9.00	$45.00	1990-1995
85	RAYMOND VINEYARD AND CELLAR	Napa Valley Rutherford	9,300	$12.00	$20.00	1990-1992
85	SILVER OAK CELLARS	Alexander Valley	12,500	$16.00	$65.00	1992-1999
85	STERLING VINEYARDS	Napa Valley Reserve	6,538	$27.50	$32.00	1990-1995
84	LOUIS M. MARTINI WINERY	Sonoma Valley Monte Rosso Lot 2	2,490	$10.00	$19.00	1991-1996
84	STONEGATE WINERY	Napa Valley	2,757	$12.00	$24.00	1993-1997
82	CAKEBREAD CELLARS	Napa Valley	3,300	$13.00	$45.00	1990-1995
82	DIAMOND CREEK VINEYARD	Napa Valley Diamond Mountain Volcanic Hill, Second Pick	415	$15.00	$40.00	1993-1999
82	EBERLE WINERY	San Luis Obispo	1,000	$10.00	$25.00	1990-1995
82	CHARLES KRUG WINERY	Napa Valley Vintage Select	2,177	$12.50	$20.00	1990-1995
82	SILVER OAK CELLARS	Napa Valley Calistoga	4,400	$18.00	$55.00	1995-2005
80	GUNDLACH BUNDSCHU WINERY	Sonoma Valley Batto Ranch	900	$8.00	$22.00	1990-1993
79	CHAPPELLET VINEYARD	Napa Valley	6,400	$13.00	$26.00	1990-1995
79	FRANCISCAN VINEYARDS	Napa Valley Oakville	9,000	$8.50	$18.00	1990
79	JORDAN VINEYARD AND WINERY	Alexander Valley Estate	47,000	$16.00	$50.00	1990-1992
79	SANTA CRUZ MOUNTAIN VYD	Santa Cruz Mountains Bates Ranch	1,225	$12.00	$35.00	1993-2000
78	VILLA MT. EDEN WINERY	Napa Valley Oakville Estate	2,773	$12.00	$21.00	1990-1993
77	CONN CREEK WINERY	Napa Valley	6,270	$13.00	$25.00	1993-1998
77	INGLENOOK-NAPA VALLEY	Napa Valley Rutherford Cask	2,672	$10.75	$23.00	1990
75	CLOS DU BOIS WINERY	Alexander Valley Marlstone Vineyard	3,395	$16.00	$30.00	1990-1994
75	CUVAISON WINERY	Napa Valley	5,000	$11.00	$20.00	1993-2000
75	NIEBAUM-COPPOLA ESTATE	Napa Valley Rutherford Rubicon	3,100	$25.00	$40.00	1990-1994
75	VILLA MT. EDEN WINERY	Napa Valley Oakville Reserve	500	$20.00	$30.00	1994-2000
74	ROBERT KEENAN WINERY	Napa Valley	2,460	$12.00	$30.00	1994-2000
72	SILVER OAK CELLARS	Napa Valley Oakville Bonny's Vineyard	1,200	$30.00	$55.00	1992-1998
69	MOUNT EDEN VINEYARDS	Santa Cruz Mountains	641	$25.00	$30.00	Avoid
68	STAG'S LEAP WINE CELLARS	Napa Valley Stags Leap District Stag's Leap Vineyards	6,000	$15.00	$32.00	Avoid
59	RAVENSWOOD	California	875	$8.00	$10.00	Avoid

VINTAGE: 1978

Score	Winery	Appellation/Vineyard	Case Prod.	Release Price	Current Price	Drink
99	DIAMOND CREEK VINEYARD	Napa Valley Diamond Mountain Lake	25	$25.00	$250.00	1994-2002
97	CAYMUS VINEYARDS	Napa Valley Rutherford Special Selection	600	$30.00	$90.00	1994-2005
97	JOSEPH PHELPS VINEYARDS	Napa Valley Calistoga Eisele Vineyard	755	$30.00	$75.00	1995-2010
95	DIAMOND CREEK VINEYARD	Napa Valley Diamond Mountain Volcanic Hill	503	$12.50	$75.00	1993-2006
95	WILLIAM HILL WINERY	Napa Valley Mount Veeder Gold Label	4,451	$16.25	$60.00	1991-1997
94	CLOS DU VAL WINE CO.	Napa Valley Stags Leap District Reserve	2,400	$30.00	$55.00	1993-2010
94	MAYACAMAS VINEYARDS	Napa Valley Mount Veeder	1,820	$18.00	$60.00	1994-2004
93	BURGESS CELLARS	Napa Valley Vintage Selection	2,800	$14.00	$34.00	1992-2000
93	CHATEAU MONTELENA WINERY	Napa Valley Calistoga Estate	7,500	$16.00	$60.00	1993-2005
93	DIAMOND CREEK VINEYARD	Napa Valley Diamond Mountain Gravelly Meadow	315	$12.50	$75.00	1995-2005

NA — not available.   NR — not released.   * — Beaulieu production figures are estimates.

Score	Winery	Appellation/Vineyard	Case Prod.	Release Price	Current Price	Drink
93	FREEMARK ABBEY WINERY	Napa Valley Rutherford Bosche	3,908	$12.50	$35.00	1990-1995
93	SILVER OAK CELLARS	Alexander Valley	8,500	$16.00	$100.00	1992-2002
92	BERINGER VINEYARDS	Napa Valley St. Helena Private Reserve Lemmon Ranch Vineyard	3,000	$15.00	$44.00	1990-1998
92	CLOS DU VAL WINE CO.	Napa Valley Stags Leap District Estate	14,000	$12.00	$40.00	1990-2000
92	CONN CREEK WINERY	Napa Valley Lot 2	2,500	$13.00	$35.00	1990-2000
92	DIAMOND CREEK VINEYARD	Napa Valley Diamond Mountain Red Rock Terrace	468	$12.50	$75.00	1992-2004
92	DUCKHORN VINEYARDS	Napa Valley	800	$10.50	$85.00	1990-1998
92	ROBERT MONDAVI WINERY	Napa Valley Oakville Reserve	11,000	$40.00	$58.00	1990-1998
92	STAG'S LEAP WINE CELLARS	Napa Valley Stags Leap District Cask 23	1,000	$35.00	$90.00	1990-1995
91	BEAULIEU VINEYARD	Napa Valley Rutherford Georges de Latour Private Reserve	15,000	$19.00	$45.00	1990-2000
91	HEITZ WINE CELLARS	Napa Valley Oakville Martha's Vineyard	5,000	$22.00	$75.00	1994-2002
91	RIDGE VINEYARDS	Santa Cruz Mountains Monte Bello	1,820	$30.00	$60.00	1993-2003
91	STONEGATE WINERY	Napa Valley	1,797	$12.00	$30.00	1991-2000
90	BUENA VISTA WINERY	Sonoma Valley Carneros Special Selection	2,020	$18.00	$60.00	1992
90	KENWOOD VINEYARDS	Sonoma Valley Artist Series	1,000	$20.00	$100.00	1990-1995
90	SANTA CRUZ MOUNTAIN VYD	Santa Cruz Mountains Bates Ranch	750	$12.00	$35.00	1990-1998
90	STERLING VINEYARDS	Napa Valley Reserve	5,016	$27.50	$35.00	1992-1998
89	DE MOOR WINERY	Napa Valley (Napa Cellars)	1,700	$10.00	$28.00	1990-2000
89	HEITZ WINE CELLARS	Napa Valley Rutherford Bella Oaks Vineyard	4,837	$15.00	$40.00	1990-1998
89	MOUNT VEEDER WINERY	Napa Valley Mount Veeder Bernstein Vineyards	3,500	$12.75	$40.00	1992-2002
89	PINE RIDGE WINERY	Napa Valley Rutherford Rutherford District	3,950	$7.50	$50.00	1990-1995
89	JOSEPH PHELPS VINEYARDS	Napa Valley Oakville Backus Vineyard	1,100	$16.50	$55.00	1991-1997
89	STAG'S LEAP WINE CELLARS	Napa Valley Stags Leap District Stag's Leap Vineyards	3,000	$13.50	$45.00	1990-1995
88	CHAPPELLET VINEYARD	Napa Valley	7,000	$13.00	$40.00	1992-1998
88	NIEBAUM-COPPOLA ESTATE	Napa Valley Rutherford Rubicon	1,700	$25.00	$45.00	1990-2000
88	MOUNT EDEN VINEYARDS	Santa Cruz Mountains	650	$25.00	$45.00	1995-2003
88	ST. CLEMENT VINEYARDS	Napa Valley	400	$10.00	$40.00	1990-1997
88	VILLA MT. EDEN WINERY	Napa Valley Oakville Reserve	761	$20.00	$42.00	1994-2004
87	BUEHLER VINEYARDS	Napa Valley	224	$10.00	$35.00	1990-1998
87	CAYMUS VINEYARDS	Napa Valley Rutherford Estate	2,600	$12.00	$60.00	1990-1996
87	CHATEAU MONTELENA WINERY	Alexander Valley Sonoma	1,560	$12.00	$50.00	1990-1996
87	JOSEPH PHELPS VINEYARDS	Napa Valley Insignia	1,175	$25.00	$65.00	1990-1997
87	RIDGE VINEYARDS	Napa County Spring Mountain York Creek	5,983	$12.00	$35.00	1990-1998
87	STELTZNER VINEYARDS	Napa Valley Stags Leap District	500	$14.00	$50.00	1990-1996
86	CAKEBREAD CELLARS	Napa Valley Rutherford Lot 2	80	$12.00	$100.00	1991-2000
86	CONN CREEK WINERY	Napa Valley Lot 1	3,000	$12.00	$30.00	1990-2000
86	GRACE FAMILY VINEYARD	Napa Valley St. Helena Estate	48	$20.00	$275.00	1990-1995
86	INGLENOOK-NAPA VALLEY	Napa Valley Rutherford Cask	11,969	$9.25	$26.00	1990-1994
86	LOUIS M. MARTINI WINERY	California Special Selection	21,388	$9.00	$23.00	1990-1996
86	MOUNT VEEDER WINERY	Napa Valley Mount Veeder Sidehill Ranch	375	$13.50	$40.00	1990-2000
85	CAKEBREAD CELLARS	Napa Valley	900	$12.00	$60.00	1992-2000
85	MARKHAM VINEYARDS	Napa Valley Yountville Markham Vineyard	2,560	$13.00	$35.00	1992-2000
85	SHAFER VINEYARDS	Napa Valley Stags Leap District	1,000	$11.00	$50.00	1992-2000
84	SMITH-MADRONE VINEYARD	Napa Valley Spring Mountain	200	$14.00	$25.00	1990-1995
83	RAVENSWOOD	Sonoma Valley (Olive Hill)	530	$11.25	$28.00	1990-1998
83	SPRING MOUNTAIN VINEYARDS	Napa Valley Rutherford	10,236	$12.00	$25.00	1990-1996
82	RAYMOND VINEYARD AND CELLAR	Napa Valley Rutherford	5,300	$10.00	$21.00	1990-1993
82	RUTHERFORD HILL WINERY	Napa Valley	16,471	$12.00	$22.00	1990-1993
81	JORDAN VINEYARD AND WINERY	Alexander Valley Estate	58,000	$16.00	$70.00	1990-1993
81	RAVENSWOOD	California	536	$10.50	$20.00	1991-1998
81	TREFETHEN VINEYARDS	Napa Valley Yountville	3,764	$10.00	$45.00	1991-1995
80	ALEXANDER VALLEY VINEYARDS	Alexander Valley	3,734	$6.50	$20.00	1990-1993
80	IRON HORSE VINEYARDS	Alexander Valley	1,250	$12.00	$25.00	1990-1994
78	FRANCISCAN VINEYARDS	Napa Valley Oakville Reserve	4,000	$15.00	$20.00	1990-1992
78	CHARLES KRUG WINERY	Napa Valley Vintage Select	14,353	$11.00	$22.00	1990-1995

NA — not available.   NR — not released.   * — Beaulieu production figures are estimates.

Score	Winery	Appellation/Vineyard	Case Prod.	Release Price	Current Price	Drink
78	VILLA MT. EDEN WINERY	Napa Valley Oakville Estate	2,421	$8.00	$25.00	1990-1994
74	ROBERT KEENAN WINERY	Napa Valley	2,044	$12.00	$40.00	1994-2000
72	CLOS DU BOIS WINERY	Alexander Valley Marlstone Vineyard	3,129	$16.00	$30.00	1990
72	CUVAISON WINERY	Napa Valley	5,000	$10.00	$20.00	1995-2002
72	SIMI WINERY	Alexander Valley Reserve	2,700	$17.00	$26.00	1990

VINTAGE: 1977

Score	Winery	Appellation/Vineyard	Case Prod.	Release Price	Current Price	Drink
94	CHATEAU MONTELENA WINERY	Napa Valley Calistoga	3,800	$12.00	$65.00	1995-2005
94	RIDGE VINEYARDS	Santa Cruz Mountains Monte Bello	840	$40.00	$80.00	1995-2005
93	STERLING VINEYARDS	Napa Valley Reserve	3,500	$27.50	$32.00	1992-2000
92	BURGESS CELLARS	Napa Valley Vintage Selection	3,000	$12.00	$45.00	1992-2000
92	MAYACAMAS VINEYARDS	Napa Valley Mount Veeder	1,510	$15.00	$60.00	1992-2000
91	CHATEAU MONTELENA WINERY	Alexander Valley Sonoma	3,298	$12.00	$65.00	1992-1999
91	HEITZ WINE CELLARS	Napa Valley Rutherford Bella Oaks Vineyard	4,185	$30.00	$57.00	1991-1997
91	MOUNT EDEN VINEYARDS	Santa Cruz Mountains	200	$20.00	$50.00	1995-2005
91	JOSEPH PHELPS VINEYARDS	Napa Valley Insignia	1,900	$25.00	$75.00	1990-1996
91	STAG'S LEAP WINE CELLARS	Napa Valley Stags Leap District Cask 23	1,000	$30.00	$75.00	1990-1993
90	CONN CREEK WINERY	Napa Valley	2,000	$12.00	$40.00	1991-1998
90	HEITZ WINE CELLARS	Napa Valley Oakville Martha's Vineyard	2,800	$30.00	$75.00	1991-2000
90	STAG'S LEAP WINE CELLARS	Napa Valley Stags Leap District Lot 2	2,000	$10.00	$50.00	1990-1996
90	ST. CLEMENT VINEYARDS	Napa Valley	650	$10.00	$45.00	1990-1999
89	CLOS DU VAL WINE CO.	Napa Valley Stags Leap District Estate	14,700	$10.00	$40.00	1990-2000
89	DIAMOND CREEK VINEYARD	Napa Valley Diamond Mountain Gravelly Meadow	422	$10.00	$55.00	1994-2000
89	GUNDLACH BUNDSCHU WINERY	Sonoma Valley Batto Ranch	900	$8.00	$24.00	1990-1995
88	BERINGER VINEYARDS	Napa Valley St. Helena Private Reserve Lemmon Ranch Vineyard	2,500	$12.00	$50.00	1990-1995
88	DIAMOND CREEK VINEYARD	Napa Valley Diamond Mountain Red Rock Terrace, First Pick	238	$10.00	$50.00	1994-2003
88	FREEMARK ABBEY WINERY	Napa Valley Rutherford Bosche	3,532	$12.50	$25.00	1990-1994
88	MOUNT VEEDER WINERY	Napa Valley Rutherford Niebaum-Coppola	1,225	$9.75	$60.00	1996-2006
88	RIDGE VINEYARDS	Napa County Spring Mountain York Creek	1,780	$12.00	$35.00	1990-1996
88	SILVER OAK CELLARS	Alexander Valley	7,350	$14.00	$85.00	1990-1997
87	CLOS DU VAL WINE CO.	Napa Valley Stags Leap District Reserve	2,900	$20.00	$53.00	1990-2001
86	JOSEPH PHELPS VINEYARDS	Napa Valley Oakville Backus Vineyard	530	$15.00	$60.00	1990-1995
86	TREFETHEN VINEYARDS	Napa Valley Yountville	3,687	$8.50	$45.00	1990-1995
86	VILLA MT. EDEN WINERY	Napa Valley Oakville Estate	2,383	$8.00	$36.00	1991-2002
85	MOUNT VEEDER WINERY	Napa Valley Mount Veeder Bernstein Vineyards	1,350	$11.00	$50.00	1994-2002
85	SPRING MOUNTAIN VINEYARDS	Napa Valley Rutherford	5,986	$9.50	$20.00	1990-1995
85	STAG'S LEAP WINE CELLARS	Napa Valley Stags Leap District Stag's Leap Vineyards	2,000	$9.00	$35.00	1990-1992
85	STELTZNER VINEYARDS	Napa Valley Stags Leap District	500	$14.00	$45.00	1990-1995
84	DIAMOND CREEK VINEYARD	Napa Valley Diamond Mountain Volcanic Hill	591	$10.00	$45.00	1990-1992
84	INGLENOOK-NAPA VALLEY	Napa Valley Rutherford Cask	6,291	$8.75	$23.00	1990-1994
84	ROBERT MONDAVI WINERY	Napa Valley Oakville Reserve	9,500	$35.00	$40.00	1990-1993
84	RAYMOND VINEYARD AND CELLAR	Napa Valley Rutherford	4,300	$8.50	$27.00	1990-1992
82	CHAPPELLET VINEYARD	Napa Valley	4,500	$12.00	$33.00	1990-1994
82	KENWOOD VINEYARDS	Sonoma Valley Artist Series	1,000	$15.00	$120.00	1990-1993
82	JOSEPH PHELPS VINEYARDS	Napa Valley Calistoga Eisele Vineyard	1,160	$25.00	$55.00	1991-1998
82	RAVENSWOOD	El Dorado County (Madrona Vineyards)	800	$8.50	$22.00	1990-1995
81	STONEGATE WINERY	Napa Valley	1,060	$10.00	$25.00	1993-1999
79	BEAULIEU VINEYARD	Napa Valley Rutherford Georges de Latour Private Reserve	15,000	$16.00	$46.00	1990-1991
79	CUVAISON WINERY	Napa Valley	6,000	$10.00	$35.00	1992-1998
77	CAYMUS VINEYARDS	Napa Valley Rutherford Estate	1,700	$10.00	$40.00	1990-1994
77	JORDAN VINEYARD AND WINERY	Alexander Valley	35,000	$14.00	$70.00	1990-1992
75	DIAMOND CREEK VINEYARD	Napa Valley Diamond Mountain Red Rock Terrace, Second Pick	60	$10.00	$40.00	1993-1996

NA — not available.　　NR — not released.　　* — Beaulieu production figures are estimates.

Score	Winery	Appellation/Vineyard	Case Prod.	Release Price	Current Price	Drink
74	CHARLES KRUG WINERY	Napa Valley Vintage Select	4,029	$10.00	$22.00	1990-1994
72	BUENA VISTA WINERY	Sonoma Valley Carneros Cask 34	2,146	$12.00	$40.00	1990
72	RUTHERFORD HILL WINERY	Napa Valley	11,337	$10.00	$18.00	1990
70	LOUIS M. MARTINI WINERY	Napa Valley Special Selection	5,464	$9.00	$20.00	1990
70	SIMI WINERY	Alexander Valley Special Selection	1,700	$20.00	$23.00	1990
69	ROBERT KEENAN WINERY	Napa Valley	843	$12.00	$50.00	Avoid

VINTAGE: 1976

Score	Winery	Appellation/Vineyard	Case Prod.	Release Price	Current Price	Drink
93	JOSEPH PHELPS VINEYARDS	Napa Valley Insignia	785	$20.00	$90.00	1994-2004
90	CAYMUS VINEYARDS	Napa Valley Rutherford Special Selection	270	$35.00	$150.00	1993-1998
90	CHATEAU MONTELENA WINERY	North Coast	5,769	$10.00	$75.00	1990-1995
87	BURGESS CELLARS	Napa Valley Vintage Selection	2,200	$12.00	$41.00	1991-1997
87	DIAMOND CREEK VINEYARD	Napa Valley Diamond Mountain Volcanic Hill	428	$9.00	$90.00	1991-1999
86	BEAULIEU VINEYARD	Napa Valley Rutherford Georges de Latour Private Reserve	15,000	$19.00	$60.00	1990-1996
86	CONN CREEK WINERY	Napa Valley	2,000	$12.00	$45.00	1990-1995
86	LOUIS M. MARTINI WINERY	California Special Selection	2,693	$9.00	$35.00	1990-1997
86	SILVER OAK CELLARS	Alexander Valley	6,600	$12.00	$70.00	1992-2002
85	DIAMOND CREEK VINEYARD	Napa Valley Diamond Mountain Gravelly Meadow	96	$9.00	$90.00	1990-1999
85	DIAMOND CREEK VINEYARD	Napa Valley Diamond Mountain Red Rock Terrace	283	$9.00	$90.00	1990-1999
85	CAYMUS VINEYARDS	Napa Valley Rutherford Estate	1,600	$10.00	$60.00	1990-1995
85	FREEMARK ABBEY WINERY	Napa Valley Rutherford Bosche	3,109	$12.50	$45.00	1990-1994
85	HEITZ WINE CELLARS	Napa Valley Rutherford Bella Oaks Vineyard	895	$30.00	$62.00	1991-1996
85	HEITZ WINE CELLARS	Napa Valley Oakville Martha's Vineyard	1,664	$30.00	$75.00	1995-2004
84	MAYACAMAS VINEYARDS	Napa Valley Mount Veeder	1,380	$15.00	$50.00	1992-1998
84	ROBERT MONDAVI WINERY	Napa Valley Oakville Reserve	8,500	$25.00	$40.00	1990-1994
83	MOUNT EDEN VINEYARDS	Santa Cruz Mountains	175	$20.00	$50.00	1993-2000
83	RIDGE VINEYARDS	Santa Cruz Mountains Monte Bello	1,577	$15.00	$65.00	1990-1998
82	CLOS DU VAL WINE CO.	Napa Valley	6,800	$9.00	$55.00	1990-1995
80	STAG'S LEAP WINE CELLARS	Napa Valley Stags Leap District Lot 2	1,000	$11.00	$60.00	1990-1992
79	CUVAISON WINERY	Napa Valley	6,000	$10.00	$35.00	1992-1996
79	JORDAN VINEYARD AND WINERY	Alexander Valley	35,000	$10.00	$70.00	1990-1992
78	RAYMOND VINEYARD AND CELLAR	Napa Valley Rutherford	3,000	$6.00	$27.00	1990
77	KENWOOD VINEYARDS	Sonoma County Artist Series	1,000	$10.00	$120.00	1990
77	MOUNT VEEDER WINERY	Napa Valley Mount Veeder Bernstein Vineyards	775	$11.00	$45.00	1994-2000
76	CHAPPELLET VINEYARD	Napa Valley	4,500	$12.00	$37.00	1990
76	STERLING VINEYARDS	Napa Valley Reserve	3,690	$25.00	$40.00	1994-1998
76	TREFETHEN VINEYARDS	Napa Valley Yountville	2,098	$7.50	$45.00	1990-1996
73	RUTHERFORD HILL WINERY	Napa Valley	5,505	$9.00	$17.00	1990
73	STAG'S LEAP WINE CELLARS	Napa Valley Stags Leap District Stag's Leap Vineyards	2,000	$10.00	$40.00	1990
72	INGLENOOK-NAPA VALLEY	Napa Valley Rutherford Cask	4,147	$8.75	$19.00	1990
70	VILLA MT. EDEN WINERY	Napa Valley Oakville Estate	860	$7.00	$38.00	1990-1994
68	RIDGE VINEYARDS	Napa County Spring Mountain York Creek	1,150	$10.00	$30.00	Avoid
66	BUENA VISTA WINERY	Sonoma Valley Carneros	994	$12.00	$40.00	Avoid
60	ALEXANDER VALLEY VINEYARDS	Alexander Valley	2,080	$5.50	$18.00	Avoid

VINTAGE: 1975-1976

Score	Winery	Appellation/Vineyard	Case Prod.	Release Price	Current Price	Drink
87	ST. CLEMENT VINEYARDS	Napa Valley	650	$8.00	$50.00	1992-2000

VINTAGE: 1975

Score	Winery	Appellation/Vineyard	Case Prod.	Release Price	Current Price	Drink
97	JOSEPH PHELPS VINEYARDS	Napa Valley Calistoga Eisele Vineyard	720	$15.00	$115.00	1992-2005
93	DIAMOND CREEK VINEYARD	Napa Valley Diamond Mountain Volcanic Hill	571	$7.50	$80.00	1993-2000
92	CAYMUS VINEYARDS	Napa Valley Rutherford Special Selection	180	$22.00	$175.00	1992-2000
92	HEITZ WINE CELLARS	Napa Valley Oakville Martha's Vineyard	4,895	$25.00	$100.00	1993-2003
90	FREEMARK ABBEY WINERY	Napa Valley Rutherford Bosche	2,632	$10.00	$48.00	1990-1995

NA — not available.   NR — not released.   * — Beaulieu production figures are estimates.

Score	Winery	Appellation/Vineyard	Case Prod.	Release Price	Current Price	Drink
90	MOUNT EDEN VINEYARDS	Santa Cruz Mountains	255	$20.00	$70.00	1994-2004
89	CAYMUS VINEYARDS	Napa Valley Rutherford Estate	1,300	$8.50	$80.00	1990-1998
89	CLOS DU VAL WINE CO.	Napa Valley Stags Leap District Estate	9,300	$9.00	$65.00	1990-2000
89	MAYACAMAS VINEYARDS	Napa Valley Mount Veeder	2,315	$12.00	$60.00	1990-1995
89	VILLA MT. EDEN WINERY	Napa Valley Oakville Estate	616	$7.00	$50.00	1990-2000
88	BURGESS CELLARS	Napa Valley Vintage Selection	1,800	$9.00	$45.00	1990-2000
88	CUVAISON WINERY	Napa Valley Philip Togni Signature	400	$40.00	$60.00	1992-1998
88	DIAMOND CREEK VINEYARD	Napa Valley Diamond Mountain Red Rock Terrace	286	$7.50	$75.00	1992-1997
88	RIDGE VINEYARDS	Santa Cruz Mountains Monte Bello	1,850	$10.00	$85.00	1990-1999
88	SILVER OAK CELLARS	Alexander Valley	6,000	$10.00	$95.00	1990-1996
87	RIDGE VINEYARDS	Napa County Spring Mountain York Creek	800	$10.00	$45.00	1992-2000
86	CHATEAU MONTELENA WINERY	North Coast	6,675	$9.00	$100.00	1993-2000
86	ROBERT MONDAVI WINERY	Napa Valley Oakville Reserve	7,000	$30.00	$75.00	1990-1992
85	DIAMOND CREEK VINEYARD	Napa Valley Diamond Mountain Gravelly Meadow	95	$7.50	$55.00	1991-2000
85	JOSEPH PHELPS VINEYARDS	Napa Valley Insignia	473	$15.00	$90.00	1990-1995
85	SIMI WINERY	Alexander Valley	11,000	$6.00	$32.00	1990
83	MOUNT VEEDER WINERY	Napa Valley Mount Veeder Bernstein Vineyards	850	$11.00	$50.00	1995-2004
83	TREFETHEN VINEYARDS	Napa Valley Yountville	783	$7.50	$55.00	1990-1994
82	FRANCISCAN VINEYARDS	Napa Valley Oakville Reserve	3,000	$12.00	$32.00	1990
79	BEAULIEU VINEYARD	Napa Valley Rutherford Georges de Latour Private Reserve	15,000	$16.00	$50.00	1990-1992
79	CUVAISON WINERY	Napa Valley	5,000	$10.00	$40.00	1990-1995
78	CHAPPELLET VINEYARD	Napa Valley	5,000	$10.00	$45.00	1990
78	STERLING VINEYARDS	Napa Valley Reserve	3,800	$20.00	$55.00	1994-2000
75	ALEXANDER VALLEY VINEYARDS	Alexander Valley	3,416	$5.50	$20.00	1990-1992
74	STAG'S LEAP WINE CELLARS	Napa Valley Stags Leap District Stag's Leap Vineyards	2,300	$8.50	$50.00	1990
73	KENWOOD VINEYARDS	Sonoma County Artist Series	1,000	$6.50	$250.00	1990
69	RUTHERFORD HILL WINERY	Napa Valley	4,984	$9.00	$18.00	Avoid
64	BUENA VISTA WINERY	Sonoma Valley Carneros	3,864	$12.00	$30.00	Avoid

VINTAGE: 1974

Score	Winery	Appellation/Vineyard	Case Prod.	Release Price	Current Price	Drink
99	HEITZ WINE CELLARS	Napa Valley Oakville Martha's Vineyard	4,543	$25.00	$200.00	1994-2008
95	MAYACAMAS VINEYARDS	Napa Valley Mount Veeder	2,300	$9.50	$115.00	1992-2004
94	CONN CREEK WINERY	Napa Valley Calistoga	900	$9.00	$70.00	1990-1998
93	RIDGE VINEYARDS	Santa Cruz Mountains Monte Bello	1,260	$12.00	$140.00	1990-1998
93	SILVER OAK CELLARS	North Coast	4,000	$8.00	$135.00	1990-2000
92	ROBERT MONDAVI WINERY	Napa Valley Oakville Reserve	9,000	$30.00	$95.00	1990-1996
91	CLOS DU VAL WINE CO.	Napa Valley Stags Leap District Estate	7,600	$7.50	$75.00	1990-2000
91	FREEMARK ABBEY WINERY	Napa Valley Rutherford Bosche	4,127	$7.75	$75.00	1990-1998
90	CHATEAU MONTELENA WINERY	Napa Valley Calistoga	1,100	$9.00	$100.00	1993-2003
90	JOSEPH PHELPS VINEYARDS	Napa Valley Insignia	670	$12.00	$130.00	1990-1998
90	STERLING VINEYARDS	Napa Valley Reserve	3,600	$20.00	$80.00	1992-2002
90	VILLA MT. EDEN WINERY	Napa Valley Oakville Estate	219	$7.00	$60.00	1990-1997
88	DIAMOND CREEK VINEYARD	Napa Valley Diamond Mountain Gravelly Meadow	105	$7.50	$135.00	1990-1997
88	CHARLES KRUG WINERY	Napa Valley Stags Leap District Lot F-1 Vintage Select	8,246	$9.00	$50.00	1990-1993
88	STAG'S LEAP WINE CELLARS	Napa Valley Stags Leap District Cask 23	100	$12.00	$135.00	1990-1993
87	CAYMUS VINEYARDS	Napa Valley Rutherford Estate	950	$7.00	$110.00	1990-1996
87	CHATEAU MONTELENA WINERY	Alexander Valley Sonoma	6,000	$9.00	$100.00	1992-2000
87	DIAMOND CREEK VINEYARD	Napa Valley Diamond Mountain Volcanic Hill	485	$7.50	$135.00	1992-2000
87	MOUNT EDEN VINEYARDS	Santa Cruz Mountains	437	$20.00	$120.00	1994-2002
87	RIDGE VINEYARDS	Napa County Spring Mountain York Creek	536	$6.75	$50.00	1990-1997
87	SIMI WINERY	Alexander Valley Reserve Vintage	14,000	$20.00	$45.00	1990-1996
87	STAG'S LEAP WINE CELLARS	Napa Valley Stags Leap District Stag's Leap Vineyards	450	$8.00	$110.00	1990-1992

NA — not available.   NR — not released.   ∗ — Beaulieu production figures are estimates.

Score	Winery	Appellation/Vineyard	Case Prod.	Release Price	Current Price	Drink
86	BURGESS CELLARS	Napa Valley Vintage Selection	1,100	$9.00	$50.00	1990-1996
86	INGLENOOK-NAPA VALLEY	Napa Valley Rutherford Cask	11,864	$9.00	$45.00	1990-1995
84	TREFETHEN VINEYARDS	Napa Valley Yountville	835	$8.00	$65.00	1990-1997
83	SIMI WINERY	Alexander Valley Special Reserve	2,000	$25.00	$65.00	1990
80	MOUNT VEEDER WINERY	Napa Valley Mount Veeder	650	$8.00	$50.00	1996-2004
79	BEAULIEU VINEYARD	Napa Valley Rutherford Georges de Latour Private Reserve	15,000	$12.00	$70.00	1990-1991
78	RAYMOND VINEYARD AND CELLAR	Napa Valley Rutherford	800	$5.50	$40.00	1990
77	LOUIS M. MARTINI WINERY	California Special Selection	5,411	$10.00	$45.00	1990-1992
70	CHAPPELLET VINEYARD	Napa Valley	3,500	$7.50	$45.00	1990
68	BUENA VISTA WINERY	Sonoma Valley Carneros Cask 25	3,046	$12.00	$40.00	Avoid

VINTAGE: 1973

Score	Winery	Appellation/Vineyard	Case Prod.	Release Price	Current Price	Drink
93	CAYMUS VINEYARDS	Napa Valley Rutherford Estate	850	$6.00	$120.00	1990-2000
92	CONN CREEK WINERY	Napa Valley Stags Leap District	400	$9.00	$70.00	1990-2000
92	HEITZ WINE CELLARS	Napa Valley Oakville Martha's Vineyard	2,329	$11.00	$120.00	1991-2000
91	MOUNT EDEN VINEYARDS	Santa Cruz Mountains	391	$14.00	$140.00	1995-2005
90	CLOS DU VAL WINE CO.	Napa Valley Stags Leap District Reserve	100	$10.00	$100.00	1990-2000
90	MOUNT VEEDER WINERY	Napa Valley Mount Veeder	400	$8.00	$80.00	1993-2005
89	STERLING VINEYARDS	Napa Valley Reserve	3,850	$10.00	$70.00	1992-1998
88	FREEMARK ABBEY WINERY	Napa Valley Rutherford Bosche	3,495	$8.00	$70.00	1990-1993
87	CHATEAU MONTELENA WINERY	Alexander Valley Sonoma	3,000	$8.50	$100.00	1990-2001
87	MAYACAMAS VINEYARDS	Napa Valley Mount Veeder	2,050	$9.00	$90.00	1990-1996
87	RIDGE VINEYARDS	Santa Cruz Mountains Monte Bello	1,094	$10.00	$110.00	1990-1994
86	CLOS DU VAL WINE CO.	Napa Valley Stags Leap District Estate	2,760	$6.00	$70.00	1990-1995
86	STAG'S LEAP WINE CELLARS	Napa Valley Stags Leap District Stag's Leap Vineyards	400	$6.00	$135.00	1990
82	ROBERT MONDAVI WINERY	Napa Valley Oakville Reserve	4,500	$12.00	$80.00	1990-1994
81	SILVER OAK CELLARS	North Coast	1,800	$7.00	$130.00	1990-1994
80	DIAMOND CREEK VINEYARD	Napa Valley Diamond Mountain Volcanic Hill	150	$7.50	$200.00	1990-1996
79	BEAULIEU VINEYARD	Napa Valley Rutherford Georges de Latour Private Reserve	15,000	$9.00	$50.00	1990
73	CHARLES KRUG WINERY	Napa Valley Vintage Select	5,846	$9.00	$40.00	1990
72	SIMI WINERY	Alexander Valley	10,000	$6.00	$25.00	1990
69	CHAPPELLET VINEYARD	Napa Valley	2,500	$7.50	$65.00	Avoid
67	INGLENOOK-NAPA VALLEY	Napa Valley Rutherford Cask	6,494	$8.00	$39.00	Avoid

VINTAGE: 1972

Score	Winery	Appellation/Vineyard	Case Prod.	Release Price	Current Price	Drink
90	CLOS DU VAL WINE CO.	Napa Valley Stags Leap District Estate	3,500	$6.00	$100.00	1990-1998
86	CAYMUS VINEYARDS	Napa Valley Rutherford Estate	230	$4.50	$110.00	1990-1993
86	SILVER OAK CELLARS	North Coast	1,100	$6.00	$160.00	1990-1995
85	DIAMOND CREEK VINEYARD	Napa Valley Diamond Mountain Volcanic Hill	40	$7.50	$200.00	1990-1995
84	MOUNT EDEN VINEYARDS	Santa Cruz Mountains	89	$20.00	$60.00	1990-1995
84	RIDGE VINEYARDS	Santa Cruz Mountains Monte Bello	740	$10.00	$100.00	1990-1992
82	MAYACAMAS VINEYARDS	Napa Valley	1,620	$8.00	$70.00	1990-1993
80	FREEMARK ABBEY WINERY	Napa Valley Rutherford Bosche	3,183	$6.00	$30.00	1990-1992
80	SIMI WINERY	Alexander Valley	10,000	$5.00	$25.00	1990
79	HEITZ WINE CELLARS	Napa Valley Oakville Martha's Vineyard	1,445	$12.75	$100.00	1990-1994
77	CHARLES KRUG WINERY	Napa Valley Vintage Select	3,787	$9.00	$45.00	1990
75	ROBERT MONDAVI WINERY	Napa Valley Oakville	NA	$6.00	$45.00	1990
74	DIAMOND CREEK VINEYARD	Napa Valley Diamond Mountain Red Rock Terrace	25	$7.50	$200.00	1990-1992
73	BEAULIEU VINEYARD	Napa Valley Rutherford Georges de Latour Private Reserve	15,000	$6.00	$40.00	1990
70	STAG'S LEAP WINE CELLARS	Napa Valley Stags Leap District Stag's Leap Vineyards	100	$5.50	$80.00	1990
67	CHAPPELLET VINEYARD	Napa Valley	1,500	$6.50	$40.00	Avoid
67	INGLENOOK-NAPA VALLEY	Napa Valley Rutherford Cask	7,278	$7.00	$44.00	Avoid

NA — not available.   NR — not released.   * — Beaulieu production figures are estimates.

Score	Winery	Appellation/Vineyard	Case Prod.	Release Price	Current Price	Drink
63	LOUIS M. MARTINI WINERY	California Special Selection	2,055	$5.00	$65.00	Avoid

VINTAGE: 1971

Score	Winery	Appellation/Vineyard	Case Prod.	Release Price	Current Price	Drink
93	ROBERT MONDAVI WINERY	Napa Valley Oakville Reserve	4,000	$12.00	$130.00	1990-1996
86	FREEMARK ABBEY WINERY	Napa Valley Rutherford Bosche	1,015	$6.75	$40.00	1990
86	MAYACAMAS VINEYARDS	Napa Valley Mount Veeder	1,490	$8.00	$80.00	1990-1995
85	RIDGE VINEYARDS	Santa Cruz Mountains Monte Bello	630	$10.00	$145.00	1990-1993
79	CHARLES KRUG WINERY	Napa Valley Vintage Select	7,993	$7.50	$35.00	1990
75	SIMI WINERY	Alexander Valley	8,000	$5.00	$30.00	1990
73	INGLENOOK-NAPA VALLEY	Napa Valley Rutherford Cask	2,978	$6.50	$50.00	1990-1991
67	BEAULIEU VINEYARD	Napa Valley Rutherford Georges de Latour Private Reserve	15,000	$8.00	$60.00	Avoid
65	CHAPPELLET VINEYARD	Napa Valley	1,000	$7.50	$80.00	Avoid

VINTAGE: 1970

Score	Winery	Appellation/Vineyard	Case Prod.	Release Price	Current Price	Drink
98	HEITZ WINE CELLARS	Napa Valley Oakville Martha's Vineyard	866	$12.75	$275.00	1993-2005
96	MAYACAMAS VINEYARDS	Napa Valley Mount Veeder	1,325	$8.00	$130.00	1996-2008
96	RIDGE VINEYARDS	Santa Cruz Mountains Monte Bello	540	$10.00	$190.00	1994-2005
95	BEAULIEU VINEYARD	Napa Valley Rutherford Georges de Latour Private Reserve	15,000	$8.00	$130.00	1990-1995
93	CHAPPELLET VINEYARD	Napa Valley	700	$7.50	$160.00	1990-1995
91	FREEMARK ABBEY WINERY	Napa Valley Rutherford Bosche	424	$8.75	$100.00	1990
89	ROBERT MONDAVI WINERY	Napa Valley Oakville Unfined	4,000	$12.00	$120.00	1990-1996
88	LOUIS M. MARTINI WINERY	California Special Selection Mountain	7,845	$8.00	$90.00	1990-1995
85	INGLENOOK-NAPA VALLEY	Napa Valley Rutherford Cask	8,109	$6.50	$75.00	1990-1995
75	CHARLES KRUG WINERY	Napa Valley Vintage Select	11,825	$7.50	$60.00	1990
73	SIMI WINERY	Alexander Valley	5,000	$4.50	$50.00	1990

VINTAGE: 1969

Score	Winery	Appellation/Vineyard	Case Prod.	Release Price	Current Price	Drink
93	HEITZ WINE CELLARS	Napa Valley Oakville Martha's Vineyard	1,016	$12.75	$275.00	1990-1995
92	RIDGE VINEYARDS	Santa Cruz Mountains Monte Bello	300	$7.50	$200.00	1990-2000
90	BEAULIEU VINEYARD	Napa Valley Rutherford Georges de Latour Private Reserve	15,000	$6.50	$120.00	1990-1995
89	MAYACAMAS VINEYARDS	California	1,080	$6.50	$100.00	1990-1995
87	CHAPPELLET VINEYARD	Napa Valley	400	$10.00	$150.00	1990-1995
86	ROBERT MONDAVI WINERY	Napa Valley Oakville Unfined	3,000	$12.00	$155.00	1990-1995
81	CHARLES KRUG WINERY	Napa Valley Vintage Select	8,262	$6.50	$65.00	1990
80	INGLENOOK-NAPA VALLEY	Napa Valley Rutherford Cask	12,508	$6.50	$80.00	1990-1992

VINTAGE: 1968

Score	Winery	Appellation/Vineyard	Case Prod.	Release Price	Current Price	Drink
99	HEITZ WINE CELLARS	Napa Valley Oakville Martha's Vineyard	749	$9.50	$375.00	1990-1995
91	BEAULIEU VINEYARD	Napa Valley Rutherford Georges de Latour Private Reserve	15,000	$6.00	$150.00	1990-1996
90	LOUIS M. MARTINI WINERY	California Special Selection	1,926	$6.00	$95.00	1990-1994
88	CHAPPELLET VINEYARD	Napa Valley	200	$5.50	$100.00	1990-1996
88	MAYACAMAS VINEYARDS	California	680	$4.50	$125.00	1990-1995
87	RIDGE VINEYARDS	Santa Cruz Mountains Monte Bello	200	$7.50	$190.00	1990-1997
85	INGLENOOK-NAPA VALLEY	Napa Valley Rutherford Cask	5,218	$6.00	$90.00	1990-1995
83	ROBERT MONDAVI WINERY	Napa Valley Oakville Unfined	2,000	$8.50	$135.00	1990-1994
80	CHARLES KRUG WINERY	Napa Valley Vintage Select	7,668	$6.50	$90.00	1990

VINTAGE: 1967

Score	Winery	Appellation/Vineyard	Case Prod.	Release Price	Current Price	Drink
86	HEITZ WINE CELLARS	Napa Valley Oakville Martha's Vineyard	2,208	$7.50	$300.00	1990-1996
85	BEAULIEU VINEYARD	Napa Valley Rutherford Georges de Latour Private Reserve	15,000	$5.25	$120.00	1990-1993
84	ROBERT MONDAVI WINERY	Napa Valley Oakville	NA	$5.00	$100.00	1990
73	INGLENOOK-NAPA VALLEY	Napa Valley Rutherford Cask	4,194	$6.00	$60.00	1990
65	MAYACAMAS VINEYARDS	California	800	$4.00	$125.00	Avoid

VINTAGE: 1966

Score	Winery	Appellation/Vineyard	Case Prod.	Release Price	Current Price	Drink
92	HEITZ WINE CELLARS	Napa Valley Oakville Martha's Vineyard	392	$8.00	$425.00	1990-1997
87	BEAULIEU VINEYARD	Napa Valley Rutherford Georges de Latour Private Reserve	15,000	$5.25	$140.00	1990-1994

NA — not available.   NR — not released.   * — Beaulieu production figures are estimates.

Score	Winery	Appellation/Vineyard	Case Prod.	Release Price	Current Price	Drink
87	LOUIS M. MARTINI WINERY	California Special Selection	2,023	$6.00	$110.00	1990-1992
80	ROBERT MONDAVI WINERY	Napa Valley Oakville	1,500	$5.00	$165.00	1990
75	MAYACAMAS VINEYARDS	California	530	$3.50	$125.00	1990-1993
73	INGLENOOK-NAPA VALLEY	Napa Valley Rutherford Cask	3,190	$5.75	$95.00	1990
VINTAGE: 1965						
87	CHARLES KRUG WINERY	Napa Valley Vintage Select	8,643	$5.00	$80.00	1990-1993
86	RIDGE VINEYARDS	Santa Cruz Mountains Monte Bello	90	$6.50	$275.00	1990-1993
85	BEAULIEU VINEYARD	Napa Valley Rutherford Georges de Latour Private Reserve	15,000	$5.25	$120.00	1990-1993
65	MAYACAMAS VINEYARDS	California	475	$2.75	$150.00	Avoid
VINTAGE: 1964						
90	RIDGE VINEYARDS	Santa Cruz Mountains Monte Bello	70	$6.50	$310.00	1990-1995
86	CHARLES KRUG WINERY	Napa Valley Vintage Select	5,780	$4.00	$85.00	1990
85	LOUIS M. MARTINI WINERY	California Special Selection	1,582	$6.00	$100.00	1990-1992
84	BEAULIEU VINEYARD	Napa Valley Rutherford Georges de Latour Private Reserve	15,000	$4.25	$145.00	1990-1994
VINTAGE: 1963						
74	CHARLES KRUG WINERY	Napa Valley Vintage Select	3,599	$3.50	$70.00	1990
70	BEAULIEU VINEYARD	Napa Valley Rutherford Georges de Latour Private Reserve	15,000	$3.50	$145.00	1990
70	RIDGE VINEYARDS	Santa Cruz Mountains Monte Bello	100	$5.00	$130.00	1990
69	MAYACAMAS VINEYARDS	California	420	$2.00	$150.00	Avoid
VINTAGE: 1962						
78	CHARLES KRUG WINERY	Napa Valley Vintage Select	2,137	$3.50	$70.00	1990
73	BEAULIEU VINEYARD	Napa Valley Rutherford Georges de Latour Private Reserve	15,000	$3.50	$140.00	1990
73	LOUIS M. MARTINI WINERY	California Private Reserve	1,151	$3.50	$80.00	1990
68	MAYACAMAS VINEYARDS	California	350	$2.00	$150.00	Avoid
VINTAGE: 1961						
89	CHARLES KRUG WINERY	Napa Valley Vintage Select	1,958	$3.50	$135.00	1990
80	LOUIS M. MARTINI WINERY	California Special Selection	1,092	$4.00	$180.00	1990-1994
78	BEAULIEU VINEYARD	Napa Valley Rutherford Georges de Latour Private Reserve	15,000	$3.50	$200.00	1990-1992
VINTAGE: 1960						
80	INGLENOOK-NAPA VALLEY	Napa Valley Rutherford Cask	2,500	$2.75	$140.00	1990
79	CHARLES KRUG WINERY	Napa Valley Vintage Select	1,516	$2.25	$70.00	1990
VINTAGE: 1959						
89	BEAULIEU VINEYARD	Napa Valley Rutherford Georges de Latour Private Reserve	15,000	$3.50	$350.00	1990-1992
87	LOUIS M. MARTINI WINERY	Napa Valley Special Selection	1,500	$4.50	$140.00	1990-1992
85	CHARLES KRUG WINERY	Napa Valley Vintage Select	7,832	$2.25	$150.00	1990
VINTAGE: 1958						
96	BEAULIEU VINEYARD	Napa Valley Rutherford Georges de Latour Private Reserve	15,000	$3.00	$400.00	1990-1994
94	INGLENOOK-NAPA VALLEY	Napa Valley Rutherford Cask	2,500	$2.50	$300.00	1990
88	CHARLES KRUG WINERY	Napa Valley Vintage Select	868	$2.00	$465.00	1990
88	LOUIS M. MARTINI WINERY	Napa Valley Special Selection	1,750	$4.50	$220.00	1990-1992
VINTAGE: 1957						
91	LOUIS M. MARTINI WINERY	Napa Valley Special Selection	1,994	$3.50	$175.00	1990-1992
VINTAGE: 1956						
90	CHARLES KRUG WINERY	Napa Valley Vintage Select	1,250	$1.40	$590.00	1990
88	BEAULIEU VINEYARD	Napa Valley Rutherford Georges de Latour Private Reserve	15,000	$2.50	$600.00	1990-1991
77	LOUIS M. MARTINI WINERY	California Private Reserve Mountain	1,500	$2.50	$90.00	1990-1991

NA — not available.   NR — not released.   * — Beaulieu production figures are estimates.

Vintage	Winery	Appellation/Vineyard	Case Prod.	Release Price	Current Price	Drink
VINTAGE: 1955						
93	INGLENOOK-NAPA VALLEY	Napa Valley Rutherford Cask	2,500	$1.85	$375.00	1990
87	LOUIS M. MARTINI WINERY	Napa Valley Special Selection	1,035	$2.50	$190.00	1990-1992
VINTAGE: 1952						
93	LOUIS M. MARTINI WINERY	Napa Valley Special Selection	1,000	$2.50	$450.00	1990-1992
92	CHARLES KRUG WINERY	Napa Valley Vintage Select	1,028	$1.26	$750.00	1990
VINTAGE: 1951						
90	BEAULIEU VINEYARD	Napa Valley Rutherford Georges de Latour Private Reserve	15,000	$1.82	$950.00	1990-1992
87	LOUIS M. MARTINI WINERY	Napa Valley Special Selection	1,000	$2.00	$275.00	1990-1992
85	CHARLES KRUG WINERY	Napa Valley Vintage Select	1,553	$1.25	$700.00	1990
VINTAGE: 1950						
79	CHARLES KRUG WINERY	Napa Valley Vintage Select	1,553	$1.25	$500.00	1990
VINTAGE: 1949						
92	INGLENOOK-NAPA VALLEY	Napa Valley Rutherford Cask	2,000	$1.49	$750.00	1990-1993
VINTAGE: 1948						
85	BEAULIEU VINEYARD	Napa Valley Rutherford Georges de Latour Private Reserve	15,000	$1.82	$800.00	1990-1992
VINTAGE: 1947						
93	BEAULIEU VINEYARD	Napa Valley Rutherford Georges de Latour Private Reserve	15,000	$1.82	$1000.00	1990-1995
90	LOUIS M. MARTINI WINERY	Napa Valley Special Selection	1,151	$1.50	$750.00	1990-1992
VINTAGE: 1946						
88	BEAULIEU VINEYARD	Napa Valley Rutherford Georges de Latour Private Reserve	15,000	$1.47	$1000.00	1990-1994
88	CHARLES KRUG WINERY	Napa Valley Vintage Select	1,452	$1.00	$750.00	1990
87	INGLENOOK-NAPA VALLEY	Napa Valley Rutherford	8,000	$1.49	$1100.00	1990-1995
VINTAGE: 1945						
75	LOUIS M. MARTINI WINERY	Napa Valley Special Selection	1,000	$1.50	$400.00	1990
VINTAGE: 1944						
88	CHARLES KRUG WINERY	Napa Valley	857	$0.95	$800.00	1990
87	BEAULIEU VINEYARD	Napa Valley Rutherford Georges de Latour Private Reserve	15,000	$1.47	$1100.00	1990-1992
VINTAGE: 1943						
91	INGLENOOK-NAPA VALLEY	Napa Valley Rutherford	7,000	$1.49	$1000.00	1990-1995
70	LOUIS M. MARTINI WINERY	Napa Valley Private Reserve Villa del Rey	1,000	$1.50	$400.00	1990
VINTAGE: 1942						
87	BEAULIEU VINEYARD	Napa Valley Rutherford Georges de Latour Private Reserve	15,000	$1.45	$1200.00	1990-1992
VINTAGE: 1941						
100	INGLENOOK-NAPA VALLEY	Napa Valley Rutherford	5,000	$1.49	$1400.00	1990-2005
85	BEAULIEU VINEYARD	Napa Valley Rutherford Georges de Latour Private Reserve	15,000	$1.45	$1200.00	1990-1992
VINTAGE: 1939						
90	LOUIS M. MARTINI WINERY	Napa Valley Special Reserve	1,000	$1.25	$1000.00	1990-1992
82	BEAULIEU VINEYARD	Napa Valley Rutherford Georges de Latour Private Reserve	15,000	$1.45	$1500.00	1990
VINTAGE: 1933						
95	INGLENOOK-NAPA VALLEY	Napa Valley Rutherford	5,000	$1.30	$1600.00	1990
VINTAGE: 1897						
87	INGLENOOK-NAPA VALLEY	Napa Valley Rutherford Claret-Medoc Type	2,000	NA		1990-1995

NA — not available.   NR — not released.   * — Beaulieu production figures are estimates.

APPENDIX 4

Cabernet Vintage Chart, 1988-1933

The following appendix lists all vintages reviewed between 1988 and 1933 in chronological order. The number next to the vintage is its score based on *The Wine Spectator's* 100-point scale.

1980s

1988	85	Very Good
1987	92	Excellent
1986	95	Classic
1985	97	Classic
1984	94	Excellent
1983	81	Very Good
1982	78	Good
1981	85	Very Good
1980	84	Very Good

1970s

1979	88	Very Good
1978	93	Excellent
1977	82	Very Good
1976	75	Good
1975	86	Very Good
1974	91	Excellent
1973	87	Very Good
1972	67	Fair
1971	68	Fair
1970	95	Classic

1960s

1969	92	Excellent
1968	96	Classic
1967	82	Very Good
1966	91	Excellent
1965	83	Very Good
1964	91	Excellent
1963	69	Fair
1962	69	Fair
1961	71	Good
1960	84	Very Good

1950s

1959	87	Very Good
1958	95	Classic
1957	78	Good
1956	86	Very Good
1955	89	Very Good
1954	85	Very Good
1953	67	Fair
1952	85	Very Good
1951	94	Excellent
1950	90	Excellent

1940s

1949	86	Very Good
1948	69	Fair
1947	85	Very Good
1946	91	Excellent
1945	84	Very Good
1944	78	Good
1943	79	Good
1942	88	Very Good
1941	89	Very Good
1940	90	Excellent

1930s

1939	87	Very Good
1938	80	Very Good
1937	80	Very Good
1936	90	Excellent
1935	79	Good
1934	91	Excellent
1933	91	Excellent

Classic	**(95-100 points)**
Excellent	**(90-94)**
Very Good	**(80-89)**
Good	**(70-79)**
Fair	**(60-69)**
Poor	**(50-59)**

APPENDIX 5
Cabernet Vintages by Score

The following appendix lists all vintages reviewed between 1988 and 1933 and ranks them in order of the scores based on *The Wine Spectator's* 100-point scale.

Classic (95-100)

1.	1985	97
2.	1968	96
3.	1986	95
4.	1970	95
5.	1958	95

Excellent (90-94)

6.	1984	94
7.	1951	94
8.	1978	93
9.	1987	92
10.	1969	92
11.	1974	91
12.	1966	91
13.	1964	91
14.	1946	91
15.	1934	91
16.	1933	91
17.	1950	90
18.	1940	90
19.	1936	90

Very Good (80-89)

20.	1955	89
21.	1941	89
22.	1979	88
23.	1942	88
24.	1973	87
25.	1959	87
26.	1939	87
27.	1975	86
28.	1956	86
29.	1949	86
30.	1988	85
31.	1981	85
32.	1954	85
33.	1952	85
34.	1947	85
35.	1980	84
36.	1960	84
36.	1952	83
37.	1945	84
38.	1965	83
39.	1977	82
40.	1967	82
41.	1983	81
42.	1938	80
43.	1937	80

Good 70-79)

44.	1943	79
45.	1935	79
46.	1982	78
47.	1957	78
48.	1944	78
49.	1976	75
50.	1961	71

Fair (60-69)

51.	1963	69
52.	1962	69
53.	1948	69
54.	1971	68
55.	1972	67
56.	1953	67

Classic	(95-100 points)
Excellent	(90-94)
Very Good	(80-89)
Good	(70-79)
Fair	(60-69)
Poor	(50-59)

INDEX

INDEX

THE
WINE SPECTATOR

Much of the research and tasting analysis in this book by James Laube has been done in conjunction with his duties as senior editor of *The Wine Spectator*.

The Wine Spectator, America's best-selling consumer wine magazine, is edited for those who are serious about wine. Published twice a month, each issue offers a unique 'insider's view' of the world of wine featuring current news, wine ratings, personality profiles, and wine and food articles as well as pieces on entertainment and travel, all of which are written by the world's leading wine journalists.

A one-year subscription to *The Wine Spectator* is $35 for U.S. delivery, $45 for Canada, and $75 for delivery anywhere in the world. To subscribe call 1-800-622-2062, or send your check, payable to The Wine Spectator in U.S. funds to *The Wine Spectator*, 387 Park Avenue South, New York, NY 10016.